RECREATION

CONSERVATION IN THE UNITED STATES

A Documentary History

General Editor: **Frank E. Smith**

RECREATION

Phillip O. Foss
Colorado State University

New York
CHELSEA HOUSE PUBLISHERS
In association with
VAN NOSTRAND REINHOLD CO.
New York, Cincinnati, Toronto, London, Melbourne
1971

EDITORIAL STAFF:

Editor-In-Chief: **Fred L. Israel**

Project Editor: **Kim Siegel**

Managing Editor: **William P. Hansen**

Associate Editors: **Joan Tapper**
Nina Flannery

Editorial Assistants: **Jane Fuller**
Maxine Krasnow
Jaffray Cuyler

Book Designer: **Connie Frey**

PREFACE

This study is intended to be an analysis of the development of outdoor recreation policy in the United States through documents. It is only peripherally concerned with the outdoor recreation activities themselves. The term "policy" is understood to mean public policy. In compiling this or any other documentary collection, major emphasis and attention is inevitably given to written and official policy statements. This emphasis on formalized or legitimatized policy statements tends to distort the realities of policy formation, because it ignores the fact that policies may exist which are not formalized into official statements. Thus although it was the policy of the United States for approximately a century that hunting, fishing, and lumbering should be almost completely unrestricted, there exists no official declaration of such a policy. There can be no such thing as a policy vacuum; a policy always exists, even if it is not formalized in a public document.

Presumably one could trace the antecedents of American outdoor recreation policy far back in time, but this volume is restricted to the development of outdoor recreation policy within the United States.

It is difficult to organize outdoor recreation policies according to activities, since frequently several activities are interdependent or adjunctive and dependent on other policy decisions. A single day's recreation might involve driving for pleasure, sight-seeing, hiking, boating, fishing, and picnicking. The availability of fishing opportunities will affect the amount of boating, and so on. Furthermore, the quality and number of outdoor recreation opportunities is frequently dependent upon other policy determinations in which recreation considerations play a minor or insignificant role. Thus policy decisions on working hours, highway construction, flood control, and water pollution may have a direct effect on fishing. These difficulties notwithstanding, it has been decided to divide this volume according to recreational activities and institutions in order to facilitate its use as a reference work.

The opening section will attempt to compensate somewhat for the inevitable deficiencies of such compartmentalization by presenting a chronological overview of the development of outdoor recreational practices and policies in the United States.

Phillip O. Foss
Colorado State University
Fort Collins, Colorado

CONTENTS

City Parks and Open Spaces   291

Water Pollution and Outdoor Recreation

The Race for Inner Space

RECREATION

DEVELOPMENT OF OUTDOOR RECREATION POLICY IN THE UNITED STATES

OUR COLONIAL HERITAGE

EXPLOITING THE INEXHAUSTIBLE AND FORBIDDING WILDERNESS

Settlers who arrived along the Atlantic Seaboard in the early seventeenth century found a continent whose resources appeared to be inexhaustible. The wilderness they encountered appeared to some of them to be dangerous and forbidding. To others it was of no value until it could be tamed or used. Forests were useful for producing lumber but they were generally thought to be a nuisance because they had to be cleared before farming could begin and because they sheltered hostile Indians. Wild game and fish had some value for food—at least until farm crops and domestic livestock could be produced.

As the original settlements became more populated, some of the original resources were depleted but the same general attitudes toward the wilderness persisted along the edges of the moving frontier and, indeed, they remained strong long after the frontier had passed by. According to Edward Crafts:

> For three centuries before the conservation movement, this Nation had been engaged in the battle to "conquer the wilderness," to "win the West," to "build an empire." As a policy the Nation gave its natural resources free, or nearly so, to those who would risk their lives to develop them. The great American heroes, both legendary and real, were the Daniel Boones, the Paul Bunyans, the Buffalo Bills, and the James J. Hills, who fought the wilderness and its original inhabitants and built a civilization upon it. "Manifest destiny" meant conquest and development of the Continent.*

This original impulse to tame, subdue, and exploit remains strong today. The feeling that America possesses inexhaustible resources is still present, but somewhat modified, in the belief that "science will find a way" to supply all our wants and needs.

THE WORK ETHIC

The Puritans and some of the other early settlers brought with them a concept of the nobility of work and the sinfulness of idleness. At that time long hours of work were necessary to maintain a subsistence living, but the Puritans made a

---

*Edward C. Crafts, "The Evolution of Outdoor Recreation Policy," *Proceedings of the National Conference on Policy Issues in Outdoor Recreation,* Ogden, Utah, 1966, 14.

virtue of necessity. Of course, this work ethic did not originate with the Puritans. In the words of Thomas Woody, the early Christians had

> learned from Genesis: "in the sweat of thy face shalt thou eat bread, till thou return unto the ground." Work was conducive to piety. Manual tasks were idealized. Spinning, weaving, hoeing, carpentry, and like employments were urged by St. Jerome, St. Basil, Cassian, and St. Benedict. St. Augustine wrote a treatise, *Concerning the Work of Monks,* to correct the error of some of the "religious" who favored the "lilies of the field, that toil not. . . ."
>
> Leisure (idleness) was condemned: It hindered godliness; it was a snare of the devil. "Idle hands are the devil's workshop." "All the ulcers," says Cassian, "Which spring from idleness, are healed by work. A monk who labors contends with one devil; idlers face innumerable ones."*

This is not the place to analyze the role of the churches in the development of the work ethic except to note that exhortations to work were common in sermons and hymns. One old hymn reads in part:

> Work, for the night is coming, Work thro' the morning hours; Work while the dew is sparkling, Work, 'midspringing flow'rs; Work, when the day grows brighter, Work in the glowing sun; Work, for the night is coming, When man's work is done.†

The work ethic was supported by colonial governments as well. Richard B. Morris points out that:

> Not alone in Puritan New England was idleness stigmatized as "the parent of all Vices," but throughout the length and breadth of the North Atlantic seaboard idleness was discountenanced. As in the Elizabethan code, Rhode Island classified together, "any Rougs, vagabonds, Sturdy beggars, masterless men, or other Notorious offenders whatsoever." Penn's Frame of Government provided that "all children within this province of the age of twelve years, shall be Taught some useful trade or skill, to the end none may be idle, but the poor may work to live, and the rich, if they become poor, may not want." Colonial almanacs were studded with aphorisms on the sinfulness of being unemployed.‡

Perhaps Benjamin Franklin best expressed the central ideas of the work ethic in his *Father Abraham's Speech,* a portion of which is reproduced below.

> I stopt my Horse lately where a great Number of People were collected at a Vendue of Merchant Goods. The Hour of Sale not being come, they were conversing on the Badness of the Times, and one of the Company call'd to a plain clean old Man, with white locks, PRAY, FATHER Abraham, WHAT THINK YOU OF THE TIMES? WON'T THESE HEAVY TAXES QUITE RUIN THE COUNTRY? HOW SHALL WE BE EVER ABLE TO PAY THEM? WHAT WOULD YOU ADVISE US TO? Father ABRAHAM stood up and reply'd.
>
> * * *
>
> "Friends, says he, and Neighbours, the Taxes are indeed very heavy, and if those laid on by the Government were the only Ones we had to pay, we might more easily discharge them; but we have many others, and much more grievous to some of us. We are taxed twice as much by

*Thomas Woody, "Leisure in the Light of History," *The Annals of the American Academy of Political and Social Science,* Vol. 313 (Sept., 1957), 5–6.
†Anna L. Walker, "Work for the Night is Coming," *Hymns of Praise* (Chicago: Hope Publishing Co., 1948), Hymn No. 442.
‡Richard B. Morris, *Government and Labor in Early America* (New York: Columbia University Press, 1947), 4–6.

our IDLENESS, three times as much by our PRIDE, and four times as much by our FOLLY, and from these Taxes the Commissioners cannot ease or deliver us by allowing an Abatement. However, let us hearken to good Advice, and something may be done for us. GOD HELPS THEM THAT HELP THEMSELVES, as POOR RICHARD says, in his Almanack of 1733.

It would be thought a hard Government that should tax its People one tenth Part of their TIME, to be employed in its Service. But IDLENESS taxes many of us much more, if we reckon all that is spent in absolute SLOTH or doing of NOTHING. SLOTH, LIKE RUST, CONSUMES FASTER THAN LABOUR WEARS, WHILE THE USED KEY IS ALWAYS BRIGHT, as POOR RICHARD says. But DOST THOU LOVE LIFE? THEN DO NOT SQUANDER TIME, FOR THAT'S THE STUFF LIFE IS MADE OF as POOR RICHARD says.

* * *

Me thinks I hear some of you say, MUST A MAN AFFORD HIMSELF NO LEISURE? I will tell thee, my Friend, what POOR RICHARD says, EMPLOY THY TIME WELL IF THOU MEANEST TO GAIN LEISURE; and, SINCE THOU ARE NOT SURE OF A MINUTE, THROW NOT AWAY AN HOUR. Leisure, is Time for doing something useful; . . . all which is well said by POOR RICHARD.*

The Puritan belief in the value of work persisted on into the nineteenth century and still retains great vitality. As Sebastian de Grazia has pointed out, "The latest version of the bill of rights for mankind, the UNESCO Declaration of Human Rights . . . proclaims, 'Everyone has the right to work.'"†

STATES RIGHTS AND ASSUMED RESPONSIBILITIES

At the outbreak of the Revolutionary War most of the population of the colonies was of English descent. People thought of themselves as Englishmen, not as Americans. Beyond that their loyalties and identifications were to a particular colony, rather than to the colonies as a whole. On the other hand, one of the basic reasons for the rebellion was resentment against the strong central government of Great Britain. Presumably this feeling carried over to include a distrust of any highly centralized government. Given these attitudes it is not surprising that the newly independent confederation of states would establish a government in which most power was retained by the individual states (formerly colonies). The national government under the Articles of Confederation was really a league of independent states, each one sending ambassadors or delegates to the national congress. Laws passed by that congress were not necessarily enforced by the individual states, nor was there a national executive or national court system. It seems obvious to us now that such a system could not work very well, but these early Americans had had too much strong central government to try anything else.

When it became apparent that the new government had serious deficiencies, a convention was called in 1781 to *revise* the old Articles of Confederation and this convention drafted the present constitution. The new document attempted

*Benjamin Franklin, *Father Abraham's Speech* (Boston: G. K. Hall and Co., 1963), 4–8.
†Sebastian de Grazia, *Of Time, Work, and Leisure* (New York: The Twentieth Century Fund, 1962), 47.

to strike some kind of compromise between a strong central government and a confederacy of independent states. It established a national government, but nevertheless placed considerable restrictions and prohibitions against the central power. The 10th Amendment summarized these restrictions on the national government in these oft-quoted words:

> The powers not delegated to the United States by the Constitution, nor prohibited by it to the States, are reserved to the States respectively, or to the people.

Colonial and early American attitudes on states' rights have exerted a tremendous impact on outdoor recreation policy throughout our history. In general, outdoor recreation has historically been considered as a responsibility of state, local, or private organizations and no concern of the national government. Most wildlife, for example, is considered to be the property of the state and consequently hunting and fishing are regulated by state governments. Recreation activities made possible by federal water impoundments have commonly been turned over to state or local organizations when it was practical to do so. The national parks were originally created to preserve unique natural "wonders" of national interest and not primarily for outdoor recreation. Moreover, while national parks may receive more publicity, people visit state and city parks far more often. Indeed, from a legal point of view, since the Constitution does not delegate the responsibility for outdoor recreation to the national government nor prohibits it to the states, one might conclude that the national government has no business in outdoor recreation. Using the single 10th Amendment criterion, a similar conclusion might be advanced for all conservation activities.

THE NINETEENTH CENTURY: EXPANSION AND EXPLOITATION

The nineteenth century was a period of tremendous territorial expansion. In 1802 the United States consisted of the original 13 colonies and the first public domain (which included the present states of Ohio, Illinois, Indiana, Michigan, Wisconsin, Alabama, Mississippi, Tennessee, and part of Pennsylvania and Minnesota). In 1803 the United States bought French claims to the Mississippi and its western drainage system—a purchase of nearly one million square miles —which virtually doubled the land area of the United States.

In 1819 the United States bought Florida, adding another 72,000 square miles to its area. Spain had held that territory since the days of the early explorers, but she was fearful of the growing power of the United States, and discouraged by her own unsuccessful attempts at colonization. A vast area in the Southwest (including the present states of California, Nevada, and Utah, and parts of New Mexico, Arizona, Colorado, and Wyoming) was ceded to the United States in 1848, after a successful military campaign against Mexico.

Texas had also been Mexican territory but the Americans who had settled there had successfully revolted against Mexico, and in 1836, declared Texas an independent state. Texas was then admitted into the Union in 1845, claiming lands outside its present boundaries. To satisfy these claims, the United States, in 1850, purchased an area of approximately 123,270 square miles from Texas.

The last large acquisition of territory in the contiguous United States was the addition of the present states of Washington, Oregon, and Idaho by agreement with Great Britain. Finally, the United States added the Gadsden Purchase area in southern Arizona and New Mexico and the states of Alaska and Hawaii.

The last century was not only a period of rapid territorial expansion, it was a period of rapid population growth and industrial expansion as well. In 1800 the population of the country was 5,308,000, by 1900 it had risen to 75,995,000. Part of this increase was caused by the influx of immigrants: in the period between 1820 and 1900, about 19 million immigrants were admitted to the United States. Moreover, during this period the center of population moved steadily westward. In 1800 it was 18 miles west of Baltimore, Maryland; by 1900 it had moved to Columbus, Indiana.

The nineteenth century also saw a transformation in production, and in the society generally, caused by the Industrial Revolution. We need not attempt to recapitulate here all the changes which occurred in American society as a result of the move from an agricultural-handcraft society to an industrial one. However, we should notice that territorial and population expansion, and the advent of the Industrial Revolution, as well as the concepts developed during colonial times, were factors in the rapid exploitation and waste of the nation's resources. This process has been best described by Stewart Udall:

> The Big Raid on resources began, in a sense, with mountain men and their beaver traps, and reached a series of high points in the last decades of the nineteenth century. Its first phase involved only the harm caused by primitive tools, but the second was linked to machines of the industrial revolution, which made possible large-scale harvesting of resources—and large-scale land damage.
>
> It was the intoxicating profusion of the American continent which induced a state of mind that made waste and plunder inevitable. A temperate continent, rich in soils and minerals and forests and wildlife, enticed men to think in terms of infinity rather than facts, and produced an overriding fallacy that was nearly our undoing—the Myth of Superabundance. According to the myth, our resources were inexhaustible. It was an assumption that made wise management of the land and provident husbandry superfluous.
>
> A growing nation needed wood for housing and fuel and shipbuilding, and the biggest of the Big Raids began in the woods. The virgin forests of North America were among the masterpieces of the natural world: east of the Great Plains nearly every acre was covered by trees; to the west softwood stands flourished on the slopes and in the valleys of the Rocky Mountains; and rising above the Pacific shore line, in the most productive timber zone in the world, redwood and fir stands provided a crescendo of arboreal splendor.
>
> * * *
>
> Lumbering, in its raider phase, was a strip-and-run business: the waste of wood was enormous, and when the best stands had been cut, the operator dismantled his mill and moved it farther west, letting the raped land go back into public ownership because the taxes went unpaid. In some areas sawmill ghost towns still clutter the landscape. Trees, like gold or silver, were "mined," for the landskinners wanted the quickest profits the system would allow.

It was an era, too, of human heroics, and the Paul Bunyan loggers and lumberjacks who took on and tamed the howling wilderness had a prowess that still commands our respect. Their feats of main strength, however, somehow symbolized the mindless, planless approach that ruined vast sections of our land.

* * *

Most of the raids on wildlife, like those on other resources, were carried out in a devil-take-the-hindmost spirit under the deadly assumption that the supply was unending. No matter how many bufflao were shot, there would always be more. Bemused by the Myth of Superabundance, Americans ignored the elementary laws of nature. They realized too late that the Atlantic salmon would never come leaping up the rivers again, the sky would never again be filled with passenger pigeons, and the buffalo would no longer make men pause in awe at the thunder of their passing.*

THE BEGINNINGS OF A CONSERVATION CONSCIENCE

During the 1800's a few persons became alarmed by this plunder of a continent. Thoreau pleaded for "national reserves, in which the bear, and the panther, and some even of the hunter race may still exist, and not be civilized off the face of the earth—not for idle sport or food, but for inspiration and our own true recreation."† Horace Greeley, who advised young men to "go West" was also aware of the dangers of "cut out and get out." In his words:

Strip "John Brown's Tract" of its timber, and the Hudson will, from June to October, cease to be navigable by floating palaces to Albany; while desolating floods, especially in Spring, will do immense damage from Utica down to Castleton.

* * *

I hope our children will see, though I shall not, the greater portion of Pike and Monroe Counties, with other sterile mountain districts of eastern Pennsylvania, converted into spacious deerparks of fifty to five hundred square miles each, enclosed by massive stone walls, intersected by belts of grass traversing each tiny valley (so as speedily to stop the running of any fires that might chance to be started), planted with the best timber, and held by large companies of shareholders for sporting, under proper regulations.‡

Perhaps George Perkins Marsh best understood the consequences of ruthless and unthinking destruction of natural resources. Marsh wrote:

Apart from the hostile influence of man, the organic and the inorganic world are, as I have remarked, bound together by such mutual relations and adaptations as secure, if not the absolute permanence and equilibrium of both, a long continuance of the established conditions of each at any given time and place, or at least, a very slow and gradual succession of changes in those conditions. But man is everywhere a disturbing agent. Wherever he plants his foot, the harmonies of nature are turned to discords. The proportions and accomodations which insured the stability of existing arrangements are overthrown. Indigenous vegetable and animal species are extirpated, and supplanted by others of foreign origin, spontaneous production is forbidden or restricted, and the face of the earth is either laid bare or covered with a new and reluctant growth of vegetable forms and with alien tribes of animal life.

* * *

The ravages committed by man subvert the relations and destroy the balance which nature had established between her organized and her inorganic creations, and she avenges herself

*Stewart L. Udall, *The Quiet Crisis* (New York: Avon Books, 1963), 66–80. Copyright © 1963 by Stewart L. Udall. Reprinted by permission of Holt, Rinehart and Winston, Inc.
†Henry David Thoreau, "Chesuncook," *Atlantic Monthly,* Vol. 2, No. 10 (Aug., 1858), 317.
‡Horace Greeley, *Recollections of a Busy Life* (New York: J. B. Ford and Co., 1868), 119–20.

upon the intruder, by letting loose upon her defaced provinces destructive energies hitherto kept in check by organic forces destined to be his best auxiliaries, but which he has unwisely dispersed and driven from the field of action. When the forest is gone, the great reservoir of moisture stored up in its vegetable mould is evaporated, and returns only in deluges of rain to wash away the parched dust into which that mould has been converted. The well-wooded and humid hills are turned to ridges of dry rock, which encumber the low grounds and choke the watercourses with their debris, and—except in countries favored with an equable distribution of rain through the seasons, and a moderate and regular inclination of surface—the whole earth, unless rescued by human art from the physical degradation to which it tends, becomes an assemblage of bald mountains, of barren, turfless hills, and of swampy and malarious plains. . . . The earth is fast becoming an unfit home for its noblest inhabitants, and another era of equal human crime and human improvidence, and of like duration with that through which traces of that crime and that improvidence extend, would reduce it to such a condition of impoverished productiveness, of shattered surface, of climatic excess, as to threaten the depravation, barbarism and perhaps even extinction of the species.*

THE TWENTIETH CENTURY:
CONSERVATION AND OUTDOOR RECREATION

This discussion has so far devoted little specific attention to outdoor recreation. There was, in fact, little outdoor recreation, as we think of it, until the twentieth century. Hours of work were long: the average work week in 1850 was 69.8 hours and productivity was low (33.7 cents per hour in 1950 dollars). By 1900 the work week had dropped to 60.2 hours and productivity had more than doubled to 75.5 cents per hour. During the nineteenth century most recreation was sedentary by nature, consisted of socializing activities, or was spectator-oriented. One would not expect a person who worked 70 hours per week in manual labor (at low wages) to actively engage in outdoor recreation. Even by 1900 there still appeared to be little need for positive efforts in support of outdoor recreation. As Edward Crafts has stated:

> In the setting of our forebears, outdoor recreation could not properly be considered a serious public purpose. What need was there for the Government to provide camping, picnicking, swimming, boating, hiking, hunting or fishing. To the 76 million largely rural Americans of 1900, nature provided free all the opportunities the population could ever possibly use. People camped and picnicked of necessity. They hiked to get from place to place. Many hunted and fished,—but for food, not for fun.†

Nevertheless some notable events had occurred. Yosemite Valley had been ceded to the state of California (1864) "for public use, resort and recreation." Yellowstone, the first national park, was established in 1872 as a "pleasuring ground." In 1891 a law was passed which allowed the President to establish reservations of forest lands on the public domain. Six years later the Organic Forestry Act of 1897 provided for administering the forest "reserves." Central

*George P. Marsh, *The Earth as Modified by Human Action* (New York: Charles Scribner's Sons, 1885), 33–43.
†Edward C. Crafts, "The Evolution of Outdoor Recreation Policy," *Proceedings of the National Conference on Policy Issues in Outdoor Recreation,* Ogden, Utah, 1966, 15.

Park in New York City was established in 1853 and the county park movement originated in Essex County, New Jersey, in 1895. Several state parks and state forests were established, including the Adirondack Forest Preserve in 1885 and the Palisades Interstate Park in 1895. Most of these landmark events had only an indirect effect on outdoor recreation but they provided the basic resources for later recreation use.

THE CONSERVATION DECADE, 1900–1910

Under the leadership of President Theodore Roosevelt and Gifford Pinchot, the ten years between 1900 and 1910 produced more significant conservation actions than all previous American history. As had been the case in the past, most of these actions were not directed toward outdoor recreation but helped provide the resource base for future recreation. Forests were acquired and timber was conserved; dams were built for flood control and irrigation; national parks were established to preserve natural wonders. Hunting laws and the beginning of wildlife refuges had a more direct recreation orientation but in many cases they were last ditch efforts to protect a threatened species from extinction. Probably of most relevance to outdoor recreation was the rapid increase in municipal and county parks.

Gifford Pinchot is generally acknowledged to have been the nation's most influential person in conservation activities during this period. In fact, Pinchot is credited with developing and popularizing the concept and use of the term "conservation." He also recognized the interrelatedness of natural ecosystems just as Marsh had done a half-century earlier. According to Pinchot:

> It was my great good luck that I had more to do with the work of more bureaus than any other man in Washington. This was partly because the Forest Service was dealing not only with trees but with public lands, mining, agriculture, irrigation, stream flow, soil erosion, fish, game, animal industry, and a host of other matters with which other bureaus also were concerned. The main reason, however, was that much of T. R.'s business with the natural resources bureaus was conducted through me.
>
> It was therefore the most natural thing in the world that the relations of forests, waters, lands, and minerals, each to each, should be brought strongly to my mind. But for a long time my mind stopped there.
>
>   *   *   *
>
> The forest and its relation to streams and inland navigation, to water power and flood control; to soil and its erosion; to coal and oil and other minerals; to fish and game; and many another possible use or waste of natural resources. . . . what had all these to do with Forestry? And what had Forestry to do with them?
>
> Here were not isolated and separate problems. My work had brought me into touch with all of them. But what was the basic link between them?
>
> Suddenly the idea flashed through my head that there was a unity in this complication—that the relation of one resource to another was not the end of the story. Here were no longer a lot of different, independent, and often antagonistic questions, each on its own separate little island, as we had been in the habit of thinking. In place of them, here was one single question with many parts. Seen in this new light, all these separate questions fitted into and made up the one great central problem of the use of the earth for the good of man.

To me it was a good deal like coming out of a dark tunnel. I had been seeing one spot of light ahead. Here, all of a sudden, was a whole landscape. Or it was like lifting the curtain on a great new stage.

* * *

When the use of all the natural resources for the general good is seen to be a common policy with a common purpose, the chance for the wise use of each of them becomes infinitely greater than it had ever been before.

The Conservation of natural resources is the key to the future. It is the key to the safety and prosperity of the American people, and all the people of the world, for all time to come. The very existence of our Nation, and of all the rest, depends on conserving the resources which are the foundations of its life. That is why Conservation is the greatest material question of all.*

Pinchot not only gained public acceptance for the general concept of forest conservation but he was instrumental in expanding forest reserves and creating the present United States Forest Service. He was at least partially responsible for President Roosevelt's vigorous conservation efforts, including the Governor's Conference on the Conservation of Natural Resources in 1908, the North American Conservation Conference of 1909, and the National Conservation Commission of 1908–9, which Pinchot chaired.

Theodore Roosevelt placed 148 million acres of public land under federal supervision during the years 1901–9. During his administration the Act for the Preservation of American Antiquities became law (1906), the first national wildlife refuge was established (Pelican Island, 1903) and the Reclamation Act was passed (1902).

THE NEW DEAL

The second Roosevelt exceeded even the first in pushing the conservation of natural resources. Only a few of the landmark policies of that period can be summarized here. The Tennessee Valley Authority was established in 1933 as a regional resource development agency. It was based on the concept that all the resources of a river basin are interrelated and should be developed under one unified plan for maximum effectiveness.

The original TVA Act made no specific reference to recreation. But it authorized surveys and plans "for the general purpose of fostering an orderly and proper physical, economic, and social development" of the Tennessee basin and adjoining territory. It was evident from the start that the region was well suited, in climate and scenic beauty, for outdoor recreation. The only missing element was water, and the program of reservoir construction was designed to supply that on a large scale. It became obvious that the recreation potential should be seriously considered as a part of the development program.

Even before TVA could finish setting up a headquarters organization at Knoxville, a member of its Washington staff was gathering data on the Valley's scenic and recreation resources. Soon after construction began on Norris Dam, the first TVA project, a small staff in Knoxville began studying the project plans to find ways to make the lakes available to the public.

Recreation potentials were carefully considered at all stages of reservoir construction and

*Gifford Pinchot, *Breaking New Ground* (New York: Harcourt, Brace and Co., 1947), 320–24. Copyright © 1947 by Harcourt Brace Jovanovich and reprinted with their permission.

planning. As field engineers set the stakes to mark future shorelines, recreation technicians followed them closely, seeking likely spots for parks, boat harbors, bathing beaches, and camps.

Recognition of the lakes' recreation potential resulted in a decision to acquire such lands as might be necessary to guarantee public access to the impounded waters. Acquisition policies varied from project to project but never departed from the principle of including lands for public access.*

In 1933 the Civilian Conservation Corps was established and the following year Congress finally passed the Taylor Grazing Act which provided for the regulation of the formerly "open" public domain, established a system of grazing districts, and halted the unrestricted homesteading of the vacant public lands. The act recognized the right of the public to hunt and fish on public lands, enjoined the Secretary of Interior to cooperate with state agencies engaged in conservation or propagation of wildlife, provided for wildlife representation on advisory boards, and prohibited any interference with access to the public lands.

In 1935 a Soil Conservation Service was created under the leadership of H. H. Bennett. The resulting benefits to the nation in soil and water conservation and in improved habitat for wildlife are incalculable. During this same period the Duck Stamp Act was enacted in 1934, the Historic Sites Act was passed in 1935 and the National Resources Planning Board was organized. In 1937 Congress passed the Pittman-Robertson Act which levied a tax on guns and ammunition to provide funds for state wildlife projects. That same year Franklin D. Roosevelt allocated $37 million to purchase 11 million acres of eastern forest lands under the old Weeks Act and a migratory bird treaty with Mexico was ratified. Finally in 1939 the United States Fish and Wildlife Service was established.

THE AFFLUENT SOCIETY

In the period following World War II the United States enjoyed an unparalleled period of high production and prosperity. This prosperity was accompanied by a rising demand for outdoor recreation facilities of all kinds. Outdoor recreation was officially recognized as a legitimate policy objective, whereas prior to this period, most outdoor recreation had been an incidental, and sometimes accidental, result of other "primary" objectives.

Under the Flood Control Act of 1944, the Corps of Engineers has been authorized "to construct, maintain, and operate public park and recreational facilities in reservoir areas . . ." as part of multiple-purpose projects. Thus the Corps of Engineers may have come to be the largest outdoor recreation organization in the world. The Bureau of Reclamation also included recreation as a purpose of project construction during this period and encouraged recreation

*Remarks of General Herbert D. Vogel, Chairman of the Board, Tennessee Valley Authority, at the Conference on Access to Recreational Waters, cosponsored by the Sport Fishing Institute and the Outdoor Boating Club of America, Chicago, Mar. 29, 1961.

use of previously constructed projects mainly through agreements with other governmental agencies. TVA continued, and indeed accelerated, its outdoor recreation activities and came to be the largest outdoor recreation project in the eastern United States—perhaps in the world. The National Park Service launched "Mission 66" to improve facilities in the parks, and the Forest Service carried out "Operation Outdoors" for substantially the same reasons. Both of these campaigns were massive efforts to cope with the rapidly accelerating use of parks and forests for recreation.

The Department of Agriculture (excluding the Forest Service) engaged in a wide variety of programs which had outdoor recreation as either a primary or secondary objective. Thousands of farm ponds were constructed and additional larger reservoirs were constructed under the Watershed Protection and Flood Prevention Act (1954). Various farm programs provided improved habitats for wildlife, and Secretary Freeman launched a vigorous program to encourage the recreational use of farm lands.

"Multiple Use" (including recreation) became the official policy of the Forest Service and the Bureau of Land Management in the Multiple Use Acts of 1960 and 1964 respectively. Additional national recreation areas, national seashores and lakeshores were added to the domain of the National Park Service in what Secretary Udall called the "race for inner space." Fish and game were emphasized in the Fish and Wildlife Coordination Act (1958), which provided that "wildlife conservation shall receive equal consideration and be coordinated with other features of water development programs. . . ." Drainage of wetlands was controlled through an act of 1962 which barred the Secretary of Agriculture from providing technical or financial assistance for wetland drainage on any farm if the Secretary of Interior (Bureau of Sport Fisheries and Wildlife) found that such drainage would "materially" harm wildlife preservation.

With rapid population growth and even more rapid industrial expansion polluted waters came to be the greatest single threat to fish, wildlife, and outdoor recreation generally. Municipal and industrial wastes caused rivers to become open sewers, and lakes to become cesspools, and even portions of the oceans became too filthy for recreational use. Since most outdoor recreation takes place in or near water, a succession of federal actions, accompanied by substantial appropriations, attempted to cope with the pollution problem. In general, however, the rate of pollution increase exceeded the rate of pollution abatement.

By 1958, outdoor recreation had become of sufficient importance in the United States to cause the formation of the Outdoor Recreation Resources Review Commission. This was the first substantial national effort to study the planning, use, and coordination of public recreation needs and resources. The ORRRC report recommended several policy changes, including the creation of a new Bureau of Outdoor Recreation which "would have over-all responsibility

[13]

for leadership of a nationwide effort by coordinating the various Federal programs and assisting other levels of government to meet the demands for outdoor recreation." The recommended new bureau was established in 1962.

In 1964, Congress passed the Land and Water Conservation Fund Act to provide revenues for recreational planning, land acquisition, and development. Funds were received mainly from sales of a windshield sticker which acted as an admission ticket to federal recreation properties. The act was regarded as one of the major pieces of conservation legislation of the sixties and perhaps the most important single congressional action on outdoor recreation.

In the post-war era Americans became increasingly sensitive to the "quality of their environment." Conservation efforts were substantial enough to call the 1960's the "Third Wave" of conservation in the United States; and outdoor recreation came of age. Raleigh Barlow aptly summarized the history of outdoor recreation in the United States by speaking in the manner of a sachem of an Indian tribe:

> We have walked in the way where the world is narrow. Our journey has brought us past the thicket of theory and through a bog of statistics. Now we are leaving the forest, the sky overhead is blue again. Let us gather for a moment by a fire at the edge of the forest while we puff a pipe, and you contemplate my message. I have not spoken with a forked tongue, nor thrown ashes in your eyes. My words have been those of one who talks of a dream.
>
> Many winters ago, the redman roamed across this land. He loved the forests, the prairies, and the open spaces. When the paleface came, he shared his heritage. But the paleface wanted land. He said it was destiny that the forests and meadows change to a domain of fields and work. Today we Indians are few and you have the land. But you also found the joy that comes when one lives and plays with nature. More and more, your fields look like the hunting grounds of my people. May the time you spend outdoors bring you new life and contentment. May your affections for the beauties of nature blossom and grow with the coming of each new day.*

OUTDOOR RECREATION AND THE AUTOMATED SOCIETY

Barring a national catastrophe, it seems reasonable to assume that:
   Population will continue to increase;
   Mobility will increase at an accelerating rate;
   Real incomes will continue to rise;
   Increasing longevity and earlier retirement will
      lengthen the time spent in retirement; and
   The trend toward reduced hours of work will be
      sharply accelerated by increased automation.
All of these factors will bring increased demand for outdoor recreation and most of them will result in increased leisure time for most Americans. The question of how best to use that leisure could very well be the most crucial

---

*Raleigh Barlow, "Land for Recreation," *Land Use Policy and Problems in the United States,* Howard W. Ottoson, ed. (Lincoln, Nebraska: University of Nebraska Press, 1963), 279–80.

problem of our time. We may have gotten too much too soon. The words of Aristotle, in speaking of Sparta, may be appropriate to our situation.

> So long as they were at war, therefore, their power was preserved, but when they had attained empire they fell, for of the arts of peace they knew nothing, and had never engaged in any employment higher than war.*

Will some future historian say of the United States:

> So long as they were at work, therefore, their power was preserved, but when they had attained leisure they fell, for of the arts of leisure they knew nothing, and had never engaged in any employment higher than work.†

*Aristotle, *Politics,* Book II, Ch. 9 (New York: The Modern Library, 1943), 113.
†This analogy was suggested by Sebastian de Grazia in *Of Time, Work, and Leisure* (New York: The Twentieth Century Fund, 1962).

HUNTING

In the not so distant past men lived mainly by hunting, but even when sustenance patterns changed from hunting and food-gathering to cultivation and the raising of domestic animals, hunting still provided an important supplementary source of food. As American society became more urbanized and farming more commercialized, hunting for food became increasingly rare. It has therefore come to be mainly symbolic ritual and sport, and as such it may properly be termed outdoor recreation.

In 1965, over 14 million persons paid $75 million for hunting licenses, and during that year these hunters spent over $1 billion on hunting, driving over eight billion miles and spending 186 million recreation days in that sport.

I shall not repeat here the stories of early game abundance, except to note that when white men first came to North America they found tremendous numbers of wildlife in great variety. Over the years this wildlife population was drastically reduced—and some species eliminated—by hunting and trapping or by the destruction of suitable habitats. By the time the first wave of settlers had reached a given area, market hunters and trappers had already taken most of the marketable game and what remained was hunted heavily by farmers and others. Market hunters killed 3.7 million buffalo in three years. Trainloads of smaller game were shipped to metropolitan centers, and "game hogs" killed thousands of additional animals. Throughout most of our history the prevalent attitude has been that all birds and animals, except domestic livestock, were "fair game."

As forests were removed and lands were used for cropping and grazing for domestic livestock, much of the wildlife habitat disappeared. Water pollution, drainage of wetlands, and pesticides have reduced these areas even more.

While hunters were partly responsible for the tragic loss of wildlife, it was also hunters who were mainly responsible for attempts to maintain or reestablish wildlife populations. Early attempts at control rested on state laws which restricted hunting in some manner. T. S. Palmer made a compilation of game laws in 1912.* Some of the "firsts" listed by Palmer are rather interesting: Connecticut passed the first state game law in 1677. The first closed season on deer was established by Massachusetts in 1694. Virginia enacted the first law to protect does in 1738. New York in 1788 was the first state to prohibit deer hunting with hounds. Spring shooting of migratory waterfowl was first prohibited by Rhode

*T. S. Palmer, *Chronology and Index of the More Important Events in American Game Protection: 1776–1911,* U.S. Dept. of Agriculture, Biological Survey Bulletin No. 41 (Washington, D.C.: Government Printing Office, Mar. 21, 1912).

Island in 1846. Iowa set the first game bag limit in 1878. State game wardens were first employed by New Hampshire and California in 1878. Hunting licenses were first required by Michigan and North Dakota in 1895. Palmer added, however, that most of the laws were passed after the game had been all but eliminated, or else they were so poorly enforced as to have little effect.

Most of the controversies and policy decisions on hunting have centered around three general areas: federal-state cooperation; laws and treaties regarding migratory waterfowl; and the protection of wildlife by the establishment of various kinds of refuges. Each of these areas will be considered briefly here.

FEDERAL-STATE COOPERATION IN HUNTING

Since colonial times wildlife had been considered the property of the state and thus, as we have noted, the early game laws were state laws. The principle of state ownership of wild game was finally formalized in the United States Supreme Court case of *Geer* v. *Connecticut*. However the Federal Government played a subordinate role by attempting to limit market hunting, by coordinating the activities of various agencies to protect wildlife, by levying a tax on sporting arms and ammunition with the proceeds going to state fish and game departments, by transferring surplus property to the states for wildlife conservation purposes, and by providing that hunting and fishing on military reservations be carried out in accordance with state game laws.

WATERFOWL AND WETLANDS

Over the years migratory waterfowl have provided hunting opportunities for millions of people. Originally the supply seemed inexhaustible and even after the country was settled, waterfowl continued to reproduce in substantial quantities. But because waterfowl migrate seasonally, state regulation of hunting cannot in itself be adequate. Similarly, since some waterfowl migrate into Canada and Mexico, optimum control can be accomplished only by the cooperative efforts of all three countries. As with other game, suitable habitat is as important to the preservation of waterfowl as are restrictions on hunting. Unless adequate nesting, feeding, and resting areas are provided, numbers will decline even though hunting may be sharply reduced.

In terms of outdoor recreation, waterfowl are valuable not only for hunting but also because they are a wonderful sight—there are few people who do not respond with interest when a flock of Canadian geese flies overhead.

WILDLIFE REFUGES

The National Wildlife Refuge System of the United States is easily the largest in the world. As of July 1, 1966, there were 312 separate wildlife refuges covering

[17]

about 28.5 million acres located in all but five states. In simplest terms a wildlife refuge is an area that is ordinarily closed to hunting, a sanctuary for one or more kinds of wildlife. If the refuge is intelligently selected, it will, of course, provide suitable habitat for the species to be protected. Furthermore, it should be surrounded by habitat favorable for the outflow from the refuge.

Refuges are established for two primary purposes: to preserve species in danger of extinction—the buffalo, for example; and to provide breeding grounds to help maintain or replenish game populations.

Although national parks, most state parks, some municipal parks, and some private holdings may also be regarded as wildlife refuges, this section will concentrate on wildlife refuges that have been so designated.

Wildlife refuges probably existed in some form long before recorded history. According to Aldo Leopold, the earliest known instance of food and cover control combined with hunting restrictions occurred in the Mongol Empire of Kublai Khan.* Marco Polo had written:

> Near this city is a valley frequented by great numbers of partridges and quail, for whose food the Great Khan causes millet and other grains that attract such birds to be sown along the sides of it every season, and gives strict command that no person shall reap the seed. Many keepers are also stationed there to see that the game is not taken or destroyed, as well as to spread the millet for the birds during the winter. So accustomed are they to this feeding, that when the grain is scattered and the man whistles, they immediately assemble from every quarter. The Great Khan also directs that a number of small buildings be prepared for their shelter during the night; in consequence of these attentions, he always finds abundant sport when he visits this country. Even in the winter, when on account of the severity of the cold he does not stay there, he has camel loads of the birds sent wherever his court may happen to be.†

One of the earliest records of game reservations was a "charter of the forest" granted by Canute the Dane, King of England and Denmark (1017–36). Canute's "forest" was essentially a game reserve for himself and other members of royalty. William the Conqueror and his successors continued this policy, and reserved considerable acreage for his exclusive enjoyment.

Some colonial Americans maintained private game refuges on their properties. George Washington, for example, attempted to maintain such a reservation for deer but apparently had the perennial problem of poachers. In 1787 he wrote to Archibald Johnston:

Mount Vernon, October 30, 1787.

Sir:
My fixed determination is, that no person whatever shall hunt upon my grounds or waters. To grant leave to one, and refuse another, would not only be drawing a line of discrimination which would be offensive, but would subject one to great inconvenience; for my strict, and positive orders to all my people are, if they hear a gun fired upon my Land to go immediately

*Aldo Leopold, *Game Management* (New York: Charles Scribner's Sons, 1937), 6.
†*The Book of Sir Marco Polo,* Vol. I, Ch. 60.

in pursuit of it. Permission therefore to any one would keep them either always in pursuit, or make them inattentive to my orders under the supposition of its belonging to a licensed person by which means I should be obtruded upon by others who to my cost I find had other objects in view. Besides, as I have not lost my relish for this sport when I can find time to indulge myself in it, and Gentlemen who come to the House are pleased with it, it is my wish not to have the game within my jurisdiction disturbed. For these reasons I beg you will not take my refusal amiss, because I would give the same to my brother if he lived off my land. I am, &c.*

Again, in 1799, he wrote to the Mr. Chichesters with some annoyance:

Mount Vernon, April 25, 1799.

Gentlemen:

I shall be obliged to you, or either of you, who may be in the practice of hunting, or driving Deer on my land, for desisting from that practice.

My Lands have been Posted, according to Law, many years; and never has, nor while I possess them, will be revoked. Besides this, in order to have the notification better understood by those who bordered on me, I had (as you will perceive by the enclosed copy thereof) a number of hand bills struck and put up at my Mill and other places, to prevent the plea of want of information, that such trespasses were disagreeable to me.

I have been at much expence, and was at a good deal of trouble, to procure Deer, both of the Country and English kind; and have never yet killed one for my own table, altho' they come into my yard and Gardens, while they are hunted and destroyed by others; and often driven, wounded and maimed into the river by me [sic], and have been found drifted on the shores.

I had them once in a Paddock, but during my absence the fencing was neglected, and getting out, they have run at large ever since. The old ones are now partly wild, and partly tame; their descendant are more wild, but associate with them; and seldom go beyond the limits of my own woodland. But admitting they exceed these, the English deer, more especially, are very distinguishable by the darkness of their colour, and their horns; and I should have hoped, that upon the principle of doing as one would be done by, they would not have been injured by my Neighbours.

You must be sensible, that at the stand where I receive the most injury, you can have no right to hunt; for between Mr. Chichester's fence (which is close to my line) and the tenement of the Widow Gray, there is no woodland but what belongs to Mr. Fairfax or myself; and unless that Gentleman has changed his sentiments very materially of late, he, equally with myself, is averse to having his Lands of Belvoir driven for Deer.

I should not have supposed then, had there not been strong evidence to the contrary, that any Gentleman would poach upon the grounds, and on the rights of another, contrary to Law, and to repeated admonition.

After this notice, as it respects my own Land, and request that you will desist from further injury to my Game, I persuade myself that I shall not, in future, have cause to complain; nor be under the disagreeable necessity of resorting to other means for the preservation of it. I am etc.†

Half a century later, Henry Thoreau saw a need for another kind of game reserve.

*The Writings of George Washington, Vol. 29, John C. Fitzpatrick, ed. (Washington, D.C.: Government Printing Office, 1939), 295–96.
†The Writings of George Washington, Vol. 37, John C. Fitzpatrick, ed. (Washington, D.C.: Government Printing Office, 1940), 194–95.

RECREATION

The kings of England formerly had their forests "to hold the king's game," for sport or food . . . and I think that they were impelled by a true instinct. Why should not we, who have renounced the king's authority, have our national preserves . . . in which the bear and panther, and some even of the hunter race, may still exist, and not be "civilized off the face of the earth"—our forests, not to hold the king's game merely, but to hold and preserve the king himself also, the lord of creation—not for idle sport or food, but for inspiration, and our own true recreation? Or shall we, like villains, grub them all up, poaching on our own national domains?*

As game became scarce the practice of establishing private game reserves became more widespread. Hotels and resorts purchased hunting lands, and shooting or gun clubs also acquired property which was reserved for their members. Writing in 1893, Theodore Roosevelt commented on this trend:

From its very nature, the life of the hunter is in most places evanescent; and when it has vanished there can be no real substitute in old settled countries. Shooting in a private game preserve is but a dismal parody; the manliest and healthiest features of the sport are lost with the change of conditions. We need, in the interest of the community at large, a rigid system of game laws rigidly enforced, and it is not only admissible, but one may almost say necessary, to establish, under the control of the State, great national forest reserves, which shall also be breeding grounds and nurseries for wild game; but I should much regret to see grow up in this country a system of large private game preserves, kept for the enjoyment of the very rich. One of the chief attractions of the life of the wilderness is its rugged and stalwart democracy; there every man stands for what he actually is, and can show himself to be.†

---

*Henry David Thoreau, "Chesuncook," *Atlantic Monthly,* Vol. 2, No. 10 (Aug., 1858), 317.
†Theodore Roosevelt, *The Wilderness Hunter* (New York: G. P. Putnam's Sons, 1893), 449.

LAKE MERRITT WILDLIFE SANCTUARY ACT*
March 18, 1870

The first official wildlife refuge was established by the State of California in 1870 when it set aside Lake Merritt as a wildlife sanctuary in what is now downtown Oakland. No other state followed California's example for 33 years until Indiana (1903) became the second state to establish a wildlife refuge. Pennsylvania (1905), Alabama (1907), Massachusetts (1908), Idaho (1909), and Louisiana (1911) followed.

An Act to prevent the destruction of Fish and Game in, upon and around the waters of Lake Merritt, or Peralta, in the County of Alameda.

The People of the State of California Represented in Senate and Assembly do enact as follows:

SECTION ONE. From and after the passage of this Act it shall be unlawful for any person to take, catch, kill, capture, or in any manner destroy any fish in the waters of Lake Merritt, or Peralta in the County of Alameda, except by the use of a hook and line; but it shall be unlawful to use any "set lines", "night lines", or crawls in said Lake.

SECTION TWO. And be it further enacted that from, and after the passage of this Act if shall be unlawful for any person to take, kill or destroy in any manner whatever, any grouse, any species of wild duck, crane, heron, swan, pelican, snipe or any wild animal or game of any kind or species whatever upon, in or around Lake Merritt, or Peralta in the County of Alameda, and within one hundred rods from high water mark upon the land around said Lake.

SECTION THREE. Any person violating any of the provisions of this Act shall be deemed guilty of a misdemeanor and upon conviction thereof before any Justice of the Peace of said County or Police Judge of any city within said County, shall be punished by a fine of not exceeding five hundred dollars and in default of payment of such fine shall be imprisoned in the County Jail of said County or within a city Prison within said County not more than six months nor less than one month.

SECTION FOUR. The fines collected under this Act shall be paid into the County Treasury in all cases prosecuted before a Justice of the Peace, and into the City Treasury in all cases of prosecution before a Police Judge of any City within the County.

SECTION FIVE. This Act shall take effect and be in full force on and after its passage. Approved March 18, 1870.

*Journal of the Senate (California), 18th sess. (1869–70), 421.

JOHN MORTIMER MURPHY ON
AMERICAN GAME BIRD SHOOTING*
1882

Early descriptions of waterfowl were vague and abounded in superlatives. Writers spoke of "dark clouds of ducks" and marshes "teeming" with waterfowl. John M. Murphy's comments on hunting geese are a good example of this sort of description.

The easiest method for shooting geese on the plains is to approach them gradually under cover of a horse or an ox, and open fire on them with a huge weapon, known locally, as a "scatter cannon," until they seek safer quarters. Market hunters have been known to earn as much as a hundred dollars a day by this system of wild-fowling and sometimes more, as the birds are valued at from fifty cents to a dollar each, and from ten to forty are bagged at every discharge of the western piece of ordnance. I have seen flocks which were so indifferent to the noise of firing that they would merely rise or "climb," as the professional hunters have it, a few feet in the air, and, after honking their alarm and their sense of annoyance at being disturbed, return to the ground again, and remain there until the shooting made them take to the wing once more. Some persons manage to secure large bags by digging holes in the stubble-fields and covering them with straw, and then blazing away at the geese when they come to feed. These men tie the birds which they have wounded to stakes driven in the ground, and use them as decoys to lure their congeners to destruction, for they are exceedingly clamorous callers. Dead geese, if properly grouped, are also useful decoys, but their attitudes should be as natural as possible, or they may do more harm than good.

If the ground is covered with snow, the wild-fowler either screens his "gopher hole" with a white sheet, makes a blind of the same material, and lies in ambush behind it, or else dons it as a garment and fastens a handkerchief around his hat, and then throws himself flat on the earth, until the unsuspicious birds come near enough to be shot. A person whose dress does not harmonize with the landscape in hue, rarely gets an opportunity of bagging them, unless he is concealed in a blind made of straw, in a thicket, or in a sink-box, for the goose, notwithstanding its supposed doltish intellect, is one of the most vigilant creatures that traverse the air, and is almost sure to notice any unusual color on the ground, and to give it a wide berth. This is why experienced hunters wear white clothing in winter, and drab or buff at other times of the year. Large numbers of geese are killed near air holes in the early part of winter, by making blinds of ice blocks, but this system is so much like pot-hunting that few sportsmen care for it. Where the

*John Mortimer Murphy, *American Game Bird Shooting* (New York: Orange Judd Co., 1882), 242–46, 256.

birds are not molested much, they become so tame that a man may ride to within shooting distance and bang away at them, for they seem to consider that a person on horseback or in a wagon is much less dangerous than one afoot.

Geese are generally found feeding on the plains and stubble-fields during the day, especially in wet or murky weather, but they return to the sand bars of rivers or the sea-shore, and the margins of ponds and lakes, in the evening. Many are slaughtered on their roosting grounds on moonlit nights, as they will often stand a good deal of shooting before they decide upon leaving for safer quarters. This is particularly the case if food is scarce, if they have been shot at much in the fields, or if the weather is cold and boisterous. "Fire-hunting" them is a favorite method with some persons, who prefer large bags to sport. These men build fires on the roosting grounds of the birds on dark nights, using the driest wood they can find, in order to produce as much glare as possible. When the geese see this, they rise in the air in vast clouds and honk their alarm, but, instead of fleeing, they hover over the treacherous beacons until many of them are brought down by the concealed fowlers, or the noise of the prolonged shooting scares them away. I heard of a man in Dakota who filled his wagon with birds in two hours by this method; and of another, in Minnesota, who killed three thousand in ten days; but such work is slaughter, not sport, and I refer to it simply to show how numerous the geese are in some portions of the country. Killing the birds in this manner is heavy labor, and often the cause of disease, as the men are liable to catch severe colds, or be seized with an attack of rheumatism that may cling to them for life. Sink-box shooting is also most disagreeable work, as the weather is often severe enough to almost freeze the wild-fowlers into inanimate statues, and they dare not lift hand or foot for fear of scaring the birds away. The result is, that they are sometimes so benumbed that they cannot handle their weapons, and so stiff from lying in a cramped position on a very hard bed, that they can hardly move for some time after emerging from their coffin.

Wild geese are exceedingly abundant along the Missouri River from October to December, but about the first or the middle of the latter month they begin to seek a more genial climate. Their honking may then be heard at all hours of the day and night, as they move southward in heavy V and W-shaped lines. They are, as a rule, in their winter quarters by Christmas, and from that time until the following spring the bays, lakes, and rivers of Florida, Texas, California, Arizona, New Mexico, and the contiguous regions, fairly teem with them.

* * *

The abundance of geese in the West and Southwest may be inferred from the fact that a man has been known to kill a thousand in a week with a muzzle-loading gun, and that another had to use a cart to take what he shot in two days to market. This was in Minnesota. A mean way of destroying them is practised in some portions of the Northwest. This is to soak corn in whiskey and scatter it in fields which they frequent. When they eat this they become helplessly intoxicated, and the men then go among them and knock them on the head with clubs. They often load cart after cart with them by this method, and send them to market, where they meet with a ready sale. I have known men to kill two hundred geese in a day with a muzzle-loader, by stalking them in a field under cover of a well-trained horse. These men did not bear directly down on the birds, but approached them obliquely, and very slowly, in order to lead them to suppose that no harm was intended, and when they got within shooting range they opened fire with huge weapons loaded with BB shot, and frequently bagged from ten to thirty in one round.

GEER v. CONNECTICUT*
1896

The states, like the individual colonies before them, enacted game laws on the premise that wildlife was the property and responsibility of the state in which it existed. However, many people reasoned that wild game belonged to no one and did not become property until it was captured or killed. Then, they claimed, it became the property of the captor or hunter, to be disposed of as he wished. This issue was never squarely faced and decided in the courts until the case of Geer v. Connecticut in 1896. In this landmark decision the U.S. Supreme Court ruled that the protection and regulation of wildlife was within the police power of the state. The opinion of the Court follows.

Mr. JUSTICE WHITE delivered the opinion of the court:

By the statutes of the state of Connecticut, referred to in the statement of facts, the open season for the game birds mentioned therein was from the first day of October to the first day of January. The birds which the defendant was charged with unlawfully having in his possession on the 19th of October, for the purpose of unlawful transportation beyond the state, were alleged to have been killed within the state after the first day of October. They were therefore killed during the open season. There was no charge that they had been unlawfully killed for the purpose of being transported outside of the state. The offense therefore charged was the possession of game birds for the purpose of transporting them beyond the state, which birds had been lawfully killed within the state. The court of last resort of the state held, in interpreting the statute already cited by the light afforded by previous enactments, that one of its objects was to forbid the killing of birds within the state during the open season for the purpose of transporting them beyond the state, and also additionally as a distinct offense to punish the having in possession, for the purpose of transportation beyond the state, birds lawfully killed within the state. The court found that the information did not charge the first of these offenses, and therefore that the sole offense which it covered was the latter. It then decided that the state had power to make it an offense to have in possession, for the purpose of transportation beyond the state, birds which had been lawfully killed within the state during the open season, and that the statute, in creating this offense, did not violate the interstate commerce clause of the Constitution of the United States. The correctness of this latter ruling is the question for review. In other words, the sole issue which the case presents is, Was it lawful under U.S. Const. art 1, § 8, for the state of

*161 U.S. 519 (1896).

[25]

Connecticut to allow the killing of birds within the state during a designated open season, to allow such birds, when so killed, to be used, to be sold, and to be bought for use within the state, and yet to forbid their transportation beyond the state? Or, to state it otherwise, had the state of Connecticut the power to regulate the killing of game within her borders so as to confine its use to the limits of the state and forbid its transmission outside of the state?

In considering this inquiry we of course accept the interpretation affixed to the state statute by the court of last resort of the state. The solution of the question involves a consideration of the nature of the property in game and the authority which the state had a right lawfully to exercise in relation thereto.

From the earliest traditions the right to reduce animals *ferae naturae* to possession has been subject to the control of the law-giving power.

The writer of a learned article in the Repertoire of the Journal du Palais mentions the fact that the law of Athens forbade the killing of game (5 Rep. Gen. J. P. 307), and Merlin says (4 Repertoire de Jurisprudence, 128) that "Solon, seeing that the Athenians gave themselves up to the chase to the neglect of the mechanical arts, forbade the killing of game."

Among other subdivisions, things were classified by the Roman law into public and common. The latter embraced animals *ferae naturae* which, having no owner, were considered as belonging in common to all the citizens of the state. After pointing out the foregoing subdivision, the Digest says:

"There are things which we acquire the dominion of, as by the law of nature, which the light of natural reason causes every man to see, and others we acquire by the civil law, that is to say, by methods which belong to the government. As the law of nature is more ancient, because it took birth with the human race, it is proper to speak first of the latter. 1. Thus, all the animals which can be taken upon the earth, in the sea, or in the air, that is to say, wild animals, belong to those who take them. . . . Because that which belongs to nobody is acquired by the natural law by the person who first possesses it. We do not distinguish the acquisition of these wild beasts and birds by whether one has captured them on his own property or on the property of another; but he who wishes to enter into the property of another to hunt can be readily prevented if the owner knows his purpose to do so." Digest, book 41, tit. 1, *De Adquir. Rer. Dom.*

No restriction, it would hence seem, was placed by the Roman law upon the power of the individual to reduce game of which he was the owner, in common with other citizens, to possession, although the Institutes of Justinian recognized the right of an owner of land to forbid another from killing game on his property, as indeed this right was impliedly admitted by the Digest in the passage just cited. Inst. book 2, tit. 1, § 12.

This inhibition was, however, rather a recognition of the right of ownership in land than an exercise by the state of its undoubted authority to control the taking and use of that which belonged to no one in particular, but was common to all. In the feudal as well as the ancient law of the continent of Europe, in all countries, the right to acquire animals *ferae naturae* by possession was recognized as being subject to the governmental authority and under its power, not only as a matter of regulation, but also of absolute control. Merlin, *ubi supra,* mentions the fact that although tradition indicates that from the earliest day in France every citizen had a right to reduce a part of the common property in game to ownership by possession, yet it was also true that, as early as the Salic law, that right was regulated in certain particulars. Pothier in his treatise on Property speaks as follows:

"In France, as well as in all other civilized countries of Europe, the civil law has restrained the liberty which the pure law of nature gave to every one to capture animals who, being *in naturali laxitate,* belong to no person in particular. The sovereigns have reserved to themselves and to those to whom they judge proper to transmit it the right to hunt all game, and have forbidden hunting to other persons. Some ancient doctors have doubted if sovereigns had the right to reserve hunting to themselves and to forbid it to their subjects. They contend that as God has given to man dominion over the beasts, the prince had no authority to deprive all his subjects of a right which God had given them. The natural law, say they, permitted hunting to each individual. The civil law which forbids it is contrary to the natural law and exceeds, consequently, the power of the legislator, who, being himself submitted to the natural law, can ordain nothing contrary to that law. It is easy to reply to these objections. From the fact that God has given to human kind dominion over wild beasts, it does not follow that each individual of the human race should be permitted to exercise this dominion. The civil law, it is said, cannot be contrary to the natural law. This is true as regards those things which the natural law commands or which it forbids; but the civil law can restrict that which the natural law only permits. The greater part of all civil laws are nothing but restrictions of those things which the natural law would otherwise permit. It is for this reason, although by the pure law of nature hunting was permitted to each individual, the prince had the right to reserve it in favor of certain persons and forbid it to others." Pothier, Traité du Droit de Proprieté, Nos. 27, 28.

"The right belongs to the king to hunt in his dominion; his quality of sovereign gives him the authority to take possession above all others of the things which belong to no one, such as wild animals; the lords and those who have a right to hunt hold such right but from his permission, and he can affix to this permission such restrictions and modifications as may seem to him good." No. 32.

In tracing the origin of the classification of animals *ferae naturae* as things common. Pothier moreover says:

"The first of mankind had in common all those things which God had given to the human race. This community was not a positive community of interest, like that which exists between several persons who have the ownership of a thing in which each have their particular portion. It was a community which those who have written on this subject have called a negative community, which resulted from the fact that those things which were common to all belonged no more to one than to the others, and hence no one could prevent another from taking of these common things that portion which he judged necessary in order to subserve his wants. Whilst he was using them others could not disturb him, but when he had ceased to use them, if they were not things which were consumed by the fact of use, the things immediately re-entered into the negative community, and another could use them. The human race having multiplied, men partitioned among themselves the earth and the greater part of those things which were on its surface. That which fell to each one among them commenced to belong to him in private ownership, and this process is the origin of the right of property. Some things, however, did not enter into this division, and remain therefore to this day in the condition of the ancient and negative community." No. 21.

Referring to those things which remain common, or in what he qualified as the negative community, this great writer says:

"These things are those which the jurisconsults called *res communes.* Marcien refers to several kinds—the air, the water which runs in the rivers, the sea and its shores. . . . As regards wild animals *ferae naturae,* they have remained in the ancient state of negative community."

In both the works of Merlin and Pothier, *ubi supra,* will be found a full reference to the history of the varying control exercised by the lawgiving power over the right of a citizen to acquire a qualified ownership in animals *ferae naturae* evidenced by the regulation thereof by the Salic law, already referred to, exemplified by the legislation of Charlemagne, and continuing through all vicissitudes of governmental authority. This unbroken line of law and precedent is summed up by the provisions of the Napoleon Code, which declare (arts. 714, 715): "There are things which belong to no one, and the use of which is common to all. Police regulations direct the manner in which they may be enjoyed. The faculty of hunting and fishing is also regulated by special laws." Like recognition of the fundamental principle upon which the property in game rests has led to similar history and identical results in the common law of Germany, in the law of Austria, Italy, and, indeed, it may be safely said in the law of all the countries of Europe. 1 St. Joseph Concordance, 58.

The common law of England also based property in game upon the principle of common ownership, and therefore treated it as subject to governmental authority.

Blackstone, whilst pointing out the distinction between things private and those which are common, rests the right of an individual to reduce a part of this common property to possession, and thus acquire a qualified ownership in it, on no other or different principle from that upon which the civilians based such rights. 2 Bl. Com. 1, 12.

Referring especially to the common ownership of game he says:

"But, after all, there are some few things which, notwithstanding the general introduction and continuance of property, must still unavoidably remain in common, being such wherein nothing but an usufructuary property is capable of being had; and therefore they still belong to the first occupant during the time he holds possession of them, and no longer. Such (among others) are the elements of light, air, and water, which a man may occupy by means of his windows, his gardens, his mills, and other conveniences; such also are the generality of those animals which are said to be *ferae naturae,* or of a wild and untamable disposition, which any man may seize upon or keep for his own use or pleasure." 2 Bl. Com. 14.

"A man may lastly have a qualified property in animals *ferae naturae, propter privilegium;* that is, he may have the privilege of hunting, taking, and killing them in exclusion of other persons. Here he has a transient property in these animals usually called game so long as they continue within his liberty, and he may restrain any stranger from taking them therein; but the instant they depart into another liberty, this qualified property ceases. . . . A man can have no absolute permanent property in these, as he may in the earth and land; since these are of a vague and fugitive nature, and therefore can only admit of a precarious and qualified ownership, which lasts so long as they are in actual use and occupation, but no longer." 2 Bl. Com. 394.

In stating the existence and scope of the royal prerogative, Blackstone further says:

"There still remains another species of prerogative property, founded upon a very different principle from any that have been mentioned before; the property of such animals *ferae naturae,* as are known by the denomination of game, with the right of pursuing, taking, and destroying them; which is vested in the King alone and from him derived to such of his subjects as have received the grants of a chase, a park, a free warren, or free fishery. . . . In the first place, then, we have already shown, and indeed it cannot be denied, that by the law of nature every man from the prince to the peasant has an equal right of pursuing and taking to his own use all such creatures as are *ferae naturae* and therefore the property of nobody, but liable to be seized by the first occupant, and so it was held by the imperial law as late as Justinian's time. . . . But it follows from the very end and constitution of society that this natural right, as well as many others belonging to man as an individual, may be restrained by positive laws enacted for reasons of state or for the supposed benefit of the community." 2 Bl. Com. 410.

The practice of the government of England from the earliest time to the present has put into execution the authority to control and regulate the taking of game.

Undoubtedly this attribute of government to control the taking of animals *ferae naturae,* which was thus recognized and enforced by the common law of England, was vested in the colonial governments, where not denied by their charters, or in conflict with grants of the royal prerogative. It is also certain that the power which the colonies thus possessed passed to the states with the separation from the mother country, and remains in them at the present day, in so far as its exercise may be not incompatible with, or restrained by, the rights conveyed to the Federal government by the Constitution. Kent, in his Commentaries, states the ownership of animals *ferae naturae* to be only that of a qualified property. 2 Kent, Com. 347. In most of the states laws have been passed for the protection and preservation of game. We have been referred to no case where the power to so legislate has been questioned, although the books contain cases involving controversies as to the meaning of some of the statutes. *Com.* v. *Hall,* 128 Mass. 410, 35 Am. Rep. 387; *Com.* v. *Wilkinson,* 139 Pa. 298; *People* v. *O'Neil,* 71 Mich. 325. There are also cases where the validity of some particular method of enforcement provided in some of the statutes has been drawn in question. *State* v. *Saunders,* 19 Kan. 127, 27 Am. Rep. 98; *Territory* v. *Evans,* 2 Idaho, 634, 7 L. R. A. 288.

The adjudicated cases recognizing the right of the state to control and regulate the common property in game are numerous. In *McCready* v. *Virginia,* 94 U.S. 395 [24: 248], the power of the state of Virginia to prohibit citizens of other states from planting oysters within the tide waters of that state was upheld by this court. In *Manchester* v. *Massachusetts,* 139 U.S. 240 [35: 159], the authority of the state of Massachusetts to control and regulate the catching of fish within the bays of that state was also maintained. See also *Phelps* v. *Racey,* 60 N.Y. 10, 19 Am. Rep. 140; *Magner* v. *People,* 97 Ill. 320; *American Exp. Co.* v. *People,* 133 Ill. 649, 9 L. R. A. 138; *State* v. *Northern P. Exp. Co.* 58 Minn. 403; *State* v. *Rodman,* 58 Minn. 393; *Ex parte Maier,* 103 Cal. 476; *Organ* v. *State,* 56 Ark. 270; *Allen* v. *Wyckoff,* 48 N.J. L. 93; *Roth* v. *State,* 51 Ohio St. 209; *Gentile* v. *State,* 29 Ind. 415; *State* v. *Farrell,* 23 Mo. App. 176, and cases there cited; *State* v. *Saunders* and *Territory* v. *Evans, ubi supra.*

Whilst the fundamental principles upon which the common property in game rests have undergone no change, the development of free institutions has led to the recognition of the fact that the power or control lodged in the state, resulting from this common ownership, is to be exercised like all other powers of government as a trust for the benefit of the people, and not as a prerogative for the advantage of the government as distinct from the people, or for the benefit of private individuals as distinguished from the public good. Therefore, for the purpose of exercising this power, the state, as held by this court in *Martin* v. *Waddell,* 41 U.S. 16 Pet. 410 [10: 1012], represents its people, and the ownership is that of the people in their united sovereignty. The common ownership, and its resulting responsibility in the state, are thus stated in a well considered opinion of the supreme court of California: "The wild game within a state belongs to the people in their collective sovereign capacity. It is not the subject of private ownership, except in so far as the people may elect to make it so; and they may, if they see fit, absolutely prohibit the taking of it, or any traffic and commerce in it, if deemed necessary for its protection or preservation, or the public good." *Ex parte Maier, ubi supra.*

The same view has been expressed by the supreme court of Minnesota as follows:

"We take it to be the correct doctrine in this country that the ownership of wild animals, so far as they are capable of ownership, is in the state, not as proprietor but in its sovereign capacity, as the representative and for the benefit of all its people in common." *State* v. *Rodman, supra.*

The foregoing analysis of the principles upon which alone rests the right of an individual to acquire a qualified ownership in game, and the power of the state, deduced therefrom, to control such ownership for the common benefit, clearly demonstrates the validity of the statute of the state of Connecticut here in controversy. The sole consequence of the provision forbidding the transportation of game killed within the state, beyond the state, is to confine the use of such game to those who own it, the people of that state. The proposition that the state may not forbid carrying it beyond her limits involves, therefore, the contention that a state cannot allow its own people the enjoyment of the benefits of the property belonging to them in common, without at the same time permitting the citizens of other states to participate in that which they do not own. It was said in the discussion at bar, although it be conceded that the state has an absolute right to control and regulate the killing of game as its judgment deems best in the interest of its people, inasmuch as the state has here chosen to allow the people within her borders to take game, to dispose of it, and thus cause it to become an object of state commerce, as a resulting necessity such property has become the subject of interstate commerce, hence controlled by the provisions of U.S. Const. art. 1, § 8. But the errors which this argument involves are manifest. It presupposes that where the killing of game and its sale within the state are allowed, it thereby becomes commerce in the legal meaning of that word. In view of the authority of the state to affix conditions to the killing and sale of game, predicated as is this power on the peculiar nature of such property and its common ownership by all the citizens of the state, it may well be doubted whether commerce is created by an authority given by a state to reduce game within its borders to possession, provided such game be not taken, when killed, without the jurisdiction of the state. The common ownership imports the right to keep the property, if the sovereign so chooses, always within its jurisdiction for every purpose. The qualification which forbids its removal from the state necessarily entered into and formed part of every transaction on the subject, and deprived the mere sale or exchange of these articles of that element of freedom of contract and of full ownership which is an essential attribute of commerce.

Passing, however, as we do, the decision of this question, and granting that the dealing in game killed within the state, under the provision in question, created internal state commerce, it does not follow that such internal commerce became necessarily the subject matter of interstate commerce, and therefore under the control of the Constitution of the United States. The distinction between internal and external commerce and interstate commerce is marked, and has always been recognized by this court. In *Gibbons* v. *Ogden,* 22 U.S. 9 Wheat. 194 [6: 69], *Mr. Chief Justice* Marshall said:

"It is not intended to say that these words comprehend that commerce which is completely internal, which is carried on between man and man in a state, or between different parts of the same state, and which does not extend to or affect other states. Such a power would be inconvenient and is certainly unnecessary. Comprehensive as the word 'among' is, it may very properly be restricted to that commerce which concerns more states than one. The phrase is not one which would probably have been selected to indicate the completely interior traffic of a state, because it is not an apt phrase for that purpose; and the enumeration of the particular classes of commerce to which the power was to be extended would not have been made, had the intention been to extend the power to every description. The enumeration presupposes something not enumerated; and that something, if we regard the language or the subject of the sentence, must be the exclusively internal commerce of a state. The genius and character of the whole government seem to be that its action is to be applied to all the external concerns of the nation, and to those internal concerns which affect the states generally, but not to those which are completely within a particular state, which do not affect other states, and with which it is not necessary to interfere, for the purpose of executing some of the general powers of the government. The completely internal commerce of a state, then, may be considered as reserved for the state itself."

So, again, in *The Daniel Ball* v. *United States,* 77 U.S. 10 Wall. 564 [19: 1001], this court, speaking through *Mr. Justice* Field, said:

"There is undoubtedly an internal commerce which is subject to the control of the states. The power delegated to Congress is limited to commerce 'among the several states,' with foreign nations, and with the Indian tribes. This limitation necessarily excludes from Federal control all commerce not thus designated, and of course that commerce which is carried on entirely within the limits of a state and does not extend to or affect other states."

The fact that internal commerce may be distinct from interstate commerce destroys the whole theory upon which the argument of the plaintiff in error proceeds. The power of the state to control the killing of and ownership in game being admitted, the commerce in game, which the state law permitted was necessarily only internal commerce since the restriction that it should not become the subject of external commerce went along with the grant and was a part of it.

All ownership in game killed within the state came under this condition, which the state had the lawful authority to impose, and no contracts made in relation to such property were exempt from the law of the state consenting that such contracts be made, provided only they were confined to internal and did not extend to external commerce.

The case in this respect is identical with *Kidd* v. *Pearson,* 128 U.S. 1 [32: 346], 2 Inters. Com. Rep. 232. The facts there considered were briefly as follows: The state of Iowa permitted the distillation of intoxicating liquors for "mechanical, medicinal, culinary, and sacramental purposes." The right was asserted to send out of the state intoxicating liquors made therein on the ground that, when manufactured in the state, such liquors became the subject of interstate commerce, and were thus protected by the Constitution of the United States; but this court, through *Mr. Justice* Lamar, pointed out the vice in the reasoning, which consisted in presupposing that the state had authorized the manufacture of intoxicants, thereby overlooking the exceptional purpose for which alone such manufacture was permitted. So here the argument of the plaintiff in error substantially asserts that the state statute gives an unqualified right to kill game, when in fact it is only given upon the condition that the game killed be not transported beyond the state limits. It was upon this power of the state to qualify and restrict the ownership in game killed within its limits that the court below rested its conclusion, and similar views have been expressed by the courts of last resort of several of the states. In *State* v. *Rodman,* 58 Minn. 393, the supreme court of Minnesota said:

"The preservation of such animals as are adapted to consumption as food or to any other useful purpose, is a matter of public interest, and it is within the police power of the state, as the representative of the people in their united sovereignty, to make such laws as will best preserve such game, and secure its beneficial use in the future to the citizens, and to that end it may adopt any reasonable regulations, not only as to time and manner in which such game may be taken and killed, but also imposing limitations upon the right of property in such game after it has been reduced to possession. Such limitations deprive no person of his property, because he who takes or kills game had no previous right to property in it, and when he acquires such right by reducing it to possession he does so subject to such conditions and limitations as the legislature has seen fit to impose." See also *State* v. *Northern P. Exp. Co.* 58 Minn. 403.

So also in *Magner* v. *People,* 97 Ill. 320, the supreme court of Illinois said:

"So far as we are aware, it has never been judicially denied that the government under its police powers may make regulations for the preservation of game and fish, restricting their taking and molestation to certain seasons of the year, although laws to this effect, it is believed, have been in force in many of the older states since the organization of the Federal government. . . . The ownership being in the people of the state, the repository of the sovereign authority, and no individual having any property rights to be affected, it necessarily results that the legislature, as the representative of the people of the state, may withhold or grant to individuals the right to hunt and kill game or qualify or restrict, as in the opinions of its members will best subserve the public welfare. Stated in other language, to hunt and kill game is a boon or privilege, granted either expressly or impliedly by the sovereign authority, not a right inherent in each individual, and consequently nothing is taken away from the individual when he is denied the privilege at stated seasons of hunting and killing game. It is perhaps accurate to say that the ownership of the sovereign authority is in trust for all the people of the state, and hence by implication it is the duty of the legislature to enact such laws as will best preserve the subject of the trust and secure its beneficial use in the future to the people of the state. But in any view, the question of individual enjoyment is one of public policy and not of private right."

See also *Ex parte Maier,* 103 Cal. 476; *Organ* v. *State,* 56 Ark. 270. It is indeed true that in *State* v. *Saunders,* 19 Kan. 127, 27 Am. Rep. 98, and *Territory* v. *Evans,* 2 Idaho, 634, 7 L. R. A. 288, it was held that a state law prohibiting the shipment outside of the state of game killed therein violated the interstate commerce clause of the Constitution of the United States, but the reasoning which controlled the decision of these cases is, we think, inconclusive, from the fact that it did not consider the fundamental distinction between the qualified ownership in game and the perfect nature of ownership in other property, and thus overlooked the authority of the state over property in game killed within its confines, and the consequent power of the state to follow such property into whatever hands it might pass with the conditions and restrictions deemed necessary for the public interest.

Aside from the authority of the state, derived from the common ownership of game and the trust for the benefit of its people which the state exercises in relation thereto, there is another view of the power of the state in regard to the property in game, which is equally conclusive. The right to preserve game flows from the undoubted existence in the state of a police power to that end, which may be none the less efficiently called into play because by doing so interstate commerce may be remotely and indirectly affected. *Kidd* v. *Pearson,* 128 U.S. 1 [32: 346], 2 Inters. Com. Rep. 232; *Hall* v. *De Cuir,* 95 U.S. 485 [24: 547]; *Sherlock* v. *Alling,* 93 U.S. 99, 103 [23: 819, 820]; *Gibbons* v. *Ogden,* 22 U.S. 9 Wheat. 194 [6: 69]. Indeed, the source of the police power as to game birds (like those covered by the statute here called in question) flows from the duty of the state to preserve for its people a valuable food supply. *Phelps* v. *Racey,* 60 N.Y. 10, 19 Am. Rep. 140; *Ex parte Maier, ubi supra; Magner* v. *People, ubi supra,* and cases there cited. The exercise by the state of such power therefore comes directly within the principle of *Plumley* v. *Massachusetts,* 155 U.S. 461, 473 [39: 223, 227]. The power of a state to protect by adequate police regulation its people against the adulteration of articles of food (which was in that case maintained), although in doing so commerce might be remotely affected, necessarily carries with it the existence of a like power to preserve a food supply which belongs in common to all the people of the state, which can only become the subject of ownership in a qualified way, and which can never be the object of commerce except with the consent of the state and subject to the conditions which it may deem best to impose for the public good.

Judgment affirmed.

THE LACEY ACT*
May 25, 1900

Market hunting could never be completely halted as long as there was sufficient game to make it profitable. The Lacey Act, however, drastically reduced the markets (and hence the profits) by prohibiting the interstate shipment of game taken or possessed in violation of the laws of the state from which, or to which, it was shipped.

An Act to enlarge the powers of the Department of Agriculture, prohibit the transportation by interstate commerce of game killed in violation of local laws, and for other purposes.

Be it enacted by the Senate and House of Representatives of the United States of America in Congress assembled, That the duties and powers of the Department of Agriculture are hereby enlarged so as to include the preservation, distribution, introduction, and restoration of game birds and other wild birds. The Secretary of Agriculture is hereby authorized to adopt such measures as may be necessary to carry out the purposes of this Act and to purchase such game birds and other wild birds as may be required therefor, subject, however, to the laws of the various States and Territories. The object and purpose of this Act is to aid in the restoration of such birds in those parts of the United States adapted thereto where the same have become scarce or extinct, and also to regulate the introduction of American or foreign birds or animals in localities where they have not heretofore existed.

The Secretary of Agriculture shall from time to time collect and publish useful information as to the propagation, uses, and preservation of such birds.

And the Secretary of Agriculture shall make and publish all needful rules and regulations for carrying out the purposes of this Act, and shall expend forsaid purposes such sums as Congress may appropriate therefor.

SEC. 2. That it shall be unlawful for any person or persons to import into the United States any foreign wild animal or bird except under special permit from the United States Department of Agriculture: *Provided,* That nothing in this section shall restrict the importation of natural history specimens for museums or scientific collections, or the importation of certain cage birds, such as domesticated canaries, parrots, or such other species as the Secretary of Agriculture may designate.

The importation of the mongoose, the so-called "flying foxes" or fruit bats, the English sparrow, the starling, or such other birds or animals as the Secretary

*31 *Statutes at Large,* 187.

[36]

of Agriculture may from time to time declare injurious to the interest of agriculture or horticulture is hereby prohibited, and such species upon arrival at any of the ports of the United States shall be destroyed or returned at the expense of the owner. The Secretary of the Treasury is hereby authorized to make regulations for carrying into effect the provisions of this section.

SEC. 3. That it shall be unlawful for any person or persons to deliver to any common carrier, or for any common carrier to transport from one State or Territory to another State or Territory, or from the District of Columbia or Alaska to any State or Territory, or from any State or Territory to the District of Columbia or Alaska, any foreign animals or birds the importation of which is prohibited, or the dead bodies or parts thereof of any wild animals or birds, where such animals or birds have been killed in violation of the laws of the State, Territory, or District in which the same were killed: *Provided,* That nothing herein shall prevent the transportation of any dead birds or animals killed during the season when the same may be lawfully captured, and the export of which is not prohibited by law in the State, Territory, or District in which the same are killed.

SEC. 4. That all packages containing such dead animals, birds, or parts thereof, when shipped by interstate commerce, as provided in section one of this Act, shall be plainly and clearly marked, so that the name and address of the shipper and the nature of the contents may be readily ascertained on inspection of the outside of such packages. For each evasion or violation of this Act the shipper shall, upon conviction, pay a fine of not exceeding two hundred dollars; and the consignee knowingly receiving such articles so shipped and transported in violation of this Act shall, upon conviction, pay a fine of not exceeding two hundred dollars; and the carrier knowingly carrying or transporting the same shall, upon conviction, pay a fine of not exceeding two hundred dollars.

SEC. 5. That all dead bodies, or parts thereof, of any foreign game animals, or game or song birds, the importation of which is prohibited, or the dead bodies, or parts thereof, of any wild game animals, or game or song birds transported into any State or Territory, or remaining therein for use, consumption, sale, or storage therein, shall upon arrival in such State or Territory be subject to the operation and effect of the laws of such State or Territory enacted in the exercise of its police powers, to the same extent and in the same manner as though such animals or birds had been produced in such State or Territory, and shall not be exempt therefrom by reason of being introduced therein in original packages or otherwise. This Act shall not prevent the importation, transportation, or sale of birds or bird plumage manufactured from the feathers of barnyard fowl.

Approved, May 25, 1900.

AN ACT TO ESTABLISH A NATIONAL BISON RANGE*
May 23, 1908

The first national wildlife refuge was Pelican Island off the coast of Florida. This small (5.5 acres) island was reserved by presidential order on March 14, 1903 to protect a colony of brown pelicans. During the next five years a few other small refuges were established, mainly for the protection of colony-nesting birds.

During 1908 the first two sizeable migratory waterfowl refuges were established: one at Klamath Lake and one at Malheur Lake in the State of Oregon. In the same year the first of Alaska's wildlife refuges was established and for the first time Congress authorized a big game range—the National Bison Range in Montana. The National Bison Range Act which follows also marks the first time that Congress appropriated funds for the acquisition of a wildlife refuge, and as a result 37 buffalo were released on the bison range on October 17, 1909.

NATIONAL BISON RANGE

The President is hereby directed to reserve and except from the unallotted lands now embraced within the Flathead Indian Reservation, in the State of Montana, not to exceed twelve thousand eight hundred acres of said lands, near the confluence of the Pend d'Oreille and Jocko rivers, for a permanent national bison range for the herd of bison to be presented by the American Bison Society. And there is hereby appropriated the sum of thirty thousand dollars, or so much thereof as may be necessary, to enable the Secretary of the Interior to pay the confederated tribes of the Flathead, Kootenai, and Upper Pend d'Oreille, and such other Indians and persons holding tribal relations or may rightfully belong on said Flathead Indian Reservation, the appraised value of said lands as shall be fixed and determined under the provisions of the Act of Congress approved April twenty-third, nineteen hundred and four, entitled "An Act for the survey and allotment of lands now embraced within the limits of the Flathead Indian Reservation, in the State of Montana, and the sale and disposal of all surplus lands after allotment." And the Secretary of Agriculture is hereby authorized and directed to inclose said lands with a good and substantial fence and to erect thereon the necessary sheds and buildings for the proper care and maintenance of the said bison; and there is hereby appropriated therefor the sum of ten thousand dollars or so much thereof as may be necessary; in all, forty thousand dollars.

Approved, May 23, 1908.

*35 *Statutes at Large,* 267.

THE WEEKS-McLEAN ACT*
March 4, 1913

Since colonial times it had been generally recognized that wild game was the property and responsibility of the state in which it existed, and this concept was legitimatized in 1896 by the United States Supreme Court in Geer v. *Connecticut. By 1910 the states were making substantial progress in regulating hunting— except for migratory game birds. Ducks, geese, and shorebirds hatched and matured in Canada and in the northern states and then migrated southward, passing over one state line after another. No single state could claim them and few states would impose restrictions on their own hunters when neighboring states had wide-open seasons and no bag limits. The Weeks-McLean Act sought to remedy this problem by declaring migratory game birds to be under "the custody and protection of the United States" by virtue of the power of Congress to regulate interstate commerce. Pertinent sections of the law, signed by President Taft on his last day in office, appear below.*

All wild geese, wild swans, brant, wild ducks, snipe, plover, woodcock, rail, wild pigeons, and all other migratory game and insectivorous birds which in their northern and southern migrations pass through or do not remain permanently the entire year within the borders of any State or Territory, shall hereafter be deemed to be within the custody and protection of the Government of the United States, and shall not be destroyed or taken contrary to regulations hereinafter provided therefor.

The Department of Agriculture is hereby authorized and directed to adopt suitable regulations to give effect to the previous paragraph by prescribing and fixing closed seasons, having due regard to the zones of temperature, breeding habits, and times and line of migratory flight, thereby enabling the department to select and designate suitable districts for different portions of the country, and it shall be unlawful to shoot or by any device kill or seize and capture migratory birds within the protection of this law during said closed seasons, and any person who shall violate any of the provisions or regulations of this law for the protection of migratory birds shall be guilty of a misdemeanor and shall be fined not more than $100 or imprisoned not more than ninety days, or both, in the discretion of the court.

The Department of Agriculture, after the preparation of said regulations, shall cause the same to be made public, and shall allow a period of three months in which said regulations may be examined and considered before final adoption, permitting, when deemed proper, public hearings thereon, and after final adop-

*37 *Statutes at Large,* 828.

tion shall cause the same to be engrossed and submitted to the President of the United States for approval: *Provided, however,* That nothing herein contained shall be deemed to affect or interfere with the local laws of the States and Territories for the protection of nonmigratory game or other birds resident and breeding within their borders, nor to prevent the States and Territories from enacting laws and regulations to promote and render efficient the regulations of the Department of Agriculture provided under this statute.

There is hereby appropriated, out of any moneys in the Treasury not otherwise appropriated, for the purpose of carrying out these provisions, the sum of $10,000.

THE MIGRATORY BIRD TREATY ACT
August 16, 1916* & July 3, 1918†

The Weeks-McLean law was of questionable constitutionality because it rested on the power of Congress to regulate interstate commerce. While birds themselves clearly moved across state lines, the hunting of such birds would not appear to constitute interstate commerce. At any rate the Weeks-McLean law was ignored by some states, and two federal district courts declared it to be unconstitutional; it seems likely that the Supreme Court would have concurred if a case had risen to that level. In the meantime, however, resolutions had been introduced in the Senate authorizing the President to negotiate a treaty with Great Britain on migratory birds. The treaty, signed in 1916, and the resulting enabling act of 1918, follow.

Convention between the United States and Great Britain for the protection of migratory birds. Signed at Washington, August 16, 1916; ratification advised by the Senate, August 29, 1916; ratified by the President, September 1, 1916; ratified by Great Britain, October 20, 1916; ratifications exchanged at Washington, December 7, 1916; proclaimed, December 8, 1916.

BY THE PRESIDENT OF THE UNITED STATES OF AMERICA
A PROCLAMATION

Whereas a Convention between the United States of America and the United Kingdom of Great Britain and Ireland for the protection of migratory birds in the United States and Canada was concluded and signed by their respective Plenipotentiaries at Washington, on the sixteenth day of August, one thousand nine hundred and sixteen, the original of which Convention is word for word as follows:

Whereas, Many species of birds in the course of their annual migrations traverse certain parts of the United States and the Dominion of Canada; and

Whereas, Many of these species are of great value as a source of food or in destroying insects which are injurious to forests and forage plants on the public domain, as well as to agricultural crops, in both the United States and Canada, but are nevertheless in danger of extermination through lack of adequate protection during the nesting season or while on their way to and from their breeding grounds;

The United States of America and His Majesty the King of the United King-

---

*39 *Statutes at Large,* Part 2, 1702.
†40 *Statutes at Large,* 755.

dom of Great Britain and Ireland and of the British Dominions beyond the Seas, Emperor of India, being desirous of saving from indiscriminate slaughter and of insuring the preservation of such migratory birds as are either useful to man or are harmless, have resolved to adopt some uniform system of protection which shall effectively accomplish such objects and to the end of concluding a convention for this purpose have appointed as their respective Plenipotentiaries:

The President of the United States of America, Robert Lansing, Secretary of State of the United States; and

His Britannic Majesty, the Right Honorable Sir Cecil Arthur Spring Rice, G.C.V.O., K.C.M.G., etc., His Majesty's Ambassador Extraordinary and Plenipotentiary at Washington;

Who, after having communicated to each other their respecitve full powers which were found to be in due and proper form, have agreed to and adopted the following articles:

ARTICLE I

The High Contracting Powers declare that the migratory birds included in the terms of this Convention shall be as follows:

1. Migratory Game Birds:

(a) Anatidae or waterfowl, including brant, wild ducks, geese, and swans.

(b) Gruidae or cranes, including little brown, sandhill, and whooping cranes.

(c) Rallidae or rails, including coots, gallinules and sora and other rails.

(d) Limicolae or shorebirds, including avocets, curlew, dowitchers, godwits, knots, oyster catchers, phalaropes, plovers, sandpipers, snipe, stilts, surf birds, turnstones, willet, woodcock and yellowlegs.

(e) Columbidae or pigeons, including doves and wild pigeons.

2. Migratory Insectivorous Birds: Bobolinks, catbirds, chickadees, cuckoos, flickers, flycatchers, grosbeaks, humming birds, kinglets, martins, meadowlarks, nighthawks or bull bats, nut-hatches, orioles, robins, shrikes, swallows, swifts, tanagers, titmice, thrushes, vireos, warblers, wax-wings, whippoorwills, woodpeckers and wrens, and all other perching birds which feed entirely or chiefly on insects.

3. Other Migratory Nongame Birds: Auks, auklets, bitterns, fulmars, gannets, grebes, guillemots, gulls, herons, jaegers, loons, murres, petrels, puffins, shearwaters, and terns.

ARTICLE II

The High Contracting Powers agree that, as an effective means of preserving migratory birds there shall be established the following close seasons during which no hunting shall be done except for scientific or propagating purposes under permits issued by proper authorities.

1. The close season on migratory game birds shall be between March 10 and

September 1, except that the close season on the Limicolae or shorebirds in the Maritime Provinces of Canada and in those States of the United States bordering on the Atlantic Ocean which are situated wholly or in part north of Chesapeake Bay shall be between February 1 and August 15, and that Indians may take at any time scoters for food but not for sale. The season for hunting shall be further restricted to such period not exceeding three and one-half months as the High Contracting Powers may severally deem appropriate and define by law or regulation.

2. The close season on migratory insectivorous birds shall continue throughout the year.

3. The close season on other migratory nongame birds shall continue throughout the year, except that Eskimos and Indians may take at any season auks, auklets, guillemots, murres and puffins, and their eggs, for food and their skins for clothing, but the birds and eggs so taken shall not be sold or offered for sale.

ARTICLE III

The High Contracting Powers agree that during the period of ten years next following the going into effect of this Convention, there shall be a continuous close season on the following migratory game birds, to wit: —

Band-tailed pigeons, little brown, sandhill and whooping cranes, swans, curlew and all shorebirds (except the black-breasted and golden plover, Wilson or jack snipe, woodcock, and the greater and lesser yellowlegs); provided that during such ten years the close seasons on cranes, swans and curlew in the Province of British Columbia shall be made by the proper authorities of that Province within the general dates and limitations elsewhere prescribed in this Convention for the respective groups to which these birds belong.

ARTICLE IV

The High Contracting Powers agree that special protection shall be given the wood duck and the eider duck either (1) by a close season extending over a period of at least five years, or (2) by the establishment of refuges, or (3) by such other regulations as may be deemed appropriate.

ARTICLE V

The taking of nests or eggs of migratory game or insectivorous or nongame birds shall be prohibited, except for scientific or propagating purposes under such laws or regulations as the High Contracting Powers may severally deem appropriate.

ARTICLE VI

The High Contracting Powers agree that the shipment or export of migratory birds or their eggs from any State or Province, during the continuance of the close season in such State or Province, shall be prohibited except for scientific or propagating purposes, and the international traffic in any birds or eggs at such time captured, killed, taken, or shipped at any time contrary to the laws of the State or Province in which the same were captured, killed, taken, or shipped shall be likewise prohibited. Every package containing migratory birds or any parts thereof or any eggs of migratory birds transported, or offered for transportation from the United States into the Dominion of Canada or from the Dominion of Canada into the United States, shall have the name and address of the shipper and an accurate statement of the contents clearly marked on the outside of such package.

ARTICLE VII

Permits to kill any of the above-named birds which, under extraordinary conditions, may become seriously injurious to the agricultural or other interests in any particular community, may be issued by the proper authorities of the High Contracting Powers under suitable regulations prescribed therefor by them respectively, but such permits shall lapse, or may be cancelled, at any time when, in the opinion of said authorities, the particular exigency has passed, and no birds killed under this article shall be shipped, sold or offered for sale.

ARTICLE VIII

The High Contracting Powers agree themselves to take, or propose to their respective appropriate law-making bodies, the necessary measures for insuring the execution of the present Convention.

ARTICLE IX

The present Convention shall be ratified by the President of the United States of America, by and with the advice and consent of the Senate thereof, and by His Britannic Majesty. The ratifications shall be exchanged at Washington as soon as possible and the Convention shall take effect on the date of the exchange of the ratifications. It shall remain in force for fifteen years and in the event of neither of the High Contracting Powers having given notification, twelve months before the expiration of said period of fifteen years, of its intention of terminating its operation, the Convention shall continue to remain in force for one year and so on from year to year.

In faith whereof, the respective Plenipotentiaries have signed the present Convention in duplicate and have hereunto affixed their seals.

Done at Washington this sixteenth day of August, one thousand nine hundred and sixteen.

[SEAL.]   *Robert Lansing*
[SEAL.]   *Cecil Spring Rice*

And whereas the said Convention has been duly ratified on both parts, and the ratifications of the two Governments were exchanged in the City of Washington, on the seventh day of December, one thousand nine hundred and sixteen;

Now, therefore, be it known that I, Woodrow Wilson, President of the United States of America, have caused the said Convention to be made public, to the end that the same and every article and clause thereof may be observed and fulfilled with good faith by the United States and the citizens thereof.

In testimony whereof, I have hereunto set my hand and caused the seal of the United States to be affixed.

Done at the City of Washington this eighth day of December in the year of our Lord one thousand nine hundred and sixteen, and of the Independence of the United States of America the one hundred and forty-first.

[SEAL.]

Woodrow Wilson

By the President:
Robert Lansing
Secretary of State

An Act to give effect to the convention between the United States and Great Britain for the protection of migratory birds concluded at Washington, August sixteenth, nineteen hundred and sixteen, and for other purposes.

Be it enacted by the Senate and House of Representatives of the United States of America in Congress assembled, That this Act shall be known by the short title of the "Migratory Bird Treaty Act."

SEC. 2. That unless and except as permitted by regulations made as hereinafter provided, it shall be unlawful to hunt, take, capture, kill, attempt to take, capture or kill, possess, offer for sale, sell, offer to purchase, purchase, deliver for shipment, ship, cause to be shipped, deliver for transportation, transport, cause to be transported, carry or cause to be carried by any means whatever, receive for shipment, transportation or carriage, or export, at any time or in any manner, any migratory bird, included in the terms of the convention between the United States and Great Britain for the protection of migratory birds concluded August sixteenth, nineteen hundred and sixteen, or any part, nest or egg of any such bird.

SEC. 3. That subject to the provisions and in order to carry out the purposes of the convention, the Secretary of Agriculture is authorized and directed, from time to time, having due regard to the zones of temperature and to the distribution, abundance, economic value, breeding habits, and times and lines of migratory flight of such birds, to determine when, to what extent, if at all, and by what means, it is compatible with the terms of the convention to allow hunting, taking, capture, killing, possession, sale, purchase, shipment, transportation, carriage, or export of any such bird, or any part, nest, or egg thereof, and to adopt suitable regulations permitting and governing the same, in accordance with such determinations, which regulations shall become effective when approved by the President.

SEC. 4. That it shall be unlawful to ship, transport, or carry, by any means whatever, from one State, Territory, or District to or through another State, Territory, or District, or to or through a foreign country, any bird, or any part, nest, or egg thereof, captured, killed, taken, shipped, transported, or carried at any time contrary to the laws of the State, Territory, or District in which it was captured, killed, or taken, or from which it was shipped, transported, or carried. It shall be unlawful to import any bird, or any part, nest, or egg thereof, captured, killed, taken, shipped, transported, or carried contrary to the laws of any Province of the Dominion of Canada in which the same was captured, killed, or taken, or from which it was shipped, transported, or carried.

SEC. 5. That any employee of the Department of Agriculture authorized by the Secretary of Agriculture to enforce the provisions of this Act shall have power, without warrant, to arrest any person committing a violation of this Act in his presence or view and to take such person immediately for examination or trial before an officer or court of competent jurisdiction; shall have power to execute any warrant or other process issued by an officer or court of competent jurisdiction for the enforcement of the provisions of this Act; and shall have authority, with a search warrant, to search any place. The several judges of the courts established under the laws of the United States, and United States commissioners may, within their respective jurisdictions, upon proper oath or affirmation showing probable cause, issue warrants in all such cases. All birds, or parts, nests, or eggs thereof, captured, killed, taken, shipped, transported, carried, or possessed contrary to the provisions of this Act or of any regulations made pursuant thereto, when found, be seized by any such employee, or by any marshal or deputy marshal, and, upon conviction of the offender or upon judgment of a court of the United States that the same were captured, killed, taken, shipped, transported, carried, or possessed contrary to the provisions of this Act or of any regulation made pursuant thereto, shall be forfeited to the United States and disposed of as directed by the court having jurisdiction.

SEC. 6. That any person, association, partnership, or corporation who shall violate any of the provisions of said convention or of this Act, or who shall violate or fail to comply with any regulation made pursuant to this Act, shall be deemed guilty of a misdemeanor and upon conviction thereof shall be fined not more than $500 or be imprisoned not more than six months, or both.

SEC. 7. That nothing in this Act shall be construed to prevent the several States and Territories from making or enforcing laws or regulations not inconsistent with the provisions of said convention or of this Act, or from making or enforcing laws or regulations which shall give further protection to migratory birds, their nests, and eggs, if such laws or regulations do not extend the open seasons for such birds beyond the dates approved by the President in accordance with section three of this Act.

SEC. 8. That until the adoption and approval, pursuant to section three of this Act, of regulations dealing with migratory birds and their nests and eggs, such migratory birds and their nests and eggs as are intended and used exclusively for scientific or propagating purposes may be taken, captured, killed, possessed, sold, purchased, shipped, and transported for such scientific or propagating purposes if and to the extent not in conflict with the laws of the State, Territory, or District in which they are taken, captured, killed, possessed, sold, or purchased, or in or from which they are shipped or transported if the packages containing the dead bodies or the nests or eggs of such birds when shipped and transported shall be marked on the outside thereof so as accurately and clearly to show the name and address of the shipper and the contents of the package.

SEC. 9. That the unexpended balances of any sums appropriated by the agricultrual appropriation Acts for the fiscal years nineteen hundred and seventeen and nineteen hundred and eighteen, for enforcing the provisions of the Act approved March fourth, nineteen hundred and thirteen, relating to the protection of migratory game and insectivorous birds, are hereby reappropriated and made available until expended for the expenses of carrying into effect the provisions of this Act and regulations made pursuant thereto, including the payment of such rent, and the employment of such persons and means, as the Secretary of Agriculture may deem necessary, in the District of Columbia and elsewhere, cooperation with local authorities in the protection of migratory birds, and necessary investigations connected therewith: *Provided,* That no person who is subject to the draft for service in the Army or Navy shall be exempted or excused from such service by reason of his employment under this Act.

SEC. 10. That if any clause, sentence, paragraph, or part of this Act shall, for any reason, be adjudged by any court of competent jurisdiction to be invalid, such judgment shall not affect, impair, or invalidate the remainder thereof, but shall be confined in its operation to the clause, sentence, paragraph, or part thereof directly involved in the controversy in which such judgment shall have been rendered.

SEC. 11. That all Acts or parts of Acts inconsistent with the provisions of this Act are hereby repealed.

SEC. 12. Nothing in this Act shall be construed to prevent the breeding of migratory game birds on farms and preserves and the sale of birds so bred under proper regulation for the purpose of increasing the food supply.

SEC. 13. That this Act shall become effective immediately upon its passage and approval.

Approved, July 3, 1918.

MISSOURI v. HOLLAND*
1919

The Migratory Bird Treaty Act of 1918 contained essentially the same provisions as the Weeks-McLean Act but it rested on an international treaty rather than the disputed power of Congress to regulate interstate commerce. Shortly after the later act was passed the State of Missouri brought suit against Ray P. Holland, a United States game warden, to prevent him from attempting to enforce the Migratory Bird Treaty Act and the Agriculture Secretary's regulation concerning that act. The State of Missouri based its case principally on contentions that the individual states had sole power to legislate on wild game and that, according to the Tenth Amendment the powers not delegated to the United States or prohibited to the states "are reserved to the States respectively, or to the people." Needless to say, the Constitution does not mention migratory birds and therefore, by this reasoning, such power is reserved to the states. By denying the state's claim, Missouri v. Holland had implications far beyond the question of power to legislate on migratory birds. The opinion of the court is reproduced here.

Mr. JUSTICE HOLMES delivered the opinion of the court:

This is a bill in equity, brought by the state of Missouri to prevent a game warden of the United States from attempting to enforce the Migratory Bird Treaty Act of July 3, 1918, chap. 128, 40 Stat. at L. 755, Comp. Stat. § 8837a, Fed. Stat. Anno. Supp. 1918, p. 196, and the regulations made by the Secretary of Agriculture in pursuance of the same. The ground of the bill is that the statute is an unconstitutional interference with the rights reserved to the states by the 10th Amendment, and that the acts of the defendant, done and threatened under that authority, invade the sovereign right of the state and contravene its will manifested in statutes. The state also alleges a pecuniary interest, as owner of the wild birds within its borders and otherwise, admitted by the government to be sufficient, but it is enough that the bill is a reasonable and proper means to assert the alleged quasi-sovereign rights of a state. Kansas v. Colorado, 185 U.S. 125, 142, 46 L. ed. 838, 844, 22 Sup. Ct. Rep. 552; Georgia v. Tennesse Copper Co. 206 U.S. 230, 237, 51 L. ed. 1038, 1044, 27 Sup. Ct. Rep. 618, 11 Ann. Cas. 488; Marshall Dental Mfg. Co. v. Iowa, 226 U.S. 460, 462, 57 L. ed. 300, 302, 33 Sup. Ct. Rep. 168. A motion to dismiss was sustained by the district court on the ground that the act of Congress is constitutional. 258 Fed. 479. United States v. Thompson, 258 Fed. 257; United States v. Rockefeller, 260 Fed. 346. The state appeals.

*252 U.S. 416 (1919).

On December 8, 1916, a treaty between the United States and Great Britain was proclaimed by the President. It recited that many species of birds in their annual migrations traversed many parts of the United States and of Canada, that they were of great value as a source of food and in destroying insects injurious to vegetation, but were in danger of extermination through lack of adequate protection. It therefore provided for specified close seasons and protection in other forms, and agreed that the two powers would take or propose to their lawmaking bodies the necessary measures for carrying the treaty out. 39 Stat. at L. 1702. The above-mentioned Act of July 3, 1918, entitled, "An Act to Give Effect to the Convention," prohibited the killing, capturing, or selling any of the migratory birds included in the terms of the treaty except as permitted by regulations compatible with those terms, to be made by the Secretary of Agriculture. Regulations were proclaimed on July 31, and October 25, 1918. 40 Stat. at L. 1812, 1863. It is unnecessary to go into any details, because, as we have said, the question raised is the general one whether the treaty and statute are void as an interference with the rights reserved to the states.

To answer this question it is not enough to refer to the 10th Amendment, reserving the powers not delegated to the United States, because by article 2, § 2, the power to make treaties is delegated expressly, and by article 6, treaties made under the authority of the United States, along with the Constitution and laws of the United States, made in pursuance thereof, are declared the supreme law of the land. If the treaty is valid, there can be no dispute about the validity of the statute under article 1, § 8, as a necessary and proper means to execute the powers of the government. The language of the Constitution as to the supremacy of treaties being general, the question before us is narrowed to an inquiry into the ground upon which the present supposed exception is placed.

It is said that a treaty cannot be valid if it infringes the Constitution; that there are limits, therefore, to the treaty-making power; and that one such limit is that what an act of Congress could not do unaided, in derogation of the powers reserved to the states, a treaty cannot do. An earlier act of Congress that attempted by itself, and not in pursuance of a treaty, to regulate the killing of migratory birds within the states, had been held bad in the district court. United States v. Shauver, 214 Fed. 154; United States v. McCullagh, 221 Fed. 288. Those decisions were supported by arguments that migratory birds were owned by the states in their sovereign capacity, for the benefit of their people, and that under cases like Geer v. Connecticut, 161 U.S. 519, 40 L. ed. 793, 16 Sup. Ct. Rep. 600, this control was one that Congress had no power to displace. The same argument is supposed to apply now with equal force.

Whether the two cases cited were decided rightly or not, they cannot be accepted as a test of the treaty power. Acts of Congress are the supreme law of the land only when made in pursuance of the Constitution, while treaties are declared to be so when made under the authority of the United States. It is open to question whether the authority of the United States means more than the formal acts prescribed to make the convention. We do not mean to imply that there are no qualifications to the treaty-making power; but they must be ascertained in a different way. It is obvious that there may be matters of the sharpest exigency for the national well-being that an act of Congress could not deal with, but that a treaty followed by such an act could, and it is not lightly to be assumed that, in matters requiring national action, "a power which must belong to and somewhere reside in every civilized government" is not to be found. Andrews v. Andrews, 188 U.S. 14, 33, 47 L. ed. 366, 370, 23 Sup. Ct. Rep. 237. What was said in that case with regard to the powers of the states applies with equal force to the powers of the nation in cases where the states individually are incompetent to act. We are not yet discussing the particular case before us, but only are considering the validity of the test proposed. With regard to that, we may add that when we are dealing with words that also are a constituent act, like the Constitution of the United States, we must realize that they have called into life a being the development of which could not have been foreseen completely by the most gifted of its begetters. It was enough for them to realize or to hope that they had created an organism; it has taken a century and has cost their successors much sweat and blood to prove that they created a nation. The case before us must be considered in the light of our whole experience, and not merely in that of what was said a hundred years ago. The treaty in question does not contravene any prohibitory words to be found in the Constitution. The only question is whether it is forbidden by some invisible radiation from the general terms of the 10th Amendment. We must consider what this country has become in deciding what that amendment has reserved.

The state, as we have intimated, founds its claim of exclusive authority upon an assertion of title to migratory birds,—an assertion that is embodied in statute. No doubt it is true that, as between a state and its inhabitants, the state may regulate the killing and sale of such birds, but it does not follow that its authority is exclusive of paramount powers. To put the claim of the state upon title is to lean upon a slender reed. Wild birds are not in the possession of anyone; and possession is the beginning of ownership. The whole foundation of the state's rights is the presence within their jurisdiction of birds that yesterday had not arrived, tomorrow may be in another state, and in a week a thousand miles away. If we are to be accurate, we cannot put the case of the state upon higher ground than that the treaty deals with creatures that for the moment are within the state borders, that it must be carried out by officers of the United States within the same territory, and that, but for the treaty, the state would be free to regulate this subject itself.

As most of the laws of the United States are carried out within the states, and as many of them deal with matters which, in the silence of such laws, the state might regulate, such general grounds are not enough to support Missouri's claim.

Valid treaties, of course, "are as binding within the territorial limits of the states as they are effective throughout the dominion of the United States." Baldwin v. Franks, 120 U.S. 678, 683, 30 L. ed. 766, 767, 7 Sup. Ct. Rep. 656, 763. No doubt the great body of private relations usually falls within the control of the state, but a treaty may override its power. We do not have to invoke the later developments of constitutional law for this proposition; it was recognized as early as Hopkirk v. Bell, 3 Cranch, 454, 2 L. ed. 497, with regard to statutes of limitation, and even earlier, as to confiscation, in Ware v. Hylton, 3 Dall. 199, 1 L. ed. 568. It was assumed by Chief Justice Marshall with regard to the escheat of land to the state in Chirac v. Chirac, 2 Wheat. 259, 275, 4 L. ed. 234, 238; Hauenstein v. Lynham, 100 U.S. 483, 25 L. ed. 628; Geofroy v. Riggs, 133 U.S. 258, 33 L. ed. 642, 10 Sup. Ct. Rep. 295; Blythe v. Hinckley, 180 U.S. 333, 340, 45 L. ed. 557, 561, 21 Sup. Ct. Rep. 390. So, as to a limited jurisdiction of foreign consuls within a state. Wildenhus's Case (Mali v. Keeper of Common Jail) 120 U.S. 1, 30 L. ed. 565, 7 Sup. Ct. Rep. 383. See Re Ross, 140 U.S. 453, 35 L. ed. 581, 11 Sup. Ct. Rep. 897. Further illustration seems unnecessary, and it only remains to consider the application of established rules to the present case.

Here a national interest of very nearly the first magnitude is involved. It can be protected only by national action in concert with that of another power. The subject-matter is only transitorily within the state, and has no permanent habitat therein. But for the treaty and the statute, there soon might be no birds for any powers to deal with. We see nothing in the Constitution that compels the government to sit by while a food supply is cut off and the protectors of our forests and of our crops are destroyed. It is not sufficient to rely upon the states. The reliance is vain, and were it otherwise, the question is whether the United States is forbidden to act. We are of opinion that the treaty and statute must be upheld. Cary v. South Dakota, 250 U.S. 118, 63 L. ed. 886, 39 Sup. Ct. Rep. 403.

Decree affirmed.

Mr. JUSTICE VAN DEVANTER and Mr. JUSTICE PITNEY dissent.

AN ACT TO ESTABLISH THE UPPER MISSISSIPPI RIVER WILDLIFE AND FISH REFUGE*
June 7, 1924

Prior to 1924 wildlife refuges had been created mainly from public lands, although an act of 1916 (39 Stat., 446, 476) authorized the President to establish refuges on forest lands purchased under terms of the Weeks Act of 1911. However, such lands were presumably not bought for the primary purpose of founding refuges. The first act of Congress to appropriate substantial funds for the purchase of a wildlife reservation from private owners was the Upper Mississippi River Wildlife and Fish Refuge Act of 1924. This legislation authorized the appropriation of $1.5 million for the purchase of bottom lands along the Upper Mississippi River, and thus helped to preserve the core of the Upper Mississippi flyway for migratory waterfowl.

Be it enacted by the Senate and House of Representatives of the United States of America in Congress assembled, That this Act may be cited as "The Upper Mississippi River Wild Life and Fish Refuge Act."

SEC. 2. The Secretary of Agriculture is authorized and directed to acquire by purchase, gift, or lease, such areas of land, or of land and water, situated between Rock Island, Illinois, and Wabasha, Minnesota, on either side of or upon islands in the Mississippi River which are subject to overflow by such river and which are not used for agricultural purposes, as he determines suitable for the purposes of this Act.

SEC. 3. Any such area, when acquired in accordance with the provisions of this Act, shall become a part of the Upper Mississippi River Wild Life and Fish Refuge (hereinafter in this Act referred to as the "refuge"). The refuge shall be established and maintained (a) as a refuge and breeding place for migratory birds included in the terms of the convention between the United States and Great Britain for the protection of migratory birds, concluded August 16, 1916, and (b) to such extent as the Secretary of Agriculture may by regulations prescribe, as a refuge and breeding place for other wild birds, game animals, fur-bearing animals, and for the conservation of wild flowers and aquatic plants, and (c) to such extent as the Secretary of Commerce may by regulations precribe as a refuge and breeding place for fish and other aquatic animal life.

SEC. 4. (a) No such area shall be acquired by the Secretary of Agriculture until the legislature of each State in which is situated any part of the areas to be acquired under this Act has consented to the acquisition of such part by the United States for the purposes of this Act, and, except in the case of a lease, no payment

*43 *Statutes at Large,* 650.

shall be made by the United States for any such area until title thereto is satisfactory to the Attorney General and is vested in the United States.

(b) The existence of a right of way, easement, or other reservation or exception in respect of such area shall not be a bar to its acquisition (1) if the Secretary of Agriculture determines that any such reservation or exception will in no manner interfere with the use of the area for the purposes of this Act, or (2) if in the deed or other conveyance it is stipulated that any reservation or exception in respect of such area, in favor of the person from whom the United States receives title, shall be subject to regulations prescribed under authority of this Act.

SEC. 5. Except where it is specifically provided otherwise, the Secretary of Agriculture and the Secretary of Commerce shall jointly prescribe such regulations, exercise such functions, and perform such duties as may be necessary to carry out the purposes of this Act.

SEC. 6. No person shall, except in accordance with regulations prescribed by the Secretary of Agriculture in respect of wild birds, game animals, fur-bearing animals, wild flowers, and aquatic plants, or by the Secretary of Commerce in respect of fish and other aquatic-animal life—

(a) Enter the refuge for any purpose; or

(b) Disturb, injure, kill, or remove, or attempt to disturb, injure, kill, or remove any wild bird, game animal, fur-bearing animal, fish or other aquatic-animal life on the refuge; or

(c) Remove from the refuge, or injure or destroy thereon any flower, plant, tree, or other natural growth, or the nest or egg of any wild bird; or

(d) Injure or destroy any notice, sign board, fence, building, or other property of the United States thereon.

SEC. 7. Commercial fishing may be conducted in the waters of this refuge under regulation by the Secretary of Commerce.

SEC. 8. (a) Any employee of the Department of Agriculture authorized by the Secretary of Agriculture to enforce the provisions of this Act, and any employee of the Department of Commerce so authorized by the Secretary of Commerce (1) shall have power, without warrant, to arrest any person committing in the presence of such employee a violation of this Act or of any regulation made pursuant to this Act, and to take such person immediately for examination or trial before an officer or court of competent jurisdiction, (2) shall have power to execute any warrant or other process issued by an officer or court of competent jurisdiction to enforce the provisions of this Act or regulations made pursuant thereto, and (3) shall have authority, with a search warrant issued by an officer or court of competent jurisdiction to make a search in accordance with the terms of such warrant. Any judge of a court established under the laws of the United States, or any United States commissioner may, within his respective jurisdiction, upon proper oath or affirmation showing probable cause, issue warrants in all such cases.

(b) All birds, animals, fish, or parts thereof captured, injured, or killed, and all flowers, plants, trees, and other natural growths, and nests and eggs of birds removed, and all implements or paraphernalia, including guns, fishing equipment, and boats used or attempted to be used contrary to the provisions of this Act or any regulations made pursuant thereto, shall, when found by such employee or by any marshal or deputy marshal, be summarily seized by him and placed in the custody of such persons as the Secretary of Agriculture and the Secretary of Commerce may jointly by regulation prescribe.

(c) A report of the seizure shall be made to the United States attorney for the judicial district in which the seizure is made, for forfeiture either (1) upon conviction of the offender under section 11, or (2) by proceedings by libel in rem. Such libel proceedings shall conform as near as may be to civil suits in admiralty, except that either party may demand trial by jury upon any issue of fact when the value in controversy exceeds $20. In case of a jury trial the verdict of the jury shall have the same effect as the finding of the court upon the facts. Libel proceedings shall be at the suit and in the name of the United States. If such forfeiture proceedings are not instituted within a reasonable time, the United States attorney shall give notice thereof, and the custodian shall thereupon release the articles seized.

SEC. 9. (a) The Secretary of Agriculture and the Secretary of Commerce are authorized to make such expenditures for construction, equipment, maintenance, repairs, and improvements, including expenditures for personal services at the seat of government and elsewhere, as may be necessary to execute the functions imposed upon them by this Act and as may be provided for by Congress from time to time.

(b) For such expenditures there is hereby authorized to be appropriated, out of any money in the Treasury not otherwise appropriated, the sum of $50,000, to be available until expended, $25,000 of such sum to be available for expenditure by the Secretary of Agriculture and $25,000 by the Secretary of Commerce.

SEC. 10. There is hereby authorized to be appropriated, out of any money in the Treasury not otherwise appropriated, and to be available until expended, the sum of $1,500,000, or so much thereof as may be necessary for the acquisition of any areas authorized by this Act to be acquired for such refuge and for all necessary expense incident to the acquisition of such areas; but no money shall be available for the acquisition of any area until the Secretary of Agriculture has acertained that all of the areas to be acquired under this Act will be acquired within the amounts appropriated or authorized to be appropriated therefor and at an average price not in excess of $5 per acre, and not in excess of the average selling price, during the years 1921, 1922, and 1923, of comparable lands within the vicinity of such areas.

SEC. 11. Any person who shall violate or fail to comply with any provision of or any regulation made pursuant to this Act shall be deemed guilty of a misdemeanor, and upon conviction thereof shall be fined not more than $500 or be imprisoned not more than six months, or both.

SEC. 12. As used in this Act the term "person" includes an individual, partnership, association, or corporation.

SEC. 13. Nothing in this Act shall be construed as exempting any portion of the Mississippi River from the provisions of Federal laws for the improvement, preservation, and protection of navigable waters, nor as authorizing any interference with the operations of the War Department in carrying out any project now or hereafter adopted for the improvement of said river.

Approved, June 7, 1924.

AN ACT TO ESTABLISH THE BEAR RIVER
MIGRATORY-BIRD REFUGE*
April 23, 1928

In 1928 Congress appropriated $350,000 to establish a migratory waterfowl refuge in Utah, on the delta where the Bear River flows into the Great Salt Lake. Although this area ordinarily produced thousands of waterfowl, in some years the marshes dried up. The act was particulary significant since it was the first time funds were appropriated for the construction of dikes and other structures to develop and maintain a marsh.

Be it enacted by the Senate and House of Representatives of the United States of America in Congress assembled, That the Secretary of Agriculture is hereby authorized to construct, at Bear River Bay and vicinity, Utah, such dikes, ditches, spillways, buildings, and improvements as may be necessary, in his judgment, for the establishment of a suitable refuge and feeding and breeding grounds for migratory wild fowl; also to acquire, by purchase, gift, or lease, water rights and privately-owned lands, including the improvements thereon, deemed necessary by him for the purpose, or, in lieu of purchase, to compensate any owner for any damage sustained by reason of the submergence of his lands.

SEC. 2. That such lands, when acquired in accordance with the provisions of this Act, together with such lands of the United States as may be designated for the purpose by proclamations or Executive orders of the President, shall constitute the Bear River Migratory Bird Refuge and shall be maintained as a refuge and breeding place for migratory birds included in the terms of the convention between the United States and Great Britain for the protection of migratory birds, concluded August 16, 1916.

SEC. 3. That no such area shall be acquired by the Secretary of Agriculture unless or until the Legislature of the State of Utah has consented to the acquisition of lands by the United States for use as a refuge for migratory wild fowl, and shall have provided for the use as a refuge for migratory wild fowl by the United States of any lands owned or controlled by the State in Bear River Bay, Utah, and vicinity, which the Secretary of Agriculture may deem necessary for such purpose, and which the Secretary of Agriculture is hereby authorized to accept on behalf of the United States; and, except in the case of a lease, no payments shall be made by the United States for any such area until title thereto is satisfactory to the Attorney General.

SEC. 4. That the existence of a right-of-way easement or other reservation or exception in respect of such area shall not be a bar to its acquisiton (1) if the Sec-

*45 *Statutes at Large,* 448.

retary of Agriculture determines that any such reservation or exception will in no manner interfere with the use of the area for the purposes of this Act, or (2) if in the deed or other conveyance it is stipulated that any reservation or exception in respect of such area, in favor of the person from whom the United States receives title, shall be subject to regulations prescribed under authority of this Act.

SEC. 5. That no person shall take, injure, or disturb any bird, or nest or egg thereof, or injure or destroy any notice, signboard, fence, dike, ditch, dam, spillway, improvement, or other property of the United States on any area acquired or received under this Act, or remove therefrom or cut, burn, injure, or destroy any grass or other natural growth thereon, or enter, use, or occupy the refuge for any purpose, except in accordance with regulations prescribed by the Secretary of Agriculture: *Provided,* That at no time shall less than 60 per centum of the total acreage of the said refuge be maintained as an inviolate sanctuary for such migratory birds.

SEC. 6. (a) Any employee of the Department of Agriculture authorized by the Secretary of Agriculture to enforce the provisions of this Act (1) shall have power, without warrant, to arrest any person committing in the presence of such employee a violation of this Act or of any regulation made pursuant thereto, and to take such person immediately for examination or trial before an officer or court of competent jurisdiction, and (2) shall have power to execute any warrant or other process issued by an officer or court of competent jurisdiction to enforce the provisions of this Act or regulations made pursuant thereto. Any judge of a court established under the laws of the United States, or any United States commissioner may, within his respective jurisdiction, upon proper oath or affirmation showing probable cause, issue warrants in all such cases.

(b) All birds or animals, or parts thereof, captured, injured, or killed, and all grass and other natural growths, and nests and eggs of birds removed contrary to the provisions of this Act or any regulation made pursuant thereto, shall, when found by such employee or by any marshal or deputy marshal, be summarily seized by him, and upon conviction of the offender or upon judgment of a court of the United States that the same were captured, killed, taken, or removed contrary to the provisions of this Act or of any regulation made pursuant thereto, shall be forfeited to the United States and disposed of as directed by the court having jurisdiction.

SEC. 7. That the Secretary of Agriculture is authorized to make such expenditures for construction, equipment, maintenance, repairs, and improvements, including necessary investigations, and expenditures for personal services and office expenses at the seat of government and elsewhere, and to employ such means as may be necessary to execute the functions imposed upon him by this Act and as may be provided for by Congress from time to time.

SEC. 8. That there is hereby authorized to be appropriated, out of any money in the Treasury not otherwise appropriated, the sum of $350,000, or so much thereof as may be necessary to effectuate the provisions of this Act: *Provided,* That not to exceed $50,000 may be expended for the purchase of land, including improvements thereon.

SEC. 9. That any person who shall violate or fail to comply with any provision of, or any regulation made pursuant to, this Act, shall be deemed guilty of a misdemeanor, and upon conviction thereof shall be fined not more than $500 or be imprisoned not more than six months, or both.

SEC. 10. That as used in this Act the term "person" includes an individual, partnership, association, or corporation.

Approved, April 23, 1928.

THE MIGRATORY BIRD CONSERVATION ACT*
February 18, 1929

The Norbeck-Andresen Act, also known as the Migratory Bird Conservation Act, established a permanent Migratory Bird Conservation Commission but, more importantly, it provided for a continuing program for acquisition of refuges. Prior to this time each refuge was reserved or purchased through a separate act of Congress or a separate Executive order of the President. The Norbeck-Andresen Act was therefore the first law that looked toward the establishment of a system of refuges.

An Act to more effectively meet the obligations of the United States under the migratory bird treaty with Great Britain by lessening the dangers threatening migratory game birds from drainage and other causes, by the acquisition of areas of land and of water to furnish in perpetuity reservations for the adequate protection of such birds; and authorizing appropriations for the establishment of such areas, their maintenance and improvement, and for other purposes.

Be it enacted by the Senate and House of Representatives of the United States of America in Congress assembled, That this Act shall be known by the short title of "Migratory Bird Conservation Act."

SEC. 2. That a commission to be known as the Migratory Bird Conservation Commission, consisting of the Secretary of Agriculture, as chairman, the Secretary of Commerce, the Secretary of the Interior, and two Members of the Senate, to be selected by the President of the Senate, and two Members of the House of Representatives to be selected by the Speaker, is hereby created and authorized to consider and pass upon any area of land, water, or land and water that may be recommended by the Secretary of Agriculture for purchase or rental under this Act, and to fix the price or prices at which such area may be purchased or rented; and no purchase or rental shall be made of any such area until it has been duly approved for purchase or rental by said commission. Any Member of the House of Representatives who is a member of the commission, if reelected to the succeeding Congress, may serve on the commission notwithstanding the expiration of a Congress. Any vacancy on the commission shall be filled in the same manner as the original appointment. The ranking officer of the branch or department of a State to which is committed the administration of its game laws, or his authorized representative, and in a State having no such branch or department, the governor thereof, or his authorized representative,

*45 *Statutes at Large,* 1222.

shall be a member ex officio of said commission for the purpose of considering and voting on all questions relating to the acquisition, under this Act, of areas in his State.

SEC. 3. That the commission hereby created shall, through its chairman, annually report in detail to Congress, not later than the first Monday in December, the operations of the commission during the preceding fiscal year.

SEC. 4. That the Secretary of Agriculture shall recommend no area for purchase or rental under the terms of this Act except such as he shall determine is necessary for the conservation of migratory game birds.

SEC. 5. That the Secretary of Agriculture is authorized to purchase or rent such areas as have been approved for purchase or rental by the commission, at the price or prices fixed by said commission, and to acquire by gift or devise, for use as inviolate sanctuaries for migratory birds, areas which he shall determine to be suitable for such purposes, and to pay the purchase or rental price and expenses incident to the location, examination, and survey of such areas and the acquisition of title thereto, including options when deemed necessary by the Secretary of Agriculture, from moneys to be appropriated hereunder by Congress from time to time: *Provided,* That no lands acquired, held, or used by the United States for military purposes shall be subject to any of the provisions of this Act.

SEC. 6. That the Secretary of Agriculture may do all things and make all expenditures necessary to secure the safe title in the United States to the areas which may be acquired under this Act, but no payment shall be made for any such areas until the title thereto shall be satisfactory to the Attorney General, but the acquisition of such areas by the United States shall in no case be defeated because of rights of way, easements, and reservations which from their nature will in the opinion of the Secretary of Agriculture in no manner interfere with the use of the areas so encumbered for the purposes of this Act; but such rights of way, easements, and reservations retained by the grantor or lessor, from whom the United States receives title, shall be subject to rules and regulations prescribed from time to time by the Secretary of Agriculture for the occupation, use, operation, protection, and administration of such areas as inviolate sanctuaries for migratory birds; and it shall be expressed in the deed or lease that the use, occupation, and operation of such rights of way, easements, and reservations shall be subordinate to and subject to such rules and regulations.

SEC. 7. That no deed or instrument of conveyance shall be accepted by the Secretary of Agriculture under this Act unless the State in which the area lies shall have consented by law to the acquisition by the United States of lands in that State.

SEC. 8. That the jurisdiction of the State, both civil and criminal, over persons upon areas acquired under this Act shall not be affected or changed by reason of their acquisition and administration by the United States as migratory bird reservations, except so far as the punishment of offenses against the United States is concerned.

SEC. 9. That nothing in this Act is intended to interfere with the operation of the game laws of the several States applying to migratory game birds in so far as they do not permit what is forbidden by Federal law.

SEC. 10. That no person shall knowingly disturb, injure, or destroy any notice, signboard, fence, building, ditch, dam, dike embankment, flume, spillway, or other improvement or property of the United States on any area acquired under this Act, or cut, burn, or destroy any timber, grass, or other natural growth, on said area or on any area of the United States which heretofore has been or which hereafter may be set apart or reserved for the use of the Department of Agriculture as a game refuge or as a preserve or reservation and breeding ground for native birds, under any law, proclamation, or Executive order, or occupy or use any part thereof, or enter thereon for any purpose, except in accordance with regulations of the Secretary of Agriculture; nor shall any person take any bird, or nest or egg thereof on any area acquired under this Act, except for scientific or propagating purposes under permit of the Secretary of Agriculture; but nothing in this Act or in any regulation thereunder shall be construed to prevent a person from entering upon any area acquired under this Act for the purpose of fishing in accordance with the law of the State in which such area is located: *Provided,* That such person complies with the regulations of the Secretary of Agriculture covering such area.

SEC. 11. That for the purposes of this Act, migratory birds are those defined as such by the treaty between the United States and Great Britain for the protection of migratory birds concluded August 16, 1916.

SEC. 12. For the acquisition, including the location, examination, and survey, of suitable areas of land, water, or land and water, for use as migratory bird reservations, and necessary expenses incident thereto, and for the administration, maintenance, and development of such areas and other preserves, reservations, or breeding grounds frequented by migratory game birds and under the administration of the Secretary of Agriculture, including the construction of dams, dikes, ditches, flumes, spillways, buildings, and other necessary improvements, and for the elimination of the loss of migratory birds from alkali poisoning, oil pollution of waters, or other causes, for cooperation with local authorities in wild life conservation, for investigations and publications relating to North American birds, for personal services, printing, engraving, and issuance of circulars, posters, and other necessary matter and for the enforcement of the provisions of this Act, there are authorized to be appropriated, in addition to all other amounts authorized by law to be appropriated, the following amounts for the fiscal years specified—

$75,000 for the fiscal year ending June 30, 1930;
$200,000 for the fiscal year ending June 30, 1931;
$600,000 for the fiscal year ending June 30, 1932;
$1,000,000 for the fiscal year ending June 30, 1933;
$1,000,000 for each fiscal year thereafter for a period of six years;
and
$200,000 for the fiscal year ending June 30, 1940, and for each fiscal year thereafter. Not more than 20 per centum of the amounts appropriated pursuant to this authorization for the fiscal year beginning July 1, 1930, and for each fiscal year to and including the fiscal year ending June 30, 1939, shall be expended for personal services in the District of Columbia and elsewhere incident to the administration and maintenance of acquired areas, printing, engraving, and issuance of circulars and posters. No part of any appropriation authorized by this section shall be used for payment of the salary, compensation, or expenses of any United States game protector, except reservation protectors for the administration, maintenance, and protection of such reservations and the birds thereon: *Provided,* That reservation protectors appointed under the provisions of this Act shall be selected, when practicable, from qualified citizens of the State in which they are to be employed. The Secretary of Agriculture is authorized and directed to make such expenditures and to employ such means, including personal services in the District of Columbia and elsewhere, as may be necessary to carry out the foregoing objects.

SEC. 13. That for the efficient execution of this Act, the judges of the several courts established under the laws of the United States, United States commissioners, and persons appointed by the Secretary of Agriculture to enforce this Act, shall have, with respect thereto, like powers and duties as are conferred by section 5 of the Migratory Bird Treaty Act (title 16, section 706 of the United States Code) upon said judges, commissioners, and employees of the Department of Agriculture appointed to enforce the Act last aforesaid. Any bird, or part, nest or egg thereof, taken or possessed contrary to this Act, when seized shall be disposed of as provided by section 5 of said Migratory Bird Treaty Act.

SEC. 14. That any person, association, partnership, or corporation who shall violate or fail to comply with any of the provisions of this Act shall be deemed guilty of a misdemeanor and upon conviction thereof shall be fined not less than $10 nor more than $500, or be imprisoned not more than six months, or both.

SEC. 15. That for the purposes of this Act the word "take" shall be construed to mean pursue, hunt, shoot, capture, collect, kill, or attempt to pursue, hunt, shoot, capture, collect, or kill, unless the context otherwise requires.

SEC. 16. Nothing in this Act shall be construed as authorizing or empowering the Migratory Bird Conservation Commission herein created, the Secretary of Agriculture, or any other board, commission, or officer, to declare, withdraw, or determine, except heretofore designated, any part of any national forest or power site, a migratory bird reservation under any of the provisions of this Act, except by and with the consent of the legislature of the State wherein such forest or power site is located.

SEC. 17. That when any State shall, by suitable legislation, make provision adequately to enforce the provisions of this Act and all regulations promulgated thereunder, the Secretary of Agriculture may so certify, and then and thereafter said State may cooperate with the Secretary of Agriculture in the enforcement of this Act and the regulations thereunder.

SEC. 18. That a sum sufficient to pay the necessary expenses of the commission and its members, not to exceed an annual expenditure of $5,000, is hereby authorized to be appropriated out of any money in the Treasury not otherwise appropriated. Said appropriation shall be paid out on the audit and order of the chairman of said commission, which audit and order shall be conclusive and binding upon the General Accounting Office as to the correctness of the accounts of said commission.

SEC. 19. That if any provision of this Act or the application thereof to any person or circumstance is held invalid the validity of the remainder of the Act and of the application of such provision to other persons and circumstances shall not be affected thereby.

SEC. 20. That this Act shall take effect upon its passage and approval.

Approved, February 18, 1929.

THE MIGRATORY BIRD HUNTING STAMP ACT*
March 16, 1934

This piece of legislation, popularly labelled the "Duck Stamp Act" required hunters to purchase a stamp which was good for one year, in order to hunt waterfowl. The proceeds were set aside for the acquisition and management of waterfowl refuges and for research. Subsequent amendments raised the price of the stamp from $1 to $2 and later to $3.

An Act to supplement and support the Migratory Bird Conservation Act by providing funds for the acquisition of areas for use as migratory-bird sanctuaries, refuges, and breeding grounds, for developing and administering such areas, for the protection of certain migratory birds, for the enforcement of the Migratory Bird Treaty Act and regulations thereunder, and for other purposes.

Be it enacted by the Senate and House of Representatives of the United States of America in Congress assembled, That after the expiration of ninety days after the date of enactment of this Act no person over sixteen years of age shall take any migratory waterfowl unless at the time of such taking he carries on his person an unexpired Federal migratory-bird hunting stamp issued to him in the manner hereinafter provided; except that no such stamp shall be required for the taking of migratory waterfowl by Federal or State institutions or official agencies, for propagation purposes or by the resident owner tenant or share cropper of the property or officially designated agencies of the Department of Agriculture for the killing of such waterfowl when found injuring crops or other property, under such restrictions as the Secretary of Agriculture may by regulation prescribe. The Secretary of Agriculture shall, immediately upon the passage of this Act, adopt and promulgate such regulations as are pertinent to the protection of private property in the injury of crops. Any person to whom a stamp has been issued under this Act shall upon request exhibit such stamp for inspection to any officer or employee of the Department of Agriculture authorized to enforce the provisions of this Act or to any officer of any State or any political subdivision thereof authorized to enforce game laws.

SEC. 2. That the stamps required under this Act shall be issued, and the fees therefor collected, by the Post Office Department, under regulations prescribed jointly by the Secretary of Agriculture and the Postmaster General: *Provided,* That stamps shall be issued at the post office or post offices of all county seats in the several States, at all post offices in all cities with a population of two thou-

*48 *Statutes at Large,* 451.

[64]

sand five hundred or over and at such other post offices as said officers may by regulation prescribe. Each such stamp shall, at the time of issuance, be affixed adhesively to the game license issued to the applicant under State law, if the applicant is required to have a State license, or, if the applicant is not required to have a State license, to a certificate furnished for that purpose by the Post Office Department at the time of issuance of such stamp. For each such stamp issued under the provisions of this Act, there shall be collected by the postmaster the sum of $1. Each stamp shall expire and be void after the 30th day of June next succeeding its issuance.

SEC. 3. Nothing in this Act shall be construed to authorize any person to take any migratory waterfowl otherwise than in accordance with regulations adopted and approved pursuant to any treaty heretofore or hereafter entered into between the United States and any other country for the protection of migratory birds, nor to exempt any person from complying with the game laws of the several States.

SEC. 4. All moneys received for such stamps shall be accounted for by the postmaster and paid into the Treasury of the United States, and shall be reserved and set aside as a special fund to be known as the migratory bird conservation fund, to be administered by the Secretary of Agriculture. All moneys received into such fund are hereby appropriated for the following objects and shall be available therefor until expended:

(a) Not less than 90 per centum shall be available for the location, ascertainment, acquisition, administration, maintenance, and development of suitable areas for inviolate migratory-bird sanctuaries, under the provisions of the Migratory Bird Conservation Act, to be expended for such purposes in all respects as moneys appropriated pursuant to the provisions of such Act; for the administration, maintenance, and development of other refuges under the administration of the Secretary of Agriculture, frequented by migratory game birds; and for such investigations on such refuges and elsewhere in regard to migratory waterfowl as the Secretary of Agriculture may deem essential for the highest utilization of the refuges and for the protection and increase of these birds.

(b) The remainder shall be available for administrative expenses under this Act and the Migratory Bird Conservation Act, including reimbursement to the Post Office Department of funds expended in connection with the printing, engraving, and issuance of migratory-bird hunting stamps, and including personal services in the District of Columbia and elsewhere: *Provided,* That the protection of said inviolate migratory-bird sanctuaries shall be, so far as possible, under section 17 of the Migratory Bird Conservation Act, passed February 18, 1929.

(c) The remainder shall be available for administrative expenses under this Act, including reimbursement to the Post Office Department of funds expended in connection with the issuance of stamps, and printing and engraving of the same, and for administration expenses under the Migratory Bird Treaty Act and any other Act to carry into effect any treaty for the protection of migratory birds, and the Migratory Bird Conservation Act.

SEC. 5. (a) No person shall alter, mutilate, loan, or transfer to another any stamp issued to him pursuant to this Act, nor shall any person other than the person to whom such stamp is issued use the same for any purpose.

(b) No person shall imitate or counterfeit any stamp authorized by this Act, or any die, plate, or engraving therefor, or make, print, or knowingly use, sell, or have in his possession any such counterfeit, license, die, plate, or engraving.

SEC. 6. For the efficient execution of this Act, the judges of the several courts, established under the laws of the United States, United States commissioners, and persons appointed by the Secretary of Agriculture to enforce the provisions of this Act, shall have, with respect thereto, like powers and duties as are conferred upon said judges, commissioners, and employees of the Department of Agriculture by the Migratory Bird Treaty Act or any other Act to carry into effect any treaty for the protection of migratory birds with respect to that Act. Any bird or part thereof taken or possessed contrary to such Acts shall, when seized, be disposed of as provided by the Migratory Bird Treaty Act, or Acts aforesaid.

SEC. 7. Any person who shall violate any provision of this Act or who shall violate or fail to comply with any regulation made pursuant thereto shall be subject to the penalties provided in section 6 of the Migratory Bird Treaty Act.

SEC 8. The Secretary of Agriculture is authorized to cooperate with the several States and Territories in the enforcement of the provisions of this Act.

SEC. 9. (a) Terms defined in the Migratory Bird Treaty Act, or the Migratory Bird Conservation Act, shall, when used in this Act, have the meaning assigned to such terms in such Acts, respectively.

(b) As used in this Act (1) the term "migratory waterfowl" means the species enumerated in paragraph (a) of subdivision 1 of article I of the treaty between the United States and Great Britain for the protection of migratory birds concluded August 16, 1916; (2) the term "State" includes the several States and Territories of the United States and the District of Columbia; and (3) the term "take" means pursue, hunt, shoot, capture, collect, kill, or attempt to pursue, hunt, shoot, capture, collect, or kill.

Approved, March 16, 1934.

THE FISH AND WILDLIFE COORDINATION ACT*
March 10, 1934

One of the most important wildlife conservation acts of the 1930's was the passage of the Fish and Wildlife Coordination Act of 1934. It authorized the Secretary of Agriculture and the Secretary of Commerce to cooperate with federal, state, and other agencies in developing a nationwide program of wildlife conservation and rehabilitation. The two departments were also to determine the effects of pollution on wildlife, and make recommendations for remedial measures. The act also provided that whenever the Federal Government impounds water for any use, the Bureau of Fisheries or the Bureau of Biological Survey (now combined in the Fish and Wildlife Service) would be given an opportunity to use the impounded waters, as long as their aims were consistent with the waters' primary use. In connection with any future dam construction, either by the Federal Government or by any agency under government permit, any economically practicable provision would be made for the migration of fish life between the upper and lower waters by means of fish lifts, ladders, or other devices.

This act with its subsequent amendments appears on pp. 98–99 in the chapter on Fishing.

---

*48 *Statutes at Large,* 401.

A MEXICAN-AMERICAN TREATY FOR THE
PROTECTION OF MIGRATORY BIRDS*
February 7, 1936

Since a considerable number of migratory waterfowl spend the winter in Mexico, both countries have a stake in the treatment the birds receive in their respective countries. In 1936 a treaty was negotiated with Mexico which was similar to the 1916 treaty with Great Britain. One difference, however, is a provision in the Mexican treaty which prohibits hunting from aircraft. The treaty with Mexico was put into effect by the passage of an amendment (49 Stat., 1555) to the old Migratory Bird Treaty Act of 1918.

Convention between the United States of America and Mexico for the protection of migratory birds and game mammals. Signed at Mexico City, February 7, 1936; ratification advised by the Senate, April 30, 1936; ratified by the President, October 8, 1936; ratified by Mexico, February 12, 1937; ratifications exchanged at Washington, March 15, 1937; proclaimed, March 15, 1937.

BY THE PRESIDENT OF THE UNITED STATES OF AMERICA
A PROCLAMATION

Whereas a convention between the United States of America and The United Mexican States providing for the protection of migratory birds and game mammals was concluded and signed by their respective plenipotentiaries at the city of Mexico on the seventh day of February, one thousand nine hundred and thirty-six, the original of which convention, being in the English and Spanish languages, is word for word as follows:

CONVENTION BETWEEN THE UNITED STATES OF AMERICA
AND THE UNITED MEXICAN STATES FOR THE PROTECTION OF
MIGRATORY BIRDS AND GAME MAMMALS

Whereas, some of the birds denominated migratory, in their movements cross the United States of America and the United Mexican States, in which countries they live temporarily;

Whereas it is right and proper to protect the said migratory birds, whatever may be their origin, in the United States of America and the United Mexican States, in order that the species may not be exterminated;

Whereas, for this purpose it is necessary to employ adequate measures which will permit a rational utilization of migratory birds for the purposes of sport as well as for food, commerce and industry;

*50 *Statutes at Large,* Part 2, 1311.

[68]

HUNTING

The Governments of the two countries have agreed to conclude a Convention which will satisfy the above mentioned need and to that end have appointed as their respective plenipotentiaries: The Honorable Josephus Daniels representing the President of the United States of America, Franklin D. Roosevelt and the Honorable Eduardo Hay, representing the President of the United Mexican States, General Lazaro Cardenas, who, having exhibited to each other and found satisfactory their respective full powers, conclude the following Convention:

ARTICLE I

In order that the species may not be exterminated, the high contracting parties declare that it is right and proper to protect birds denominated as migratory, whatever may be their origin, which in their movements live temporarily in the United States of America and the United Mexican States, by means of adequate methods which will permit, in so far as the respective high contracting parties may see fit, the utilization of said birds rationally for purposes of sport, food, commerce and industry.

ARTICLE II

The high contracting parties agree to establish laws, regulations and provisions to satisfy the need set forth in the preceding Article, including:

A)—The establishment of close seasons, which will prohibit in certain periods of the year the taking of migratory birds, their nests or eggs, as well as their transportation or sale, alive or dead, their products or parts, except when proceeding, with appropriate authorization, from private game farms or when used for scientific purposes, for propagation or for museums.

B)—The establishment of refuge zones in which the taking of such birds will be prohibited.

C)—The limitation of their hunting to four months in each year, as a maximum, under permits issued by the respective authorities in each case.

D)—The establishment of a close season for wild ducks from the tenth of March to the first of September.

E)—The prohibition of the killing of migratory insectivorous birds, except when they become injurious to agriculture and constitute plagues, as well as when they come from reserves or game farms: provided however that such birds may be captured alive and used in conformity with the laws of each contracting country.

F)—The prohibition of hunting from aircraft.

ARTICLE III

The high contracting parties respectively agree, in addition, not to permit the transportation over the American-Mexican border of migratory birds, dead or alive, their parts or products, without a permit of authorization provided for that purpose by the government of each country, with the understanding that in the case that the said birds, their parts or products are transported from one country to the other without the stipulated authorization, they will be considered as contraband and treated accordingly.

ARTICLE IV

The high contracting parties declare that for the purposes of the present Convention the following birds shall be considered migratory:

MIGRATORY GAME BIRDS.

Familia Anatidae.	Familia Scolopacidae.
Familia Gruidae.	Familia Recurvirostridae.
Familia Rallidae.	Familia Phalaropodidae.
Familia Charadriidae.	Familia Columbidae.

MIGRATORY NON-GAME BIRDS.

Familia Cuculidae.	Familia Turdidae.
Familia Caprimulgidae.	Familia Mimidae.
Familia Micropodidae.	Familia Sylviidae.
Familia Trochilidae.	Familia Motacillidae.
Familia Picidae.	Familia Bombycillidae.
Familia Tyrannidae.	Familia Ptilogonatidae.
Familia Alaudidae.	Familia Laniidae.
Familia Hirundinidae.	Familia Vireonidae.
Familia Paridae.	Familia Compsothlypidae.
Familia Certhiidae.	Familia Icteridae.
Familia Troglodytidae.	Familia Thraupidae.
Familia Fringillidae.	

Others which the Presidents of the United States of America and the United Mexican States may determine by common agreement.

ARTICLE V

The high contracting parties agree to apply the stipulations set forth in Article III with respect to the game mammals which live in their respective countries.

ARTICLE VI

This Convention shall be ratified by the high contracting parties in accordance with their constitutional methods and shall remain in force for fifteen years and shall be understood to be extended from year to year if the high contracting parties have not indicated twelve months in advance their intention to terminate it.

The respective plenipotentiaries sign the present Convention in duplicate in English and Spanish, affixing thereto their respective seals, in the City of Mexico, the seventh day of February of 1936.

Josephus Daniels
[SEAL]

Secretaría de Relaciones Exteriores
Estados Unidos Mexicanos
Mexico

México, 10 de febrero de 1936

Señor Encargado de Negocios:

Tengo la honra de manifestar a usted, en relación con el Convenio entre los Estados Unidos Mexicanos y los Estados Unidos de Norteamérica para la Protección de Aves Migratorias y de Mamíferos Cinegeticos, firmado en esta ciudad el 7 del mes en curso, que esta Secretaría se permite proponer la ciudad de Washington para los efectos del canje de ratificaciones a que se refiere el artículo VI del Convenio mencionado, tan pronto como sea practicable.

Aprovecho la oportunidad para renovar a usted las seguridades de mi atenta consideración.

Eduardo Hay

Señor Henry R. Norweb
Encargado de Negocios ad-ínterim
de los Estados Unidos de América
Presente[1]

---

[1]Following is translation:
Department of Foreign Relations
United Mexican States
Mexico City

México City, February 10, 1936

Mr. Chargé d'Affaires:

I have the honor to advise you, with regard to the Convention between the United Mexican States and the United States of North America for the protection of Migratory Birds and Game Mammals, signed in this city on the 7th instant, that this Department takes the liberty of proposing the city of Washington for the purpose of the exchange of ratifications referred to by Article VI of the said Convention as soon as may be practicable.

I avail myself of the opportunity to renew to you the assurances of my high consideration.

Eduardo Hay

Mr. Henry R. Norweb
Chargé d'Affaires ad interim
of the United States of America,
City

No. 1488   Embassy of the United States of America
Mexico, February 11, 1936

Excellency:

I have the honor to acknowledge with appreciation Your Excellency's courteous note No. 3, Ref. III/, of February 10, 1936, in which it is suggested with reference to the Convention between the United States of America and the United Mexican States for the Protection of Migratory Birds and Game Mammals signed in this city on the 7th of this month that the ratifications provided for in Article VI of the above-mentioned Convention be exchanged in Washington. It is understood that this proposal is satisfactory to my Government and that the treaty shall take effect on the date of the exchange of ratifications.

Please accept, Excellency, the renewed assurances of my highest and most distinguished consideration.

R. Henry Norweb
Chargé d'Affaires ad interim

His Excellency
Señor General Eduardo Hay
Minister for Foreign Affairs
Mexico

And whereas the said convention has been duly ratified on both parts and the ratifications of the two Governments were exchanged in the city of Washington on the fifteenth day of March, one thousand nine hundred and thirty-seven, on which day the convention entered into force in accordance with an understanding reached by an exchange of notes signed on February 10 and February 11, 1936, by the Minister for Foreign Affairs of the United Mexican States and the Chargé d'Affaires of the United States of America at the city of Mexico.

Now, therefore, be it known that I, Franklin D. Roosevelt, President of the United States of America, have caused the said convention to be made public to the end that the same and every article and clause thereof may be observed and fulfilled with good faith by the United States of America and the citizens thereof.

In testimony whereof, I have hereunto set my hand and caused the Seal of the United States of America to be affixed.

Done at the city of Washington this fifteenth day of March, in the year of our Lord one thousand nine hundred and thirty-seven, and of the Independence of the United States of America the one hundred and sixty-first.

[SEAL]   *Franklin D. Roosevelt*

By the President:
Cordell Hull
Secretary of State

THE PITTMAN-ROBERTSON ACT*
September 2, 1937

Perhaps the outstanding example of federal aid to the states for wildlife conservation was the Pittman-Robertson Act of September 2, 1937. Under authority of this legislation, an 11 percent excise tax on the manufacturers' price of sporting arms and ammunition was apportioned to state fish and game departments. From 1938 to 1966 about $30 million was allocated to the states from this source and during this period the lands purchased with these federal funds amounted to 2,774,214 acres.†

An Act to provide that the United States shall aid the States in wildlife-restoration projects, and for other purposes.

Be it enacted by the Senate and House of Representatives of the United States of America in Congress assembled, That the Secretary of Agriculture is authorized to cooperate with the States, through their respective State fish and game departments, in wildlife-restoration projects as hereinafter set forth; but no money apportioned under this Act to any State shall be expended therein until its legislature, or other State agency authorized by the State constitution to make laws governing the conservation of wildlife, shall have assented to the provision of this Act and shall have passed laws for the conservation of wildlife which shall include a prohibition against the diversion of license fees paid by hunters for any other purpose than the administration of said State fish and game department, except that, until the final adjournment of the first regular session of the legislature held after the passage of this Act, the assent of the Governor of the State shall be sufficient. The Secretary of Agriculture and the State fish and game department of each State accepting the benefits of this Act shall agree upon the wildlife-restoration projects to be aided in such State under the terms of this Act and all projects shall conform to the standards fixed by the Secretary of Agriculture.

SEC. 2. For the purposes of this Act the term "wildlife-restoration project" shall be construed to mean and include the selection, restoration, rehabilitation, and improvement of areas of land or water adaptable as feeding, resting, or breeding places for wildlife, including acquisition by purchase, condemnation, lease, or gift of such areas or estates or interests therein as are suitable or capable of being made suitable therefor, and the construction thereon or therein of such works as may be necessary to make them available for such purposes and also including such research into problems of wildlife management as may be

---

*50 *Statutes at Large,* 917.
†Bureau of Sport Fisheries and Wildlife, *Federal Aid in Wildlife Restoration* (Washington, D.C.: Government Printing Office, 1967), 8–9.

necessary to efficient administration affecting wildlife resources, and such preliminary or incidental costs and expenses as may be incurred in and about such projects; the term "State fish and game department" shall be construed to mean and include any department or division of department of another name, or commission, or official or officials, of a State empowered under its laws to exercise the functions ordinarily exercised by a State fish and game department.

SEC. 3. An amount equal to the revenue accruing during the fiscal year ending June 30, 1939, and each fiscal year thereafter, from the tax imposed by section 610, title IV, of the Revenue Act of 1932 (47 Stat. 169), as heretofore or hereafter extended and amended, on firearms, shells, and cartridges, is hereby authorized to be set apart in the Treasury as a special fund to be known as "The Federal aid to wildlife-restoration fund" and is hereby authorized to be appropriated and made available until expended for the purposes of this Act. So much of such appropriation apportioned to any State for any fiscal year as remains unexpended at the close thereof is authorized to be made available for expenditure in that State until the close of the succeeding fiscal year. Any amount apportioned to any State under the provisions of this Act which is unexpended or unobligated at the end of the period during which it is available for expenditure on any project is authorized to be made available for expenditure by the Secretary of Agriculture in carrying out the provisions of the Migratory Bird Conservation Act.

SEC. 4. So much, not to exceed 8 per centum, of the revenue covered into said fund in each fiscal year as the Secretary of Agriculture may estimate to be necessary for his expenses in the administration and execution of this Act and the Migratory Bird Conservation Act shall be deducted for that purpose, and such sum is authorized to be made available therefor until the expiration of the next succeeding fiscal year, and within sixty days after the close of such fiscal year the Secretary of Agriculture shall apportion such part thereof as remains unexpended by him, if any, and make certificate thereof to the Secretary of the Treasury and to the State fish and game departments on the same basis and in the same manner as is provided as to other amounts authorized by this Act to be apportioned among the States for such current fiscal year. The Secretary of Agriculture, after making the aforesaid deduction, shall apportion the remainder of the revenues in said fund for each fiscal year among the several States in the following manner, that is to say, one-half in the ratio which the area of each State bears to the total area of all the States and one-half in the ratio which the number of paid hunting-license holders of each State in the preceding fiscal year, as certified to said Secretary by the State fish and game departments, bears to the total number of paid hunting-license holders of all the States: *Provided,* That the apportionment for any one State shall not exceed the sum of $150,000 annually: *Provided further,* That where the apportionment to any State under this section is less than $15,000 annually, the Secretary of Agriculture may allocate not more

[74]

than $15,000 of said fund to said State to carry out the purposes of this Act when said State certifies to the Secretary of Agriculture that it has set aside not less than $5,000 from its fish and game funds or has made, through its legislature, an appropriation in this amount, for said purposes.

SEC. 5. Within sixty days after the approval of this Act the Secretary of Agriculture shall certify to the Secretary of the Treasury and to each State fish and game department the sum which he has estimated to be deducted for administering and executing this Act and the Migratory Bird Conservation Act and the sum which he has apportioned to each State for the fiscal year ending June 30, 1939, and on or before February 20 next preceding the commencement of each succeeding fiscal year shall make like certificates for such fiscal year. Any State desiring to avail itself of the benefits of this Act shall notify the Secretary of Agriculture to this effect within sixty days after it has received the certification referred to in this section. The sum apportioned to any State which fails to notify the Secretary of Agriculture as herein provided is authorized to be made available for expenditure by the Secretary of Agriculture in carrying out the provisions of the Migratory Bird Conservation Act.

SEC. 6. Any State desiring to avail itself of the benefits of this Act shall by its State fish and game department submit to the Secretary of Agriculture full and detailed statements of any wildlife-restoration project proposed for that State. If the Secretary of Agriculture finds that such project meets with the standards set up by him and approves said project, the State fish and game department shall furnish to him such surveys, plans, specifications, and estimates therefor as he may require: *Provided, however,* That the Secretary of Agriculture shall approve only such projects as may be substantial in character and design and the expenditure of funds hereby authorized shall be applied only to such approved projects and if otherwise applied they shall be replaced by the State before it may participate in any further apportionment under this Act. Items included for engineering, inspection, and unforeseen contingencies in connection with any works to be constructed shall not exceed 10 per centum of the cost of such works and shall be paid by the State as a part of its contribution to the total cost of such works. If the Secretary of Agriculture approves the plans, specifications, and estimates for the project, he shall notify the State fish and game department and immediately certify the fact to the Secretary of the Treasury. The Secretary of the Treasury shall thereupon set aside so much of said fund as represents the share of the United States payable under this Act on account of such project, which sum so set aside shall not exceed 75 per centum of the total estimated cost thereof. No payment of any money apportioned under this Act shall be made on any project until such statement of the project and the plans, specifications, and estimates thereof shall have been submitted to and approved by the Secretary of Agriculture.

SEC. 7. When the Secretary of Agriculture shall find that any project approved by him has been completed or, if involving research relating to wildlife, is being conducted, in compliance with said plans and specifications, he shall cause to be paid to the proper authority of said State the amount set aside for said project: *Provided,* That the Secretary of Agriculture may, in his discretion, from time to time, make payments on said project as the same progresses; but these payments, including previous payments, if any, shall not be more than the United States' pro-rata share of the project in conformity with said plans and specifications. Any construction work and labor in each State shall be performed in accordance with its laws and under the direct supervision of the State fish and game department, subject to the inspection and approval of the Secretary of Agriculture and in accordance with rules and regulations made pursuant to this Act. The Secretary of Agriculture and the State fish and game department of each State may jointly determine at what times and in what amounts payments, as work progresses, shall be made under this Act. Such payments shall be made by the Secretary of the Treasury, on warrants drawn by the Secretary of Agriculture against the said fund to such official or officials, or depository, as may be designated by the State fish and game department and authorized under the laws of the State to receive public funds of the State.

SEC. 8. To maintain wildlife-restoration projects established under the provisions of this Act shall be the duty of the States according to their respective laws.

SEC. 9. Out of the deductions set aside for administering and executing this Act and the Migratory Bird Conservation Act, the Secretary of Agriculture is authorized to employ such assistants, clerks, and other persons in the city of Washington and elsewhere, to be taken from the eligible lists of the Civil Service; to rent or construct buildings outside of the city of Washington; to purchase such supplies, materials, equipment, office fixtures, and apparatus; and to incur such travel and other expenses, including purchase, maintenance, and hire of passenger-carrying motor vehicles, as he may deem necessary for carrying out the purposes of this Act.

SEC. 10. The Secretary of Agriculture is authorized to make rules and regulations for carrying out the provisions of this Act.

SEC. 11. The Secretary of Agriculture shall make an annual report to the Congress of the sum set apart in "The Federal aid to wildlife restoration fund", giving detailed information as to the projects and expenditures therefor.

Approved, September 2, 1937.

AN ACT CONCERNING WILDLIFE ON MILITARY RESERVATIONS*
February 28, 1958

Over the years, the various military departments have owned or controlled several million acres of land. In 1956, for example, the total was about 25 million acres. Sportsmen complained that unnecessarily large sections were frequently reserved, that wildlife values were ignored, and that civilian sportsmen were restricted from military reservations. Moreover state officials were not admitted to these reservations to carry out proper game conservation and management practices, and state game laws were commonly ignored. Congress responded to these criticisms by passing Public Law 85–337, which required that reservations of over 5,000 acres must be approved by an act of Congress, and that hunting and fishing on military reservations must be in accordance with state game laws.

An Act to provide that withdrawals, reservations, or restrictions of more than five thousand acres of public lands of the United States for certain purposes shall not become effective until approved by Act of Congress, and for other purposes.

Be it enacted by the Senate and House of Representatives of the United States of America in Congress assembled, That, notwithstanding any other provisions of law, except in time of war or national emergency hereafter declared by the President or the Congress, on and after the date of enactment of this Act the provisions hereof shall apply to the withdrawal and reservation for, restriction of, and utilization by, the Department of Defense for defense purposes of the public lands of the United States, including public lands in the Territories of Alaska and Hawaii: *Provided,* That—

(1) for the purposes of this Act, the term "public lands" shall be deemed to include, without limiting the meaning thereof, Federal lands and waters of the Outer Continental Shelf, as defined in section 2 of the Outer Continental Shelf Lands Act (67 Stat. 462), and Federal lands and waters off the coast of the Territories of Alaska and Hawaii;

(2) nothing in this Act shall be deemed to be applicable to the withdrawal or reservation of public lands specifically as naval petroleum, naval oil shale, or naval coal reserves;

(3) nothing in this Act shall be deemed to be applicable to the warning areas over the Federal lands and waters of the Outer Continental Shelf and Federal lands and waters off the coast of the Territory of Alaska reserved for use of the military departments prior to the enactment of the Outer Continental Shelf Lands Act (67 Stat. 462); and

*72 *Statutes at Large,* 27.

(4) nothing in sections 1, 2, or 3 of this Act shall be deemed to be applicable either to those reservations or withdrawals which expired due to the ending of the unlimited national emergency of May 27, 1941, and which subsequent to such expiration have been and are now used by the military departments with the concurrence of the Department of the Interior, or to the withdrawal of public domain lands of the Marine Corps Training Center, Twentynine Palms, California, and the naval gunnery ranges in the State of Nevada designated as Basic Black Rock and Basic Sahwave Mountain.

SEC. 2. No public land, water, or land and water area shall, except by Act of Congress, hereafter be (1) withdrawn from settlement, location, sale, or entry for the use of the Department of Defense for defense purposes; (2) reserved for such use; or (3) restricted from operation of the mineral leasing provisions of the Outer Continental Shelf Lands Act (67 Stat. 462), if such withdrawal, reservation, or restriction would result in the withdrawal, reservation, or restriction of more than five thousand acres in the aggregate for any one defense project or facility of the Department of Defense since the date of enactment of this Act or since the last previous Act of Congress which withdrew, reserved, or restricted public land, water, or land and water area for that project or facility, whichever is later.

SEC. 3. Any application hereafter filed for a withdrawal, reservation, or restriction, the approval of which will, under section 2 of this Act, require an Act of Congress, shall specify—

(1) the name of the requesting agency and intended using agency;

(2) location of the area involved, to include a detailed description of the exterior boundaries and excepted areas, if any, within such proposed withdrawal, reservation, or restriction;

(3) gross land and water acreage within the exterior boundaries of the requested withdrawal, reservation, or restriction, and net public land, water, or public land and water acreage covered by the application;

(4) the purpose or purposes for which the area is proposed to be withdrawn, reserved, or restricted, or if the purpose or purposes are classified for national security reasons, a statement to that effect;

(5) whether the proposed use will result in contamination of any or all of the requested withdrawal, reservation, or restriction area, and if so, whether such contamination will be permanent or temporary;

(6) the period during which the proposed withdrawal, reservation, or restriction will continue in effect;

(7) whether, and if so to what extent, the proposed use will affect continuing full operation of the public land laws and Federal regulations relating to conservation, utilization, and development of mineral resources, timber and other material resources, grazing resources, fish and wildlife resources, water resources and scenic, wilderness, and recreation and other values; and

(8) if effecting the purpose for which the area is proposed to be withdrawn, reserved, or restricted, will involve the use of water in any State, whether, subject to existing rights under law, the intended using agency has acquired, or proposes to acquire, rights to the use thereof in conformity with State laws and procedures relating to the control, appropriation, use, and distribution of water.

SEC. 4. Chapter 159 of title 10, United States Code, is amended as follows:

(1) By adding the following new section at the end:

"§ 2671. Military reservations and facilities: hunting, fishing, and trapping

"(a) The Secretary of Defense shall, with respect to each military installation or facility under the jurisdiction of any military department in a State or Territory—

"(1) require that all hunting, fishing, and trapping at that installation or facility be in accordance with the fish and game laws of the State or Territory in which it is located;

"(2) require that an appropriate license for hunting, fishing, or trapping on that installation or facility be obtained, except that with respect to members of the Armed Forces, such a license may be required only if the State or Territory authorizes the issuance of a license to a member on active duty for a period of more than thirty days at an installation or facility within that State or Territory, without regard to residence requirements, and upon terms otherwise not less favorable than the terms upon which such a license is issued to residents of that State or Territory; and

"(3) develop, subject to safety requirements and military security, and in cooperation with the Governor (or his designee) of the State or Territory in which the installation or facility is located, procedures under which designated fish and game or conservation officials of that State or Territory may, at such time and under such conditions as may be agreed upon, have full access to that installation or facility to effect measures for the management, conservation, and harvesting of fish and game resources.

"(b) The Secretary of Defense shall prescribe regulations to carry out this section.

"(c) Whoever is guilty of an act or omission which violates a requirement prescribed under subsection (a) (1) or (2), which act or omission would be punishable if committed or omitted within the jurisdiction of the State or Territory in which the installation or facility is located, by the laws thereof in effect at the time of that act or omission, is guilty of a like offense and is subject to a like punishment.

"(d) This section does not modify any rights granted by treaty or otherwise to any Indian tribe or to the members thereof."

(2) By adding the following new item at the end of the analysis:

"2671. Military reservations and facilities: hunting, fishing, and trapping."

SEC. 5. The Federal Property and Administrative Services Act of 1949 (63 Stat.

377), as amended, is hereby further amended by revising section 3 (d) to read as follows:

"(d) The term 'property' means any interest in property except (1) the public domain; lands reserved or dedicated for national forest or national park purposes; minerals in lands or portions of lands withdrawn or reserved from the public domain which the Secretary of the Interior determines are suitable for disposition under the public land mining and mineral leasing laws; and lands withdrawn or reserved from the public domain except lands or portions of lands so withdrawn or reserved which the Secretary of the Interior, with the concurrence of the Administrator, determines are not suitable for return to the public domain for disposition under the general public-land laws because such lands are substantially changed in character by improvements or otherwise; (2) naval vessels of the following categories: Battleships, cruisers, aircraft carriers, destroyers, and submarines; and (3) records of the Federal Government."

SEC. 6. All withdrawals or reservations of public lands for the use of any agency of the Department of Defense, except lands withdrawn or reserved specifically as naval petroleum, naval oil shale, or naval coal reserves, heretofore or hereafter made by the United States, shall be deemed to be subject to the condition that all minerals, including oil and gas, in the lands so withdrawn or reserved are under the jurisdiction of the Secretary of the Interior and there shall be no disposition of, or exploration for, any minerals in such lands except under the applicable public land mining and mineral leasing laws: *Provided,* That no disposition of, or exploration for, any minerals in such lands shall be made where the Secretary of Defense, after consultation with the Secretary of the Interior, determines that such disposition or exploration is inconsistent with the military use of the lands so withdrawn or reserved.

Approved February 28, 1958.

AN ACT TO LIMIT WETLANDS DRAINAGE*
October 2, 1962

Waterfowl and some other varieties of wildlife require substantial areas of wetlands (swamps, marshes, potholes, ponds, and lakes) to survive and reproduce. It is estimated that when white men first came to the North American continent, there were 127 million acres of natural wetlands in what is now the United States. Through various drainage or flood control operations, this acreage has now been reduced to about 80 million acres, and only about 22.5 million is considered to be good wildlife habitat. Throughout most of our history wetlands have been regarded as waste areas because they were incapable of producing agricultural crops; consequently, the emphasis has been on drainage to produce lands suitable for cultivation. The Swamp Land Acts of 1849 and 1850 (documented in Land and Water: 1492–1900, *pp. 404–405) were grants to the states for the purpose of "reclaiming" such lands by construction of levees and drainage devices. While some of these lands were not in fact swamp lands, about 65 million acres were transferred to the states. Nearly all of these are now privately owned and a considerable proportion of them have indeed been drained.*

It is only recently that Americans have come to realize that wetlands are among the most valuable habitat for the production of waterfowl and some other wildlife. The pioneering acts of 1929 and 1934 initiated a system of acquisition of wetlands for waterfowl refuges. An act of October 4, 1961 (75 Stat., *813) augmented these funds by providing an advance of $105 million against the migratory bird conservation fund.*

The rapid decrease in wetlands was especially crucial in the "prairie pothole" region of Minnesota, North Dakota, and South Dakota. This 56,000-square-mile area contained the most valuable waterfowl production acreage in the coterminous United States, and at peak produced about 15 million ducks per year. During the period 1943–1960 an estimated 1,027,000 acres was destroyed as wildlife habitat through the expenditure of some $25 million by the Federal Government for farm drainage.

President Kennedy referred to this particular situation when he said in his Special Message on Natural Resources *on February 23, 1961:*

> I am also hopeful that consistent and coordinated Federal leadership can expand our fish and wildlife opportunities without the present conflicts of agencies and interests: One department paying to have wetlands drained for agricultural purposes while another is purchasing such lands for wildlife or water fowl refuges. . . .

The following act was an effort to rectify these contradictory policies of the Federal Government.

*76 Statutes at Large, 696.

An Act to amend the Soil Conservation and Domestic Allotment Act, as amended, to add a new section 16A to limit financial and technical assistance for drainage of certain wetlands.

Be it enacted by the Senate and House of Representatives of the United States of America in Congress assembled, That the Soil Conservation and Domestic Allotment Act, as amended, is further amended by inserting after section 16 thereof the following new section:

"SEC. 16A. The Secretary of Agriculture shall not enter into an agreement in the States of North Dakota, South Dakota, and Minnesota to provide financial or technical assistance for wetland drainage on a farm under authority of this Act, if the Secretary of the Interior has made a finding that wildlife preservation will be materially harmed on that farm by such drainage and that preservation of such land in its undrained status will materially contribute to wildlife preservation and such finding, identifying specifically the farm and the land on that farm with respect to which the finding was made, has been filed with the Secretary of Agriculture within ninety days after the filing of the application for drainage assistance: *Provided,* That the limitation against furnishing such financial or technical assistance shall terminate (1) at such time as the Secretary of the Interior notifies the Secretary of Agriculture that such limitation should not be applicable, (2) one year after the date on which the adverse finding of the Secretary of the Interior was filed unless during that time an offer has been made by the Secretary of the Interior or a State government agency to lease or to purchase the wetland area from the owner thereof as a waterfowl resource, or (3) five years after the date on which such adverse finding was filed if such an offer to lease or to purchase such wetland area has not been accepted by the owner thereof: *Provided further,* That upon any change in the ownership of the land with respect to which such adverse finding was filed, the eligibility of such land for such financial or technical assistance shall be redetermined in accordance with the provisions of this section."

Approved October 2, 1962.

OUTDOOR RECREATION ON WILDLIFE REFUGES*
September 28, 1962

While recreation visits to some refuges were permitted from the beginning, funds, facilities, and personnel were ordinarily not available to accomodate the visitors or to enhance the recreation experience. An act passed in 1962 gave official recognition and approval to recreation on the refuges and authorized appropriations for that purpose.

An Act to assure continued fish and wildlife benefits from the national fish and wildlife conservation areas by authorizing their appropriate incidental or secondary use for public recreation to the extent that such use is compatible with the primary purposes of such areas, and for other purposes.

Be it enacted by the Senate and House of Representatives of the United States of America in Congress assembled, That in recognition of mounting public demands for recreational opportunities on national wildlife refuges, game ranges, national fish hatcheries, and other conservation areas administered by the Secretary of the Interior for fish and wildlife purposes; and in recognition also of the resulting imperative need, if such recreational opportunities are provided, to assure that any present or future recreational use will be compatible with, and will not prevent accomplishment of, the primary purposes for which the said conservation areas were acquired or established, the Secretary of the Interior is authorized, as an appropriate incidental or secondary use, to administer such areas or parts thereof for public recreation when in his judgment public recreation can be an appropriate incidental or secondary use: *Provided,* That such public recreation use shall be permitted only to the extent that is practicable and not inconsistent with other previously authorized Federal operations or with the primary objectives for which each particular area is established: *Provided further,* That in order to insure accomplishment of such primary objectives, the Secretary, after consideration of all authorized uses, purposes, and other pertinent factors relating to individual areas, shall curtail public recreation use generally or certain types of public recreation use within individual areas or in portions thereof whenever he considers such action to be necessary: *And provided further,* That none of the aforesaid refuges, hatcheries, game ranges, and other conservation areas shall be used during any fiscal year for those forms of recreation that are not directly related to the primary purposes and functions of the individual areas until the Secretary shall have determined—

*76 *Statutes at Large,* 653.

(a) that such recreational use will not interfere with the primary purposes for which the areas were established, and

(b) that funds are available for the development, operation, and maintenance of these permitted forms of recreation. This section shall not be construed to repeal or amend previous enactments relating to particular areas.

SEC. 2. In order to avoid adverse effects upon fish and wildlife populations and management operations of the said areas that might otherwise result from public recreation or visitation to such areas, the Secretary is authorized to acquire limited areas of land for recreational development adjacent to the said conservation areas in existence or approved by the Migratory Bird Conservation Commission as of the date of enactment of this Act: *Provided,* That the acquisition of any land or interest therein pursuant to this section shall be accomplished only with such funds as may be appropriated therefor by the Congress or donated for such purposes, but such property shall not be acquired with funds obtained from the sale of Federal migratory bird hunting stamps. Lands acquired pursuant to this section shall become a part of the particular conservation area to which they are adjacent.

SEC. 3. In furtherance of the purposes of this Act, the Secretary is authorized to cooperate with public and private agencies, organizations, and individuals, and he may accept and use, without further authorization, donations of funds and real and personal property. Such acceptance may be accomplished under the terms and conditions of restrictive covenants imposed by donors when such covenants are deemed by the Secretary to be compatible with the purposes of the wildlife refuges, games ranges, fish hatcheries, and other fish and wildlife conservation areas.

SEC. 4. The Secretary may establish reasonable charges and fees and issue permits for public use of national wildlife refuges, game ranges, national fish hatcheries, and other conservation areas administered by the Department of the Interior for fish and wildlife purposes. The Secretary may issue regulations to carry out the purposes of this Act. A violation of such regulations shall be a petty offense (18 U.S.C.1) with maximum penalties of imprisonment for not more than six months, or a fine of not more than $500, or both.

SEC. 5. There is authorized to be appropriated such funds as may be necessary to carry out the purposes of this Act, including the construction and maintenance of public recreational facilities.

Approved September 28, 1962.

AN ACT TO PROTECT ENDANGERED SPECIES
FROM EXTINCTION*
October 15, 1966

When a particular species has been in danger of extinction, the government has sometimes tried to protect it either by hunting restrictions, as with the Bald Eagle (54 Stat., 25), or by the establishment of a refuge mainly for that species. In the latter instance it had usually been necessary to pass separate legislation for each individual species, but in 1966 the Secretary of the Interior was authorized to establish such refuges, and funds were provided for that purpose.

An Act to provide for the conservation, protection, and propagation of native species of fish and wildlife, including migratory birds, that are threatened with extinction; to consolidate the authorities relating to the administration by the Secretary of the Interior of the National Wildlife Refuge System; and for other purposes.

Be it enacted by the Senate and House of Representatives of the United States of America in Congress assembled, That (a) the Congress finds and declares that one of the unfortunate consequences of growth and development in the United States has been the extermination of some native species of fish and wildlife; that serious losses in other species of native wild animals with educational, historical, recreational, and scientific value have occurred and are occurring; and that the United States has pledged itself, pursuant to migratory bird treaties with Canada and Mexico and the Convention on Nature Protection and Wildlife Preservation in the Western Hemisphere, to conserve and protect, where practicable, the various species of native fish and wildlife, including game and nongame migratory birds, that are threatened with extinction. The purposes of this Act are to provide a program for the conservation, protection, restoration, and propagation of selected species of native fish and wildlife, including migratory birds, that are threatened with extinction, and to consolidate, restate, and modify the present authorities relating to administration by the Secretary of the Interior of the National Wildlife Refuge System.

(b) It is further declared to be the policy of Congress that the Secretary of the Interior, the Secretary of Agriculture, and the Secretary of Defense, together with the heads of bureaus, agencies, and services within their departments, shall seek to protect species of native fish and wildlife, including migratory birds, that are threatened with extinction, and, insofar as is practicable and consistent with

*80 *Statutes at Large,* 926.

[85]

the primary purposes of such bureaus, agencies, and services, shall preserve the habitats of such threatened species on lands under their jurisdiction.

(c) A species of native fish and wildlife shall be regarded as threatened with extinction whenever the Secretary of the Interior finds, after consultation with the affected States, that its existence is endangered because its habitat is threatened with destruction, drastic modification, or severe curtailment, or because of overexploitation, disease, predation, or because of other factors, and that its survival requires assistance. In addition to consulting with the States, the Secretary shall, from time to time, seek the advice and recommendations of interested persons and organizations including, but not limited to, ornithologists, ichthyologists, ecologists, herpetologists, and mammalogists. He shall publish in the Federal Register the names of the species of native fish and wildlife found to be threatened with extinction in accordance with this paragraph.

SEC. 2. (a) The Secretary of the Interior shall utilize the land acquisition and other authorities of the Migratory Bird Conservation Act, as amended, the Fish and Wildlife Act of 1956, as amended, and the Fish and Wildlife Coordination Act to carry out a program in the United States of conserving, protecting, restoring, and propagating selected species of native fish and wildlife that are threatened with extinction.

(b) In addition to the land acquisition authorities in such Acts, the Secretary is hereby authorized to acquire by purchase, donation, or otherwise, lands or interests therein needed to carry out the purpose of this Act relating to the conservation, protection, restoration, and propagation of selected species of native fish that are threatened with extinction.

(c) Funds made available pursuant to the Land and Water Conservation Fund Act of 1965 (78 Stat. 897) may be used for the purpose of acquiring lands, waters, or interests therein pursuant to this section that are needed for the purpose of conserving, protecting, restoring, and propagating selected species of native fish and wildlife, including migratory birds, that are threatened with extinction. Not to exceed $5,000,000 may be appropriated annually pursuant to that Act for such purpose for any fiscal year, and the total sum appropriated for such purpose shall not exceed $15,000,000: *Provided,* That the Secretary shall, to the greatest extent possible, utilize funds from the Land and Water Conservation Fund Act of 1965 for such purpose. Such sums shall remain available until expended. The Secretary shall not use more than $750,000 to acquire lands, waters, or interests therein for any one area for such purpose unless authorized by Act of Congress.

(d) The Secretary shall review other programs administered by him and, to the extent practicable, utilize such programs in furtherance of the purpose of this Act. The Secretary shall also encourage other Federal agencies to utilize, where practicable, their authorities in furtherance of the purpose of this Act and shall consult with and assist such agencies in carrying out endangered species program.

SEC. 3. (a) In carrying out the program authorized by this Act, the Secretary shall cooperate to the maximum extent practicable with the several States. Such cooperation shall include consultation before the acquisition of any land for the purpose of conserving, protecting, restoring, or propagating any endangered species of native fish and wildlife.

(b) The Secretary may enter into agreements with the States for the administration and management of any area established for the conservation, protection, restoration, and propagation of endangered species of native fish and wildlife. Any revenues derived from the administration of such areas under these agreements shall be subject to the provisions of section 401 of the Act of June 15, 1935 (49 Stat. 383), as amended (16 U.S.C. 715s).

SEC. 4.(a) For the purpose of consolidating the authorities relating to the various categories of areas that are administered by the Secretary of the Interior for the conservation of fish and wildlife, including species that are threatened with extinction, all lands, waters, and interests therein administered by the Secretary as wildlife refuges, areas for the protection and conservation of fish and wildlife that are threatened with extinction, wildlife ranges, game ranges, wildlife management areas, or waterfowl production areas are hereby designated as the "National Wildlife Refuge System" (referred to herein as the "System"), which shall be subject to the provisions of this section. Nothing contained in this Act shall restrict the authority of the Secretary to modify or revoke public land withdrawals affecting lands in the System as presently constituted, or as it may be constituted, whenever he determines that such action is consistent with the public interest.

(b) In administering the System, the Secretary is authorized—

(1) to enter into contracts with any person or public or private agency through negotiation for the provision of public accommodations when, and in such locations, and to the extent that the Secretary determines will not be inconsistent with the primary purpose for which the affected area was established.

(2) to accept donations of funds and to use such funds to acquire or manage lands or interests therein, and

(3) to acquire lands or interests therein by exchange (a) for acquired lands or public lands under his jurisdiction which he finds suitable for disposition, or (b) for the right to remove, in accordance with such terms and conditions as the Secretary may prescribe, products from the acquired or public lands within the System. The values of the properties so exchanged either shall be approximately equal, or if they are not approximately equal the values shall be equalized by the payment of cash to the grantor or to the Secretary as the circumstances require.

(c) No person shall knowingly disturb, injure, cut, burn, remove, destroy, or possess any real or personal property of the United States, including natural growth, in any area of the System; or take or possess any fish, bird, mammal, or other wild vertebrate or invertebrate animals or part or nest or egg thereof within any such area; or enter, use, or otherwise occupy any such area for any purpose; unless such activities are performed by persons authorized to manage such area, or unless such activities are permitted either under subsection (d) of this section or by express provision of the law, proclamation, Executive order, or public land order establishing the area, or amendment thereof: *Provided,* That the United States mining and mineral leasing laws shall continue to apply to any lands within the System to the same extent they apply prior to the effective date of this Act unless subsequently withdrawn under other authority of law. Nothing in this Act shall be construed to authorize the Secretary to control or regulate hunting or fishing of resident fish and wildlife, including endangered species thereof, on lands not within the System. The regulations permitting hunting and fishing of resident fish and wildlife within the System shall be, to the extent practicable, consistent with State fish and wildlife laws and regulations. The provisions of this Act shall not be construed as affecting the authority, jurisdiction, or responsibility of the several States to manage, control, or regulate fish and resident wildlife under State law or regulations in any area within the System.

(d) The Secretary is authorized, under such regulations as he may prescribe, to—

> (1) permit the use of any area within the System for any purpose, including but not limited to hunting, fishing, public recreation and accommodations, and access whenever he determines that such uses are compatible with the major purposes for which such areas were established: *Provided,* That not to exceed 40 per centum at any one time of any area that has been, or hereafter may be acquired, reserved, or set apart as an inviolate sanctuary for migratory birds, under any law, proclamation, Executive order, or public land order may be administered by the Secretary as an area within which the taking of migratory game birds may be permitted under such regulations as he may prescribe; and

> (2) permit the use of, or grant easements in, over, across, upon, through, or under any areas within the System for purposes such as but not necessarily limited to, powerlines, telephone lines, canals, ditches, pipelines, and roads, including the construction, operation, and maintenance thereof, whenever he determines that such uses are compatible with the purposes for which these areas are established.

(e) Any person who violates or fails to comply with any of the provisions of this Act or any regulations issued thereunder shall be fined not more than $500 or be imprisoned not more than six months, or both.

(f) Any person authorized by the Secretary of the Interior to enforce the provisions of this Act or any regulations issued thereunder, may, without a warrant, arrest any person violating this Act or regulations in his presence or view, and may execute any warrant or other process issued by an officer or court of competent jurisdiction to enforce the provisions of this Act or regulations, and may with a search warrant search for and seize any property, fish, bird, mammal, or other wild vertebrate or invertebrate animals or part or nest or egg thereof, taken or possessed in violation of this Act or the regulations issued thereunder. Any property, fish, bird, mammal, or other wild vertebrate or invertebrate animals or part or egg thereof seized with or without a search warrant shall be held by such person or by a United States marshal, and upon conviction, shall be forfeited to the United States and disposed of by the court.

(g) Regulations applicable to areas of the System that are in effect on the date of enactment of this Act shall continue in effect until modified or rescinded.

(h) Nothing in this section shall be construed to amend, repeal, or otherwise modify the provision of the Act of September 28, 1962 (76 Stat. 653; 16 U.S.C. 460K — 460K–4) which authorizes the Secretary of the Interior to administer the areas within the System for public recreation. The provisions of this section relating to recreation shall be administered in accordance with the provisions of said Act.

(i) Nothing in this Act shall constitute an express or implied claim or denial on the part of the Federal Government as to exemption from State water laws.

SEC. 5. (a) The term "person" as used in this Act means any individual, partnership, corporation, or association.

(b) The terms "take" or "taking" or "taken" as used in this Act mean to pursue, hunt, shoot, capture, collect, kill, or attempt to pursue, hunt, shoot, capture, collect, or kill.

(c) The terms "State" and the "United States" as used in this Act mean the several States of the United States, the Commonwealth of Puerto Rico, American Samoa, the Virgin Islands, and Guam.

SEC. 6. Section 4(b) of the Act of March 16, 1934 (48 Stat. 451), as amended (16 U.S.C. 718d (b)), is further amended by changing the colon after the word "areas" to a period and striking the provisos, which relate to hunting at certain wildlife refuges and which are now covered by section 4 of this Act.

SEC. 7. (a) Sections 4 and 12 of the Migratory Bird Conservation Act (45 Stat. 1222), as amended (16 U.S.C. 715c and 715k), are further amended by deleting the word "game" wherever it appears.

(b) Section 10 of the Migratory Bird Conservation Act (45 Stat. 1224), as amended (16 U.S.C. 715i), which relates to the administration of certain wildlife refuges, is amended to read as follows:

"SEC. 10. (a) Areas of lands, waters, or interests therein acquired or reserved pursuant to this Act shall, unless otherwise provided by law, be administered by the Secretary of the Interior under rules and regulations prescribed by him to conserve and protect migratory birds in accordance with treaty obligations with Mexico and Canada, and other species of wildlife found thereon, including species that are threatened with extinction, and to restore or develop adequate wildlife habitat.

"(b) In administering such areas, the Secretary is authorized to manage timber, range, and agricultural crops; to manage other species of animals, including but not limited to fenced range animals, with the objectives of perpetuating, distributing, and utilizing the resources; and to enter into agreements with public and private agencies."

(c) Section 11 of the Migratory Bird Conservation Act (45 Stat. 1224 16 U. S.C. 715j) is amended by striking the period at the end thereof and adding the following: "(39 Stat. 1702) and the treaty between the United States and the United Mexican States for the protection of migratory birds and game mammals concluded February 7, 1936 (50 Stat. 1311)."

(d) Sections 13 and 14 of the Migratory Bird Conservation Act (45 Stat. 1225), as amended (16 U.S.C. 7151 and 715m), which provide for the enforcement of said Act and for penalties for violations thereof and which are covered by section 4 of this Act, are repealed.

SEC. 8. (a) Sections 302 and 303 of title III of the Act of June 15, 1935 (40 Stat. 382), as amended (16 U.S.C. 715d–1 and 715d–2), which authorize exchanges at wildlife refuges and which are covered by section 4 of this Act, are repealed.

(b) The last sentence of section 401 (a) of the Act of June 15, 1935 (49 Stat. 383), as amended (16 U.S.C. 715s), is amended by inserting after the term "wildlife refuges", the following: "lands acquired or reserved for the protection and conservation of fish and wildlife that are threatened with extinction,".

SEC. 9. The first clause in section 1 of the Act of September 28, 1962 (76 Stat. 653), is amended by deleting the words "national wildlife refuges, game ranges," and inserting therein "areas within the National Wildlife Refuge System,".

SEC. 10. (a) The first sentence in section 1 of the Act of August 22, 1957 (71 Stat. 412; 16 U.S.C. 696), is amended to read as follows:

"SEC. 1. In order to protect and preserve in the national interest the key deer and other wildlife resources in the Florida Keys, the Secretary of the Interior is authorized to acquire by purchase, lease, exchange, and donations, including the use of donated funds, such lands or interests therein in townships 65 and 66 south, ranges 28, 29, and 30 east, Monroe County, Florida, as he shall find to be suitable for the conservation and management of the said key deer and other wildlife: *Provided,* That no lands within a one thousand-foot zone adjacent to either side of United States Highway Numbered 1 in Monroe County shall be acquired for the Key Deer National Wildlife Refuge by condemnation. The Secretary, in the exercise of his exchange authority, may accept title to any non-Federal property in townships 65 and 66 south, ranges 28, 29, and 30 east, Monroe County, Florida, and in exchange therefor convey to the grantor of such property any federally owned property in the State of Florida under his jurisdiction which he classifies as suitable for exchange or other disposal. The values of the properties so exchanged either shall be approximately equal, or if they are not approximately equal the values shall be equalized by the payment of cash to the grantor or to the Secretary as the circumstances require."

(b) Section 3 of such Act of August 22, 1957 (16 U.S.C. 696b), is amended by striking out the second and third sentences and inserting in lieu thereof the following: "The Secretary shall not utilize more than $2,035,000 from appropriated funds for the acquisition of land and interests in land for the purposes of this Act."

Approved October 15, 1966

FISHING

In 1965 there were 28,348,000 sport fishermen who traveled 22.7 billion miles and spent $2.9 billion during 523 million recreation days. Plainly, sport fishing is one of America's favorite forms of outdoor recreation. Our knowledge of aquatic life is meager, however, compared to our knowledge of flora and fauna on land. The basic reason for this discrepancy is, of course, that it is much more difficult to study and observe plant and animal life under water. For this reason government fishery agencies at both the national and the state level have been greatly concerned with the development of research. Their other major efforts have involved stocking streams and lakes, reduction of "trash" and certain predatory fish, and manipulation of the aquatic environment.

Sport fish, like wild game, are presumed to be the property and responsibility of the individual states. Consequently, much of the management of fish and fishermen has been carried on by state fish and game agencies. For example, as early as 1678 Virginia prohibited the use of "jack lights" in fishing and in 1734 the Common Council of New York City prohibited fishing in fresh water ponds except by rod, hook, and line.

As fishing declined around heavily populated areas, sportsmen's organizations were formed to rehabilitate fishing grounds. These groups were mainly responsible for the creation of state fish commissions in the latter half of the nineteenth century and now all 50 states have fish and game departments that enforce regulations and carry on fishery research and management functions.

The early efforts of such state fish management agencies were devoted primarily to restrictions on fishing through licenses, restricted seasons, creel limits, and restocking. Between 1870 and 1900 there was also considerable experimentation in introducing new species into certain areas. Carp were brought from Europe in 1872. Largemouth bass were moved north. Striped bass were introduced in Pacific Coast drainages. Rainbow trout were transported to eastern states. Not all of these "transplants" were successful. For example, attempts to establish Pacific salmon and steelhead trout in the Great Lakes failed.

All these management methods (restrictions on catch, restocking, and transplants) have lately come to be questioned. It now appears that providing suitable habitat is the most effective management tool and that restrictions on fishing and restocking have little effect unless the environment is suitable for reproduction and growth.

The states were not always prepared to adequately discharge their responsibilities of fishing regulation and fishery management, however, because they were either unwilling or unable to provide sufficient funds. For this reason the Federal Government came to the aid of the states by passing the Dingell-Johnson Act of 1950 and the Anadromous Fish Act of 1965.

It is not generally understood that water resources developments (for flood control, irrigation, navigation, or power) often destroy or injure fish and wildlife unless certain safety measures are built into the project. Four important congressional acts have been designed to better integrate the water projects with the aim of fish and wildlife preservation: the Fish and Wildlife Coordination Act of 1934; a substantial amendment to strengthen that act in 1946 (60 *Stat.* 1080); a second amendment called the Fish and Wildlife Coordination Act of 1958; and the Federal Water Project Recreation Act of 1965.

Finally, as it has come to be recognized that common sense and casual observation are inadequate to deal with problems of fish management and manipulation of habitat, increasing effort has gone into systematic research. As long as we continue to change the aquatic environment through pollution, dam-building, highway construction, drainage, and canal-building, research activities must be continued and accelerated if fishing opportunities are to be maintained or improved.

HORACE GREELEY'S "PLAY DAYS"*
1868

Horace Greeley described fishing opportunities and experiences in the early 1800's in this excerpt from Recollections of a Busy Life.

Fifty years have passed since I first stole down, one foggy morning, to the brook that ran through the west side of my father's farm in New Hampshire, and, dropping my line off the bridge, felt a bite almost instantly, and, hauling up, drew in a nice speckled trout. I had tried to fish before, but without success; henceforth, through boyhood, I was an enthusiastic, persevering fisherman, though never a master of the art. The modern sophistications of fly and reel were unknown in rural New England in those days; hook, line, and sinker gave adequate warning to every considerate, wary fish of what he had to expect if he bit; but fishermen were fewer and brooks more shady, less capricious in volume, than the clearing away of woods has since made them, while intellectual delights were rarer and less inviting: so fishing was largely the pleasure of the gay and the business of the grave. Our rivers, unvexed by mill-dams, swarmed in their season with shad, lamprey-eels, &c., and afforded some salmon, as well as fish of less consideration. Even the sea was not too far to be visited by adventurous parties, intent on a week's profitable sport. Winter brought its sleigh-loads of fresh cod, frozen as soon as fairly out of water, and so retaining the sweetness which soon vanishes forever; and I reckon that, down to 1800, the people of New England had eaten many more pounds of fish than of beef and mutton together,—perhaps of all meats save those obtained by the chase.

In Vermont, the clay soil of the Champlain Valley discolors the brooks when full and repels the trout; but the abundant lakes and lakelets used to abound in perch, bass, and sunfish, while the larger streams afforded, in addition, eels and pike. East Bay—the common estuary of the Poultney and Castleton creeks, and dividing Westhaven from Hampton, N.Y.—is, in Spring, the resort of a small, peculiar shad, which, with a few pike, bass, mullet, &c., come up from the Lake to spawn, and are caught with seines drawn by two fishermen, who wade through the swollen stream,—one of them sometimes obliged to swim,—while great blocks of ice, left aground by the receding floods, often lie slowly wasting along the bank. The melted snow from the mountains eastward stings like a hornet as you enter it; so that, if this were not sport, it would be disagreeable; but I have often, when ten to twelve years old, carried the in-shore staff while my father took the deeper track, which immersed him up to his neck; we dipping together at his word of command, and then gathering up our net and carrying out therein,

*Horace Greeley, *Recollections of a Busy Life* (New York: J.B. Ford and Co., 1868), 114–16.

from no fish at all up to six or eight. I have known a dozen taken at one haul; but this was most extraordinary.

In Summer, we sometimes caught a fine pike or eel with hook and line in the basin beneath the fifty-foot cataract by which the blended creeks tumble into the Bay; but fishing here was too slow for any sportsman less persistent than I then was. I have sat here alone in the dense darkness of a wooded abyss, where the fall drowned all sounds but its own, from 8 to 11 P. M., without being blest with a bite, and then felt my way up through the Egyptian darkness of the forest hillside to the road, and so home, pondering on the fickleness of fortune; yet eager to try again whenever opportunity should favor. I always had my week's work allotted me when I could, and generally succeeded in redeeming at least the Saturday afternoon for my favorite pastime.

JOINT RESOLUTION TO ESTABLISH A COMMISSION
OF FISH AND FISHERIES*
February 9, 1871

The first federal agency devoted to fisheries was the United States Fish and Fisheries Commission which was established in 1871.

No. 22.—Joint Resolution for the Protection and Preservation of Food Fishes of the Coast of the United States.

Whereas it is asserted that the most valuable food fishes of the coast and the lakes of the United States are rapidly diminishing in number, to the public injury, and so as materially to affect the interests of trade and commerce: Therefore,

Be it resolved by the Senate and House of Representatives of the United States of America in Congress assembled, That the President be, and he hereby is, authorized and required to appoint, by and with the advice and consent of the Senate, from among the civil officers or employees of the Government, one person of proved scientific and practical acquaintance with the fishes of the coast, to be commissioner of fish and fisheries, to serve without additional salary.

SEC. 2. *And be it further resolved,* That it shall be the duty of said commissioner to prosecute investigations and inquiries on the subject, with the view of ascertaining whether any and what diminution in the number of the food fishes of the coast and the lakes of the United States has taken place; and, if so, to what causes the same is due; and also whether any and what protective, prohibitory, or precautionary measures should be adopted in the premises; and to report upon the same to Congress.

SEC. 3. *And be it further resolved,* That the heads of the Executive Departments be, and they are hereby, directed to cause to be rendered all necessary and practicable aid to the said commissioner in the prosecution of the investigations and inquiries aforesaid.

SEC. 4. *And be it further resolved,* That it shall be lawful for said commissioner to take, or cause to be taken, at all times, in the waters of the sea-coast of the United States, where the tide ebbs and flows, and also in the waters of the lakes, such fish or specimens thereof as may in his judgment, from time to time, be needful or proper for the conduct of his duties as aforesaid, any law, custom, or usage of any State to the contrary notwithstanding.

Approved, February 9, 1871.

---

*Cong. Globe, 41st Cong., 3rd sess. (Feb. 9, 1871), 398.

AN APPROPRIATION FOR FISHERIES RESEARCH*
June 21, 1916

One of the earliest congressional acts appropriating funds for fisheries research concerned the damage to fisheries by predatory fishes and acquatic animals.

An Act to conduct investigations and experiments for ameliorating the damage wrought to the fisheries by predacious fishes and aquatic animals.

Be it enacted by the Senate and House of Representatives of the United States of America in Congress assembled, That the Commissioner of Fisheries be, and he is hereby, authorized and directed to conduct investigations and experiments for the purpose of ameliorating the damage wrought to the fisheries by dogfish and other predacious fishes and aquatic animals.

SEC. 2. That the said investigations and experiments shall be such as to develop the best and cheapest means of taking such fishes and aquatic animals, of utilizing them for economic purposes, especially for food and to encourage the establishment of fisheries and markets for them.

SEC. 3. That the sum of $25,000, or so much thereof as may be necessary, is hereby appropriated, out of any money in the Treasury not otherwise appropriated, to enable the Commissioner of Fisheries to carry out the provisions of this Act, the same to be immediately available.

Approved, June 21, 1916.

*39 *Statutes at Large,* 232.

THE FISH AND WILDLIFE COORDINATION ACT*
March 10, 1934

By 1934 it had come to be recognized that the construction of dams and other water improvements could have harmful, as well as beneficial, effects on fish and wildlife. The Fish and Wildlife Coordination Act of 1934 provided a mechanism for minimizing the harmful effects of these water projects.

An Act to promote the conservation of wild life, fish, and game, and for other purposes.

Be it enacted by the Senate and House of Representatives of the United States of America in Congress assembled, That the Secretary of Agriculture and the Secretary of Commerce are authorized to provide expert assistance to and to cooperate with Federal, State, and other agencies in the rearing, stocking, and increasing the supply of game and fur-bearing animals and fish, in combating diseases, and in developing a Nation-wide program of wild-life conservation and rehabilitation.

SEC. 2. The Secretary of Agriculture and the Secretary of Commerce are authorized to make such investigations as they may deem necessary to determine the effects of domestic sewage, trade wastes, and other polluting substances on wild life, with special reference to birds, mammals, fish, and shellfish, and to make reports to the Congress of their investigations with recommendations for remedial measures. Such investigations shall include studies of methods for the recovery of wastes and the collation of data on the progress being made in these fields for the use of Federal, State, municipal, and private agencies.

SEC. 3. (a) Whenever the Federal Government through the Bureau of Reclamation or otherwise, impounds water for any use, opportunity shall be given to the Bureau of Fisheries and/or the Bureau of Biological Survey to make such uses of the impounded waters for fish-culture stations and migratory-bird resting and nesting areas as are not inconsistent with the primary use of the waters and/or the constitutional rights of the States. In the case of any waters heretofore impounded by the United States, through the Bureau of Reclamation or otherwise, the Bureau of Fisheries and/or the Bureau of Biological Survey may consult with the Bureau of Reclamation or other governmental agency controlling the impounded waters, with a view to securing a greater biological use of the waters not inconsistent with their primary use and/or the constitutional rights of the States and make such proper uses thereof as are not inconsistent with the primary use of the waters and/or the constitutional rights of the States.

*48 Statutes at Large, 401.

(b) Hereafter, whenever any dam is authorized to be constructed, either by the Federal Government itself or by any private agency under Government permit, the Bureau of Fisheries shall be consulted, and before such construction is begun or permit granted, when deemed necessary, due and adequate provision, if economically practicable, shall be made for the migration of fish life from the upper to the lower and from the lower to the upper waters of said dam by means of fish lifts, ladders, or other devices.

SEC. 4. The Office of Indian Affairs, the Bureau of Fisheries, and the Bureau of Biological Survey are authorized, jointly, to prepare plans for the better protection of the wild-life resources, including fish, migratory waterfowl and upland game birds, game animals and fur-bearing animals, upon all the Indian reservations and unallotted Indian lands coming under the supervision of the Federal Government. When such plans have been prepared they shall be promulgated by the Secretary of the Interior, the Secretary of Commerce, and the Secretary of Agriculture, who are authorized to make the necessary regulations for enforcement thereof and from time to time to change, alter, or amend such regulations.

SEC. 5. The Bureau of Biological Survey and the Bureau of Fisheries are hereby authorized to make surveys of the wild-life resources of the public domain, or of any lands owned or leased by the Government, to conduct such investigations as may be necessary for the development of a program for the maintenance of an adequate supply of wild life in these areas, to establish thereon game farms and fish-cultural stations commensurate with the need for replenishing the supply of game and fur-bearing animals and fish, and, in cooperation with the National Park Service, The Forest Service, or other Federal agencies, the State agencies, to coodinate and establish adequate measures for wild-life control on such game farms and fish-cultural stations: *Provided,* That no such game farm shall hereafter be established in any State without the consent of the legislature of that State.

SEC. 6. In carrying out the provisions of this Act the Federal agencies charged with its enforcement may cooperate with other Federal agencies and with States, counties, municipalities, individuals, and public and private agencies, organizations, and institutions, and may accept donations of lands, funds, and other aids to the development of the program authorized in this Act: *Provided, however,* That no such donations of land shall be accepted without consent of the legislature of the State in which such land may be situated: *Provided,* That no authority is given in this Act for setting up any additional bureau or division in any department or commission, and shall not authorize any additional appropriation for carrying out its purposes.

Approved, March 10, 1934.

AN ACT TO TRANSFER THE BUREAU OF FISHERIES TO THE DEPARTMENT OF THE INTERIOR*
May 9, 1939

The United States Commission of Fish and Fisheries had been established in 1871. However, an act of February 14, 1903 (32 Stat. 825,827) created the Department of Commerce and Labor and incorporated the old commission, renamed the Bureau of Fisheries, into the new department. In 1939 there was another organizational change—one which proved to be highly significant for sport fishermen in particular. The Bureau of Fisheries was transferred from the Department of Commerce to the Department of the Interior since the general orientation of the Department of Commerce had allowed for scant attention to fishing except for commercial purposes. The relevant portion of the act follows.

(e) *Bureau of Fisheries.* — The Bureau of Fisheries in the Department of Commerce and its functions are hereby transferred to the Department of the Interior and shall be administered in that Department under the direction and supervision of the Secretary of the Interior. The functions of the Secretary of Commerce relating to the protection of fur seals and other fur-bearing animals, to the supervision of the Pribilof Islands and the care of the natives thereof, and to the Whaling Treaty Act, are hereby transferred to, and shall be exercised by, the Secretary of the Interior.

---

*53 *Statutes at Large,* 1433, pursuant to 53 *Statutes at Large,* 561.

AN ACT TO CONSOLIDATE THE BUREAU OF FISHERIES WITH THE BUREAU OF BIOLOGICAL SURVEY*
April 2, 1940

By 1940 it was obvious that many of the functions of the Bureau of Fisheries and the Bureau of Biological Survey were complementary. Part of Reorganization Plan 3, which consolidated these two agencies to form the Fish and Wildlife Service, is reproduced below.

SEC. 3. *Fish and Wildlife Service.* — The Bureau of Fisheries and the Bureau of Biological Survey in the Department of the Interior with their respective functions are consolidated into one agency in the Department of the Interior to be known as the Fish and Wildlife Service. The functions of the consolidated agency shall be administered under the direction and supervision of the Secretary of the Interior by a Director and not more than two Assistant Directors, who shall be appointed by the Secretary and perform such duties as he shall prescribe. The offices of Commissioner and Deputy Commissioner of Fisheries and the offices of Chief and Associate Chief of the Bureau of Biological Survey are abolished and their functions transferred to the consolidated agency.

*54 *Statutes at Large,* 1232.

A SURVEY OF FISHERY RESOURCES,*
May 11, 1944

The act of 1944 recognized the need for the collection of data on fishery resources and the use of such data as a basis for regulation.

> Joint Resolution authorizing and directing the Fish and Wildlife Service of the Department of the Interior to conduct a survey of the marine and fresh-water fishery resources of the United States, its Territories, and possessions.

Whereas the fishery resources of the United States and its contiguous waters are so varied and so abundant that the fishery industries at the beginning of the Second World War had assumed a world position with respect to the production of fishery commodities, second only to the position occupied by Japan; and

Whereas despite the magnitude of these fishery resources and the economic importance of the fishing industry, the United States has failed to develop, to utilize, and to conserve her marine and fresh-water fishery resources to the fullest possible extent and to a degree commensurate with the development, utilization, and conservation of the resources of the land; and

Whereas the wartime demands for fishery products as food, for fishery by-products for industrial uses, and upon the fisheries as a recreational pursuit, far exceed even the most optimistic production estimates; and

Whereas it is in the interest of all of the people of the United States to insure the fullest permanent development, utilization, and protection of the marine fishery resources of the high seas which may be subject to utilization by United States nationals, and of the marine and fresh-water fishery resources within the limits of territorial jurisdiction prosecuted both commercially and recreationally: Therefore be it

Resolved by the Senate and House of Representatives of the United States of America in Congress assembled, That the Fish and Wildlife Service of the Department of the Interior is hereby authorized and directed to conduct a survey of the character, extent, and condition of all of the marine and fresh-water fishery resources and other aquatic resources of the United States, its Territories, and possessions, including high-seas resources in which the United States may have interests or rights; and the economic organization and status of the industry based thereon; such survey is to include but is not to be limited to the following:

(a) The current methods, practices, facilities, and equipment used in producing commercial fishery products.

(b) The methods, practices, facilities, and equipment used in processing, dis-

*58 *Statutes at Large,* 220.

tributing, transporting, marketing, and storing fishery products, including an assessment of measures required for the protection of these perishable commodities.

(c) The methods, practices, facilities, and equipment which may be practicable for expanding the utilization of the existing or potential marine and fresh-water fishery resources, inclusive of recreational fishing.

(d) The laws and regulations that govern the commercial and recreational fisheries.

SEC. 2. The Fish and Wildlife Service of the Department of the Interior is directed to submit a report to the Congress as soon as practicable, but not later than January 1, 1945, concerning the results of the survey mentioned in the preceding section, and also shall submit recommendations with respect to the following:

(a) New or revised regulations or precautionary measures deemed to be necessary or advisable for the protection, conservation, and management on a sustained-yield basis of the fishery and other renewable marine and fresh-water resources.

(b) New or revised regulations or precautionary measures deemed to be necessary or desirable to insure adequate protection of the fishery and other biological resources from contamination by pollution or other hazards, and to prevent spoilage or deterioration of fishery products; such recommendations to apply to catching, landing, processing, transporting, marketing, or storing fishery products or commodities derived from the fisheries.

(c) The opportunities for, and the advisability of further arrangements for, coordinating fishery administration and management through State fishery compacts with the consent of the Congress (as authorized by article I, section 10, of the Constitution of the United States of America), and opportunities for, and the advisability of additional coordinated management and administration of, international fisheries.

(d) The means of effecting the maximum utilization, consistent with their continued preservation at an optimum level of productivity, of the marine and fresh-water fishery resources utilized or potentially capable of utilization for commercial and recreational fishing, giving special consideration to methods of managing and increasing the fishery production of interior waters, including artificial impoundments and farm ponds.

(e) New and improved methods of capturing, landing, processing, storing, distributing, and marketing fishery products or commodities, including increasing consumption as food and the industrial utilization of fishery products through public education, or other activities; such recommendations to contemplate the full and cooperative use of the personnel and facilities of appropriate State, Territorial, county, local, or other organizations, as well as those of private and industrial or other organizations and enterprises.

(f) A program of economic stabilization of the fisheries and of Federal, State, or other assistance needed during the post-war period and thereafter to effect orderly development and expansion of the commercial fisheries and allied enterprises, and to secure and provide for the fisheries benefits comparable to those afforded the food production activities and industries dependent upon the lands.

(g) A comprehensive statistical and market-reporting system to provide complete, accurate, and current data on production and fishing intensity in the commercial and recreational fisheries, to facilitate the most efficient utilization of the aquatic resources and the greatest possible benefits and returns therefrom, as well as for the purpose of providing fundamental information on rates of withdrawal in order that the effects of utilization upon the basic resources may always be known.

(h) Special and regular appropriations necessary to establish a national policy and to carry out a program for the optimum utilization of the marine and freshwater commercial and recreational fishery resources such as may be necessary to accomplish the specific purposes and objectives hereinbefore mentioned, including funds for the publication and dissemination of technical and practical information.

SEC. 3. There is authorized to be appropriated, out of moneys in the Treasury not otherwise appropriated, such funds as may be necessary for the purpose of carrying out the provisions of this joint resolution, but not to exceed $20,000.

Approved May 11, 1944.

ERADICATION OF THE SEA LAMPREY*
August 8, 1946

The most valuable fish in the Great Lakes was once the lake trout. At peak production, about 10 million pounds of lake trout were taken annually. Partly because of the invasion of the predatory sea lamprey, however, the lake trout catch was sharply reduced. This act attempted to alleviate the situation.

Joint Resolution authorizing and directing the Director of the Fish and Wildlife Service of the Department of the Interior to investigate and eradicate the predatory sea lampreys of the Great Lakes.

Resolved by the Senate and House of Representatives of the United States of America in Congress assembled, That the Director of the Fish and Wildlife Service of the Department of the Interior is hereby authorized and directed to prosecute, for a period of not to exceed ten years from the date of approval of this joint resolution, investigations of the abundance and distribution of sea lampreys, experiments to develop control measures, and a vigorous program for the elimination and eradication of sea lamprey populations of the Great Lakes.

SEC. 2. In carrying out the foregoing purposes and objectives the Director of the Fish and Wildlife Service is authorized to cooperate with the official conservation agencies of the States bordering on the Great Lakes, with the commercial fishing industry, and with other governmental or private agencies, organizations, or individuals having jurisdiction over or an interest in the fisheries of the Great Lakes.

SEC. 3. There is authorized to be appropriated from time to time, out of any moneys in the Treasury not otherwise appropriated, such sums as may be necessary not to exceed $20,000 per annum to carry out the purposes and objectives of this joint resolution.

Approved August 8, 1946.

*60 *Statutes at Large*, 930.

THE DINGELL-JOHNSON ACT*
August 9, 1950

The Dingell-Johnson Act of 1950 was patterned after the Pittman-Robertson (Federal Aid in Wildlife Restoration) Act of 1937. (See pp. 73–76.) It provided for a 10 percent manufacturer's excise tax on fishing rods, creels, reels, and artificial lures, baits, and flies. The proceeds were to go to the states for fish restoration and management purposes, and it goes without saying that these funds have greatly increased capabilities in these areas.

An Act to provide that the United States shall aid the States in fish restoration and management projects, and for other purposes.

Be it enacted by the Senate and House of Representatives of the United States of America in Congress assembled, That the Secretary of the Interior is authorized and directed to cooperate with the States through their respective State fish and game departments in fish restoration and management projects as hereinafter set forth: No money apportioned under this Act to any State, except as hereinafter provided, shall be expended therein until its legislature, or other State agency authorized by the State constitution to make laws governing the conservation of fish, shall have assented to the provisions of this Act and shall have passed laws for the conservation of fish, which shall include a prohibition against the diversion of license fees paid by fishermen for any other purposes than the administration of said State fish and game department, except that, until the final adjournment of the first regular session of the legislature held after passage of this Act, the assent of the governor of the State shall be sufficient. The Secretary of the Interior and the State fish and game department of each State accepting the benefits of this Act shall agree upon the fish restoration and management projects to be aided in such State under the terms of this Act, and all projects shall conform to the standards fixed by the Secretary of the Interior.

SEC. 2. For the purpose of this Act the term "fish restoration and management projects" shall be construed to mean projects designed for the restoration and management of all species of fish which have material value in connection with sport or recreation in the marine and/or fresh waters of the United States and include—

(a) such research into problems of fish management and culture as may be necessary to efficient administration affecting fish resources;

(b) the acquisition of such facts as are necessary to guide and direct the regulation of fishing by law, including the extent of the fish population, the drain on the fish supply from fishing and/or natural causes, the necessity of legal regulation of fishing and the effects of any measures of regulation that are applied;

*64 Statutes at Large, 430.

(c) the formulation and adoption of plans of restocking waters with food and game fishes according to natural areas or districts to which such plans are applicable, together with the acquisition of such facts as are necessary to the formulation, execution, and testing the efficacy of such plans;

(d) the selection, restoration, rehabilitation, and improvement of areas of water or land adaptable as hatching, feeding, resting, or breeding places for fish, including acquisition by purchase, condemnation, lease, or gift of such areas or estates or interests therein as are suitable or capable of being made suitable therefor, and the construction thereon or therein of such works as may be necessary to make them available for such purposes, and such preliminary or incidental costs and expenses as may be incurred in and about such works; the term "State fish and game department" shall be construed to mean and include any department or division of department of another name, or commission, or official or officials, of a State empowered under its laws to exercise the functions ordinarily exercised by a State fish and game department.

SEC. 3. To carry out the provisions of this Act, there is hereby authorized to be appropriated an amount equal to the revenue accruing from tax imposed by section 3406 of the Internal Revenue Code, as heretofore or hereafter extended and amended, on fishing rods, creels, reels, and artificial lures, baits, and flies during the fiscal year ending June 30, 1951, and each fiscal year thereafter. The appropriation made under the provisions of this section for each fiscal year shall continue available during the succeeding fiscal year. So much of such appropriation apportioned to any State for any fiscal year as remains unexpended at the close thereof is authorized to be made available for expenditure in that State until the close of the succeeding fiscal year. Any amount apportioned to any State under the provisions of this Act which is unexpended or unobligated at the end of the period during which it is available for expenditure on any project is authorized to be made available for expenditure by the Secretary of the Interior in carrying on the research program of the Fish and Wildlife Service in respect to fish of material value for sport and recreation.

SEC. 4. So much, not to exceed 8 per centum, of each annual appropriation made in pursuance of the provisions of section 3 of this Act as the Secretary of the Interior may estimate to be necessary for his expenses in the conduct of necessary investigations, administration, and the execution of this Act and for aiding in the formulation, adoption, or administration of any compact between two or more States for the conservation and management of migratory fishes in marine or fresh waters shall be deducted for that purpose, and such sum is authorized to be made available therefor until the expiration of the next succeeding fiscal year. The Secretary of the Interior, after making the aforesaid deduction, shall apportion the remainder of the appropriation for each fiscal year among the several States in the following manner, that is to say, 40 per centum in the ratio which the area of each State including coastal and Great Lakes waters (as determined by the Secretary of the Interior) bears to the total area of all the

States and 60 per centum in the ratio which the number of persons holding paid licenses to fish for sport or recreation in the State in the second fiscal year preceding the fiscal year for which such apportionment is made, as certified to said Secretary by the State fish and game departments, bears to the number of such persons in all the States: *Provided,* That such apportionments shall be adjusted equitably so that no State shall receive less than 1 per centum nor more than 5 per centum of the total amount apportioned to all of the States: *Provided further,* That where the apportionment to any State under this section is less than $4,500 annually, the Secretary of the Interior may allocate not more than $4,500 of said appropriation to said State to carry out the purposes of this Act when said State certifies to the Secretary of the Interior that it has set aside not less than $1,500 from its fish-and-game funds or has made, through its legislature, an appropriation in this amount for said purposes. So much of any sum not allocated under the provisions of this section for any fiscal year is hereby authorized to be made available for expenditure to carry out the purposes of this Act until the close of the succeeding fiscal year, and if unexpended or unobligated at the end of such year such sum is hereby authorized to be made available for expenditure by the Secretary of the Interior in carrying on the research program of the Fish and Wildlife Service in respect to fish of material value for sport or recreation.

SEC. 5. For each fiscal year beginning with the fiscal year ending June 30, 1951, the Secretary of the Interior shall certify to the Secretary of the Treasury, and to each State fish and game department, the sum which he has estimated to be deducted for administering and executing this Act and the sum which he has apportioned to each State for such fiscal year. Any State desiring to avail itself of the benefits of this Act shall notify the Secretary of the Interior to this effect within sixty days after it has received the certification referred to in this section. The sum apportioned to any State which fails to notify the Secretary of the Interior as herein provided is authorized to be made available for expenditure by the Secretary of the Interior in carrying out the provisions of the fish-research program of the Fish and Wildlife Service.

SEC. 6. Any State desiring to avail itself of the benefits of this Act shall, by its State fish and game department, submit to the Secretary of the Interior full and detailed statements of any fish-restoration and management project proposed for that State. If the Secretary of the Interior finds that such project meets with the standards set up by him and approves said project, the State fish and game department shall furnish to him such surveys, plans, specifications, and estimates therefor as he may require: *Provided, however,* That the Secretary of the Interior shall approve only such projects as may be substantial in character and design, and the expenditure of funds hereby authorized shall be applied only to such approved projects and if otherwise applied they shall be replaced by the State before it may participate in any further apportionment under this Act.

Items included for engineering, inspection, and unforeseen contingencies in connection with any works to be constructed shall not exceed 10 per centum of the cost of such works and shall be paid by the State as a part of its contribution to the total cost of such works. If the Secretary of the Interior approves the plans, specifications, and estimates for the project, he shall notify the State fish and game department and immediately certify the fact to the Secretary of the Treasury. The Secretary of the Treasury shall thereupon set aside so much of said appropriation as represents the share of the United States payable under this Act on account of such project, which sum so set aside shall not exceed 75 per centum of the total estimated cost thereof. No payment of any money apportioned under this Act shall be made on any project until such statement of the project and the plans, specifications, and estimates thereof shall have been submitted to and approved by the Secretary of the Interior.

SEC. 7. When the Secretary of the Interior shall find that any project approved by him has been completed or, if involving research relating to fish, is being conducted, in compliance with said plans and specifications, he shall cause to be paid to the proper authority of said State the amount set aside for said project: *Provided,* That the Secretary of the Interior may, in his discretion, from time to time, make payments on said project as the same progresses; but these payments, including previous payments, if any, shall not be more than the United States pro rata share of the project in conformity with said plans and specifications. Any construction work and labor in each State shall be performed in accordance with its laws and under the direct supervision of the State fish and game department, subject to the inspection and approval of the Secretary of the Interior and in accordance with the rules and regulations made pursuant to this Act. The Secretary of the Interior and the State fish and game department of each State may jointly determine at what times and in what amounts payments, as work progresses, shall be made under this Act. Such payments shall be made against the said appropriation to such official or officials, or depository, as may be designated by the State fish and game department and authorized under the laws of the State to receive public funds of the State.

SEC. 8. To maintain fish-restoration and management projects established under the provisions of this Act shall be the duty of the States according to their respective laws: *Provided,* That beginning July 1, 1953, maintenance of projects heretofore completed under the provisions of this Act may be considered as projects under this Act: *Provided further,* That not more than 25 per centum of the allocation from Federal funds in any one year after July 1, 1953, may be set aside for such maintenance projects. Title to any real or personal property acquired by any State, and to improvements placed on State-owned lands through the use of funds paid to the State under the provisions of this Act, shall be vested in such State.

SEC. 9. Out of the deductions set aside for administering and executing this

Act the Secretary of the Interior is authorized to employ such assistants, clerks, and other persons in the District of Columbia and elsewhere, to be taken from the eligible lists of the civil service; to rent or construct buildings outside of the District of Columbia; to purchase such supplies, materials, equipment, office fixtures, and apparatus; and to incur such travel and other expenses, including publication of technical and administrative reports, purchase, maintenance, and hire of passenger-carrying motor vehicles, as he may deem necessary for carrying out the provisions of this Act.

SEC. 10. The Secretary of the Interior is authorized to make rules and regulations for carrying out the provisions of this Act.

SEC. 11. The Secretary of the Interior shall make an annual report to the Congress giving detailed information as to the projects established under the provisions of this Act and expenditures therefor.

SEC. 12. The Secretary of the Interior is authorized to cooperate with the Alaska Game Commission, the Division of Game and Fish of the Board of Commissioners of Agriculture and Forestry of Hawaii, the Commissioner of Agriculture and Commerce of Puerto Rico, and the Governor of the Virgin Islands, in the conduct of fish restoration and management projects, as defined in section 2 of this Act, upon such terms and conditions as he shall deem fair, just, and equitable, and is authorized to apportion to said Territories, Puerto Rico, and the Virgin Islands, out of money available for apportionment under this Act, such sums as he shall determine, not exceeding $75,000 for Alaska, not exceeding $25,000 for Hawaii, and not exceeding $10,000 each for Puerto Rico, and the Virgin Islands, in any one year, which apportionments, when made, shall be deducted before making the apportionments to the States provided for by this Act; but the Secretary shall in no event require any of said cooperating agencies to pay an amount which will exceed 25 per centum of the cost of any project. Any unexpended or unobligated balance of any apportionment made pursuant to this section shall be available for expenditure in the Territories, Puerto Rico, or the Vigin Islands, as the case may be, in the succeeding year, on any approved project, and if unexpended or unobligated at the end of such year is authorized to be made available for expenditure by the Secretary of the Interior in carrying on the research program of the Fish and Wildlife Service in respect to fish of material value for sport recreation.

SEC. 13. The effective date of this Act shall be July 1, 1950.

Approved August 9, 1950.

THE FISH AND WILDLIFE ACT*
August 8, 1956

The Fish and Wildlife Act of August 8, 1956 established within the Department of the Interior a United States Fish and Wildlife Service, consisting of two separate agencies, each of which was to have the status of a federal bureau. One of the agencies was to be known as the Bureau of Commercial Fisheries and the other as the Bureau of Sport Fisheries and Wildlife. The creation of a separate bureau with primary jurisdiction over sport fishing and wild game was partly the result of pressures from sportsmen's organizations which believed that sport fishing was being neglected in favor of commercial fishing. Whether or not such fears were justified, it would appear that a separate bureau with a primary responsibility for sport fishing and hunting would be most responsive to the demands of outdoor recreation.

An Act to establish a sound and comprehensive national policy with respect to fish and wildlife; to strengthen the fish and wildlife segments of the national economy; to establish within the Department of the Interior the position of Assistant Secretary for Fish and Wildlife; to establish a United States Fish and Wildlife Service; and for other purposes.

Be it enacted by the Senate and House of Representatives of the United States of America in Congress assembled, That this Act may be cited as the "Fish and Wildlife Act of 1956".

DECLARATION OF POLICY

SEC. 2. The Congress hereby declares that the fish, shellfish, and wildlife resources of the Nation make a material contribution to our national economy and food supply, as well as a material contribution to the health, recreation, and well-being of our citizens; that such resources are a living, renewable form of national wealth that is capable of being maintained and greatly increased with proper management, but equally capable of destruction if neglected or unwisely exploited; that such resources afford outdoor recreation throughout the Nation and provide employment, directly or indirectly, to a substantial number of citizens; that the fishing industries strengthen the defense of the United States through the provision of a trained seafaring citizenry and action-ready fleets of seaworthy vessels; that the training and sport afforded by fish and wildlife resources strengthen the national defense by contributing to the general health and physical fitness of millions of citizens; and that properly developed, such

*70 *Statutes at Large,* 1119.

[111]

fish and wildlife resources are capable of steadily increasing these valuable contributions to the life of the Nation.

The Congress further declares that the fishing industry, in its several branches, can prosper and thus fulfill its proper function in national life only if certain fundamental needs are satisfied by means that are consistent with the public interest and in accord with constitutional functions of governments. Among these needs are:

(1) Freedom of enterprise—freedom to develop new areas, methods, products, and markets in accordance with sound economic principles, as well as freedom from unnecessary administrative or legal restrictions that unreasonably conflict with or ignore economic needs;

(2) Protection of opportunity—maintenance of an economic atmosphere in which domestic production and processing can prosper; protection from subsidized competing products; protection of opportunity to fish on the high seas in accordance with international law;

(3) Assistance—assistance consistent with that provided by the Government for industry generally, such as is involved in promoting good industrial relations, fair trade standards, harmonious labor relations, better health standards and sanitation; and including, but not limited to—

(a) services to provide current information on production and trade, market promotion and development, and an extension service,

(b) research services for economic and technologic development and resource conservation, and

(c) resource management to assure the maximum sustainable production for the fisheries.

The Congress further declares that the provisions of this Act are necessary in order to accomplish the objective of proper resource development, and that this Act shall be administered with due regard to the inherent right of every citizen and resident of the United States to engage in fishing for his own pleasure, enjoyment, and betterment, and with the intent of maintaining and increasing the public opportunities for recreational use of our fish and wildlife resources, and stimulating the development of a strong, prosperous, and thriving fishery and fish processing industry.

REORGANIZATION WITHIN THE DEPARTMENT OF THE INTERIOR

Sec. 3. (a) There is hereby established within the Department of the Interior the position of Assistant Secretary for Fish and Wildlife, and the position of Commissioner of Fish and Wildlife. Such Assistant Secretary shall be appointed by the President, by and with the advice and consent of the Senate, and shall be compensated at the same rate as other Assistant Secretaries. The Commissioner shall be appointed by the President by and with the advice and consent of the Senate. He shall receive compensation at the same rate as that provided for

Grade GS—18. There is also established a United States Fish and Wildlife Service within the Department, consisting of two separate agencies, each of which shall have the status of a Federal bureau. There shall be a Director of each of said Bureaus appointed by the Secretary at Grades GS—17 each. One of the agencies shall be known as the "Bureau of Commercial Fisheries" and the other agency shall be known as the "Bureau of Sport Fisheries and Wildlife". The United States Fish and Wildlife Service, except as prescribed by this Act, shall succeed to and replace the presently existing Fish and Wildlife Service of the Department.

(b) The functions of the United States Fish and Wildlife Service hereby established shall be administered under the supervision of the said Commissioner of Fish and Wildlife, who shall be subject to the supervision of the Assistant Secretary for Fish and Wildlife.

(c) All functions and responsibilities placed in the Department of the Interior or any official thereof by this Act shall be included among the functions and responsibilities of the Secretary of the Interior, as the head of the Department, and shall be carried out under his direction pursuant to such procedures or delegations of authority as he may deem advisable and in the public interest.

(d) In order to make a proper distribution between the two Bureaus of the United States Fish and Wildlife Service established by this Act, the previously existing functions, powers, duties, authority, liabilities, commitments, personnel, records, and other properties or matters previously handled by or administered through the former Fish and Wildlife Service of the Department, shall be distributed as follows:

(1) The Bureau of Commercial Fisheries shall be responsible for those matters to which this Act applies relating primarily to commercial fisheries, whales, seals, and sea-lions, and related matters;

(2) The Bureau of Sport Fisheries and Wildlife shall be responsible for those matters to which this Act applies relating primarily to migratory birds, game management, wildlife refuges, sport fisheries, sea mammals (except whales, seals and sea-lions), and related matters; and the funds and allocations, appropriated or otherwise, relating to the matters covered by paragraphs (1) and (2) of this subsection shall be distributed between such Bureaus as the Secretary of the Interior shall determine.

(e) Except as changed by the terms of this Act or by subsequent laws or regulations, all laws and regulations now in effect relating to matters heretofore administered by the Department of the Interior through the former Fish and Wildlife Service as heretofore existing, shall remain in effect.

(f) In recognition of the need for authority to execute the purposes of this Act effectively, the Secretary of the Interior shall exercise such general administrative authority consistently with the terms of this Act as he shall find to be necessary to carry out the provisions of this Act effectively and in the public interest.

[113]

In order to allow sufficient time to place the reorganizations under this Act into effect, the Secretary is authorized to establish an effective procedure and date of such reorganizations, notice of which shall be published in the Federal Register. Such reorganization shall be accomplished as soon as practicable after the approval of this Act, but not later than ninety (90) calendar days after such approval.

LOAN PROCEDURES

SEC. 4. (a) The Secretary is authorized under rules and regulations and under terms and conditions prescribed by him, to make loans for financing and refinancing of operations, maintenance, replacement, repair, and equipment of fishing gear and vessels, and for research into the basic problems of fisheries.

(b) Any loans made under the provisions of this section shall be subject to the following restrictions:

(1) Bear an interest rate of not less than 3 per centum per annum;

(2) Mature in not more than ten years;

(3) No financial assistance shall be extended pursuant to this section unless reasonable financial assistance applied for is not otherwise available on reasonable terms.

(c) There is hereby created a fisheries loan fund, which shall be used by the Secretary as a revolving fund to make loans for financing and refinancing under this section. Any funds received by the Secretary on or before June 30, 1965, in payment or principal or interest on any loans so made, shall be deposited in the fund and be available for making additional loans under this section. Any funds so received after June 30, 1965, and any balance remaining in the fund at the close of June 30, 1965 (at which time the fund shall cease to exist), shall be covered into the Treasury as miscellaneous receipts. There are hereby authorized to be appropriated to the fund the sum of $10,000,000 to provide initial capital.

(d) The Secretary, subject to the specific limitations in this section, may consent to the modification, with respect to the rate of interest, time of payment of any installment of principal, or security, of any loan contract to which he is a party.

INVESTIGATIONS, INFORMATION, REPORTS

SEC. 5. (a) The Secretary shall conduct continuing investigations, prepare and disseminate information, and make periodical reports to the public, to the President, and to Congress, with respect to the following matters:

(1) The production and flow to market of fish and fishery products domestically produced, and also those produced by foreign producers which affect the domestic fisheries;

(2) The availability and abundance and the biological requirements of the fish and wildlife resources;

(3) The competitive economic position of the various fish and fishery products with respect to each other, and with respect to competitive domestic and foreign-produced commodities;

(4) The collection and dissemination of statistics on commercial and sport fishing;

(5) The collection and dissemination of statistics on the nature and availability of wildlife, progress in acquisition of additional refuges and measures being taken to foster a coordinated program to encourage and develop wildlife values;

(6) The improvement of production and marketing practices in regard to commercial species and the conduct of educational and extension services relative to commercial and sport fishing, and wildlife matters;

(7) Any other matters which in the judgment of the Secretary are of public interest in connection with any phases of fish and wildlife operations.

TRANSFER OF FUNCTIONS
ASSISTANCE OF OTHER AGENCIES

SEC. 6. (a) There shall be transferred to the Secretary all functions of the Secretary of Agriculture, the Secretary of Commerce, and the head of any other department or agency, as determined by the Director of the Bureau of the Budget to relate primarily to the development, advancement, management, conservation, and protection of commercial fisheries; but nothing in this section shall be construed to modify the authority of the Department of State or the Secretary of State to negotiate or enter into any international agreements, or conventions with respect to the development, management, or protection of any fisheries and wildlife resources or with respect to international commissions operating under conventions to which the United States is a party.

(b) There shall be transferred to the Department of the Interior so much of the personnel, property, facilities, records, and unexpended balances of appropriations, allocations, and other funds (available or to be made available) as the Director of the Bureau of the Budget determines to be necessary in connection with the exercise of any functions transferred to the Secretary pursuant to subsection (a) of this section.

(c) The Secretary may request and secure the advice or assistance of any department or agency of the Government in carrying out the provisions of this Act, and any such department or agency which furnishes advice or assistance to the Secretary may expend its own funds for such purposes, with or without reimbursement from the Secretary as may be agreed upon between the Secretary and the department or agency.

POLICIES, PROCEDURES, RECOMMENDATIONS

SEC. 7. (a) The Secretary of the Interior, with such advice and assistance as he may require from the Assistant Secretary for Fish and Wildlife, shall consider and determine the policies and procedures that are necessary and desirable in carrying out efficiently and in the public interest the laws relating to fish and wildlife. The Secretary, with the assistance of the departmental staff herein authorized, shall—

(1) develop and recommend measures which are appropriate to assure the maximum sustainable production of fish and fishery products and to prevent unnecessary and excessive fluctuations in such production;

(2) study the economic condition of the industry, and whenever he determines that any segment of the domestic fisheries has been seriously disturbed either by wide fluctuation in the abundance of the resource supporting it, or by unstable market or fishing conditions or due to any other factors he shall make such recommendations to the President and the Congress as he deems appropriate to aid in stabilizing the domestic fisheries;

(3) develop and recommend special promotional and informational activities with a view to stimulating the consumption of fishery products whenever he determines that there is a prospective or actual surplus of such products;

(4) take such steps as may be required for the development, advancement, management, conservation, and protection of the fisheries resources; and

(5) take such steps as may be required for the development, management, advancement, conservation, and protection of wildlife resources through research, acquisition of refuge lands, development of existing facilities, and other means.

STATE DEPARTMENT— COOPERATION

Sec. 8. (a) The Secretary shall cooperate to the fullest practicable extent with the Secretary of State in providing representation at all meetings and conferences relating to fish and wildlife in which representatives of the United States and foreign countries participate.

The Secretary of State shall designate the Secretary of the Interior or the Assistant Secretary for Fish and Wildlife, or a person designated by the Secretary of the Interior to represent the Department of the Interior, as a member of the United States delegation attending such meetings and conferences and also as a member of the negotiating team of any such delegation.

(b) The Secretary of State and all other officials having responsibilities in the fields of technical and economic aid to foreign nations shall consult with the Secretary in all cases in which the interests of fish and wildlife are involved, with a view to assuring that such interests are adequately represented at all times.

(c) Notwithstanding any other provision of law, the Secretary shall be represented in all international negotiations conducted by the United States pursuant to section 350 of the Tariff Act of 1930, as amended, in any case in which fish products are directly affected by such negotiations.

(d) The Secretary shall consult periodically with the various governmental, private nonprofit, and other organizations and agencies which have to do with any phase of fish and wildlife with respect to any problems that may arise in connection with such fish and wildlife.

REPORTS ON ACTIVITIES AND IMPORTS

SEC. 9. (a) The Secretary of the Interior shall make an annual report to the Congress with respect to activities of the United States Fish and Wildlife Service under this Act, and shall make such recommendations for additional legislation as he deems necessary.

(b) The Secretary is authorized to make a report to the President and the Congress, and, when requested by the United States Tariff Commission in connection with section 7 of the Trade Agreements Extension Act of 1951, as amended (67 Stat. 72, 74), or when an investigation is made under the Tariff Act of 1930 (19 U.S.C. 1332), the Secretary is authorized to make a report to such Commission, concerning the following matters with respect to any fishery product which is imported into the United States, or such reports may be made upon a request from any segment of the domestic industry producing a like or directly competitive product—

> (1) whether there has been a downward trend in the production, employment in the production, or prices, or a decline in the sales, of the like or directly competitive product by the domestic industry; and
>
> (2) whether there has been an increase in the imports of the fishery products into the United States, either actual or relative to the production of the like or directly competitive product produced by the domestic industry.

THE RIGHTS OF STATES

SEC. 10. Nothing in this Act shall be construed (1) to interfere in any manner with the rights of any State under the Submerged Lands Act (Public Law 31, Eighty-third Congress) or otherwise provided by law, or to supersede any regulatory authority over fisheries exercised by the States either individually or under interstate compacts; or (2) to interfere in any manner with the authority exercised by any International Commission established under any treaty or convention to which the United States is a party.

AUTHORIZATION FOR APPROPRIATION

SEC. 11. There are hereby authorized to be appropriated such sums as may be necessary to carry out the provisions of this Act.

SEC. 12. (a) The authorization for the transfer of certain funds from the Secretary of Agriculture to the Secretary of the Interior and their maintenance in a separate fund as contained in section 2 (a) of the Act of August 11, 1939, as amended July 1, 1954 (68 Stat. 376), shall be continued for the year ending June 30, 1957, and each year thereafter.

(b) Subsection (e) of section 2 of the aforesaid Act of August 11, 1939, as amended, is hereby amended to read as follows:

"(e) The separate fund created for the use of the Secretary of the Interior under section 2 (a) of this Act and the annual accruals thereto shall be available for each year hereafter until expended by the Secretary."

Approved August 8, 1956.

THE FISH AND WILDLIFE COORDINATION ACT*
August 12, 1958

The Fish and Wildlife Coordination Act of 1958 provided that ". . . wildlife conservation . . . receive equal consideration and be coordinated with other features of water-resource development programs. . . ." Recognizing that the two problems were closely related, the act required that federal agencies constructing or licensing water-development projects consult with the Fish and Wildlife Service and the corresponding state agency prior to the construction of such projects, in order to better protect fish and wildlife resources.

An Act to amend the Act of March 10, 1934, to provide for more effective integration of a fish and wildlife conservation program with Federal water-resource developments, and for other purposes.

Be it enacted by the Senate and House of Representatives of the United States of America in Congress assembled, That the Act of March 10, 1934, as amended, and as further amended by this Act may be cited as the "Fish and Wildlife Coordination Act".

SEC. 2. The first four sections of the Act entitled "An Act to promote the conservation of wildlife, fish, and game, and for other purposes", approved March 10, 1934 (16 U. S. C., secs. 661–664, inclusive) are amended to read as follows:

"For the purpose of recognizing the vital contribution of our wildlife resources to the Nation, the increasing public interest and significance thereof due to expansion of our national economy and other factors, and to provide that wildlife conservation shall receive equal consideration and be coordinated with other features of water-resource development programs through the effectual and harmonious planning, development, maintenance, and coordination of wildlife conservation and rehabilitation for the purposes of this Act in the United States, its Territories and possessions, the Secretary of the Interior is authorized (1) to provide assistance to, and cooperate with, Federal, State, and public or private agencies and organizations in the development, protection, rearing, and stocking of all species of wildlife, resources thereof, and their habitat, in controlling losses of the same from disease or other causes, in minimizing damages from overabundant species, in providing public shooting and fishing areas, including easements across public lands for access thereto, and in carrying out other measures necessary to effectuate the purposes of this Act; (2) to make surveys and investigations of the wildlife of the public domain, including lands and waters or interests therein acquired or controlled by any agency of the United States; and (3) to ac-

*72 *Statutes at Large,* 563.

cept donations of land and contributions of funds in furtherance of the purposes of this Act.

"SEC. 2. (a) Except as hereafter stated in subsection (h) of this section, whenever the waters of any stream or other body of water are proposed or authorized to be impounded, diverted, the channel deepened, or the stream or other body of water otherwise controlled or modified for any purpose whatever, including navigation and drainage, by any department or agency of the United States, or by any public or private agency under Federal permit or license, such department or agency first shall consult with the United States Fish and Wildlife Service, Department of the Interior, and with the head of the agency exercising administration over the wildlife resources of the particular State wherein the impoundment, diversion, or other control facility is to be constructed, with a view to the conservation of wildlife resources by preventing loss of and damage to such resources as well as providing for the development and improvement thereof in connection with such water-resource development.

"(b) In furtherance of such purposes, the reports and recommendations of the Secretary of the Interior on the wildlife aspects of such projects, and any report of the head of the State agency exercising administration over the wildlife resources of the State, based on surveys and investigations conducted by the United States Fish and Wildlife Service and such State agency for the purpose of determining the possible damage to wildlife resources and for the purpose of determining means and measures that should be adopted to prevent the loss of or damage to such wildlife resources, as well as to provide concurrently for the development and improvement of such resources, shall be made an integral part of any report prepared or submitted by any agency of the Federal Government responsible for engineering surveys and construction of such projects when such reports are presented to the Congress or to any agency or person having the authority or the power, by administrative action or otherwise, (1) to authorize the construction of water-resource development projects or (2) to approve a report on the modification or supplementation of plans for previously authorized projects, to which this Act applies. Recommendations of the Secretary of the Interior shall be as specific as is practicable with respect to features recommended for wildlife conservation and development, lands to be utilized or acquired for such purposes, the results expected, and shall describe the damage to wildlife attributable to the project and the measures proposed for mitigating or compensating for these damages. The reporting officers in project reports of the Federal agencies shall give full consideration to the report and recommendations of the Secretary of the Interior and to any report of the State agency on the wildlife aspects of such projects, and the project plan shall include such justifiable means and measures for wildlife purposes as the reporting agency finds should be adopted to obtain maximum overall project benefits.

"(c) Federal agencies authorized to construct or operate water-control projects are hereby authorized to modify or add to the structures and operations of such projects, the construction of which has not been substantially completed on the date of enactment of the Fish and Wildlife Coordination Act, and to acquire lands in accordance with section 3 of this Act, in order to accommodate the means and measures for such conservation of wildlife resources as an integral part of such projects: *Provided,* That for projects authorized by a specific Act of Congress before the date of enactment of the Fish and Wildlife Coordination Act (1) such modification or land acquisition shall be compatible with the purposes for which the project was authorized; (2) the cost of such modifications or land acquisition, as means and measures to prevent loss of and damage to wildlife resources to the extent justifiable, shall be an integral part of the cost of such projects; and (3) the cost of such modifications or land acquisition for the development or improvement of wildlife resources may be included to the extent justifiable, and an appropriate share of the cost of any project may be allocated for this purpose with a finding as to the part of such allocated cost, if any, to be reimbursed by non-Federal interests.

"(d) The cost of planning for and the construction or installation and maintenance of such means and measures adopted to carry out the conservation purposes of this section shall constitute an integral part of the cost of such projects: *Provided,* That such cost attributable to the development and improvement of wildlife shall not extend beyond those necessary for (1) land acquisition, (2) modification of the project, and (3) modification of project operations; but shall not include the operation of wildlife facilities nor the construction of such facilities beyond those herein described: *And provided further,* That, in the case of projects authorized to be constructed, operated, and maintained in accordance with the Federal reclamation laws (Act of June 17, 1902, 32 Stat. 388, and Acts amendatory thereof or supplementary thereto), the Secretary of the Interior, in addition to allocations made under section 9 of the Reclamation Project Act of 1939 (53 Stat. 1187), shall make findings on the part of the estimated cost of the project which can properly be allocated to means and measures to prevent loss of and damage to wildlife resources, which costs shall not be reimbursable, and an appropriate share of the project costs may be allocated to development and improvement of wildlife resources, with a finding as to the part of such allocated costs, if any, to be reimbursed by non-Federal fish and wildlife agencies or interests.

"(e) In the case of construction by a Federal agency, that agency is authorized to transfer to the United States Fish and Wildlife Service, out of appropriations or other funds made available for investigations, engineering, or construction, such funds as may be necessary to conduct all or part of the investigations required to carry out the purposes of this section.

"(f) In addition to other requirements, there shall be included in any report submitted to Congress supporting a recommendation for authorization of any new project for the control or use of water as described herein (including any new division of such project or new supplemental works on such project) an estimation of the wildlife benefits or losses to be derived therefrom including benefits to be derived from measures recommended specifically for the development and improvement of wildlife resources, the cost of providing wildlife benefits (including the cost of additional facilities to be installed or lands to be acquired specifically for that particular phase of wildlife conservation relating to the development and improvement of wildlife), the part of the cost of joint-use facilities allocated to wildlife, and the part of such costs, if any, to be reimbursed by non-Federal interests.

"(g) The provisions of this section shall be applicable with respect to any project for the control or use of water as prescribed herein, or any unit of such project authorized before or after the date of enactment of the Fish and Wildlife Coordination Act for planning or construction, but shall not be applicable to any project or unit thereof authorized before the date of enactment of the Fish and Wildlife Coordination Act if the construction of the particular project or unit thereof has been substantially completed. A project or unit thereof shall be considered to be substantially completed when sixty percent or more of the estimated construction cost has been obligated for expenditure.

"(h) The provisions of this Act shall not be applicable to those projects for the impoundment of water where the maximum surface area of such impoundments is less than ten acres, nor to activities for or in connection with programs primarily for land management and use carried out by Federal agencies with respect to Federal lands under their jurisdiction.

"Sec. 3. (a) Subject to the exceptions prescribed in section 2 (h) of this Act, whenever the waters of any stream or other body of water are impounded, diverted, the channel deepened, or the stream or other body of water otherwise controlled or modified for any purpose whatever, including navigation and drainage, by any department or agency of the United States, adequate provision, consistent with the primary purposes of such impoundment, diversion, or other control, shall be made for the use thereof, together with any areas of land, water, or interests therein, acquired or administered by a Federal agency in connection therewith, for the conservation, maintenance, and management of wildlife resources thereof, and its habitat thereon, including the development and improvement of such wildlife resources pursuant to the provisions of section 2 of this Act.

"(b) The use of such waters, land, or interests therein for wildlife conservation purposes shall be in accordance with general plans approved jointly (1) by the head of the particular department or agency exercising primary administration in each instance, (2) by the Secretary of the Interior, and (3) by the head of the agency exercising the administration of the wildlife resources of the particular State wherein the waters and areas lie. Such waters and other interests shall be made available, without cost for administration, by such State agency, if the management of the properties relate to the conservation of wildlife other than migratory birds, or by the Secretary of the Interior, for administration in such manner as he may deem advisable, where the particular properties have value in carrying out the national migratory bird management program: *Provided,* That nothing in this section shall be construed as affecting the authority of the Secretary of Agriculture to cooperate with the States or in making lands available to the States with respect to the management of wildlife and wildlife habitat on lands administered by him.

"(c) When consistent with the purposes of this Act and the reports and findings of the Secretary of the Interior prepared in accordance with section 2, land, waters, and interests therein may be acquired by Federal construction agencies for the wildlife conservation and development purposes of this Act in connection with a project as reasonably needed to preserve and assure for the public benefit the wildlife potentials of the particular project area: *Provided,* That before properties are acquired for this purpose, the probable extent of such acquisition shall be set forth, along with other data necessary for project authorization, in a report submitted to the Congress, or in the case of a project previously authorized, no such properties shall be acquired unless specifically authorized by Congress, if specific authority for such acquisition is recommended by the construction agency.

"(d) Properties acquired for the purposes of this section shall continue to be used for such purposes, and shall not become the subject of exchange or other transactions if such exchange or other transaction would defeat the initial purpose of their acquisition.

"(e) Federal lands acquired or withdrawn for Federal water-resource purposes and made available to the States or to the Secretary of the Interior for wildlife management purposes, shall be made available for such purposes in accordance with this Act, notwithstanding other provisions of law.

"(f) Any lands acquired pursuant to this section by any Federal agency within the exterior boundaries of a national forest shall, upon acquisition, be added to and become national forest lands, and shall be administered as a part of the forest within which they are situated, subject to all laws applicable to lands acquired under the provisions of the Act of March 1, 1911 (36 Stat. 961), unless such lands are acquired to carry out the National Migratory Bird Management Program.

"Sec. 4. Such areas as are made available to the Secretary of the Interior for the purposes of this Act, pursuant to sections 1 and 3 or pursuant to any other authorization, shall be administered by him directly or in accordance with cooperative agreements entered into pursuant to the provisions of the first section of this Act and in accordance with such rules and regulations for the conservation, maintenance, and management of wildlife, resources thereof, and its habitat thereon, as may be adopted by the Secretary in accordance with general plans approved jointly by the Secretary of the Interior and the head of the department or agency exercising primary administration of such areas: *Provided,* That such rules and regulations shall not be inconsistent with the laws for the protection of fish and game of the States in which such area is situated (16 U. S. C., sec. 664): *Provided further,* That lands having value to the National Migratory Bird Management Program may, pursuant to general plans, be made available without cost directly to the State agency having control over wildlife resources, if it is jointly determined by the Secretary of the Interior and such State agency that this would be in the public interest: *And provided further,* That the Secretary of the Interior shall have the right to assume the management and administration of such lands in behalf of the National Migratory Bird Management Program if the Secretary finds that the State agency has withdrawn from or otherwise relinquished such management and administration."

Sec. 3. The Watershed Protection and Flood Prevention Act, as amended (16 U. S. C., secs. 1001–1007, inclusive), is amended by adding at the end thereof the following new section:

"Sec. 12. When the Secretary approves the furnishing of assistance to a local organization in preparing a plan for works of improvement as provided for in section 3:

"(1) The Secretary shall so notify the Secretary of the Interior in order that the latter, as he desires, may make surveys and investigations and prepare a report with recommendations concerning the conservation and development of wildlife resources and participate, under arrangements satisfactory to the Secretary of Agriculture, in the preparation of a plan for works of improvement that is acceptable to the local organization and the Secretary of Agriculture.

"(2) Full consideration shall be given to the recommendations contained in any such report of the Secretary of the Interior as he may submit to the Secretary of Agriculture prior to the time the local organization and the Secretary of Agriculture have agreed on a plan for works of improvement. The plan shall include such of the technically and economically feasible works of improvement for wildlife purposes recommended in the report by the Secretary of the Interior as are acceptable to, and agreed to by, the local organization and the Secretary of Agriculture, and such report of the Secretary of the Interior shall, if requested by the Secretary of the Interior, accompany the plan for works of improvement when it is submitted to the Secretary of Agriculture for approval or transmitted to the Congress through the President.

"(3) The cost of making surveys and investigations and of preparing reports concerning the conservation and development of wildlife resources shall be borne by the Secretary of the Interior out of funds appropriated to his Department."

Sec. 4. There is authorized to be appropriated and expended such funds as may be necessary to carry out the purposes of this Act.

Approved August 12, 1958.

THE MARINE GAME FISH RESEARCH ACT*
September 22, 1959

By 1959 there had been considerable research on commercial ocean fishes but very little on marine game fish. The act below moved to plug this gap in the understanding of migratory marine game fish, by providing for research.

An Act authorizing and directing the Secretary of the Interior to undertake continuing research on the biology fluctuations, status, and statistics of the migratory marine species of game fish of the United States and contiguous waters.

Be it enacted by the Senate and House of Representatives of the United States of America in Congress assembled, That the Secretary of the Interior is hereby directed to undertake a comprehensive continuing study of the migratory marine fish of interest to recreational fishermen of the United States, including species inhabiting the offshore waters of the United States and species which migrate through or spend a part of their lives in the inshore waters of the United States. The study shall include, but not be limited to, research on migrations, identity of stocks, growth rates, mortality rates, variations in survival, environmental influences, both natural and artificial, including pollution, and effects of fishing on the species, for the purpose of developing wise conservation policies and constructive management activities.

Sec. 2. For the purpose of carrying out the provisions of this Act, the Secretary of the Interior is authorized (1) to acquire lands, construct laboratory or other buildings, purchase boats, acquire such other equipment and apparatus, and to employ such officers and employees as he deems necessary; (2) to cooperate or contract with State and other institutions and agencies upon such terms and conditions as he determines to be appropriate; and (3) to make public the results of such research conducted pursuant to the first section of this Act.

Sec. 3. There are hereby authorized to be appropriated such sums as may be necessary to carry out the provisions of this Act: *Provided,* That no more than $2,700,000 be appropriated for this purpose in any one fiscal year.

Approved September 22, 1959.

*73 *Statutes at Large,* 642.

THE FEDERAL WATER PROJECT RECREATION ACT*
July 9, 1965

The Water Project Recreation Act generally reiterated the coordination requirements of the Fish and Wildlife Coordination Act of 1958, but it added guidelines for financing recreation and fish and wildlife measures on federal multiple-purpose water-resource projects. The act is of particular significance because it recognizes recreation as a legitimate purpose of water-resource projects. From the point of view of the recreationist, it should produce substantial enlargement and better facilities both at future water projects and for those that have already been constructed. Because most outdoor recreation takes place in, on, or near water the act is of great importance.

An Act to provide uniform policies with respect to recreation and fish and wildlife benefits and costs of Federal multiple-purpose water resource projects, and for other purposes.

Be it enacted by the Senate and House of Representatives of the United States of America in Congress assembled, That it is the policy of the Congress and the intent of this Act that (a) in investigating and planning any Federal navigation, flood control, reclamation, hydroelectric, or multiple-purpose water resource project, full consideration shall be given to the opportunities, if any, which the project affords for outdoor recreation and for fish and wildlife enhancement and that, wherever any such project can reasonably serve either or both of these purposes consistently with the provisions of this Act, it shall be constructed, operated, and maintained accordingly; (b) planning with respect to the development of the recreation potential of any such project shall be based on the coordination of the recreational use of the project area with the use of existing and planned Federal, State, or local public recreation developments; and (c) project construction agencies shall encourage non-Federal public bodies to administer project land and water areas for recreation and fish and wildlife enhancement purposes and operate, maintain, and replace facilities provided for those purposes unless such areas or facilities are included or proposed for inclusion within a national recreation area, or are appropriate for administration by a Federal agency as a part of the national forest system, as a part of the public lands classified for retention in Federal ownership, or in connection with an authorized Federal program for the conservation and development of fish and wildife.

SEC. 2. (a) If, before authorization of a project, non-Federal public bodies indicate their intent in writing to agree to administer project land and water areas for recreation or fish and wildlife enhancement or for both of these pur-

*79 *Statutes at Large,* 213.

poses pursuant to the plan for the development of the project approved by the head of the agency having administrative jurisdiction over it and to bear not less than one-half the separable costs of the project allocated to either or both of said purposes, as the case may be, and all the costs of operation, maintenance, and replacement incurred therefor—

(1) the benefits of the project to said purpose or purposes shall be taken into account in determining the economic benefits of the project;

(2) costs shall be allocated to said purpose or purposes and to other purposes in a manner which will insure that all project purposes share equitably in the advantages of multiple-purpose construction: *Provided,* That the costs allocated to recreation or fish and wildlife enhancement shall not exceed the lesser of the benefits from those functions or the costs of providing recreation or fish and wildlife enhancement benefits of reasonably equivalent use and location by the least costly alternative means; and

(3) not more than one-half the separable costs and all the joint costs of the project allocated to recreation and fish and wildlife enhancement shall be borne by the United States and be non-reimbursable.

Projects authorized during the calendar year 1965 may include recreation and fish and wildlife enhancement on the foregoing basis without the required indication of intent. Execution of an agreement as a foresaid shall be a prerequisite to commencement of construction of any project to which this subsection is applicable.

(b) The non-Federal share of the separable costs of the project allocated to recreation and fish and wildlife enhancement shall be borne by non-Federal interests, under either or both of the following methods as may be determined appropriate by the head of the Federal agency having jurisdiction over the project: (1) payment, or provision of lands, interests therein, or facilities for the project; or (2) repayment, with interest at a rate comparable to that for other interest-bearing functions of Federal water resource projects, within fifty years of first use of project recreation or fish and wildlife enhancement facilities: *Provided,* That the source of repayment may be limited to entrance and user fees or charges collected at the project by non-Federal interests if the fee schedule and the portion of fees dedicated to repayment are established on a basis calculated to achieve repayment as aforesaid and are made subject to review and renegotiation at intervals of not more than five years.

SEC. 3. (a) No facilities or project modifications which will furnish recreation or fish and wildlife enhancement benefits shall be provided in the absence of the indication of intent with respect thereto specified in subsection 2(a) of this Act unless (1) such facilities or modifications serve other project purposes and are justified thereby without regard to such incidental recreation or fish and wildlife enhancement benefits as they may have or (2) they are minimum facilities which are required for the public health and safety and are located at access points provided by roads existing at the time of project construction or constructed for the administration and management of the project. Calculation of the recreation and fish and wildlife enhancement benefits in any such case shall be based on the number of visitor-days anticipated in the absence of recreation and fish and wildlife enhancement facilities or modifications except as hereinbefore provided and on the value per visitor-day of the project without such facilities or modifications. Project costs allocated to recreation and fish and wildlife enhancement on this basis shall be nonreimbursable.

(b) Notwithstanding the absence of an indication of intent as specified in subsection 2(a), lands may be provided in connection with project construction to preserve the recreation and fish and wildlife enhancement potential of the project:

(1) If non-Federal public bodies execute an agreement within ten years after initial operation of the project (which agreement shall provide that the non-Federal public bodies will administer project land and water areas for recreation or fish and wildlife enhancement or both pursuant to the plan for the development of the project approved by the head of the agency having administrative jurisdiction over it and will bear not less than one-half the costs of lands, facilities, and project modifications provided for either or both of those purposes, as the case may be, and all costs of operation, maintenance, and replacement attributable thereto) the remainder of the costs of lands, facilities, and project modifications provided pursuant to this paragraph shall be nonreimbursable. Such agreement and subsequent development, however, shall not be the basis for any reallocation of joint costs of the project to recreation or fish and wildlife enhancement.

(2) If, within ten years after initial operation of the project, there is not an executed agreement as specified in paragraph (1) of this subsection, the head of the agency having jurisdiction over the project may utilize the lands for any lawful purpose within the jurisdiction of his agency, or may offer the land for sale to its immediate prior owner or his immediate heirs at its appraised fair market value as approved by the head of the agency at the time of offer or, if a firm agreement by said owner or his immediate heirs is not executed within ninety days of the date of the offer, may transfer custody of the lands to another Federal agency for use for any lawful purpose within the jurisdiction of that agency, or may lease the lands to a non-Federal public body, or may transfer the lands to the Administrator of General Services for disposition in accordance with the surplus property laws of the United States. In no case shall the lands be used or made available for use for any purpose in conflict with the purposes for which the project was constructed, and in every case except that of an offer to purchase made, as hereinbefore provided, by the prior owner or his heirs preference shall be given

[129]

to uses which will preserve and promote the recreation and fish and wildlife enhancement potential of the project or, in the absence thereof, will not detract from that potential.

SEC. 4. At projects, the construction of which has commenced or been completed as of the effective date of this Act, where non-Federal public bodies agree to administer project land and water areas for recreation and fish and wildlife enhancement purposes and to bear the costs of operation, maintenance, and replacement of existing facilities serving those purposes, such facilities and appropriate project lands may be leased to non-Federal public bodies.

SEC. 5. Nothing herein shall be construed as preventing or discouraging post-authorization development of any project for recreation or fish and wildlife enhancement or both by non-Federal public bodies pursuant to agreement with the head of the Federal agency having jurisdiction over the project. Such development shall not be the basis for any allocation or reallocation of project costs to recreation or fish and wildlife enhancement.

SEC. 6. (a) The views of the Secretary of the Interior developed in accordance with section 3 of the Act of May 28, 1963 (77 Stat. 49), with respect to the outdoor recreation aspects shall be set forth in any report of any project or appropriate unit thereof within the purview of this Act. Such views shall include a report on the extent to which the proposed recreation and fish and wildlife development conforms to and is in accord with the State comprehensive plan developed pursuant to subsection 5(d) of the Land and Water Conservation Fund Act of 1965 (78 Stat. 897).

(b) The first proviso of subsection 2(d) of the Act of August 12, 1958 (72 Stat. 563; 16 U.S.C. 662(d)), is amended to read as follows: *"Provided,* That such cost attributable to the development and improvement of wildlife shall not extend beyond that necessary for (1) land acquisition, (2) facilities as specifically recommended in water resource project reports, (3) modification of the project, and (4) modification of project operations, but shall not include the operation of wildlife facilities." The second proviso of subsection 2(d) of said Act is hereby repealed.

(c) Expenditures for lands or interests in lands hereafter acquired by project construction agencies for the establishment of migratory waterfowl refuges recommended by the Secretary of the Interior at Federal water resources projects, when such lands or interests in lands would not have been acquired but for the establishment of a migratory waterfowl refuge at the project, shall not exceed $28,000,000: *Provided,* That the aforementioned expenditure limitation in this subsection shall not apply to the costs of mitigating damages to migratory waterfowl caused by such water resource project.

(d) This Act shall not apply to the Tennessee Valley Authority, nor to projects constructed under authority of the Small Reclamation Projects Act, as amended, or under authority of the Watershed Protection and Flood Prevention Act, as amended.

(e) Sections 2, 3, 4, and 5 of this Act shall not apply to nonreservoir local flood control projects, beach erosion control projects, small boat harbor projects, hurricane protection projects, or to project areas or facilities authorized by law for inclusion within a national recreation area or appropriate for administration by a Federal agency as a part of the national forest system, as a part of the public lands classified for retention in Federal ownership, or in connection with an authorized Federal program for the conservation and development of fish and wildlife.

(f) As used in this Act, the term "nonreimbursable" shall not be construed to prohibit the imposition of entrance, admission, and other recreation user fees or charges.

(g) Subsection 6(a) (2) of the Land and Water Conservation Fund Act of 1965 (78 Stat. 897) shall not apply to costs allocated to recreation and fish and wildlife enhancement which are borne by the United States as a nonreimbursable project cost pursuant to subsection 2(a) or subsection 3(b) (1) of this Act.

(h) All payments and repayment by non-Federal public bodies under the provisions of this Act shall be deposited in the Treasury as miscellaneous receipts, and revenue from the conveyance by deed, lease, or otherwise, of lands under subsection 3(b) (2) of this Act shall be deposited in the Land and Water Conservation Fund.

SEC. 7. (a) The Secretary is authorized, in conjunction with any reservoir heretofore constructed by him pursuant to the Federal reclamation laws or any reservoir which is otherwise under his control, except reservoirs within national wildlife refuges, to investigate, plan, construct, operate and maintain, or otherwise provide for public outdoor recreation and fish and wildlife enhancement facilities, to acquire or otherwise make available such adjacent lands or interests therein as are necessary for public outdoor recreation or fish and wildlife use, and to provide for public use and enjoyment of project lands, facilities, and water areas in a manner coordinated with the other project purposes: *Provided,* That not more than $100,000 shall be available to carry out the provisions of this subsection at any one reservoir. Lands, facilities and project modifications for the purposes of this subsection may be provided only after an agreement in accordance with subsection 3(b) of this Act has been executed.

(b) The Secretary of the Interior is authorized to enter into agreements with Federal agencies or State or local public bodies for the administration of project land and water areas and the operation, maintenance, and replacement of facilities and to transfer project lands or facilities to Federal agencies or State or local public bodies by lease agreement or exchange upon such terms and conditions as will best promote the development and operation of such lands or facilities in the public interest for recreation and fish and wildlife enhancement purposes.

(c) No lands under the jurisdiction of any other Federal agency may be included for or devoted to recreation or fish and wildlife purposes under the authority of this section without the consent of the head of such agency; and the head of any such agency is authorized to transfer any such lands to the jurisdiction of the Secretary of the Interior for purposes of this section. The Secretary of the Interior is authorized to transfer jurisdiction over project lands within or adjacent to the exterior boundaries of national forests and facilities thereon to the Secretary of Agriculture for recreation and other national forest system purposes; and such transfer shall be made in each case in which the project reservoir area is located wholly within the exterior boundaries of a national forest unless the Secretaries of Agriculture and Interior jointly determine otherwise. Where any project lands are transferred hereunder to the jurisdiction of the Secretary of Agriculture, the lands involved shall become national forest lands: *Provided,* That the lands and waters within the flow lines of any reservoir or otherwise needed or used for the operation of the project for other purposes shall continue to be administered by the Secretary of the Interior to the extent he determines to be necessary for such operation. Nothing herein shall limit the authority of the Secretary of the Interior granted by existing provisions of law relating to recreation or fish and wildlife development in connection with water resource projects or to disposition of public lands for such purposes.

SEC. 8. Effective on and after July 1, 1966, neither the Secretary of the Interior nor any bureau nor any person acting under his authority shall engage in the preparation of any feasibility report under reclamation law with respect to any water resource project unless the preparation of such feasibility report has been specifically authorized by law, any other provision of law to the contrary notwithstanding.

SEC. 9. Nothing contained in this Act shall be taken to authorize or to sanction the construction under the Federal reclamation laws or under any Rivers and Harbors or Flood Control Act of any project in which the sum of the allocations to recreation and fish and wildlife enhancement exceeds the sum of the allocations to irrigation, hydro-electric power, municipal, domestic and industrial water supply, navigation, and flood control, except that this section shall not apply to any such project for the enhancement of anadromous fisheries, shrimp, or for the conservation of migratory birds protected by treaty, when each of the other functions of such a project has, of itself, a favorable benefit-cost ratio.

SEC. 10. As used in this Act:

(a) The term "project" shall mean a project or any appropriate unit thereof.

(b) The term "separable costs," as applied to any project purpose, means the difference between the capital cost of the entire multiple-purpose project and the capital cost of the project with the purpose omitted.

(c) The term "joint costs" means the difference between the capital cost of the entire multiple-purpose project and the sum of the separable costs for all project purposes.

(d) The term "feasibility report" shall mean any report of the scope required by the Congress when formally considering authorization of the project of which the report treats.

(e) The term "capital cost" includes interest during construction, wherever appropriate.

SEC. 11. Section 2, subsection (a) of the Land and Water Conservation Fund Act of 1965 (78 Stat. 897) is hereby amended by striking out the words "notwithstanding any provision of law that such proceeds shall be credited to miscellaneous receipts of the Treasury:" and inserting in lieu thereof the words "notwithstanding any other provision of law:" and by striking out the words "or any provision of law that provides that any fees or charges collected at particular Federal areas shall be used for or credited to specific purposes or special funds as authorized by that provision of law" and inserting in lieu thereof "or affect any contract heretofore entered into by the United States that provides that such revenues collected at particular Federal areas shall be credited to specific purposes".

SEC. 12. This Act may be cited as the "Federal Water Project Recreation Act".

Approved July 9, 1965.

THE ANADROMOUS AND GREAT LAKES FISH ACT*
October 30, 1965

Anadromous fish hatch in fresh water, migrate to salt water for most of their lives, and return to fresh water to spawn. Because of their migratory habits such fish are comparatively easy to catch during their "runs," and have been sharply reduced in numbers both from heavy catches and because of the presence of dams and other obstructions in the spawning streams. The Anadromous and Great Lakes Fish Act of 1965, introduced by Congressman Dingell, provided for a five-year program to match state funds with federal funds for the purpose of conserving and developing the anadromous fishery resources of the nation.

An Act to authorize the Secretary of the Interior to initiate with the several States a cooperative program for the conservation, development, and enhancement of the Nation's anadromous fish, and for other purposes.

Be it enacted by the Senate and House of Representatives of the United States of America in Congress assembled, That (a) for the purpose of conserving, developing, and enhancing within the several States the anadromous fishery resources of the Nation that are subject to depletion from water resources developments and other causes, or with respect to which the United States has made conservation commitments by international agreements, and for the purpose of conserving, developing, and enhancing the fish in the Great Lakes that ascend streams to spawn, the Secretary of the Interior is authorized to enter into cooperative agreements with one or more States, acting jointly or severally, that are concerned with the development, conservation, and enhancement of such fish, and, whenever he deems it appropriate, with other non-Federal interests. Such agreements shall describe (1) the actions to be taken by the Secretary and the cooperating parties, (2) the benefits that are expected to be derived by the States and other non-Federal interests, (3) the estimated cost of these actions, (4) the share of such costs to be borne by the Federal Government and by the States and other non-Federal interests: *Provided,* That the Federal share, including the operation and maintenance costs of any facilities constructed by the Secretary pursuant to this Act, which he annually determines to be a proper Federal cost, shall not exceed 50 per centum of such costs exclusive of the value of any Federal land involved: *Provided further,* That the non-Federal share may be in the form of real or personal property, the value of which will be determined by the Secretary, as well as money, (5) the term of the agreement, (6) the terms and conditions for disposing of any real or personal property acquired by the Secre-

*79 *Statutes at Large,* 1125.

tary during or at the end of the term of the agreement, and (7) such other terms and conditions as he deems desirable.

(b) The Secretary may also enter into agreements with the States for the operation of any facilities and management and administration of any lands or interests therein acquired or facilities constructed pursuant to this Act.

SEC. 2. The Secretary, in accordance with any agreements entered into pursuant to section 1 (a) of this Act, is authorized (1) to conduct such investigations, engineering and biological surveys, and research as may be desirable to carry out the program; (2) to carry out stream clearance activities; (3) to construct, install, maintain, and operate devices and structures for the improvement of feeding and spawning conditions, for the protection of fishery resources, and for facilitating the free migration of the fish; (4) to construct, operate, and maintain fish hatcheries whereever necessary to accomplish the purposes of this Act; (5) to conduct such studies and make such recommendations as the Secretary determines to be appropriate regarding the development and management of any stream or other body of water for the conservation and enhancement of anadromous fishery resources and the fish in the Great Lakes that ascend streams to spawn: *Provided,* That the reports on such studies and the recommendations of the Secretary shall be transmitted to the States, the Congress, and the Federal water resources construction agencies for their information: *Provided further,* That this Act shall not be construed as authorizing the formulation or construction of water resources projects, except that water resources projects which are determined by the Secretary to be needed solely for the conservation, protection, and enhancement of such fish may be planned and constructed by the Bureau of Reclamation in its currently authorized geographic area of responsibility, or by the Corps of Engineers, or by the Department of Agriculture, or by the States, with funds made available by the Secretary under this Act and subject to the cost-sharing and appropriations provisions of this Act; (6) to acquire lands or interests therein by purchase, lease, donation, or exchange for acquired lands or public lands under his jurisdiction which he finds suitable for disposition: *Provided,* That the lands or interests therein so exchanged shall involve approximately equal values, as determined by the Secretary: *Provided further,* That the Secretary may accept cash from, or pay cash to, the grantor in such an exchange in order to equalize the values of the properties exchanged; (7) to accept donations of funds and to use such funds to acquire or manage lands or interests therein; and (8) to administer such lands or interests therein for the purposes of this Act. Title to lands or interests therein acquired pursuant to this Act shall be in the United States.

SEC. 3. Activities authorized by this Act to be performed on lands administered by other Federal departments or agencies shall be carried out only with the prior approval of such departments or agencies.

SEC. 4. (a) There is authorized to be appropriated for the period ending on June 30, 1970, not to exceed $25,000,000 to carry out the purposes of this Act.

(b) Not more than $1,000,000 of the funds appropriated under this section in any one fiscal year shall be obligated in any one State.

SEC. 5. This Act shall not be construed to affect, modify, or apply to the same area as the provisions of the Act of May 11, 1938 (52 Stat. 345), as amended (16 U.S.C. 755–757).

SEC. 6. The Secretary of the Interior shall, on the basis of studies carried out pursuant to this Act and section 5 of the Fish and Wildlife Coordination Act (48 Stat. 402), as amended (16 U.S.C. 665), make recommendations to the Secretary of Health, Education, and Welfare concerning the elimination or reduction of polluting substances detrimental to fish and wildlife in interstate or navigable waters or the tributaries thereof. Such recommendations and any enforcement measures initiated pursuant thereto by the Secretary of Health, Education, and Welfare shall be designed to enhance the quality of such waters, and shall take into consideration all other legitimate uses of such waters.

Approved October 30, 1965.

FISHING RESOURCES*
1962

In its report of 1962 the Outdoor Recreation Resources Review Commission summarized the outlook for sport fishing in the United States.

The supply of fishing opportunities is a special problem involving a variety of environments—public and private areas, salt and fresh water, natural lakes and streams, and artificial impoundments.

A large amount of water is now available for angling. Inland fresh waters within the 48 States cover some 95,000 square miles, an area comparable to the State of Oregon. This water is in almost a million miles of streams and rivers and more than 100,000 natural lakes; 10 million surface acres of it is in artificial impoundments; and over half of the total area is in the Great Lakes.

These fresh waters produced 522 million pounds of fish for sportsmen in 1960. Salt and tidal waters yielded another 590 million pounds.

The demand for fishing opportunities is expected to increase over the coming years—50 percent by 1976 and 150 percent by 2000. Commercial fishing needs must also be met. There may be a slight reduction in the amount of fish each angler will be able to land, but opportunities can generally be adequate if the needed action is taken.

Supply can be increased by a number of means—

1. An increase of inland fishing water. It is estimated that new impoundments over the next 40 years will create 10 million new surface acres of fishing waters. These waters may not all be opportunely located to meet the needs of fishermen, but they will go a long way toward providing the additional supply needed.

2. Better management of existing waters. Applying techniques now known and that can be developed during the coming years can substantially increase the supply. These measures include pollution abatement, better control of environment and undesired fish species, improved hatchery and stocking procedures, promotion of species not now utilized as sport fish, improved reservoir management, and improved information programs.

3. An increase in salt-water fishing. Ocean waters can provide an almost unlimited increase in fishing opportunities, and some of the increase in demand could be absorbed by a shift to salt-water fishing if problems of management and access can be solved.

---

*Outdoor Recreation Resources Review Commission, *Outdoor Recreation for America* (Washington, D.C.: Government Printing Office, 1962), 71–72.

THE WATER CRISIS*
1967

Senator Frank E. Moss has aptly summarized the extent of fishing resources and some of the problems involved in providing sport fishing opportunities for 28 million fishermen:

Sport fishing has been a delight to Americans since the first settlers reached our shores. The colonists emigrated from European countries that, in the main, reserved streams and fields for landed gentry. Most of the charters of the original thirteen colonies granted the settlers the right to fish and hunt freely on lands not in private ownership. These rights were highly prized, and our zest for these pursuits has never waned.

A 1955 survey showed that a fisherman or hunter lived in one of every three U.S. households, that one-fourth of all males fished, and one-fifth of them hunted. Fishing and hunting now account for as much consumer expenditure as household electricity.

The United States had a population of 146 million in 1946, when 14 million fishing licenses were issued. Ten years later, the population had grown to 174 million, but the number of fishing permits had increased to 20 million—an increase of 43 per cent in fishing licenses against a population growth of 19 per cent. By 1980, there will be 47 million fishermen looking for fishing waters, and by the century's end there will be some 63 million. Sports fishing alone will account for 930 million man-days of recreation and $4.5 billion of expenditure annually.

Such demands for fish can never be met unless we protect our aquatic resources. The 95,500 square miles of U.S. inland fresh waters are—or were—nearly all suitable for fish. By types of waters, the total is divided as follows: public streams, 4,985,000 acres; private streams, 917,000 acres; public natural lakes, 9,130,000 acres; private natural lakes, 200,000 acres; public reservoirs, 8,095,000 acres; private reservoirs, 2,068,000 acres (principally farm ponds averaging slightly more than one acre each in area). In addition, Alaska has 12,400,000 acres of fresh water. Virtually all of it is in public ownership. In Hawaii, 4,647 acres—more than three-fourths of the state's total—is in private ownership.

Fishing waters are classified as cold and warm. There are variations in definition, but cold water usually means that below about 65° F. Trout, salmon, and whitefish live in cold waters; bass, muskellunge, northern pike, and yellow perch prefer warm. Slightly more than half of our 707,000 miles of public streams are

*Frank E. Moss, *The Water Crisis* (New York: Praeger Publishers, 1967), 140–45. Copyright © 1967, reprinted by permission of Praeger Publishers.

cold water. All the Great Lakes contain both cold and warm water habitats. Two-thirds of our natural lakes and almost seven-eighths of man-made reservoirs are managed for warm-water fish. Alaska's waters are all cold; Hawaii's nearly all warm.

Productive waters for fishing are those that maintain nature's biological balance. To support fish, three physical factors must be present in a body of water—a tolerable range of temperatures, sufficient light penetration for production of energy by photosynthesis, and currents to transport nutrients and carry off waste. In addition, there must be the chemicals to nourish plants and organisms to feed the fish.

We have seen that there is an intimate relationship between the quality of stream and the care of its watershed. In the same way, the fertility of a stream reflects that of the watershed. Excessive land clearing, farming, and grazing cause siltation that deteriorates water quality and injures fish-breeding grounds. Flooding washes away foods upon which fish depend. Nonselective timber cutting, fire, and overgrazing reduce fish production as well as the yield of land crops.

Building dams and diverting water through canals can injure the capability of streams to support fish life, although (as will be shown) the building of a reservoir often increases fishing opportunities. Reduced streamflows and silt from returned irrigation flows cut the quantity of pure water, which fish need.

In any consideration of fish habitat, the brackish water of the coastal estuaries deserve special mention. These are the tidewater and saltmarsh regions of the river mouths, a zone of interplay between the margins of the sea and the land.

We have noted the ease with which these acres can become infested with pollution, and the dire consequences of such contamination both to fish habitat and to other beneficial uses of the bays and sounds. The estuaries are of great value because of their fertility and the unique character of the life they support. The example of the Sapelo marshes of Georgia, which produce nearly seven times as much organic matter per unit area as the water of the continental shelf, has been cited. Many of our most prized sea foods—oysters, soft clams, crabs, and diamondback terrapins—come from there. The zone is a nursing ground for prawns, menhaden, bluefish, croaker, mullet, and channel bass. Numerous forms of sea life feed on the plentiful plankton in the shallow waters, and, in turn, provide food for the larger fish.

Migratory fish, such as the salmon, enter the estuaries during their journey upstream to fresh-water spawning grounds. Of the great fish harvest of our continental shelf, nearly two-thirds is composed of species that live in the estuaries at least part of their lives or must pass through on their way to spawning grounds.

These wetlands also provide winter feeding grounds for our most valued waterfowl species—ducks, geese, swans. They support marsh birds such as herons, ibises, and cranes, and shore birds and fish-eaters such as pelicans, loons, cormorants, and sandpipers.

In other words, there is no substitute for the unique aquatic environment of the salt-water estuary. Destruction of this environment by pollution and depletion has had most undesirable consequences for many species and for the industries dependent on them. Planning for the future must include effective measures to preserve large areas of this resource.

Since early times, Americans have shown concern for the protection of fish and the waters they inhabit. Before 1750, local laws had been enacted: Middlesex County, Virginia, prohibited the use of "jack lights" for night fishing; New York City permitted the taking of fish from fresh-water ponds with "angle rod, hook and line only." Today all fifty states maintain fish conservation programs, at least for their inland waters.

In 1871, Congress appointed the Commissioner of Fish and Fisheries; in 1903, the Bureau of Fisheries was designated. In 1956, the Fish and Wildlife Act was passed, Congress declaring that fish, shellfish, and wildlife resources are a "living, renewable form of wealth" that can be maintained and increased with good management, but destroyed if neglected or unwisely exploited.

The act created the Fish and Wildlife Service within the Department of the Interior. The service has two bureaus: Commercial Fisheries and Sport Fisheries and Wildlife, which together employ about 5,000 persons. Aided by the state fish and game agencies, they exhort and educate in a valiant effort to maintain the nation's outdoor resources. But the accomplishments of the conservationist are limited by the means placed at his disposal. In 1962, the Bureau of Sport Fisheries and Wildlife stated: "The fishery biologist is largely dependent upon the sanitary engineer, the construction engineer, the industrialist, and the politician, to provide the quality and quantity of waters he believes essential to maintain fish life."

Of all these, the most important is probably the politician. Only if the conflicts for use of water are resolved—if laws are enacted to keep streams clean, forests and watersheds planted and estuaries protected—can the scientists and technicians do their part.

Despite the act, conservation has failed to keep up with the destructive forces of our industrial society. Water pollution, unwise exploitation of land and forest resources, draining of wetlands and other commercial encroachment have continued to deplete our stock of fish and wildlife.

A decade ago, fishermen lined the banks of the lovely Connecticut River during shad runs. River pollution has ended sports fishing in the stream, which was termed the world's best landscaped sewer by conservationists who surveyed it in 1965. Pollution and dams have all but destroyed anadromous fish in the East. The Atlantic salmon is almost extinct in U.S. rivers; the shad runs have all but ceased; the alewives are almost gone. As we have seen, dams on the Columbia, Snake, and other western streams have been equipped with fishladders, but these have produced less than spectacular results.

One cause for optimism, however, is that most of our cold-water streams are still clean, even though all major river systems suffer from pollution.

Just as good watershed management can restore the land for other purposes, it can improve fishing and bring back wildlife habitat. A prominent example is the Spring Creek watershed of Missouri, which was logged out, burnt over, and badly eroded at the time 5,000 acres were purchased for addition to the Missouri National Forest in the mid-1930's. Good management has made Spring Creek, which flowed only sporadically, a year-round stream. Trees, grasses, and shrubs have been planted, and insects have returned to feed hungry fish. In 1954, after three years of drought, the creek still contained enough water to support sports fishing.

On the Roanoke River, cooperation has minimized the impact of serious pollution and saved both commercial and sports fishing. The Roanoke is a major source of municipal water supply. Its lower reaches are spawning ground, nursery, and migration area for striped bass, alewives, menhaden, white perch, and shad. Low oxygen content and toxic wastes have caused serious fish kills. In 1959, a steering commitee made recommendations for cooperation among the Corps of Engineers, private utilities, state agencies, and the Fish and Wildlife Service. Regulated discharges of water from behind Kerr federal dam and two private utility dams have maintained minimum streamflow; submerged weirs have increased the water's oxygen content.

Resources for the Future, a private, nonprofit research organization, has proposed an experiment on the Potomac that could have important implications for sports fishing. It calls for mass aeration of the river by 100 anchored barges, each equipped with a propeller to churn up the water. New oxygen would burn up pollution and permit the fish population to flourish.

Paradoxically, it is possible to increase the amount of available sports fishing even while habitats are being destroyed. For one thing, reservoirs create vast new fishing opportunities. The TVA is a sports-fishing playground second only to the Great Lakes. A great new fishery was established in Utah and Arizona when the Glen Canyon Dam was built and backed up water for 180 miles to form Lake Powell. Lake Mead, farther down the Colorado River, behind Hoover Dam, has long been famous for its stock of bass and trout.

Usually, the creation of a reservoir does not reduce fishing in adjacent streams. The same number of stream fishermen use the reduced stream acreage, while a new, more numerous group of fishermen come to use the reservoir. Private reservoirs, especially farm ponds, are of increasing significance to sports fishing. Their greatest growth has been in southern and midwestern states.

As is true with all aspects of recreation, accessibility can make larger areas of desirable water available to fishermen. Many remote streams and wetlands are still reached by only a few. Pressure on inland waters, combined with the availability of larger and better boats, is rapidly expanding ocean fishing. Zoning of waters may help solve the problem of fast motor boats, water skiers, and spearfishermen competing for water use with sportsmen using angle rod, hook, and line.

Fish hatcheries, both state and federal, are already an important element in maintaining supply. Undesirable fish species can be replaced by species attractive to fishermen, and the population of fisheries can be expanded, particularly as our knowledge grows.

NATIONAL PARKS

More words have been written about national parks than about any other out-door recreation base or activity. This voluminous literature has not only in-creased park attendance but has also aroused wider public interest in park pol-icies and, at times, intense controversy over such policies.

National, state, and local parks are probably the only institutions that were originally established to provide outdoor recreation for the public. Other re-source-based recreational facilities have emerged as incidental, or accidental, by-products of forestry, irrigation, or other "primary activities."

In January 1915 (before the National Park Service was formed), the national park system consisted of 13 national parks with an area of 4,666,261 acres and 18 national monuments with an area of 85,731 acres, making a grand total of 4,751,992 acres. By 1968 there were 33 national parks and allied areas under the supervision of the National Park Service and a total acreage of 28,048,629 acres.

YELLOWSTONE, YOSEMITE, AND REDWOODS NATIONAL PARKS

Yellowstone and Yosemite National Parks were created before the National Park Service was established. Not only was Yellowstone the first national park, but it embodied and legitimatized the national park concept itself. The objec-tives expressed in the Yellowstone National Park Act laid the basis for all the parks that followed and, in fact, established a central theme for the National Park Service.

Yosemite National Park evolved through a curious set of circumstances. The Yosemite Valley and Mariposa Big Tree Grove had been first ceded to the State of California for park purposes in 1864. The present Yosemite National Park was formed in 1890, and consisted of lands that completely surrounded the 1864 California cession. Finally, in 1906, the State of California ceded back to the United States the lands it had originally obtained in 1864.

The Redwoods National Park is one of the most recent additions to the Na-tional Park Service (October 2, 1968) and it may very well be the most contro-versial of any of the national park proposals.

Over the years, a highly emotional and controversial issue has been the prob-lem of dams in parks. One of the earliest such controversies was a proposal by the city of San Francisco to build a dam in Yosemite National Park. The Hetch-Hetchy dam was built, but six decades later the battle rages on.

As we have noted, the National Park Service administers several different kinds of areas and establishments in addition to the national parks. While this chapter will be mainly concerned with the parks, we cannot completely ignore the parent organization; consequently, some of the documents deal with the creation of the National Park Service. These include statements by Horace M. Albright (second director of the National Park Service), by the Commissioner of the General Land Office in his 1901 report, by Secretary of the Interior Richard A. Ballinger in his 1910 report, and by President Taft in 1911 and 1912, and, finally, there is the act establishing the National Park Service in 1916.

The statements of directors of the National Park Service tend to reflect the current policies of the service and the manner in which such policies have evolved. The statements of three directors in particular, Stephen T. Mather (Director, 1917–1928), Newton P. Drury (Director, 1940–1951), and George B. Hartzog (Director, 1964), have been selected to document the evolution of park policy from 1916 to 1968.

PRESERVATION VERSUS USE

There has probably always been disagreement on whether the primary purpose of parks is preservation of natural wonders or use by the people. The various congressional acts relating to parks have not clarified this situation. Thus the act creating Yellowstone Park in 1872 directed the Secretary of the Interior to publish regulations which ". . . shall provide for the preservation, from injury or spoliation . . . wonders within said park, and their retention in their natural condition." At the same time, the act established the park as ". . . a pleasuring-ground for the benefit and enjoyment of the people. . . ." The act of 1916 creating the NPS reiterated the same dual objective: ". . . to conserve the scenery and the natural and historic objects and the wildlife therein and to provide for the enjoyment of the same in such manner . . . as will leave them unimpaired for the enjoyment of future generations." Similar conflicting sentiments have been expressed in other legislation establishing specific parks. The intent of Congress has plainly been that the parks shall be devoted to both preservation *and* use; the disagreement is over the relative emphasis to be given to each. The so-called "purists," represented by such organizations as the National Parks Association, the Wilderness Society, and the Sierra Club, have emphasized preservation and have sometimes criticized the NPS for its "recreation orientation." Former NPS directors Albright, Arno B. Cammerer, and Conrad L. Wirth have all been censured by these or similar groups, for allegedly departing from "true park standards."

At the same time many recreationists, including sportsmen's organizations and mining, timber, and grazing interests, have objected to the "overemphasis" given to preservation and the "park concept." This reaction is probably partially responsible for the mixed success of the NPS under the Park, Parkway, and Recreation Area Study Act of 1936. Groups opposed to the park preservation concept naturally are not interested in giving the NPS additional territoral jurisdiction nor are they interested in recreation plans and studies undertaken by the NPS.

A third criticism stems from the fact that the NPS cannot make up its mind between preservation and use, and that it vacillates between the two or tries to go in opposite directions at the same time. Given the dual statutory directives this controversy seems inevitable and is likely to continue indefinitely. Shifts of emphasis will depend on public sentiment as reflected in Congress and on the personal views and influence of executives in the Department of the Interior and the NPS.

Past directors of the NPS would probably have agreed to the general proposition that public use of the parks should be allowed and encouraged until it begins to impair non-renewable resources. There would, however, be some differences in the application of this principle to specific situations. Such differences might include variations of opinion on what constitutes "suitable" recreation activities in the parks; on what constitutes serious impairment of resources; and on what is meant by the term "renewable" resources. For example, the Grand Canyon and Mount Ranier are obviously not renewable but neither are they likely to be destroyed by over-use. The ruins in Mesa Verde National Park are also non-renewable, but their "use" is almost certain to cause some deterioration. Timber is ordinarily regarded as a renewable resource but in some instances, Sequoia National Park, for example, it would take hundreds of years to replace the present stand. These few examples are offered only as indications of the complexity of the question of preservation versus use.

These differing views are represented by the statements of Secretary of the Interior Harold L. Ickes, author Bernard DeVoto, and Park Service Director Conrad L. Wirth.

The table below is a summary of the areas administered by the National Park Service in 1968.

By 1915 there were 335,000 visits to the national park system. By 1967 this figure had risen to 139,676,000. While the area of the park system had increased roughly six times, the number of visits increased by a factor of 417. This has obviously created management problems, but it has also raised questions about injury to park resources and given rise to allegations that the parks were becoming "resorts."

Since each of the national parks has been created by a separate act of Con-

No. 289. National Parks, Monuments, and Allied Areas: 1968*

[As of January 1. Includes data for 5 areas in Puerto Rico and Virgin Islands. See also *Historical Statistics, Colonial Times to 1957, series H 455–470*]

Type of Area	Number of areas	Total acreage	Type of Area	Number of areas	Total acreage
National Park System	263	28,048,629	Memorials	21	5,650
National parks	33	13,890,350	Cemeteries	10	220
Historical parks	13	44,689	Seashores	7	345,557
Military parks	11	31,947	Parkways	5	125,231
Memorial park	1	70,436	Recreation areas	12	3,688,827
National Capital Parks [1]	1	7,711	White House	1	18
Battlefield parks	4	9,268	Lakeshores	2	75,721
Monuments	82	9,596,169	Scenic Riverways	1	85,000
Battlefields	5	4,229	Parks, other	4	25,601
Battlefield sites	3	786	International park	1	10
Historic sites	45	8,709	Scientific Reserve	1	32,500

[1]Includes portion of Chesapeake and Ohio Canal among the 730 units administered, as of Dec. 27, 1967.

Source: Dept. of the Interior, National Park Service; annual report, *National Parks & Landmarks.*

gress, it is obviously impossible to document all the acts which established national parks in this chapter. Instead we shall be concerned with the genesis of the national park idea, the establishment of the first two national parks (Yellowstone and Yosemite) and the recent highly controversial Redwood National Park, the battle over the Hetch-Hetchy dam in Yosemite National Park, and the establishment of a National Park Service. We shall include a review of national park policies as enunciated by various Park Service directors and finally, some statements on the perennial controversy of preservation versus use.

*U.S. Bureau of the Census, *Statistical Abstract of the United States, 1968,* 89th ed. (Washington, D.C.: Government Printing Office), 200.

THE BIRTH OF AN IDEA: NATHANIEL P. LANGFORD ON THE YELLOWSTONE PARK REGION*
1870

The Yellowstone Park region was first described in writing by David E. Folsom who, with C. W. Cook, had explored part of the area in 1869. Prior to that time some prospectors and mountain men—among them Jim Bridger and John Colter—had penetrated the park area. Colter had been a member of the Lewis and Clark Expedition and remained in the Upper Missouri River area until 1810. His fantastic stories about the Yellowstone region were generally disbelieved but gained enough publicity to cause the area to become known as "Colter's Hell."

In 1870 a small party of distinguished Montana residents accompanied by a cavalry detachment undertook an exploration of what later became Yellowstone National Park. It was during this expedition that the national park idea was conceived. Nathaniel P. Langford, a member of the exploration party and later the first superintendent of the Park, recorded the genesis of the national park concept in his diary.

TUESDAY, SEPTEMBER 20, 1870

We broke camp at half past nine o'clock, traveling along the rocky edge of the river bank by the rapids, passing thence through a beautiful pine wood and over a long stretch of fallen timber, blackened by fire, for about four miles, when we again reached the river, which here bends in a westerly direction. Lieutenant Doane and I climbed to the top of one of the two prominent hills on our course, and had a fine view of the country for the distance of thirty miles.

Last night, and also this morning in camp, the entire party had a rather unusual discussion. The proposition was made by some member that we utilize the result of our exploration by taking up quarter sections of land at the most prominent points of interest, and a general discussion followed. One member of our party suggested that if there could be secured by pre-emption a good title to two or three quarter sections of land opposite the lower fall of the Yellowstone and extending down the river along the canon, they would eventually become a source of great profit to the owners. Another member of the party thought that it would be more desirable to take up a quarter section of land at the Upper Geyser Basin, for the reason that that locality could be more easily reached by tourists and pleasure seekers. A third suggestion was that each member of the party pre-empt a claim, and in order that no one should have an advantage over the others, the whole should be thrown into a common pool for the benefit of the entire party.

*Nathaniel Pitt Langford, *The Discovery of the Yellowstone Park, 1870* (Saint Paul: J. E. Haynes, 1905), 179–80.

Mr. Hedges then said that he did not approve of any of these plans—that there ought to be no private ownership of any portion of that region, but that the whole of it ought to be set apart as a great National Park, and that each one of us ought to make an effort to have this accomplished. His suggestion met with an instantaneous and favorable response from all—except one—of the members of our party, and each hour since the matter was first broached, our enthusiasm has increased. It has been the main theme of our conversation today as we journeyed. I lay awake half of last night thinking about it;—and if my wakefulness deprived my bed-fellow (Hedges) of any sleep, he has only himself and his disturbing National Park proposition to answer for it.

Our purpose to create a park can only be accomplished by untiring work and concerted action in a warfare against the incredulity and unbelief of our National legislators when our proposal shall be presented for their approval. Nevertheless, I believe we can win the battle.

I do not know of any portion of our country where a national park can be established furnishing to visitors more wonderful attractions than here. These wonders are so different from anything we have ever seen—they are so various, so extensive—that the feeling in my mind from the moment they began to appear until we left them has been one of intense surprise and of incredulity. Every day spent in surveying them has revealed to me some new beauty, and now that I have left them, I begin to feel a skepticism which clothes them in a memory clouded by doubt.

THE CREATION OF YELLOWSTONE NATIONAL PARK*
March 1, 1872

Reports of the Washburn-Langford expedition might have gone unnoticed if one of the member of the party, Truman C. Everts, had not become lost and not been found for over a month. Without a gun or a knife, Everts survived by eating roots and catching an occasional fish or bird with his bare hands. He built fires by kindling tinder with his field glasses. The Everts story received nationwide publicity and this extended to the findings of the Washburn-Langford Expedition as well. Also, Nathaniel Langford conducted a lecture tour on the wonders of the Upper Yellowstone.

In December 1871, William H. Claggett, the delegate from Montana, introduced a bill in the House of Representatives for the reservation of a national park near the headwaters of the Yellowstone River. A similar bill was introduced in the Senate by S. C. Pomeroy of Kansas. The bill passed without amendment and was approved on March 1, 1872.

An Act to set apart a certain tract of land lying near the headwaters of the Yellowstone River as a public park.

Be it enacted by the Senate and House of Representatives of the United States of America in Congress assembled, That the tract of land in the Territories of Montana and Wyoming lying near the headwaters of the Yellowstone River, and described as follows, to wit: commencing at the junction of the Gardiner's River with the Yellowstone River and running east to the meridian passing ten miles to the eastward of the most eastern point of Yellowstone Lake; thence south along the said meridian to the parallel of latitude passing ten miles south of the most southern point of Yellowstone Lake; thence west along said parallel to the meridian passing fifteen miles west of the most western point of Madison Lake; thence north along said meridian to the latitude of the junction of the Yellowstone and Gardiner's Rivers; thence east to the place of beginning, is hereby reserved and withdrawn from settlement, occupancy, or sale under the laws of the United States, and dedicated and set apart as a public park or pleasure ground for the benefit and enjoyment of the people; and all persons who shall locate, settle upon, or occupy the same or any part thereof, except as hereinafter provided, shall be considered trespassers and removed therefrom.

SEC. 2. That said public park shall be under the exclusive control of the Secretary of the Interior, whose duty it shall be, as soon as practicable, to make and publish such rules and regulations as he may deem necessary or proper for the care and management of the same. Such regulations shall provide for the preser-

*17 *Statutes at Large,* 32.

vation from injury or spoliation of all timber, mineral deposits, natural curiosities, or wonders within said park, and their retention in their natural condition.

The Secretary may, in his discretion, grant leases for building purposes, for terms not exceeding ten years, of small parcels of ground, at such places in said park as shall require the erection of buildings for the accommodation of visitors; all of the proceeds of said leases, and all other revenues that may be derived from any source connected with said park, to be expended under his direction in the management of the same and the construction of roads and bridle-paths therein. He shall provide against the wanton destruction of the fish and game found within said park and against their capture or destruction for the purpose of merchandise or profit. He shall also cause all persons trespassing upon the same after the passage of this act to be removed therefrom, and generally shall be authorized to take all such measures as shall be necessary or proper to fully carry out the objects and purposes of this act.

Approved March 1, 1872

CESSION OF THE YOSEMITE VALLEY AND MARIPOSA BIG TREE GROVE TO CALIFORNIA*
May 17, 1864

Yellowstone was the first national park to be created but the two outstanding attractions of the present Yosemite National Park (Yosemite Valley and the Mariposa Big Tree Grove) had been ceded to the State of California eight years earlier in 1864. The bill to transfer the valley and the grove to the State of California apparently met with little opposition. The following passage describes the bill and includes a brief discussion in the Senate.

Mr. CONNESS. I now move that the Senate proceed to the consideration of Senate bill No. 203, reported by the Senator from Vermont [Mr. Foot] this morning from the Committee on Public Lands.

There being no objection, the Senate, as in Committee of the Whole, proceeded to consider the bill (S. No. 203) authorizing a grant to the State of California of the "Yosemite valley" and of the land embracing the "Mariposa Big Tree Grove."

The first section of the bill provides that there shall be granted to the State of California the "cleft" or "gorge" in the Granite peak of the Sierra Nevada mountains, situated in the county of Mariposa and the headwaters of the Merced river, and known as the Yosemite valley, with its branches or spurs in estimated length fifteen miles, and in average width one mile back from the main edge of the precipice on each side of the valley, with the stipulation, nevertheless, that the State is to accept this grant upon the express conditions that the premises are to be held for public use, resort, and recreation, and are to be inalienable for all time; but leases, not exceeding ten years, may be granted for portions of the premises. All incomes derived from leases of privileges are to be expended in the preservation and improvement of the property, or the roads leading thereto; the boundaries to be established at the cost of the State by the United States surveyor general of California, whose official plat, when affirmed by the Commissioner of the General Land Office, is to constitute the evidence of the *locus,* extent, and limits of the cleft or gorge. The premises are to be managed by the Governor of the State, with eight other commissioners, to be appointed by the Executive of California, and who are to receive no compensation for their services.

The second section provides that there shall likewise be granted to the State of California the tracts embracing what is known as the "Mariposa Big Tree Grove," not to exceed the area of four sections, and to be taken in legal subdivisions of one quarter section each, with the like stipulation as expressed in the

*Cong. Globe, 38th Cong., 1st sess. (May 17, 1864), 2300.

first section of this act as to the State's acceptance, with like conditions as to in-alienability, yet with the same lease privilege; the income to be expended in the preservation, improvement, and protection of the property; the premises to be managed by commissioners, as stipulated in the first section, and to be taken in legal subdivisions, and the official plat of the United States surveyor general, when affirmed by the Commissioner of the General Land Office, to be the evi-dence of the *locus* of the "Mariposa Big Tree Grove."

Mr. CONNESS. I will state to the Senate that this bill proposes to make a grant of certain premises located in the Sierra Nevada mountains, in the State of Cali-fornia, that are for all public purposes worthless, but which constitute, perhaps, some of the greatest wonders of the world. The object and purpose is to make a grant to the State, on the stipulations contained in the bill, that the property shall be inalienable forever, and preserved and improved as a place of public resort, to be taken charge of by gentlemen to be appointed by the Governor, who are to receive no compensation for their services, and who are to undertake the man-agement and improvement of the property by making roads leading thereto and adopting such other means as may be necessary for its preservation and improve-ment. It includes a grant of a few sections of ground upon which one of the cele-brated big tree groves of that State is located, of which most Senators doubtless have heard. The trees contained in that grove have no parallel, perhaps, in the world. They are subject now to damage and injury; and this bill, as I have before stated, proposes to commit them to the care of the authorities of that State for their constant preservation, that they may be exposed to public view, and that they may be used and preserved for the benefit of mankind. It is a matter involv-ing no appropriation whatever. The property is of no value to the Government. I make this explanation that the Senate may understand what the purpose is.

The bill was reported to the Senate without amendment.

Mr. FOSTER. I should like to ask the Senator from California whether the State of California—

The PRESIDENT *pro tempore*. The Chair must interrupt the Senator to call up the special order of the day, the time fixed for its consideration having arrived.

Mr. CONNESS. I hope it will lie over for the present.

Mr. WILSON. Let it go over informally for a few minutes.

The PRESIDENT *pro tempore*. That course will be taken if there be no objec-tion.

Mr. FOSTER. I should like to ask the Senator from California whether the State of California has intimated any wish that we should thus make this grant to them, and how it comes about that we propose making it.

Mr. CONNESS. I will state to the Senator from Connecticut and to the Senate, that they may understand it, that the application comes to us from various gen-tlemen in California, gentlemen of fortune, of taste, and of refinement, and the plan proposed in this bill has been suggested by them, that this property be committed to the care of the State. I submitted the plan as presented by these gentlemen to the Land Office, and the bill now before the Senate has been prepared by the Commissioner of the General Land Office, who also takes a great interest in the preservation both of the Yosemite valley and the Big Tree Grove. Such was the origin of the measure, and such are its purposes.

Mr. FOSTER. I did not by any means mean to intimate any opposition to the bill; but it struck me as being rather a singular grant, unprecedented so far as my recollection goes, and unless the State through her appropriate authorities signified some wish in the matter, it might be deemed by the State officious on our part to make a grant of this kind.

Mr. CONNESS. Ordinarily I should hope I spoke for the State of California here. I feel authorized to do so under existing circumstances. There is no parallel, and can be no parallel for this measure, for there is not, as I stated before, on earth just such a condition of things. The Mariposa Big Tree Grove is really the wonder of the world, containing those magnificent monarchs of the forest that are from thirty to forty feet in diameter.

Mr. DAVIS. How old?

Mr. CONNESS. Well, sir, they are estimated to reach an age of three thousand years. There are two such groves in the State. One is known as the Mariposa grove, the one contemplated in this bill; and the other is known as the Calaveras grove. From the Calaveras grove some sections of a fallen tree were cut during and pending the great World's Fair that was held in London some years since. One joint of the tree was sectionized and transported to that country in sections, and then set up there. The English who saw it declared it to be a Yankee invention, made from beginning to end; that it was an utter untruth that such trees grew in the country; that it could not be; and, although the section of the tree was transported there at an expense of several thousand dollars, we were not able to convince them that it was a specimen of American growth. They would not believe us. The purpose of this bill is to preserve one of these groves from devastation and injury. The necessity of taking early possession and care of these great wonders can easily be seen and understood.

Mr. FOSTER. I certainly did not mean to say anthing which implied that the honorable Senator from California had not the most perfect and entire right to speak for his State, and I am at a loss to understand what I was so unfortunate as to say which led him to suppose that I doubted it.

The bill was ordered to be engrossed for a third reading, and was read the third time, and passed.

AN ACT TO ESTABLISH YOSEMITE NATIONAL PARK*
October 1, 1890

Yosemite National Park was established as a "forest reservation" in 1890. It originally included only those lands surrounding Yosemite Valley, which still belonged to the State of California.

An Act to set apart certain tracts of land in the State of California as forest reservations.

Be it enacted by the Senate and House of Representatives of the United States of America in Congress assembled, That the tracts of land in the State of California known as described as follows: Commencing at the northwest corner of township two north, range nineteen east Mount Diablo meridian, thence eastwardly on the line between townships two and three north, ranges twenty-four and twenty-five east; thence southwardly on the line between ranges twenty-four and twenty-five east to the Mount Diablo base line; thence eastwardly on said base line to the corner to township one south, ranges twenty-five and twenty-six east; thence southwardly on the line between ranges twenty-five and twenty-six east to the southeast corner of township two south, range twenty-five east; thence eastwardly on the line between townships two and three south, range twenty-six east to the corner to townships two and three south, ranges twenty-six and twenty-seven east; thence southwardly on the line between ranges twenty-six and twenty-seven east to the first standard parallel south; thence westwardly on the first standard parallel south to the southwest corner of township four south, range nineteen east; thence northwardly on the line between ranges eighteen and nineteen east to the northwest corner of township two south, range nineteen east; thence westwardly on the line between townships one and two south to the southwest corner of township one south, range nineteen east; thence northwardly on the line between ranges eighteen and nineteen east to the northwest corner of township two north, range nineteen east, the place of beginning, are hereby reserved and withdrawn from settlement, occupancy, or sale under the laws of the United States, and set apart as reserved forest lands; and all persons who shall locate or settle upon, or occupy the same or any part thereof, except as hereinafter provided, shall be considered trespassers and removed therefrom: *Provided, however,* That nothing in this act shall be construed as in anywise affecting the grant of lands made to the State of California by virtue of the act entitled "An act authorizing a grant to the State of California of the Yosemite Valley, and of the land embracing the Mariposa Big-Tree Grove, ap-

*26 *Statutes at Large,* 650.

proved June thirtieth, eighteen hundred and sixty-four; or as affecting any bona-fide entry of land made within the limits above described under any law of the United States prior to the approval of this act.

SEC. 2. That said reservation shall be under the exclusive control of the Secretary of the Interior, whose duty it shall be, as soon as practicable, to make and publish such rules and regulations as he may deem necessary or proper for the care and management of the same. Such regulations shall provide for the preservation from injury of all timber, mineral deposits, natural curiosities, or wonders within said reservation, and their retention in their natural condition. The Secretary may, in his discretion, grant leases for building purposes for terms not exceeding ten years of small parcels of ground not exceeding five acres; at such places in said reservation as shall require the erection of buildings for the accommodation of visitors; all of the proceeds of said leases and other revenues that may be derived from any source connected with said reservation to be expended under his direction in the management of the same and the construction of roads and paths therein. He shall provide against the wanton destruction of the fish, and game found within said reservation, and against their capture or destruction, for the purposes of merchandise or profit. He shall also cause all persons trespassing upon the same after the passage of this act to be removed therefrom, and, generally, shall be authorized to take all such measures as shall be necessary or proper to fully carry out the objects and purposes of this act.

SEC. 3. There shall also be and is hereby reserved and withdrawn from settlement, occupancy or sale under the laws of the United States, and shall be set apart as reserved forest lands, as hereinbefore provided, and subject to all the limitations and provisions herein contained, the following additional lands, to wit; Township seventeen, south, range thirty east of the Mount Diablo meridian, excepting sections thirty-one, thirty-two, thirty-three, and thirty-four of said township, included in a previous bill. And there is also reserved and withdrawn from settlement, occupancy or sale under the laws of the United States, and set apart as forest lands, subject to like limitations, conditions and provisions, all of townships fifteen and sixteen, south, of ranges twenty-nine and thirty east of the Mount Diablo meridian. And there is also hereby reserved and withdrawn from settlement, occupancy or sale under the laws of the United States, and set apart as reserved forest lands under like limitations, restrictions and provisions, Sections five and six in township fourteen, south, range twenty-eight, east of Mount Diablo meridian, and also Sections thirty-one and thirty-two of township thirteen, south, range twenty-eight east of the same meridian. Nothing in this act shall authorize rules or contracts touching the protection and improvement of said reservations, beyond the sums that may be received by the Secretary of the Interior under the foregoing provisions, or authorize any charge against the Treasury of the United States.

Approved, October 1, 1890.

JOINT RESOLUTION ADDING LAND TO YOSEMITE PARK*
June 11, 1906

In 1906 the Yosemite Valley and the Mariposa Big Tree Grove, which had been given to California in 1864, were re-ceded to the United States and became part of Yosemite National Park.

> Joint Resolution accepting the recession by the State of California of the Yosemite Valley grant and the Mariposa Big Tree Grove, and including the same, together with fractional sections five and six, township five south, range twenty-two east, Mount Diablo meridian, California, within the metes and bounds of the Yosemite National Park, and changing the boundaries thereof.

Resolved by the Senate and House of Representatives of the United States of America in Congress assembled, That the recession and regranting unto the United States by the State of California of the cleft or gorge in the granite peak of the Sierra Nevada Mountains, situated in the county of Mariposa, State of California, and the headwaters of the Merced River, and known as the Yosemite Valley, with its branches or spurs, granted unto the State of California in trust for public use, resort, and recreation by the Act of Congress entitled "An Act authorizing a grant to the State of California of the Yosemite Valley and of the land embracing the Mariposa Big Tree Grove," approved June thirtieth, eighteen hundred and sixty-four (Thirteenth Statutes, page three hundred and twenty-five), as well as the tracts embracing what is known as the "Mariposa Big Tree Grove," likewise granted unto the State of California by the aforsaid Act of Congress, is hereby ratified and accepted, and the tracts of land embracing the Yosemite Valley and the Mariposa Big Tree Grove, as described in the Act of Congress approved June thirtieth, eighteen hundred and sixty-four, together with that part of fractional sections five and six, township five south, range twenty-two east, Mount Diablo meridian, California, lying south of the South Fork of Merced River and almost wholly between the Mariposa Big Tree Grove and the present south boundary of the Yosemite National Park, be, and the same are hereby, reserved and withdrawn from settlement, occupancy, or sale under the laws of the United States and set apart as reserved forest lands, subject to all the limitations, conditions, and provisions of the Act of Congress approved October first, eighteen hundred and ninety, entitled "An Act to set apart certain tracts of land in the State of California as forest reservations," as well as the limitations, conditions, and provisions of the Act of Congress approved February seventh, nineteen hundred and five, entitled "An Act to exclude from the Yosemite National Park, California, certain lands therein described, and to attach

*34 *Statutes at Large,* 841.

and include the said lands in the Sierra Forest Reserve," and shall hereafter form a part of the Yosemite National Park.

The south and west boundary lines of the Yosemite National Park are hereby changed as follows: Beginning at the point on the line between sections thirty-five and thirty-six, township four south, range twenty-one east, where same intersects the middle of the channel of the South Fork of the Merced River; thence north on section line to the southwest corner of section twenty-five; thence west on section lines to the southwest corner of section twenty-eight; thence north on section line to the northwest corner of section twenty-eight; thence west on section line to the quarter-section corner between sections twenty and twenty-nine; thence north through the middle of section twenty to the center thereof; thence east through the middle of section twenty to the quarter-section corner between sections twenty and twenty-one; thence north on section line to the quarter-section corner between sections sixteen and seventeen; thence west through middle of section seventeen to the center thereof; thence north through the middle of sections seventeen, eight, and five to the quarter-section corner of north boundary of section five on township boundary, all in township four south, range twenty-one east; thence north through the middle of section thirty-two, township three south, range twenty-one east, to the center thereof; thence west through the middle of section thirty-two, said township, and section thirty-six, township three south, range twenty east, to the quarter-section corner, between sections thirty-five and thirty-six; thence north on section line to the quarter-section corner between sections twenty-five and twenty-six; thence east through the middle of section twenty-five to the center thereof; thence north through the middle of sections twenty-five and twenty-four to the center of section twenty-four; thence west through the middle of sections twenty-four, twenty-three, and twenty-two to the quarter-section corner between sections twenty-one and twenty-two, township three south, range twenty east, on the present western boundary of the Yosemite National Park. And all that portion of the Yosemite National Park lying between the boundary line last above mentioned and the present boundary line of said national park is excluded from said park; and the said lands so excluded, and all thereof, are added to and made a part of the Sierra Forest Reserve, and shall hereafter form a part of said Sierra Forest Reserve, and shall be subject to all of the Acts of Congress with relation thereto: *Provided,* That the Secretary of the Interior may require the payment of such price as he may deem proper for privileges on the land herein segregated from the Yosemite National Park and made a part of the Sierra Forest Reserve accorded under the Act approved February fifteenth, nineteen hundred and one, relating to rights of way over certain parks, reservations, and other lands, and other Acts concerning rights of way over public lands: *And provided further,* That in the grant of any right of way for railway purposes across the lands placed under this measure within the Sierra Forest Reserve it shall be stipulated that no logs or timber shall be hauled over the same without the consent of the Secretary of the Interior, and under regulations to be promulgated by him.

SEC. 2. That none of the lands patented and in private ownership in the area hereby included in the Sierra Forest Reserve shall have the privileges of the lieu-land scrip provisions of the land laws, but otherwise to be in all respects under the laws and regulations affecting the forest reserves, and immediately upon the passage of this Act all laws, rules, and regulations affecting forest reservations, including the right to change the boundaries thereof by Executive proclamation, shall take effect and be in force within the limits of the territory excluded by this Act from the Yosemite National Park, except as herein otherwise provided.

SEC. 3. That all revenues derived from privileges in the park authorized under the Act of October first, eighteen hundred and ninety, the Act of February seventh, nineteen hundred and five, as well as under this measure, or from privileges accorded on the lands herein segregated from said park and included within the Sierra Forest Reserve, shall be paid into the Treasury of the United States, to be expended under the direction of the Secretary of the Interior in the management, protection, and improvement of the Yosemite National Park.

Approved, June 11, 1906.

THE BATTLE OVER HETCH-HETCHY*
1913

No controversy involving a national park has been fought so long or with such emotional intensity as the battle of Hetch-Hetchy. The plan to build a dam in the Hetch-Hetchy Valley of Yosemite National Park was to provide a water supply for the city of San Francisco through a 175-mile aqueduct. The dam would generate electricity and provide some flood control benefits, but the reservoir would also flood Hetch-Hetchy Valley—a part of the park.

The bill to authorize this project contained a controversial amendment, written by Congressman William Kent of California, which provided that the city of San Francisco distribute the electric power generated by the project directly to consumers. In other words, the bill would put San Francisco into the electric power business. Consequently the bill was opposed by privately-owned power utilities and their supporters.

The public electric power versus private electric power controversy in the United States has continued for many years and includes such incidents as the Muscle Shoals, Hell's Canyon, and Dixon-Yates disputes. If anything, it has been more emotional than disagreements over the proper role of national parks and has been fought even more bitterly.

The Hetch-Hetchy proposal thus contained two basic controversies: the public versus private control of electric power, and conservation (wise use) versus preservation role for parks. It also happened that the issue divided the major exponents of conservation. William Kent had a reputation as a conservationist. He had personally purchased Muir Woods and dedicated it to the State of California as a state park. He was joined by Gifford Pinchot and Secretary of the Interior James R. Garfield against John Muir of the Sierra Club and J. Horace McFarland, president of the American Civic Association.

John Muir led opponents to the plan. He had fallen in love with the Yosemite region years before and had done much both to publicize and protect the area. Muir worshipped the wilds and his followers apparently almost worshipped him. He founded the Sierra Club in 1892 and was influential in causing the Yosemite Valley to be re-ceded to the United States in 1906.

Some insight into the tone of the congressional debates on Hetch-Hetchy may be obtained from the following exerpts from the Congressional Record of 1913.

AUGUST 29, 1913

Mr. [JOHN E.] RAKER [Calif.] . . . I want particularly to call the attention of gentlemen to the fact that the world-wide famed Yosemite Valley, which is in

*Cong. Rec., 63rd Cong., 1st sess., (Aug. 29, 1913) 3902; (Aug. 30, 1913) 3973–74; (Aug. 30, 1913) 4004.

the Yosemite National Park, lies south in the neighborhood of 20 to 25 miles, on a different divide and in a different watershed from that in which the Hetch Hetchy Valley is located. The Merced River heads in the Yosemite Valley, and the Tuolumne River heads in the Hetch Hetchy. There is not an attempt, there is not an effort, to in any way interfere with or to come within less than 20 miles of the Yosemite Valley.

Take now the Hetch Hetchy, which is owned practically, half of it, by the city and county of San Francisco, the other half being owned by the Government. The city and county of San Francisco, without the consent of the Government to use it as a dam, can not use it unless the Government condemns the city's property, upon which it has expended $1,750,000 in various ways; about $700,000 for land alone. The city and county can not use this land that they now have for a reservoir site unless the Government gives its consent, and there we see this natural reservoir site unused, with the waters of the Tuolumne River, that from the beginning of time have been running to waste as flood waters in the Pacific Ocean, causing devastation in the spring, flooding part of the San Joaquin Valley, around Stockton, up to the steps of the depot, as I have seen myself, and from then on to Sacramento, flooded, and even from there on up to Red Bluff, or Tehama Junction in conjunction with the Sacramento River, and now this permission is asked to build this dam in order that these flood waters may be restrained in flood times, and in order that the city and county of San Francisco may use the flood water, not the natural flow of the stream, because in the bill they concede the prior right to the irrigationists below, but for the purpose of supplying the natural wants of the city.

I want, Mr. Chairman, to call the attention of the committee further to this fact that this bill provides for roads to be built by the city and county of San Francisco, from the public highway into the valley, the Hetch Hetchy Valley. They say there is a trail around the Hetch Hetchy Valley. The city and county of San Francisco under this grant are to build the road up to the dam, around the lake, and from there north to the Tioga Road, which is a public road leading across the mountains to the State of Nevada. It will also build a trail up to the Tiltill Valley, where the city and county of San Francisco now own 160 acres of land, an ideal place for hotels and camp sites. They will build a road from there through the valley to Smiths Peak, and a trail from the main road around the Hetch Hetchy on to Lake Eleanor and then to Cherry Creek. The city and county of San Francisco will keep up these roads from now until the crack of doom. Today about 25 to 75 people per year visit the Hetch Hetchy Valley. You must go in on the trail and on burro back to get there. Instead of that, you will have one of the scenic roads of the world built to this valley, and instead of having barren cliffs on either side you will have boulevards around this lake, so that the people may see the wonders of the Hetch Hetchy Valley and also the remainder of this territory that is in the watershed of this valley. They will make it accessible, and make accessible the Tuolumne meadows, which are about 40 miles beyond, where there are about 1,500 acres which will be accessible to campers. That part of the floor of the valley which is now owned by the city and county of San Francisco, about 780 acres in extent, could now be fenced, and the Government could be prevented from using any of that part of the floor of the valley. But instead of that, they say they will build roads where people can go and see this beautiful lake, as well as the rest of the park.

They will turn over the 160 acres of land which they now own at the Tiltill Valley for camping purposes. They will make accessible Lake Eleanor, which is today inaccessible, except to a few who go there by trail. They will turn over the Cherry Creek Valley in the same way, all that they do not use for reservoir purposes, and there is a good deal of it. So that instead of destroying the scenery and preventing the people going in there, this valley will be made more beautiful with a road in, through, and about it, with the camping ground made accessible and turned over to the use of the public instead of being, as now, controlled by a municipal corporation. Those who have seen lakes in the mountains can not but believe that Lake Hetch Hetchy will be more beautiful than anything there today. Lake Louise, in Canada, which is but a pond of water with a snow-capped mountain in front of it, a rugged mountain on one side and a rugged mountain covered with trees on the other, is one of the most famous bits of scenery in the world. The very colors of the rainbow are reflected in that lake, and people go from all over the world to behold its beauty. It will be the same with this lake in the Hetch Hetchy Valley, which is today inaccessible. As for the rocks, there are grander and larger rocks to be seen in the Yosemite Valley. You can see them almost anywhere; but this bill proposes to make accessible that which today is inaccessible. Prof. Grant said in relation to Lake Louise, "I would like to go to heaven. I do not want to go to hell; but if I can not go to heaven, send me to Lake Louise." And it will be the same with Lake Hetch Hetchy when it is completed

AUGUST 30, 1913

Mr. [HALVOR] STEENERSON, [Minn.] . . . It is said by some that this improvement will not injure the park. Here is a national park, created by Congress, belonging to the whole people.

It is, no doubt, a rare beauty spot. I have never had the good fortune to visit California and behold its beautiful scenery. I have stored up that pleasure for some future day, and I hope to be able to see the Hetch Hetchy Valley in its pristine glory and beauty before the destroying hand of greed and commerce shall have been laid upon it.

I can not speak from personal knowledge as to the scenic value of the land here in question, but I take it that no better authority on that subject could be found than Mr. John Muir, the naturalist. In a letter addressed to me, dated June 27, 1913, he says:

> The Yosemite National Park is not only the greatest and most wonderful national playground in California, but in many of its features it is without a rival in the whole world. It belongs to the American people, and in world-wide interest ranks with the Yellowstone and the Grand Canyon of Colorado. It embraces the headwaters of two rivers—the Merced and the Tuolumne. The Yosemite Valley is in the Merced Basin; the Hetch Hetchy Valley, the grand canyon of the Tuolumne, and the Tuolumne Meadows are in the Tuolumne Basin. Excepting only the Yosemite Valley, the Tuolumne Basin in its general features is the more wonderful and larger half of the park.
>
> The Hetch Hetchy Valley is a wonderfully exact counterpart of the great Yosemite, not only in its cliffs and waterfalls and peaceful river, but in the gardens, groves, meadows, and camp grounds of its flowery, parklike floor.

[Applause.]
Why, Dr. Johnson, the editor of the Century Magazine, says:

> The Hetch Hetchy is a veritable temple of the living God, and again the money changers are in the temple to desecrate it.

Mr. FERRIS. Will the gentleman yield?

Mr. STEENERSON. I will yield to the gentleman.

Mr. FERRIS. These letters ought not to go unchallenged. Doubtless the gentleman knows that this park is 20 miles away from the main Yosemite National Park. There are 719,000 acres in the park. This will only flood 3,000 acres, and two-thirds of the 3,000 acres are owned in fee simple by the city of San Francisco.

Mr. STEENERSON. That has been stated several times.

Mr. FERRIS. Compared to the size of the whole park this is no more than a pimple on your back.

Mr. STEENERSON. It has been stated several times that this is not the main part of the Yosemite Park, but it is a part of the park, and as Mr. Muir, the naturalist, who ought to be a good judge of such things, says, as I have read, that valley is the most wonderful part of the park. So I will put up Mr. Muir against the judgment of men who want to destroy the park.

As I have already remarked, this is not a local question. The people of the whole United States are interested in it. If the entire New York delegation should come here unanimously demanding that Niagara Falls be destroyed for the purpose of creating power, would we from the other portions of the United States stand here indifferent? Could we recognize the claim that nobody except the State of New York is interested? This question is exactly analogous.

Mr. STEENERSON. I believe, as I have already stated, that my duty to my constituents and to the whole people of the United States requires me to oppose this bill. There is nothing in the argument that the flooding of this valley will improve upon nature. One gentleman from California, who spoke in favor of the bill yesterday, had the temerity to make that argument, and he was indorsed by the gentleman from Idaho. You might as well try to improve upon the lily of the field by hand painting it. The idea that a reservoir for water supply will make a beautiful lake is absurd. Of course, you understand that in a dry time when water is needed the reservoir will probably be empty, as all reservoirs are at those times, and you will have in place of the beautiful floor of the Hetch Hetchy Valley, as described by Mr. Muir, a dirty, muddy pond, with the water drained off to supply San Francisco, and probably some dead fish and frogs in it. [Laughter.] Will that be beautiful? And then there will be perhaps large generating works, with rolling wheels and buzzing machinery and transmission wires with a devilish, hissing noise echoing and reechoing sounds strange and cacophonous. [Laughter.] That is what you will offer us in place of the temple of the gods that has been made ready for our admiration.

The gentleman from California [Mr. Knowland] yesterday pointed out the wonderful increase in population in the cities on San Francisco Bay, and he took great pride in it. He said that influx from the country to the city was very strong in that region, the same as it is elsewhere in the world. Instead of taking pride in that fact I deplore it. All the greatest statesmen of our time are deploring the fact of the influx to the city from the country. They are putting forth efforts for Government encouragement of rural life. We hear on every hand futile complaints against the rising cost of living. Some gentlemen have discovered that the way to cheapen the cost of living is to import beef and foodstuffs from abroad, but that is a vain remedy, because, when you discourage the farm and country life here in the United States, the foreign farmer will have you in his power and charge you even higher prices than you now pay.

I am opposed to the eternal drawing upon the Federal Government resources and of the people to make cities more attractive at the expense of the country. Rather would I encourage the people to go to the national parks, where they can admire nature in its pristine beauty and glory and become imbued with the love of nature become second Burbanks in knowledge and practice and science of plant breeding and all the secrets of animal and vegetable life.

Mr. FERRIS. Will the gentlemen yeild?

Mr. STEENERSON. I speak for myself only as a member of the Republican Party and not the whole party.

Mr. FERRIS. Of course the gentleman is aware, he having mentioned some of the political phases of the question, that California is a Republican State; that San Francisco is a Republican city; that the Members who will be benefited by it locally, if any particular partisanship should be injected into it, are Republicans; and, furthermore, does the gentleman now set his own judgment up against the combined judgment of the California delegation, of 11 in number; and does he set his judgment up against the Secretary of the Interior, the Secretary of Agriculture; the Chief Forester, Gifford Pinchot; F. H. Newell, the head of the Reclamation Service; the head of the Geological Survey; the unanimous report of our Public Lands Committee? Every other arm of the Government that has anything to do with or knows anything about it has been consulted. They have appeared in person and by letter, and they are all earnestly for it.

Mr. STEENERSON. In answer to that, I will say I will set up my judgment with Secretary Hitchcock and Secretary Garfield and Secretary Fisher as against the present Secretary; and as to the judgment of the present Representatives from California, for whom I have great respect, you must admit they are interested parties, and they can not act as judges in a matter of this kind. As to the question of politics, I acquit the gentleman from Oklahoma from trying to work any political scheme in this bill. I acknowledge his generosity to the California delegation—and it is a very great generosity—but it is impossible for the majority of this House to escape the responsibility for this bill. You can not throw it on the Representatives from California, because, being in control, you are responsible. As to Gifford Pinchot, I will say that I go by his first stand, which I am advised was against taking Hetch Hetchy Valley.

Mr. FERRIS. He has always been for the bill.

Mr. STEENERSON. This bill? He was opposed to this idea a few years ago.

Mr. FERRIS. He has always been for the bill.

Mr. STEENERSON. Well, even if he now is for this bill, I do not take him as an authority. I can not follow blindly, but must know his reasons. Some four years ago he and other conservationists stated that they were in favor of free lumber, because by getting free lumber supplied from abroad we would save our own forests—a plain proposition, that could not be contradicted—yet only a few hours after conferring with a few lumber barons he changed about and wrote a letter to the Committee on Ways and Means and said that the way to conserve the forests of the United States was to put on a duty and make lumber high priced to the farmers. A man who can make a somersault like that can not command my confidence either in economics or polities. [Laughter and applause.]

AUGUST 30, 1913

Mr. [MARTIN] DIES, [Texas] . . . I only rise, Mr. Chairman, to call the attention of those gentlemen who were so vociferous for free lumber in the Sixty-first and Sixty-second Congresses to the fact that they had better conserve the resources of the country in the matter of wheat, oats, and corn, and mules, than in the matter of trees in this country. But I sympathize with my friends in California who want to take a part of the public domain now, notwithstanding all their declamations for conservation of resources. I am willing to let them have it. I am willing to let them have it when they take it in California and San Francisco for the public good.

That is what the great resources of this country are for. They are for the American people. I want them to open the coal mines in Alaska. I want them to open the reservations in this country. I am not for reservations and parks. I would have the great timber and mineral and coal resources of this country opened to the people, and I only want to say, Mr. Chairman, that your Pinchots and your conservationists generally are theorists who are not, in my humble judgment, making a propaganda in the interest of the American people.

Let California have it, and let Alaska open her coal mines. God Almighty has located the resources of this country in such a form as that His children will not use them in disproportion, and your Pinchots will not be able to controvert and circumvent the laws of God Almighty. [Applause and cries of "Vote!" "Vote!"]

THE HETCH-HETCHY ACT*
December 19, 1913

The Hetch-Hetchy bill was finally passed and approved.

An Act granting to the city and county of San Francisco certain rights of way in, over, and through certain public lands, the Yosemite National Park, and Stanislaus National Forest, and certain lands in the Yosemite National Park, the Stanislaus National Forest, and the public lands in the State of California, and for other purposes.

Be it enacted by the Senate and House of Representatives of the United States of America in Congress assembled, That there is hereby granted to the city and county of San Francisco, a municipal corporation in the State of California, all necessary rights of way along such locations and of such width, not to exceed two hundred and fifty feet, as in the judgment of the Secretary of the Interior may be required for the purposes of this Act, in, over, and through the public lands of the United States in the counties of Tuolumne, Stanislaus, San Joaquin, and Alameda, in the State of California, and in, over, and through the Yosemite National Park and the Stanislaus National Forest, or portions thereof, lying within the said counties, for the purpose of constructing, operating, and maintaining aqueducts, canals, ditches, pipes, pipe lines, flumes, tunnels, and conduits for conveying water for domestic purposes and uses to the city and county of San Francisco and such other municipalities and water districts as, with the consent of the city and county of San Francisco, or in accordance with the laws of the State of California in force at the time application is made, may hereafter participate in the beneficial use of the rights and privileges granted by this Act; for the purpose of constructing, operating, and maintaining power and electric plants, poles, and lines for generation and sale and distribution of electric energy; also for the purpose of constructing, operating, and maintaining telephone and telegraph lines, and for the purpose of constructing, operating, and maintaining roads, trails, bridges, tramways, railroads, and other means of locomotion, transportation, and communication, such as may be necessary or proper in the construction, maintenance, and operation of the works constructed by the grantee herein; together with such lands in the Hetch Hetchy Valley and Lake Eleanor Basin within the Yosemite National Park, and the Cherry Valley within the Stanislaus National Forest, irrespective of the width or extent of said lands, as may be determined by the Secretary of the Interior to be actually necessary for surface or underground reservoirs, diverting and storage dams; together with such lands as the Secretary of the Interior may determine to be actually necessary for power houses, and all other structures or buildings necessary or properly inci-

*38 *Statutes at Large,* 242.

dent to the construction, operation, and maintenance of said water-power and electric plants, telephone and telegraph lines, and such means of locomotion, transportation, and communication as may be established; together with the right to take, free of cost, from the public lands, the Yosemite National Park, and the Stanislaus National Forest adjacent to its right of way, within such distance as the Secretary of the Interior and the Secretary of Agriculture may determine, stone, earth, gravel, sand, tufa, and other materials of like character actually necessary to be used in the construction, operation, and repair of its said water-power and electric plants, its said telephone and telegraph lines, and its said means of locomotion, transportation, or communication, under such conditions and regulations as may be fixed by the Secretary of the Interior and the Secretary of Agriculture, within their respective jurisdictions, for the protection of the public lands, the Yosemite National Park, and the Stanislaus National Forest: *Provided,* That said grantee shall file, as hereinafter provided, a map or maps showing the boundaries, location, and extent of said proposed rights of way and lands for the purposes hereinabove set forth: *Provided further,* That the Secretary of the Interior shall approve no location or change of location in the national forests unless said location or change of location shall have been approved in writing by the Secretary of Agriculture.

SEC. 2. That within three years after the passage of this Act said grantee shall file with the registers of the United States land offices, in the districts where said rights of way or lands are located, a map or maps showing the boundaries, locations, and extent of said proposed rights of way and lands required for the purposes stated in section one of this Act; but no permanent construction work shall be commenced on said land until such map or maps shall have been filed as herein provided and approved by the Secretary of the Interior: *Provided, however,* That any changes of location of any of said rights of way or lands may be made by said grantee before the final completion of any of said work permitted in section one hereof, by filing such additional map or maps as may be necessary to show such changes of location, said additional map or maps to be filed in the same manner as the original map or maps; but no change of location shall become valid until approved by the Secretary of the Interior, and the approval by the Secretary of the Interior of said map or maps showing changes of location of said rights of way or lands shall operate as an abandonment by the city and county of San Francisco to the extent of such change or changes of any of the rights of way or lands indicated on the original maps: *And provided further,* That any rights inuring to the grantee under this Act shall, on the approval of the map or maps referred to herein by the Secretary of the Interior, relate back to the date of the filing of said map or maps with the register of the United States Land Office as provided herein, or to the date of the filing of such maps as they may be copies of as provided for herein: *And provided further,* That with reference to any map or maps heretofore filed by said city and county of San Francisco or its grantor with any officer of the Department of the Interior or the Department of Agriculture, and approved by said department, the provisions hereof will be considered complied with by the filing by said grantee of copies of any of such map or maps with the register of the United States Land Office as provided for herein, which said map or maps and locations shall as in all other cases be subject to the approval of the Secretary of the Interior.

SEC. 3. That the rights of way hereby granted shall not be effective over any lands upon which homestead, mining, or other existing valid claim or claims shall have been filed or made and which now in law constitute prior rights to any claim of the grantee until said grantee shall have purchased such portion or portions of such homestead, mining, or other existing valid claims as it may require for right-of-way purposes and other purposes herein set forth, and shall have procured proper relinquishments of such portion or portions of such claims, or acquired title by due process of law and just compensation paid to said entrymen or claimants, and caused proper evidence of such fact to be filed with the Commissioner of the General Land Office, and the right of such entrymen or claimants to sell and of said grantee to purchase such portion or portions of such claims are hereby granted: *Provided, however,* That this Act shall not apply to any lands embraced in rights of way heretofore approved under any Act of Congress for the benefit of any parties other than said grantee or its predecessors in interest.

SEC. 4. That the said grantee shall conform to all regulations adopted and prescribed by the Secretary of the Interior governing the Yosemite National Park and by the Secretary of Agriculture governing the Stanislaus National Forest, and shall not take, cut, or destroy any timber within the Yosemite National Park or the Stanislaus National Forest, except such as may be actually necessary in order to construct, repair, and operate its said reservoirs, dams, power plants, water-power and electric works, and other structures above mentioned, but no timber shall be cut or removed from lands outside of the right of way until designated by the Secretary of the Interior or the Secretary of Agriculture, respectively; and it shall pay to the United States the full value of all timber and wood cut, injured, or destroyed on or adjacent to any of the rights of way and lands, as required by the Secretary of the Interior or the Secretary of Agriculture: *Provided,* That no timber shall be cut by the grantee in the Yosemite National Park except from land to be submerged or which constitutes an actual obstruction to the right or rights of way or to any road or trail provided in this Act: *Provided further,* That for and in consideration of the rights and privileges hereby granted to it the said grantee shall construct and maintain in good repair such bridges or other practicable crossings over its rights of way within the Stanislaus National Forest as may be prescribed in writing by the Secretary of Agriculture, and elsewhere on public lands along the line of said works, and within the Yosemite National Park as may be prescribed in writing by the Secretary of the Interior; and said grantee shall, as said waterworks are completed, if directed in writing by the Secretary of the Interior or the Secretary of Agriculture, construct and maintain along each side of said right of way a lawful fence of such character as may be prescribed by the proper Secretary, with such suitable lanes or crossing as the aforesaid officers shall prescribe: *And provided further,* That the said grantee shall clear its rights of way within the Yosemite National Park and the Stanislaus National Forest and over any public land of any debris or inflammable material as directed by the Secretary of the Interior and the Secretary of Agriculture, respectively; and said grantee shall permit any road or trail which it may construct over the public lands, the Yosemite National Park, or the Stanislaus National Forest to be freely used by the officials of the Government and by the public, and shall permit officials of the Government, for official business only, the free use of any telephone or telegraph lines, or equipment, or railroads that it may construct and maintain within the Yosemite National Park and the Stanislaus National Forest, or on the public lands, together with the right to connect with any such telephone or telegraph lines private telephone wires for the exclusive use of said Government officials: *And provided further,* That all reservoirs, dams, conduits, power plants, water power and electric work, bridges, fences, and other structures not of a temporary character shall be sightly and of suitable exterior design and finish so as to harmonize with the surrounding landscape and its use as a park; and for this purpose all plans and designs shall be submitted for approval to the Secretary of the Interior.

Sec. 5. That all lands over which the rights of way mentioned in this Act shall pass shall be disposed of only subject to such easements: *Provided, however,* That the construction of the aforesaid works shall be prosecuted diligently, and no cessation of such construction shall continue for a period of three consecutive years, and in the event that the Secretary of the Interior shall find and determine that there has not been diligent prosecution of the work or of some integral and essential part thereof, or that there has been a cessation of such construction for a period of three consecutive years, then he may declare forfeited all rights of the grantee herein as to that part of the works not constructed, and request the Attorney General, on behalf of the United States, to commence suit in the United States District Court for the Northern District of California for the purpose of procuring a judgment declaring all such rights to that part of the works not constructed to be forfeited to the United States, and upon such request it shall be the duty of the said Attorney General to cause to be commenced and prosecuted to a final judgment such suit: *Provided further,* That the Secretary of the Interior shall make no such finding and take no such action if he shall find that the construction or progress of the works has been delayed or prevented by the act of God or the public enemy, or by engineering or other difficulties that could not have been reasonably foreseen and overcome, or by other special or peculiar difficulties beyond the control of the said grantee: *Provided further,*

That, in the exercise of the rights granted by this Act, the grantee shall at all times comply with the regulations herein authorized, and in the event of any material departure therefrom the Secretary of the Interior or the Secretary of Agriculture, respectively, may take such action as may be necessary in the courts or otherwise to enforce such regulations.

SEC. 6. That the grantee is prohibited from ever selling or letting to any corporation or individual, except a municipality or a municipal water district or irrigation district, the right to sell or sublet the water or the electric energy sold or given to it or him by the said grantee: *Provided,* That the rights hereby granted shall not be sold, assigned, or transferred to any private person, corporation, or association, and in case of any attempt to so sell, assign, transfer, or convey, this grant shall revert to the Government of the United States.

SEC. 7. That for and in consideration of the grant by the United States as provided for in this Act the said grantee shall assign, free of cost to the United States, all roads and trails built under the provisions hereof; and further, after the expiration of five years from the passage of this Act the grantee shall pay to the United States the sum of $15,000 annually for a period of ten years, beginning with the expiration of the five-year period before mentioned, and for the next ten years following $20,000 annually, and for the remainder of the term of the grant shall, unless in the discretion of Congress the annual charge should be increased or diminished, pay the sum of $30,000 annually, said sums to be paid on the first day of July of each year. Until otherwise provided by Congress, said sums shall be kept in a separate fund by the United States, to be applied to the building and maintenance of roads and trails and other improvements in the Yosemite National Park and other national parks in the State of California. The Secretary of the Interior shall designate the uses to be made of sums paid under the provisions of this section under the conditions specified herein.

SEC. 8. That the word "grantee" as used herein shall be understood as meaning the city and county of San Francisco and such other municipalities or water district or water districts as may, with the consent of the city and county of San Francisco or in accordance with the laws of the State of California, hereafter participate in or succeed to the beneficial rights and privileges granted by this Act.

SEC. 9. That this grant is made to the said grantee subject to the observance on the part of the grantee of all the conditions hereinbefore and hereinafter enumerated:

(a) That upon the completion of the Hetch Hetchy Dam or the Lake Eleanor Dam, in the Yosemite National Park, by the grantee, as herein specified, and upon the commencement of the use of any reservoirs thereby created by said grantee as a source of water supply for said grantee, the following sanitary regulations shall be made effective within the watershed above and around said reservoir sites so used by said grantee:

First. No human excrement, garbage, or other refuse shall be placed in the waters of any reservoir or stream or within three hundred feet thereof.

Second. All sewage from permanent camps and hotels within the watershed shall be filtered by natural percolation through porous earth or otherwise adequately purified or destroyed.

Third. No person shall bathe, wash clothes or cooking utensils, or water stock in, or in any way pollute, the water within the limits of the Hetch Hetchy Reservoir or any reservoir constructed by the said grantee under the provisions of this grant, or in the streams leading thereto, within one mile of said reservoir; or, with reference to the Hetch Hetchy Reservoir, in the waters from the reservoir or waters entering the river between it and the "Early intake" of the aqueduct, pending the completion of the aqueduct between "Early intake" and the Hetch Hetchy Dam site.

Fourth. The cost of the inspection necessary to secure compliance with the sanitary regulations made a part of these conditions, which inspection shall be under the direction of the Secretary of the Interior, shall be defrayed by the said grantee.

Fifth. If at any time the sanitary regulations provided for herein shall be deemed by said grantee insufficient to protect the purity of the water supply, then the said grantee shall install a filtration plant or provide other means to guard the purity of the water. No other sanitary rules or restrictions shall be demanded by or granted to the said grantee as to the use of the watershed by campers, tourists, or the occupants of hotels and cottages.

(b) That the said grantee shall recognize the prior rights of the Modesto Irrigation District and the Turlock Irrigation District as now constituted under the laws of the State of California, or as said districts may be hereafter enlarged to contain in the aggregate not to exceed three hundred thousand acres of land, to receive two thousand three hundred and fifty second-feet of the natural daily flow of the Tuolumne River, measured at the La Grange Dam, whenever the same can be beneficially used by said irrigation districts, and that the grantee shall never interfere with said rights.

(c) That whenever said irrigation districts receive at the La Grange Dam less than two thousand three hundred and fifty second-feet of water, and when it is necessary for their beneficial use to receive more water the said grantee shall release free of charge, out of the natural daily flow of the streams which it has intercepted, so much water as may be necessary for the beneficial use of said irrigation districts not exceeding an amount which, with the waters of the Tuolumne and its tributaries, will cause a flow at La Grange Dam of two thousand three hundred and fifty second-feet; and shall also recognize the rights of the said irrigation districts to the extent of four thousand second-feet of water out of the natural daily flow of the Tuolumne River for combined direct use and collection into storage reservoirs as may be provided by said irrigation districts, during the period of sixty days immediately following and including April fifteenth of each year, and shall during such period release free of charge such quantity of water as may be necessary to secure to the said irrigation districts such four thousand second-feet flow or portion thereof as the said irrigation districts are capable of beneficially directly using and storing below Jawbone Creek: *Provided, however,* That at such times as the aggregate daily natural flow of the watershed of the Tuolumne and its tributaries measured at the La Grange Dam shall be less than said districts can beneficially use and less than two thousand three hundred and fifty second-feet, then and in that event the said grantee shall release, free of charge, the entire natural daily flow of the streams which it has under this grant intercepted.

(d) That the said grantee whenever the said irrigation districts desire water in excess of that to which they are entitled under the foregoing, shall on the written demand of the said irrigation districts sell to the said irrigation districts from the reservoir or reservoirs of the said grantee such amounts of stored water as may be needed for the beneficial use of the said irrigation districts at such a price as will return to the grantee the actual total costs of providing such stored water, such costs to be computed in accordance with the currently accepted practice of public cost accounting as may be determined by the Secretary of the Interior, including, however, a fair proportion of the cost to said grantee of the conduit, lands, dams, and water-supply system included in the Hetch Hetchy and Lake Eleanor sites; upon the express condition, however, that the said grantee may require the said irrigation districts to purchase and pay for a minimum quantity of such stored water, and that the said grantee shall be entitled to receive compensation for a minimum quantity of stored water and shall not be required to sell and deliver to the said irrigation districts more than a maximum quantity of such stored water to be released during any calendar year: *Provided, however,* That if the said irrigation districts shall develop sufficient water to meet their own needs for beneficial use and shall so notify in writing the Secretary of the Interior, the said grantee shall not be required to sell or deliver to said irrigation districts the maximum or minimum amount of stored waters hereinbefore provided for, and shall release the said districts from the obligation to pay for such stored water: *And provided further,* That said grantee shall without cost to said irrigation districts return to the Tuolumne River above the La Grange Dam for the use of the said irrigation districts all surplus or waste water resulting from the development of hydroelectric energy generated by the said grantee.

(e) That such minimum and maximum amounts of such stored water to be so released during any calendar year as hereinbefore provided and the price to be paid therefor by the said irrigation districts are to be determined and fixed by the Secretary of the Interior in accordance with the provisions of the preceding paragraph.

(f) That the Secretary of the Interior shall revise the maximum and minimum amounts of stored water to be supplied to said irrigation districts by said grantee as hereinbefore provided, whenever the said irrigation districts have properly developed the facilities of the Davis Reservoir of the Turlock Irrigation District and the Warner-Dallas Reservoir of the Modesto Irrigation District to the fullest practicable extent up to a development not exceeding in cost $15 per acre-foot storage capacity, and whenever additional storage has been provided by the said irrigation districts which is necessary to the economical utilization of the waters of said watershed, and also after water losses and wastes have been reduced to such reasonable minimum as will assure the economical and beneficial use of such water.

(g) That the said grantee shall not be required to furnish more than the said minimum quantity of stored water hereinbefore provided for until the said irrigation districts shall have first drawn upon their own stored water to the fullest practicable extent.

(h) That the said grantee shall not divert beyond the limits of the San Joaquin Valley any more of the waters from the Tuolumne watershed than, together with the waters which it now has or may hereafter acquire, shall be necessary for its beneficial use for domestic and other municipal purposes.

(i) That the said grantee shall, at its own expense, locate and construct, under the direction of the Secretary of the Interior, such weirs or other suitable structures on sites to be granted, if necessary, by the United States, for accurately measuring the flow in the said river at or above La Grange Dam, and measuring the flow into and out from the reservoirs or intakes of said districts, and into and out from any reservoirs constructed by the said grantee, and at any other point on the Tuolumne River or its tributaries, which he may designate, and fit the same with water-measuring apparatus satisfactory to said Secretary and keep such hydrographic records as he may direct, such apparatus and records to be open to inspection by any interested party at any time.

(j) That by "the flow," "natural daily flow," "aggregate daily natural flow," and "what is naturally flowing," as are used herein, is meant such flow as on any given day would flow in the Tuolumne River or its tributaries if said grantee had no storage or diversion works on the said Tuolumne watershed.

(k) That when the said grantee begins the development of the Hetch Hetchy Reservoir site, it shall undertake and vigorously prosecute to completion a dam at least two hundred feet high, with a foundation capable of supporting said dam when built to its greatest economic and safe height.

(l) That the said grantee shall, upon request, sell or supply to said irrigation districts, and also to the municipalities within either or both said irrigation districts, for the use of any land owner or owners therein for pumping subsurface water for drainage or irrigation, or for the actual municipal public purposes of said municipalities (which purposes shall not include sale to private persons or corporations) any excess of electrical energy which may be generated, and

[173]

which may be so beneficially used by said irrigation districts or municipalities, when any such excess of electric energy may not be required for pumping the water supply for said grantee and for the actual municipal public purposes of the said grantee (which purposes shall not include sale to private persons or corporations) at such price as will actually reimburse the said grantee for developing and maintaining and transmitting the surplus electrical energy thus sold; and no power plant shall be interposed on the line of the conduit except by the said grantee, or the lessee, as hereinafter provided, and for the purposes and within the limitations in the conditions set forth herein: *Provided,* That said grantee shall satisfy the needs of the landowners in said irrigation districts for pumping subsurface water for drainage or irrigation, and the needs of the municipalities within such irrigation districts for actual municipal public purposes, after which it may dispose of any excess electrical energy for commercial purposes.

(m) That the right of said grantee in the Tuolumne water supply to develop electric power for either municipal or commercial use is to be made conditional for twenty years following the completion of any portion of the works adapted to the generation of electrical energy, as follows: The said grantee shall within three years from the date of completion of said portion of the works install, operate, and maintain apparatus capable of developing and transmitting not less than ten thousand horsepower of electric power for municipal and commercial use, said ten thousand horsepower to be actually used or offered for use; and within ten years from the completion of said portion of the works not less than twenty thousand horsepower; and within fifteen years therefrom not less than thirty thousand horsepower; and within twenty years therefrom not less than sixty thousand horsepower, unless in the judgment of the Secretary of the Interior the public interest will be satisfied with a lesser development. The said grantee shall develop and use hydroelectric power for the use of its people and shall, at prices to be fixed under the laws of California or, in the absence of such laws, at prices approved by the Secretary of the Interior, sell or supply such power for irrigation, pumping, or other beneficial use, said prices not to be less than will return to said grantee the actual total costs of providing and supplying said power, which costs shall be computed in accordance with the currently accepted practice of public cost accounting, as shall be determined by the Secretary of the Interior, including, however, a fair proportion of cost of conduit, lands, dams, and water-supply system; and further, said grantee shall, before using any of said water for the purpose of developing hydroelectric power, file such maps, surveys, field notes, or other data as may be required by law, and shall conform to any law existing and applicable to said subject of development of said hydroelectric power for municipal or commercial uses.

(n) That after the period of twenty years hereinbefore provided for the development, transmission, use, and sale of electric power, the Secretary of the Interior, under authorization hereby given, may require the grantee, within a time fixed by the Secretary, to develop, transmit, and use, or offer for sale, such additional power, and also such power less than sixty thousand horsepower as the grantee may have failed to develop, transmit, use, or sell, within the twenty years aforesaid, as in the judgment of said Secretary the grantee may or ought to develop under this grant, and which in his judgment the public interest demands or convenience requires; and in case of the failure of the grantee to carry out any such requirements of the Secretary of the Interior the latter is hereby authorized so to do, and he may, in such manner and form and upon such terms and conditions as he may determine, provide for the development, transmission, use, and sale of such additional power and such power not so developed, transmitted, or used by the grantee at the end of said twenty years up to sixty thousand horsepower; and for that purpose the Secretary of the Interior may take possession of and lease to such person or persons as he may designate such portion of the rights of way, structures, dams, conduits, and other property acquired or constructed by the grantee hereunder as may be necessary for the development, transmission, use, and sale of such power.

(o) That the rates or charges to be made by the grantee or by any lessee under the last preceding paragraph for the use of power for commercial purposes shall at all times conform to the laws of the State of California or, in the absence of any such statutory law, be subject to the approval of the Secretary of the Interior, and in the absence of such law no rates or charges shall be made, fixed, or collected without such approval, and the grantee shall at any time, upon the demand of the Secretary of the Interior allow the latter or such person or persons as he may designate full and free access, right, and opportunity to examine and inspect all of the grantee's books, records, and accounts, and all the works constructed and property occupied hereunder by the grantee.

(p) That this grant is upon the further condition that the grantee shall construct on the north side of the Hetch Hetchy Reservoir site a scenic road or trail, as the Secretary of the Interior, may determine, above and along the proposed lake to such point as may be designated by the said Secretary, and also leading from said scenic road or trail a trail to the Tiltill Valley and to Lake Vernon, and a road or trail to Lake Eleanor and Cherry Valley via McGill Meadow; and likewise the said grantee shall build a wagon road from Hamilton or Smiths Station along the most feasible route adjacent to its proposed aqueduct from Groveland to Portulaca or Hog Ranch and into the Hetch Hetchy Dam site, and a road along the southerly slope of Smiths Peak from Hog Ranch past Harden Lake to a junction with the old Tioga Road, in section four, township one south, range twenty-one east, Mount Diablo base and meridian, and such roads and trails made necessary by this grant, and as may be prescribed by the Secretary of the Interior. Said grantee shall have the right to build and maintain such other necessary roads or trails through the public lands, for the construction and operation of its works, subject, however, to the approval of the Secretary of Agriculture in the Stanislaus National Forest, and the Secretary of the Interior in the Yosemite National Park. The said grantee shall further lay and maintain a water pipe, or otherwise provide a good and sufficient supply of water for camp purposes at the Meadow, one-third of a mile, more or less, southeasterly from the Hetch Hetchy Dam site.

That all trail and road building and maintenance by the said grantee in the Yosemite National Park and the Stanislaus National Forest shall be done subject to the direction and approval of the Secretary of the Interior or the Secretary of Agriculture according to their respective jurisdictions.

(q) That the said grantee shall furnish water at cost to any authorized occupant within one mile of the reservoir and in addition to the sums provided for in section seven it shall reimburse the United States Government for the actual cost of maintenance of the above roads and trails in a condition of repair as good as when constructed.

(r) That in case the Department of the Interior is called upon, by reason of any of the above conditions, to make investigations and decisions respecting the rights, benefits, or obligations specified in this Act, which investigations or decisions involve expense to the said Department of the Interior, then such expense shall be borne by said grantee.

(s) That the grantee shall file with the Secretary of the Interior, within six months after the approval of this Act, its acceptance of the terms and conditions of this grant.

(t) That the grantee herein shall convey to the United States, by proper conveyance, a good and sufficient title free from all liens and encumbrances of any nature whatever, to any and all tracts of land which are now owned by said grantee within the Yosemite National Park or that part of the national forest adjacent thereto not actually required for use under the provisions of this Act, said conveyance to be approved by and filed with the Secretary of the Interior within six months after the said grantee ceases to use such lands for the purpose of construction or repair under the provisions of this Act.

(u) That the city and county of San Francisco shall sell to the United States, for the use of the War Department, such water as the War Department may elect to take, and shall deliver the same through its system in or near the city of San Francisco to the mains or systems of such military reservations in that vicinity as may be designated by the Secretary of War, under such rules and regulations as he may prescribe. In payment for such water and the delivery thereof the United States shall pay to the said city and county of San Francisco a rental, to be calculated at a fixed rate per one thousand gallons, said rate not to exceed the actual cost of said water to said city and county for all the water so furnished, as determined by meter measurements: *And provided further,* That payment of said rental shall be made by the local disbursing officer of the War Department in the usual manner: *Provided, however,* That the grantee shall at all times

[176]

comply with and observe on its part all the conditions specified in this Act, and in the event that the same are not reasonably complied with and carried out by the grantee, upon written request of the Secretary of the Interior, it is made the duty of the Attorney General in the name of the United States to commence all necessary suits or proceedings in the proper court having jurisdiction thereof, for the purpose of enforcing and carrying out the provisions of this Act.

SEC. 10. That this grant, so far as it relates to the said irrigation districts, shall be deemed and held to constitute a binding obligation upon said grantee in favor of the said irrigation districts which said districts, or either of them, may judicially enforce in any court of competent jurisdiction.

SEC. 11. That this Act is a grant upon certain express conditions specifically set forth herein, and nothing herein contained shall be construed as affecting or intending to affect or in any way to interfere with the laws of the State of California relating to the control, appropriation, use, or distribution of water used in irrigation or for municipal or other uses, or any vested right acquired thereunder, and the Secretary of the Interior, in carrying out the provisions of this Act, shall proceed in conformity with the laws of said State.

Approved, December 19, 1913.

HORACE M. ALBRIGHT ON THE
EARLY NATIONAL PARKS*
1928

Horace M. Albright, second director of the National Park Service, described the lack of direction and control of the National Parks in the early years in the following passage.

It will be seen that in the early days national parks were created from time to time by Congress without any particular policy governing their establishment. Some of the parks were established as a part of local activites of the states. It was many years before the idea evolved that the greatest of these scenic wonders should be gathered together by the federal government under one management guided by a broad policy. There was no bureau in Washington to govern the parks according to a comprehensive plan and policy until 1916. Previous to that time the parks were looked after by the Secretary of the Interior as a part of the miscellaneous activities of his department. To keep order in the parks, the Secretary of the Interior called upon the War Department for troops, which were stationed in Yellowstone, Yosemite, and Sequoia parks each summer.

In the parks where the troops were on patrol, the acting superintendent was a military officer, usually changed each year. He reported to the Secretary of the Interior as well as to the War Department. In Yellowstone there was still further division of authority in that all improvements were under the army engineering corps and of course no engineer officer would be required to report to the superintendent, who was a cavalry officer. Consequently, there were times when the park roads were not available to the public because the engineers would not take instructions from the superintendent who was chiefly responsible for provisions for the traveling public. On the other hand, it is only fair to say that there were some remarkably able army officers in charge of the parks from time to time, men deeply interested in their work and eager to render every possible service to the public.

A superintendent who deserves special mention was Nathaniel P. Langford, who had charge of Yellowstone during the first five years after the creation of the park. Mr. Langford not only served without remuneration, but paid all his own expenses as well. He had no assistance and lacked adequate authority, and in his constant struggle to protect the park from depredations he had little to aid him except persuasion and discussion. Yet he was able to do much to protect the park in those early days and kept visitors from carrying away valuable exhibits.

In parks not placed under military control, the superintendents were often po-

*Horace M. Albright and Frank J. Taylor, *"Oh Ranger!"* (Stanford: Stanford University Press, 1928), 122–24.

litical appointees, chosen because of favors to their parties rather than because of particular qualification for their work. Fortunately, some of these men were very good executives. In some cases, they made miserable failures of their tasks of preserving the park wonders for the future. Appropriations were small, and with the exception of the Yellowstone, Crater Lake, and Mount Rainier National parks, where road systems were built by the army engineers, very little road building was done at all. There was little money for the maintenance and protection of the parks. In the early days, following Mr. Langford's administration and preceding the coming of the military, protectors of the Yellowstone received little compensation and their earnings came principally from dividing fines and fees with justices of the peace who were appointed for the territories in which the park lay. This system was particularly vicious because the visitors to the parks were harassed and fined for minor infractions of the rules or for no breach of conduct at all, in order that the justice of the peace and the arresting officer might increase their incomes.

The politicians who followed the public-spirited Langford and his successor, Colonel P. W. Norris, in Yellowstone, were so careless and inefficient in the performance of their duties that employment of troops was necessary to preserve the park from despoliation. Fort Yellowstone was built at Mammoth Hot Springs, not so much to combat redskins, as was commonly supposed, as to keep the "white Indians," the grafters, and exploiters out of the nation's playground.

When Yosemite and Sequoia parks were created in 1890, troops were assigned to them at once. These parks never had civilian administrations the year around until 1914, when troops were removed and National Park Service officials assumed their duties. In Yellowstone, the cavalry stayed until 1918; likewise the army engineers.

As a rule, it took from three to seven years after the creation of a national park before funds for its care and upkeep were provided, and up to 1910 there was little that a non-military park superintendent could do. In that year, following the formation of Glacier National Park, the American Civic Association, led by its vigorous and able president, Dr. J. Horace McFarland, who had carefully watched the growth of the national park idea for years, launched a campaign for the creation of a national park bureau. The Secretary of the Interior, Walter L. Fisher, and President Taft himself, urged Congress to set up a central bureau for the administration of the parks. The President sent a special message to Congress on the subject. Senator Reed Smoot of Utah and Congressman John E. Raker of California introduced identical bills in the Senate and the House creating such a bureau.

That was the situation when Franklin K. Lane became Secretary of the Interior in 1913 upon the inauguration of President Wilson. The parks were the orphans of the federal government. They were nobody's charge and anybody's worry.

THE COMMISSIONER OF THE GENERAL LAND OFFICE
ON A NATIONAL PARK SERVICE*
1901

As early as 1901 the Commissioner of the General Land Office urged general legislation concerning national parks.

I have in former reports to the Department stated that I am impressed with the need for legislation which shall authorize the President to set apart and reserve, as national parks, by public proclamation, tracts of public land, which, for their scenic beauty, natural wonders, ancient ruins and relics or other objects of scientific or historic interest, or springs of medicinal or other properties, it is desirable to protect and utilize in the interest of the general public.

Owing to the want of some such general provision of law, each case, as it arises now, has to be made a matter for special legislation, and, in consequence, becomes subject to frequent delays and postponements, extending in some cases over years, which is a serious matter, since the need for promptness of action is frequently emergent, as testified to by such organizations as the Smithsonian Institution, the National Geographic Society, etc.

Since Congress has empowered the President to set apart tracts of public land for forest-reservation purposes, affecting interests much more far-reaching and of far greater importance than those involved in cases of national parks, it appears altogether reasonable, and in a line with the policy already adopted, that the same power should be vested in the President in respect to reserving tracts of public land for national park purposes. This course, by materially expediting the work of reserving these tracts, would undoubtedly greatly further the interest of science.

*Annual Reports of the Department of the Interior for the Fiscal Year ended June 30, 1901 (Washington, D.C.: Government Printing Office, 1901), 154–55.

RICHARD A. BALLINGER ON A
NATIONAL PARK SERVICE*
1910

By 1910, Secretary of the Interior Richard A. Ballinger recommended that a bureau of national parks be established.

In order that creditable progress may be made in each of the national parks, after the development of all necessary plans for road and other construction for the convenience of travel and tourists, liberal appropriations will be required and a departmental organization for administrative purposes perfected, capable of efficient field administration and of careful inspection of all public works and the conduct of concessionaires. It will doubtless be necessary in the accomplishment of these purposes to create a bureau of national parks and resorts, under the supervision of a competent commissioner, with a suitable force of superintendents, supervising engineers, and landscape architects, inspectors, park guards, and other employees.

The creation of such a bureau and the planning under it of a consistent and broadly considered scheme for national parks and resorts to fit the future needs of the United States of America would be in line with the policy under which our first President planned, in 1803, the federal city which now bears his name, without which planning no such civic convenience, beauty, impressiveness, and national dignity as the city of Washington now enjoys would have been possible.

The volume and importance of the work of the supervision of the national parks and resorts under the Secretary of the Interior has passed beyond the stage of satisfactory control by operations carried on with the small force available in the Secretary's office.

Report of the Secretary of the Interior, 1910 (Washington, D.C.: Government Printing Office, 1911), 58.

PRESIDENT WILLIAM H. TAFT ON A NATIONAL PARK SERVICE
1911* & 1912†

In a speech before the American Civic Association in 1911 President Taft noted the lack of organization among the national parks.

Now we have in the United States a great many natural wonders, and in that lazy way we have in our government of first taking up one thing and then another, we have set aside a number of national parks, of forest reservations covering what ought to be national parks, and what are called "national monuments." We have said to ourselves, "Those cannot get away. We have surrounded them by a law which makes them necessarily government property forever, and we will wait in our own good time to make them useful as parks to the people. Since the Interior Department is the 'lumber room' of the government, into which we put everything that we don't know how to classify, and don't know what to do with, we will just put them under the Secretary of the Interior." That is the condition of the national parks today.

Taft followed up this statement in a special message to Congress on February 2, 1912.

I earnestly recommend the establishment of a Bureau of National Parks. Such legislation is essential to the proper management of those wonderful manifestations of nature, so startling and so beautiful that everyone recognizes the obligations of the government to preserve them for the edification and recreation of the people. The Yellowstone Park, the Yosemite, the Grand Canyon of the Colorado, the Glacier National Park, and the Mount Rainier National Park and others furnish appropriate instances. In only one case have we made anything like adequate preparation for the use of a park by the public. That case is the Yellowstone National Park. Every consideration of patriotism and the love of nature and of beauty and of art requires us to expend money enough to bring all these natural wonders within easy reach of our people. The first step in that direction is the establishment of a responsible bureau, which shall take upon itself the burden of supervising the parks and of making recommendations as to the best method of improving their accessibility and usefulness.

---

*President William H. Taft, quoted by Robert Shankland in *Steve Mather of the National Parks* (New York: Alfred A. Knopf, 1951), 52.
†*Cong. Rec.,* 62nd Cong., 2nd sess., 1661.

AN ACT TO ESTABLISH A NATIONAL PARK SERVICE*
August 25, 1916

President Taft and other influential Americans had recommended the establishment of a national park service or bureau for several years, but Congress took no immediate action. In 1913, however, Secretary of the Interior Franklin Lane placed the Assistant to the Secretary in charge of park administration. Then on June 5, 1914 a General Superintendent and Landscape Engineer was appointed for the national parks. A deficiency appropriation act of February 28, 1916 gave the Secretary authority to appoint a General Superintendent with such clerical or other assistants (not exceeding four persons) as were needed.

In the interim, hearings had been held by the Public Lands Committees in 1912, 1914, and 1916 and a small group of park enthusiasts had also been active. This group included Stephen Mather, Horace Albright, R. B. Marshall, Sterling Lord, Gilbert Grosvener, Frederick Law Olmsted, and J. Horace McFarland. Finally, a bill, introduced in the House of Representatives by Congressman Kent of California, passed the House, and under the auspices of Senator Reed Smoot of Utah, it cleared the Senate with minor amendments. President Wilson signed the bill on August 25, 1916. The pen Wilson used still hangs in the office of the Director of the National Park Service.

Be it enacted by the Senate and House of Representatives of the United States of America in Congress assembled. That there is hereby created in the Department of the Interior a service to be called the National Park Service, which shall be under the charge of a director, who shall be appointed by the Secretary and who shall receive a salary of $4,500 per annum. There shall also be appointed by the Secretary the following assistants and other employees at the salaries designated: One assistant director, at $2,500 per annum; one chief clerk, at $2,000 per annum; one draftsman, at $1,800 per annum; one messenger, at $600 per annum; and, in addition thereto, such other employees as the Secretary of the Interior shall deem necessary: *Provided,* That not more than $8,100 annually shall be expended for salaries of experts, assistants, and employees within the District of Columbia not herein specifically enumerated unless previously authorized by law. The service thus established shall promote and regulate the use of the Federal areas known as national parks, monuments, and reservations hereinafter specified by such means and measures as conform to the fundamental purpose of the said parks, monuments, and reservations, which purpose is to conserve the scenery and the natural and historic objects and the wild life therein and to provide for the enjoyment of the same in such manner and by such means as will leave them unimpaired for the enjoyment of future generations.

*39 *Statutes at Large,* 535.

SEC. 2. That the director shall, under the direction of the Secretary of the Interior, have the supervision, management, and control of the several national parks and national monuments which are now under the jurisdiction of the Department of the Interior, and of the Hot Springs Reservation in the State of Arkansas, and of such other national parks and reservations of like character as may be hereafter created by Congress: *Provided,* That in the supervision, management, and control of national monuments contiguous to national forests the Secretary of Agriculture may cooperate with said National Park Service to such extent as may be requested by the Secretary of the Interior.

SEC. 3. That the Secretary of the Interior shall make and publish such rules and regulations as he may deem necessary or proper for the use and management of the parks, monuments, and reservations under the jurisdiction of the National Park Service, and any violations of any of the rules and regulations authorized by this Act shall be punished as provided for in section fifty of the Act entitled "An Act to codify and amend the penal laws of the United States," approved March fourth, nineteen hundred and nine, as amended by section six of the Act of June twenty-fifth, nineteen hundred and ten (Thirty-sixth United States Statutes at Large, page eight hundred and fifty-seven). He may also, upon terms and conditions to be fixed by him, sell or dispose of timber in those cases where in his judgment the cutting of such timber is required in order to control the attacks of insects or diseases or otherwise conserve the scenery or the natural or historic objects in any such park, monument, or reservation. He may also provide in his discretion for the destruction of such animals and of such plant life as may be detrimental to the use of any of said parks, monuments, or reservations. He may also grant privileges, leases, and permits for the use of land for the accommodation of visitors in the various parks, monuments, or other reservations herein provided for, but for periods not exceeding twenty years; and no natural curiosities, wonders, or objects of interest shall be leased, rented, or granted to anyone on such terms as to interfere with free access to them by the public: *Provided, however,* That the Secretary of the Interior may, under such rules and regulations and on such terms as he may prescribe, grant the privilege to graze live stock within any national park, monument, or reservation herein referred to when in his judgment such use is not detrimental to the primary purpose for which such park, monument, or reservation was created, except that this provision shall not apply to the Yellowstone National Park.

SEC. 4. That nothing in this Act contained shall affect or modify the provisions of the Act approved February fifteenth, nineteen hundred and one, entitled "An Act relating to rights of way through certain parks, reservations, and other public lands."

Approved, August 25, 1916.

LETTER FROM FRANKLIN LANE TO STEVEN MATHER*
May 13, 1918

Mather had been Assistant to the Secretary of the Interior, in charge of parks, when the National Park Service Act was passed. He then became its first director and remained in that office until 1928. More than anyone else, Mather is responsible for formulating the basic policies which have guided the operation of the national parks. He was truly the father of the national park system.

The policy guidelines for the new National Park Service were set forth in a letter from Secretary of the Interior Franklin K. Lane to Director Mather, but it seems likely that this letter was actually prepared by Mather for the Secretary's signature.

Department of the Interior,
Washington, May 13, 1918.

Mr. Stephen T. Mather,
Director National Park Service.

Dear Mr. Mather:

The National Park Service has been established as a bureau of this department just one year. During this period our efforts have been chiefly directed toward the building of an effecitve organization while engaged in the performance of duties relating to the administration, protection, and improvement of the national parks and monuments, as required by law. This constructive work is now completed. The new Service is fully organized; its personnel has been carefully chosen; it has been conveniently and comfortably situated in the new Interior Department Building; and it has been splendidly equipped for the quick and effective transaction of its business.

For the information of the public an outline of the administrative policy to which the new Service will adhere may now be announced. This policy is based on three broad principles: "First, that the national parks must be maintained in absolutely unimpaired form for the use of future generations as well as those of our own time; second, that they are set apart for the use, observation, health, and pleasure of the people; and third, that the national interest must dictate all decisions affecting public or private enterprise in the parks."

Every activity of the Service is subordinate to the duties imposed upon it to faithfully preserve the parks for posterity in essentially their natural state. The commercial use of these reservations, except as specially authorized by law, or such as may be incidental to the accommodation and entertainment of visitors, will not be permitted under any circumstances.

Report of the Secretary of the Interior, 1918 (Washington, D.C.: Government Printing Office, 1918), 110–13.

In all of the national parks except Yellowstone you may permit the grazing of cattle in isolated regions not frequented by visitors, and where no injury to the natural features of the parks may result from such use. The grazing of sheep, however, must not be permitted in any national park.

In leasing lands for the operation of hotels, camps, transportation facilities, or other public service under strict Government control, concessioners should be confined to tracts no larger than absolutely necessary for the purposes of their business enterprises.

You should not permit the leasing of park lands for summer homes. It is conceivable, and even exceedingly probable, that within a few years under a policy of permitting the establishment of summer homes in national parks, these reservations might become so generally settled as to exclude the public from convenient access to their streams, lakes, and other natural features, and thus destroy the very basis upon which this national playground system is being constructed.

You should not permit the cutting of trees except where timber is needed in the construction of buildings or other improvements within the park and can be removed without injury to the forests or disfigurement of the landscape, where the thinning of forests or cutting of vistas will improve the scenic features of the parks, or where their destruction is necessary to eliminate insect infestations or diseases common to forests and shrubs.

In the construction of roads, trails, buildings, and other improvements, particular attention must be devoted always to the harmonizing of these improvements with the landscape. This is a most important item in our program of development and requires the employment of trained engineers who either possess a knowledge of landscape architecture or have a proper appreciation of the esthetic value of park lands. All improvements will be carried out in accordance with a preconceived plan developed with special reference to the preservation of the landscape, and comprehensive plans for future development of the national parks on an adequate scale will be prepared as funds are available for this purpose.

Wherever the Federal Government has exclusive jurisdiction over national parks it is clear that more effective measures for the protection of the parks can be taken. The Federal Government has exclusive jurisdiction over the national parks in the States of Arkansas, Oklahoma, Wyoming, Montana, Washington, and Oregon, and also in the Territories of Hawaii and Alaska. We should urge the cession of exclusive jurisdiction over the parks in the other States, and particularly in California and Colorado.

There are many private holdings in the national parks, and many of these seriously hamper the administration of these reservations. All of them should be eliminated as far as it is practicable to accomplish this purpose in the course of time, either through congressional appropriation or by acceptance of donations of these lands. Isolated tracts in important scenic areas should be given first consideration, of course, in the purchase of private property.

Every opportunity should be afforded the public, wherever possible, to enjoy the national parks in the manner that best satisfies the individual taste. Automobiles and motorcycles will be permitted in all of the national parks; in fact, the parks will be kept accessible by any means practicable.

All outdoor sports which may be maintained consistently with the observation of the safeguards thrown around the national parks by law will be heartily indorsed and aided wherever possible. Mountain climbing, horseback riding, walking, motoring, swimming, boating, and fishing will ever be the favorite sports. Winter sports will be developed in the parks that are accessible throughout the year. Hunting will not be permitted in any national park.

The educational, as well as the recreational, use of the national parks should be encouraged in every practicable way. University and high-school classes in science will find special facilities for their vacation-period studies. Museums containing specimens of wild flowers, shrubs, and trees, and mounted animals, birds, and fish native to the parks, and other exhibits of this character will be established as authorized.

Low-priced camps operated by concessioners should be maintained, as well as comfortable and even luxurious hotels wherever the volume of travel warrants the establishment of these classes of accommodations. In each reservation, as funds are available, a system of free camp sites will be cleared, and these grounds will be equipped with adequate water and sanitation facilities.

As concessions in the national parks represent in most instances a large investment, and as the obligation to render service satisfactory to the department at carefully regulated rates is imposed, these enterprises must be given a large measure of protection, and, generally speaking, competitive business should not be authorized where a concession is meeting our requirements, which, of course, will as nearly as possible coincide with the needs of the traveling public.

All concessions should yield revenue to the Federal Government, but the development of the revenues of the parks should not impose a burden upon the visitor.

Automobile fees in the parks should be reduced as the volume of motor travel increases.

For assistance in the solution of administrative problems in the parks relating both to their protection and use the scientific bureaus of the Government offer facilities of the highest worth and authority. In the protection of the public health, for instance, the destruction of insect pests in the forests, the care of wild animals, and the propagation and distribution of fish, you should utilize their hearty cooperation to the utmost.

You should utilize to the fullest extent the opportunity afforded by the Rail-

[187]

road Administration in appointing a committee of western railroads to inform the traveling public how to comfortably reach the national parks; you should diligently extend and use the splendid cooperation developed during the last three years among chambers of commerce, tourist bureaus, and automobile-highway associations for the purpose of spreading information about our national parks and facilitating their use and enjoyment; you should keep informed of park movements and park progress, municipal, county, and State, both at home and abroad, for the purpose of adapting, whenever practicable, the world's best thought to the needs of the national parks. You should encourage all movements looking to outdoor living. In particular, you should maintain close working relationship with the Dominion parks branch of the Canadian department of the interior and assist in the solution of park problems of an international character.

The department is often requested for reports on pending legislation proposing the establishment of new national parks or the addition of lands to existing parks. Complete data on such park projects should be obtained by the National Park Service and submitted to the department in tentative form of report to Congress.

In studying new park projects you should seek to find "scenery of supreme and distinctive quality or some natural feature so extraordinary or unique as to be of national interest and importance." You should seek "distinguished examples of typical forms of world architecture," such, for instance, as the Grand Canyon, as exemplifying the highest accomplishment of stream erosion, and the high, rugged portion of Mount Desert Island as exemplifying the oldest rock forms in America and the luxuriance of deciduous forests.

The national park system as now constituted should not be lowered in standard, dignity, and prestige by the inclusion of areas which express in less than the highest terms the particular class or kind of exhibit which they represent.

It is not necessary that a national park should have a large area. The element of size is of no importance as long as the park is susceptible of effective administration and control.

You should study existing national parks with the idea of improving them by the addition of adjacent areas which will complete their scenic purposes or facilitate administration. The addition of the Teton Mountains to the Yellowstone National Park, for instance, will supply Yellowstone's greatest need, which is an uplift of glacier-bearing peaks; and the addition to the Sequoia National Park of the Sierra summits and slopes to the north and east, as contemplated by pending legislation, will create a reservation unique in the world, because of its combination of gigantic trees, extraordinary canyons, and mountain masses.

In considering projects involving the establishment of new national parks or the extension of existing park areas by delimitation of national forests, you should observe what effect such delimitation would have on the administration of adjacent forest lands, and, wherever practicable, you should engage in an investigation of such park projects jointly with officers of the Forest Service, in order that questions of national park and national forest policy as they affect the lands involved may be thoroughly understood.

Cordially yours,

Franklin K. Lane

A SPEECH BY NEWTON B. DRURY ON
NATIONAL PARK POLICIES*
September 1948

Newton Drury, director of the National Park Service from 1940 to 1951, had been the executive-secretary for the Save-the-Redwoods League and an executive in the California State Park Commission. Since his two immediate predecessors, Arno B. Cammerer and Horace Albright, had worked in the Park Service since its inception, Drury was therefore the first director who was not a "Mather-man."

Drury's administration spanned World War II—with its attendant problems of shortages of appropriations and personnel for park purposes—and those years following the war which saw a sensational increase in park visits.

After eight years as director, Drury set forth the policies and functions of the Park Service in a speech to the Inter-American Conference on Conservation of Renewable Natural Resources in Denver in September 1948.

This Conference has rightly emphasized the land as the basis of man's material existence. But here and there through the discussions has run a thread of thought that, as a spokesman of the National Park Service of the Department of the Interior, I might be expected to pick up and emphasize.

Phrases like "nature protection," "recreation," "wilderness values," "the unity of nature," "sanctuaries for native animals and plants," imply the recognition, by those concerned with the good earth and the fullness thereof, of the fact that land is used to minister not only to man's physical well-being, but also to his mind and spirit—that man "does not live by bread alone"; that some lands, in the Americas and throughout the world, should be preserved for what they are, as well as for what they will produce; preserved with all their wealth of flora and fauna and geological formations, with all their beauty and wonder and significance, in the perfection that nature gave them, unchanged by man.

It is this thought that, with us, is the basis of the national park concept. In these meetings it has been evident that this concept is growing in other American republics. Our government has had a cordial cooperative relation with the Mexican government looking toward international parks to include lands across the border from Big Bend National Park in Texas and the proposed Coronado National Memorial in Arizona. Glacier-Waterton Lakes International Park on either side of the Canadian border has long been an accomplished fact. We are gratified that encouragement has been given here in this conference to further ratification of the Convention on Nature Protection and Wildlife in the Amer-

*National Parks Magazine, Vol. 23, No. 97 (Apr.-June, 1949), 28–34.

icas, and that hope has been expressed that we are ready for a similar World Convention.

On Sunday many of you will visit one of our greatest national park areas, the near-by Rocky Mountain National Park. You will see there one of the grandest landscapes of America and learn something of the policies and procedures under which we are trying to maintain its greatness, so that millions today and in the future may enjoy it.

It is our hope that you will visit others of our national parks—Grand Canyon, with its colorful strata that tell dramatically the story of time; Yosemite, with its sheer granite cliffs and the thunder and mist of its waterfalls; Carlsbad, with its gleaming caverns; Yellowstone, with its geysers and its abundance of wildlife— bison, elk and antelope and the rare trumpeter swan; Grand Teton, with its spectacular mountain range and the historic and geologically-significant Jackson Hole; Olympic, with its rain forests; Rainier, with its glaciers; Mesa Verde, with its ruined habitations of long-forgotten peoples; Sequoia, with its giant trees that were saplings before the birth of Christ.

There are many more that we would be proud to have you see.

These are lands so unique and precious that our nation has decreed that they should be preserved inviolate for public inspiration and enjoyment.

The Act of our Congress of August 24, 1916, establishing the National Park Service, specified the purpose of national parks. It is: ". . . to conserve the scenery and the natural and historic objects and the wild life therein and to provide for the enjoyment of the same in such manner and by such means as will leave then unimpaired for the enjoyment of future generations."

The national park system in the United States, built on this foundation, now includes 174 reservations with a total public land area of 20,775,082 acres. It was visited last year by 25,265,229 people. This year we expect 27,000,000 visitors. In addition to the national parks, monuments and historic sites, other kinds of reservations such as military parks, historical parks, memorial parks, parkways and battlefield sites—mere subspecies of national parks, to use a biological term—have been established. Their common denominator lies in the fact that they are all lands and objects considered to be of national significance, set apart to be conserved unimpaired for public enjoyment.

A further unifying element in the system is that body of policies, principles, and procedures, based on law, under which the areas are administered. Essential policies that govern our administration of this national trust include:

(1) Inviolate protection: No resources should be. consumed or features destroyed through lumbering, grazing, mining, hunting, water-control developments or other industrial uses.

This is a cardinal point, which park agencies and executives have learned must be adhered to as closely as possible. Nearly always there is arrayed against it the multiple-use philosophy of public resource management which holds that scenic and recreational resources may be used for numerous other purposes without sacrificing the scenic and recreational values; that selective logging will save timber from decay and waste and will leave a forest that will be "just as good" for park purposes; that grazing by livestock will reduce the fire hazard and make a more attractive park; that the damming of streams and lakes for irrigation and power will make them more useful for recreation, will do little real harm, and will bring great economic benefits. This is an attractive philosophy to the utilitarians, but it misses the point, so far as the purposes of national park areas are concerned. The simple fact is that the natural forest is more satisfying, more inspiring, than the cutover forest; the virgin mountain meadow with its clean streams, wild flowers and native wildlife is more pleasing and interesting than the cow pasture; the natural streams and lakes with their normal seasonal variations are more satisfying to people for recreation than the fluctuating reservoir with its unsightly shoreline of dead vegetation or the stream that has for all practical purposes been dried up by diversion structures.

If we are going to succeed in preserving the greatness of the national parks, they must be held inviolate. They represent the last stand of primitive America. If we are going to whittle away at them, we should recognize, at the very beginning, that all such whittlings are cumulative and that the end product will be mediocrity. Greatness will be gone.

(2) Planned development: Modifications for human use or for protective purposes should be kept to the minimum necessary to accomplish their object, should be designed to harmonize with their setting, and should be carefully planned and located so as to effect the minimum change in natural conditions. Our guiding motto is "Restraint."

To forestall hasty and ill-advised developments, as well as to arrive at the best possible plan, we have developed what we call a master plan for each park. The plan is not static; it is reexamined annually, reviewed by the administrators and their technical advisors, and is revised when desirable. The master plan shows all existing and proposed developments in a particular park, together with a concise statement of the objectives to be attained in the administration of the park. No development is permitted until it has been included in the approved master plan. This is intentionally a conservative instrument, devised to screen out unworthy projects and to retain in graphic form the plan as a whole for the development of each park.

(3) Public accommodations: Such accommodations essential to a reasonably full enjoyment of the parks should be provided, when near-by outside enterprises do not adequately meet public needs. The aim is to provide these at moderate rates, under regulation by the government. This is done through contracts with concessioners. Periodic review is made of contracts to determine that they are in the interest of the government, the parks and the public, and are fair to the concessioners.

We have tried to provide a fairly wide range of accommodations in the national parks, including campgrounds, trailer camps, housekeeping cabins, lodges, and de luxe hotels. The prices of meals, lodging and all other commodities and services provided by the concessioners are subject to approval by the Secretary of the Interior.

(4) Natural presentation of natural features: There should be no attempt to "gild the lily" or try to improve on nature's design. Forests should be allowed to evolve naturally. All wildlife should be displayed in a natural manner, interfering as little as possible with the normal habits of all animals, refraining from their artificial "management" (except for their protection, and then only as a last resort), avoiding the pauperizing or domestication of wild animals, and avoiding also the herding of these animals in "shows." Exotic flora and fauna should not be brought into the parks.

This policy is especially applicable to the preservation of great natural areas, such as national parks and some state parks. It is, of course, not applicable to the development of recreational facilities for local communities, where the promotion of sports, games and large numbers of participants are the ends sought. But in the great natural parks there is opportunity to preserve for all time outdoor museums, natural laboratories, in which the normal processes of nature may be observed and studied. As the surface of the earth is increasingly changed by man, these relatively small islands of nature become increasingly important as scientific check plots.

(5) Interpretive aids: Visitors should be afforded such guidance and exhibits as are desirable for the full appreciation of the parks, but in as simple and natural a manner as possible. These services should not be forced upon visitors, but should be made available for those who want them.

The national parks, both historic and natural, can be of great public educational value, but people, as a rule, do not go to them for the purpose of being educated. They go for such pleasurable experiences as getting in touch with the out-of-doors, the enjoyment of scenic beauty, the inspiration that comes from viewing great works of nature or sites of significant historic events. In a word, they go for recreation in the broad sense. Understanding increases enjoyment. We have found that park visitors generally appreciate such interpretive aids as museums, wayside exhibits, informal talks by naturalists or historians, illustrated lectures on park topics, guided field parties, pamphlets and books. The sense of time, for instance, of turning the pages of earth's history back through millions of years, which one gets at the Grand Canyon, when its geological story is unfolded at the observation station on the rim, immeasurably adds to the significance and enjoyment of the visit.

Our concept of land management—the national park concept—we realize can be applied to only a small fraction of our territory. The national park system is only 85/100ths of one percent of the area of the United States. We know that in

Latin America similar reserves have been set up, and that there are movements to establish more of them. We know that the pressures to consume the resources in these parks are growing year by year. They must be resisted. When 27,000,000 visit our national parks in one year, it is obvious that here are cultural institutions that must not be destroyed. We know that you are with us in the hope that, while we wrestle with the problem of man's subsistence from the land, we can continue, in proper proportion, to maintain for knowledge and for inspiration, these special areas where centuries of new forests will grow and evolve naturally; where plant and wildlife species remain in harmonious relationship to themselves and to their environment, and where nature and all of her works in their magnificent beauty can still be studied in their original design.

GEORGE B. HARTZOG ON
NATIONAL PARK POLICIES*
1964

George B. Hartzog who has directed the National Park Service since 1964, expressed his views on park policies in this statement to the House Subcommittee on National Parks.

Congress has assigned the National Park Service a vital mission in the total conservation effort. May I say, Mr. Chairman, and members of the committee, with pardonable pride, we think it is one of the most fulfilling, satisfying, and personally rewarding missions assigned to any Government bureau.

Primarily the National Park Service is a people-serving agency. In addition to that, it is also a resource-managing agency. Congress has given us the mission of managing resources for the continuing benefit of all of the people.

The scope of the national park system has been spelled out by the Congress in six landmark pieces of legislation, beginning with the act of 1872, establishing Yellowstone National Park—the first of its kind in the world—in which the Congress laid down a new public land policy; namely, that portions of the public lands were to be dedicated and set apart in perpetuity, not for material gain or riches, but rather for the benefit and enjoyment of the people as ". . . a public park or pleasuring ground . . ."

The second landmark piece of legislation is the 1906 act, the Antiquities Act. When, by an expanding population, the Indian and prehistoric ruins in the Southwest were in jeopardy, the Congress enacted the 1906 act to preserve a part of America's historic landmarks, historic and prehistoric structures, and other objects of historic or scientific interest situated on lands owned or controlled by the United States, and provided that the President, by proclamation, should set these aside as national monuments.

In addition to this, in 1916, the Congress transferred a number of parks into central administration as well as national monuments, and created the National Park Service. But it did more than this—by the act of 1916 the Congress gave form and substance to a specific type of land use and decreed a management philosophy for its administration; namely, that the Service shall promote and regulate the use of the national parks and monuments by such means and measures as conform to the fundamental purpose of the said parks and monuments, which purpose is to conserve the scenery and the natural and historic objects and the

*House Subcommittee on National Parks of the Committee on Interior and Insular Affairs, *Review of National Park Service Policies,* Serial No. 16, 88th Cong., 2nd sess. (Washington, D.C.: Government Printing Office, 1964), 23–30.

wildlife therein, and to provide for the enjoyment of the same in such manner and by such means as will leave them unimpaired for the enjoyment of future generations.

Further consolidation of the administration of the Nation's parks was accomplished pursuant to law in 1933 when numerous military parks, memorials, and national monuments were transferred from other governmental agencies to the Department of the Interior.

The Historic Sites Act of 1935 established a national policy of preserving historic sites and buildings. It also directed the Secretary to carry out wide-ranging programs in the field of history and placed with the Secretary responsibility for national leadership in the field of historic preservation.

Another important provision of the act, which has had strong influence upon the development of the national park system, was the establishment of the Advisory Board on National Parks, Historic Sites, Buildings, and Monuments.

The Park, Parkway, and Recreation Area Study Act of 1936, authorized the Secretary to cooperate with other Federal agencies, and with the States and their political subdivisions, in carrying out a comprehensive study of the public parks, parkway, and recreation area resources of the United States. A valuable result of this act has been to strengthen the capabilities of the State park systems.

With the establishment of the Bureau of Outdoor Recreation in the Department of the Interior last year, the nationwide recreation planning function was transferred to the new agency. The National Park Service, however, continues to make available its professional skills and experience in such activities as land use planning, design, and construction, and interpretation to Federal and State agencies, and we are working very closely with the new Bureau in furthering the mission assigned to it by the Congress.

The act of 1961 authorizing Cape Cod National Seashore marked a new concept in the development of the national park system; namely, the use of appropriated funds at the outset to purchase a natural area in its entirety for public enjoyment as a park. Prior to this enactment, areas, for the most part, were established either by setting aside portions of the public lands or from lands donated to the Federal Government initially by the States and private parties.

As will be observed, the national park system is not and has not been a static institution. It has continued to evolve for almost a century. With each new congressional enactment it has taken on a new vitality and meaning. Even so, our original mission remains unchanged; namely, to manage park resources for the continuing benefit and enjoyment of all the people.

I have been asked, specifically, by the committee to discuss the criteria used for the selection of national parks.

At the outset, I wish to say, Mr. Chairman, that the Congress is the ultimate judge of the criteria which shall be used for the establishment of national parks, since national parks are established only by the Congress.

Former Director Newton B. Drury referred to our national parks as the "crown jewels" of our country and, indeed, they are because in them the Congress has set aside outstanding examples of our Nation's scenic grandeur. They are in a class by themselves.

Secretary Udall's Advisory Board on Wildlife Management, sometimes referred to as the Leopold committee, has underscored the basic criterion in saying that the national parks should represent vignettes of primitive America.

In general, the criteria, though admittedly not absolute since factors of human judgment are involved, are these:

1. National parks are spacious land and water areas, so outstandingly superior in quality and beauty to average examples of their several types as to make imperative their preservation by the Federal Government for the enjoyment, education, and inspiration of all the people.

2. They should embrace a sufficiently comprehensive unit to permit public use and enjoyment and effective management of a continuing representation of its flora and fauna.

Subject to the policy laid down by the Congress for the management of each national park, it is the purpose of the Service to manage each park in such a manner as will give the visitors the most satisfying experience the park can provide without material impairment of the characteristics that merited its establishment.

Historical areas must meet similar criteria. For example, the historical personage or event must have had sufficient influence upon the course of national history as to warrant the preservation of the site by the Federal Government.

National recreation areas are selected on the basis of the criteria outlined in Policy Circular No. 1 of the Recreation Advisory Council. A copy of this circular either has or will be distributed to you. The primary criteria include: size, location, interstate significance, and recreational opportunities.

All new area proposals for additions to the national park system are submitted to the Secretary's Advisory Board on National Parks, Historic Sites, Buildings, and Monuments for evaluation. This Board, as mentioned earlier, was authorized by the Congress in 1935, and is composed of eminent citizens competent in the professional fields encompassed by the programs of the Service. The Board consists of 11 members, appointed by the Secretary for terms of 6 years each. A list of the present members of the Board has been provided the committee.

Ours is a civilization hurtling with breathtaking speed through a revolutionary period in our history—in large part a scientific revolution. Automation, shorter working hours, and other factors have greatly improved our standard of living. We stand at the threshold of a new era. An era in which leisure is rapidly moving from the fringe to the core of life.

Our population continues to grow. For the most part, this growing population is concentrated in our great metropolitan areas, and this trend is continuing.

All of these factors continue to place pressure upon us to provide healthful outdoor recreational opportunities for all the people. For example, visitation to the areas of the national park system amounted to more than 90 million in 1963. We predict that this visitation will double by 1980.

May I call the committee's particular attention to the fact that this broken dotted line was a projection of travel for Mission 66, and this solid black line is actually what has happened from 1956 to 1963, and you will note there is hardly any deviation.

To meet this mounting need, the administration now has pending before your committee, Mr. Chairman, a number of proposed additions to the national park system.

It will be noted that, for the most part, these additions are proposed to serve the needs of our rapidly emerging strip cities with their millions of urban citizens to whom outdoor recreation is becoming an increasingly precious element of their total environment.

It has been my privilege and pleasure during the past year to work with this committee. In this work, I have learned of your great and deep interest in meeting this challenge. Indeed, Mr. Chairman and members of the committee, we share the justifiable pride of all Americans in the way in which the Congress has responded to this great challenge. For example, in the past 5 years 16 new areas have been authorized by the Congress for addition to the national park system.

The answer to this mounting need for expanding outdoor recreational opportunities does not lie wholly, however, in our view, in an expanded system. Part of the answer lies in improved management.

For example, traditionally the Service has followed a policy of protection, allowing plant and animal life an opportunity to freely adapt to changing natural conditions. But the pressures and influences of a constantly increased visitation, coupled with an expanding urban society—in many instances in close proximity to the national parks—interfere with this freedom and make protection alone insufficient for proper management.

This problem was studied last year by the Secretary's Advisory Board on Wildlife Management and placed in clear focus in its brilliant report, a copy of which has been given to the committee. In brief, the Board recommended:

> That the biotic associations within each park be maintained, and where necessary recreated, as nearly as possible in the condition that prevailed when the areas were first visited by the white man. A national park should represent a vignette of primitive America.

The Academy of Sciences, in its report, has underscored the need for additional natural history research as a basis upon which to improve our overall management. These reports influenced our decision to coordinate all resources studies within the Service under the supervision of a single assistant director.

The Secretary's Advisory Board on Wildlife Management, independent researchers, conservationists, and many others have called attention to the factor of human use and the physical developments therefor, and the resultant impact of both upon the preservation of park values.

To approach the complex task of providing for increased park use and reducing its impact upon park resources on the broadest possible front, we need to undertake programs of comprehensive land planning with other agencies which will provide for the optimum man-land ratio and result in the highest and best use of the land.

In the atmosphere of mutual confidence and cooperation recently established by Secretary Udall and Secretary Freeman, we are pleased to tell you, Mr. Chairman, that we have recently begun a concerted effort toward such joint and improved land use planning with our sister Federal agency, the U.S. Forest Service. On March 5 of this year, we and the Forest Service will hold a joint meeting of our regional directors and regional foresters. It shall be our purpose to discuss areas where such joint planning possibilities exist.

We expect to undertake joint planning for public use with the Forest Service on two pilot areas this year; the southern portion of Mount Rainier and the adjacent national forest, and at Yellowstone National Park in cooperation with the national forests that surround it. We are hopeful that these pilot projects will lay a successful foundation upon which this effort may be extended in the future.

Additionally, at Glen Canyon and at Whiskeytown National Recreation Areas we are developing joint visitor center and interpretive facilities with the Bureau of Reclamation. These joint facilities will present a unified story covering development of our natural resources and of outdoor recreational opportunities.

This is another example of the type of cooperation that brings into sharp focus the total broad conservation program. And, it saves the taxpayer's money!

Over the past century the Congress has included within the national park system—national parks and monuments, historical parks and battlefields, national seashores and recreation areas.

They have been established in perpetuity to serve a common purpose; namely, to be used and enjoyed by the people. Yet each has individual significance and value.

The protection of these irreplaceable values, while serving the common purpose, requires that our management practices, rules, and regulations vary between the types and kinds of areas that make up this national park system. Thus, it is that we are now in the process of defining our management practices for each major category of areas within the system; the natural, the historical, and the recreational.

As Assistant Secretary Carver has pointed out in connection with his discussion of the land and water conservation fund bill, the preservation of America's scenic, scientific, and historic heritage, and the providing of healthful outdoor recreational opportunities for all of our people, cannot be done by the Federal Government alone.

To encourage other agencies, States, local governments, and private parties to recognize and preserve important sites representative of our Nation's historic heritage, the Service has undertaken a national survey of historic sites. Such sites are identified and, upon agreement of the owner, are marked with a national landmark plaque. The Federal Government, in this program, can officially recognize and encourage support for the preservation of these important historic sites, although it does not provide the funds necessary for their preservation.

The national parks and the national park idea have great significance not only for us but also for people all around the world. We can be rightfully proud, we believe, that this truly American philosophy is being embraced by more and more nations. We welcome the growing opportunity to share our management know-how with other nations in the development of their park and recreation programs.

As park people and as conservationists, our primary responsibility is the preservation of America's scenic, scientific, and historic heritage represented in the national park system.

We are pleased, however, with the obvious economic benefits which accrue from the establishment of parks and recreation areas at all levels of government—local, State, and Federal. We must admit that they do represent a mighty handsome benefit to many local communities and to the overall economy of the Nation.

For example, in a study of tourism in 1957 by the Department of Commerce it was concluded that the visit of a couple of dozen tourists per day throughout the year to a community was the equivalent of a $100,000 annual industrial payroll.

Beyond the material benefits received from tourism, however, are the priceless contributions these parks make to the inner strength of our Nation. The American people are now far removed from the old frontiers when everyone lived close to the earth on farms, ranches, and in small communities. In those days, there was unlimited space and the out of doors was always within easy reach. But today when most people have cut their roots and moved off the land, they find less and less opportunity to enjoy what once was taken for granted.

With a swiftly burgeoning population, an industrial and urban expansion without parallel, life has changed and areas that once provided recreational opportunity are gone.

Spiritually, our people need reminders of their past. Without them, they lose the sense of being part of the old America. This is a major need and it is our opportunity to meet it by providing the areas necessary and protecting them so that future generations may always gain strength and stability from them. Without these reminders of our great national heritage, we are without roots. Without roots we cannot understand the past, enjoy the present, or build for the future.

Mr. Chairman, this concludes our statement.

We shall be pleased to answer any questions you may have. Thank you very much.

Mr. MORRIS. Mr. Hartzog, thank you for a very comprehensive and informative statement.

"KEEP IT A WILDERNESS"*
August 26, 1938

Secretary of the Interior Harold L. Ickes set forth his views on national parks and the preservation versus use issue in this address at Seattle, Washington shortly after Olympic National Park was authorized.

I can say without the slightest hesitation that the Olympic National Park, when rounded out by proclamation under the power given to the President to add additional territory, will take its place with the greatest parks in our national system. It will be a worthy rival of your famous Mt. Rainier National Park. It will be inferior to none, and at the same time it will be different from all others.

A region of tumbled mountains, of far-spreading glaciers, of trees of unimaginable size—the wet forest tropics of North America—lies here on the Olympic peninsula, near the great city of Seattle, without acclaim, without recognition, almost unknown. Bring it into the national park system, place the signet of government recognition upon it, and it will speedily spring forward to its rightful place. Visitors will come to it from all over the world.

In view of this it is timely to reflect that fame has its drawbacks as well as its compensations. A national park, praised by everybody, thronged to by the great traveling public, needs the same protection from its too enthusiastic admirers that a man needs when fame descends upon him. Society offers little, if any, protection to the man seeking to escape from those who adulate today only to forget tomorrow. It is simpler and easier to protect a national park, provided the right kind of a start is made. In the case of a wilderness area like the Olympic National Park, the solution can be stated in four words. Keep it a wilderness.

When a national park is established, the insistent demand is to build roads everywhere, to build broad easy trails, to build air fields, to make it possible for everybody to go everywhere—*without effort.*

These last two words are what cause the trouble. It is characteristic of the American people that they want everything to be attainable *without effort.* Too many of us want a predigested breakfast food for our stomachs and a previewed national park for our eyes. Nine people out of ten, visiting our national parks, stay within half a mile of the motor roads and the hotels. Some of these people appreciate and love the parks, but are physically handicapped. For these we should show the greatest possible consideration. Others feel that they are roughing it if they twist their necks in a sightseeing bus, or expose their adenoids to the crisp air while gazing through field glasses at some distant scene. And these are the vast majority. Only a few days ago I was told of a man and his wife who

*Harold L. Ickes, "Keep It a Wilderness," *National Park Bulletin,* Vol. 14, No. 66 (Dec., 1938), 9–13, 29.

stopped at a park entrance, bought a sticker which they placed on their windshield and then proceeded happily and triumphantly on their way. They had "seen" another national park.

You know what happens when too many elk or deer are herded in a small space. They overbrowse it and destroy the foliage. Well, wherever we open a motor road in a national park, that part of the park tends to become overbrowsed by human beings. This is something we have to accept, and allow for, because the parks are for everybody, but we do not have to expose the entire park to overbrowsing by its human visitors.

I am in favor of opening a liberal and representative section of every national park to those who, because of physical limitations, are confined to motor roads. I am even willing to make this same concession to those who cling to motor roads as a matter of choice. But let us preserve a still larger representative area in its primitive condition, for all time, by excluding roads. *Limit the roads.* Make the trails safe but not too easy, and you will preserve the beauty of the parks for untold generations. Yield to the thoughtless demand for easy travel, and in time the few wilderness areas that are left to us will be nothing but the back yards of filling stations.

This is a fitting occasion to speak of the general policies of our Government in expanding and administering its national park system.

There have been two stages in the creation of national parks. During the first stage, national parks were established on lands already owned by the government on which there were striking natural phenomena—mountains, glaciers, waterfalls, lakes, geysers, hot springs, etc. Such lands were created into national parks without much opposition, provided the lands had no commercial value. The boundary lines were drawn so as to exclude all commercial timber, all mineral deposits, all lands suitable for grazing.

Sometimes these early national parks preserved only what could not well be destroyed, such as mountains and glaciers, but, even so, they served a great purpose in establishing the national park idea and in holding these areas in public ownership for the benefit of future generations.

In this second stage of creating a national park system, we have come to realize that even though a land area may have commercial value, it may have an even greater value for national park purposes. We have discovered that, in special instances, the commercial value of a given area may be enhanced by staying the woodman's ax. There are instances where the preserving of a notable forest, especially if the forest is only one feature of an outstanding scenic region, not only enhances the commercial value of the region but makes this value a continuing one.

An example of this is the Great Smoky Mountains National Park in the southern Appalachians, where, through the cordial and close cooperation of the states of North Carolina and Tennessee and the Government of the United States, the

[203]

greatest of our eastern national parks has been set up. This park was created to preserve for all time the last of the virgin hardwood forests of the East. Here forests, of great commercial value, were acquired by the states of North Carolina and Tennessee and presented as a gift to the nation. The United States Government has also made a considerable investment in this park, as have two or three interested citizens, notably John D. Rockefeller, Jr. The Great Smoky Mountains National Park was opposed by local lumber interests, but was overwhelmingly supported by the people who saw the virgin forests of the East disappearing before the saw and ax. Today this park has the favor of practically all of those who at first opposed its creation.

That is the universal history of national parks. Those who fight them become their ardent supporters and defenders after they are created.

This new Olympic National Park in the state of Washington has the characteristics of both of the two general types of national parks. It has the mountains and glaciers of the first type, and it has commercially valuable forests which place it in the second type. Because of its valuable forests, this park was established over the vigorous opposition of the lumber interests, which would have been quite willing to see a small park restricted to the treeless snowfields of the high mountains.

As I have traveled, mile after mile, around the Olympic peninsula, and seen mile after mile of gigantic stumps, the blackened logs of slash firings, and the scattered dead shags that tower skywards, gaunt specters of once noble trees, I have marveled that any man or woman in the state of Washington could oppose the proposal of Congress to place in trust for all the people for all time this outstanding area as a national park, thus preserving a fragment of this wonderful primeval forest from otherwise certain destruction. Yet it is natural that there should have been opposition.

Wherever a commercial interest conflicts, or even merely seems to conflict, with a non-commercial public purpose, you will find men fighting for commercialization regardless of every other consideration. Throughout the United States, the record of private timber exploitation has been one of ruthless destruction, not by bad citizens, but by men caught in a system they could not control; by men so engrossed in the struggle for survival and supremacy that they have not stopped to count the cost of wasting a national heritage.

All thoughtful men recognize that, when natural resources are wasted, there must be a reordering of economic life or disaster will ensue. In fact, many sections of our land have not escaped disaster more or less complete. An almost demoniac onslaught upon our forests, beginning at the Atlantic seaboard and spreading ever westward until this greatest stand of all along the Pacific Coast has been reached, has been followed by destructive forest fires, the inevitable result of which has been to burn out the soil while consuming the trees, to dry the source streams of our rivers and to make uninhabitable for our wild life a once teeming land. Following the woodman with his indiscriminate ax, his trail lighted by raging forest fires, there came in their turn destructive floods that have cost in the aggregate thousands of human lives, as well as an uncalculable property loss; water erosion of rich and irreplaceable top soil and its sinister twin, wind erosion.

The vicious circle has repeated itself in practically every part of the country where great forests once made gracious the land and held forth beckoning hands to those who, if they had been regardful, could have won riches for themselves without destroying the source of a wealth that was capable of reproducing itself. Fires, floods, droughts; fires, floods, droughts, resulting in wanton wastage and ruthless destruction; resulting in the disinheritance of thousands of American families of a heritage on which they could have supported themselves in comfort. By the cutting of the trees a forest was lost; by the cutting of a forest a land was lost—all for the lack of foresight and self-restraint on the part of our rugged individualists; all for a failure on the part of our Government to insist upon sound conservation policies before conservation assumed the characteristics of a rummage sale.

The prevention of further demolition of our timber resources with its resulting disorganization of our economic and social life, depends upon the new system of forest management which was forced upon the Federal Government some years ago. This government undertaking is in charge of the Department of Agriculture and with it I am in hearty accord. National park policies touch this question of forest management at various points, but chiefly in this particular. It is the function of the national parks to preserve specimens of the primeval forest, so that coming generations may see portions of this land as it was when the Pilgram Fathers landed at Plymouth, when Daniel Boone pushed westward across the Appalachians, and when Lewis and Clarke made their way through the towering conifers of the Pacific Coast.

We have created national parks, or added to them, to protect the giant sequoias and the sugar pines of California, and the hardwoods of the East. Now, in the state of Washington, we are protecting a fragment of the Pacific Coast rain forest with its magnificent Douglas fir, Sitka spruce, western hemlock and giant cedar.

On the Olympic peninsula cedar trees are standing that are forty-five feet in circumference, trees from which Indian women stripped inner bark for clothing a hundred years before Columbus discovered America. In this new park there will be Douglas fir forty feet in circumference and a thousand years old.

The reservation of this area is not exclusive of or inconsistent with the right of the lumber industry to a proper and legitimate exploitation of the lumber resources of this area. The manufacture of lumber is necessary to our prosperity and well being as a nation. There is room on this peninsula for forests for both the people and the saw mill. Assuming that the self-interest of the lumbermen is an intelligent one, we have a right to look forward to a willingness on their part to cooperate with the Government to the end that this wonderful section of our country may be put to the wisest and best use for all concerned.

Under any system of timber exploitation, whether that of profligate destruction by unregulated private operation or that of the sustained yield method of scientific forestry, all of these great trees were doomed before the establishment of this national park. It is the function of the national park to save a part of the primeval forest for us and our children and our children's children that we may gaze upon it in awe, and wonder at the majesty of Nature's handiwork.

One would think that it might be taken for granted that every Government agency having to do with the conservation of our natural resources, particularly as it relates to our forests, would gladly cooperate in any effort to preserve sections of our primeval forests for future generations. It is not to be denied that this can be done only through the setting up of national monuments and national parks. And yet, as you in the state of Washington know, this outstanding Olympic National Park was not opposed alone by those who cannot see a glorious tree for the board feet of lumber that it contains; a magnificent forest for its pulp wood. More bitterly even than by those whose interest lies in sawing a tree, not in saving it, this park was fought by local men in the Government service whose lives are supposed to be dedicated to the principle of the highest possible use of our forests. Yet to what higher possible use could this outstanding area on the Olympic peninsula have been dedicated than to that of a national park where our descendants, for all the generations to come, might be able to see with their own eyes some of the finest miracles of the master craftsman, Nature?

Nor has the National Park Service been immune to overt attack and sinister propaganda from similar groups when other outstanding areas little, if any, inferior to that, the acquisition of which we are here tonight to celebrate, have been proposed for national park purposes. The Department of the Interior for years has gladly cooperated with the Forest Service. Without demur we have handed over millions of acres of the public domain desired by that service. Only in rare instances, and then for insignificant tracts as to size when compared with the forest lands as a whole, have we, on behalf of the public, asked for the re-dedication of a negligible number of outstanding areas for creation into national parks. Both services are arms of the Federal Government that, in theory at least, are devoted to the same ideals respecting our natural resources. It is a pity that any branch of the Federal Government, for any reason, should oppose the acquisition by another of an area that cries aloud for any disinterested ear to hear for dedication as a national park in order that its beauties and its wonders may be preserved for all time as only they can be preserved without risk of future exploitation. Fortunately, as the Olympic National Park event proved, there is a statesmanship in the departments in Washington that will not brook local, petty jealousies on the part of subordinates.

The commercialism or selfishness that stands against such an undertaking by the people, through their government, is doomed to defeat. It met defeat in the Congress of the United States when this Olympic National Park was established, and the President was given power to determine its final boundaries. This commercialism and selfishness met a greater defeat, however, in the state of Washington itself, where a public opinion that would not be denied rose up behind Congressman Wallgren and your representatives in both branches of Congress who favored this enterprise, and demanded the creation of a real park. I want to say that the fine thing about Congressman Wallgren's attitude is that he stood for this park before, not after, public sentiment rallied to it so overwhelmingly. Congressman Wallgren was statesman enough to look ahead and courageous enough to lead when leadership was needed. Fortunately there were here in the state of Washington, as is evidenced by this fine occasion, forward-looking and enterprising citizens who wanted to be led and whom it was an inspiration to lead.

The greatest function of national parks is to preserve what civilization, lacking them, would destroy. The increasing destructiveness of civilization must be counter-balanced by a steady growth in our national park system. A part of this function of conservation through the park system, and this is increasingly important, is the preservation of wildlife. As most people know, hunting is forbidden in all national parks. Fishing is permitted and encouraged.

There are many sound reasons for the policy of our Government in closing all national park lands to hunting. First, the forces of civilized society are set so heavily against the survival of the larger mammals that they can be preserved only in large sanctuaries. For these the large national parks are ideal. In the second place, living wild animals form one of the chief attractions of our national parks. People from all over the United States go to Yellowstone to see bears and bison, as they will come to the Olympic National Park to see the Roosevelt elk. Wild animals and good fishing are powerful magnets to draw the public. In the third place, hunting in national parks would be dangerous to all park visitors. Yet even the hunter benefits from this policy of wildlife protection, for when a national park is maintained as a wildlife sanctuary, surplus game spreads into nearby regions, thus providing a constant supply for the sportsman. For the sound reasons enumerated, national parks are permanently closed to hunting.

Fishing is in a different category. Fishing brings enjoyment to millions, endangers nobody with stray bullets, and can be maintained indefinitely. The United States Government encourages fishing in the national parks. Whenever a state passes a law ceding complete jurisdiction over park lands to the United States, so that fishing licenses are not required, the Federal Government stands ready to assume the full cost of keeping the lakes and streams of such parks stocked with fish. One of the effects of this policy, of course, is to make the parks far more attractive to visitors from outside the state. This is one of the legitimate commercial advantages which a state may derive from the national park system.

It is entirely up to the state to decide whether it shall or shall not cede exclusive jurisdiction over park lands to the Federal Government. If complete jurisdiction is not ceded, control is concurrent. It thus requires the combined action of the state and Federal government to open a park to hunting or fishing, but either government can prevent it. Since the Federal Government at all times forbids hunting, the only practical questions are whether the state or the Federal Government shall pay for stocking the park waters with fish, and whether visitors may fish without a license. The real problem to decide, in this connection, is how attractive you want to make the park to the traveling public. The park that does not require a license pulls visitors from the parks, and consequently from the states, that do require licenses. To make a park most attractive to the public, we prefer to have jurisdiction ceded, but this is not vitally necessary. The Federal Government possesses ample power, even under concurrent jurisdiction, to protect game animals in national parks. But it is unwilling to spend Federal funds to maintain good fishing if the state insists on collecting license fees in the parks.

Let me point out, in this connection, that there is a broad community of interests between a national park and the region surrounding it. When as many as 600,000 people visit one national park in a year, how much money do you suppose they leave in the surrounding country? And this money spent by tourists is a steady source of income. It may even be an increasing source of income.

In the case of the Olympic National Park, practically the entire financial return will be to those who live in the surrounding communities. Since this is to be a wilderness park, the Department of the Interior will neither build nor approve the building of hotels on public lands.

It is our intention to build overnight trail shelters for hikers and horseback parties, but those who want all the comforts of home, including facilities for reading while taking a bath, will have to look for them in the communities that encircle this park, at the base of the mountains.

It is in the directions that I have indicated that we hope to expand and develop the national park system, in order to protect the beautiful and majestic works of Nature that should be held in perpetuity as a heritage of the people. No greater step toward this end has been taken in the twentieth century, no greater step could be taken, than, as the result of the work of Monrad C. Wallgren and Franklin D. Roosevelt in creating the Olympic National Park has been done. I ask cooperation of the state of Washington, as I pledge the sincere efforts of the Department of the Interior, in making this new park a notable addition to a great national park system.

"LET'S CLOSE THE NATIONAL PARKS"*
October 1953

During World War II the parks suffered from lack of appropriations and competent personnel, but immediately after the war park visitations soared upward at an unprecedented rate. Facilities which were hardly adequate in 1940 were overtaxed and prompted Bernard DeVoto to propose that the parks be closed.

The chief official of a national park is called the Superintendent. He is a dedicated man. He is also a patient, frustrated, and sorely harassed man. Sit in his office for an hour some morning and listen to what is said to him by the traveling public and by his administrative assistant, the Chief Ranger.

Some of his visitors are polite; some aren't; all have grievances. A middle-aged couple with a Cadillac make a formal protest: it is annoying that they must wait three-quarters of an hour to get a table at Lookout Point Lodge, but when it comes to queuing up in order to use the toilets at the Point—well, really! A woman in travel-stained denim is angry because Indian Creek Camp Ground is intolerably dusty. Clouds of dust hang over it, dust sifts into the sleeping bags at night, dust settles on the food and the children and the foliage, she has breathed dust throughout her two-weeks stay. Another woman reports that the toilet at Inspiration Cliff Camp Ground has been clogged since early last evening and that one of the tables there went to pieces at breakfast time. A man pounds the desk and shouts that he hit a chuck-hole on Rimrock Drive and broke a spring; the Drive, he says, is a car-killer and will soon be a man-killer. Another enraged tourist reports that a guardrail collapsed when his little girl leaned against it and that she nearly fell into the gorge. The representative of a nature society sums up his observations. He has hardly seen a ranger since he reached the park. (One reason is that most of the rangers are up in the high country fighting a forest fire.) Tourists have picked all the bear grass at Eyrie Overlook and the observer doubts if the species will come back there. Fifty-one names have been freshly carved in the vicinity of Cirque Falls, some of them actually on the famous Nine Centuries Tree itself. All but one of the camp grounds look like slums; in the observer's opinion, the reason why they look that way is that they are slums.

Such complaints must be distinguished from the irrational ones voiced to the Superintendent by tourists who are cantankerous, crackbrained, tired, or merely bewildered. They must be so distinguished because they are factual and true. (The Superintendent, not having a plumber, will send a ranger to clean out the toilet but replacing the guardrail will leave him too little money to buy lumber

*Bernard DeVoto, "Let's Close the National Parks," *Harper's Magazine,* Vol. 207, No. 1241 (Oct., 1953), 49–52. Copyright © 1953 by *Harper's Magazine,* Inc. Reprinted by permission of Mrs. Bernard DeVoto.

for a new table. He squeezed $1,200 from his budget to enlarge Indian Creek Camp Ground and so reduce the dust there but Brawling River undercut fifty feet of main road and the emergency repairs cost $1350.) He answers all complaints courteously, as a representative of the National Park Service and the United States Government, but he has no effective answer. He is withheld from saying what would count, "Build a fire under your Congressman." He cannot go on and explain that the Service is suffering from financial anemia, that it is the impoverished stepchild of Congress, and that the lack of money has now brought our national park system to the verge of crisis. He cannot say this and neither can his superiors in the Washington office, but it is true.

Between visitors the Chief Ranger has been developing this theme. He got together a crew yesterday and put them to work on the decaying bridge inside the north entrance; it can be shored up for the rest of this season but next year it will be beyond help and the north entrance will have to be closed. He also went over Beaver Creek Trail again yesterday and he is scared; unless some work can be done on it at once it must be closed as unsafe. Costs on last week's rescue job are now in. Fourteen men worked three shifts a day for two days to bring that climber with a broken hip down from Deception Peak. A doctor had to be summoned from eighty miles away and an ambulance from a hundred and seventy-five miles. The episode cost just over a thousand dollars, which will have to come out of the budget, and this means one summer ranger less next year. (In 1936 the park had two more summer rangers than it has this year—and only one-twelfth as many visitors.) Furthermore, Ranger Doakes, an expert alpinist, has demanded overtime pay for that rescue—sacrilege in the Service, but the Chief Ranger cannot blame him. The recent increase in rents hit Ranger Doakes hard. He got only a 137 per cent increase, which was less than some others, but it brought his rent to 23.5 per cent of his annual salary.

Let's leave the Chief Ranger's remaining woes unprinted and look at this latest device for reducing pay by compelling personnel to subsidize the National Park Service budget. The most valuable asset the Service has even had is the morale of its employes. I have said that the Superintendent is a dedicated man; all his permanent staff and all the temporary rangers and ranger-naturalists are dedicated men, too—they are all lovers and all fanatics or they would have quit long since. Ever since it was organized the Service has been able to do its difficult, complex, and highly expert job with great distinction because it could count on this ardor and devotion. The forty-hour week means nothing in a national park. Personnel have always worked sixteen hours a day and seven days a week whenever such labor was necessary. Superintendent, rangers, engineers, summer staff, fire lookouts—they all drop their specialties to join a garbage-disposal crew or a rescue party, to sweep up tourist litter, to clean a defouled spring, to do anything else that has to be done but can't be paid for. They are the most courteous and the most patient men in the United States and maybe once a week several of them get a full night's sleep. If you undermine their morale, you will destroy the Service. Well, the latest increase in rents has begun to undermine it.

By decree of the Bureau of the Budget the rents of government housing must be equalized with those of comparable housing in the same locality. In the end this amounts to some sleight of hand in the bookkeeping of the U.S. Treasury but it is probably sound in theory. Sound, that is, for a lot of government housing—but not for that which, to a varying degree, shields NPS employees from the weather. In the first place, the locality with which rents must be equalized is the nearest resort town outside the park, where rents are two or three times as high as in the nearest non-parasitical town. In the second place, there is practically no comparable housing. These are not the massive dwellings of a military installation, the imposing and luxurious ones that the Bureau of Reclamation erects, or the comfortable cabins of the Forest Service that were built by the CCC. Apart from a few such cabins by the CCC and a few new structures which the Service has been able to pay for from the pin-money that passes as its appropriation, they are either antiques or shacks. The best of them are usually inadequate—one-bedroom houses for couples with two or more small children, two-bedroom houses for couples with two or more adolescent children. Many of the rest of them belong in the Hoovervilles of 1931—CCC barracks built of tar-paper in 1934 and intended to last no more than five years, old warehouses and cook shacks built of slabs, curious structures hammered together from whatever salvaged lumber might be at hand. I have seen adobe huts in damp climates that were melting away from the rain, other quarters that were race-courses for rats, still others that would produce an egg shortage if you kept chickens in them.

Park Service employes are allowed an "isolation deduction" of from five to forty per cent, intended to compensate them for being forced to live at a galling and expensive distance from the services of civilization. Even so, the already high rents have been cruelly increased by the last directive from the Bureau of the Budget. On a list I have at hand of seventeen dwellings in Grand Teton National Park, the lowest increase (*after* the isolation deduction) is one hundred per cent, the highest two hundred per cent, the average one hundred and fifty-plus.

At this park there is an associated ingenuity. The park pays Teton County, Wyoming, $26,000 a year in lieu of taxes; it produces God knows how much for the state in gasoline and sales taxes; the business brought in by its visitors is all that keeps the town of Jackson solvent or even alive. But a hangover from the controversy over Jackson Hole National Monument, a controversy created for profit by local politicians and the gamblers and land-speculators allied with them, has enabled the town of Jackson to pressure the state administration. By decree of the state Attorney General, park personnel are not residents of Wyoming, though any itinerant Okie who paused there would be, and must therefore pay for the transportation and tuition of their children who attend public schools. They total $158 per pupil. It makes quite an item in the family finance of an underpaid public servant who has now had his rent increased, the rent of a leaky and rat-ridden crate which he cannot slect but must take as assigned — and in which he gets no equity though he pays a fifth of his salary or more.

This last summer I visited some fifteen NPS areas. It was a commonplace to meet a park employee who had had to bring a son or daughter back from college, as a result of the rent increase. It was even commoner to find one who had decided that the kids could not go to college when they finished high school. In many places, wives of park personnel are working for the private firms licensed to operate businesses in the parks, and this is a highly undesirable practice. The chief clerk of one of the most important parks works weekends in a grocery store in order to stay fed while retaining the job he loves. I could add to these specimens indefinitely but let it go with the end-product: the most valuable asset of the National Park Service is beginning to erode away.

So are the parks and national monuments themselves. The deterioration of roads and plants that began with the war years, when proper maintenance was impossible, has been accelerated by the enormous increase in visitors, by the shrinkage of staffs, and by miserly appropriations that have prevented both repair and expansion of facilities. The Service is like a favorite figure of American legendry, the widow who scrapes and patches and ekes out, who by desperate expedients succeeds in bringing up her children to be a credit to our culture. (The boys work the graveyard shift in the mills; the girls' underwear is made of flour sacking.) Its general efficiency, the astonishingly good condition of its areas, its success at improvising and patching up is just short of miraculous. But it stops there, short of the necessary miracle. Congress did not provide money to rehabilitate the parks at the end of the war, it has not provided money to meet the enormously increased demand. So much of the priceless heritage which the Service must safeguard for the United States is beginning to go to hell.

Like a number of other small areas in the system, the Black Canyon of the Gunnison has *no* NPS personnel assigned to it. On one rim of this spectacular gorge there are a few inadequate guard rails, on the other and more precipitous rim there are none. When I visited it, one of the two registers for visitors and all the descriptive pamphlets had been stolen. The ranger force at Mesa Verde National Park is the same size it was in 1932; seven times as many people visited it in 1952; the figures for June 1953 were up 38 per cent from last year's. The park can man the entrance station for only one shift; automobiles which arrive in late afternoon cannot be charged the modest entrance fee. It cannot assign a ranger exclusively to fire-duty at headquarters, though it is in an arid region where destructive fire is a constant danger; the headquarters ranger must keep the fire-alert system operating while he attends to a dozen other jobs. All park facilities are strained to the utmost. Stretches of the main road keep sinking and must be repaired at excessive cost because there is not money enough to relocate them where the underlying strata are more stable. There is not even money enough to replace broken guard-rail posts along the edge of the canyon. Colorado and New Mexico are about to construct a new highway past the park to the famous Four Corners. On the day it is completed visitors to Mesa Verde will double in number and the park will be unable to take care of them. It will be paralyzed.

Last year Senator Hunt of Wyoming made a pleasure trip to Yellowstone Park, at least a trip that was intended to be peasureable. He was so shocked by the condition of the roads that he wrote a letter of protest to President Truman. (It got buried under the election campaign.) And yet, considering the handicaps, Yellowstone has done magnificently with its roads; those of many other parks are in worse conditions. (Of the *main* road system in the park 15 per cent is of pre-1920 standard, 42 per cent of pre-1930 standard, and only 27 per cent of 1930–1940 standard. Exactly three miles of new road have been constructed since 1945 and those three complete a project that was begun before the war.) This is the oldest, most popular, and most important national park. In 1932, when 200,000 people visited it, its uniformed staff was large enough to perform just over 6,000 man-hours of work per week; last year, with one and one-third million visitors, the shrunken staff performed just over 4,000 man-hours per week. Like nearly every other popular park, it has reached the limit of performance and begun to slide downhill. There are not enough rangers to protect either the scenic areas from the depredations of tourists or the tourists from the consequences of their own carelessnes—or to gather up the litter or to collect all the entrance fees that should be paid. Water and garbage and sewage systems are beginning to break down under the load put on them; already some sewage is being discharged in Yellowstone Lake. The park's high plateaus covered with lodgepole pine are natural fire-traps which some day will be burned out because the budget will not permit adequate fire-protection.

I have touched on only a few of Yellowstone's critical problems. What I have said is true also of all the most popular areas administered by the Service and in some degree of almost all the less accessible areas. There are true slum districts in Yellowstone, Rocky Mountain, Yosemite, Mesa Verde, various other parks. The National Park Service does a far better job on its starvation rations than it could reasonably be expected to do, but it falls increasingly short of what it must do. It is charged with the preservation, protection, maintenance, development, and administration of 28 national parks, 5 national historical parks, 85 national monuments, 56 areas of various other classifications, and 785 National Capital parks. Their importance to the American present and future is simply incalculable; they are inestimably valuable. But Congress made no proper provision for rehabilitating the areas at the end of the war or for preparing them for the enormous increase in use—more than thirty million people visited them last

[213]

year. It could have provided for renovation and expansion at about a fourth or a fifth of what the job would cost now—but it didn't. It requires the Service to operate a big plant on a hot-dog-stand budget.

The crisis is now in sight. Homeopathic measures will no longer suffice; thirty cents here and a dollar-seventy-five there will no longer keep the national park system in operation. I estimate that an appropriation of two hundred and fifty million dollars, backed by another one to provide the enlarged staff of experts required to expend it properly in no more than five years, would restore the parks to what they were in 1940 and provide proper facilities and equipment to take care of the crowds and problems of 1953. After that we could take action on behalf of the expanding future—and save from destruction the most majestic scenery in the United States, and the most important field areas of archeology, history, and biological science.

No such sums will be appropriated. Therefore only one course seems possible. The national park system must be temporarily reduced to a size for which Congress is willing to pay. Let us, as a beginning, close Yellowstone, Yosemite, Rocky Mountain, and Grand Canyon National Parks—close and seal them, assign the Army to patrol them, and so hold them secure till they can be reopened. They have the largest staffs in the system but neither those staffs nor the budgets allotted them are large enough to maintain the areas at a proper level of safety, attractiveness, comfort, or efficiency. They are unable to do the job in full and so it had better not be attempted at all. If these staffs—and their respective budgets—were distributed among other areas, perhaps the Service could meet the demands now put on it. If not, additional areas could be temporarily closed and sealed, held in trust for a more enlightened future—say Zion, Big Bend, Great Smoky, Shenandoah, Everglades, and Gettysburg. Meanwhile letters from constituents unable to visit Old Faithful, Half Dome, the Great White Throne, and Bright Angel Trail would bring a nationally disgraceful situation to the really serious attention of the Congress which is responsible for it.

"PARKS ARE FOR PEOPLE"*
June 1959

The Park Service's answer to the run-down condition of the parks was Mission 66. This was a 10–year program started in 1956, which was designed to:

1. Wipe out the deficit in park staffs, facilities, and maintenance that had been accumulating since World War II, and move ahead to cope with rising public use;

2. Encourage appreciation and enjoyment of NPS areas in ways that would leave them unimpaired;

3. Study America's outdoor recreation resources in cooperation with other public agencies so that a national recreation plan might be formulated for the United States and its territories.

It was estimated that the cost of rehabilitating the parks would be $800 million in 1955 dollars.

Whether or not Mission 66 accomplished its objective is to some extent a matter of opinion, but conditions did improve even though park visits continued to surge upward. The "preservationists" continued to worry about damage from overuse while the "recreationists" continued to clamor for more and better roads and facilities. In this context Conrad L. Wirth, director of the Park Service at that time, wrote his now famous article.

Every once in a while I like to take time out from the rush and pressure of day to day duties just to think and to ask myself questions about our objectives and where we are going in our park work. One of these questions that is basic to all of our plans and operations has to do with the purpose of parks and what they stand for.

What are parks for? Are they pretty places to look at? Are they places of historic or scientific interest? Are they open spaces for active recreation only, or are they places for those who prefer quiet and solitude and the enjoyment of nature? Parks include all of these things. They provide opportunities for relaxation, for enjoyment of natural beauty and objects and places of historic interest, for healthful outdoor recreation, and for leisure-time activities. The over-all purpose of any park system as I see it, is to fulfill a need of the people.

What is this need that parks should provide for? Is it the same for all people and in all locations? Can a single set of standards guide park executives of city, state, and federal parks? I think not. The determination of where parks should be and how they should be developed requires the best thinking and the combined skills of a number of professional people such as the architect, landscape architect, engineer, biologist, and recreation director, but their efforts will fall

*Conrad L. Wirth, "Parks Are for People," *Parks and Recreation,* Vol. 42, No. 6 (June, 1959), 262–65.

[215]

short of the goal unless they keep in mind the needs of the people the park system is to serve. The city, county, state, and federal governments have responsibilities—and limitations—in meeting park needs and no one division of government can satisfy them all. Each can supply certain kinds of lands. Sound park philosophy requires that they all work closely together to determine land requirements, and to establish guidelines and policies for carrying out plans to meet the needs of the people.

I often turn to a letter I received from the late Frederick Law Olmsted shortly after the death of my father because of the sound thinking and philosophy expressed in the following paragraphs:

> At some time, when we can get together for a quiet chat, I want to talk with you about him and about something difficult to describe which I think he and my father had very much in common and which was, I believe, largely responsible for the great accomplishments of both of them in park work. It is something to which my attention has been strongly drawn of late by reading certain old letters of my father—and something of much more profound importance in park work than is generally recognized. At bottom, it depends on a deep-seated, constant and compelling personal interest in, and simply with, the *PEOPLE* using the parks—and finding one's chief satisfaction in appreciative friendly observation and study of the ways in which those people actually use, and derive pleasure and benefit from any given park, and in helping and guiding them by every available means to get the best value from their use of it, in the long run, that are made possible by the inherent characteristics of that particular park AND by the widely various PERSONAL CHARACTERISTICS OF THE PEOPLE THEMSELVES.
>
> Unless a park man's interest in, and use of, the techniques of designing, constructing and operating parks are dominated and motivated by such a fundamental and observing interest in the PEOPLE who use the parks and in all the details of how they use them and how they can be induced to use them with greater benefit to themselves in the long run—as was the case with my father and yours—mere technical skill in any or all of these phases of park work tends to become academic and sterile, except so far as that man is used as a subordinate technician assistant by a master mind who has a broader human interest in the people as such, and can to some degree inspire his assistants with the same absorbing interest in them. Isn't that the most important thing that park men ought to learn from your father's life work and that of my father?

I believe firmly in Mr. Olmsted's forceful statement that all of the technical skill will become academic and sterile unless it is applied to the park needs of the people. City, state, and national parks are truly a recognized requirement of the people and for the people.

Automation, labor saving devices in the home, faster transportation, the shorter workweek, longer and more frequent vacations, longer life expectancy mean increased leisure time. The way the people use this time will determine the kind of nation we will become. A properly developed national program of parks at all levels of government is an essential element in the building of the character of our nation of the future.

Our park programs are way behind schedule. We need only look about us to see evidence that our present facilities are inadequate. But it is not enough that our plans aim to meet current needs; we must project our thinking ahead toward future demands.

* * *

If we subscribe to the basic philosophy that parks are for people and their value lies in meeting demands for service, then our course is clear. We must plan for and work for more lands and better developments to meet the increasing needs. Our plans should provide for all of the outdoor recreation needs of all the people—not just for the fortunate few. To accomplish this, each level of government must do its proper share.

We must also be constantly alert to the pressures of encroachment for other purposes and especially, in these days, for highway construction. We must not divert park lands to uses not in keeping with the outdoor recreation needs of the people.

* * *

One final thought. The everyday rush to attend meetings, take part in celebrations, prepare budgets, defend legislative proposals, and many other things fall heavily on the shoulders of park executives. Special pressure groups, crash programs, and deadlines to meet day after day can, in the long run, ruin a good park organization and its people. I know full well that we cannot avoid these pressures: they are with us to stay. However, I do feel that we must arrange for time out to analyze what has happened, what is happening, and what might happen if definite plans and objectives are not fully enunciated in policy and adhered to. We must always keep in mind that parks are for people and are to be preserved and administered in such a way as to satisfy their needs.

AN ACT TO ESTABLISH REDWOOD NATIONAL PARK*
October 2, 1968

Probably no other national park proposal has generated as much opposition, over such a long time period, as the move to establish a Redwood National Park in California. As early as 1852 a joint resolution was submitted to the California State Assembly citing the rapidly increasing demand for redwood timber and urging the passage of a law which would prohibit settlement of public lands where redwoods grew.

The first successful effort to conserve the redwoods was the establishment of Big Basin Redwoods State Park in 1902. Muir Woods National Monument, a gift of Congressman William Kent, followed in 1908. Next came the organization of the Save-the-Redwoods League in 1918 and the consequent establishment of the 2,000-acre Humbolt Redwoods State Park in 1921. Eventually there came to be some 28 redwood state parks.

President Johnson urged establishment of a redwood national park in his Natural Beauty message to Congress on February 8, 1965. In another message to Congress on February 23, 1966, he again stressed the need for early action to preserve the redwoods.

After extensive congressional hearings, a compromise bill finally passed both houses and was signed by the President on October 2, 1968.

Be it enacted by the Senate and House of Representatives of the United States of America in Congress assembled, That, in order to preserve significant examples of the primeval coastal redwood (Sequoia sempervirens) forests and the streams and seashores with which they are associated for purposes of public inspiration, enjoyment, and scientific study, there is hereby established a Redwood National Park in Del Norte and Humboldt Counties, California.

Sec. 2. (a) The area to be included within the Redwood National Park is that generally depicted on the maps entitled "Redwood National Park," numbered NPS–RED–7114–A and NPS–RED–7114–B, and dated September 1968, copies of which maps shall be kept available for public inspection in the offices of the National Park Service, Department of the Interior, and shall be filed with appropriate officers of Del Norte and Humboldt Counties. The Secretary of the Interior (hereinafter referred to as the "Secretary") may from time to time, with a view to carrying out the purpose of this Act and with particular attention to minimizing siltation of the streams, damage to the timber, and assuring the preservation of the scenery within the boundaries of the national park as depicted on said maps, modify said boundaries, giving notice of any changes involved therein by

*82 *Statutes at Large,* 931.

publication of a revised drawing or boundary description in the Federal Register and by filing said revision with the officers with whom the original maps were filed, but the acreage within said park shall at no time exceed fifty-eight thousand acres, exclusive of submerged lands.

(b) The Secretary is authorized to acquire by donation only all or part of existing publicly owned highways and roads within the boundaries of the park as he may deem necessary for park purposes. Until such highways and roads have been acquired, the Secretary may cooperate with appropriate State and local officials in patroling and maintaining such roads and highways.

SEC. 3. (a) The Secretary is authorized to acquire lands and interests in land within the boundaries of the Redwood National Park and, in addition thereto, not more than ten acres outside of those boundaries for an administrative site or sites. Such acquisition may be by donation, purchase with appropriated or donated funds, exchange, or otherwise, but lands and interests in land owned by the State of California may be acquired only by donation.

(b) (1) Effective on the date of enactment of this Act, there is hereby vested in the United States all right, title, and interest in, and the right to immediate possession of, all real property within the park boundaries designated in maps NPS–RED–7114–A and NPS–RED–7114–B, except real property owned by the State of California or a political subdivision thereof and except as provided in paragraph (3) of this subsection. The Secretary shall allow for the orderly termination of all operations on real property acquired by the United States under this subsection, and for the removal of equipment, facilities, and personal property therefrom.

(2) The United States will pay just compensation to the owner of any real property taken by paragraph (1) of this subsection. Such compensation shall be paid either: (A) by the Secretary of the Treasury from money appropriated from the Land and Water Conservation Fund, including money appropriated to the Fund pursuant to section 4(b) of the Land and Water Conservation Fund Act of 1965, as amended, subject to the appropriation limitation in section 10 of this Act, upon certification to him by the Secretary of the agreed negotiated value of such property, or the valuation of the property awarded by judgment, including interest at the rate of 6 per centum per annum from the date of taking the property to the date of payment therefor; or (B) by the Secretary, if the owner of the land concurs, with any federally owned property available to him for purposes of exchange pursuant to the provisions of section 5 of this Act; or (C) by the Secretary using any combination of such money or federally owned property. Any action against the United States for the recovery of just compensation for the land and interests therein taken by the United States by this subsection shall be brought in the Court of Claims as provided in title 28, United States Code, section 1491.

(3) Subsection 3(b) shall apply to ownerships of fifty acres or less only if such

ownerships are held or occupied primarily for nonresidential or nonagricultural purposes, and if the Secretary gives notice to the owner within sixty days after the effective date of this Act of the application of this subsection. Notice by the Secretary shall be deemed to have been made as of the effective date of this Act. The district court of the United States for that district in which such ownerships are located shall have jurisdiction to hear and determine any action brought by any person having an interest therein for damages occurring by reason of the temporary application of this paragraph, between the effective date of this Act and the date upon which the Secretary gives such notice. Nothing in this paragraph shall be construed as affecting the authority of the Secretary under subsections (a) and (c) of this section to acquire such areas for the purposes of this Act.

(c) If any individual tract or parcel of land acquired is partly inside and partly outside the boundaries of the park or the administrative site the Secretary may, in order to minimize the payment of severance damages, acquire the whole of the tract or parcel and exchange that part of it which is outside the boundaries for land or interests in land inside the boundaries or for other land or interests in land acquired pursuant to this Act, and dispose of so much thereof as is not so utilized in accordance with the provisions of the Federal Property and Administrative Services Act of 1949 (63 Stat. 377), as amended (40 U.S.C. 471 et seq.). The cost of any land so acquired and disposed of shall not be charged against the limitation on authorized appropriations contained in section 10 of this Act.

(d) The Secretary is further authorized to acquire, as provided in subsection (a) of this section, lands and interests in land bordering both sides of the highway between the present southern boundary of Prairie Creek Redwoods State Park and a point on Redwood Creek near the town of Orick to a depth sufficient to maintain or to restore a screen of trees between the highway and the land behind the screen and the activities conducted thereon.

(e) In order to afford as full protection as is reasonably possible to the timber, soil, and streams within the boundaries of the park, the Secretary is authorized, by any of the means set out in subsections (a) and (c) of this section, to acquire interests in land from, and to enter into contracts and cooperative agreements with, the owners of land on the periphery of the park and on watersheds tributary to streams within the park designed to assure that the consequences of forestry management, timbering, land use, and soil conservation practices conducted thereon, or of the lack of such practices, will not adversely affect the timber, soil, and streams within the park as aforesaid. As used in this subsection, the term "interests in land" does not include fee title unless the Secretary finds that the cost of a necessary less-than-fee interest would be disproportionately high as compared with the estimated cost of the fee. No acquisition other than by donation shall be effectuated and no contract or cooperative agreement shall be executed by the Secretary pursuant to the provisions of this subsection until sixty days after he has notified the President of the Senate and the Speaker of the House of Representatives of his intended action and of the costs and benefits to the United States involved therein.

SEC. 4. (a) The owner of improved property on the date of its acquisition by the Secretary under this Act may, as a condition of such acquisition, retain for himself and his heirs and assigns a right of use and occupancy of the improved property for noncommercial residential purposes for a definite term of not more than twenty-five years or, in lieu thereof, for a term ending at the death of the owner or the death of his spouse, whichever is later. The owner shall elect the term to be reserved. Unless the property is wholly or partially donated to the United States, the Secretary shall pay the owner the fair market value of the property on the date of acquisition minus the fair market value on that date of the right retained by the owner. A right retained pursuant to this section shall be subject to termination by the Secretary upon his determination that it is being exercised in a manner inconsistent with the purpose of this Act, and it shall terminate by operation of law upon the Secretary's notifying the holder of the right of such determination and tendering to him an amount equal to the fair market value of that portion of the right which remains unexpired.

(b) The term "improved property", as used in this section, means a detached, noncommercial residential dwelling, the construction of which was begun before October 9, 1967, together with so much of the land on which the dwelling is situated, the said land being in the same ownership as the dwelling, as the Secretary shall designate to be reasonably necessary for the enjoyment of the dwelling for the sole purpose of noncommercial residential use, together with any structures accessory to the dwelling which are situated on the land so designated.

(c) The Secretary shall have, with respect to any real property acquired by him in sections 5 and 8, township 13 north, range 1 east, Humboldt meridian, authority to sell or lease the same to the former owner under such conditions and restrictions as will assure that it is not utilized in a manner or for purposes inconsistent with the national park.

SEC. 5. In exercising his authority to acquire property by exchange, the Secretary may accept title to any non-Federal property within the boundaries of the park, and outside of such boundaries within the limits prescribed in this Act. Notwithstanding any other provision of law, the Secretary may acquire such property from the grantor by exchange for any federally owned property under the jurisdiction of the Bureau of Land Management in California, except property needed for public use and management, which he classifies as suitable for exchange or other disposal, or any federally owned property he may designate within the Northern Redwood Purchase Unit in Del Norte County, California, except that section known and designated as the Yurok Experimental Forest, consisting of approximately nine hundred and thirty-five acres. Such federally owned property shall also be available for use by the Secretary in lieu of, or together with, cash in payment of just compensation for any real property taken pursuant to section 3(b) of this Act. The values of the properties so exchanged either shall be approximately equal or, if they are not approximately equal, the value shall be equalized by the payment of cash to the grantor or to the Secretary as the circumstances require. Through the exercise of his exchange authority, the Secretary shall, to the extent possible, minimize economic dislocation and the disruption of the grantor's commercial operations.

Sec. 6. Notwithstanding any other provision of law, any Federal property located within any of the areas described in sections 2 and 3 of this Act may, with the concurrence of the head of the agency having custody thereof, be transferred without consideration to the administrative jurisdiction of the Secretary for use by him in carrying out the provisions of this Act.

Sec. 7. (a) Notwithstanding any other provision of law, the Secretary shall have the same authority with respect to contracts for the acquisition of land and interests in land for the purposes of this Act as was given the Secretary of the Treasury for other land acquisitions by section 34 of the Act of May 30, 1908 (35 Stat. 545; 40 U.S.C. 261), and the Secretary and the owner of land to be acquired under this Act may agree that the purchase price will be paid in periodic installments over a period that does not exceed ten years, with interest on the unpaid balance thereof at a rate which is not in excess of the current average market yield on outstanding marketable obligations of the United States with remaining periods to maturity comparable to the average maturities on the installments.

(b) Judgments against the United States for amounts in excess of the deposit in court made in condemnation actions shall be subject to the provisions of section 1302 of the Act of July 27, 1956 (70 Stat. 694), as amended (31 U.S.C. 724a), and the Act of June 25, 1948 (62 Stat. 979), as amended (28 U.S.C. 2414, 2517).

Sec. 8. The present practice of the California Department of Parks and Recreation of maintaining memorial groves of redwood trees named for benefactors of the State redwood parks shall be continued by the Secretary in the Redwood National Park.

Sec. 9. The Secretary shall administer the Redwood National Park in accordance with the provisions of the Act of August 25, 1916 (39 Stat. 535; 16 U.S.C. 1-4), as amended and supplemented.

Sec. 10. There are hereby authorized to be appropriated $92,000,000 for land acquisition to carry out the provisions of this Act.

Approved October 2, 1968.

STATE PARKS

State parks do not receive as much publicity as national parks, and most of them do not possess the superlative scenic qualities or the unique features of the national parks. Nevertheless, state parks entertain more visitors than national parks, presumably because most are within easy driving distance of major population centers.

The following table of attendance figures indicates the rapid growth in the recreational use of state parks.

1941	97,488,000
1954	166,427,000
1959	255,310,000
1961	273,484,000
1962	285,000,000
1964	421,000,000*

While most of the national parks were created from lands already in federal ownership, the state parks had varying origins. Some were established by private donors; some by the reclassification of state forests as state parks. Many were donated by the Federal Government or purchased for token prices; others exist through long-term leases with federal agencies or other state agencies.

Beginning with the Northwest Ordinance of 1785, the new states were granted lands for schools, roadbuilding, and other purposes, but there were no grants for parks. Most of these lands have been sold over the years but even in those states which still possess considerable holdings state land boards ordinarily understand that they are to maximize the return on the lands through sale or lease.

Probably the first official act to reserve areas of substantial size for outdoor recreation occurred in 1641 with the passage of an ordinance by the Massachusetts Bay Colony to set aside the "Great Ponds" for "fishing and fowling." The "Great Ponds" were bodies of fresh water over 10 acres in size. It is estimated that there are about 2,000 of these "Great Ponds" with a total area of about 90,000 acres.

For the next two centuries there was almost no action toward the establishment of state parks. The lone exception appears to be a message by Governor DeWitt Clinton to the legislature of New York in 1820 in which he urged that

*Derived from U.S. Dept. of the Interior, National Park Service, *State Park Statistics, 1961;* U.S. Bureau of the Census, *Statistical Abstract of the United States, 1967;* and National Recreation and Park Association, *Recreation and Park Yearbook, 1966.*

sale of state lands in the Adirondacks be discontinued. These land sales were indeed stopped, but not until 65 years later, when the Adirondack State Forest was authorized. In that same year (1885) Niagara State Reservation was established as New York's first state park. In 1895 Mackinac Island was transferred to the state of Michigan by the Federal Government. This 2,000-acre island had originally been a military reservation and dated back to an old fort built by the British in 1780. In the meantime, the first state park in the United States had been established at Yosemite in 1864.

Minnesota began its system of state parks in 1893 with the acquisition of Birch Coulie, scene of a battle with the Sioux Indians, and with the beginnings of Itasca State Park at the headwaters of the Mississippi River.

During the 1890's timber cutting and leases to private parties were prohibited in the Adirondacks and Catskills making them, in effect, wildland parks. The Adirondack Preserve comprised some 3.3 million acres and was the nation's largest state park in 1968.

In 1895 the nucleus of Palisades Interstate Park was acquired. Over the years, J. P. Morgan, John D. Rockefeller, Jr., and Mrs. E. H. Harriman have contributed several million dollars toward the purchase of land for this park, which includes land in both New York and New Jersey and is especially significant because of its proximity to large population centers.

In the twentieth century the Federal Government continued to encourage the states to develop and operate their own parks. The Recreation and Public Purposes Act of 1926 authorized transfer of "unreserved public lands" to states, counties, and municipalities for recreation purposes. The Park, Parkway, and Recreation Area Act of 1936 provided assistance to the states in planning and management studies in outdoor recreation. An act of 1944 authorized the transfer of certain surplus real estate to the states for park and recreation purposes, and the Land and Water Conservation Fund Act of 1965 provided matching funds to the states for planning, acquisition, and development of state parks and other outdoor recreation areas.

In the meantime some states had made substantial advances on their own. Of particular significance was North Carolina's "model" state recreation law and Indiana's system of nature preserves.

SALT SPRINGS AND HOT SPRINGS IN
THE ARKANSAS TERRITORY*
April 20, 1832

Throughout our history the Federal Government has provided intermittent assistance to the states in outdoor recreation. Perhaps the first such action was the reservation of certain salt springs in the territory of Arkansas. This reservation is ordinarily thought of as the forerunner of the National Park system but the original purpose of the act was to give the governor of the territory authority to lease certain lands for recreational (or medicinal) purposes. As such, it was really the beginning of federal assistance to states for outdoor recreation.

An Act authorizing the Governor of the Territory of Arkansas
to lease the Salt Springs, in said Territory, and for other purposes.

Be it enacted, &c. That the Salt Springs, lying on the Washita river, on Little river, and on Saline creek, in said Territory of Arkansas, together with as many contiguous sections to each of said Springs as shall be equal to one township, and every other salt spring which may be discovered in said Territory, with the section of one mile square which includes it, shall be reserved for the future disposal of the United States, and shall not be liable to be entered, located, or appropriated, for any other purpose whatever.

SEC. 2. *And be it further enacted,* That the Governor of said Territory shall be, and is hereby, authorized to let out or lease said springs, for a term not exceeding five years; and the rents and profits arising from said Springs shall be applied, by the Legislature of said Territory, to the opening and improving such roads in said Territory as said Legislature may direct, and to no other purpose whatever.

SEC. 3. *And be it further enacted,* That the Hot Springs in said Territory, together with four sections of land, including said Springs, as near to the centre thereof as may be, shall be reserved for the future disposal of the United States, and shall not be entered, located, or appropriated, for any other purpose whatever.

Approved: April 20, 1832.

*4 *Statutes at Large,* 505.

AN ACT GRANTING YOSEMITE VALLEY AND THE MARIPOSA BIG TREE GROVE TO CALIFORNIA*
June 30, 1864

The first real state park was Yosemite Valley and the Mariposa Big Tree Grove in California. This area was later re-ceded to the United States to become a part of the present Yosemite National Park. (See pp. 156–58).

An Act authorizing a grant to the State of California of the Yosemite Valley, and of the land embracing the Mariposa Big Tree Grove.

Be it enacted by the Senate and House of Representatives of the United States of America in Congress assembled, That there shall be, and is hereby, granted to the State of California the Cleft or Gorge in the granite peak of the Sierra Nevada mountains, situated in the county of Mariposa, in the State aforesaid, and the headwaters of the Merced river, and known as the Yo-Semite Valley, with its branches or spurs, in estimated length fifteen miles, and in average width one mile back from the main edge of the precipice, on each side of the valley, with the stipulation, nevertheless, that the said State shall accept this grant upon the express conditions that the premises shall be held for public use, resort, and recreation; shall be inalienable for all time; but leases not exceeding ten years may be granted for portions of said premises. All incomes derived from leases of privileges to be expended in the preservation and improvement of the property, or the roads leading thereto; the boundaries to be established at the cost of said State by the United States surveyor general of California, whose official plat, when affirmed by the Commissioner of the General Land Office, shall constitute the evidence of the locus, extent, and limits of the said Cleft or Gorge; the premises to be managed by the Governor of the State with eight other commissioners, to be appointed by the Executive of California, and who shall receive no compensation for their services.

SEC. 2. *And be it further enacted,* That there shall likewise be, and there is hereby, granted to the said State of California the tracts embracing what is known as the Mariposa Big Tree Grove, not to exceed the area of four sections, and to be taken in legal subdivisions of one quarter section each, with the like stipulation as expressed in the first section of this act as to the State's acceptance, with like conditions as in the first section of this act as to inalienability, yet with same lease privilege; the income to be expended in preservation, improvement, and protection of the property; the premises to be managed by commis-

Cong. Globe, 38th Cong., 1st sess. (July 1, 1864), 240.

sioners as stipulated in the first section of this act, and to be taken in legal subdivisions as aforesaid; and the official plat of the United States surveyor general, when affirmed by the Commissioner of the General Land Office, to be the evidence of the locus of the said Mariposa Big Tree Grove.

Approved, June 30, 1864.

MINNESOTA STATE PARKS: ITASCA* AND BIRCH COULIE†
1893

The State of Minnesota began its system of state parks in 1893 with the acquisition of lands in the headwaters of the Mississippi River which formed the beginnings of Itasca State Park. These lands were granted to the state by the Federal Government "for perpetual use as a public park." In the same year, Minnesota appropriated funds for the purchase of land at Birch Coulie which had been the scene of a battle with the Sioux Indians in 1862.

An Act to accept the grant of lands made to the state of Minnesota by the congress of the United States by the act approved August third, one thousand eight hundred and ninety-two, entitled "An act to grant certain public lands to the State of Minnesota for perpetual use as a public park," and to provide for the protection of timber thereon.

Be it enacted by the Legislature of the state of Minnesota:

SECTION 1. The state of Minnesota hereby accepts the grant of lands, together with the conditions thereof, made to it by an act of the congress of the United States approved August third, one thousand eight hundred and ninety-two, entitled "An act to grant certain public lands to the state of Minnesota for perpetual use as a public park," and assents to the purpose of said grant, as in said act set forth.

SEC. 2. All persons, companies and corporations are, by this act, prohibited from cutting, destroying, mutilating or injuring any timber, tree, or evergreen standing or growing upon any of the lands within the limits of the Itasca state park, granted to the state of Minnesota by the congress of the United States, as set forth in the first section of this act. Any person who shall willfully cut, destroy, mutilate or injure, or who shall cause to be cut, destroyed, mutilated or injured, any timber, tree or evergreen standing or growing upon any of the lands aforesaid within the limits of said park, shall be guilty of a misdemeanor, and, upon conviction thereof, shall be fined for the first offense fifty dollars, for the second offense two hundred dollars, and for the third or further offenses he shall be fined the sum of five hundred dollars and imprisonment not less than ninety days or more than one year in the county jail. All offenses charged for misdemeanors as hereinbefore provided shall be tried and determined under the general laws of this state applicable to the trial of criminal actions.

SEC. 3. The secretary of state shall file certified copies of this act, under seal, with the secretary of the interior and the commissioner of the general land office at the city of Washington.

General Laws of Minnesota (1893), ch. 15, 111.
†*General Laws of Minnesota* (1893), ch. 231, 381.

SEC. 4. This act shall take effect and be in force from and after its passage. Approved April 19, 1893.

An Act appropriating money for the purchase of the battle field of Birch Coulie and the erection of a suitable monument thereon.

Be it enacted by the Legislature of the state of Minnesota:

SECTION 1. That there be and is hereby appropriated the sum of twenty-five hundred dollars or so much thereof as may be necessary for the purchase of and conveyance to the state of the land on which was fought the battle of Birch Coulie on the second and third days of September, 1862, in the county of Renville, not exceeding an area of five acres, and suitably enclosing the same, and for erecting thereon a granite monument which shall not only commemorate the event, but the state's appreciation of the services of the men who there sacrificed their lives in its defense.

SEC. 2. That Charles D. Gilfillan of Redwood county, Dr. Stoddard, R. B. Henton and Jerry Patton of Renville county, J. W. Daniels of Rice county, Samuel C. Arbuckle and William H. Grant of Ramsey county, be and hereby are constituted commissioners, without compensation, to carry out the provisions of this act.

MACKINAC ISLAND STATE PARK*
May 31, 1895

Mackinac Island, located in Lake Huron near the straits between Lake Michigan and Lake Huron, was transferred from the Federal Government to the State of Michigan in 1895 with the stipulation that it be used for state park purposes only. The island was originally a military reservation and historically dates back to an old fort built by the British in 1780. Automobiles are prohibited on Mackinac Island and the Michigan State Park Commission has, in other ways, attempted to preserve historical buildings and other landmarks.

An Act to provide for the appointment of a board of commissioners who shall have the management and control of the Mackinac Island State Park, and defining its powers and duties.

SECTION 1. *The People of the State of Michigan enact,* That pursuant to an act of congress, authorizing the secretary of war on application of the Governor of the State of Michigan, to turn over to the State of Michigan, for use as a State park, and for no other purpose, the military reservation and buildings, and the lands, of the national park on Mackinac Island, Michigan: *Provided,* That whenever the State ceases to use the lands for the purpose aforesaid, it shall revert to to the United States; the Governor be and he is hereby authorized and directed to make application to the secretary of war as aforesaid; and that upon the turning over to the State of Michigan of said military reservation and buildings and the lands of the national park on Mackinac Island, the same shall thereafter be known as the Mackinac Island State Park.

SEC. 2. Within thirty days after the passage of this act there shall be appointed by the Governor, by and with the consent of the Senate, five commissioners, who shall be citizens of the State of Michigan, and who shall constitute a board of commissioners to be known as the Mackinac Island State Park Commission. The Governor shall be *ex officio* a member of said board. One of said commissioners shall be appointed for a term of two years, one for a term of four years, one for a term of six years, one for a term of eight years, and one for a term of ten years. Within thirty days after the expiration of the term of a commissioner his successor shall be appointed, who shall hold office for the term of ten years, and until his successor has been appointed and qualified. No member of the board shall receive any compensation for his services as commissioner, but each commissioner shall be entitled to receive his actual disbursement for his expense in connection with the duties of his office, not exceeding for one week in any one

Public Acts of Michigan (1895), No. 222, 514.

year, to be paid out of the park fund. In case of any vacancy upon said board such vacancy shall be filled by the Governor.

SEC. 3. The Mackinac Island State Park shall be under the control and management of said Mackinac Island State Park Commission, and the majority of same shall constitute a quorum for the transaction of business. The commissioners shall have power out of said fund to lay out, manage and maintain said park, and preserve the old fort, and to make and enforce by-laws, rules and regulations necessary to carry out the purposes thereof, not inconsistent with the laws of the State; to effect leases, and to fix prices for rentals or privileges upon the property of said park; to employ a superintendent and such persons as may be needed. And it is hereby provided that the sheriff of the county of Mackinac shall, upon the application of said commission, appoint one or more persons to be by said commission designated, and who shall be employés, as provided in this act, as deputy sheriffs in and for said county, but who shall receive no fees or emoluments for services as deputy sheriffs. Said commissioners shall have the power to fix the compensation of the persons employed by them, but no debt or obligations shall be created by them exceeding the amount of moneys at their disposal at the time. All money received from rentals or privileges may be applied by the commissioners to the maintenance and improvement of said park. Said commissioners shall make to the Governor an annual report and statement of receipts and expenditures, and such recommendations and suggestions as may seem to them proper.

SEC. 4. It shall be the duty of the superintendent of said Mackinac Island State Park to see to it that the United States flag is kept floating from the flag-staff at Fort Mackinac, the rules relative thereto being the same as those that have governed in that matter when the fort was in possession and occupancy by the United States troops.

This act is ordered to take immediate effect.

Approved May 31, 1895.

FREDERICK LAW OLMSTED, JR. ON STATE PARKS*
1929

The Olmsteds, father and son, are among the great figures in park planning and management. This prophetic article by Frederick Law Olmsted, Jr. is still generally valid 40 years later.

The magnitude and importance, socially and economically, in California, of the values arising directly and indirectly from the enjoyment of scenery and from related pleasures of non-urban outdoor life, considered in the aggregate and without regard to the means by which they are made available, are incalculably great, and in this summary are taken for granted.

Some conception of the variety and extent of the means by which these values are sought, and of the aggregate price at which they are valued by those who seek them, may be derived from a brief and partial enumeration:

(1) *Automobile pleasure trips and tours.* Riding for no other purpose than enjoyment of the pleasant out-of-doors through which one passes, or with that as a controlling motive combined with some other purpose or excuse, is one of the "major sports" of California. Statistical measurement of its extent is impossible but no less an authority than a member of the State Highway Commission has indicated his belief that half the travel on California highways is of this class. If so, substantially half the annual expenditures on the purchase, operation, and servicing of California's 1,880,000 automobiles, and on the construction and maintenance of some 7000 miles of public highways, is one item gladly paid for obtaining values of the sort we are considering.

(2) *Other means of locomotion through pleasant scenery for the sake of enjoyment,* as by rail, by boat, on horseback, or on foot.

(3) *Commercially operated hotels, resorts, camps, eating-places, stores, etc.,* used and supported by automobilists and others on their pleasure trips, and in localities where they stop for the prime purpose of enjoying outdoor life. Of this business also there are no adequate statistics, but it is enormous.

(4) *Private vacationist dwelling-places* established and used solely or primarily because of the enjoyment obtainable by means of them, and mainly from the pleasantness of their outdoor environment, ranging from tents and little week-end and vacation cabins in canyon or forest or at the seashore to palatial country estates.

(5) *That share of the passenger and freight business of common carriers, and that share of mercantile, manufacturing, agricultural, and miscellaneous service*

*Frederick Law Olmsted, Jr. "Present-Day Outdoor Recreation and the Relation of State Parks to It," *A State Park Anthology,* Herbert Evison, ed. (Washington, D.C.: National Conference on State Parks, 1930), 18–27.

businesses required for the creation, maintenance and operation of the above facilities.

(6) *Other confessedly recreational uses* (i.e. other than by automobile and by occupation of pleasantly situated temporary domiciles as above) of scenically agreeable places on the coast, in the mountains, in the forests, on streams and lakes, etc. (bathing, boating, fishing, and other outdoor sports, nature study, and just plain quiet enjoyment of one's outdoor surroundings) *through substantially gratuitous use of lands not privately owned by the users.* This includes (a) lands held publicly for such use (as parks), and (b) lands held primarily for other purposes with which such use is not inconsistant (such as public forests and watershed lands, and such as timber or grazinglands, or vacant areas) which have agreeable landscapes and which the public enjoy either from neighboring roads or public places, or through being permitted to wander on them by sufferance.

Lands held as public parks thus appear only as one minor subdivision, fractionally minute in area, of the vast aggregate of lands from which these scenic and recreational values are even now derived in so large a measure as to make regard for them an important factor in management.

The kinds of values sought by such means have always been part of the joy of living for many people, but in our time, in America, there has been an enormous increase in the proportion of people who have time left for the pursuit of such values after earning the bare necessities of existence.

These values, together with others which directly make life worth living, as distinguished from things which are valued only because they can be exchanged for something one really wants, are the final things which economic prosperity enables people to buy. In California, today, people are using their economic wealth in the ways above indicated to buy values of this particular kind enormously—incredibly to anyone of a former age or another country. And they will probably seek to buy this kind of values more and more.

How far such values *can* be bought, at any price, by succeeding generations in California will depend largely on the degree to which the physical conditions which make them possible are permanently conserved or are destroyed by the first comers through their wasteful methods of exploiting them.

The enormous development in California of the use of these scenic and recreational values of the out-of-doors has resulted in part from the economic prosperity of the people, leaving them time and means for such enjoyment, and in part from the lavish abundance of naturally favorable conditions of landscape and climate.

But there are signs on every hand that because of this very abundance (and of the increasing rate at which the favorable conditions are being put to use), careless, hasty, shortsightedly selfish methods of exploiting the natural assets of scenic value are rapidly killing the geese that lay the golden eggs.

To take a single type of this destructive exploitation: Every year thousands of "cabin-site subdivisions" and other residential and pleasure resort developments of the types listed as (3) and (4) above are being laid out in the pleasantest spots readily available as private speculations, with the sole motive of making quick sales and "getting out from under"; and in a considerable proportion of cases *in such a crowded and unsatisfactory manner that before half of the lots are actually put to use the natural advantages of the spot for such use are in large part permanently destroyed and the place tends to become a rural slum* in which the occupants fail to get in any satisfactory measure what they hoped and paid for. In every such case a good opportunity is wrecked, the more enterprising lot-owners gradually abandon the blighted spot for a new venture in virgin territory, which in turn is apt to become similarly blighted because those who determine what is done to it lack either the *will* or the *skill* to use the opportunity other than destructively.

The procedure is identical in principle with such destructive exploitation of natural timber resources as converts lands of potentially permanent timber productivity into useless barrens.

The most urgent concerns of the State in this connection are: (1) *To teach the great mass of well-intentioned people how to get what they want* in enjoyment of scenic and recreational values, *how to get it successfully* for themselves now and on their own initiative, and *how to get it without destroying the natural assets* on which the continued enjoyment of such values depends; and (2) *to curb and limit the activities of exploiters* who would destroy the birthright of their successors, no matter what its value, for the sake of a quick turn of profit to themselves.

The first concern of the State, then, is one of *public education,* including:

(*a*) Study and research as to the various good and bad methods by which the use of scenic and recreational resources is and can be carried on, and (*b*) getting the results of such knowledge across to the people.

The second concern of the State in this matter, *direct prevention of unwarrantably destructive exploitation* of such resources, has many ramifications. The chief means of prevention are these:

(a) BY PROPRIETARY CONTROL

(1) *Parks.* Peculiarly valuable scenic and recreational resources of many kinds, which under private ownership and management are specially subject either to destructive exploitation or to a narrow monopolization which makes their enjoyment by the ordinary citizen impossible, can most simply and effectively be protected against wasteful abuse by means of their public ownership and management in perpetuity as parks. To acquire and manage such parks is the prime function of the State Park Commission.

(2) *Other public holdings.* Lands now held, or which may come to be held by the State and its subdivisions and agencies, and by the Federal Government,

primarily for other purposes than the conservation and use of their scenic and recreational resources, can, and obviously should, be protected against the unnecessary and wasteful impairment of such elements of scenic and recreational value as they contain by a proper and businesslike regard for these values as by-products in their public management; and, in case of the alienation of such lands, by establishing reasonable conditions and restrictions for ensuring a continuance of the same general policy. This is now the policy of the U.S. Forest Service, in management of the National Forests, constituting the largest areas of publicly owned land in the State, amounting to nearly one-fifth of its entire territory.

But there are many other valuable public lands to which the principle should be systematically applied. The most familiar and widespread of these are the lands of the highway system, the location and boundaries of which, as well as their physical treatment, should be determined in considerable measure, as is now well recognized by the Department of Public Works, by regard for the scenic enjoyment to be derived by the public from their use concurrently with their use for purely economic transportation.

Another notable example, as to which the principle has not yet been officially recognized, is to be found in the tidelands. The State received from the United States, in trust for the people, the entire coast of California up to "ordinary high water," and still owns most of it. This is a vastly important area of publicly owned land, the administration of which intimately affects the scenic and recreational resources of the State.

In this connection the State Park Commission can and should collaborate, in a consulting and advisory capacity, with the various responsible public agencies in charge of such public lands.

(3) *Protective restrictions or easements on private land.* In connection with the creation of the better class of residential subdivisions in America there has occurred within the last thirty years a notable development in the methods of applying a very old legal device, that of covenants entered into by the owners of land in regard to the manner of use of the land, to the end of guarding against forms of exploitation injurious to the community. Methods have been found for making such covenants reasonably elastic and adaptable to changing conditions, instead of attempting to impose a rigid arbitrary control by a "dead hand" as in the old days; and with these improvements in technique the method has become a far more valuable and practical device. There have been some beginnings here and there of the use of this device by agreement between private land-owners and public authorities; as where a park, parkway, or pleasure drive is laid out and constructed at public expense on a public right-of-way in a manner beneficial to the owners of abutting lands and the latter agree voluntarily, as a matter of public spirit, or of enlightened selfishness, to subject their land along the borders of this public improvement to certain covenants. These covenants pro-

vide that the land will not be used in certain specified ways detrimental to the value of the public improvement and to the general attractiveness of the region through which it runs, but are so drawn as not to interfere with uses of the land appropriate to the local conditions. Such covenants have often been entered into, for example, by landowners along a given stretch of highway, requiring any buildings to be set back certain distances from the highway. In many cases, such agreements have been entered into for a nominal consideration, sometimes upon condition that similar easements are secured throughout the unit of highway in question; and in the latter case the required easements have sometimes been acquired from a recalcitrant minority by condemnation in order to make the whole project effective.

By patience and tact in negotiation and by the application of adequate technical skill, a great many land-owners in California can, I believe, be induced to enter voluntarily into agreements with public authorities that will safeguard the scenic and recreational resources of their neighbors from all the most seriously threatening dangers that attend wholly individualistic management.

(b) BY REGULATION UNDER THE POLICE POWER

To some extent, and under proper circumstances, it is practicable by public regulation to check certain unnecessary and unreasonable impairments of the State's natural resources, such as are often caused by methods of exploiting private property which are needlessly wasteful or destructive of those resources.

In relation to scenic and recreational resources this can sometimes be done by more effective use of the now well-established method of public regulation of subdivision platting, and by extending and perfecting the operation of reasonable zoning regulations in regions where the permanent welfare of the community is clearly dependent on conserving its general scenic and recreational attractions and where the ill-advised exploitation of a few properties may not only conflict with the larger interest of the State in the region but seriously depreciate the aggregate of private property values in the region itself. It is only the more flagrant cases of misuse of private property which can thus be definitely prevented, for it would be contrary to our American political and legal principles to emasculate individual initiative under guise of police power regulation. But it often happens that the deliberate review and consideration of plans prepared on private initiative which is brought about by wholly reasonable police regulations of the kinds above mentioned gives opportunity for constructive education and leads to the voluntary adoption by the individual of much better development plans than would have been followed in the absence of such review.

It is worth while to examine here in some detail two[1] notable opportunities for

[1] Only one is reproduced here, as having more general application than the second, the Lower Sacramento River.

the intelligent use of existing public proprietary control, existing primarily for other than park purposes (a2 preceding), and of proper police regulation over related private property (b above).

First opportunity: The tidelands.

The State of California and municipalities created by and holding from it, broadly speaking, *now possess title, in trust for the people, to the entire coast of California between ordinary high tide and low tide, and to the submerged lands beyond so far as that ownership can be made effective.* These so-called tidelands are held in trust for the people's use in various ways, primarily in navigation. But the vast majority of them are so exposed and so conditioned that without prejudice to navigation they can and should be administered largely in the interest of protecting the scenic and recreational resources so intimately associated with them. These public tidelands embrace a large and sometimes the major part of the area directly used for recreation at beaches all along the coast. The manner in which their use is controlled and regulated, or left free from regulation, can profoundly influence not only the manner of use of these public lands but also the manner of use and development of the immediately abutting upland even when not publicly owned. At present, except in a few localities, no precise determination has been made of the landward limit of the State's tideland ownership, and no detailed supervision and control are exerted over the actions of abutting owners, who have in some cases, without permission from or supervision by the State, encroached upon its tideland property with pilings and buildings and artificial fillings to the detriment of the interests of the people for whom the State holds those lands in trust.

It should be made the duty of some suitable agency, presumably the Department of Natural Resources, actively and systematically to protect the proprietary interests of the State in all tidelands not yet definitely assigned to specialized uses under specialized agencies, such as the Harbor Commissioners, to ascertain, survey and firmly establish the maximum legal limits of the State's proprietary control; to study the use to which the various parts of these lands can most wisely and properly be put—some for commerce, some for fisheries, some for mineral wealth, some for combinations of uses in which recreation is an important part; and to provide for their proper administration and for the proper regulation of their use and prevention of their abuse by the general public and by abutting riparian owners. To that end there is need of legislation and of appropriations for actively protecting the State's proprietary rights. The values at stake along a thousand miles of almost unwatched tideland boundary, with many thousands of aggressive private neighbors ready to take an ell where they can get an inch, are too vast to be left longer without vigorous safeguarding.

Moreover, it is the right and the duty of the State to bring about the establishment and enforcement of suitable police regulations governing the use of private land abutting on the public tidelands and the public highway of the ocean so far as is necessary to prevent those unreasonable dangers to the "safety, health, morals or general welfare of the people," which are, in fact, liable to occur in the unregulated competitive use of separate parcels of ocean-front land.

For example, an ocean beach, considered either as a geological structure adjusted by nature to withstand the impact of storm-waves or as a place of human recreation, extends as a unit from beyond the seaward side of low-water surf to the upper limit or crest of the wave-washed material that forms the beach. But ordinarily this unit is owned partly by the State and partly by upland owners, with some very real overlapping of rights. When an attempt is made to fix a sharp boundary of these two "ownerships," the dividing-line has traditionally been described by the courts, broadly, as the line of "ordinary high water," usually interpreted as being the imaginary line of a mathematically computed "mean high tide"; but the rights of the two parties are not as sharply separated by this line as are the rights of two owners of upland real estate by the joint boundary. Where recreational uses of the coastal lands as a whole, including in such uses private dwelling-places and commercial resorts, afford or are likely to afford the maximum values obtainable, as they largely do on the California coast, the natural resources of the locality can generally be used to far better advantage, at less economic cost, with less danger to property and life and with larger returns to all concerned, if buildings and other structures are kept to the landward and safe side of the crest of the beach and if the entire natural unit of the beach is kept free to absorb the impact of storm waves and for recreational uses. Private developments along a beach usually begin in this sensible way, leaving the whole of the beach proper free from fixed structures. But when a subdivision separates ownership of the riparian edge from ownership of the back land, unregulated competition tempts to expansion of structures on the riparian edge seaward, occupying part of the beach, inviting danger and high construction costs, and greatly reducing the total values obtainable from the beach *and* the hinterland.

In such situations a police regulation fixing in advance a reasonable "front building-line" for all private land-owners, in the common interest and with proper provision for adaptation by a competent central authority to meet special local conditions, would prevent an immense final waste of natural resources.

To decree, as a condition of approving subdivision plats, that the now private portion of all ocean shores (that is to say, above "ordinary high water") shall be dedicated to public use for street or park purposes might be confiscatory and unconstitutional. But to decree that such private marginal lands along the beaches shall not be used for certain purposes to which they are naturally ill adapted, which invite danger to property and life, and which tend to impair the potential aggregate values of property in the region as a whole, would be a reasonable and farsighted use of the State's police power; and in connection with suitable regulation of the public use of the State's portion of all beaches would leave it open to the State, at proper times and places, to acquire by gift, purchase or condemnation so much of the upper portions of the beaches, now privately owned, as it may prove expedient to have in public rather than in private ownership.

PARK, PARKWAY, AND RECREATIONAL AREA STUDIES
1936* & 1937†

During the 1930's a considerable portion of the work done by the Civilian Conservation Corps was carried out in the national parks and on state-owned parklands. At the peak of CCC activity, there were 561 camps assigned to national, state, and local parks. Thirty years later, many of the roads, trails, campsites, and other facilities developed by the CCC were still in use. The availability of CCC funds and manpower made it possible for some states to embark on park programs which would not otherwise have been feasible.

The CCC and other Depression programs were probably the first cases of large-scale cooperative enterprises in outdoor recreation between the states and the Federal Government. One outgrowth of this cooperative endeavor was the passage of the Park, Parkway, and Recreational Area Study Act on June 23, 1936. At that time very few of the states had personnel competent to undertake inventory, planning, or management studies in outdoor recreation. The act is reproduced below along with the National Park Service report of its first year's activities under the new law.

An Act to authorize a study of the park, parkway, and recreational-area programs in the United States, and for other purposes.

Be it enacted by the Senate and House of Representatives of the United States of America in Congress assembled, That the Secretary of the Interior (hereinafter referred to as the "Secretary") is authorized and directed to cause the National Park Service to make a comprehensive study, other than on lands under the jurisdiction of the Department of Agriculture, of the public park, parkway, and recreational-area programs of the United States, and of the several States and political subdivisions thereof, and of the lands throughout the United States which are or may be chiefly valuable as such areas, but no such study shall be made in any State without the consent and approval of the State officials, boards, or departments having jurisdiction over such lands and park areas. The said study shall be such as, in the judgment of the Secretary, will provide data helpful in developing a plan for coordinated and adequate public park, parkway, and recreational-area facilities for the people of the United States. In making the said study and in accomplishing any of the purposes of this Act, the Secretary is authorized and directed, through the National Park Service, to seek and accept the cooperation and assistance of Federal departments or agencies having jurisdiction of lands belonging to the United States, and may cooperate and make agreements with and seek and accept the assistance of other Federal agencies

*49 *Statutes at Large,* 1894.
†U.S. Dept. of the Interior, National Park Service, *1937 Yearbook—Park and Recreation Progress* (Washington, D.C.: Government Printing Office, 1938), 7.

and instrumentalities, and of States and political subdivisions thereof and the agencies and instrumentalities of either of them.

SEC. 2. For the purpose of developing coordinated and adequate public park, parkway, and recreational-area facilities for the people of the United States, the Secretary is authorized to aid the several States and political subdivisions thereof in planning such areas therein, and in cooperating with one another to accomplish these ends. Such aid shall be made available through the National Park Service acting in cooperation with such State agencies or agencies of political subdivisions of States as the Secretary deems best.

SEC. 3. The consent of Congress is hereby given to any two or more States to negotiate and enter into compacts or agreements with one another with reference to planning, establishing, developing, improving, and maintaining any park, parkway, or recreational area. No such compact or agreement shall be effective until approved by the legislatures of the several States which are parties thereto and by the Congress of the United States.

SEC. 4. As used in sections 1 and 2 of this Act the term "State" shall be deemed to include Hawaii, Alaska, Puerto Rico, the Virgin Islands, and the District of Columbia.

Approved, June 23, 1936.

THE PARK, PARKWAY, AND RECREATIONAL-AREA STUDY

When Federal emergency funds were applied to recreation and conservation work for the first time 5 years ago, the Federal Government and the States entered into a partnership which has led to a permanent system of cooperation in a Nation-wide program through which it is hoped ultimately to fill the whole park and recreational area needs of the American people.

The foundation of this permanent cooperative working arrangement was provided in the Park, Parkway, and Recreation Study Act passed by Congress as Public 770½[1] and approved by President Roosevelt on June 23, 1936. This act authorized the Park, Parkway, and Recreational-Area Study which is being conducted by the National Park Service with the cooperation of other Federal agencies and the States and their civil divisions, and it further authorizes the Secretary of the Interior, through the National Park Service, to aid the States and their civil divisions in the planning of park and recreational areas.

The need for coordinated, Nation-wide study of the country's park, parkway, and recreational area requirements has been recognized by Federal and State authorities for many years. The situation became especially acute under the impetus of the widespread park development projects financed by emergency funds which unexpectedly threw the whole park and recreation movement into

[1] Text of act appended to this article.

high gear. States which had given little if any attention to developing park systems awakened quickly to the importance of recreation service as a function of government. Since 1933, seven States have established their first State parks and 37 States have acquired 350 new park areas, totaling 600,000 acres, which, exclusive of the Adirondack and Catskill Forest Preserves in New York, represents an increase in State park acreage of approximately 70 percent. Simultaneously, public interest in outdoor recreation has developed to the point where park administrative agencies are hard pressed to keep up with the demand for adequate areas and facilities.

Those in charge of planning, developing, and administering park and recreational areas were quick to learn several important things: that Federal and State cooperation in this field is a sound, workable arrangement productive of excellent results; that people regard the provision of park and recreational areas and facilities as a responsibility of government; and that no State or regional system can be really adequate unless related to the Nation-wide movement, though planned basically to meet the local requirements.

It was realized that in order to plan on a national scale to meet the park and recreational needs of the people, planners must know the extent of areas and facilities already existing and how much and in what way they are being used; the recreational needs of people in different parts of the country and their inclinations in this respect as indicated by their experience, type of employment, and financial condition; the extent of potential areas and facilities, and the ability (financially and otherwise) of the State and local governments to develop such resources. It is the purpose of the Park, Parkway, and Recreational-Area Study to assemble such information and formulate State master plans designed to insure proper and adequate development of the State and local park and recreational area systems.

The Study, then, has three major objectives: (1) to obtain all available information concerning existing recreational facilities, areas and systems, and to analyze legislation, existing plans, population, and other factors affecting the recreational problem; (2) to determine requirements for recreation over a period of years on a Nation-wide scale; and (3) to formulate definite plans and recommendations for adequately meeting the present and future recreational requirements.

In accordance with this procedure, the Study is divided into two phases: first, the inventory phase which includes the collection and organization of factual material essential to sound recreational planning, and, second, the study phase which involves analysis and appraisal of these data and the formulation of plans and recommendations.

The act authorizing the Study provides that "no such study shall be made in any State without the consent and approval of the State officials, boards, or departments having jurisdiction over such lands and park areas." In order to assure

[241]

every cooperation, the Governor of each State was requested to designate some established State agency, such as conservation department, planning board, or the park authority already functioning for emergency work, to act as State study authority and be responsible for directing and conducting the Study within the State in cooperation with National Park Service representatives. In most States such a functional working relationship has been established with appropriate State agencies, and work has proceeded on the inventory phase of the Study. The collection of data from Federal agencies is handled through the Washington office of the National Park Service either by obtaining the information directly or by negotiating an agreement under which Service field men may work with the field men of the agency involved. A regional supervisor for the Study in each of the four regions of the National Park Service coordinates the Study work in his respective territory.

As information is assembled on existing and potential recreational areas and facilities, data are also being gathered on such important matters as legislation, financing, and administration, and on social and economic factors such as distribution and trends of population, needs of Negro and other distinct racial groups, per capita income and per capita wealth. State budgets are being examined to see how the amount set up for park and recreation purposes compares with the budget as a whole and the State's revenue and tax rate.

Sufficient information has already been assembled to make possible analysis of data and preparation of preliminary master plans for several States. The task of analysis is a difficult one, because in developing this new common sense approach to recreational planning there is little precedent on which to base conclusions and recommendations. There are few experts in this field fully qualified to make such analyses from the standpoint of the social and economic aspects of recreation and how park and recreation planning is affected by population distribution and trends, the per capita income, occupation, education, age, habits and interests, resources, land ownership status, sources of recreational funds, and the ability of individuals to reach recreational areas. Their study must take into consideration also such physical factors as geological and physiographic conditions, flora and fauna, climate, history, transportation, and land use. In the recreation situation they must consider legislation, involving authorization for recreational activities on the part of an agency and the provision of funds therefor, and administration, including the type of departmental structure, personnel, and standards and policies concerning acquisition, development, operation, and the recreational program.

THE SURPLUS PROPERTY ACT*
1944

Prior to and during World War II the Federal Government acquired parcels of real estate of various sizes for military or defense purposes. Some of these properties were later declared to be outside the needs of the government and were made available for disposal under provisions of the Surplus Property Act of 1944. Section 13 (h) of this long and complex law provided that real property which was found to be suitable for park or recreation purposes could be sold to states or subdivisions thereof for 50 percent of its appraised market value. It further provided that property for historic-monument purposes could be transferred without cost to the states.

The Surplus Property Act of 1944 was repealed by Sec. 602 of the Federal Property and Administrative Services Act of 1949 (63 Stat., 377) but the original Section 13 (h) was excepted from repeal.

SECTION 13 (h) (50 U. S. C. App. 1622 (h):

"(h) (1) Notwithstanding any other provision of this Act, any disposal agency designated pursuant to this Act may, with the approval of the Administrator, convey to any State, political subdivision, instrumentalities thereof, or municipality, all of the right, title, and interest of the United States in and to any surplus land, including improvements and equipment located thereon, which in the determination of the Secretary of the Interior, is suitable and desirable for use as a public park, public recreational area, or historic monument, for the benefit of the public. The Administrator, from funds appropriated to the War Assets Administration, shall reimburse the Secretary of the Interior for the costs incurred in making any such determination.

"(2) Conveyances for park or recreational purposes made pursuant to the authority contained in this subsection shall be made at a price equal to 50 per centum of the fair value of the property conveyed, based on the highest and best use of the property at the time it is offered for disposal, regardless of its former character or use, as determined by the Administrator. Conveyances of property for historic-monument purposes under this subsection shall be made without monetary consideration: *Provided,* That no property shall be determined under this paragraph to be suitable or desirable for use as an historic monument except in conformity with the recommendation of the Advisory Board on National Parks, Historic Sites, Buildings and Monuments established by section 3 of the Act entitled 'An Act for the preservation of historic American sites, buildings, objects, and antiquities of national significance, and for other purposes', approved August 21, 1935 (49 Stat. 666), and no property shall be so determined to

*58 *Statutes at Large,* 765.

[243]

be suitable or desirable for such use if (A) its area exceeds that necessary for the preservation and proper observation of the historic monument situated thereon, or (B) it was acquired by the United States at any time subsequent to January 1, 1900.

"(3) The deed of conveyance of any surplus real property disposed of under the provisions of this subsection—

"(A) shall provide that all such property shall be used and maintained for the purpose for which it was conveyed for a period of not less than twenty years, and that in the event that such property ceases to be used or maintained for such purpose during such period, all or any portion of such property shall in its then existing condition, at the option of the United States, revert to the United States; and

"(B) may contain such additional terms, reservations, restrictions, and conditions as may be determined by the Administrator to be necessary to safeguard the interests of the United States."

NORTH CAROLINA'S RECREATION ENABLING LAW*
March 31, 1945

In 1945 the North Carolina legislature amended a 1923 law to produce a Recreation Enabling Law which is sometimes cited as a "model" state recreation law. Among other things it declared recreation to be a responsibility of state government, authorized condemnation proceedings for acquisition of park lands, provided funding methods through bonding and taxation, established methods for participation of local governments, and authorized the establishment of recreation boards or commissions.

An Act to rewrite Article 12 of Chapter 160 of the General Statutes of North Carolina, authorizing the governing bodies of the state's political subdivisions to establish and provide for a recreation system.

The General Assembly of North Carolina do enact:

SECTION 1. Article twelve of Chapter one hundred and sixty of the General Statutes of North Carolina is hereby rewritten to read as follows:

ARTICLE 12. *Recreation Systems and Playgrounds.*

SECTION 160–155 Title—This article shall be known and may be cited as the "Recreation Enabling Law."

SECTION 160–156. *Declaration of State Public Policy*—As a guide to the interpretation and application of this article, the policy of this state is declared to be as follows:

The lack of adequate recreational programs and facilities is a menace to the morals, happiness and welfare of the people of this state in times of peace as well as in times of war. Making available recreational opportunities for citizens of all ages is a subject of general interest and concern, and a function requiring appropriate action by the governing bodies of the several political and educational subdivisions of the state. The legislature, therefore, declares that in its considered judgment the public good and the general welfare of the citizens of this state require an adequate recreation program and that the creation, establishment and operation of a recreation system is a governmental function and a necessary expense as defined by Article VII, Section seven, of the Constitution of North Carolina.

SECTION 160–157. *Definitions*—(1) Recreation, for the purposes of this article, is defined to mean those activities which are diversionary in character and which aid in promoting entertainment, pleasure, relaxation, instruction and other physical, mental, and cultural developments and experiences of a leisure-time nature.

(2) Unit, for the purposes of this article, means county, city and town.

*Vol. 3D, *General Statutes of North Carolina, 1964,* 141–44.

SECTION 160–158. *Powers*—The governing body of any unit, as defined in Section 160–157, may exercise the following powers for recreational purposes:

(1) Establish and conduct a system of supervised recreation for such unit.

(2) Set apart for use as parks or playgrounds, recreational centers or facilities, any land or building owned by or leased to such unit and may improve and equip such lands or buildings.

(3) Acquire lands or buildings by gift, purchase, lease or loan, or by condemnation as provided by Chapter forty, eminent domain, of the General Statutes.

(4) Accept any gift or bequest of money, or other personal property, or any donation to be applied principal or income for recreational use.

(5) Provide, construct, equip, operate and maintain parks, playgrounds, recreation centers and recreation facilities, and all buildings and structures necessary or useful in connection therewith.

(6) Appropriate funds for the purpose of carrying out the provisions of this article.

SECTION 160–159. *Funds*—If the governing body of any unit, as defined in Section 160–157, finds it necessary for the purpose of carrying out the provisions of this article, the governing body is hereby authorized to call a special election without a petition for that purpose as provided by Section 160–163, and submit as therein provided to the qualified voters of said unit the question of whether or not a special tax shall be levied and/or bonds issued for the purpose of acquiring lands for parks, playgrounds and buildings, and the improvement thereof, and for equipping and operating same.

SECTION 160–160. *System Conducted by Unit or Recreation Board*—If a recreational system is established, it may be conducted by the unit as any other department of the unit is conducted, or if the governing body of the unit determines that it is for the best interest of the system that it be supervised and directed by a recreation board or commission, then such governing body may create such board or commission by ordinance or resolution to be known as the "Recreation Board or Commission of the unit," and may vest such board or commission with the authority to provide, maintain, conduct and operate the recreational system with authority to employ directors, supervisors and play leaders and such other officers or employees as may be deemed best within the budget provided for the commission or board by the unit or from other funds in the hands of the commission or board. The board or commission may be vested with such powers and duties as the governing body may deem proper.

SECTION 160–161. *Appointment of Members to Board*—The board or commission shall be appointed by the governing body of the unit and shall consist of at least five members, one of whom shall be affiliated with the government of the unit, one with the school system, one with the health department and one with the welfare department. The term of at least one member of those first

[246]

appointed shall expire in each of the first five years and until successors are appointed and qualified. The members shall serve without compensation. Vacancies in the board or commission shall be filled for the unexpired term by appointment of the governing body of the unit. The recreation board or commission at its first meeting shall appoint a chairman and such other officers as may be deemed proper for the conduct of its business, and shall adopt rules and regulations to govern its procedure. Rules and regulations may be adopted from time to time for the purpose of governing the use of parks, playgrounds, recreation centers and facilities.

SECTION 160–162. *Power to Accept Gifts and Hold Property*—The recreation board or commission may accept any grant, lease, loan or devise of real estate or any gift or bequest of money or other personal property, or any donation to be applied, principal or income, for either temporary, immediate or permanent recreational use; but if the acceptance of any grant or devise of real estate, or gift or bequest of money or other personal property will subject the unit to expense for improvement or maintenance, the acceptance thereof shall be subject to the approval of the governing body of such unit. Lands or devises, gifts or bequests, may be accepted and held subject to the terms under which such land or devise, gift or bequest, is made, given or received.

SECTION 160–163. *Petition for Establishment of System and Levy of Tax; Election*—A petition signed by at least fifteen percent of the qualified and registered voters in the unit may be filed in the office of the clerk or other proper officer of such unit requesting the governing body of such unit to do any one or all of the following things:

(1) Provide, establish, maintain and conduct a supervised recreation system for the unit.

(2) Levy an annual tax of not less than three cents (3¢) nor more than ten cents (10¢) on each one hundred dollars of assessed valuation of the taxable property within such unit for providing, conducting and maintaining a supervised recreation system.

(3) Issue bonds of the unit in an amount specified therein and levy a tax for the payment thereof, for the purpose of acquiring, improving and equipping lands or buildings or both for parks, playgrounds, recreation centers and other recreational facilities.

When the petition is filed, it shall be the duty of the governing body of such unit to cause the question petitioned for to be submitted to the voters at a special election to be held in such unit within ninety days from the date of the filing, which election shall be held as now provided by law for the holding of general elections in such units, except in all such elections a special registration shall be provided.

If the proposition submitted at such election shall receive a majority vote of the qualified registered electors at such election, the governing body of the unit shall, by appropriate ordinance or resolution, put into effect such proposition as soon as practicable.

SECTION 160–164. *Joint Playgrounds or Neighborhood Recreation Centers—* Any two or more units may jointly provide and establish, operate and conduct and maintain a supervised recreation system and acquire, operate, improve and maintain property, both real and personal, for parks, playgrounds, recreation centers and other recreational facilities and activities, the expense thereof to be proportioned between the units participating as may to them seem just and proper.

SECTION 2. All laws or parts of laws inconsistent herewith are hereby repealed: Provided, that nothing in this Act shall have the effect of replacing Public-Local or Private Acts creating or authorizing the creation of any recreational system by a unit or relating to the management thereof.

SECTION 3. This Act shall be in full force and effect from and after its ratification.

In the General Assembly read three times and ratified this the 31st day of March, 1945.

* * *

THE RECREATION AND PUBLIC PURPOSES ACT*
1954

The act of June 14, 1926 (44 Stat., 741) authorized the Secretary of the Interior to make available to states, counties, or municipalities, by exchange, sale, or lease, unreserved non-mineral public lands considered valuable mainly for recreational purposes. The "unreserved" public lands totaling about 475 million acres, were the remains of the old public domain and were located almost altogether in the western states and Alaska.

The purpose of the act was to encourage states and their local subdivisions to acquire land for recreational purposes at low cost (the 1961 price schedule was $2.50 per acre). Land for historic monuments could be transferred without charge. The 1926 act was completely revised in this amendment of 1954.

To amend the Recreation Act of June 14, 1926, to include other public purposes and to permit nonprofit organizations to purchase or lease public lands for certain purposes.

Be it enacted by the Senate and House of Representatives of the United States of America in Congress assembled, That the Act approved June 14, 1926 (44 Stat. 741; 43 U.S.C., sec. 869), entitled "An Act to authorize acquisition or use of public lands by States, counties, or municipalities for recreational purposes", is hereby amended to read as follows:

"SECTION 1. (a) The Secretary of the Interior upon application filed by a duly qualified applicant under section 2 of this Act may, in the manner prescribed by this Act, dispose of any public lands to a State, Territory, county, municipality, or other State, Territorial, or Federal instrumentality or political subdivision for any public purposes or to a nonprofit corporation or nonprofit association for any recreational or any public purpose consistent with its articles of incorporation or other creating authority. Before the land may be disposed of under this Act it must be shown to the satisfaction of the Secretary that the land is to be used for an established or definitely proposed project. The Secretary may classify public lands in Alaska for disposition under this Act. Lands so classified may not be appropriated under any other public land law unless the Secretary revises such classification or authorizes the disposition of an interest in the lands under other applicable law. If, within eighteen months following such classification, no application has been filed for the purpose for which the lands have been so classified, then the Secretary shall restore such lands to appropriation under the applicable public land laws.

"(b) Conveyances made in any one calendar year shall be limited as follows:

*68 *Statutes at Large,* 173.

"(i) For recreational purposes:

"(A) To any State or the State park agency or any other agency having jurisdiction over the State park system of said State designated by the Governor of that State as its sole representative for acceptance of lands under this provision, for not more than three sites, six thousand four hundred acres in all, except that during each of the calendar years 1960, 1961, and 1962, conveyances may be made for not more than six sites, comprising a total of not more than twelve thousand eight hundred acres and, in addition thereto, such acreage as may be needed for small roadside parks and rest sites of not more than ten acres each.

"(B) To any political subdivision of a State, six hundred and forty acres.

"(C) To any nonprofit corporation or nonprofit association, six hundred and forty acres.

"(ii) For public purposes other than recreation:

"(A) To any State or agency or instrumentality thereof, for any one program, six hundred and forty acres.

"(B) To any political subdivision of a State, six hundred and forty acres.

"(C) To any nonprofit corporation or nonprofit association, six hundred and forty acres.

"(c) Where the lands have been withdrawn in aid of a function of a Federal department or agency other than the Department of the Interior, or of a State, Territory, county, municipality, water district, or other local governmental subdivision or agency, the Secretary of the Interior may make disposals under this Act only with the consent of such Federal department or agency, or of such State, Territory, or local governmental unit. Nothing in this Act shall be construed to apply to lands in any national forest, national park, or national monument, or national wildlife refuge, or to any Indian lands or lands set aside or held for the use or benefit of Indians, including lands over which jurisdiction has been transferred to the Department of the Interior by Executive order for the use of Indians, or, except insofar as this Act applies to leases of land to States and counties and to State and Federal instrumentalities and political subdivisions and to municipal corporations, to the revested Oregon and California Railroad grant lands and the reconveyed Coos Bay Wagon Road grant lands in the State of Oregon. Nor shall any disposition be made under this Act for any use authorized under any other law, except for a use authorized under the Act of June 1, 1938 (52 Stat. 609; 43 U.S.C., sec. 682a), as amended.

"SEC. 2. The Secretary of the Interior may after due consideration as to the power value of the land, whether or not withdrawn therefor, (a) sell such land to the State, Territory, county, or other State, Territorial, or Federal instrumentality or political subdivision in which the lands are situated, or to a nearby municipal corporation in the same State or Territory, for the purpose for which the land has been classified, and conveyances of such land for historic-monument purposes under this subsection shall be made without monetary consideration, while conveyances for any other purpose under this subsection shall be made at a price to be fixed by the Secretary of the Interior through appraisal or otherwise, after taking into consideration the purpose for which the lands are to be used; (b) lease such land to the State, Territory, county, or other State, Territorial, or Federal instrumentality or political subdivision in which the lands are situated, or to a nearby municipal corporation in the same State or Territory, for the purpose for which the land has been classified, at a reasonable annual rental, for a period up to twenty years, and, at the discretion of the Secretary, with a privilege of renewal for a like period, (c) sell such land to a nonprofit corporation or nonprofit association, for the purpose for which the land has been classified, at a price to be fixed by the Secretary of the Interior through appraisal, after taking into consideration the purpose for which the lands are to be used, or (d) lease such land to a nonprofit corporation or nonprofit association at a reasonable annual rental, for a period up to twenty years, and, at the discretion of the Secretary, with a privilege of renewal for a like period. Each patent or lease so issued shall contain a reservation to the United States of all mineral deposits in the lands conveyed or leased and of the right to mine and remove the same, under applicable laws and regulations to be established by the Secretary. Each lease shall contain a provision for its termination upon a finding by the Secretary that the land has not been used by the lessee for the purpose specified in the lease for such a period, not over five years, as may be specifed in the lease, or that such land or any part thereof is being devoted to another use.

"SEC. 3. Title to lands conveyed by the Government under this Act may not be transferred by the grantee or its successor except, with the consent of the Secretary of the Interior, to a transferee which would be a qualified grantee under section 2 (a) or (c) and subject to the acreage limitation contained in section 1 (b) of this Act. A grantee or its successor may not change the use specified in the conveyance to another or additional use except, with the consent of the Secretary, to a use for which such grantee or its successor could obtain a conveyance under this Act. If at any time after the lands are conveyed by the Government, the grantee or its successor attempts to transfer title to or control over these lands to another or the lands are devoted to a use other than that for which the lands were conveyed, without the consent of the Secretary, title to the lands shall revert to the United States.

"SEC. 4. The Secretary may authorize transfers of title or changes in use in accordance with the provisions of section 3 of this Act with respect to any patent heretofore issued under any Act upon application by a patentee qualifed to obtain a conveyance under section 2 (a) or (c) of this Act. If the Secretary, pursuant to such an application, authorizes such transfer or use, all reverter provisions and other limitations on transfer or use, under this or any other Act affecting the lands involved, shall cease to be in effect twenty-five years after the Secretary authorizes the transfer or use for a changed or additional purpose under the provisions of this section.

"Sec. 5. The Act of September 30, 1890, entitled 'An Act to authorize entry of the public lands by incorporated cities and towns for cemetery and park purposes', and the Act of October 17, 1940, entitled 'An Act to authorize the Secretary of the Interior to sell or lease for park or recreational purposes, and to sell for cemetery purposes, certain public lands in Alaska', are hereby repealed.

"Sec. 6. All moneys received from or on account of any revested Oregon and California Railroad grant lands or reconveyed Coos Bay Wagon Road grant lands under this Act shall be deposited respectively in the Oregon and California land-grant fund and the Coos Bay Wagon Road grant fund, and shall be applied in the manner prescribed respectively by title II of the Act of August 28, 1937 (50 Stat. 875), as amended (43 U.S.C. 1181f), and by the Act of May 24, 1939 (53 Stat. 753)."

WILLIAM O. DOUGLAS ON COUNTY CONSERVATION PARKS*
1964

Since county governments are legally considered to be arms or extensions of the state, it seems appropriate to include some discussion of county parks in this chapter on state parks. Supreme Court Justice William O. Douglas has long been an ardent conservationist. In this article he makes a plea for county parks and, in particular, for County Conservation Parks.

The park has become a main recreational adjunct of the American community. City parks, state parks, national parks and county parks, as well, help people escape asphalt and traffic and imprisonment in their modern cliff houses of steel and concrete.

The county park system is widespread. As of 1960, all states but eleven had some county parks. About one-ninth of all local parks today are county parks. Of the area in local parks, over 40 per cent of the acreage is in county units. While municipal parks average 26.5 acres, county parks average 165 acres. Most of these are recreational, as distinguished from conservation, parks. They offer facilities that run from arboretums to zoos, from bowling greens to handball courts, from dance pavilions to shuffleboard—softball, baseball, picnic centers, tennis and horseshoe courts leading the list. There are, however, some strictly conservation uses. Thus the 24,710 local parks have 450 devoted to nature trails and centers, though the total acreage dedicated to that use is small (210 acres). It is for a vast revolutionary expansion of that kind of county park that I speak today.

A CONSERVATION COUNTY PARK

I commend to you this other kind of county park to supplement, not to replace existing ones. A conservation county park may have to be created on what at present is wasteland. But it will fill a need supplied by few city, county, or state parks presently existing.

A century ago we had no national, state, or county parks and no forests—local or national. At that time few cities had any parks. The "Village Green" of New England was the Town Square of Europe. Thus was the Boston Common set aside in 1634 and until 1830 used simply as a place where cows grazed and the militia drilled. Philadelphia established its first parks in 1682, Fairmont Park of

*William O. Douglas, "A Role for Counties in Recreation," *County Parks and Recreation . . . A Basis for Action,* Philip Warren, ed. (New York: National Association of Counties and the National Recreation Association, 1964), 16–24.

[253]

4,000 acres still being the largest within the limits of any American city. The plans approved by Washington in 1791 for Washington, D.C. included many parks. But these were among the few exceptions. City parks even a century ago were scarce.

NEW YORK'S CENTRAL PARK

At that time New York City had a huge open backyard north of 23rd Street on Manhattan Island. Efforts to preserve parts of it in their natural state engendered bitter fights.

William Cullen Bryant and Frederick Law Olmsted were responsible for Central Park in New York City, the creation of which was authorized in 1853. At the same time an effort was also made to set aside Jones' Woods along the East River. But commercial interests carried the day. Two parks were thought to be one too many. New York's Mayor stated the case against Jones' Woods:

"The ground spoken of is on one side of the island, and too remote for what must ever remain the centre of population, to be generally available to the masses as a place of recreation and healthful exercise. . . . It occupies some thousands of feet of the margin of the East River, none of which ought ever to be taken from the purposes of commerce."

WILDERNESS WAS EVERYWHERE

The restless, roving American of those days, who could leave his city, needed no preserve for his outings. Wilderness seemed to be everywhere. Rivers ran clear and lakes had no sewage or industrial waste. The hunter and fisherman—and the canoeist and backpacker too—could reach the promised land of wild country, no matter what point of the compass he followed.

Thoreau (1817–1862) and Emerson (1803–1882) lived near the hub of an expanding industrialism and saw the damage done by the robber barons who thought of trees only in terms of board feet. They sounded the alarms that still ring true and ominous; but there was little heed to their warnings.

The great leveling of the wilderness went forward by men with axes, by sheep over-grazing land, by cattle pounding prairies to dust. Whole townships were made desolate; hillsides were eroded; precious topsoil was swept toward the ocean; watersheds were cruelly despoiled.

By the 1870's public opinion was aroused. Congress created Yellowstone Park in 1872. The Redwoods of California were an early and easy target. But in spite of Carl Schurz's warnings and pleadings, starting in the 1870's the first measures to protect them did not come until 1890. John Muir and others continued the crusade for protection of our primitive areas against commercial exploitation. But the lobbies, then as now, were powerful; and conservation progress was slow.

STATE FORESTS

By the turn of the century we had no forestry profession. State foresters were practically unknown. Forestry as a science was in its infancy. Had we traveled the world we would have seen the managed woodlands of Europe; and we would have realized that predatory man from China to the Mediterranean had stripped the land of trees and left the earth largely bald and bare, apart from jungle areas. By the opening of this century, Gifford Pinchot and Teddy Roosevelt were taking practical measures to do something about the American problem. The Forest Service was created in 1905 with Pinchot its first Chief Forester.

While national parks and national forests were latecomers, state parks and state forests were even later. In the beginning state forestry was for the most part an educational agency and one that gave state aid to owners of forest lands. By 1909, eleven states (all in the northeast, middle west and Atlantic area) had forest preserves—New York leading with the Adirondacks and Catskills.

Today about nineteen million acres are in state forests; but they are seldom of the dimensions or character of the national forests. The Kettle-Moraine State Forest of Wisconsin is unusual in some respects—it offers inviting trails for hiking in the summer and skiing in the winter, as well as fishing. Very few of these state forests are wilderness areas, practically all of them being penetrated by roads and heavily traveled by vehicles. State forests indeed have practically no wilderness value in the cultural sense of the word. They have campsites or roadside picnic spots. They satisfy recreational needs for those who seek recreation by motor vehicles.

STATE PARKS

State parks embrace a smaller acreage than state forests; but they occupy a more important role by recreational standards than do state forests. Our state parks, indeed, perform a very critical role in meeting recreational needs. Although in size they are only one fifth of the acreage of the national parks, three times the number of people use them. The reason is two-fold: first, the state parks are close to metropolitan areas while the large national parks are distant from most large centers, being located mainly in the far west; second, the state parks, with few exceptions, are picnic areas or camp grounds where tents can be pitched or where cabins can be rented.

There are not many, certainly not more than a dozen, state parks that contain in whole or even in part primeval forests or that have been locked up against the invasion of roads. One such place is Baxter State Park in the Katahdin area of Maine. It bears the name of Percival P. Baxter, former Governor of Maine, who was the donor. Out of his own funds he acquired nearly 200,000 acres and presented them to the State of Maine on condition that they "shall forever be left in the natural wild state." No roads are allowed; the park is a sanctuary for animals and birds. Baxter State Park includes not only Mt. Katahdin but at least thirty other peaks and several dozens of lakes. This was land that the lumbermen mutilated. Yet the area has great recuperative powers. While the glories of ancient forests have gone, the hardwoods have come back. The climax forests will in time return. Several hundred years from now American youngsters, who walk those forests, will feel the ecstasy of Americans who saw the majestic primeval stands of New England at the time of our revolution.

A few state parks have alcoves that cars cannot reach, where a few hours of quiet and solitude can be found. Occasionally a state park advertises a wilderness area that is made by blocking off all existing roads to vehicular traffic. These projects are not many in number or great in acreage.

State parks cater primarily to the motorists. Those who have a summer day to spend and those who want to drive to an overnight camp can either put up their own tent or rent a public facility. Those parks often have tramways and other facilities customary in amusement parks. As Richard Lieber, famous in Indiana's park system, wrote in 1939, "today there is an ill-starred tendency to scramble all recreational eggs and call the result a state park." Like city parks and county parks, state parks are a far cry from the wilderness. Yet they serve an important function in a society that wants to preserve wilderness values. The reason is obvious: the more state parks are multiplied the less the pressure will be on wilderness areas.

STATE PARKWAYS

The idea of state parks has spread to state parkways. Two great parkways in the National Park System have been a contagious example—the Blue Ridge Parkway that connects the Shenandoah with the Great Smokies and the Natchez Trace Parkway that extends from Nashville, Tennessee, to Natchez, Mississippi. These federal arteries have essential facilities for picnic and campgrounds, trails that lead to wilderness bowls or ravines, trails that follow ridges looking down into deep valleys. The states have similar parkways. New York has vast parkways throughout its length. New Jersey also has some. So have Virginia and Connecticut. All of these, like the great federal parkways, are recreational in a sense, because they provide landscape arteries, picnic grounds, and scenic views. But one who uses them rarely escapes the roaring cars that seem to be the fate of all woodlands.

Yet by modern standards these parkways perform an important recreational function. By modern definition, recreation is being in the outdoors. That is, indeed, the way the Rockefeller Commission defines it and that is the popular concept. If demand for recreation is measured by the number of days per year devoted to a particular activity, driving for pleasure heads the list. Walking for pleasure—which of course includes strolling in the city park—is second. If days of sightseeing are added to driving for pleasure a total of 26.64 days per year per person of recreation by automobile are obtained. That is a conservative figure, for recreation by automobile is hidden in almost every category of the recreational list in the Rockefeller Report. The automobile brings even the hunter and fisherman to the places where they hunt or fish. Roads extend so far these days that they often do not stop until they reach the very edge of a wilderness area.

RECREATION PARTICIPATION INCREASING

By the year 2000 A.D. the nation's population is expected to double over what it was in 1960; and the Rockefeller Report shows that by that time participation in outdoor recreation will nearly triple. By 1976 passenger cars will have increased to one hundred million, which is an 80 per cent increase over 1959; by the year 2000 A.D. they will have increased another 80 per cent. This means that motor vehicle pressure on all outdoor recreational areas will vastly increase. More cars will demand more roads. More roads will threaten the very existence of the few pockets of wilderness area left. So it is that lovers of wilderness, as well as state and county planners, must get busy and use their imagination for the building and construction of ten times—yes, twenty times—the amount of recreational facilities presently provided by the states and counties. Only in that way can the appetite of the majority of the people for areas that are reachable by car and the appetite of the minority of the people for wilderness sanctuaries be satisfied. We must start looking for sites where no one ever dreamed of creating a park. The natural sites for city, county, or state parks are mostly all gone. Many stretches of wasteland, however, can be reclaimed. Let me give you a few examples of what has been done.

One is the Umstead State Park in the Piedmont area of North Carolina. It has reclaimed land that was once rich but finally lost to cultivation by crop production, poor farming methods, and deforestation. It is now set aside and locked up against commercial use and it is truly flourishing as a bit of wilderness sanctuary.

Dead Horse Point in Utah is a headland which offers a panoramic spectacle and was ordained to be a park whether or not it had commercial value.

I can think of at least one lookout point—now a garbage dump—that in time will be destined for conversion into a park.

Golden Gate Park in San Francisco was created out of sand dunes and a noisome marshland.

Crowley's Ridge State Park in Eastern Arkansas served 450,000 people last year. Not many years ago it was heavily eroded with deep banks and gullies and entirely unfit for any type of agriculture or for commercial reforestation. It is now a beautiful park.

Many of Mississippi's fifteen state parks were created from depleted cut-over lands. The Corps of Engineers, as part of its flood control work, erected four large reservoirs in North Mississippi on lands that were badly eroded and consisted mostly of unsightly washed-out gullies. On three of these, Mississippi has created parks that are now major areas of beauty and recreational use.

24,710 LOCAL PARKS

Of the 24,710 local parks there are 951 having bathing beaches. These can be greatly expanded by the conversion of polluted beaches to usable ones. At least twenty miles of lake front at Cleveland, Ohio, can be reclaimed and made into healthy beaches—places where no one dares swim today.

Stretches in Virginia and Maryland along the Potomac could be converted into swimming holes for young and old—if the sewage that now pollutes it were adequately treated. The same can be said for dozens of other rivers across our broad land.

Minnesota, that has over three million visitors a year to its state parks, half of them being out-of-state—has made parks out of wastelands. Many state parks were created out of logged-off and burnt-over land, Itasca State Park's 32,000 acres and Gooseberry Falls being typical. In southeast Minnesota, some state parks, of which Beaver Creek Valley is representative, were created on lands largely unused because of the frequency of flash floods. As a result of soil conservation practices on farmed hilltops, flooding was greatly reduced and attractive parks came into being.

A park can be made almost anywhere. In areas of substantial rainfall the recuperative powers of nature are great, once the soil is stabilized. New growth comes quickly and soon the original glories of the area reappear. It is the recreation of those sylvan wonders that qualifies a piece of ground for a park.

Conrad Wirth, until recently Director of the National Park System, wrote (*National Geographic,* November 1963) that while state parks originally were conceptions of naturalists, they have become more and more places to play, ". . . gymnasium and athletic fields for the young; the checkerboard painted on the table and the bowling green for the old; the square-dancing classes, the ceramics and hobby shops for everybody." At Jones Beach State Park in New York there are not only handball courts, deck tennis, roller skating, shuffleboard, archery, miniature golf courses, softball diamonds, picnic grounds, fishing dock, two miles of boardwalk, and an outdoor dancing pavilion, but also diaper-changing rooms with electric bottle warmers and kindergartens. And the people love these facilities.

CONSERVATION PARKS NEEDED

We need, however, another kind of park at the local level—a conservation park, if you please.

A conservation park is not a playground. It is not an amusement center. The Disneyland approach is at war with the idea of conservation parks. Those who want to play tennis or basketball or practice on bars need a gymnasium or a stadium. Those who want to play Bingo or cards need a room. Those who want music need an auditorium. Those who hanker for a merry-go-round or slot machines need an amusement center. The conservation park (as Olmsted maintained in his long struggle to keep New York City's Central Park free of commercial interests) should return man to the environment from which he came. Central Park, in Olmsted's words, was designed "to supply to the hundreds of thousands of tired workers, who have no opportunity to spend their summers in the country, a specimen of God's handiwork that shall be to them, inexpensively, what a month or two in the White Mountains or the Adirondacks is, at great cost, to those in easier circumstances."

He pointed up how its value as a bit of woodland would increase over the years: "The time will come when New York will be built up, when all the grading and filling will be done, and when the picturesquely varied, rocky formations of the island will have been converted into formations for rows of monotonous straight streets, and piles of erect buildings."

A conservation park, as distinguished from the ordinary city, state, or county park, gives man an introduction to the quiet order of nature.

Richard Lieber wrote in 1939:

> State parks are meant to be the show windows of a state, but more than that, state parks are a dedication to the soul of the land. . . . It is the land on which we all depend in the last essence. It is the land and the very soil, the trees and waters, the dales and glens which we love. Without vision a land will die. Without inspiration we remain disconnected from the immortal order of all things.

Even with that concept as the standard, a conservation park is heavily pounded and often nearly ruined as a sanctuary.

AVOID CONVERSION INTO AMUSEMENT CENTERS

The battle to keep a conservation park from being an amusement center has not always succeeded. Olmsted described his experience with Central Park.

> During the last twenty years Europe has been swept by a mania for sacrificing natural scenery to coarse manufactures of brilliant and gaudy decoration under the name of specimen gardening; bedding, carpet, embroidery, and ribbon gardening, or other terms suitable to the house-furnishing and millinery trades. . . .
> It ran into all park management, the only limit often being that fixed by annual appropriations. Long ago, for example, it seized Hyde Park, and put completely out of countenance the single charm of broad homely sylvan and pastoral simplicity which the fogs and smoke of London, and its weary miles of iron hurdles, had left to it. Why? I asked the old superintendent. "Well, you know the fashion must have its run, and it just tickles the nursery maids."

If there is to be camping in a park, pure water supplies are necessary. Pressure of population often makes toilet facilities necessary. A shed where firewood can be purchased may at times be needed if camping is authorized. In that event campsites, each with an outdoor fireplace and an area for car parking, will frequently be demanded. In other words, if an area is open to camping, the volume of visitors will often threaten to transform a sanctuary into a thoroughfare. A sanctuary can be destroyed that way as easily as by industrial cruelty.

CAREFUL PLANNING NECESSARY

So careful planning with long-range interests in mind is necessary. A small tract like Glover-Archbold in the District of Columbia (186 acres) can tolerate no structure and no improvement beyond a trail.

Bartholomew's Cobble—a few hundred acres near Lenox, Massachusetts—has beauty and charm because of the absence of structures; outcroppings of limestone above the purling Housatonic make it a bit of heaven on earth.

Green Oaks—a 600-acre tract near Galesburg, Illinois—is owned by Knox College and is under the management of its biology department. Ugly scars of strip mining have partially healed; ponds that followed the mining have filled and been planted with fish; the primeval prairie grasses of Illinois that once stood six feet high are coming back.

The Dierson Refuge in Maryland is so small that a silver dollar could be thrown across it. Yet it is a place of quiet wonder and mystery where wildlife is abundant.

The Pleasant Valley Sanctuary in Western Massachusetts is a mile square and more pretentious. But it too, has swamps disturbed by nothing but trails, woodlands removed from the roar of traffic, and glades and ridges where all of nature's diversity unfolds.

Haverford College has an untamed corner of its campus dedicated to wildness.

Near Pittsfield, Massachusetts, are ponds where city folks, having an hour for lunch, can spend half of it in quiet repose under an elm or in a stand of white birch.

The examples could be multiplied. I use them on this occasion to illustrate the kind of areas that counties and cities should set aside and protect.

SERVE LOCAL NEEDS

State parks, like national parks and national forests, are being pulled more and more into the vortex of tourism. County parks can aim at local needs and cater to them.

County planners are usually engineers and architects. But when the county moves to find or to create as sanctuaries nearby wooded alcoves or swamp areas or meadowland, the biologist, botanist, agronomist, and ornithologist need to have a voice in the original planning and in the long-range management as well. For the areas of which I speak have their full attraction in the flora and fauna found there, in the music of the wind in the treetops, in the orchestration of birds, in the magic wrought by the wands of sunrise and sunset.

An unmolested pond may be worth more to the high school class in biology than any number of textbooks.

Bird calls can be learned by children five years old. A sanctuary of the kind I describe can be highly useful to parents and teachers alike who are interested in unlocking the mysteries of life to children when they are small.

Classes in botany can make a woodland meadow a laboratory. Some sanctuaries, like Bartholomew's Cobble will be a geologist's classroom.

TIE-IN WITH EDUCATIONAL SYSTEM

In other words, the county park which I envision should be a useful adjunct to the county's educational system.

But it will serve adults as well. The healing effects of wilderness are well known. Cares slough off; the conscious and unconscious springs that create tension are relaxed; man comes to an understanding of his relation to the earth from which he came and to which he returns. The idea has been variously put.

Richard Lieber stated: "Converse with nature restores happiness; communion with its mysterious forces, Antaeus-like, fills us with renewed strength and rids us of fear. It is the land and all it contains which performs the miracle."

Wordsworth, Thoreau, Muir, Leopold, Murie—each experienced the healing effects of the wildness of nature, and together they constitute an illustrious list of witnesses in its favor.

The beneficiaries of a nearby sanctuary will be all those who yearn for an occasional retreat—old folks, working men, clerks, housewives, teachers, everyone who needs respite from tensions or from the humdrum of a job. Those who come to scoff will in time walk this place with reverence.

This county park program will not concern itself with amusement devices—or soft drinks—or hostels—or playgrounds. This county park program will try to provide sylvan areas for man's solace and repose.

CALL FOR LOCAL LEADERSHIP

The other day, near dusk, I came by taxi from La Guardia Airport in New York via the Triboro Bridge to Manhattan. Lights were going on in the vast expanse of modern apartments now filling the area near the western abutments of the bridge. Thousands upon thousands of children live there. Yet there are no thickets, no woodlands, no meadows in which to play—only a patch of grass, a few scraggly trees growing in concrete, and an occasional pigeon. "What opportunities will they ever have," I asked my wife, "to learn the mysteries of the earth of which they are a part?"

What a tragedy, I thought, that Jones' Woods along the East River were abandoned to industrialism a century ago.

We cannot live by industrialism alone. By spiritual standards, jam-packed

[261]

cities soon become uninhabitable. What is true of our metropolitan areas will be increasingly true even of many county seats by the time 2000 A.D. arrives.

Now is the time to make park plans that will keep us ahead of the population pressure. Now is the time to promote the conservation type park and to introduce it at the local level. We create refuges for birds, for deer, for antelope. Man, too, needs one. The noisy, smoky city where asphalt has supplanted grass, and concrete has taken the place of woods and thickets, is suffocating. Every city dweller needs a refuge where he can periodically find repose and resume his elemental relation with the earth. Man has wholeness only when he has an understanding relation with the universe.

A NATIONAL POLICY FOR COUNTY PARKS AND RECREATION*
1964

For some years the National Association of Counties has devoted increasing attention to outdoor recreation in general and to county parks in particular. In August 1964, the Board of Directors of the organization adopted a formal policy statement on county parks and recreation. The draft copy of this statement had previously been sent to some 25,000 county officials for review and comment.

PREAMBLE

A major goal of civilized societies everywhere has historically been leisure— the progressive diminishment of the effort required to provide the necessities of human physical and economic survival. In the 20th century, we are approaching the attainment of this goal. It is the purpose of the National Policy for County Parks and Recreation to suggest some guidelines by which county governments in the United States may contribute toward effective utilization of leisure by participating in the provision of a balanced program of public parks and recreation.

Such a balanced program will involve every level of government, as well as the private sector, and will serve every segment of society. Our youth will be helped to develop physically, mentally and spiritually, and youth problems may be lessened. Our young and middle-aged adults will have an outlet from the tensions of a competitive and industrialized urban environment, and a chance to express their individuality and creativity. Our senior citizens will find meaning and purpose in their retirement years.

THE ROLE OF THE COUNTY

The special role of the county is to acquire, develop and maintain parks and to administer public recreation programs that will serve the needs of communities broader than the local neighborhood or municipality, but less than state-wide or national in scope.

In addition, the county should plan and coordinate local neighborhood and community facilities with the cooperation of the cities, townships, and other intra-county units, and should itself cooperate in state and federal planning and coordinative activities.

Where there is no existing unit of local government except the county to provide needed local neighborhood or municipal facilities and programs, the county should provide such facilites and programs, utilizing county service districts,

*Trends in Parks and Recreation, Vol. 3, No. 2 (Apr., 1966), 31–32.

local assessments and other methods by which those benefitted will pay the cost. Coordination with local boards of education should include the park-school concept of building park sites adjacent to schools.

Internal Organization—Counties have an obligation to create organizational structures for meeting their park and recreation responsibilities.

Internally, such organizational structures should fix responsibility for the county park and recreation program clearly with the elected county governing body.

Counties are urged to employ a Parks and Recreation Director and staff qualified by education and experience to administer, implement, manage and assist in planning the park and recreation program. In addition, they should fully utilize the wide range of technical services that are available through various state and federal departments and the several national park, recreation and conservation organizations.

County park and recreation responsibilities involve several facets of county government. Other county departments should be kept fully informed and requested to cooperate in the development of these programs, and share mutual responsibilities and interests.

External Organization—Park and recreation facilities and programs serving a community larger than an individual county, but of less than a state-wide scope, should be administered jointly through cooperative arrangements between two or more counties. In the event that creation of a new unit of government is necessary to attain an effective and economically feasible solution of regional park and recreation problems, the final responsibility for its administration should be vested in the elected county governing bodies involved.

Financing County Programs—County park and recreation programs should be financed principally through general taxation. This may be supplemented by such sources as general obligation and revenue bonding, donations of money, land and services from private individuals and groups, and user fees.

County government strongly supports the concept that users of certain kinds of public park and recreation facilities and programs should pay fees for such use. Revenue from this source should be applied toward the acquisition, development, maintenance and administration of parks and recreation programs. Fees should be regulated so as to insure that persons with modest incomes will not be denied the privilege and benefits of public park and recreation programs or facilities.

Planning Responsibility—Parks and recreation should be an integral element of all county land use planning and zoning. Such planning and zoning should embrace not only areas to be acquired for the county park or recreation system, but maximum use should also be made of zoning and other regulatory powers to preserve open space, protect scenic values and otherwise enhance recreational opportunities in private developments.

Counties should jealously protect existing park and recreation areas against both public and private encroachment, and should yield such areas for other purposes only upon the condition that areas lost are replaced by others of comparable value which serve the same population.

THE COUNTY AND OTHER LOCAL GOVERNMENTS

Counties should encourage, through planning, consultation and other services, the providing of adequate local neighborhood and community facilities and programs by municipalities, townships and other intra-county units of government. Municipal governments should be encouraged to step up their efforts to secure open space and recreation areas, particularly in and around urban centers.

Municipal, township and other intra-county units should coordinate their programs with existing county plans. Their requests for technical and financial assistance should be made first to their county governments. If the county is unable to provide such assistance, it should forward the request to the appropriate state agency and should support the local unit in its request. All such requests should be restricted to those instances in which the county lacks the resources to provide the requested services on its own behalf.

Counties should also, where appropriate, enter into inter-governmental contracts or agreements with municipalities, townships and other intra-county units for the joint use of personnel and for joint administration of park and recreation facilities and programs.

THE COUNTY AND STATE GOVERNMENTS

Every state should acquire, develop, maintain and administer park and recreation facilities and programs which provide values for the benefit of the entire state. In addition, every state should authorize appropriate enabling legislation so that counties and other local governments will have full authority to provide a balanced program of park and recreation services and to finance it adequately. The states should also provide technical assistance to local governments in their park and recreation endeavors and, where possible, financial incentives to assist them in accelerating their park and recreation programs.

The states should consult formally with the local governments involved, from the inception of their planning process, before deciding to acquire or withdraw lands from tax rolls for state park and recreation programs.

Where state or federal recreation or park areas are being used primarily by residents of a single county, the state and federal governments should give consideration to offering such areas to the county government for operation.

THE COUNTY AND THE FEDERAL GOVERNMENT

The excellent Report to the President and to the Congress in January, 1962, entitled "Outdoor Recreation for America," by the Outdoor Recreation Resource Review Commission, is strongly recommended as a source of information of lasting usefulness. County government endorses the basic recommendation of this bi-partisan group that the primary responsibility for adequately meeting the nation's recreation and park demands lies with "private enterprise, the states, and local government" and that the role of the Federal government should not be one of domination, but of cooperation and assistance in meeting the nation's park and recreation challenge.

The Federal government should acquire, develop and maintain park and recreation areas which have scenic, scientific, historic or special recreation values of significance to the entire nation. Federal agencies responsible for multiple-use management of federal lands should integrate recreation land use, wherever feasible, with other federal land uses. In all federal land use planning for management, withdrawal or disposal of federally-designated recreation areas and general multiple-use lands, county governments should be consulted and invited to participate from the earliest stages of investigation.

In the disposition of federal surplus land, including military reservations or bases, the states and local governments should be given a preference if they are able and willing to accept and manage such lands for public park and recreation purposes. In such cases, the Federal government should transfer these lands to the state or local agencies for a nominal consideration. Acquisition of surplus federal land by states and local governments for park and recreation purposes should be in accordance with long range plans and with the ability of the states or local units to finance the maintenance and administration of the facilities and program.

County government supports a program of federal grants-in-aid to states and local governments for planning, acquiring and developing park and recreation facilities, along the lines recommended by the Outdoor Recreation Resources Review Commission. Federal laws should require that the county governments involved be formally consulted before federal grant funds are used by federal agencies or states to acquire park and recreation areas.

THE COUNTY AND THE PRIVATE SECTOR

Some two-thirds of the nation's land is privately owned. Collectively, these lands have an enormous potential for park and recreation development, at private expense, which has been only partially realized. Counties should seek opportunities to stimulate such development. County cooperation should include the provision of access roads, where feasible and traffic volume will justify, to permit the park and recreation development of private lands.

Counties should support state legislation exempting private owners of land from tort liability where lands are opened for general public recreational use without charge to the public.

Counties should encourage their agricultural extension agents to provide advice and demonstrations of the recreational development of private lands for profit.

Public agencies should acquire conservation easements over private lands, where feasible, to preserve open spaces in and around urban areas.

Counties should cooperate with and support in every way possible the efforts of private businesses and of charitable, service and civic organizations to acquire and appropriately manage recreation and park sites which serve public needs.

THE LAND AND WATER CONSERVATION FUND ACT*
September 3, 1964

The most important step toward the acquisition and development of state parks was the passage of the Land and Water Conservation Fund Act. The Fund was to be obtained from sales of a windshield sticker, "the golden eagle," motorboat fuel taxes, and surplus property sales. A substantial part (normally about 60 percent) of the Fund could be used to match state expenditures for planning, acquisition, and development of state parks and other outdoor recreation areas.

This act will be considered in more detail in the chapter on ORRRC and BOR but the section of the act dealing with financial assistance to the states is reproduced below. The total amount apportioned to the states from January 1, 1965 to February 1, 1967 was $144,782,407.

FINANCIAL ASSISTANCE TO STATES

SEC. 5. GENERAL AUTHORITY; PURPOSES. — (a) The Secretary of the Interior (hereinafter referred to as the "Secretary") is authorized to provide financial assistance to the States from moneys available for State purposes. Payments may be made to the States by the Secretary as hereafter provided, subject to such terms and conditions as he considers appropriate and in the public interest to carry out the purposes of this Act, for outdoor recreation: (1) planning, (2) acquisition of land, waters, or interests in land or waters, or (3) development.

(b) APPORTIONMENT AMONG STATES; NOTIFICATION. — Sums appropriated and available for State purposes for each fiscal year shall be apportioned among the several States by the Secretary, whose determination shall be final, in accordance with the following formula:

(1) two-fifths shall be apportioned equally among the several States; and

(2) three-fifths shall be apportioned on the basis of need to individual States by the Secretary in such amounts as in his judgment will best accomplish the purposes of this Act. The determination of need shall include among other things a consideration of the proportion which the population of each State bears to the total population of the United States and of the use of outdoor recreation resources of individual States by persons from outside the State as well as a consideration of the Federal resources and programs in the particular States.

The total allocation to an individual State under paragraphs (1) and (2) of this subsection shall not exceed 7 per centum of the total amount allocated to the several States in any one year.

The Secretary shall notify each State of its apportionments; and the amounts thereof shall be available thereafter for payment to such State for planning, acquisition, or development projects as hereafter prescribed. Any amount of any

*78 *Statutes at Large,* 900.

apportionment that has not been paid or obligated by the Secretary during the fiscal year in which such notification is given and for two fiscal years thereafter shall be reapportioned by the Secretary in accordance with paragraph (2) of this subsection.

The District of Columbia, Puerto Rico, the Virgin Islands, Guam, and American Samoa shall be treated as States for the purposes of this title, except for the purpose of paragraph (1) of this subsection. Their population also shall be included as a part of the total population in computing the apportionment under paragraph (2) of this subsection.

(c) MATCHING REQUIREMENTS.—Payments to any State shall cover not more than 50 per centum of the cost of planning, acquisition, or development projects that are undertaken by the State. The remaining share of the cost shall be borne by the State in a manner and with such funds or services as shall be satisfactory to the Secretary. No payment may be made to any State for or on account of any cost or obligation incurred or any service rendered prior to the date of approval of this Act.

(d) COMPREHENSIVE STATE PLAN REQUIRED; PLANNING PROJECTS.—A comprehensive statewide outdoor recreation plan shall be required prior to the consideration by the Secretary of financial assistance for acquisition or development projects. The plan shall be adequate if, in the judgment of the Secretary, it encompasses and will promote the purposes of this Act. The plan shall contain—

(1) the name of the State agency that will have authority to represent and act for the State in dealing with the Secretary for purposes of this Act;

(2) an evaluation of the demand for and supply of outdoor recreation resources and facilities in the State;

(3) a program for the implementation of the plan; and

(4) other necessary information, as may be determined by the Secretary. The plan shall take into account relevant Federal resources and programs and shall be correlated so far as practicable with other State, regional, and local plans. Where there exists or is in preparation for any particular State a comprehensive plan financed in part with funds supplied by the Housing and Home Finance Agency, any statewide outdoor recreation plan prepared for purposes of this Act shall be based upon the same population, growth, and other pertinent factors as are used in formulating the Housing and Home Finance Agency financed plans.

The Secretary may provide financial assistance to any State for projects for the preparation of a comprehensive statewide outdoor recreation plan when such plan is not otherwise available or for the maintenance of such plan.

(e) PROJECTS FOR LAND AND WATER ACQUISITION; DEVELOPMENT.—In addition to assistance for planning projects, the Secretary may provide financial assistance to any State for the following types of projects or combinations thereof if they are in accordance with the State comprehensive plan:

(1) ACQUISITION OF LAND AND WATERS.—For the acquisition of land, waters, or interests in land or waters (other than land, waters, or interests in land or waters acquired from the United States for less than fair market value), but not including incidental costs relating to acquisition.

(2) DEVELOPMENT.—For development, including but not limited to site planning and the development of Federal lands under lease to States for terms of twenty-five years or more.

(f) REQUIREMENTS FOR PROJECT APPROVAL; CONDITION.—Payments may be made to States by the Secretary only for those planning, acquisition, or development projects that are approved by him. No payment may be made by the Secretary for or on account of any project with respect to which financial assistance has been given or promised under any other Federal program or activity, and no financial assistance may be given under any other Federal program or activity for or on account of any project with respect to which such assistance has been given or promised under this Act. The Secretary may make payments from time to time in keeping with the rate of progress toward the satisfactory completion of individual projects: *Provided,* That the approval of all projects and all payments, or any commitments relating thereto, shall be withheld until the Secretary receives appropriate written assurance from the State that the State has the ability and intention to finance its share of the cost of the particular project, and to operate and maintain by acceptable standards, at State expense, the particular properties or facilities acquired or developed for public outdoor recreation use.

Payments for all projects shall be made by the Secretary to the Governor of the State or to a State official or agency designated by the Governor or by State law having authority and responsibility to accept and to administer funds paid hereunder for approved projects. If consistent with an approved project, funds may be transferred by the State to a political subdivision or other appropriate public agency.

No property acquired or developed with assistance under this section shall, without the approval of the Secretary, be converted to other than public outdoor recreation uses. The Secretary shall approve such conversion only if he finds it to be in accord with the then existing comprehensive statewide outdoor recreation plan and only upon such conditions as he deems necessary to assure the substitution of other recreation properties of at least equal fair market value and of reasonably equivalent usefulness and location.

No payment shall be made to any State until the State has agreed to (1) provide such reports to the Secretary, in such form and containing such information, as may be reasonably necessary to enable the Secretary to perform his duties under this Act, and (2) provide such fiscal control and fund accounting procedures as may be necessary to assure proper disbursement and accounting for Federal funds paid to the State under this Act.

Each recipient of assistance under this Act shall keep such records as the Secretary of the Interior shall prescribe, including records which fully disclose the amount and the disposition by such recipient of the proceeds of such assistance, the total cost of the project or undertaking in connection with which such assistance is given or used, and the amount and nature of that portion of the cost of the project or undertaking supplied by other sources, and such other records as will facilitate an effective audit.

The Secretary of the Interior, and the Comptroller General of the United States, or any of their duly authorized representatives, shall have access for the purpose of audit and examination to any books, documents, papers, and records of the recipient that are pertinent to assistance received under this Act.

(g) COORDINATION WITH FEDERAL AGENCIES.—In order to assure consistency in policies and actions under this Act, with other related Federal programs and activities (including those conducted pursuant to title VII of the Housing Act of 1961 and section 701 of the Housing Act of 1954) and to assure coordination of the planning, acquisition, and development assistance to States under this section with other related Federal programs and activities, the President may issue such regulations with respect thereto as he deems desirable and such assistance may be provided only in accordance with such regulations.

THE INDIANA NATURE PRESERVES ACT*
1967

Many state parks have as one of their objectives the preservation of unique, natural, or wild areas. The State of Indiana has gone farther, however, in providing for a system of "nature preserves."

An Act creating a division of nature preserves establishing a state system of nature preserves providing for their acquisition, control, use, management, and protection, and making an appropriation.

Be it enacted by the General Assembly of the State of Indiana:

SECTION 1. As part of the continuing growth of the population and the development of the economy of the State of Indiana it is necessary and desirable that areas of unusual natural significance be set aside and preserved for the benefit of present and future generations before they have been destroyed; for once destroyed they cannot be wholly restored. Such areas are irreplaceable as laboratories for scientific research, as reservoirs of natural materials not all of the uses of which are now known, as habitats for plant and animal species and biotic communities whose diversity enriches the meaning and enjoyment of human life, as living museums where people may observe natural biotic and environmental systems of the earth and the interdependence of all forms of life, and as reminders of the vital dependence of the health of the human community upon the health of the natural communities of which it is an inseparable part. It is essential to the people of the State of Indiana that they retain the opportunities to maintain close contact with such living communities and environmental systems of the earth and to benefit from the scientific, esthetic, cultural and spiritual values they possess. It is therefore the public policy of the State of Indiana that a registry of such areas be established and maintained by the department, that such areas be acquired and preserved by the state and that other agencies, organizations, and individuals, both public and private, be encouraged to set aside such areas for the common benefit of the people of present and future generations.

SEC. 2. As used in this act: (a) The word "area" means an area of land or water or of both land and water, whether in public or private ownership, which either retains or has reestablished its natural character (although it need not be undisturbed) or has unusual flora or fauna or has biotic, geological, scenic or paleontological features of scientific or educational value.

(b) The term "nature preserve" means an area, any estate, interest or right in which has been formally dedicated under the provisions of this act.

Vol. 11, Pt. 1, Burn's Annotated Indiana Statutes, 1968 Supplement, 68–73.

(c) The words "dedicate" and "dedication" mean the transfer to the department, for and on behalf of the State of Indiana, of an estate, interest or right in an area in any manner permitted by section 6 of this act.

(d) The term "articles of dedication" means the writing by which any estate, interest or right in an area is formally dedicated as permitted by section 7 of this act.

(e) The word "system" means the nature preserves held under the provisions of this act.

(f) The word "division" means the division of nature preserves created by this act.

(g) The word "department" means the department of natural resources.

(h) The word "commission" means the natural resources commission.

Sec. 3. In order to secure for the people of the State of Indiana of present and future generations the benefits of an enduring resource of areas having one or more of the characteristics referred to in subsection 2 (a) of this act, the State of Indiana, acting through the department, shall acquire and hold in trust for the benefit of the people an adequate system of nature preserves for the following uses and purposes:

(a) For scientific research in such fields as ecology, taxonomy, genetics, forestry, pharmacology, agriculture, soil science, geology, paleontology, conservation and similar fields;

(b) For the teaching of biology, natural history, ecology, geology, conservation and other subjects;

(c) As habitats for plant and animal species and communities and other natural objects;

(d) As reservoirs of natural materials;

(e) As places of natural interest and beauty;

(f) As living illustrations of our natural heritage wherein one may observe and experience natural biotic and environmental systems of the earth and their processes;

(g) To promote understanding and appreciation of the esthetic, cultural, scientific and spiritual values of such areas by the people of the State of Indiana;

(h) For the preservation and protection of nature preserves against modification or encroachment resulting from occupation, development or other use which would destroy their natural or esthetic conditions.

In order to give recognition to natural areas, the Department shall establish and maintain a registry of natural areas of unusual significance, but no area so registered shall be a nature preserve unless and until it shall have been dedicated as provided for in Section 6 of this Act.

Sec. 4. There is hereby created within the Department a Division of Nature Preserves, which shall administer for the Department the provisions of this Act.

Sec. 5. In furtherance of the purposes of this act, the president of the Indiana

Academy of Science is hereby made an ex-officio member of the commission in place of one of the lay members of that commission whose term expires June 30, 1967.

SEC. 6. The department is authorized and empowered, for and on behalf of the State of Indiana, to acquire nature preserves by gift, devise, purchase, exchange, condemnation or any other method of acquiring real property or any estate, interest or right therein provided that any interest owned by the state or by any subdivision thereof may be dedicated only by voluntary act of the agency having jurisdiction thereof. The department may acquire the fee simple interest in an area of any one or more lesser estates, interests and rights therein, including (without limitation upon the generality of the foregoing by reason of specification) a leasehold estate, an easement either appurtenant or in gross and either granting the state specified rights of use or denying to the grantor specified rights of use or both, a license, a covenant and other contractual rights. A nature preserve may be acquired voluntarily for such consideration as the department deems advisable or without consideration.

An estate, interest or right in an area may be dedicated by any state agency having jurisdiction thereof, by any other unit of government within the state having jurisdiction thereof, and by any private owner thereof. A dedication shall be deemed effective, and an area shall become a nature preserve, only upon the acceptance of the articles of dedication by the department. Articles of dedication shall be placed on public record in the proper record in the county or counties in which the area is located.

With the approval of the governor and upon such terms and conditions as the department may determine, the department may, after the giving of notice and the holding of a public hearing as provided in section 9 of this act, enter into amendments of any articles of dedication upon a finding by the commission that such amendments will not permit an impairment, disturbance, use or development of the area inconsistent with the purposes of this act: Provided, however, that if the fee simple interest in the area is not held by the State of Indiana under this act, no amendment shall be made without the written consent of the owner or owners of the other interests therein.

SEC. 7. In furtherance of the purposes of this act and in implementation of the powers and duties elsewhere provided in this act, the department shall have the following additional powers and duties:

(a) To formulate policies for the selection, acquisition, use, management, and protection of nature preserves.

(b) To formulate policies for the selection of areas suitable for registration under the provisions of this Act.

(c) To formulate policies for the dedication of areas as nature preserves.

(d) To determine, supervise and control the management of nature preserves and to make, publish, and amend from time to time rules and regulations necessary or advisable for the use and protection of nature preserves.

(e) To encourage and recommend the dedication of areas as nature preserves.

(f) To make surveys and maintain registeries and records of unique natural areas within the state.

(g) To carry on interpretive programs and publish and disseminate information pertaining to nature preserves and other areas within the state.

(h) To promote and assist in the establishment, restoration and protection of, and advise in the management of, natural areas and other areas of educational or scientific value and otherwise to foster and aid in the establishment, restoration and preservation of natural conditions within the state elsewhere than in the system.

SEC. 8. The nature preserves within the system are hereby declared to be held in trust, for those uses and purposes expressed in this act which are not prohibited by the articles of dedication, for the benefit of the people of the State of Indiana of present and future generations and declared to be put to their highest, best, and most important use for the public benefit. They shall be managed and protected in the manner approved by, and subject to the rules and regulations established by, the department. They shall not be taken for any other use except another public use after a finding by the commission of the existence of an imperative and unavoidable public necessity for such other public use and with the approval of the governor. Except as may otherwise be provided in the articles of dedication, the department may grant, upon such terms and conditions as it may determine, an estate, interest or right in, or dispose of a nature preserve, but only after a finding by the commission of the existence of an imperative and unavoidable public necessity for such grant or disposition and with the approval of the governor.

SEC. 9. Before the commission shall make any finding of the existence of an imperative and unavoidable public necessity, or shall grant any estate, interest or right in a nature preserve or dispose of a nature preserve or of any estate, interest or right therein as provided in section 8 of this act, or shall enter into any amendment of any articles of dedication as provided in section 6 of this act, it shall give notice of such proposed action and an opportunity for any person to be heard. Such notice shall be published at least once in a newspaper printed in the English language with a general circulation in the county or counties wherein the nature preserve is located. The notice shall set forth the substance of the proposed action and describe, with or without legal description, the nature preserve affected, and shall specify a place and time not less than thirty (30) days after such publication for a public hearing before the commission on such proposed action. All persons desiring to be heard shall have a reasonable opportunity to be heard prior to action by the commission on such proposal.

Sec. 10. All units, departments, agencies, and instrumentalities of the state, including (without limitation upon the generality of the foregoing by reason of specification) counties, townships, municipalities, public corporation, boards, commissions, colleges and universities, are empowered and urged to dedicate as nature preserves suitable areas or portions of areas within their jurisdiction.

Sec. 11. Nothing contained in this act shall be construed as interfering with the purposes stated in the establishment of or pertaining to any state or local park, preserve, wildlife refuge or other area or the proper management and development thereof, except that any agency administering an area dedicated as a nature preserve under the provisions of this act shall be responsible for preserving the character of the area in accordance with the articles of dedication and the applicable rules and regulations with respect thereto established by the department from time to time. Neither the dedication of an area as a nature preserve nor any action taken by the department under any of the provisions of this act shall void or replace any protective status under law which the area would have were it not a nature preserve and the protective provisions of this act shall be supplemental thereto.

Sec. 12. If any provision of this act or the application thereof to any circumstance is held invalid, such invalidity shall not affect other provisions or applications of this act which can be given effect without the invalid provision or application, and to this end the provisions of this act are declared to be severable.

Sec. 13. The sum of $30,000 is hereby appropriated from the General Fund to the Department for the purposes of this Act.

Sec. 14. All laws and parts of laws in conflict herewith insofar as such conflicts exist, are hereby repealed.

Sec. 15. Whereas an emergency exists for the immediate taking effect of this act, the same shall be in full force and effect on its passage.

"THE PARKS IN YOUR BACKYARD"*
1963

In this chapter we have documented the development of state parks but we have not given any attention to what these parks are really like. In the article that follows, Conrad Wirth, director of the National Park Service when he wrote this in 1963, describes many state (and some local) parks and includes brief glimpses of their history.

Would you like to share a sack of marshmallows with wild alligators, swim with barracudas, hobnob with a gorilla? Would your children care to pet a tapir, or perhaps a guanaco?

Maybe you'd rather eat buffalo steaks on a cookout under the stars or watch Choctaw Indians play stickball. Possibly you like great symphony orchestras, Shakespearean theater, or masterpieces of painting; or maybe you go in for square dancing, lawn bowling, sailboat racing, or studying sea otters.

You can find every one of these things, plus swimming, fishing, riding, golf and baseball, skiing, picnicking, hunting, camping, nature trails—hundreds of others too, most of them free—all within easy distance of millions of Americans in this day of instant travel.

You will find them in one or another of the city, county, and state parks that dot our Nation with oases of respite from the turmoil of urban life.

RELIEF FROM STEEL AND ASPHALT

Since I administer only the National Park System, I may appear to be stepping out of my bailiwick in writing about state and local parks. I do not see it that way.

I believe in public parks, no matter who runs them. I look upon each one as part of an all-American parks system. Each supports the other in offering every citizen his just share of those special benefits found in a public park.

Of our need for all our parks with all their varied uses, there can no longer be any doubt. Along the Atlantic and Pacific, even on the plains and prairies, cities are expanding and touching each other and merging into unbroken expanses of steel, concrete, and asphalt.

This is the age in which we live, of course, and it is a good age. Without sunshine, fresh air, and open space, however, man diminishes physically, mentally, and emotionally.

*Conrad L. Wirth, "The Parks in Your Backyard," *National Geographic,* Vol. 124, No. 5 (Nov., 1963), 647–73.

We need more parks. We need them now, before the cities and the highways and the private beach cottages take all the scenic lands or drive the price out of reach. We need more national parks—but above all, we need more local parks, close to the people.

So when I talk about local parks, I am not really leaving my own field—or my own philosophy, if you wish—but only my jurisdiction.

Instead of generalizing about local parks, maybe it would be best if we set out right now to visit some. There are thousands, ranging in size from New York's two-million-acre Adirondack Park . . . to tiny green plots in the downtown sections of large cities. We cannot see them all, but those we do visit will be fun.

Take the one, for example, with the alligators that eat marshmallows. This is Highlands Hammock State Park near Sebring, Florida—3,800 acres of live-oak trees hung with Spanish moss and shy orchids, of cypress trees, of heron and egret, deer and scuttling armadillos.

A jeep with a trailer takes visitors into the heart of this true nature park. Naturally the sightseers want to see alligators. Well, there are plenty of 'gators, but it takes coaxing to bring them out of the deep swamp.

Natural bait—fish and meat—costs too much for a parks budget. One day a child dropped a marshmallow into the water. The 'gators went for it like ladies for a bargain counter.

Now the naturalist who rides the jeep carries marshmallows and need only crinkle the sack to bring the 'gators out. Once I noticed one minus a front foot.

"Caught in a trap?" I asked.

"No," was the answer. "I think that when he was a little fellow, he got a marshmallow stuck in his teeth. He tried to claw it out with his foot. A larger 'gator grabbed the marshmallow and the foot too."

The Roebling family of New Jersey donated magnificent Highlands Hammock to the people of Florida. Two talented members of this family engineered the Brooklyn Bridge, and Roebling factories made the wire cables that hold it up.

SIGHTSEEING AMONG THE BARRACUDAS

To go on with our trip and maybe swim with barracudas, folks do that in the only park in the United States that is entirely underwater except for its 2,200-acre headquarters area and boat docks. This jewel of Florida coastal waters is the John Pennekamp Coral Reef State Park, which is also known as Key Largo Coral Reef Preserve.

Most people see its gorgeous coral formations and vivid tropical fishes from a glass-bottomed boat, but a surprising number go down in swimsuits and Aqua-Lungs.

Barracudas are found there, from little ones to gaunt, sinister six-footers.

Experts say the 'cuda strikes only at something it believes to be a fish of moderate size, its natural prey. I keep thinking there might be a 'cuda with bad eyesight among all those hundreds of ghostly shapes, so I stick to the glass-bottomed boat.

Florida named the 21-mile-long reef for the veteran managing editor of the Miami *Herald,* who has long been active in conservation matters. Mr. Pennekamp, who with Senator Spessard L. Holland (then Governor) and the late Ernest Coe had helped acquire Everglades National Park for the people of the Nation, also sparked a citizens group in the movement to conserve the reef as a park.

Regarding that hobnobbing with gorillas, mine has been done with Yula, who lives with a baby chimpanzee and a youthful orangutan in the San Diego Zoo, an outstanding feature of the city's marvelous Balboa Park. Yula apparently enjoys sitting on my hip like the infant she is.

Many city zoos these days have special sections for children. They are wonderful places; every zoo should have one.

In San Diego the child can pick up dogs, cats, rabbits, baby chickens. He can slide down a chute into a corral filled with baby hoofed animals, too young to harm him. This is where he may pet a tapir and a guanaco, . . . also learn firsthand that a camel has chronic bad breath, and put his arms around the neck of an African sable antelope.

Young girl attendants teach the children not to squeeze the chicks or feed the tapir chewing gum, and of course they also watch for signs that the larger animals are getting big enough to kick or bite.

The main San Diego Zoo is one of the best in the world. Mostly the animals live behind hidden moats rather than bars. Visitors from every state ride the buses that wind through the zoo's steep, palm-lined roads.

Wild ducks drop onto the waterfowl ponds by the thousands during migrations, thus paying Director Charles R. Schroeder the greatest compliment possible: They come to his zoo because they want to.

Balboa Park also has mirror lakes, an art museum, formal gardens, even a replica of London's Old Globe theater, where Elizabethans cheered Shakespeare's plays.

While we are still in California, we had best look at another of the great Western city parks, Golden Gate in San Francisco. . . . It was created in its entirety out of sand dunes and noisome marshland.

The city bought the desolate landscape in 1868. In 1887 Golden Gate's guiding genius, John McLaren, took over, and the wonderful park with its herds of buffalo and elk, its Steinhart Aquarium, its arboretum, its botanical gardens, and its matchless trees and grassy spaces stands today as his monument.

McLaren was one of the great parks men of all times, a member of the small but dedicated group who around the turn of the century understood what parks and open spaces meant to their fellow men and had the courage to fight for their convictions. I knew him well and learned much from him.

A city park on the other side of the country from California is regarded by parks people as the most sacred place of all, for in Boston Common, in the capital city of Massachusetts, the American concept of public parks was first put into practice.

BOSTON'S "VILLAGE GREEN" STILL SERVES CITY

In Europe, originally all land was held in the name of the rulers, and about the only space that vaguely resembled a public park was the central square in a town. This was a utilitarian place, however, where people went to draw their water and sell their pigs.

The New England settlers brought the town square to the New World with them, although they put the title in the name of the people and called it a "village green." Set aside in 1634 as public property, Boston Common was simply a place where the cows grazed and the militia drilled.

There the matter stood until 1830, when the people informed their servants, the city officials, that they preferred a playground to a pasture. The officials perforce chased off the cows and planted shade trees and flowers for the people to enjoy.

Other cities initiated parks systems early. Philadelphia established its first parks in 1682, and its 4,000-acre Fairmount Park is the largest within the limits of any U.S. city. More than four and a half times the size of New York's Central Park, it would cover Manhattan from the Battery to 23d Street.

President George Washington in 1791 gave approval when Pierre Charles L'Enfant included parks in his master plan for Washington, D.C., so that today the National Capital is bejeweled with parks, forming graceful settings for public buildings and giving the city its air of spaciousness and beauty. Rock Creek Park, with its extension into Maryland, totals 3,400 acres.

COYOTES COMPETE WITH COWBOY SINGERS

I mentioned a buffalo steak cookout under the stars. I was thinking of an enchanted evening I spent in Custer State Park, in South Dakota's Black Hills country, when the cowhands sang songs of the West around the campfire and the coyotes answered in the wild tenor voices of their kind.

The buffalo steaks sizzled. Behind me a great roar drowned coyotes and guitars.

"Is that a buffalo come to avenge his brother we are cooking?" I asked.

The young ranger at my side laughed. "No, Mr. Wirth, that's a wild burro. We have about 30 head of them. They stop cars on the roads and beg for something to eat, which in the case of a burro can be almost anything.

"But the tourists love them, and heaven help us if we ever tried to get rid of them."

Since the herd must not exceed the grazing capacity of Custer's grassy hills, the park runs a commercial buffalo ranch, turning a profit on meat and hides. If there is another buffalo-ranching public park in the world, I never heard of it. Chances are that the buffalo meat you find sometimes on menus in big restaurants came from Custer.

Choctaw Indians play stickball at Chucalissa (its name means "abandoned village" in Choctaw) near Memphis, Tennessee. A wild and woolly game, related to lacrosse, it was played in the old days on the central square that most Indian villages possessed. The sport was a kind of formalized warfare, village against village, and all able-bodied men joined in. The racket was used as a weapon as much as for catching and throwing the ball, and broken bones and dislocated joints were not uncommon.

Chucalissa, inhabited for at least six centuries starting around A.D. 1000, has been lovingly restored, and the stickball games take place on the original square surrounded by mud huts with thatched roofs.

But Charles H. Nash, Chucalissa museum director, has had to set up restraining rules.

"Sometimes the players are Boy Scouts," he explained. "I'm sure they'd be proud to tell their friends a real Indian cracked their skull, but parents wouldn't understand. So we forbid using the sticks as clubs, and we bench players who become angry."

PARKS OWE DEBT TO DEPRESSION YEARS

The Civilian Conservation Corps of the depression years found the site of Chucalissa. Parks on all levels, especially state and national parks, owe a great deal to the CCC.

Everywhere you see the solid buildings constructed by the jobless young men of those difficult years, sometimes as the only buildings in an entire park. Lovely park forests stand now where they planted saplings. In my opinion the CCC was the best and most enduring investment in human and natural-resource conservation this country ever made, and I wish every young man today could similarly work with his own hands to preserve our natural heritage. He would be a better citizen for the experience.

One of my Park Service jobs in those days was finding worthwhile projects for the CCC. I well remember the enthusiasm of archeologists when they learned what the corps uncovered at Chucalissa.

Swiftly the University of Tennessee took over scientific direction of the dig.

Today Memphis State University operates Chucalissa Park; Mr. Nash is one of the professors.

Preservation of historic sites and objects is an important responsibility of all park authorities. Understanding the past is valuable and inspiring. Patrick Henry put it this way:

"I have but one lamp by which my feet are guided, and that is the lamp of experience. I know of no way of judging of the future but by the past."

A few states established parks of their own before the turn of the century, but the big year for the state parks movement was 1921. Called together by Stephen T. Mather, then Director of National Parks, some 200 conservationists met in Des Moines, Iowa, and promulgated the idea of state participation in the all-American system of parks. "There shall be public parks, forests and preserves within easy access of all the citizens of every state and territory of the United States," the group recommended.

County parks came later. Many were established near big cities whose residential suburbs had sprawled over city boundaries. In such cases the city and county parks really form a single large metropolitan park system.

State parks in general preserve areas of interest mainly to the citizens of the state and are handier to the local people than a national park might be. Some offer less scenery and more varied recreation—things like group camps, baseball, and such organized sports—than a national park provides. This is the way it should be, but many offer, as sort of a bonus, scenery that meets national park specifications so well that it makes us envious.

The city park moves still farther away from nature, furnishing a rich variety of worthwhile artificial recreational forms—zoos, swimming pools, playgrounds, museums, music, formal flower gardens, even Ferris wheels and carrousels.

The tiniest plot of land can make a useful city park. Seattle, Washington, for instance, has Pioneer Square: hardly more than a few benches clustered under an old-fashioned glass-and-iron roof. Yet it rarely is without its group of Indian and Eskimo fishermen and cannery workers, who use it as an outdoor clubhouse. Appropriately, a totem pole rises from the square's center.

The various categories of public parks have a great deal in common, and parks people have two major professional associations through which they keep in touch with each other and swap ideas. One is the National Conference of State Parks, the other the American Institute of Park Executives; the latter began in 1898 as the New England Association of Park Superintendents. Many national park officials belong to both groups.

One of the finest nature parks I know is Point Lobos Reserve State Park, a glorious bit of California's rocky Pacific coast near Monterey and Carmel. Established primarily to preserve one of two original stands of the strangely beautiful Monterey cypresses, it has become of late a haven for sea otters.

First Russian fur hunters, then others of many nationalities, almost exterminated the sea otter of northern Pacific waters. Inch-deep otter fur commanded fabulous prices in Moscow, China, and Europe.

The United States Government forbade the taking of otters in 1911, but their numbers nevertheless still declined, until naturalists, in the 1920's declared them doomed.

Then in 1938, people with field glasses spotted a few playing in the ocean off Monterey Peninsula. The graceful animals have been making a gradual recovery ever since.

Today an estimated 700 sea otters frequent the coastal waters, ranging from Carmel Bay south to Point Conception, near Santa Barbara. You can see them asleep in the kelp beds beneath the cliffs, lulled by the long Pacific swell. Sometimes, when they eat fish or clams, they lie flat on their backs and use their chests as tables.

BUTTERFLIES CLOAK ENTIRE TREES

Besides sea otters and sea lions, the Lobos forest has myriad nesting sea birds, deer, foxes, raccoons, bobcats, an occasional mountain lion, and the greatest glory of all: countless millions of monarch butterflies, resting in migration time until whole trees look like tongues of flame.

California's famous Save-the-Redwoods League helped launch the state's outstanding parks system in 1927, although it thought initially only to protect the unique coastal redwood trees of northern California from annihilation by lumbermen.

The redwood parks the league saved from the ax and turned over to the state are unmatched anywhere. The dedicated group raised millions of dollars to buy groves, then gave them to the people.

Now the primeval forest still survives along Prairie Creek, with a thriving herd of Roosevelt elk, as a crowning touch, living peacefully in the open meadows beside the main highway. There are redwood parks along the Del Norte coast, and on Smith River and Mill Creek near Crescent City.

Best of all is the Bull Creek watershed, a part of Humboldt Redwoods State Park. Humboldt's magnificent Avenue of the Giants contains the tallest trees on earth, *Sequoia sempervirens,* scores of which tower more than 360 feet high.

Once in Humboldt Park's Rockefeller Forest, night overtook us—a warm summer night musical with the sound of Bull Creek running in its rocky bed. Frederick Law Olmsted, one of the great naturalists and landscape architects of his time, was with us.

"Walk away from the campfire," he suggested. "Then lie on your back on the forest floor and look up at the sky."

[283]

Through the openings in the roof of redwood foliage the stars blazed. So bright were they, and so lofty the trees, that I could have sworn they touched. Never in my life have I felt heaven and earth so near each other.

CANYON SHELTERS RARE PALM GROVES

In Anza-Borrego Desert State Park, between San Diego and the Imperial Valley, a man also feels close to his Creator. Here are the trackless sands, the pitiless sun, and the gaunt cacti that march almost to the Mexican border. Here too are the 6,000-foot-high San Ysidro Mountains, home of bands of desert bighorn sheep, and Borrego Palm Canyon with its everlasting stream and its groves of Washingtonia palms, the only palm tree native to California.

When Juan Bautista de Anza's expedition left Sonora in 1775 bound for the founding of San Francisco and the building of its Presidio, the Spaniards rode through what is now the park. And Kit Carson led General Kearny's troops through in 1846.

A man on a horse or in a jeep sees Anza-Borrego best, for some of the roads are too rough for passenger cars. He must take water along and be careful of the sun in the summer.

The only hotter place I ever ran into was Nevada's rugged Valley of Fire State Park. We went there in a car, before the days of air-conditioning, and put a box of dry ice on the back seat, thinking it might cool us.

It helped some. Our thermometer showed only 105° F. in the car, against 115 outside.

It is always cool, on the other hand, in Longhorn Cavern near Burnet, Texas. The state developed a 708-acre park, one of a string of good local parks in the rough scruboak woods that mark this part of Texas.

I know Longhorn from CCC days. For four years the youths scraped silt and dirt from the cavern floor until they had made a two-mile underground trail. Today 35,000 people walk along it every year without bumping their heads too many times.

According to a fairly well documented story, a band of Comanche Indians raided San Antonio, captured a girl, and held her prisoner in the cave. Three Texas Rangers rescued her after a battle, and one of them later married her.

During the Civil War, the South used the cave as a gunpowder factory; its deposits of bat guano provided a handy source of saltpeter. Excavations have yielded a rusted Colt revolver made in 1852 and a skeleton in the remains of a Confederate uniform.

I wish I had room to describe more of the state parks with unusual features. There is, for example, Dry Falls in Washington State, with a great, sheer cliff over which the entire Columbia River tumbled when an Ice Age glacier changed its course.

There is Petit Jean in Arkansas, a cool, wooded plateau overlooking part of Winthrop Rockefeller's Santa Gertrudis cattle ranch, Winrock, beside the Arkansas River; and Minnesota's lovely Itasca, enshrining the birthspring of the Mississippi River. When I was 12 years old, my father took me to Itasca on my first family camping trip.

For every park of unusual grandeur, there are fifty quiet green places where people go to picnic and camp and sit in the sun. One such place is Hungry Mother State Park, in Virginia between Roanoke and Bristol.

CITY FAMILY FINDS HANDY RETREAT

I know a devoted visitor to Hungry Mother. She is a Washington secretary, a mother working to help support her family. She has neither time nor money for luxury vacations.

"So," she says, "we tried the Virginia state parks, several of them, until we found Hungry Mother, and that was for us.

"We load the old car with children and canned goods and nice old clothes. We drive down to the cabin we've reserved. We rent a boat, and my husband fishes in the lake.

"Our three kids swim, hike, and play on the beach. In the evening, the whippoorwills on the hills sing us to sleep. Sometimes my husband and I go to a little lodge where there is music, and we square dance in bare feet.

"The best thing is the knowledge that here we are, city people who don't know much about forests and animals, living here, alone but together, doing all our own chores—and all the time I know that if something goes wrong, like a skunk under the back porch, I only have to scream and a ranger will come running and chase the skunk away."

What more can you ask of a park?

FORESTS REPLACE FARMED OUT FIELDS

Another of the quiet parks, North Carolina's beloved William B. Umstead near Raleigh, stands with San Francisco's Golden Gate as an example of what persevering people can create out of practically nothing. Once it was eroded, submarginal farmland, with the sight and smell of human failure hanging heavy over treeless, gullied hills and cotton fields gone back to weeds and briars.

The CCC came in. The young men dammed Sycamore Creek to make a lake and put the trees back. Roads and nature trails were constructed. A bigger lake was built. Now the trees are forest, and under the trees are campgrounds and picnic tables.

Four city parks have had considerable influence upon my life. The first is New York's Central Park, which, more than any other place in the country, demonstrates the lengths to which Americans will go to give themselves sunshine and green grass.

Here, in the heart of the huge, congested city, lies an 840-acre park that would bring the people of New York, were they to sell it, hundreds of millions of dollars. Would they sell so much as a foot of it? Emphatically no. They have been resisting encroachments upon the park's beauty and cultural values since it was created out of a patchwork of farms in the 1860's.

BOYHOOD SPENT IN AND AROUND PARKS

When my father, Theodore Wirth, a Swiss landscape gardener, came to this country, he took a job trimming the trees in Central Park. Right after a city election the politicians laid off their tree trimmers, common practice in the 1880's. My father went out to Long Island and worked for a horticulturist whose daughter he later married.

I was born in the second city park that influenced my life. In the park superintendent's house, that is, for my father was by then superintendent of Elizabeth Park in Hartford, Connecticut. Here he designed and built the first municipal rose garden in the United States. No one has ever changed his design so far as I can find out, and experts call it one of the finest in the country.

The mounted head of a ram glared from a wall of the superintendent's house, I remember. Once it had belonged to the leader of the park's lawn-mowing flock; in those days, before power mowers, city parks invariably used sheep to cut grass. The shepherd kept telling my father the ram was getting old and cantankerous, but Dad wouldn't listen.

One day my father dropped something in the grass, and when he bent over to pick it up, the ram sent him flying into the shrubbery. So then he left the ram's fate to the shepherd, who shortly afterward sent him the mounted head of his late adversary.

In the third park I spent much of my youth, for Dad went to Minneapolis, Minnesota, as parks superintendent, and he built much of that city's outstanding system. He badgered city officials and the taxpaying citizens until he was allowed to create a string of swimming, fishing, and boating lakes out of a chain of marshes.

There was always a little trouble keeping the water level where it should be during dry years. Recently the city put in a pump with which it can keep the uppermost lake full and feed water through the chain as needed.

Loring Park, the big downtown central park, my father found forlorn and neglected. He put a fence around it, he ploughed every bit of it, he planted grass. When the grass was strong, he pulled the fence down and passed the word: "Do walk on the grass."

After the people had trampled trails, showing where it was they liked most to go, Dad paved the trails. "Let the people make their own paths." he said. "A park that is not for people is not a park."

NATION'S CAPITAL A CITY OF PARKS

The fourth city park that looms large in my life actually is in my jurisdiction. It is the District of Columbia system planned by L'Enfant. The National Park Service of the Department of the Interior runs it only because Washington is a Federal city.

Almost every American has heard of Rock Creek Park, and of Lafayette Square across Pennsylvania Avenue from the White House. . . . I doubt, however, that most people realize there are 776 pieces of park property in Washington, some of them the merest patches of greenery with room for a few benches, a few flowers, a statue, and numerous gray squirrels. We have a mule-drawn barge that takes visitors up the Chesapeake and Ohio Canal, one of our historic areas that doubles as a place for outdoor recreation.

Probably every school child in the Capital area has visited our Nature Center in Rock Creek Park, or been to the top of our Washington Monument, or seen Japanese cherry blossoms against the background of our Lincoln and Jefferson Memorials; thousands have walked along the Theodore Roosevelt Island nature trail in mid-Potomac.

Thanks to the best kind of intergovernmental cooperation, the National Capital Parks System sprawls far beyond District of Columbia boundaries, into those nearby Maryland and Virginia communities that are in reality the Capital's residential suburbs.

Thus Montgomery County, Maryland, cooperated to the full in extending Rock Creek Park upstream, and Virginia is as proud of George Washington Memorial Parkway, running south to Mount Vernon, as we are.

Good city-county cooperation exists elsewhere. Cook County, Illinois, acquired its big Forest Preserve almost solely for the people of Chicago, to give them woodland wilds they could not have in their modern city. The parks system ringing Cleveland, Ohio, does not hesitate to spill over the city-county frontier when this makes for a better park.

Dade County, Florida, runs a park system in the Miami area that benefits local people, tourists, everybody. It has some of the best beaches and marinas in the state, and also a rifle range in the nearby Keys.

TODAY'S PARK CONCEPT: A PLACE TO PLAY

A moment ago I reported that my father pulled down the "Keep off the Grass" signs. He also put community recreation buildings in his parks. This represented a major change in American park philosophy, a change that is now accepted as imperative for modern local park and recreation systems.

The old-timers in the parks business were mostly landscape gardeners and horticulturists. They liked their parks beautiful, formal, and neat. You could row on a lake in Baltimore's Druid Hill Park, or admire the flowers in Chicago's

Grant Park—but you'd better not play catch with your son on the grass or the police in those days would chase you off.

But plenty of today's parks have the necessary buildings and roads and athletic fields, and many a community has added to the title Department of Parks the words ". . . and Recreation." And why not?

After all, a park is but a piece of public land dedicated to recreation, and there are many healthy kinds of recreation. In this big country of ours we can have all sorts of parks.

Good parks can furnish an infinite variety of good things to do—gymnasium and athletic fields for the young; the checkerboard painted on the table and the bowling green for the old; the square-dancing classes, the ceramics and hobby shops for everybody.

In Houston, Texas, the park police prowl car pulled up late one night beside a floodlit basketball court. Although park rules said the court should have been closed an hour earlier, some youths still played, and the park recreation director said he would stay and keep lights on as long as the boys wanted.

"Bless you," said one of the policemen. "There's a dozen less kids for us to worry about tonight."

And in Florida's strange little Redland Fruit and Spice Park near Homestead, created originally to show the exotic commercial fruits the state can grow, I watched as some adults painted happily under a teacher's direction.

I looked over the shoulder of one gentleman who must have seen 80 summers. He was painting, without any guide or model, the portrait of a lovely young girl.

Well, if a park activity can restore an old man's memory, it has to be a good thing.

PARKLANDS NOT EASY TO GAIN AND HOLD

But the parks business has its problems.

Americans hold firmly to the principle of public parks. We realize we need parks, we want them, and we know we do not yet have enough of them to take care of present and future needs.

Parks management, meanwhile, becomes more and more efficient, and parks people are fast uniting into a professional fraternity that speaks with a single voice.

But no sooner does the parks man get down to the brass tacks of land acquisition and park management and park protection than he runs into obstacles, mostly bearing the label "in the name of progress."

He doesn't have as much trouble with commercial interests as he used to. The mining company that sought to invade the Porcupine Mountains wild area on Michigan's Upper Peninsula for instance, has quit trying, at least for now. Enlightened timber companies in the West have sold many valuable holdings to park interests at fair prices.

The people's own public agencies, usually with the best of motives, give the parks their biggest headaches these days. The military, for example, has legitimate need for large tracts of land and competes with parks systems for what is available.

Logically enough, the highway builders often decide parks offer the best routes for new roads. At this very minute, they seek to run a throughway across Prairie Creek Redwoods State Park in California. The Nation's Capital is battling this situation throughout the city, the most important test being over a proposed freeway through Glover Archbold Park, a beautiful place we promised never to let become other than a park the day we accepted it as a gracious gift.

Since good highways are eminently desirable, the parks man has trouble fighting off the throughway builder. Sometimes the roads man gives us the impression he sees a park simply as free land.

We insist, however, that the social and cultural values in a good park outweigh a road curve or detour. After all, more than 100 billion miles a year is rolled up by Americans on vaction or seeking a weekend's recreation. Why, then, destroy the very thing that people seek when they take to the road?

No doubt the highway engineer thinks us unreasonable sometimes, and maybe we are, but I do find increasing signs of better cooperation. The case of Oregon shows what can be done.

A few years back, Sam Boardman was state highway engineer. But under the Oregon system, in which parks management is vested in the highway commission, he was also chief of state parks.

Building a coastal highway, he bought for the state not only the road right-of-way, but all the land between road and sea plus strips on the other side that would screen ugly lumbering in the Douglas firs.

Now, driving this beautiful highway, you can turn off every few miles into a state park, and fish and camp and picnic and have a wonderful outdoors experience.

Taking up where Sam Boardman left off, the Parks and Recreation Division of the Oregon Highway Department last year published what I consider a model plan for the future of its parks.

Exhaustive research laid the foundation for its recommendations—in population growth, the rate at which American leisure time is increasing, trends in recreational preferences, the rise in land values, and all the other factors involved in sound planning.

Oregon in only a dozen years, the report concluded, will need at least 15 new parks. Further, park officials say, 22 of the existing 187 park units should be augmented by some 4,000 acres of adjacent lands.

You can change the figures in such recommendations, and they become valid for almost any state, county, and city park system in the Nation—and also for the National parks.

We need more parks, as I said in the beginning. In many cases, it is possible to be quite specific: Some areas seem to have been created to become public recreational grounds.

Lake Tahoe is such a place. Surely its glorious wooded shores should belong to all the people, or at least enough of these scenic shores to accommodate all who wish to visit the lake. As this is being written, California has set aside money to buy shore land, and Nevada hopes to do so. California also is acquiring land on either side of the Golden Gate.

In Louisiana, private citizens hope to persuade state officials to buy 9,000 acres at Port Hudson, 15 miles north of Baton Rouge, that are not only perfect for recreation but have archeological and historical interest as well.

About 800 acres on the Virginia side of the Potomac River at Great Falls, now under 50-year lease by the Department of Interior, should definitely be retained as parkland. Here is one of the world's finest stretches of white water, rich in scenery and history.

Here Indians came to fish, hunt, and live amid beauty. Here, too, the Potowmack Company, headed by George Washington, began in 1785 to dig the first canal past the rapids; ruins of locks and buildings still remain.

The Chesapeake and Ohio Canal, on the Maryland side of the river, is in public ownership already, and I am sure Congress will authorize purchase of the Virginia side very soon. After that, we will sit down and work out a plan for using the park to benefit the citizens of metropolitan Washington and the Nation as a whole.

PRECIOUS HERITAGE: A SPACIOUS OUTDOORS

In addition to being a bit behind on acquiring new parks, we are slow in improving those we already have—in enlarging them, in furnishing them with better equipment, in managing them better.

If we truly believe in the public parks philosophy, if we feel that parks have enriched our lives—and I am sure we do—then we must pass along to our children a full all-American park system of national, state, and local parks, their blessed heritage of open spaces. It is an obligation so long as we believe in our way of life.

CITY PARKS AND OPEN SPACES

Throughout most of our history, recreation has had last claim on land or other resources. It has been a residual use: the vacant lot became a temporary playground; land too rough or rocky for cultivation became wildlife habitat. As population became more concentrated and need for outdoor recreation increased, land values increased roughly in proportion to the degree of congestion. Coupled with the high cost of land was the pervasive notion that recreation was a waste of time and that natural resources should serve a useful, that is, commercial, purpose. Under these conditions it is not surprising that city parks and open spaces are few in number and small in area as compared with some ideal proportion of recreation areas to residential and commercial land use.

In most American cities, parks and open spaces exist mainly for several reasons: they were set aside in an earlier day when land values were low, New England Commons, for example; they were located in areas where topography or other factors made commercial or residential uses impractical; or they were established only after difficult, and sometimes prolonged, political fights. It has only been in the last half of the twentieth century that recreation has come to be generally accepted as a legitimate use of high-cost resources. Even with such general acceptance, the financial and legal problems involved in acquiring and holding property for recreation made it difficult to provide adequate areas in or near population centers. Roads, parking lots, industrial uses, shopping centers, and sprawling suburbs continued to encroach upon recreation areas.

This chapter will document the evolution of old commons and squares into parks, the creation of New York Central Park the first large *planned* urban park, and the more recent development of the concept of open space in urban areas.

"EVOLUTION OF THE NEW ENGLAND TOWN COMMON"*
1630–1966

Some present day city parks and open spaces in the eastern United States originated during colonial times as public squares or commons. David D. Brodeur explores the origins and changes in use of the New England town common in the article that follows.

The typical rural southern New England town common (or green) is an irregular grassy plot flanked by a tall, steepled church or two, and an aging Victorian-style town hall. Although many commons also have the usual park accoutrements (benches, bandstands, monuments, fountains and footpaths), it is certain that commons were not first conceived of as parks. Inquiry into the origins of these charming, informal open spaces reveals that, while a few of them do stem from the common grazing lands set aside by township proprietors in the early colonial period, the great majority actually derive from the original lot of the *first parish meetinghouse.* A few commons in the Connecticut valley are also remnants of broad survey highways laid out to follow the longitudinal contours of the flood plain terrace settlements.

The tradition of having several unfenced pasturages for the common use of certain *freemen or free townsmen* was fast disappearing in its birthplace, England, when the first Pilgrims sailed from her shores, *via* Holland, in 1620. But the system of common pasturage had a special appeal in the first decades of the Massachusetts Bay Colony, because the Pilgrims soon learned that in order to survive in a hostile wilderness with severe winters they were compelled to share and cooperate in all undertakings. Later, however, land pressures created by the constant flow of new arrivals began to force a reduction in the generous size of tracts of common grazing land that were set aside by the township proprietors. By 1700, most outlying common lands in the coastal towns had been sold to new freeholders by towns hungry for revenue. In fact it was apparent at the very beginning that the growth of population made it impractical that so much land should remain in reserve for a few privileged *freemen* (or *free townsmen*) who enjoyed rights as *proprietors.* A few once marshy tracts of common grazing land have survived, among them the well known commons in Boston, and Salem, Massachusetts.

The survival of Boston Common was assured partly because of some lingering sentiment for the ancient institution of common pasturage, but mostly because new functions were discovered for this inner pasturage as the town slowly grew

*David D. Brodeur, "Evolution of the New England Town Common: 1630–1966." Reproduced by permission from *The Professional Geographer* of the Association of American Geographers, Vol. XIX, No. 6 (Nov., 1967), 313–18.

around it. The Boston Common early served conveniently as a drill field for militia. It also attracted rope makers from the docks who needed a long open space for their work. It came to be appreciated, later, as a place for an evening stroll. Orators and evangelists flocked to Boston Common in the eighteenth century and on occasion can be heard there today. When, at various times, the town fathers made known plans to sell portions of the common for revenue, irate townsmen fell back on their right to tether a cow and the common was saved. This continued until 1830 when the city passed an ordinance forbidding grazing as an obstruction to traffic. In 1822, two years before Boston incorporated as a city, the last outlying common pastures on the neck were sold to make way for house lots. The city began to landscape her remaining forty-acre common on the flank of Beacon Hill after 1836.

Most New England village greens derive, not from common pasturage, but from the meetinghouse lot. If they are sometimes also called commons it is because they served sporadically as night corrals for the domestic animals of the community. Also, a portion of the meetinghouse lot often was reserved as a training field for local militia and this may have contributed to the "common land" concept.

Because the Puritans believed that no humanly conceived structure was worthy of being called a church, they referred to their place of worship as the *meetinghouse.* Provision for a large lot for the meetinghouse became a strict requirement of the General Court of the Massachusetts Bay Colony about 1650. For example, in 1667, the court provided that some fifty acres be set aside for the Worcester, Massachusetts, meetinghouse. As historian Cushing says, ". . . the transformation of the meetinghouse lot into a town common is part of the history of each community." Such lots were successively encroached upon by abutting private property holders, rival church sects, and even taverns. This in part explains why so many commons are only three or four acres in area today. In the seventeenth century, all town business, religious and civil, was carried on in the meetinghouse by the ecclesiastical oligarchy, and the distinction between church and state in most of these communities was largely theoretical. Because the meetinghouse was not really a "church" in the traditional sense, there was rarely any objection to this arrangement.

More research needs to be done to determine just when the term "green" came to be applied to the inevitably reduced meetinghouse common lot. It probably followed the first attempts to beautify these commons in certain towns. While records show that the first tree plantings on the green at Canton, Massachusetts, were made in 1794 and those on New Haven's Public Square (Green), in 1799, Cushing claims that ". . . most commons were barren, unsightly plots from the early days until well after 1835. Brush, stumps, stones, rubbish, dead trees, and stagnant pools . . . typified a great many. . . ." The constant stream of settlers and other visitors from England in the nineteenth century, bringing with them vivid memories of the manicured English church green so often celebrated in verse, must have had its influence on the New England brethren. The landscaping of the commons or greens began in earnest, however, after the Civil War when communities were moved by patriotic sentiment to erect monuments to the fallen. With so much communal history already tied up in the site of the first parish meetinghouse, such monuments commonly were erected on the green which by then had often become separated from the meetinghouse by the formalization of old cow trails and wagon roads into town streets. Although doubtless the New England town common or green has inspired some isolated imitations in other parts of the United States, in particular some township squares in Ohio, this phenomenon is limited not only to New England but, with few exceptions, to southern New England. The communities founded later in northern Maine, New Hampshire and Vermont were mostly the settlements of large, chartered land companies and their members were not of a Puritan cast of mind.

A survey of the communal land uses facing commons was performed by the author in 1962. As Table 1 shows, in half the 138 towns (with commons) on

Table 1. *Major Land Uses and Land Use Combinations Found on the Central Common of 138 Towns**

	Town Hall	Library	Historical Society	Church(es)
No. of commons with cited use	69	58	30	81
Use as a % of all commons cited	50%	42%	21.7%	60%

	Res.	Business	Mixed R. & B.	Other Town Bldgs.
No. of commons with cited use(es)	47	18	64	36
Use(es) as a % of all commons cited	35%	13%	47%	27%

*Source: Brodeur, *Geographic Consequences* . . . p. 68.

which land use data were collected, the town hall faced the common or stood on a portion of it. In six out of ten communities, one or more churches faced the common or stood upon it. This phenomenon of church and town hall-on-common is the result of the legal formalization of the already realized separation of church and state in Massachusetts, Connecticut, New Hampshire and Maine in the second decade of the nineteenth century. In Vermont and Rhode Island, where few Puritans settled, church and state had, in effect, never been united. The congregations of most towns continued to permit town business to be conducted in the meetinghouse. It was not until the 1840's that most New England towns got around to building a hall for the purpose of town business. When they did they usually chose, for the sake of tradition and convenience, a spot by the common. In like manner, such sects that evolved from the Puritan church, the

Congregationalists and Unitarians, as well as Methodists, Baptists and others, also preempted a place on the common.

Commons and greens in New England have served for two centuries as the conspicuous setting for finely designed churches. They have also served to attract a number of private schools whose religiously motivated founders wanted to be close to the meetinghouse. Among such common-oriented secondary schools are Governor Dummer Academy on Byfield, Massachusetts, common; Northfield Academy on the common at Northfield, Massachusetts, and Deerfield Academy, which moved to its present location on the common at Deerfield from another location in that town in 1878. Among the colleges that were founded on sites overlooking commons are Dartmouth, in Hanover, New Hampshire; Harvard, overlooking the common at Cambridge, Massachusetts, and Mount Holyoke on the small common at South Hadley, Massachusetts. Yale College, founded at Saybrook, Connecticut, removed to New Haven, overlooking the green, in 1717. The green was the site of the first meetinghouse (1640) and, later, the State House.

Towns and cities have long since acquired control of the common, the norm usually being outright ownership. An exception is found in the Public Square (or Green) at New Haven, Connecticut, which has been controlled since 1641 by an elected Proprietor's Committee. Another exception is the village green at Bedford, New York, a town that was founded as a part of Connecticut. In Bedford, the green is controlled by the descendants of the original proprietors. In Newington, New Hampshire, the town owns both the common and its meetinghouse.

In recent decades, historic district zoning and urban renewal have combined to contribute to the preservation or restoration of certain commons in Massachusetts and Connecticut. The recent transformation of Salem Square on the south fringe of the city common at Worcester, Massachusetts, illustrates what has been done for commons through urban renewal. Until 1960, an ugly three-story brick loft, a relic of the bygone textile era, could be found facing the square. The loft was demolished and eventually replaced by the relocated city public library, while dilapidated bus terminals on the south side of the square were torn down, exposing again the nave of the Catholic church. A further contribution toward making the common a community center was in the construction of a well-designed YMCA facility beside the library. At the opposite or north end of Worcester Common stands the city hall on the site of the first parish church. A plaque there commemorates the fact of the first public reading in New England of the Declaration of Independence on July 14, 1776.

EARLY OPEN SPACE RESERVATIONS IN
PHILADELPHIA, SAVANNAH, AND WASHINGTON*
1682–1791

Frederick Law Olmstead and Theordora Kimball describe other early reservations of open space in the city.

All through Massachusetts, Connecticut and New Hampshire numerous examples still exist of more or less beautiful village greens, of various origins, and in various states of preservation or retrogression from their original sizes and forms. But these commons were probably seldom, if ever, set aside by the colonists as any part of a conscious town planning scheme or predominantly for recreation.

In two of the English proprietary colonies, however, we find the same intelligent attention to the town of the future which the Spanish King and his advisers had shown in regard to their settlements in the New World. William Penn assigned five open squares in the plan for Philadelphia, drafted in 1682 by his Surveyor-General, Thomas Holme. The following description is said to be an extract from Mr. Holme's own account of his plan.

> The city, as the model shews, consists of a large *Front-street* on each river, and a *High-street,* near the middle, from river to river, of one hundred feet broad; and a *Broad-street,* in the middle of the city from side to side, of the like breadth. In the center of the city, is *a square of ten acres;* at each angle to build houses for public affairs. There is also in each quarter of the city, *a square of eight acres,* to be for the like uses, as *Moorfields,* in *London. . . .*

The early historian of Pennsylvania regrets that these beneficial regulations "whose future great importance to the city, having since not been sufficiently considered and attended to, some of them have either been neglected, or violated."

General James Oglethorpe went much further in his plans for the principal city of his ideal colony of Georgia in 1733. Mr. Robert Wright thus describes the settlement of Savannah.

> Although the first settlers were but 120 in number, Oglethorpe thought of those who were to come after them, and their descendants. Acting on the motto of the Trustees, "Not for themselves, but for others," his imagination depicted a populous city, with a large square for markets and other public purposes in every quarter, wide and regular streets crossing each other at right angles and shaded by rows of noble trees. . . . Even in his own lifetime, his expectations were in a great degree realized, but not so completely as afterwards.
>
> Knowing that man cannot live by bread alone, he made provision for future luxuries, and laid out a public garden which he designed as a nursery to supply the colonists with white mulberry trees, vines, oranges, olives and other fruits for their several plantations, and appointed a gardener to take care of it.

*Frederick Law Olmsted, Jr. and Theodora Kimball, eds., *Forty Years of Landscape Architecture, Vol. 2: Central Park 1853–1895* (New York: G. P. Putnam's Sons, 1928), 14–16.

Gen. Oglethorpe also had many of the fine forest trees spared when the site for the town was cleared.

When the proprietor re-visited his colony in 1736 he found substantial progress made in the carrying out of his plan: the streets were wide, the squares had been left, and each freeholder, besides his own town plot, had five acres outside the Common, to serve as garden and orchard. Oglethorpe was greatly pleased by the Public Gardens, which comprised ten acres of undulating ground in a delightful situation near the river. There is a charming description of this garden as he saw it in 1736 contained in Mr. Wright's *Memoir*.

A facsimile of the original plan for Savannah shows no less than twenty-four of the small squares and open spaces in addition to the Public Garden and Common. So generous a provision for future needs has hardly a parallel in the early history of town planning. It is greatly to the credit of Savannah that a hundred and fifty years later when many cities were conspicuously lacking in public grounds, she had thirty-three acres in twenty-three public places, besides a ten-acre park and a twenty-acre parade ground.

When Major L'Enfant drew up the plan for the Federal City under the guidance of Washington and Jefferson, in 1791, again there was a vision of a future city with stately parks and pleasure gardens. The plan shows fifteen squares, intended to be developed by the fifteen states, a grand cascade, a public walk, grand avenues, a President's park, and so on. In the bustle and haste of a young democracy's superabounding growth, many features of this generous plan for Washington were forgotten; and although some little attempt at park development was made in Downing's day, it was not until 1900 that the plan was rescued and given new life.

A DESCRIPTION OF BOSTON*
1631

One of the oldest city park areas in the United States is Boston Common which dates back to 1634. In the following selection, Arthur Gilman described the Boston area as it was when Mrs. Winthrop, wife of the first governor of Massachusetts, arrived in 1631.

The physical aspect of Boston when Mrs. Winthrop and her family approached it in 1631 was quite different from its appearance now, for in the march of civilization the hills have been carried into the sea, the rough places have been made smooth, and many acres of superficial area have been added to the original measure. The area at that time was about 783 acres,—less than that of the territory bought by the city of New York in 1861 for its Central Park. The present dry land in original Boston measures 1,829 acres; and the total number of acres in the city limits is more than 23,000. Mr. Blaxton recommended the place on account of its good springs of water, and Winthrop established himself near the chief of these, which gave its name to Spring Lane, the water of which though long since disused is thought to have bubbled up anew when excavations were made in 1869 for the present Post-Office.

The chief features, however, that Mrs. Winthrop noticed, as she entered the harbor, were the hills at the feet of which the straggling houses of the hamlet were nestled. At the north end of the promontory stood Windmill (now Copp's) Hill; to the south appeared Fort Hill, now completely cut away; and between them rose the three-topped Sentry Hill, which changed its name to Beacon Hill, when in 1635 the sentry who had had his post there gave place to the beacon which dominated the spot until about 1811.

The promontory itself was divided into two portions by coves which made into its boundaries; the first portion contained little more than Copp's Hill, and was separated from the rest by Mill Cove which put in at the north, and Town Cove on the south, the connection being made more complete by Mill Creek which very nearly followed the line of Blackstone Street, as now laid out. It has been supposed that at high tide the waters of the harbor may have swept quite over the slight connecting link of land, making an island of Copp's Hill and the small territory around its base.

The southerly and main portion of the promontory contained the other hills, and it was connected with the mainland by a neck much narrower even than that which has just been mentioned. Over this neck the tide sometimes flowed, making the whole promontory an island. Thus there was but one road leading from

*Arthur Gilman, *The Story of Boston: A Study of Independency* (New York: G. P. Putnam's Sons, 1889), 56–61.

the town to the neighboring villages. It was at first known simply as High or Main Street, and at a later period, when it had become of sufficient dignity to receive names, it was called Cornhill, Marlborough, Newbury, and Orange Street, at different points. These names were attached as early as 1708, when the first list of streets was placed on the town records. The name of Washington was applied to a portion of this thoroughfare in 1789, on the occasion of the visit of the first President, who entered the town by it then, as he had at the time of the evacuation of the place by the British in 1776. Until 1872 it ended at Dock Square, but in that year, after a fire which opened the way for its extension, it was continued through that square, then re-named Adams Square, to Haymarket Square, a spot within the limits of the Mill Pond of the earliest days. For more than a century— for seven-score years indeed, there were no brick sidewalks except on that part of Main Street near the Old South, called Cornhill; and the streets were paved with pebbles. Foot-passengers took the middle of the streets, where they were the smoothest. King Street had no sidewalks before the Revolution, and the pavement extended from house to house. Of course there were no street lamps.

* * *

From Mr. Winthrop's house the walk to the water's edge was not more than one third of the present distance, and he was surrounded by unoccupied territory on all sides. In fact the region beyond Milk Street was far out of town until a much later period, and was known as the "South End," for the chief portion of the town was found on the northern promontory, at the south side of Copp's Hill, and on the shore of "Town Cove," where it was under protection of a battery. The present North Street ran along the shore of this cove, and the Town Dock was at Dock Square, the site of Faneuil Hall being in early times covered with water. The appearance of the houses as they grew up on the line of the Town Cove was very agreeable from the water.

To the west from Mr. Winthrop's dwelling, a short space, was an open field running down to the waters that flowed thence quite to the higher land in Roxbury. It was the "Sentry Field," or the Common, and was, largely through the efforts of Governor Winthrop, kept open for the common use of the inhabitants. On it cows were pastured until about sixty years ago. At the time of Margaret Winthrop's arrival it was probably covered with boulders that were convenient, as building progressed, for use in the foundations. The whole promontory when Mr. Winthrop arrived was "very uneven, abounding in small hollows and swamps, covered with blueberries and other bushes," and doubtless its character had changed but little during the few months that elapsed before Margaret's arrival. There were, in fact, but a few cabins on the eastern side of the hill which sloped towards the bay.

"It being a neck and bare of wood, they are not troubled with three great annoyances of wolves, rattlesnakes, and musquitoes," writes one observer the first year, though Johnson, in his "Wonder-Working Providence," declares that at the time of Winthrop's landing the "hideous thickets" were such that "wolves and bears nursed up their young from the eyes of all beholders." It is a matter of dispute whether there was actually no wood on the peninsula, though there was but little, if any, and Winthrop wrote to his son in the winter of 1637, that Boston was "almost ready to break up for want of wood," the season being so severe, and the water about them frozen over. Most if not all of the firewood and timber was brought to the settlers by water, and so was the general supply of hay, for even when the blueberry fields had been subdued they did not prove sufficient for the agricultural purposes of the growing town.

AN EARLY HISTORY OF BOSTON COMMON*
1856

The following selection, published in 1856, summarized the history of Boston Common.

BOSTON COMMON

Contains 48 acres. The iron fence is 5,932 feet in length, and cost upwards of $100,000.

The Common has many historical associations to attach it to the hearts of the people. From the earliest settlement of Boston, it attracted attention, which has been increasing ever since. It has several times been in danger of invasion, but thanks to the wisdom which then preserved it, and which has since rendered it inaccessible. The example should be heeded by all bodies who legislate for the health and happiness of posterity. Had this delightful spot been sacrificed to satisfy the cravings of public or private cupidity, language would fail in attempting to describe the injury it would have inflicted upon the city, or the contempt that would have covered the perpetrators of the deed.

Anxiety, however, for the future welfare of the Common may well remain unaroused, as under the auspices of the City Government it must receive proper improvement. Much is now doing to render the place still more attractive. Great credit is due our worthy Mayor, for the efficiency which has been exhibited in improving it the present year. A superintendent has recently been appointed to take charge of it, whose efforts are giving it an additional beauty. Several years since, the ashes and dirt that were carted on the Mall were found to operate against the healthy condition of the trees. Plantain weeds sprang up, also, to the great injury of the grass. This year, these evils have been remedied. The ashes have been removed, and about thirty loads of the plantain carried off. The consequence is, a healthier appearance among the trees, and a more luxuriant growth of grass.

Its Early History. — Commissioners were appointed to dispose of unoccupied lands, in 1634, and were instructed to leave out portions for new comers, and the *further benefits of the town.* Among this reserved territory was our present beautiful Common, which it is believed has always been public property. For many generations it served the double purpose of a training field and pasture, for which it was laid out by the town, according to depositions of the then oldest inhabitants, taken before Gov. Bradstreet, in 1684. The city ordinance forbidding

*History of Boston from 1630 to 1856 (Boston: F. C. Moore and Co., 1856), 195–97.

its use as a pasturage bears the date of 1833. The late militia laws have rendered its use, as a "training field," in a measure obsolete; it is now used for the parades of our independent companies.

Attempts to possess the Common have been made at different times. In one instance, a citizen petitioned for half an acre, for a building lot, but these attempts were all unsuccessful. We may be permitted to record an act which came very near making it private property. The proprietors of the Rope Walks, in 1795, had the misfortune to have their property burned. The town generously offered them that portion of the Common which is now the Public Garden, rent free, for rebuilding, which offer was accepted. In 1819, the rope walks were again destroyed by fire, and the owners proposed to cut the land into building lots and sell it. To this the citizens strongly objected, and so intense was public feeling upon the subject, that it was left to referees, and as it appeared that the proprietors of the walks had *ground* for their claim, they were awarded the sum of $50,000 to relinquish it, which the town authorities paid.

A clause was inserted in the City Charter, making the Common public property for ever, and placing it beyond the power of the city to dispose of it.

The Fence. — Previous to 1836 the Common was inclosed by a plain, unpretending, wooden post, three-rail fence. The present substantial iron fence was built at this date, and makes an imposing appearance.

The Malls are wide, gravelled, and smooth, and are deemed the most delightful promenade grounds in the world. They are beautifully shaded by majestic elms and other trees, to the number of upwards of one thousand, some of which were planted over a hundred years ago.

The time-honored elm still stands, the most significant and attractive of all, and crowds on all public days pay it a special visit. It has been strengthened by the aid of art, and it is inclosed by a fence to prevent its admirers from plucking a remembrancer from its rough exterior. By its side lies the frog-pond, but not the one of yore. Cochituate Lake now pours her glistening stream upon its rocky bed, and its waters leap and seem to laugh for joy that they have come to visit the far-famed garden of liberty. The wants of visitors have been anticipated, and, to give all the privilege of drinking the pure beverage, hydrants have been placed in different parts of the Common.

In early times the name of "Crescent Pond" was given to this sheet of water, and it has been known as "Quincy Lake," but none have been in so common use as that of "Frog Pond," which now claims precedence only by custom.

The grounds of the Common have been greatly improved the last year, under the superintendence of Mr. Sherburne. The paths have been regravelled, and the trees trimmed and washed with composition. Many of the young trees have had guards placed around them. The following is a list of the kind and number of trees.

American Elms	664	Buttonwood	1
English Elms	49	Black Aspen	5
Linden Trees	65	Black Ash	7
Tulip Trees	17	White and Silver-leaf Maple	70
Oaks	8	Rock Maple	14
Sycamores	10	Arbor Vitae	20
Hemlock	1	Fir Trees	250
Jingo	1	Spruce Trees	69
Slippery Elm	1		
Total			1255

Of the above, 202 trees were set out in April and May, 1850. Many of the decayed trees were thoroughly repaired. For this purpose, 300 yards of duck and 40 barrels of composition were used. Fifteen barrels of composition were used in filling up the hollow in the "Big Elm," near the pond. Forty loads of plantain and seventy-five loads of knot-weed were carried away, and twelve bushels of grass-seed and eight bushels of oats were sown last season. There was also taken from Tremont Mall 6,104 loads of coal ashes, which were carried over to fill up near the Charles street Mall. Fifteen thousand and nine hundred bushels of Somerville gravel were used in improving Tremont and Charles Street Malls.

Iron Fences. — The Iron Fence around the Common has been thoroughly cleaned, and 552 pounds of pales were put into it. Besides the iron fence, 8,110 feet of joist were used in stopping up paths made by persons in walking across the lots.

There are on the Common 201 seats, of which 171 are wood, and thirty are stone. Of the wooden seats, 50 were put up and covered with zinc, in 1850; the remaining 121 are covered with sheet iron.

Boston Neck. — On this beautiful avenue there are 240 American elm trees.

Fort Hill. — At this place there are fifty American elms, five ash trees, and one rock maple; all of which have been trimmed and washed. The fence has also been repaired.

In Summer, Franklin, Cambridge, Charles, and other streets, the trees have been fixed up in good style, and they are now repaying us, by their vigorous appearance, for the attention bestowed upon them.

NEW YORK'S CENTRAL PARK*
1785–1853

Commons and public squares had been established in many colonial cities for various utilitarian purposes. Many of these later came to be used for parks although that was not their original intended use. One of the first substantial efforts to create a city park involved the establishment of New York's Central Park, and following New York's "breakthrough," other cities also created significant park systems.

As early as 1785 a citizen complained about the lack of public parks in New York City in this open letter to the Mayor and Aldermen.

> *It is a very general complaint that there is not in this great city, nor in its environs, any one proper spot, where its numerous inhabitants can enjoy, with convenience, the exercise that is necessary for health and amusement.*
>
> *In all cities of this magnitude, older countries have been ever attentive to contrive certain places, where the bulk of the citizens can enjoy the benefits of exercise and wholesome air. In London, the inhabitants have, at one end of the town, three extensive parks, the most convenient of which is St. James's, and at the other end of the city they have Moorfields. These places are laid out in walks, regularly planted with trees, and furnished throughout with garden benches; the walks are rolled, kept clean from grass, and the benches under the shade of venerable trees, afford a charming resting place. . . . Paris has her* Tuileries, *and the different gardens of the* Palais Royales. *And Dublin her squares, one of which (St. Stephen's green) is perhaps the largest in Europe, with a gravel walk all round, planted with full-grown elms; this green is an exact square of a mile in circumference. These places are all resorted to after the fatigues of the day. . . .*
>
> *The size and consequence that this town must one day arrive at, ought strongly to impress the necessity of attending to this object, as well from a desire to contribute to the comfort and health of the inhabitants, as from the propriety of adding to the public ornaments of the city.*
>
> *Veritas †*

*   *   *

By 1807 a Commission of Streets and Roads was appointed to map and lay out Manhattan Island. The plan they submitted in 1811 showed seven squares or "places" and a Parade Ground extending from 23rd Street to 34th Street and from Third Avenue to Seventh Avenue. These eight open spaces totalled about 450 acres. The Commission explained their reasons for leaving so little open space in this excerpt from their report of 1811.

> *It may, to many, be a matter of surprise that so few vacant spaces have been left, and those so small, for the benefit of fresh air, and consequent preservation of*

*Laws of New York (1853), Ch. 616, 1162–65.
†Printed in the New York Packet, Aug. 15, 1785, as quoted by Frederick Law Olmsted, Jr. and Theodora Kimball, Forty Years of Landscape Architecture: Vol. 2, Central Park, 1853–1895 (New York: G. P. Putnam's Sons, 1928), 18–19.

health. Certainly if the City of New York were destined to stand on the side of a small stream such as the Seine or the Thames, a great number of ample places might be needful; but those large arms of the sea which embrace Manhattan Island render its situation, in regard to health and pleasure, as well as to the convenience of commerce, peculiarly felicitous; when therefore, from the same causes the price of land is so uncommonly great, it seemed proper to admit the principles of economy to greater influence than might, under circumstances of a different kind, have consisted with the dictates of prudence and the sense of duty.

By 1853, when Central Park was authorized, this total had been reduced to about 117 acres.

Over the years park enthusiasts continued to advocate the establishment of a substantial city park. Perhaps more than any other person, William Cullen Bryant, editor of the New York Evening Post, was responsible for the eventual authorization for Central Park. Andrew Jackson Downing, one of America's first landscape architects and the editor of The Horticulturist was also a staunch park supporter and devoted much space in his columns to advocating a city park. By 1850 sufficient favorable public support had been generated so that in the mayoralty campaign of that year both major candidates favored the establishment of a city park. The successful candidate, A. C. Kingsland continued his support of the city park concept after his election. On April 5, 1851 in a message to the Common Council he observed that

> The public places of New York are not in keeping with the character of our city; nor do they in any wise subserve the purpose for which such places should be set apart. Each year will witness a certain increase in the value of real estate, out of the city proper, and I do not know that any period will be more suitable than the present one, for the purchase and laying out of a park, on a scale which will be worthy of the city.
>
> There are places on the island easily accessible, and possessing all the advantages of wood, lawn and water, which might, at a comparatively small expense, be converted into a park, which would be at once the pride and ornament of the city. Such a park, well laid out, would become the favorite resort of all classes.

By this time the Evening Post advocated the acquisition of an area known as Jones' Wood as well as "the range of parks and public gardens along the central part of the island." The Jones' Wood proposal encountered strong opposition but for varying reasons. Some persons were opposed to any park proposal; others disliked the plan because they considered the site inadequate by itself. The second group pressed for two parks. In consideration of this situation, the city did not take immediate action on Jones' Wood but instead the Board of Aldermen appointed a committee to investigate the comparative desirability of Jones' Wood and other possible park sites. The committee recommended the central site and the Board of Aldermen adopted their report on January 2, 1852. On July 21, 1853 the state legislature authorized the city to acquire the land for Central Park. This landmark act follows.

An Act to alter the map of the city of New-York by laying out thereon a public place, and to authorize the taking of the same.

Passed July 21, 1853, three-fifths being present.

The People of the State of New-York, represented in Senate and Assembly, do enact as follows:

§ 1. All that piece or parcel of land situate, lying and being in the twelfth, nineteenth and twenty-second wards of the city of New-York, bounded southerly by Fifty-ninth-street, northerly by One Hundred and Sixth-street, easterly by the Fifth-avenue, and westerly by Eighth-avenue, is hereby declared to be a public place, in like manner as if the same had been laid out by the commissioners appointed in and by the act of the Legislature, entitled "An act relative to improvements touching the laying out of streets and roads in the city of New-York, and for other purposes," passed April 3, 1807; and the map or plan of said city is hereby altered accordingly.

§ 2. The mayor, aldermen and commonalty of the city of New-York are hereby authorized to take the said piece of land for public use, as and for a public square, pursuant to the act entitled "An act to reduce several laws relating particularly to the city of New-York into one act, passed April 9th, 1813," and the several acts amendatory thereto, or such portions thereof as are now in force, so far as the same are applicable to the laying out and taking of public squares and places in the city of New-York, except as hereinafter provided; and all such portions of the said act and of the said several acts amendatory thereto as are applicable to the laying out and taking of public squares and places in said city, and as are now in force, shall apply to the taking and laying out of the piece of land above described as and for a public square, in the same manner and to the same extent as if the said piece of land had been originally laid down as and for a public square upon the map or plan aforesaid of said city, except as hereinafter provided.

§ 3. Five persons shall be appointed commissioners of estimate and assessment, instead of three; and in case of the death, resignation, disqualification or refusal to act of them, or either of them, it shall be lawful for the supreme court in the first judicial district, at a general term thereof, on the application of the said mayor, aldermen, and commonalty, and officers, as such event shall happen, to appoint a discreet and disinterested person, being a citizen of the city of New-York, in the place and stead of such commissioner so dying, resigning or refusing to act.

§ 4. In every case of the appointment of commissioners under this act, it shall be competent and lawful for any three of said commissioners, so to be appointed, to perform the trust and duties of their appointment, and their acts shall be as valid and effectual as the acts of all the commissioners so to be appointed, if they had acted therein, would have been; and in every case the proceedings and decisions of such commissioners, being three in number, as shall be acting in the premises, shall be as valid and effectual as if the said commissioners appointed for such purpose had all concurred and joined therein.

§ 5. The said commissioners may allow compensation for any building or buildings, upon the said land, which may have been built, placed or erected thereon after the time of the filing of the original maps or plan of the said city.

§ 6. Payment of the damages awarded by the said commissioners shall be made and become due and payable immediately upon the confirmation of the report of said commissioners in the premises.

§ 7. For the payment of so much of the damages awarded by the commissioners of estimate and assessment, and the expenses, disbursements and charges in the premises, as shall exceed the amounts or sums that may be assessed by the said commissioners upon the parties and persons, lands and tenements, deemed by them benefited by the opening of such public square or place, it shall be lawful for the said mayor, aldermen, and commonalty to raise the amount of such excess by loan, by the creation of a public fund or stock, to be called "The Central Park Fund," which shall bear an interest not exceeding five per centum per annum, and shall be redeemable within a period of time not exceeding forty-five years after the passage of this act, and for the payment of which the said piece of land, so as aforesaid to be taken, shall be irrevocably pledged.

§ 8. It shall be lawful for the mayor, aldermen and commonalty to determine what shall be the nominal amount or value of each share of said stock, and of what number of shares the same shall consist; and they are hereby authorized to sell and dispose of such shares at public auction, or at private sale, or by subscription for such stock, and on such terms as they shall think proper; said stock shall not be sold at less than its par value.

§ 9. In order to pay the interest upon the stock hereby authorized, the mayor, recorder and aldermen of the city and county of New-York, as the supervisors thereof, are hereby authorized and empowered to order and cause to be raised by tax on the estates, real and personal, subject to taxation according to law, within said city and county, and to be collected in addition to the ordinary taxes, yearly and every year, until the whole amount of the tax be paid, a sum of money sufficient to pay the interest annually accruing on said stock.

§ 10. The provisions of the act entitled "An act to regulate the finances of the city of New-York," passed June 8th, 1812, which are not repugnant to or incompatible with any provision in this act contained, shall apply to said stock.

§ 11. This act shall take effect immediately.

THE CONTINUING INFLUENCE OF FREDERICK LAW OLMSTED*
1871

The success of Central Park under the leadership of Olmsted and Vaux stimulated park developments in other cities. During the next half century, these two men planned, or participated in planning, some 40 city parks. All these efforts cannot be described here but a few of them deserve special notice. In New York plans were devised for Prospect Park in Brooklyn and for Riverside and Morningside Parks. Between 1863 and 1865 Olmsted designed Golden Gate Park in San Francisco, the Oakland Cemetery, and the grounds of the University of California at Berkeley.

In the next few years Olmsted and Vaux collaborated on the design of the South Side parks of Chicago and other parks in Montreal, Buffalo, and Detroit. About 1871 Olmsted planned Fairmont Park, on the banks of the Schuylkill River in Philadelphia, which became the largest city park (3,845 acres) in the United States.

The next big step was the development of the concept of a system *of city parks rather than individual non-related parks. Olmsted set out this idea in his article, "Public Parks and the Enlargement of Towns" in 1871.*

A park fairly well managed near a large town, will surely become a new centre of that town. With the determination of location, size, and boundaries should therefore be associated the duty of arranging new trunk routes of communication between it and the distant parts of the town existing and forecasted.

These may be either narrow informal elongations of the park, varying say from two to five hundred feet in width, and radiating irregularly from it, or if, unfortunately, the town is already laid out in the unhappy way that New York and Brooklyn, San Francisco and Chicago, are, and, I am glad to say, Boston is not, on a plan made years ago by a man who never saw a spring-carriage, and who had a conscientious dread of the Graces, then we must probably adopt formal Park-ways. They should be so planned and constructed as never to be noisy and seldom crowded, and so also that the straightforward movement of pleasure-carriages need never be obstructed, unless at absolutely necessary crossings, by slow-going heavy vehicles used for commercial purposes. If possible, also, they should be branched or reticulated with other ways of a similar class, so that no part of the town should finally be many minutes walk from some one of them; and they should be made interesting by a process of planting and decoration, so that in necessarily passing through them, whether in going to or from the

---

*Frederick Law Olmsted, "Public Parks and the Enlargement of Towns," *Journal of Social Science,* No. 3 (1871), 24–25.

park, or to and from business, some substantial recreative advantage may be incidentally gained. It is a common error to regard a park as something to be produced complete in itself, as a picture to be painted on canvas. It should rather be planned as one to be done in fresco, with constant consideration of exterior objects, some of them quite at a distance and even existing as yet only in the imagination of the painter.

"CENTRAL PARK: NEW YORK'S BIG BACK YARD"*
1954

Legislative authorization to acquire the land to be included in Central Park was only the beginning of a long battle that was to last for the next century. In this article Creighton Peet described the park as it was in 1954 and recalled some of its earlier difficulties.

Few visitors to New York City ever come to understand about Central Park. Too often in the movies they have seen boy meet girl in this Park, and perhaps take her riding in an old horse-drawn carriage, and concluded this is about all there is to it.

Actually, Central Park is an area of 840 acres of great trees, shrubbery, lawns, lakes, rocky crags, and even wild landscape still all but untouched in the very center of a city three hundred years old. And it is of tremendous importance in the daily lives of vast numbers of New York's millions. It gets such a terrific workout almost every fair day that calling it, "New York's Big Back Yard" as it once was in a musical show about the Park, is no exaggeration.

Two and a half miles long and half a mile wide, Central Park is easily accessible to people on both the East and West sides of town — and it has something special for everyone.

Near the entrances are a score of small, fenced-in playgrounds for small children, with swings, sandboxes, etc. Farther inside are a dozen baseball diamonds, two lakes with rowboats for rent, and an open air rink used for ice skating for six months and for roller skating or dances the rest of the time. There is also a good-sized zoo, and a cafeteria with tables on an outdoor terrace. For horseback riders there are miles of tree-shaded, traffic-free paths, and for cyclists, other miles of paved paths. On summer evenings there are band concerts, and for older visitors there is a chess and checker house with tables both inside and under the trees, as well as a number of bowling greens where senior citizens gather to make like Rip Van Winkle.

For those who merely want to stroll, there are 57 miles of paths, with 4000 benches to sit on when they become weary. And every Saturday and Sunday hundreds sit or lie under the trees reading, sleeping, or eating.

But most important of all, Central Park takes the New Yorker out into the country for a time. As a result of a hundred year-old "invention" of Frederick Law Olmsted and Calvert Vaux, the landscape architects who designed Central Park, traffic is seldom seen or heard. Even in the 1850's traffic was nerve-wracking (iron-bound wheels on cobblestones), and Olmsted decided that all commer-

*Creighton Peet, "Central Park: New York's Big Back Yard," *American Forests,* Vol. 60, No. 7 (July, 1954), 8–11, 63.

cial vehicles should use four "transverse" roads. These are stone-walled channels sunk below grade and passing directly through the Park without any connections with its roads.

Today buses, trucks and many private cars use these transverse roads, which are so hidden by artful planning that visitors are seldom aware of them. Roads and paths in the Park are carried over these transverse roads on bridges. Today we would call these grade separations, but a hundred years ago, 50 years before the automobile, the transverse road was a revolutionary idea.

The need for such a Park in a rapidly growing city was first discussed in the newspapers in 1844 by such citizens as Washington Irving, William Cullen Bryant, poet and editor, Andrew J. Dowling, editor of "The Horticulturalist," and Cyrus Field, who later laid the first Atlantic telegraph cable. However, it was many years before the customary American process of haggling over the details was finished, and work could start. The rich predicted that such a Park would be "usurped by rowdies and low people," and one newspaper feared it would be lined with saloons and grog shops whose customers would use it for sobering up. On the other hand papers representing the rank and file suspected darkly that it would be restricted "for the upper few who ride in fine carriages."

After almost a decade of argument over the site, the financing and the design, work was begun in 1856, although it was not until 1858 that a large force of men began serious operations. By 1860, however, the work had become so mired in politics that a State Senate Committee was appointed to investigate, and get things moving again. While sections of the Park were opened as early as 1857, it was not pronounced complete until 1878.

While the site selected for the Park was wild and rugged and even "way out of town," it was by no means uninhabited, nor was it attractive. The southern section, adjacent to the land on which some of New York's finest hotels stand today, was a sort of no-man's land dotted with squatter's shacks, and covered with rubbish, broken-down stone walls, loose rock and tangled vines. The land was undrained and in many places swampy, and a report of the day found it "filthy, squalid and disgusting." The squatters indulged in such occupations as "cinder sifting, rag picking and bone boiling" not ordinarily permitted within the city limits. From this jungle some 300 "dwellings" were removed as construction progressed.

The only major construction already in the Park was some distance farther north—the Reservoir, forming a large lake which had been built some 20 years before. This is an essential part of the city's water system.

The northern section of the Park, which was originally, and still is today after a hundred years, far more wild and undeveloped, with some of the largest trees, held the only building of any importance or interest. This was the Black Horse Tavern built by Jacob Dyckman, Jr., in 1748, but better known as the Widow Magowan's Tavern, located rightly enough in Magowan's Pass through which

[311]

ran the original Post Road to Boston. The Widow's tavern burned once and was torn down once, but was rebuilt and flourished until 1915.

In 1752 the Colonial Assembly met there during the smallpox epidemic, and from 1776–83 it was the headquarters for the British troops holding the rocky heights along what is now the northern boundary of Central Park.

From 1847–58 the Tavern was used by the Mt. St. Vincent Academy and Convent, and from 1861–65 it was a hospital for Civil War soldiers. In the gay 90's it was a roadhouse, and for a time the management had a custom of presenting the first sleigh load of customers to arrive after the first snow of the year, with a magnum of champagne! Today a winding road runs through Magowan's Pass, and the only reminder of the tavern is a small plaque on a bench.

That Central Park still exists in its entirety here in 1954 after almost a hundred years of diligent effort by all sorts of promoters, is something of a phenomenon.

From the very first the sight of so much "vacant" land attracted people with all sorts of projects. Those who have wanted to cut the Park up into building lots have been easy to slap down, but those operating under the guise of patriotism, civic pride, or culture, have been more of a problem.

Olmsted—a remarkable man who worked on the Capitol in Washington and designed scores of parks and public buildings all over America, had very specific ideas about Central Park. He insisted that it have as much wild, untouched terrain as possible—forests, meadows, lakes, cliffs, etc. Many of the famous parks of Europe, such as Versailles, he pointed out, had become so filled with statuary, and their planting was so geometrical and artificial, that they no longer fulfilled what he conceived was a park's greatest function for the city-dweller. This was to make it possible for him to slip temporarily into natural surroundings, where trees, grass and winding paths would make him forget the stony regularity of streets and the racket of traffic.

In laying out Central Park Olmsted used the natural contours of the land as much as possible. Swampy areas were dredged into lakes, drainage was organized, and many new types of trees were imported from all over the world, but paths were made to twist and turn, and no straightaways were permitted in the carriage roads—for a reason no longer important—to prevent the racing of trotting horses.

One of the first major assaults on Central Park was a plan to put Grant's Tomb there. If this had succeeded, following generations of military and political heroes would have been buried there until the place would have become a vast cemetery—and the football, baseball, boating, skating, dancing and horseback riding now enjoyed by millions would have been impossible.

One of the most spectacular attempts to take over Central Park was in 1892, when a group of racing operators quietly got legislation passed in Albany to allow a 70-foot wide speedway for trotting horses right through the Park. This almost succeeded, but when the newspapers got word of it they really went to town. Indignant mass meetings were held, prominent citizens denounced the idea, and when the workmen arrived to build the raceway they were threatened with physical violence by angry citizens.

Those were the days before newspapers were timid and libel-conscious, and on March 18, 1892 the New York *Times* said the project was "monsterous and intolerable," and would not be approved "by a single New Yorker of standing or intelligence." As for those sponsoring the raceway, the paper said, "a statesman who was brought up to regard a pig in the parlor as indicative of social position is not going to trouble himself about a trotting track in the park."

Important in getting the legislation repealed 39 days after it was approved, were many labor organizations from the lower East Side, whose indignation put real fear into Tammany. The Park was regarded as the poor man's summer vacation, while trotting horses were strictly for the wealthy.

At other times suggestions have been made to put a steamship and a full rigged sailing ship on the reservoir lake, hold a world's fair in the Park, cut the lower half up into building lots, move the Metropolitan Opera into the Park and, more recently, hollow it out and build a vast garage under it.

The problem of gifts of statuary presented by well-meaning patriotic or literary groups has been still harder to cope with and, it must be admitted, Central Park does have its share of long-forgotten heroes in bronze and stone—but on the whole succeeding generations of Park Commissioners have kept the landscape much as Olmsted intended it should be.

The battle to keep commercial establishments and, in fact, any sort of building at all in the Park to a minimum, also has been successful. The Metropolitan Museum of Art, on the Fifth Avenue side, has been there almost since the park was laid out, and is regarded as a special case. Another building, the Tavern on the Green, a city-operated restaurant, also meets with general approval. It was originally a sheepfold, housing sheep which kept the lawns trimmed in the days before power mowers.

Another building going back to the beginning was "The Ladies Refreshment Salon," which, down the years became a restaurant until the late Mayor Jimmy Walker turned it into the Central Park Casino an ornate and expensive nightclub. This drew so much indignant criticism that at the end of the Walker reign it was demolished and a children's playground built on the site.

Generally speaking, the idea has been that while a few buildings are essential in the Park, they should not be seen, so whenever possible they have been located in odd spots and well camouflaged with planting. Nothing must destroy the effect of the natural landscape—although, of course, since Olmsted's day the Park has become rimmed on three sides with 20-story apartment houses. Once, however, the Park had a superintendent who had other ideas. He felt that the most wonderful sight in the world was that of the Sixth Avenue Elevated trains rounding the high curve at 110th Street, and cut vistas through the trees so people could get a good look. When the Park Commissioner discovered this he was furious and started a planting program to fill in these vistas.

The Central Park terrain is extremely rocky, with many bald ridges and knobs, and a good deal of top soil was added in certain places to support the planting needed. Nevertheless a great variety of vegetation has always thrived there with very little care. Today there are some 20,000 full-grown trees, chiefly elms, maples, oaks, lindens and planes, in the Park, but many of the older trees are not doing too well, and oaks, maples and beeches, among others, will not be replaced.

While they all thrived equally well in the Park at first, the vast increase in the City's population which brought millions of children climbing through every inch of the Park, and the gases from oil burners and motor vehicles, have given the vegetation a rough time these past 50 years.

A two-track subway was tunneled diagonally under the northwest corner of the Park in 1903, a four-track line dug just outside the western boundry in the 1930's, and every few years new water, gas, electric or telephone connections pass under some portion of the Park. All of these things seem to disturb the normal course of growth, despite the best scientific care.

* * *

Possibly because of the success of Central Park we do have today many large and beautiful parks all over America—but like New York's Big Back Yard they too have had to put up a constant fight for their lives. While real estate projects and crackpot "memorials" are not as much of a menace as they once were, we now have thruway engineers threatening to lay down wide bands of concrete regardless of what they do to the natural beauty of a park which is in their way.

So the fight to preserve even a few small acres of unspoiled landscape is endless—and at times seems hopeless. The only encouraging aspect of the situation is that Americans are becoming increasingly aware of the priceless value of their heritage, and so increasingly reluctant to see it destroyed.

BERMAN v. PARKER*
1954

Parks and open spaces are similar, but not synonymous, terms: a park may be an open space but an open space need not be a park. In simplest terms, open space is simply land that is not used for commercial, industrial, or residential purposes. In most cases, farm lands do not fall into this category even though buildings, streets, and so forth may be absent. Open space is valuable mainly for outdoor recreation in the broadest meaning of the term.

We have seen that open spaces were historically set aside mainly for utilitarian purposes and that some of these areas eventually came to have the characteristics of parks. It is only very recently that the concept of open space in urban areas has come to have somewhat general acceptance. Like other developments in outdoor recreation the idea of open space developed as an adjunct to other activities—in this case urban renewal and housing policy. These programs emphasized the need for planned *development and redevelopment, and partly because of them, the concept of large-scale and long-range planning acquired more general public acceptance. After all, planned development was obviously preferable to unplanned, haphazard development and the horrendous consequences of unplanned growth were painfully evident all over the country.*

In 1954 a Supreme Court decision established the right of the District of Columbia to obtain land for redevelopment purposes under eminent domain proceedings. It further held that, "If those who govern the District of Columbia decide that the Nation's Capital should be beautiful as well as sanitary, there is nothing in the Fifth Amendment that stands in the way." A summary of the relevant portions of this decision are reproduced below.

SUMMARY OF DECISION

The District of Columbia Redevelopment Act of 1945 (60 Stat 790, DC Code 1951, §§ 5-701-5-719), the purpose of which is the redevelopment of substandard housing and blighted areas in the District of Columbia, delegates to the District of Columbia Redevelopment Land Agency power to acquire and assemble by eminent domain and otherwise real property to effect the redevelopment. An owner of property used as a department store and not as a dwelling or a place of habitation, claimed that his property might not be constitutionally taken in connection with the redevelopment of the area; he argued that the property was commercial, not residential property or slum housing; that, under the terms of the statute, it would be put into the redevelopment project under the management of a private, not a public, agency and redeveloped for private, not public,

*348 U.S. 26 (1954)

use; and that the statute thus operated to deprive him of the Fifth Amendment's guaranties of due process of law, and that private property may not be taken for public use without just compensation. The trial court ruled in favor of the constitutionality of the statute.

On Appeal, DOUGLAS, J., speaking for a unanimous Court, affirmed the decision of the court below, holding that the redevelopment of the District of Columbia was a public purpose for which Congress could properly exercise its police power, and the power of eminent domain. In addition, it was ruled that, the public purpose having been established, Congress could attain that purpose on an area, rather than a structural, basis, notwithstanding that this involved the taking, in eminent domain, of innocuous and unoffending property located in an area to be redeveloped. The act was also held to contain sufficiently definite standards to sustain the delegation of authority to the Agency, and to empower the Agency to take full title to land in redevelopment areas, as distinguished from title to the objectionable buildings located on it.

* * *

Mr. JUSTICE DOUGLAS delivered the opinion of the Court.

The power of Congress over the District of Columbia includes all the legislative powers which a state may exercise over its affairs. See District of Columbia v. John R. Thompson Co. 346 US 100, 108, 97 L ed 1480, 1488, 73 S Ct 1007. We deal, in other words, with what traditionally has been known as the police power. An attempt to define its reach or trace its outer limits is fruitless, for each case must turn on its own facts. The definition is essentially the product of legislative determinations addressed to the purposes of government, purposes neither abstractly nor historically capable of complete definition. Subject to specific constitutional limitations, when the legislature has spoken, the public interest has been declared in terms well-nigh conclusive. In such cases the legislature, not the judiciary, is the main guardian of the public needs to be served by social legislation, whether it be Congress legislating concerning the District of Columbia (see Block v. Hirsh, 256 US 135, 65 L ed 865, 41 S Ct 458, 16 ALR 165) or the States legislating concerning local affairs. See Olsen v. Nebraska, 313 US 236, 85 L ed 1305, 61 S Ct 862, 133 ALR 1500; Lincoln Federal Labor Union v. Northwestern Iron & Metal Co. 335 US 525, 93 L ed 212, 69 S Ct 251, 6 ALR2d 473; California State Auto. Asso. v. Maloney, 341 US 105, 95 L ed 788, 71 S Ct 601. This principle admits of no exception merely because the power of eminent domain is involved. The role of the judiciary in determining whether that power is being exercised for a public purpose is an extremely narrow one. See Old Dominion Land Co. v. United States, 269 US 55, 66, 70 L ed 162, 165, 46 S Ct 39; United States ex rel. Tennessee Valley Authority v. Welch, 327 US 546, 552, 90 L ed 843, 848, 66 S Ct 715.

Public safety, public health, morality, peace and quiet, law and order—these are some of the more conspicuous examples of the traditional application of the police power to municipal affairs. Yet they merely illustrate the scope of the power and do not delimit it. See Noble State Bank v. Haskell, 219 US 104, 111, 55 L ed 112, 116, 31 S Ct 186, 32 LRA NS 1062, Ann Cas 1912A 487. Miserable and disreputable housing conditions may do more than spread disease and crime and immorality. They may also suffocate the spirit by reducing the people who live there to the status of cattle. They may indeed make living an almost insufferable burden. They may also be an ugly sore, a blight on the community which robs it of charm, which makes it a place from which men turn. The misery of housing may despoil a community as an open sewer may ruin a river.

We do not sit to determine whether a particular housing project is or is not desirable. The concept of the public welfare is broad and inclusive. See DayBrite Lighting, Inc. v. Missouri, 342 US 421, 424, 96 L ed 469, 472, 72 S Ct 405. The values it represents are spiritual as well as physical, aesthetic as well as monetary. It is within the power of the legislature to determine that the community should be beautiful as well as healthy, spacious as well as clean, well-balanced as well as carefully patrolled. In the present case, the Congress and its authorized agencies have made determinations that take into account a wide variety of values. It is not for us to reappraise them. If those who govern the District of Columbia decide that the Nation's Capital should be beautiful as well as sanitary, there is nothing in the Fifth Amendment that stands in the way.

In the present case, Congress and its authorized agencies attack the problem of the blighted parts of the community on an area rather than on a structure-by-structure basis. That, too, is opposed by appellants. They maintain that since their building does not imperil health or safety nor contribute to the making of a slum or a blighted area, it cannot be swept into a redevelopment plan by the mere dictum of the Planning Commission or the Commissioners. The particular uses to be made of the land in the project were determined with regard to the needs of the particular community. The experts concluded that if the community were to be healthy, if it were not to revert again to a blighted or slum area, as though possessed of a congenital disease, the area must be planned as a whole. It was not enough, they believed, to remove existing buildings that were insanitary or unsightly. It was important to redesign the whole area so as to eliminate the conditions that cause slums—the overcrowding of dwellings, the lack of parks, the lack of adequate streets and alleys, the absence of recreational areas, the lack of light and air, the presence of out-moded street patterns. It was believed that the piecemeal approach, the removal of individual structures that were offensive, would be only a palliative. The entire area needed redesigning so that a balanced, integrated plan could be developed for the region, including not only new homes but also schools, churches, parks, streets, and shopping centers. In this way it was hoped that the cycle of decay of the area could be controlled and the birth of future slums prevented. Cf. Gohld Realty Co. v. Hartford, 141 Conn 135, 141–144, 104 A2d 365, 368–370; Hunter v. Norfolk Redevelopment & Housing Authority, 195 Va 326, 338–339, 78 SE2d 893, 900–901. Such diversification in future use is plainly relevant to the maintenance of the desired housing standards and therefore within congressional power.

*   *   *

"A PLAN TO SAVE VANISHING U.S. COUNTRYSIDE"*
1959

*Although some open space was created within large cities through urban re-
newal and other redevelopment programs, obviously the easiest and cheapest
way to acquire open space was to reserve land that was* already open. *However,
the rapid, unplanned growth of suburbia made such acquisition extremely difficult. William H. Whyte, Jr., described this problem in these excerpts from a
1959 article.*

Take a last look. Some summer's morning drive past the golf club on the edge
of town, turn off onto a back road and go for a short trip through the open countryside. Look well at the meadows, the wooded draws, the stands of pine, the
creeks and streams, and fix them in your memory. If the American standard of
living goes up another notch, this is about the last chance you will have.

Go back toward the city five or 10 miles. Here, in what was pleasant countryside only a year ago, is the sight of what is to come. No more sweep of green—
across the hills are splattered scores of random subdivisions, each laid out in the
same dreary asphalt curves. Gone are the streams, brooks, woods and forests
that the subdivisions' signs talked about. The streams are largely buried in concrete culverts. Where one flows briefly through a patch of weeds and tin cans it
is fetid with the ooze of septic tanks.

A row of stumps marks the place where sycamores used to shade the road and
if a stand of maple or walnut still exists the men with power saws will soon be at
it. Here and there a farm remains, but the "For Sale" signs are up and now even
the golf course is to be chopped into lots. What open space remains you can no
longer see. To the eye it is all a jumble, an endless succession of driving ranges,
open-air theaters, billboards, neon signs, frozen custard spas, TV aerials and
pink plaster flamingos.

This is only a foretaste of the future. The mess we have made so far has been
achieved with a population reaching 175 million. By 1970 there will be 35 million more Americans. Most of the housing to take care of the increase will be
built on the edges of our metropolitan areas. And long before that the pattern
will have been set. The new federal highway program, just now getting into gear,
will visibly accelerate the exploitation of outlying areas. With each new interchange will come a speculative land rush the like of which few communities are
prepared to resist. If any open spaces are to be saved they must be saved now.
The options are fast expiring. At best most communities have only a year of
grace.

* * *

*William H. Whyte, Jr., "A Plan to Save Vanishing U.S. Countryside," *Life,* Vol. 47, No. 7 (Aug.
17, 1959), 88–90, 92, 94, 96, 102.

Many of our past difficulties in dealing with sprawl come from some very mistaken if widely held assumptions. One is that sprawl is due to too many people and not enough land. A second is that the best way to save open space is to provide more of it for each homestead. A third, following from the others, is that zoning is therefore the main antisprawl safeguard.

But a shortage of land is *not* the problem. Indeed, many communities that have become sprawling messes could have accommodated up to half again as many people and had more usable open space to boot. Most people assume that the area close to a city is "filled up." If they were to look closely they would be surprised at how much vacant space there really is—even on the city's very edge. It looks terrible, of course—a vacant lot here, an automobile graveyard there—but if you add it all up you have quite a lot of space. The problem, simply, is that you cannot add it up. It is scattered.

There is not a shortage of land. There is a shortage of space. Ten acres have been used to do the work of one, for the pattern of suburban growth has been left almost entirely up to the speculative builder. The builder is not the villain of the piece. He is understandably interested in making money, and he can hardly be expected to double as a volunteer city planner. Where development might be best for orderly growth is generally just the place where landowners are holding out for a killing. So the builder leapfrogs, leaving behind many an unrequited cupidity, and goes out where the land is cheap.

In one year the total amount of land in an area that he and other developers finally build on may be only a fraction of the whole, but the presence of the model homes and the bulldozers has a tremendous pre-emptive effect. Because these projects have been scattered, a few casually placed developments rob the community of scores of choices that would be important to it five or 10 years from now—for parks, industrial districts, reservoirs and just plain breathing space. Already the community begins to look filled up—and the new suburbanites are only now beginning to arrive.

* * *

Let us trust our instincts. Esthetics is the driving force for action, but it is not something separate from economics. Look again at the desecration of a countryside—the buried streams, the jumble of neon signs and driving ranges, the abandoned beauty spots with those telltale signs, WILL SUBDIVIDE. Your instincts will tell you that anything that looks this terrible cannot be good economics, that it is not progress, that it is not inevitable. And that we had better get cracking.

THE RACE FOR OPEN SPACE*
1960

*In 1960 the Regional Plan Association conducted a study of open space re-
quirements for the tri-state New York metropolitan area. Since this was one of
the early comprehensive plans and since it involved one of the most heavily populated areas in the United States, a portion of the summary report is documented
here.*

Open space is a fundamental element in any decent and desirable living
environment. We are emerging, indeed we have already emerged, into an era
when parks and open space are taking on a new and vital importance for the
American people. The test of the future is not only how well we do in outer
space and in our international relations; we are also challenged to produce
healthy and happy communities for all Americans in this period of explosive
metropolitan growth. In the burgeoning Tri-State New York Metropolitan
Region the task of preserving adequate open land is a formidable one, and no
less critical than the need for schools and housing and highways. To carry out
this task, the people of the Region and their elected representatives at all levels
of government have a great responsibility to act swiftly and boldly. Time and
space are running out.

WHY A RACE FOR OPEN SPACE?

The New York Region, which extends for roughly 50 miles from its center in
Manhattan, has an area of 7,000 square miles. It is about 25 percent developed;
the rest of its terrain is in fields, woods, wetlands, mountains and beaches. Super-
ficially, there appears to be plenty of land left. But more than a third of the land
suitable for urban development has already been used up. And two powerful
forces leave no room for complacency. The first is the rising demand for outdoor
recreation; the second is the startling increase in the rate of consumption of land
for development. Both derive from the same source: a Region which is growing
dramatically in population and economic strength.

The problem of open space is magnified because we have fallen far behind in
providing parks for the Region's existing population. As shown in the accom-
panying Staff Report, the pace of park acquisition is declining relative to the Region's growing population.

INCREASING DEMAND FOR OUTDOOR RECREATION

The demand for all forms of outdoor recreation will increase at an unprecedented pace during
the next 25 years in the New York Metropolitan Region, and in the United States as a whole.

*The Race for Open Space (New York: Regional Plan Association, Inc., 1960), 8–12.

There will be a substantial rise in each of the factors which most affect the demand for recreation: population, per capita income, leisure time, and ease of travel. Growth in any one of these separate factors would be significant; when their gains are combined the impact on the need for parks and other open space becomes a major challenge of our time.[1]

Between 1955 and 1985 the change predicted in the New York Region for the four factors is as follows: population from 15 million to 24 million; per capita real personal income from $2,470 to $4,350; the work week from 40 hours to 32 hours; and passenger automobiles from 3.9 million to 8.6 million.

The directions of these underlying forces give us a notion of what is in store for us. This is confirmed by recent recreation trends. Every indicator of recreation demand—equipment sales, attendance records, licenses issued—points to an inexorable rush to the outdoors.

INCREASING CONSUMPTION OF LAND FOR DEVELOPMENT

In the early history of the Region's settlement houses were close together. The tenements of the turn of the century housed from 200 to 400 families per acre. This density was typical. Today the one-family house is the dominant type of residential construction; new suburban developments seldom have more than six of these per acre. The four-acre lot is not uncommon. Similarly, factories and shopping centers sprawl over many times the land they once did.

What is the effect of changing trends in land consumption on the Region's landscape? At present the Region has about 2,000 square miles of developed land of all kinds. This has been achieved gradually over a span of 300 years. In the next *twenty-five years,* if present trends continue, developed land will at least double and may quite possibly triple.

Because the Region's total area of 7,000 square miles includes over 1,000 square miles of land either too steeply sloped or too swampy for development, the trends described above mean that the remaining 6,000 square miles will be completely urbanized within 30 to 40 years. We can look forward to the day when all of the Region's twenty-two counties will be virtually fully developed.

HOW MUCH OPEN SPACE?

To keep pace with estimated urban growth, the Project recommends an increase in permanent open space in the Region (in round figures) from 600 to 1,700 square miles, as shown in Table 1. This amount is about 25 percent of the Region's total land area. (Only a portion of this recommended open space is in the sloped and swampy areas which are unsuitable for development; this is because these latter areas are not uniformly distributed throughout the Region nor are they appropriate topographically to provide all of the Region's open space needs.)

[1]Marion Clawson. *The Dynamics of Park Demand,* Regional Plan Association, 1960, the second report of the Park, Recreation and Open Space Project.

Table 1 Summary of Permanent Open Space[a] in the New York Region, 1958, and Proposed, 1985

| | Existing | | Total Proposed | |
	in acres	*in sq. mi.*	*in acres*	*in sq. mi.*
Public Parks and Recreation Areas	189,000	300	736,000	1,150
Public Water Supply, Institutional and Military Lands	175,000	270	175,000	270
Public or Private Conservation Land	10,000	20 }	150,000	230
Public or Private Residential Commons[b]				
Total	374,000	590	1,061,000	1,650

a. Excludes cemeteries; airfields; parkways and other highways; such private holdings as railroad yards, utility company properties, sportsmen's clubs, golf courses, and estates.
b. Defined in Staff Report.

The central concern of the Park, Recreation and Open Space Project is the preservation of open land for three major purposes: for recreation; for conservation; and for a liveable and efficient residential development pattern. These purposes are not mutually exclusive. There are many areas which serve two or all of them at the same time. But each has its own needs which the Project will attempt to define.

Recreation land emphasizes use and enjoyment by people. It is land which provides a setting for a variety of popular activities and for the satisfying of a host of basic human physical and emotional needs. The activities range from games and swimming to walking and bird-watching. The human needs include relief of tensions; keeping physically fit; satisfying the impulses to explore, to learn, to be alone, to express one's self; esthetic experience; and the need for fruitful and pleasurable leisure.

Conservation land is, of course, important for many forms of recreation. The protection of wildlife in a metropolitan area is important for the enjoyment and enlightenment of people. But conservation is an ecological need as well. Its practice is essential to such basic functions as flood prevention, water supply, insect and air pollution control and protecting agriculture and fishery resources.[2]

Residential open space is needed in addition to local recreation areas for a liveable and efficient urban development pattern. Open land gives character to the urban environment. It is relief from the monotony of urban sprawl. It is scenery which relaxes the eye and the mind. It is the counterbalance to urbanization which gives man-made development structure and order. Open space in

[2]The importance of conservation in the Tri-State New York Region is demonstrated in William A. Niering, *Nature in the Metropolis,* Regional Plan Association, 1960, the third report of the Park, Recreation and Open Space Project.

association with buildings is essential for light, air, and the assurance of quiet and privacy.

OPEN SPACE FOR RECREATION

The Project recommends that the Region's present 189,000 acres (290 square miles) of public parks be expanded to 736,000 acres (1,150 square miles). Distribution by level of government is summarized in Table 2.

Table 2 Summary of Existing Public Park Acreage[a] in the Region, 1958, and Proposed Parks, 1985, by Level of Government

	Existing		Total Proposed	
	in acres	*in sq. mi.*	*in acres*	*in sq. mi.*
Municipal Parks[b]	67,000	100	176,000	280
County Parks	28,000	40	263,000	410
State Parks	94,000[c]	150	297,000	460
Total	189,000	290	736,000	1,150

a. Includes all public park systems, but not parkways; includes state forests, fish and game lands.
b. Includes public school recreation areas and New York City.
c. Includes 2,746 acres of federally-owned parks in the Region.

LOCAL RECREATION AREAS

Less than 4 percent of the Region's population lives in communities which meet the National Recreation Association's minimum standard of 10 acres of park per 1,000 population. By this or any other reasonable standard, and in spite of noteworthy efforts in some localities, the Region's 550 municipalities are woefully deficient in recreation acreage.

In searching for realizable goals for municipal recreation acreage, a paradox presents itself. The densely populated cities which need recreation space the most have the least physical and financial potential for achieving it. The extreme example of this difficulty is Manhattan. To accommodate 10 acres of parks for every 1,000 of Manhattan's population would require an area bigger than the Island itself; site acquisition is seldom less than $500,000 an acre and is thus about 100 times greater than in most suburban locations. This situation pertains, although in less exaggerated form, in the more densely built-up communities of the Region.

The National Recreation Association's minimum standard of 10 acres of park per 1,000 population is, nevertheless, the most reliable space standard based on the recreation needs of all age groups in the population. The Association is considering an upward revision of this requirement. On the other hand, it recognizes that in applying the standard "varying local conditions . . . influence the amount and types of open space that are required."

The Project recommends that all communities strive to provide a minimum of

10 acres of recreation space per 1,000 population, but it has also set a series of goals for localities in which this standard cannot be attained.

These goals, discussed in some detail in the Staff Report, are based on density and may be summarized as follows: for the highest density multi-family area, Manhattan, the Project recommends a goal of 1.8 recreation acres per 1,000 population (which means an addition of 250 acres in small parks); for all other substantially multi-family communities, 5 to 6 acres per 1,000; for one-family communities where lot-size ranges from 5,000 to 15,000 square feet, 8 to 9 acres per 1,000; and for lower density one-family areas, over 10 acres per 1,000. Based on these goals, the Project recommends a near-tripling of local recreation areas in the Tri-State Region from 67,000 acres in 1958 to 176,000 acres by 1985.

Such a compromise of a desirable space standard can only be justified if it is accompanied by some other means of assuring that adequate recreation opportunities are available to all. Two such means are recommended.

First, the emphasis in densely populated areas should be on neighborhood playgrounds, playfields and small parks. Large parks accessible to the big cities in the center of the Region, which will necessarily have to occur outside the boundaries of these cities, should be provided by the states, although counties containing such cities (Essex, Union, Passaic, Westchester) can fulfill part of this role for their own communities.

Second, the amount of land is only part of the recreation story. How it is distributed and what facilities and programs are provided on it are also essential considerations. This applies, of course, to all municipalities. But for the most densely populated places like New York City and Newark, these factors are particularly significant. High density cities, by their very nature, must make more intensive use of all their land for all purposes. For recreation, this means better-distributed, more intensively developed parks and more active recreation programs.

A salutary trend in local recreation planning has been the growing coordination of school site acquisition programs with general municipal parks and recreation. School sites with their related play facilities should be planned in conjunction with neighborhood and community recreation areas.

A final point in connection with municipal park acreage is the Project's recommendation that all local facilities which tend to be within walking distance of the home, such as playgrounds, playfields and neighborhood and community parks, be provided by local authorities and not by higher levels of government. Municipalities should not rely on county or state parks as a substitute for needed local recreation acreage, but should seize the opportunity to provide local facilities as a legitimate exercise of local initiative.

ALL-DAY RECREATION AREAS, PUBLIC AND PRIVATE

All-day recreation areas, as the name implies, are for all-day outings requiring from ½ to 2 hours traveling time. They are generally (and properly) provided by county and state governments. With increasing income, leisure and car ownership, typical all-day activities such as swimming, boating, golf, picnicking, hiking, fishing, hunting, and nature study are rising rapidly in importance.

The Park, Recreation and Open Space Project recommends that county and state parks accommodating all-day activities be increased from their present 122,000 acres to 560,000 acres by 1985 (see Table 2).

County parks. The Project has developed a standard for county parks based on the growing demand for all-day activities which are fairly close to home. With growing leisure for the housewife as well as her husband, with increased mobility of teenagers and an earlier retirement age for older people, golf, swimming, boating and various natural area activities are engaged in throughout the week. These activities should be accommodated within 15 or 30 minutes of the home. The Project's standard calls for 12 acres of county parks per 1,000 of the county's anticipated 1985 population, or 5 percent of the county's total area, whichever is greater. The standard applies, of course, only where it is physically feasible. The reason for the 5 percent provision is that some of the Region's counties may not have reached their ultimate population by 1985 but should nevertheless begin to anticipate the time when they will.

Because county parks for the Region as a whole have been slower in developing than state parks, and because of the great rise in demand which is foreseen for facilities which can best be provided at the county level, the Project recommends a nine-fold increase in county park land from the present 28,000 acres to 263,000 acres (see Table 2).

These recommendations for county parks exclude the Core Counties (Bronx, Brooklyn, Manhattan, Queens and Hudson) whose lack of available land requires that their all-day recreation needs be satisfied in state parks.

State parks. The states have the role of providing parks whose attraction is regionwide. These are the parks to which people will travel up to two hours for an all-day or overnight outing either because the parks have a unique natural quality or because they are accessible to the densely populated cities at the Region's center.

The Region's geography dictates where state parks should be located. The Region is, in effect, a great urbanized area with a range of mountains above it to the north and a magnificent stretch of shoreline to the south. The continuous ranges of mountainous land comprise nearly 800,000 acres and the Atlantic oceanfront stretches for 150 miles. Both are highly accessible to the Region's population and it is rare good fortune that nature has provided us with such a spectacular basis for regional parks and open space. Long Island Sound and the lower Hudson River are important secondary sources for state parks.

The mountains and shoreline already provide the setting for some of our great state parks in all three states. The Project recommends that the states acquire an additional 173,000 acres in the mountains and that they acquire all of the remaining 71 miles (roughly 10,000 acres) of undeveloped oceanfront in the Region.

Oceanfront is a unique, limited and highly desirable resource. Like the air we breathe and the water we drink, it must be kept in its most natural possible state and yet be available to all. In light of the impending growth and spread of the Region's population, the ocean beaches can be of optimum recreation and conservation value only if they are publicly owned. The intensively built-up New Jersey shore is a great waste of a scarce natural asset and provides a vivid picture of the consequences of inaction.

Private all-day recreation areas. Golf and boating are two important all-day recreation activities which in the main are privately provided. Of the Region's 268 golf courses, 226 are privately owned. They cover 37,000 acres. The Region has over 650 boating facilities occupying about 5,000 acres along 65 miles of waterfront. All but a fraction of these are privately operated. It is hoped that private golf courses and other private recreation areas will grow substantially in order to alleviate the great task of preserving adequate open space. This could be achieved in part through the use of the Project's proposal for residential commons, discussed below.

OPEN SPACE FOR CONSERVATION

The Tri-State New York Region has as great a variety of natural features as any other metropolitan area in the United States. Conservation for human enjoyment is encompassed in our definition of recreation. Land for this purpose is included in the recreation goals and standards set forth above.

But there are additional conservation needs related to the Region's basic ecology. For example, there are 88,000 acres of wetlands in the Region (swamps, marshes and bogs). Only a third of this acreage is publicly owned. Counties and municipalities should examine these wetlands for their importance in controlling floods, enhancing fishing resources, providing educational benefits, as well as for their recreation value. States should assist in protecting the Region's wetlands. New York State took a step in this direction by amending its conservation law to provide for State technical and financial assistance for the management of wetlands which are already owned by counties and towns. All three states should consider how they may assist in their public acquisition, or in otherwise preserving additional needed wetlands and other conservation areas.

To make proper use of water resources as well as to prevent damage to life and property from uncontrolled runoff requires sizable tracts of land area. Water impoundments, streamside floodways and floodplains, wetland water storage areas, reservoir properties, and storm water collection areas (recharge basins) all require space. Counties and municipalities should examine these demands along with their wildlife conservation needs and take steps to meet them.

[327]

OPEN SPACE FOR RESIDENTIAL AREAS

In addition to local recreation acreage, there is a need for open space in residential areas which make them more pleasant, more convenient and efficient. There is no single formula for such open space in a metropolitan region as large and diverse as ours. We have definitely moved forward from the extreme congestion of the old-law tenement which covered 90 percent of each lot and represented the ultimate in disregard for open space. On the other hand, in most of the counties of the Tri-State Region the days of the private estate with one house to 50 or even 1,000 acres are numbered. Between these two disappearing extremes many different standards of density of population and different relations of buildings to open space are possible and desirable.

The Project recommends that each county and each community evolve its own residential open space plan for its residential districts.

For city and city-suburban areas where population densities must be high, space requirements should be based on the concept of usable open space rather than mechanistic formulae of courts, yards and set-backs. Required open space should not be preempted by parked automobiles, drying yards, delivery areas, etc., but where practicable, should include areas for outdoor living and recreation on the ground, in balconies and on roof tops. Flexibility should be given in the design of such developments so that open space may be concentrated to provide relatively large areas available to the residents of the adjacent buildings, such as were achieved years ago at Gramercy Park and Sunnyside, New York and Radburn, New Jersey.

Flexibility of design should be encouraged to avoid wasting open space in meaningless side and rear yards. For example, two dwellings with a soundproof common wall occupying a lot of 100 feet width may be preferable to two free standing houses on 50 foot lots separated by narrow side yards. Concentration of buildings and concentration of usable open space (leaving modest areas for individual privacy) are preferable to uniform spacing of dwellings resulting in wasted slivers of open space and often complete lack of outdoor privacy.

The planning principles just enumerated for more densely populated areas— namely, usable open space, concentration of building to avoid waste of open space, flexibility and variety of design—apply equally to suburbia. They apply also to commercial and industrial areas.

In areas where most building is by new subdivision of multi-acre tracts of land, every effort should be made to avoid lot-next-to-lot development unrelieved by areas of open space. Exclusive reliance on acreage zoning (even if such zoning did not break down, as it always may in the face of developmental pressures) would result in a monotony of not-quite-estates lacking the amenities of either urban or rural living.

The Project endorses the principle of requiring subdividers, in suitable areas, either to dedicate a percentage of each subdivision for park land or to pay a fee to a municipal park fund in lieu of such a land contribution.

Also endorsed is the principle of clustering dwellings in suitable areas and under adequate safeguards. By "clustering" we refer to permitting greater density of building in one part of a large tract (not less than, say, 50 acres in single ownership before subdivision) providing that the average density required by the zoning is maintained for the entire tract, that all the land not subdivided is dedicated unequivocably and irrevocably as a residential common of permanent open space and that the location of the cluster of dwellings is in harmony with the master plan of the community.

Whether the 20th Century City called suburbia is to become as obsolete in 50 years as the 19th Century City appears today depends in large part upon how our generation handles its residential open space.

MESSAGE FROM PRESIDENT JOHN F. KENNEDY ON HOUSING
AND COMMUNITY DEVELOPMENT*
March 9, 1961

Shortly after taking office, President Kennedy sent a message to Congress recommending measures to improve the nation's housing—including provision for open space land. Partly because of the President's support, a broad-scale housing bill was enacted later that year. Excerpts from President Kennedy's message follow.

To the Congress of the United States:

Our communities are what we make them. We as a nation have before us the opportunity—and the responsibility—to remold our cities, to improve our patterns of community development, and to provide for the housing needs of all segments of our population. Meeting these goals will contribute to the nation's economic recovery and its long-term economic growth.

In 1949 the Congress, with great vision, announced our national housing policy of "a decent home and a suitable living environment for every American family." We have progressed since that time; but we must still redeem this pledge to the 14 million American families who currently live in substandard or deteriorating homes, and protect the other 39 million American families from the encroachment of blight and slums.

An equal challenge is the tremendous urban growth that lies ahead. Within 15 years our population will rise to 235 million and by the year 2000 to 300 million people. Most of this increase will occur in and around urban areas. We must begin now to lay the foundations for livable, efficient and attractive communities of the future.

Land adjoining urban centers has been engulfed by urban development at the astounding rate of about one million acres a year. But the result has been haphazard and inefficient suburban expansion, and continued setbacks in the central cities' desperate struggle against blight and decay. Their social and economic base has been eroded by the movement of middle and upper income families to the suburbs, by the attendant loss of retail sales, and by the preference of many industrial firms for outlying locations.

Our policy for housing and community development must be directed toward the accomplishment of three basic national objectives:

First, to renew our cities and assure sound growth of our rapidly expanding metropolitan areas.

Second, to provide decent housing for all of our people.

H. Doc. 102, 87th Cong., 1st sess. (Mar. 9, 1961).

Third, to encourage a prosperous and efficient construction industry as an essential component of general economic prosperity and growth.

* * *

LAND RESERVES

Land is the most precious resource of the metropolitan area. The present patterns of haphazard suburban development are contributing to a tragic waste in the use of a vital resource now being consumed at an alarming rate.

Open space must be reserved to provide parks and recreation, conserve water and other natural resources, prevent building in undesirable locations, prevent erosion and floods, and avoid the wasteful extension of public services. Open land is also needed to provide reserves for future residential development, to protect against undue speculation, and to make it possible for State and regional bodies to control the rate and character of community development.

(a) I am directing the Administrator of the Housing and Home Finance Agency and the Secretary of the Interior to develop a long-range program and policy for dealing with open space and orderly development of urban land.

(b) Nevertheless, this problem is so urgent that we must make a start now. I therefore recommend legislation providing: (1) for $100 million to initiate a program of 20% grants to help public bodies finance the reservation of land—by acquisition or other means—as permanent urban open space in the form of parks and other facilities; and (2) for urban renewal loans to help local agencies finance the acquisition of open space for future public or private development. In both programs a prerequisite for Federal aid will be an effective and comprehensive plan for metropolitan or regional development.

* * *

CONCLUSION

A nation that is partly ill-housed is not as strong as a nation with adequate homes for every family. A nation with ugly, crime-infested cities and haphazard suburbs does not present the same image to the world as a nation characterized by bright and orderly urban development. To achieve our nation's housing goals, to meet our appropriate Federal responsibilities to aid private and local efforts— and at the same time helping to combat the present recession while furthering long-term growth—I commend this program to the Congress and urge its prompt consideration and enactment.

John F. Kennedy

OPEN SPACE PROVISIONS OF THE HOUSING ACT*
1961

If we are to preserve what is left of the natural majesty and beauty of America . . . and reserve land for orderly future expansion of our communities, we must protect our open spaces by law. To do otherwise is to sacrifice our heritage to the bulldozer and the concrete mixer.

. . . we are responsible not only to our present citizens but to a national population which will nearly double within the life of a 40-year mortgage.

We must, in effect, build a second United States. The question, then, is not whether we will do it, but how well it will be done. We can create a new age of prosperity and beauty for America or botch the job irretrievably.†

The need for open space as part of an integrated community plan was admirably summarized by Luther Gulick when he testified on the Housing Act of 1961.

If I judge aright, we don't want to hand over to the next generation a land condemned to become rural and suburban slums, plastered with signboards, and broken into self-destroying, inefficient, and incongruous "developments." There is a legitimate place for all the developments we shall need, but these must be fitted one into the other with suitable public services, so that we will not end up with the piano in the kitchen—speaking figuratively—and the kitchen sink in the parlor. These arrangements can be influenced through zoning and areawide plans, and controlled by public land acquisition. The developments themselves will always be designed and carried through by private enterprise, except, of course, for the public buildings and highways that are required. A good zoning and control program will in fact encourage private investment because it is the best insurance any builder can ask.

There is, however, a major need of the future that will not, and cannot, be met by private enterprise even with the best local planning and zoning. This is the fundamental requirement for open space. If it is to exist at all, open space must be nailed down before development cuts it into useless shreds or erases it completely, and before land costs soar, and water rights are alienated or drained away.

Looking into the future, we want not only open space as a heritage for our children, but also a general urban development which is efficient, comfortable, reasonably attractive, and always capable of still further advance, that is elastic. We don't expect things to stay put forever, but we do expect things to develop on a planned basis without destroying efficiency, convenience and attractiveness.‡

*75 *Statutes at Large,* 149.

†Statement of Philip Will, Jr., President, American Institute of Architects, *The Housing Act of 1961,* Hearings on H. R. 6028, H. R. 5300, and H. R. 6423, before the Subcommittee on Housing of the Committee on Banking and Currency, U.S. House of Representatives, 87th Cong., 1st sess., 862.

‡*The Housing Act of 1961,* Hearings on H.R. 6028, H.R. 5300, and H.R. 6423, before the Subcommittee on Housing of the Committee on Banking and Currency, U.S. House of Representatives, 87th Cong., 1st sess., 824–25.

The Housing Act of 1961 represented a major breakthrough in open space planning and acquisition. Title VII, which provided funds to state and local governments to "preserve open-space land which is essential to the proper long-range development and welfare of the Nation's urban areas" follows.

TITLE VII—OPEN SPACE LAND

FINDINGS AND PURPOSE

SEC. 701. (a) The Congress finds that a combination of economic, social, governmental, and technological forces have caused a rapid expansion of the Nation's urban areas, which has created critical problems of service and finance for all levels of government and which, combined with a rapid population growth in such areas, threatens severe problems of urban and suburban living, including the loss of valuable open-space land in such areas, for the preponderant majority of the Nation's present and future population.

(b) It is the purpose of this title to help curb urban sprawl and prevent the spread of urban blight and deterioration, to encourage more economic and desirable urban development, and to help provide necessary recreational, conservation, and scenic areas by assisting State and local governments in taking prompt action to preserve open-space land which is essential to the proper long-range development and welfare of the Nation's urban areas, in accordance with plans for the allocation of such land for open-space purposes.

FEDERAL GRANTS

SEC. 702. (a) In order to encourage and assist in the timely acquisition of land to be used as permanent open-space land, as defined herein, the Housing and Home Finance Administrator (hereinafter referred to as the "Administrator") is authorized to enter into contracts to make grants to States and local public bodies acceptable to the Administrator as capable of carrying out the provisions of this title to help finance the acquisition of title to, or other permanent interests in, such land. The amount of any such grant shall not exceed 20 per centum of the total cost, as approved by the Administrator, of acquiring such interests: Provided, That this limitation may be increased to not to exceed 30 per centum in the case of a grant extended to a public body which (1) exercises responsibilities consistent with the purposes of this title for an urban area as a whole, or (2) exercises or participates in the exercise of such responsibilities for all or a substantial portion of an urban area pursuant to an interstate or other intergovernmental compact or agreement. The faith of the United States is pledged to the payment of all grants contracted for under this title.

(b) The Administrator may enter into contracts to make grants under this title aggregating not to exceed $50,000,000. There are hereby authorized to be appropriated, out of any moneys in the Treasury not otherwise appropriated, the amounts necessary to provide for the payment of such grants as well as to carry out all other purposes of this title.

(c) No grants under this title shall be used to defray development costs or ordinary State or local governmental expenses, or to help finance the acquisition by a public body of land located outside the urban area for which it exercises (or participates in the exercise of) responsibilities consistent with the purpose of this title.

(d) The Administrator may set such further terms and conditions for assistance under this title as he determines to be desirable.

(e) The Administrator shall consult with the Secretary of the Interior on the general policies to be followed in reviewing applications for grants. To assist the Administrator in such review, the Secretary of the Interior shall furnish him appropriate information on the status of recreational planning for the areas to be served by the open-space land acquired with the grants. The Administrator shall provide current information to the Secretary from time to time on significant program developments.

PLANNING REQUIREMENTS

SEC. 703. (a) The Administrator shall enter into contracts to make grants for the acquisition of land under this title only if he finds that (1) the proposed use of the land for permanent open space is important to the execution of a comprehensive plan for the urban area meeting criteria he has established for such plans, and (2) a program of comprehensive planning (as defined in section 701 (d) of the Housing Act of 1954) is being actively carried on for the urban area.

(b) In extending financial assistance under this title, the Administrator shall take such action as he deems appropriate to assure that local governing bodies are preserving a maximum of open-space land, with a minimum of cost, through the use of existing public land; the use of special tax, zoning, and subdivision provisions; and the continuation of appropriate private use of open-space land through acquisition and leaseback, the acquisition of restrictive easements, and other available means.

CONVERSIONS TO OTHER USES

SEC. 704. No open-space land for which a grant has been made under this title shall, without the approval of the Administrator, be converted to uses other than those originally approved by him. The Administrator shall approve no conversion of land from open-space use unless he finds that such conversion is essential to the orderly development and growth of the urban area involved and is in accord with the then applicable comprehensive plan, meeting criteria established by him. The Administrator shall approve any such conversion only upon such conditions as he deems necessary to assure the substitution of other open-space land of at least equal fair market value and of as nearly as feasible equivalent usefulness and location.

TECHNICAL ASSISTANCE, STUDIES, AND
PUBLICATION OF INFORMATION

SEC. 705. In order to carry out the purpose of this title the Administrator is authorized to provide technical assistance to State and local public bodies and to undertake such studies and publish such information, either directly or by contract, as he shall determine to be desirable. There are hereby authorized to be appropriated, out of any moneys in the Treasury not otherwise appropriated, such amounts as may be necessary to provide for such assistance, studies, and publication. Nothing contained in this section shall limit any authority of the Administrator under any other provision of law.

DEFINITIONS

SEC. 706. As used in this title—

(1) The term "open-space land" means any undeveloped or predominantly undeveloped land in an urban area which has value for (A) park and recreational purposes, (B) conservation of land and other natural resources, or (C) historic or scenic purposes.

(2) The term "urban area" means any area which is urban in character, including those surrounding areas which, in the judgement of the Administrator, form an economic and socially related region, taking into consideration such factors as present and future population trends and patterns of urban growth, location of transportation facilities and systems, and distribution of industrial, commercial, residential, governmental, institutional, and other activities.

(3) The term "State" means any of the several States, the District of Columbia, the Commonwealth of Puerto Rico, the Virgin Islands, and Guam.

"RECREATION FOR METROPOLITAN AMERICA"*
1962

In 1962, the Outdoor Recreation Resources Review Commission submitted its report and recommendations to the President and Congress. Since many of its recommendations were carried out in the years that followed, the ORRRC report on "Recreation for Metropolitan America" is especially significant.

As long as men have clustered together in built-up communities, local governments—city and county—have been concerned with the provision of outdoor recreation for their citizens. In the United States, it dates back to the village green of colonial New England, which has remained a landmark in cities like Boston, Hartford, Providence, and New Haven.

Throughout the country, as the population density has increased, so has concern for outdoor recreation. Rural communities faced few difficulties since fishing streams, swimming holes, open fields for games, and woods for hunting were not far from Main Street. But as the open fields were replaced by houses, factories, and stores, and the swimming holes became polluted, problems mounted. Opportunities previously taken for granted as a part of the natural environment had to be consciously planned for—or lost. And as population centers grew in size and number, there was a corresponding increase in the demand for outdoor recreation.

Massive urbanization is a very recent phenomenon. In the 1880's, there were only four cities in the world with a population of over 1 million. In 1960, there were 5 cities and 16 other metropolitan areas in the United States alone with populations exceeding 1 million. Only 14 States were more than 50 percent urban in 1910; in 1960 there were 40. By the year 2000, approximately 73 percent of the country's inhabitants, or 250 million people, will live in metropolitan areas—compared with 63 percent, or 113 million people, in 1960, and 35 percent, or only 43 million people, in 1930. In 1960, the Los Angeles-Long Beach standard metropolitan statistical area had a population of 6.7 million. It is expected almost to triple to 17 million by 2000[1] a startling contrast to 1900, when only 102,500 lived in the city of Los Angeles.[2]

As cities spill out into suburbs and metropolitan areas are formed, they blend together into a "megalopolis." This interlocking will produce chains of heavily populated, built-up regions, each radiating from a central urban core. Across the

*ORRRC, *Outdoor Recreation for America* (Washington, D.C.: Government Printing Office, 1962), 145–56.

[1]*Economic Projections by States for the Years 1976 and 2000,* Part II, Statistical Appendix, table 20, "Selected Standard Metropolitan Areas in 1976 and 2000," National Planning Association, May 1961, included in ORRRC Study Report 23.

[2]Except where previously noted, statistics are from *U.S. Census of Population: 1960, U.S. Summary, Number of Inhabitants,* U.S. Dept. of Commerce, Bureau of the Census, tables G, 5, 8, 29, 36.

country, large belts of populated areas will emerge. In the East, there will be a single urbanized tract extending from Portland, Maine, to Norfolk, Virginia. A midwestern urban complex stretching from Detroit to Cleveland may extend eastward through a chain from Lake Erie along the Mohawk and Hudson Valleys and intersect the Atlantic population belt.[3]

It is not the growth itself that is the problem, but the pattern of growth. Even with the great expansion to come, there will still be a certain amount of open space within the urban areas. Because the pattern of development has been left largely to the speculative builder, it has been scattered all over the countryside — an unguided sprawl in which 10 acres have sometimes been used to do the work of one, or one acre to do the work of 10. In this leapfrogging process, open space may be left behind, but it is not effective open space; often, it is an agglomeration of bits and pieces too small or too poorly sited to use well — the residue of expired choices. What is done about shaping urban growth, then, will very largely determine the kind of outdoor recreation that will be provided for the bulk of the people.

RESPONSIBILITY OF LOCAL GOVERNMENT

Local government has an important responsibility for providing adequate outdoor recreation opportunities. Almost every community has suitable resources: small parks; places where nature is not disturbed and where grass, trees, and bushes grow, and people can walk, play, or picnic; a marsh with cattails, small mammals, and waterfowl; a clear river, stream, or pond where people can swim, fish, or boat. But many of these features are giving way to the housing subdivision, the industrial plant, the highway, the airport, or the shopping center.

The loss of natural assets narrows the opportunities for physical exercise or escape from the tensions of urban living. But thoughtful and effective local land-use planning, zoning, and programing can often restore to a community, regardless of its size or location, the natural features that contribute so much to making an urban environment a better and healthier place.

Recommendation 10–1: *Outdoor recreation should be an integral element in local land-use planning.*

Planning for public recreation must be as systematic as planning for schools, roads, and municipal water. This objective can be met by giving full recognition to outdoor recreation in local comprehensive land-use plans. Through long-

[3] *The Future of Outdoor Recreation in Metropolitan Regions of the United States,* ORRRC Study Report 21, describes the general characteristics of outdoor recreation activities and particular problems of metropolitan residents, including the problem of access. It contains separate studies of five selected metropolitan regions: New York-New Jersey-Philadelphia, Atlanta, St. Louis, Chicago, and Los Angeles.

term planning, schedules of priorities and of investment requirements can be prepared.

In order to be effective, planning must have active community support. The public must be convinced of the need for both taking full advantage of existing public areas and facilities and acquiring new ones.

There are some highly encouraging signs. There has been a marked acceleration of local planning efforts; in almost every urbanized State, planning is becoming a more important function. Many of the people involved in these efforts, furthermore, are beginning to give recreation a higher priority than in the past. In their eyes, the areas assigned to recreation are not only valuable in themselves; they are equally valuable as a basic framework for shaping and channeling the area's growth. These areas can often serve several purposes in addition to recreation. A marsh can serve as a sponge for flood protection, as a wildlife sanctuary, as a place for nature study and for hunting, and as a visual contrast to congested areas. Preservation of stream valleys can provide a region with a series of recreation areas as has been possible in the Washington, D.C. metropolitan area under the Capper-Cramton Act, which provides Federal assistance to communities in and around the Capital for stream valley acquisition.

A careful inventory of potential outdoor recreation sites should be undertaken by every community. Although not every city can boast of outstanding natural assets within its boundaries, most communities have nearby natural features which can be adapted to outdoor recreation—open fields, marshes and streams, or rocky slopes.

TOOLS FOR THE JOB

Recommendation 10–2: *Local governments should utilize all available techniques in making available for public use the land and water resources needed for outdoor recreation purposes.*

Local governments need to be both resourceful and imaginative. No one answer will suffice. The problem demands the use of all available tools, including relatively new techniques as well as the more traditional means. The tools fall into four groups: (1) Acquisition of full rights, (2) acquisition of rights less than full ownership, (3) regulatory devices, and (4) assessment and tax policies.

ACQUISITION OF FULL RIGHTS

EMINENT DOMAIN

In many cases, outright acquisition may be the only effective means of acquiring essential areas and key tracts. This may require exercise of the power of eminent domain. Eminent domain for public park acquisitions has been recognized in the United States since the middle of the 19th century. In 1874, the court of St. Louis County, Missouri, declared that "* * * private property is taken for a public use when it is appropriated for the common use of the public at large. A stronger instance cannot be given than that of the property converted into a public park."[4]

The mere existence of the power of eminent domain, even without its actual use, frequently facilitates negotiated purchase. It also increases the effectiveness of other relatively new devices discussed below. And it is often employed not to "take" land but to clear clouded titles.

NEGOTIATED PURCHASE

No legal problem is involved in acquiring lands for public use by negotiated purchase, for the courts have long affirmed outdoor recreation as a valid purpose for which public funds may be expended. However, negotiated purchase often presents a financial problem, since it is not always possible to obtain needed lands at reasonable cost.

A reserve fund for land acquisition often enables an agency to take advantage of favorable changes in the offering prices of particular tracts. Economical acquisition through negotiated purchase is more likely if agencies inform themselves about the local real estate market. The high rate of property transfers in and near many metropolitan areas indicates that recreation developers might be able to consider for purchase each year a sizable portion of lands having recreation potential. In one Connecticut county near New York City, 80 percent of 38 such tracts analyzed had been sold at least once since 1940, and almost 40 percent of them more than once.[5]

ACQUISITION OF RIGHTS LESS THAN FULL OWNERSHIP

Although the traditional method—acquiring land in fee simple and retaining it in public ownership for public use—will probably remain the basic method for public agencies, the acquisition of less-than-fee title can provide many supplementary outdoor recreation opportunities. There are several of these arrange ments, each with particular features to recommend it, and they should be considered by every community.

EASEMENTS

By the ancient device of the easement, the public does not have to buy the full bundle of property rights to land. It can acquire only the right that it needs— the right that the land be kept in its natural state or be open to the public for certain purposes like hiking. In highly congested areas, where the speculative value of land for subdivision is very high, easements might cost virtually as much

---

[4]County Court of St. Louis, *County* v. *Griswold,* 58 No. 175, 196 (1874).

[5]*Potential New Sites for Outdoor Recreation in the Northeast,* Economic Research Service, U.S. Dept. of Agriculture, ORRRC Study Report 8, table 51.

as the land itself; in relatively open land, however, they can be both reasonable and useful.

Easements provide open space and buffer zones for parks. They can preserve a natural countryside to protect the flanks of highways, as with scenic easements bordering the New York Thruway and the Great River Road in Wisconsin. Although public entry may not always be possible on land obtained through these easements, they do produce conservation values as well as recreation value for pleasure driving.

Easements can effectively provide "greenways" within and near metropolitan areas on open space now underused. Rights-of-way for high-tension transmission lines, for example, are too often considered a necessary "eyesore," and the swath they cut through an area is frequently a no-man's land littered with refuse. They can be put to work. Given public action, at very small cost, the land could be used for recreation—and the very fact that the rights-of-way are a network furnishes a readymade means of tying different recreation areas together with walkways.

There are several advantages—mostly economic—for a community in the use of these less-than-fee rights. For one thing, the land obtained through easements—as with other less-than-fee rights—is left in private ownership, usually continuing its present productive use. Moreover, the land is productive from the local government point of view since it remains on the local tax rolls, although perhaps at a reduced valuation. Finally, the acquisition of less than full rights is usually less expensive than acquisition in fee. The easements along the Great River Road in Wisconsin cost $15 per acre—one-fourth the cost of fee title.

OTHER DEVICES

Other legal devices involving less than full title to land are rights, leases, licenses, salebacks, and leasebacks. Public entry is possible with some of these less-than-fee arrangements, such as fishing rights, which have been widely used in this country. Others like leasebacks and salebacks offer an unusual opportunity for public agencies to acquire control of property and also derive an income from it.

Wherever possible an easement or other less than full title arrangement should be made perpetual. When an arrangement is not perpetual, the right of public use is lost at the termination of the contract. The property is then open for private development and use, and the cost of regaining the right of public use may be prohibitive.

REGULATORY DEVICES

The normal regulatory powers of local governments can also be used effectively.

ZONING

Zoning is the major tool in land-use control. Although zoning cannot always withstand the pressures for development and does not necessarily produce land for public outdoor recreation as does purchase, it can help preserve existing land features. Agricultural zoning, for instance, has been a means of preserving excellent agricultural land and preventing its loss to urban development in Santa Clara County, California. Flood-plain zoning can protect valleys from unsafe developments and preserve natural areas. Even within built-up areas, zoning regulations can provide for more outdoor recreation if greater flexibility in setback requirements permits the clustering of dwelling units, with increased open space in between the clusters.

Subdivision regulations, another form of zoning, can expand opportunities for a community by requiring developers to reserve a certain percent of subdivision land for recreation purposes or, in lieu of land contribution, to pay a fee to a local park fund.

CLUSTER DEVELOPMENT

This is a form of zoning and is, in effect, a change in the pattern of development itself. Until recently, communities thought big lot sizes would guarantee open space, but, in the typical subdivision, this hope proved to be an illusion; big enough to have to mow, too small to use, and a perfect amplifier of sound. Instead of forcing subdividers to chew up all of an area with rigid lot sizes, some communities have suggested that they group the houses in a tighter, more cohesive pattern. This saves money for the developer, for he does not have to provide as much asphalt and service facilities. It may pay him to leave anywhere from 40 to 60 percent of the land open and, as part of the bargain, this is deeded for common use of the residents. Instead of a miscellany of back lots, there can be bridle paths, playgrounds, wooded areas, and—that most desirable of community assets—a stream, flowing in the open and not buried in a concrete culvert.

The potential of a series of open spaces is great. The open space of each cluster development can be planned so that it can connect with others; by wise siting of publicly purchased land for parks and schools, there can be a unified network of open space in which each element contributes to the others.

ASSESSMENT POLICIES

Closely related to zoning are assessment devices. By assessing open land— such as farms and golf courses—at the value of its current use rather than at its subdivision value, this policy seeks to stem the spiral by which rising land assessment stimulates owners to sell to subdividers, thus further raising the assessment on the remaining open land. The principal defect is one of equity.

The landowners are asking that their land be taxed only on its open space value rather than on the full market value. Yet there is no assurance that they will not sell out when it suits their self-interest. Despite this, urban voters have sometimes been in favor of constitutional amendments for such special treatment, for they feel that it will help preserve the countryside about them. These devices will be a source of much debate during the next few years, but the fact that urban voters see such a stake in farmland preservation is very promising for a more comprehensive approach.

THREAT OF ENCROACHMENT

Recommendation 10–3: *Local outdoor recreation areas should not be appropriated for incompatible purposes.*

Public outdoor recreation areas face continual threat from encroachment by other public and private uses—freeways, hospitals, armories, schools, museums, memorials, and business enterprises. Throughout the country, highways have been one of the most frequent invaders. Louisville, Kentucky, will lose one park and parts of two others for highways, and Wilmington, Delaware, will gain a new expressway at the expense of 40 acres of parkland. In Toledo, Ohio, parklands have been turned over to a naval armory, a YMCA building, a police pistol range, a private yacht club, a sewage disposal plant, and factory parking lots.

Where it is necessary to build essential facilities on parklands, there should be a requirement that lands lost for park purposes be replaced with other lands of equivalent size, usability, and quality that would serve the same population.

MEETING REGIONAL NEEDS

Recommendation 10–4: *Large-scale outdoor recreation areas and facilities must be provided on a metropolitan or regional basis.*

In addition to the need for recreation within the urban environment—local parks, parkways, developed riverbanks, stream valleys, and marshes—there is need to use over-all regional resources in metropolitan areas. The regional or metropolitan day-use area—such as Jones Beach in New York, the Cook County Forest Preserve near Chicago, and Strawberry Lane in Cleveland—is quite different from the local site. Local areas cannot be expected to meet all the demands of the masses of people who live in the urban core of metropolitan areas. Urban dwellers and suburbanites are increasingly seeking recreation opportunities beyond community boundaries.

The metropolitan or regional outdoor recreation area is larger and can have a wider variety of natural features and man-made facilities than local areas. Regional sites within a 2-hour drive from the metropolitan center can provide a broad variety of day-use activities, as well as some overnight facilities.

The size of these areas and of their facilities makes them too large an undertaking for most local governments. They may be provided by a county, as in Essex County, New Jersey; by a special purpose authority, like the Cleveland Metropolitan Park District; by a regional agency, like the East Bay Regional Park District in California; by a State, as in the case of Huntington Beach State Park, California; or by an interstate agency like the Palisades Interstate Park Commission in New Jersey and New York.

NEED FOR PLANNING

A thorough understanding of areawide needs is essential to planning the location of metropolitan facilities. Adjoining metropolitan areas should also be taken into account. There are a number of outstanding examples of such planning. In Detroit and its four surrounding counties outdoor recreation is provided on a regional basis through the Huron-Clinton Metropolitan Authority. The Metropolitan District Commission has been supplying outdoor recreation in the Boston area since the end of the last century.

A key objective in planning metropolitan outdoor recreation areas is assuring their accessibility to population centers. Accessibility, rather than physical availability of land, is the serious problem. It is particularly important that recreation sites be accessible by public as well as private transportation. Access to many existing recreation areas is now largely limited to private automobiles. In the New York metropolitan area, for instance, at parks like Harriman State Park, with more than 500,000 annual visits, Bethpage State Park, with more than 400,000, and Captree State Park with more than 1 million annual visits, at least 95 percent of their visitors come by car, and approximately 5 percent by common carrier. This reliance on private automobile transportation seriously limits access to these areas for urban residents in the lower income brackets and, of course, creates parking problems.

NEED FOR ACQUISITION

Land-acquisition programs for metropolitan areas must include a broad range of land types to provide a choice of outdoor recreation opportunities. Metropolitan recreation should not be limited solely to high-density areas (Class I), although they should have high priority.

Public agencies acquiring large-scale metropolitan recreation areas will probably rely heavily on purchasing full rights to the land—either through negotiated purchase, use of the power of eminent domain, or outright gifts. Other tools and devices must be explored, however. Easements, for instance, cannot produce a beach which could be used for swimming and picnicking on a weekend day by 200,000 people, but they can provide for scenic outdoor recreation pleasures, especially along highways.

A device which may prove helpful is the land bank, public or private. Allegheny County, Pennsylvania, which includes Pittsburgh, has been able to profit from a private park-acquisition revolving fund, which has already purchased 3,600 acres of land that it will sell at cost to the county for the development of regional parks. Public funds were not available when needed to purchase the entire tract. This private acquisition is saving the county from buying land at higher prices later on. Similar arrangements have been made elsewhere in the country.

A number of experiments have been started on the basis of a private effort by landowners, particularly in stream valleys. In the end, public action may be necessary, but private initiative is valuable in stimulating the local government to act. A notable example is the "Scenic Reserve" plan pushed by residents of the Monterey Peninsula in California, an imaginative plan that dovetails park purchase with open space conservation of the prime areas in private hands. Another is the efforts of residents of the Neshaminy River watershed in Bucks County, Pennsylvania—by pledging gifts, citizens are trying to get joint county and State action for the protection of the whole valley's water and scenic resources.

The acquisition of large tracts by regional park systems within a brief period of time can present serious short-term problems to the tax base of the local communities. When large parks are acquired, which remove a major part of a township from the local tax rolls, it may be necessary to consider in-lieu tax arrangements.

PROBLEMS OF DEVELOPMENT

Recommendation 10–5: *All publicly owned recreation land should be developed to maximize its recreation potential yet maintain the quality characteristics of the area.*

In many cases—both in the local community and in the metropolitan area— intensive development can substantially increase opportunities for outdoor recreation. In metropolitan areas where land is difficult to acquire, further development of existing facilities may be the best answer to the problem. Tasteful development is not necessarily cheap and may require almost as much investment as acquisition of new areas, but expert management can increase the carrying capacity of existing areas.

In the course of intensive development, discretion must be used not to damage the resource. Too much asphalt for parking lots and play areas can destroy the natural setting. There should be a balance between intensive use and retention of natural features. Development may require heavy investment, but in areas of dense population, it may produce the greatest number of recreation opportunities at the lowest cost.

THE FEDERAL GOVERNMENT AND CITY PARKS*
1965

President Johnson's Task Force on Natural Beauty agreed in its 1965 report that more land should be acquired for city parks and open spaces. Most of the emphasis was placed, however, on the maintenance and improvement of existing sites. The section of the report dealing with city parks and open spaces follows.

Most of the city parks being created in our own time are routinely designed, incompetently detailed and perfunctorily located. Instead of being suited to modern needs, they are generally even less suited than the parks inherited from the 18th and 19th centuries.

Maintenance is wretched. It is easier to get money to create a new park than money to keep up what we already have. The Federal emphasis on funds for capital improvement has created a serious imbalance in city budgets and, as with so many other municipal activities, parks simply do not get the personnel and housekeeping money they need.

The problem is not to be solved by a program merely calling for more city parks and playgrounds. More parks are needed, to be sure, but greater quantity will not help unless we work much harder for quality.

So far the Federal Government's influence on quality of city parks has not been good. But it could be, and the following proposals are submitted to show how.

The Federal Government should use anti-poverty funds to train city park workers. — The need for more park personnel in cities is desperate, and will grow more so. A suitable training program would supply quickly trained workers for simple maintenance tasks: it would also embark young men and women upon significant lifetime careers, by providing a program of experience and training leading to construction, design, horticultural, supervisory, recreation and park-based educational work.

The "classrooms" would be entire parks, preferably located in the city neighborhoods from which most of the trainees are drawn. These parks would be leased from the city by the Federal Government.

Most trainees would enter the parks system of the city; some would staff completed training parks after these had been brought up to high standards as a by-product of the training; some would become teachers in the training program itself.

The Federal Government should contribute park operating funds to cities cooperating with the training program. —Such contributions would be for the

*The President's Task Force on Natural Beauty, *Report on the Preservation of Natural Beauty* (Washington, D.C.: Government Printing Office, 1965), 11–12.

increased personnel fed into the city parks systems by the anti-poverty training program and for the additional maintenance and operating equipment required. The city would agree to maintain at least its normal operating budget for parks, the Federal Government, via the Bureau of Outdoor Recreation, would provide an extra 30 percent contribution, as more trainees were added, the contribution would increase, with an eventual ceiling of 200 percent additional funds. To meet the need already evident the program's goal should be nothing less than a tripling of city park employment and operating resources.

The Federal Government should establish more parks of its own in cities. — At least two types are appropriate. One would be demonstration parks to introduce new ideas in equipment, design and programs, new uses, and to set standards of high quality. They could serve as training parks and would be leased from the city.

Another would be national sites. These would follow such precedents as the proposed national Ellis Island Park in New York. They would not have to be large. They would focus upon an historic event, site or structure.

The Federal Government should contribute a fair share toward operating funds for city parks. — The Federal Government takes the larger share of the city dweller's tax money. It comes back to him overwhelmingly in the form of programs that build this and build that. Practically nothing comes back, however, for keeping up what has been built.

The deteriorating maintenance of parks is only one symptom of an imbalance which is wreaking havoc on city budgets. Federal subsidies usually provide for capital expenditures but they do not provide for the lost tax funds nor do they provide anything for subsequent maintenance costs.

In its housing program the Federal Government should make a pro rata contribution to the public park and recreational capital funds of the city. — This, coupled with payment of a real estate tax equivalent on Federal properties, would make possible a great variety of new public park facilities rather than the sterile open spaces now enforced by housing regulations.

Federal regulations applying to use, arrangement or size or housing sites should be dropped. — Public Housing Administration has already taken this step, tentatively. Urban Renewal Administration and Federal Housing Administration should follow. Conformance to city codes would then be the only criterion required in FHA appraisal procedures and for URA approval of grants.

Lacking this change in policy, we will have a dual system of city parks. Alongside the public system will have grown a quasi-private system for users segregated by income and, in practical fact, by race. This incalculably destructive trend is now being encouraged by Federal agencies.

The benefits of the housing parks are, in any case, pitifully meager. Although housing projects have added considerable gross park acreage to cities, they have added little to the variety or character of their areas. The regulations governing them were hygienic in origin; they are expressed in formulae of distance of buildings setbacks, percentage of ground coverage and statistical ratios of use. Their original purpose has been outdated by revolutionary changes in the tools of public health and in building technology affecting ventilation and light.

The Federal Government should provide grants to local housing authorities and city park departments for the redesign of the dead spaces of existing housing projects. — The object would be to provide quality and variety — park facilities unique in the neighborhoods concerned and perhaps in the city. Swimming pools, ice skating rinks, digging and shack building areas are obvious possibilities.

The big obstacle is institutional, for the staffs of the PHA and local housing authorities have not been equipped to think in such terms. It might be in order that the responsibility for redesign of project spaces be vested in a different agency.

AN ACT TO ESTABLISH A DEPARTMENT
OF HOUSING AND URBAN DEVELOPMENT*
September 9, 1965

The establishment of an executive department of Housing and Urban Development in 1965 underscored the need for high-level attention to urban problems and, hopefully, escalated the priority of urban needs in the total context of national problems. The creation of the new department had no direct and immediate effect on open space policy, but the act of raising urban affairs to Cabinet-level status was considered to mean that open space, along with other urban programs, would receive increased attention and accelerated support.

Be it enacted by the Senate and House of Representatives of the United States of America in Congress assembled, That this Act may be cited as the "Department of Housing and Urban Development Act".

DECLARATION OF PURPOSE

SEC. 2. The Congress hereby declares that the general welfare and security of the Nation and the health and living standards of our people require, as a matter of national purpose, sound development of the Nation's communities and metropolitan areas in which the vast majority of its people live and work.

To carry out such purpose, and in recognition of the increasing importance of housing and urban development in our national life, the Congress finds that establishment of an executive department is desirable to achieve the best administration of the principal programs of the Federal Government which provide assistance for housing and for the development of the Nation's communities; to assist the President in achieving maximum coordination of the various Federal activities which have a major effect upon urban community, suburban, or metropolitan development; to encourage the solution of problems of housing, urban development, and mass transportation through State, county, town, village, or other local and private action, including promotion of interstate, regional, and metropolitan cooperation; to encourage the maximum contributions that may be made by vigorous private homebuilding and mortgage lending industries to housing, urban development, and the national economy; and to provide for full and appropriate consideration, at the national level, of the needs and interests of the Nation's communities and of the people who live and work in them.

ESTABLISHMENT OF DEPARTMENT

SEC. 3. (a) There is hereby established at the seat of government an executive

*79 *Statutes at Large,* 667.

department to be known as the Department of Housing and Urban Development (hereinafter referred to as the "Department"). There shall be at the head of the Department a Secretary of Housing and Urban Development (hereinafter referred to as the "Secretary"), who shall be appointed by the President by and with the advice and consent of the Senate. The Department shall be administered under the supervision and direction of the Secretary. The Secretary shall receive compensation at the rate now or hereafter prescribed by law for the heads of executive departments.

(b) The Secretary shall, among his responsibilities, advise the President with respect to Federal programs and activities relating to housing and urban development; develop and recommend to the President policies for fostering the orderly growth and development of the Nation's urban areas; exercise leadership at the direction of the President in coordinating Federal activities affecting housing and urban development; provide technical assistance and information, including a clearinghouse service to aid State, county, town, village, or other local governments in developing solutions to community and metropolitan development problems; consult and cooperate with State Governors and State agencies, including, when appropriate, holding informal public hearings, with respect to Federal and State programs for assisting communities in developing solutions to community and metropolitan development problems and for encouraging effective regional cooperation in the planning and conduct of community and metropolitan development programs and projects; encourage comprehensive planning by the State and local governments with a view to coordinating Federal, State, and local urban and community development activities; encourage private enterprise to serve as large a part of the Nation's total housing and urban development needs as it can and develop the fullest cooperation with private enterprise in achieving the objectives of the Department; and conduct continuing comprehensive studies, and make available findings, with respect to the problems of housing and urban development.

* * *

TRANSFERS TO DEPARTMENT

SEC. 5. (a) Except as otherwise provided in subsection (b) of this section, there are hereby transferred to and vested in the Secretary all of the functions, powers, and duties of the Housing and Home Finance Agency, of the Federal Housing Administration and the Public Housing Administration in that Agency, and of the heads and other officers and offices of said agencies.

(b) The Federal National Mortgage Association, together with its functions, powers, and duties, is hereby transferred to the Department. The next to the last sentence of section 308 of the Federal National Mortgage Association Charter Act and the item numbered (94) of section 303(e) of the Federal Executive Salary Act of 1964 are hereby repealed, and the position of the President of said Association is hereby allocated among the positions referred to in section 7(c) hereof.

(c) The President shall undertake studies of the organization of housing and urban development functions and programs within the Federal Government, and he shall provide the Congress with the findings and conclusions of such studies, together with his recommendations regarding the transfer of such functions and programs to or from the Department.

"PLANNING OUR OPEN SPACE LAND RESOURCES
FOR THE FUTURE"*
September 24, 1964

Arthur A. Davis best reviewed past open space policies and the outlook for the future in this speech before the Joint Annual Conference of the Illinois Association of Park Districts and the Illinois Recreation Association.

If we are to suggest how to plan our resources for the future, we will need to define first what resources we mean, and then sketch in broad strokes the shape of the future for which we are planning.

The resources I will be dealing with are those lands and waters related to or affected by the forces of urbanization now working such dramatic changes on the face of our land. We will be considering how to plan for the lands a half hour from home; of how we may use or abuse these lands and waters in such fashion as to affect the lives of all of us here, and of generations to come. What is happening to these areas, and what they can contribute to our society in the future—these I think are of central concern to us. As Dr. Weaver has said, "Our city dwellers have a need and desire to breathe, to touch the earth occasionally, and to be refreshed by beauty instead of exhausted by congestion and ugliness."

We recognize, of course, the need for the proper conservation and management of all the lands and waters of our nation—forest and range, meadow and tundra, marsh and desert. Our concern, though, is with meeting local and regional needs, and it is the resources required to meet these needs that are under the greatest pressures. It is here that great changes are taking place. Here lies the grave challenge to our ability to develop an urban society that retains a continuing association with the natural world.

Can we provide in our crowded urban areas a place for nature and a place for man? I think we can. But it presents new and difficult problems that will test the mettle of all of us. President Johnson, in his recent speech at the University of Michigan, eloquently expressed the challenge as that of creating a great society which he described as "a place where every child can find knowledge to enrich his mind and enlarge his talents. It is a place where leisure is a welcome chance to build and reflect, not a feared cause of boredom and restlessness. It is a place where the city of man serves not only the needs of the body and the demands of commerce but the desire for beauty and the hunger for community.

"It is a place where man can renew contact with nature. It is a place which honors creation for its own sake, and for what it adds to the understanding of

*Arthur A. Davis, Deputy Assistant Commissioner, Housing and Home Finance Agency, *Trends in Parks and Recreation*, Vol. 2, No. 1 (Jan., 1965), 29–32.

the race. It is a place where men are more concerned with the quality of their goals than the quantity of their goods."

The attainment of these goals will take the wit, and skill, and vision of all of us. It seems to me they especially challenge those of us concerned with parks, recreation, conservation, and the other values provided by urban open space. For over the years it has been the park administrator who has been most concerned with preserving the handiwork of nature in the city of man, and the recreationist who has fought for constructive leisure time outlets. All experts agree that it is these values in our society that are in the ascendancy.

Now we need to look briefly at the setting in which these goals will have to be realized. For what kind of future are we planning?

In a word, we must plan to meet more pressures on a shrinking natural resource base. Population by the turn of the century—400 million. Illinois, for example, is estimated to top 19 million by the year 2000—almost double the 1960 figure. Higher disposable income, greater personal mobility, available leisure time beyond that enjoyed by any society of man—these are what the experts tell us to expect. They tell us, also, that we are rapidly becoming an urban society. Soon four-fifths of us will live in urban areas. To accommodate this migration, open lands are being developed for urban uses at the rate of a million acres a year. There was a doubling of the lands given over to urban purposes between 1950 and 1960, and there will be a doubling again by the turn of the century.

And the need for parks and recreation? Over-all, it is expected that demands for public recreation opportunities will triple by the year 2000. Except that in the case of day-use recreation opportunities—the kind provided in and close to our metropolitan regions—and in the circumstances of a shrinking resource base, *the demand is estimated to increase tenfold.*

Can we possibly meet needs of this dimension? Can we do it without destroying the natural environment, and diluting the quality of the individual recreational experience? I think we can. But it will require an enormous expansion of present efforts. And it will require the application of some new approaches as well. Let's examine what needs to be done, and see how it might be accomplished.

First, and it cannot be repeated too often, we need to rededicate ourselves to preserving now, while they are still available, those lands a half hour from home where nature still predominates. Open land, undeveloped land, lands—and waters too—that have value for park, conservation, recreation, scenic, and historic purposes must be preserved for public use while they are still available. The critical need for action now is beyond argument.

Will these efforts meet future needs? Undoubtedly they will improve our position, thanks to a rebirth of interest at all levels of government, as well as among institutions and private individuals.

[353]

The Federal Open-Space Land Program, during its first three years of operation, has assisted in the acquisition of 101,947 acres of urban open-space land. Grants totaling over $32 million have been made to 219 applicants in 177 communities. Acquisitions have included regional parks and greenbelts; community and neighborhood parks, conservation areas; scenic and historic sites; and special open space uses. Here in Illinois 15 grants have been approved involving Federal funds of $5,920,806, and a total of 8,379 acres. We are proud of this record, and pleased at the increasing tempo of program activity. Yet the total acreage acquired so far under the Federal Open-Space Land Program is still only one-tenth the acreage that goes into urban uses each year. Progress to date is encouraging, but we have a long way to go.

At the State level, a number of programs assist local and regional agencies to acquire park, recreation, conservation, and other kinds of open space areas. New York, New Jersey, Pennsylvania, Massachusetts, Connecticut, and now California and Rhode Island provide grants to localities for these purposes. In many cases, there has been three-way cooperation, with the Federal, state and local governments all contributing toward the common objective of open-space preservation. Both state and local funds can be counted toward the non-Federal share of matching funds of local agencies applying for Federal open-space land grants. In addition to the states listed above, a number of states—including Wisconsin, Florida, Minnesota and Ohio have launched sizable outdoor recreation land acquisition financing programs in the last 5 years. This last election saw the voters of California, Rhode Island and Washington approve outdoor recreation-open space bond issues. California voters approved a $150 million program of park and open-space acquisition, with $40 million of the total going to local and regional agencies. Rhode Island voters approved a $5 million bond issue of which one-third will assist local communities in acquiring open space. Washington voters approved two ballot measures for open space acquisition; one, a bond issue of $10 million will provide funds to acquire state park lands, while a second, financed by the state motorboat fuel tax will provide funds for shoreline acquisition and development. This last measure may also provide local assistance for communities as well as for statewide acquisitions.

But these new efforts, while encouraging, cannot alone meet projected needs for open space areas. In fact, continuing present levels of acquiring public park and recreation areas will only assure that we will lose ground—quite literally—more slowly. Public open space acquisition programs cannot possibly match the pace at which land is being turned to urban uses. And land must be turned to such uses, in quantity, to meet the needs of millions of people for homes, schools, hospitals, stores, industries, roads, airports, and many other purposes. Let us recognize these needs as pressing and legitimate. To be in favor of conservation and recreation does not, I hope, require that we be "against" people. Bulldozers, too, serve useful purposes.

Make no mistake: I urge the preservation for public purposes of every possible acre of urban open space. But I recognize that communities cannot acquire all the park, conservation, and recreation areas they will need to meet project demands by public purchase. New approaches will be needed—and it seems to be that it is groups of this kind that should take the lead in employing them.

If I may present one fundamental idea to you let it be this: that to meet the challenge of population explosion and urbanization, conservationists and recreationists will need to broaden their roles and accept new stewardship responsibilities. Your concern for natural beauty; your dedication to the conservation ethic; your efforts to make recreation activities creative and constructive— these must be carried to the community, not alone in terms of parks and recreation areas, but as they relate to the total physical environment.

Where we have roads and highways, let's have roadside rests, foot paths, bicycle trails, landscaped areas, buffer strips, screens of trees, historical markers —let us consider these as usual concomitants of our road-building, to be included in the planning, budgeting, and construction process of normal costs of our highway system.

We will need new water supply reservoirs. Build into these projects park and recreation features. Provide access to existing areas. Municipal water supplies *can* be used for outdoor recreation. If this means certain remedial measures, as a new filtration plant, let's fight for them.

Airports are being expanded, with longer runways to handle new jets. For the good of both planes and people, approach zones should be as spacious as possible. Let's not permit unwise development, such as housing sure to be blighted by the constant din of jet engines. Dedicate these areas instead to a permanent open space use—perhaps a park, perhaps an agricultural or conservation area.

The grounds of our hospitals, libraries, court houses, municipal buildings— all can be made to contribute to breaking up the monotony of urban development, arresting blight, and giving form and identity to our communities.

The goal is to relate the natural world to the developments of man: From the flower border of the city hall lawn, to tree-shaded residential streets, imaginatively landscaped public facilities, neighborhood commons, candy-striped playgrounds, small parks that invite one to rest and chat, bicycle paths paralleling our roads, accessible lakes and reservoirs, protected stream valleys, historic sites that have been respected and restored, spacious playing fields, municipal, county, and regional parks, town forests, nature sanctuaries and conservation areas—all contributing to a continuum of nature interwoven throughout the entire fabric of our urban environment.

We need to take full advantage of every opportunity for bringing nature to the metropolis. And we need to involve the entire metropolis—the central city or cities, the surrounding towns and suburbs, the rural-urban fringe areas. All must work in some general harmony. We are too familiar with the bumpy pat-

[355]

tern of urban sprawl that accompanies unbridled growth—urban strips that mar rural countrysides, auto graveyards astride entrance highways to our cities, pockets of blight downtown, monotonous suburban sprawl near town; the list is long and sad.

Better planning is vital. Coordination, setting up common criteria, agreeing upon general priorities, looking at the city and its surroundings in terms of total needs and total resources—these are key steps in attaining our objectives.

In recognition of the importance of joint planning and acquisition programs, the law establishing the Federal Open-Space Land Program provides for increasing grants to 30% of acquisition costs where applicants have, or share, open space responsibilities for an entire urban area. Since few public agencies have authority to plan and acquire lands through the urban region in which they are located, most 30% grants (69 to 99) have been approved on the basis of intergovernmental agreements.

These agreements vary in content, but all are intended to achieve as nearly as possible the degree of coordination that could be obtained by a single agency. To accomplish this, all must have the following:

1. A statement of policy or intent concerning the functions, scope, and purpose of the agreement.
2. A method for coordinating both plans and acquisition proposals for open-space land in the urban area covered by the agreement, not limited to lands involving Federal assistance.

Intergovernmental agreements have been formed for 30 metropolitan areas, including both Chicago and Peoria in Illinois. The Chicago agreement has been entered into by 13 villages, cities, and counties, and involves 80% of the area covered by the 6-county Chicago urban region. All of the signatories of the agreements qualify for the higher grant.

Let me stress that these agreements are designed, executed, and administered by the participants. We are concerned that there is an effective mechanism for getting a total job done. The terms under which local agencies wish to accomplish this job will vary, of course.

These agreements to work together are no departure from time-honored arrangements to join forces in solving common problems. Our towns and cities often act together in the public interest and surely this is a worthy cause. No fire-boss would stand by idly with his crew until the fire had roared over the county line. Unregulated urban growth can leave a comparable blemish.

Let us turn from direct public actions of the various kinds discussed so far to other instruments for preserving open-space lands such as zoning, requirements for the set-aside of open-space lands in new developments, official maps, subdivision regulations. These, and related measures, can be powerful tools in the race for open space. And their use has a solid foundation in law. In Berman vs. Parker (Nov., 1954) the U.S. Supreme Court held that "the concept of public welfare is broad and inclusive . . . the values it represents are spiritual as well as physical, aesthetic as well as monetary. It is within the power of the legislature to determine that the community should be beautiful as well as healthy, spacious as well as clean, well-balanced as well as carefully patrolled."

Few communities would not benefit from a careful reconsideration of how these administrative and regulatory measures could be better employed to the public benefit.

Still other tools are available, often overlooked or untried because they are untested. Easements, long term leases, and development rights can often be acquired at less cost and dislocation than would be the case if lands were purchased outright. Compensable regulations offer a unique approach to keeping lands in a natural condition. Tax incentives and preferential assessments, agricultural zoning—all offer promise for helping to preserve the urban open space.

None of these devices can accomplish the job alone. Some will require a real pioneering approach. Naturally any new requirement, or constraint, or inducement, will need to be carefully thought through and responsibly administered. But we cannot afford to lose any opportunities out of timidity.

There is yet another need demanding your attention. Our efforts to preserve open-space lands will only meet with public support if they fill a public need. I ask, therefore, that you examine again how well your areas are serving human wants, how responsive they are to meeting community requirements.

Why are some parks sterile, insulated enclosures, repositories of windblown papers, the sanctuary of vagrants by day and vandals by night—while others are warm and tranquil, colorful and secure, beloved by children, young lovers, and our elders? I'm not entirely sure; no one is. There are some theories, some experience, some tentative conclusions. But we need to know more if we are not to waste natural resources that each day are harder to acquire.

Why do children forsake hardtop playgrounds to play on nearby piles of fresh dirt from construction of a new road? Or develop fascinating and complex games with discarded cardboard boxes instead of using new playground equip ment? You can get several answers—and arguments.

Why do people seldom venture further than a hundred yards into a wooded area? Are they afraid of snakes and poison ivy? Or possible attack? Why don't people take walks anymore? Is there no place to walk—no sidewalks or trails or paths? Or is there nothing left to delight the eye and nourish the spirit?

What can we do to maintain—or enhance—the quality of the individual recreational experience?

Until we can answer these kinds of questions better, our service to community will be incomplete. In turn, it will be that much more difficult to compete for limited public funds against other claimants that have convinced the community of their worth.

I am not suggesting that you become social psychologists or specialists in behavior (although you may find the services of these professionals most useful). I do suggest that we modify the injunction "Know thyself" to "Know thy community."

What kind of people live in your town? What do they really enjoy doing in their leisure time? Do you provide a choice, a wide range of enjoyment to attract all ages, sizes, and sexes? Is there opportunity for solitary pursuits, group activities, active sports, family gatherings? Or is your park a stereotype of wooden benches, concrete walks in conventional pattern, a statue attended mostly by pigeons, drinking fountains that don't quite supply enough water for a decent drink—or, alternatively, threaten to put out your eye—and well-manicured grass complete with "Keep Off" signs?

On what basis do you decide how to develop an area—or when to develop it—or how much to develop it? What assumptions guide your land purchase program? Availability? Price? Are you giving priority to acquisition, or using your funds for development?

Intelligent answers to these questions require a critical analysis of the community—as we see it now, as we project its growth over time. Assumptions about the people we will be serving should be basic to the open space planning process. How many, where, of what age distribution and income. Are the users of your parks apartment dwellers? Homeowners? Do they walk, bicycle, drive, and if the latter, how far? Data such as this adds to our understanding of demand, and helps assure that we will as nearly as possible contribute to the lives of all in our communities.

After all, that is our final goal—to contribute to the maximum extent we possibly can to the beauty of our land, and the peace and joy of our people. It is a goal easily stated, but difficult of achievement. But achieve it we can. As President Johnson told the graduates of Michigan, "Let us from this moment begin our work so that in the future men will look back and say: It was then, after a long and weary way, that man turned the exploits of his genius to the enrichment of his life."

FOREST RECREATION

In 1968 the National Forests provided 157 million visitor days of recreation use; the forests truly had become "America's Playgrounds." But forested lands attracted recreationists long before forest reserves were established. Luxurious camping expeditions by European sportsmen, complete with servants and portable bathtubs, were recorded as early as 1843. According to a Forest Service brochure:

> The lure of big game in the Rockies, fabulous scenery, and the challenge of unmapped terrain attracted generation after generation of their less affluent American counterparts. In the East, recreational use of lands became especially well entrenched in areas which were later purchased and proclaimed as National Forests. Many of the Nation's oldest families have traditionally spent leisure time in the Ozarks, the southern Appalachian ranges, the mountains of New England, and in forested areas near the northern Great Lakes.
>
> The diversity of National Forest recreation opportunity ranges from the scenic glaciers of Alaska to the tropics in Puerto Rico; from skiing in the high country to winter picnicking in the southern forests; from deep wilderness in the Northwest to highly developed campgrounds near population centers; from mountain streams to the northern lakes. The potential capacity of the National Forest System to accommodate recreation visitors is enormous.*

The National Forest System consists of 154 national forests, and 19 national grasslands with a total area of about 186 million acres. While most of these areas are located in the West, some 20 million acres of national forest lands are located east of the Mississippi River. The national forests contain one-third of the nation's big game, over 80,000 miles of fishing streams, more than 40,000 lakes and literally millions of small game animals, upland game birds, waterfowl, and song birds.

The development of the National Forest System has been documented in Volumes I and II of this series. In this chapter, we shall devote our attention mainly to those events that were significant in the growth of outdoor recreation in the forests.

EARLY RECOGNITION OF THE RECREATION POTENTIALS OF THE FORESTS

While a considerable amount of forest recreation takes place in privately-owned forests, the great bulk of recreation activity occurs in public forests.

*U.S. Forest Service, *Outdoor Recreation in the National Forests* (Washington, D.C.: Government Printing Office, 1965), 1, 16.

The creation of a system of forest reserves was therefore vital to the interests of forest recreation even though the reserves were not created for recreation purposes. One might add that if some system of reserving forested areas from exploitation had not been devised there would be little forest left for recreation or any other purpose.

In earlier times, recreation in the forests was considered to be an incidental and almost accidental use of the basic resource. Thoreau, in his inimitable fashion, spoke of "rambling through the aisles of the wood" near Walden Pond. By 1899, special use permits were authorized for "health or pleasure" in areas adjacent to mineral springs in forest reserves. The earliest known written statement on recreational use of the forests (by a member of the Forest Service) was prepared by Treadwell Cleveland, Jr. in 1910.

As early as 1912, Franklin D. Roosevelt spoke of the need for forest conservation and in the same year the Chief of the Forest Service took note of the difficulties of game preservation in his annual report. In 1915, summer homes were permitted in the National Forests and in 1916 the President was authorized to establish game refuges within forest reserves. The first systematic survey of forest recreation use was conducted by Frank A. Waugh in 1918. These early events are documented in this chapter.

THE BEGINNINGS OF ACTION:
THE 20's AND 30's

Recreation use of the national forests increased rapidly during the 1920's and 1930's, principally because of the development of more efficient automobiles and the construction of roads into the forests. These roads were built mainly for logging and fire protection purposes but they were heavily used by recreationists.

The large number of visitors created sanitary problems, among other things, at the campsites that were most heavily used. As early as 1920, the Forest Service was complaining about being "swamped" with campers. Congress took note of this situation in the Appropriations Act of May 11, 1922 (42 *Stat.,* 507) by appropriating $10,000 for the construction of camping facilities. While little could be accomplished with this small amount, it represented a "breakthrough" for the Forest Service because it was the first congressional appropriation for recreation in the national forests.

During the twenty year period from 1920–40, outdoor recreation came to be officially recognized as a legitimate use of the national forests. The Forest Service devoted considerable attention to campers and other recreationists; the first appropriation for recreation was then authorized and the first major area of a national forest was set aside for recreation purposes.

During the 30's the Civilian Conservation Corps greatly enhanced the recreation potential of the forests by building over 100,000 miles of roads and by constructing facilities for camp grounds and picnic sites. Total recreation visits to national forests soon rose from 4,660,000 in 1924 to 14,332,000 in 1939.

MULTIPLE USE

The Forest Service has generally followed the concept of multiple use since 1905 when Secretary of Agriculture Wilson directed that "all the resources of forest reserves are for use . . ." and "the dominant industry will be decided first but with as little restrictions to minor industries as may be possible. . . ." The ultimate objective was the "greatest good of the greatest number in the long run." Secretary "Tama Jim" Wilson's directive is reproduced in this chapter.

Over the years, the practice of multiple-use was refined and was perhaps best explained by Chief Forester Richard McArdle in his article "Multiple-Use—Multiple Benefits." Congress finally legitimatized the concept through passage of the Multiple Use Act of 1960 and in the last selection in this chapter, Chief of the Forest Service Edward P. Cliff discusses outdoor recreation within the context of multiple use of the forests.

WILDERNESS

Few questions on resource use have raised as much controversy as has the issue of preservation of wilderness areas. "Wilderness type" lands within the National Parks are already withdrawn and reserved so they are ordinarily not included in proposals to preserve wilderness. But some areas of the public domain, especially in Alaska, fit the wilderness category and there has been some considerable dispute over proposals to withdraw portions of these lands for various purposes which would have the effect of preserving them in their "natural" state. Some 19 million acres have been withdrawn in Alaska for wild-life ranges and refuges. However, most of the controversy in recent years has centered around wilderness areas in the National Forests.

National Forest wilderness areas were formerly designated by the Secretary of Agriculture or (for smaller units) by the Chief of the Forest Service. Hunting and fishing (subject to state laws) was permitted in wilderness areas as was prospecting and mining. Lumbering and road-building were prohibited except that owners of private property, including miners, were allowed roads for ingress and egress. Residences and commercial enterprises were prohibited, while grazing was permitted but was being gradually reduced. As of 1961, the National Forests contained 14,661,416 acres of wilderness-type areas.

One of the first persons to analyze the value of wilderness for outdoor recreation was Aldo Leopold in 1921. By 1935 a Wilderness Society had been organized and had issued "A Summons to Save the Wilderness," but it was not until 1964 that wilderness values were finally protected by an act of Congress. The three documents noted above appear in this chapter.

THOREAU'S WALDEN*
1854

Various kinds of restrictions on lumbering have existed since colonial times but such restrictions were mainly to save trees (for future harvest) and to protect watersheds—not to protect recreation. It was undoubtedly recognized in earlier times that forests provided recreational opportunities but this was taken for granted. When the forests disappeared the primary concern was for diminished timber supply, and occasionally, a recognition that denuded forest areas permitted accelerated rates of erosion. Only a few strange souls like Thoreau objected to lost recreation opportunities.

When I first paddled a boat on Walden, it was completely surrounded by thick and lofty pine and oak woods, and in some of its coves grape-vines had run over the trees next the water and formed bowers under which a boat could pass. The hills which form its shores are so steep, and the woods on them were then so high, that, as you looked down from the west end, it had the appearance of an amphitheatre for some kind of sylvan spectacle. I have spent many an hour, when I was younger, floating over its surface as the zephyr willed, having paddled my boat to the middle, and lying on my back across the seats, in a summer forenoon, dreaming awake, until I was aroused by the boat touching the sand, and I arose to see what shore my fates had impelled me to; days when idleness was the most attractive and productive industry. Many a forenoon have I stolen away, preferring to spend thus the most valued part of the day; for I was rich, if not in money, in sunny hours and summer days, and spent them lavishly; nor do I regret that I did not waste more of them in the workshop or the teacher's desk. But since I left those shores the woodchoppers have still further laid them waste, and now for many a year there will be no more rambling through the aisles of the wood, with occasional vistas through which you see the water. My Muse may be excused if she is silent henceforth. How can you expect the birds to sing when their groves are cut down?

Now the trunks of trees on the bottom, and the old log canoe, and the dark surrounding woods, are gone, and the villagers, who scarcely know where it lies, instead of going to the pond to bathe or drink, are thinking to bring its water, which should be as sacred as the Ganges at least, to the village in a pipe, to wash their dishes with!—to earn their Walden by the turning of a cock or drawing of a plug! That devilish Iron Horse, whose ear-rending neigh is heard throughout the town, has muddied the Boiling Spring with his foot, and he it is that has browsed off all the woods on Walden shore, that Trojan horse, with a thousand men in his belly, introduced by mercenary Greeks!

*Henry David Thoreau, *Walden,* Vol. 2 (Boston: Houghton, Mifflin and Co., 1854), 300–01.

AN ACT TO AUTHORIZE SPECIAL-USE PERMITS FOR LAND ADJACENT TO MINERAL SPRINGS*
February 28, 1899

Probably the first official recognition of the recreation potential of forest reserves concerned mineral springs which were thought to have medicinal values. The 1899 act however, used the words "for health or pleasure," and therefore this act is significant only because it appears to be the first governmental recognition of the recreation values of the forest reserves. Relevant portions of the act follow.

The Secretary of the Interior . . . hereby is authorized, under such rules and regulations as he from time to time may make, to enter or lease to responsible persons or corporations applying therefore suitable spaces and portions of ground near, or adjacent to, mineral, medicinal, or other springs, within any forest reserves established within the United States, or hereafter to be established, and where the public is accustomed or desires to frequent, for health or pleasure, for the purpose of erecting upon such leased ground sanitariums or hotels, to be opened for the reception of the public. And he is further authorized to make such regulations, for the convenience of people visiting such springs, with reference to spaces and locations for the erection of tents or temporary dwelling houses to be erected or constructed for the use of those visiting such springs for health or pleasure. And the Secretary of the Interior is authorized to prescribe the terms and duration and the compensation to be paid for the privileges granted under the provisions of this act.

*30 *Statutes at Large,* 908.

A LETTER FROM "TAMA JIM" WILSON TO GIFFORD PINCHOT*
1905

The establishment of forest reserves was first permitted in an act of March 3, 1891 (26 Stat., 1095) which authorized the President to withdraw timbered lands from the public domain and set them apart as forest reservations. Such lands remained under the jurisdiction of the Department of the Interior for the next 14 years and were then transferred to the Department of Agriculture by the Act of February 1, 1905 (33 Stat., 628). When the transfer was accomplished, the Secretary of Agriculture "Tama Jim" Wilson issued a letter of instructions to the head of the Forest Service, Gifford Pinchot. It is understood that Pinchot wrote the letter (to himself) and then obtained the Secretary's approval and signature. It seems rather unlikely that Pinchot had outdoor recreation in mind when he drafted this policy statement, but since it has been used by the Forest Service as the ideological basis for their outdoor recreation activities, the substantive portions of the letter are quoted here.

In the administration of the forest reserves it must be clearly borne in mind that all land is to be devoted to its most productive use for the permanent good of the whole people, and not for the temporary benefit of individuals or companies. All the resources of forest reserves are for *use*, and this use must be brought about in a thoroughly prompt and businesslike manner, under such restrictions only as will insure the permanence of these resources. The vital importance of forest reserves to the great industries of the Western States will be largely increased in the near future by the continued steady advance in settlement and development. The permanence of the resources of the reserves is therefore indispensable to continued prosperity, and the policy of this department for their protection and use will invariably be guided by this fact, always bearing in mind that the *conservative use* of these resources in no way conflicts with their permanent value.

You will see to it that the water, wood, and forage of the reserves are conserved and wisely used for the benefit of the home builder first of all, upon whom depends the best permanent use of lands and resources alike. The continued prosperity of the agricultural, lumbering, mining, and livestock interests is directly dependent upon a permanent and accessible supply of water, wood, and forage, as well as upon the present and future use of their resources under businesslike regulations, enforced with promptness, effectiveness, and common sense. In the management of each reserve local questions will be decided upon local grounds; the dominant industry will be considered first, but with as little

*Gifford Pinchot, *Breaking New Ground* (New York: Harcourt, Brace and Co., 1947), 261–62.

restriction to minor industries as may be possible; sudden changes in industrial conditions will be avoided by gradual adjustment after due notice; and where conflicting interests must be reconciled the question will always be decided from the standpoint of the greatest good of the greatest number in the long run.

These general principles will govern in the protection and use of the water supply, in the disposal of timber and wood, in the use of the range, and in all other matters connected with the management of the reserves. They can be successfully applied only when the administration of each reserve is left very largely in the hands of the local officers, under the eye of thoroughly trained and competent inspectors.

Very respectfully,

James Wilson
Secretary

"NATIONAL FORESTS AS RECREATION GROUNDS"*
1910

Perhaps the first written statement on outdoor recreation by a member of the Forest Service was this perceptive and prophetic article by Treadwell Cleveland, Jr.

In extent, in variety of attractions, and in availability to the people of the country, the national forests form as a whole by far the greatest national recreation grounds in the world. Some of them, especially those near large centers of population, draw tens of thousands every season. Altogether, some 400,000 persons visit the forests annually for recreation. Most of these come from nearby cities and towns, but many come from other states and even from other countries. Moreover, the use of the forests for recreation has only fairly begun. It is increasing very rapidly—at least ten per cent a year on the average, and in some cases one hundred per cent a year.

The national forests are maintained to conserve the vast natural resources of wood and water. These resources are located on the slopes, crests, and peaks of the Rockies and the Coast Ranges, which are the most picturesque and healthful regions in the United States. Thus, by geographic necessity, they include the highest peaks, the finest glaciers, the most interesting geological formations, and much of the best virgin forests in the United States. They are, as a rule, supplied with pure water in great abundance. They contain much of the best hunting and fishing country. Within them are many of the most striking and important historic and prehistoric landmarks, as well as natural wonders which do not suffer by comparison with those of the national parks. An endless variety of landscape and every natural charm are included in their boundaries.

Recreation in the national forests usually takes the form of summer outings devoted simply to camping out. Individuals and small parties, or clubs, come in by stage or wagon—in some cases, by automobile—bringing with them provisions for a longer or a shorter visit, make camp, and shift for themselves with true western independence and skill. Doing without many conveniences is not regarded as privation. In comparison with this western way of enjoying nature, the usual eastern summer vacations spent at boarding houses and hotels, or in camps which are camps in little more than name, appear highly artificial. In the national forests enjoyment of recreation is largely based on the absence of conditions which less sincere and capable lovers of outdoor life find quite as indispensable in the woods as in the towns. This fact explains much of the very wide

*Treadwell Cleveland, Jr., "National Forests as Recreation Grounds," *Annals of the American Academy of Political and Social Science,* Vol. 35, No. 2 (Mar., 1910), 25–26, 29–31.

use of national forests for recreation, in regions which are largely pure wilderness.

Summer cottages and hotels within the forests accommodate a large number of seekers after recreation. Many of the cottages are owned by city people who spend the summers in them. Others are rented. Railways which are interested in developing their summer business are doing much to attract visitors by providing and encouraging hotels and cottages in the forests. To mention but a single case in point, the Great Northern Railroad is developing the attractions of the Lake McDonald region, in the Blackfeet Forest. It has established a hotel on the Flathead River as headquarters for visitors, and has begun the erection of a series of Swiss chalets and cabins from point to point.

Besides just "camping out," the visitors do a great deal of fishing in a very energetic sort of way. In some forests they spend most of the season in fishing on almost a professional scale. Mountain climbing, boating, and riding are favorite pursuits. In the autumn, in the forests where game is plentiful, hunting is the chief sport.

* * *

Encouragement of Recreation.—The use of the forests for recreation is indirectly encouraged by furthering their economic use. Permanent improvements, which are made as fast as the available funds will permit, are opening up the forests to every sort of legitimate use, and these improvements greatly add to the value of the forests for recreation. Roads, trails, and bridges, built for protection and the transaction of forest business, give visitors to the forest more ready access to all their parts. But a good deal is done by the Forest Service to encourage recreation directly, and this side of the subject must be briefly touched upon.

In general, forest officers spare no pains to serve visitors in the forest. They direct them to the best camping sites and to points of interest, do what they can to make them comfortable, and explain to them the forest regulations. More specifically, where occasion warrants, care is taken to prevent unfair use of camp and summer cottage sites. Thus, in the Minnesota Forest, for example, the shores of Cass Lake have been surveyed in blocks of camp sites, between which general access is had to the water. These sites are allotted to those who desire to establish camps, while the unallotted parts of the shore are used by those visiting the lake temporarily. By this arrangement, a desirable camp site may be secured from year to year for the nominal charge made for the permit, while monopoly of the shore is prevented. The same general scheme is followed in many other forests.

To prevent the fouling of camp sites, grazing animals are kept at a proper distance. In this way campers who have horses are secured pasturage for them, since horses will not graze after sheep unless accustomed to run with them.

In some cases trails are made and bridges constructed expressly to open up places in the forests which are particularly well adapted for camps.

Assistance of this sort is keenly appreciated, and tends greatly to foster good feeling between the Service and the public.

Object Lessons in Forestry.—Visitors to the forests display keen interest in the objects and methods of forest administration. They have an opportunity to see the problems which have to be solved and the means employed for their solution. In this way the value of the work is brought home to them; they get an insight into it which only observation under skilled guidance can give. As a result, the general attitude of visitors is one of interested approval. The forest nurseries, in which seedlings are raised for reforesting, attract many, and where logging operations are in progress these are inspected and discussed. So marked is the interest shown in the practice of forestry that means will be taken, as far as practicable, to handle certain small areas in such a way as to furnish object lessons for purely education purposes—what the forester would call demonstration plots. On Star Island, in Cass Lake, Minn., for instance, it is planned to handle the forest so as to show various kinds of silvicultural practice, such as nursery work, planting, and thinning. On the whole, the educational impression made upon those who take recreation in the forests must be regarded as considerable and important.

Future Use of the Forests for Recreation.—The use of national forests for recreation is certain to increase very greatly in the future. As the country becomes more crowded, and the wilderness retreats before the frontier of settlement, the national forests will tend to become almost the only available recreation grounds on a scale commensurate with the needs of the people. It is of the utmost importance, therefore, to consider the future of the forests.

Fortunately, the objects for which the national forests were created and are maintained, will guarantee the permanence of their resources and will bring about their fullest development for every use. The national forests safeguard the integrity of the resources and place their use on a permanent basis. For the reason the recreation value of the national forests can never be destroyed. On the contrary, it must increase. The development of the various resources requires the extension and maintenance of permanent improvements in the form of roads, trails, bridges, and telephone lines, for the better protection of the forests and for the readier transaction of forest business. These improvements, in turn, benefit all users of the forests, including those who visit them for recreation. As the forests are opened up progressively by more intensive economic use, they will become more attractive, more convenient, and more accessible.

So great is the value of national forest area for recreation, and so certain is this value to increase with the growth of the country and the shrinkage of the wilderness, that even if the forest resources of wood and water were not to be required by the civilization of the future, many of the forests ought certainly to be preserved, in the interest of national health and well-being, for recreation use alone.

THE WEEKS ACT*
March 1, 1911

The Weeks Act authorized land purchases by the Federal Government in headwaters areas to protect the flow of navigable streams. Most of the land area of the eastern national forests was acquired under this legislation. The special significance of this act for outdoor recreation rests on the fact that the lands purchased are close to the heavily populated areas of the East and consequently support about 30 percent of the total recreation visits to the national forests. The Weeks Act appears on p. 221 of Land and Water: 1900–1970 *of this series.*

*36 *Statutes at Large,* 961.

FRANKLIN D. ROOSEVELT AND FOREST CONSERVATION*
March 3, 1912

Twenty years before he was elected President, Franklin D. Roosevelt set forth his ideas on forest conservation in this speech before the People's Forum at Troy, New York.

To put it another way competition has been shown to be useful up to a certain point and no further. Co-operation must begin where competition leaves off and co-operation is as good a word for the new theory as any other. The founders of the republic were groping for the idea when they tried to form a government aimed to secure the greatest good for the greatest number and it is precisely that idea which is being developed to-day along every possible walk of life.

Let us take some examples of this, in what we call to-day, Conservation. We are taking merely a theory which began to be developed in other countries many years ago. It was recognized in Germany for instance one hundred years ago that the trees on the land were necessary for the preservation of the water power and indeed for the health of the people. As a result practically all of Germany is to-day working out the theory of the liberty of the Community rather than of the liberty of the individual.

One hundred and fifty years ago in Germany the individual was not restricted from denuding his lands of the growing trees. To-day he must cut only in a manner scientifically worked out, which is calculated to serve the ends of the community and not his ends.

They passed beyond the liberty of the individual to do as he pleased with his own property and found it was necessary to check this liberty for the benefit of the freedom of the whole people.

So in New York State we are beginning to do the same thing. As a whole we are beginning to realize that it is necessary to the health and happiness of the whole people of the State that individuals and lumber companies should not go into our wooded areas like the Adirondacks and the Catskills and cut them off root and branch for the benefit of their own pocket.

There are many persons left to-day that can see no reason why if a man owns land he should not be permitted to do as he likes with it. The most striking example of what happens in such a case, that I know of, was a picture shown me by Mr. Gifford Pinchot last week. It was a photograph of a walled city in northern China. Four or five hundred years ago this city had been the center of the populous and prosperous district. A district whose mountains and ridges were

*Franklin D. Roosevelt and Conservation: 1911–1945, Vol. I, Edgar B. Nixon, ed. (Washington, D. C.: Government Printing Office, 1957), 17–19.

covered with magnificent trees. Its streams flowing without interruption and its crops in the valleys prospering. It was known as one of the most prosperous provinces in China, both as a lumber exporting center and as an agricultural community.

To-day the picture shows the walled town, almost as it stood 500 years ago. There is not a human being within the walls. There are but few human beings in the whole region. Rows upon rows of bare ridges and mountains stretch back from the city without a vestige of tree life, without a vestige of flowing streams and with the bare rocks reflecting the glare of the sun. Below in the plains the little soil which remains is parched and unable to yield more than a tiny fraction of its former crops. This is the best example I know of the liberty of the individual without anything further.

Every man 500 years ago did as he pleased with his own property. He cut the trees without affording a chance for reproduction and he thereby parched the ground, dried up the streams and ruined the valley and the sad part of it is that there are to-day men of the State who for the sake of lining their pockets during their own lifetime are willing to cause the same thing that happened in China. With them the motto is "After us the deluge."

They care not what happens after they are gone and I will go even further and say that they care not what happens even to their neighbors, to the community as a whole, during their own lifetime. The opponents of Conservation who, after all, are merely opponents of the liberty of the community, will argue that even though they do exhaust all the natural resources, the inventiveness of man and the progress of civilization will supply a substitute when the crisis comes. When the crisis came on that prosperous province of China the progress of civilization and the inventiveness of man did not find a substitute. Why will we assume that we can do it when the Chinese failed.

It is the same way with all of our other natural resources in addition to forests. Why, let me ask, are so many of the farms in the State of New York abandoned. The answer is easy. Their owners 50 or 100 years ago took from the soil without returning any equivalent to the soil. In other words they got something for nothing. Their land was rich and the work was easy. They prospered for a while until the deluge came and when it came they discovered that they lands would not produce. They had taken the richness away and did not pay for it with fertilizers and other methods of soil regeneration.

To-day the people in the cities and the people on the farms are suffering because these early farmers gave no thought to the liberty of the Community. To have suggested to a New York State farmer one hundred years ago that the government would compel him to put so much lime or so much fertilizer on every acre he cultivated would have been an impossibility. He would have stared and muttered something about taking care of his own land in his own way.

Yet there are many thinking people in the State to-day who believe that the time is not far distant when the government of the State will rightly and of necessity compel every cultivator of land to pay back to that land some quid pro quo.

I have taken the conservation of our natural resources as the first lesson that points to the necessity for seeking community freedom, because I believe it to be the most important of all our lessons. Five hundred years ago the peasants of Europe, our ancestors, were not giving much thought to use who are here to-day. But I think a good many people in the audience have often considered what kind of a country we to-day are fashioning to hand down to our descendants.

HENRY S. GRAVES ON GAME PRESERVATION*
1912

We have noted that the national forests support large game populations. Almost from the beginning wildlife conservation was a major concern of Forest Service personnel. This excerpt from the 1912 Annual Report of the Forester outlines some of the early problems and activities of wildlife management in the national forests.

There were no additions during the year to the number of game refuges or preserves within the national forests, nor was there any material change in the status of those previously existing, viz, the Wichita and the Grand Canyon national game refuges and the various State game preserves located within the Bighorn, Boise, Gallatin, Monterey, Minnesota, Superior, Teton, and Targhee National Forests. The majority of the forest officers engaged in administering these areas hold commissions as deputy State game wardens and effectively assist State officers in enforcing the local game laws. Throughout all of the national forests a vigorous effort was made to protect the game animals and birds from slaughter and molestation within their natural breeding ground, while the destruction of predatory animals and the regulated grazing of domestic live stock favored game preservation. The activities of the service contributed largely to the success of the movement to protect and perpetuate all species of game birds and animals.

No attempt has been made to stock the Grand Canyon game refuge with introduced species, and the only game animals within the refuge are those indigenous to the locality, which have multiplied encouragingly.

The buffalo herd on the Wichita, which when introduced in 1907 numbered 15 head, now contains 39 head. Nine calves were born during the year. The herd is in thriving condition, the buffalo having become thoroughly adapted to their new environment. No losses occurred. The elk herd was increased by 8 head shipped from Jacksons Hole, Wyo., in March, 1912, but 3 of these animals died shortly after their arrival at the refuge, presumably from injuries received in transit. The herd now numbers 12, of which one is a calf born in 1912. Like the buffalo, they are in splendid physical condition and free from Texas fever. The attempt to introduce antelope has met with poor success, although the country formerly was an antelope range; only 2 head survive out of a total of 10 placed within the inclosure. The cause is not defintely known. Additional animals will be secured if possible. Introduced wild turkey are doing well and give promise of large increases. The native deer are increasing rapidly, as are the quail and

*U.S. Dept. of Agriculture, U.S. Forest Service, *Report of the Forester—1912* (Washington, D.C.: Government Printing Office, 1912), 67–69.

other native game birds. The nature of the Wichita game preserve makes it most interesting, and it is visited annually by a large number of people.

The Biological Survey cooperated with the Forest Service in stocking national forests with elk shipped from Jacksons Hole, Wyo. In addition to the 8 head placed on the Wichita, 14 head were placed in the Billy Meadows grazing experiment pasture in the Wallowa National Forest, and 20 head were liberated within the Sundance National Forest in Wyoming. It is hoped that the natural increase of these small bunches will ultimately stock the forests in question. Other shipments of elk were distributed by the States of Montana and Wyoming to points where the animals will range chiefly within national forests.

* * *

The migration of elk during the winter season into the national forests surrounding the Yellowstone National Park, when the snow in the park compels them to seek food elsewhere, creates conditions that call for action. Three parties are concerned with the problem: (1) The State, represented by the State game warden; (2) the park authorities, who control the major portion of the ranges used by the elk during the summer season; and (3) the Forest Service, which controls a large part of the range used by the elk during all seasons. A census of the elk in the entire Yellowstone region was taken during the past summer. With this as a basis it is hoped to secure cooperation of the three authorities concerned in order that a definite policy for the future handling of this rather interesting problem may be formulated.

Fish secured from the Bureau of Fisheries have been used to stock streams within a number of the national forests, and this phase of game preservation receives increasing attention.

SUMMER HOMES IN NATIONAL FORESTS:
THE AGRICULTURAL APPROPRIATIONS ACT*
March 4, 1915

It appears that the first time the word "recreation" was used in national forest legislation was in the Agricultural Appropriations Act of 1915. This short statement in the act (which appears to be almost an afterthought) is important because it recognized recreation as a legitimate use of the national forests.

That hereafter the Secretary of Agriculture may, upon such terms as he may deem proper, for periods not exceeding thirty years, permit responsible persons or associations to use and occupy suitable spaces or portions of ground in the national forests for the construction of summer homes, hotels, stores, or other structures needed for recreation or public convenience, not exceeding five acres to any one person or association, but this shall not be construed to interfere with the right to enter homesteads upon agricultural lands in national forests as now provided by law.

*38 *Statutes at Large,* 1101.

GAME REFUGES IN NATIONAL FORESTS*
August 11, 1916

Public concern over diminishing wildlife was demonstrated by an act of 1916 which authorized the President to designate game refuges in national forests.

The President of the United States is authorized to designate such areas on any lands purchased by the United States under the provisions of sections 513 to 519 and 521 of this title [the Weeks Act], as should, in his opinion, be set aside for the protection of game animals, birds, or fish. Whoever shall hunt, catch, trap, willfully disturb or kill any kind of game animals, game or nongame birds, or fish, or take the eggs of any such birds on lands set aside, or in or on the waters thereof, except under such general rules and regulations as the Secretary of Agriculture may from time to time describe, shall be fined not more than $500 or imprisoned not more than six months, or both.

*39 Statutes at Large, 476.

"RECREATION USES ON THE NATIONAL FORESTS"*
1918

In 1918, Frank A. Waugh conducted the first systematic survey of national forest recreation use, problems, and needs. Excerpts from his report follow.

Long before the National Forests were established men went hunting in the woods and fishing in the streams. Camping and picnicking in the wilds had an ancient priority over the administration of those same areas by the Federal Government for the production of timber and the conservation of water. These conditions were not changed by the assignment of the lands to the care of the National Forest Service, except that such recreation uses were multiplied and intensified.

It is of course inevitable that the Forests should be so used. Outdoor recreation is a necessity of civilized life, and as civilization becomes more intensive the demand grows keener. The vast extent of our present National Forests, their enticing wildness, and the notable beauty of the native landscape lure men and women thither by hundreds of thousands. The really enormous extent and value of this kind of forest product has been generally overlooked in America.

This oversight, however, is only local and temporary. In older countries, where public forests have existed for centuries, the recreation use of such areas has always been recognized. It would be perfectly easy to show that recreation was, in fact, the original and primary purpose in the creation of public forests. The ancient law of England is most significant on this point. From before Norman days until the reign of Charles II the legal definition of a forest stood as follows:

> A certain territorie of wooddy grounds and fruitfull pasture, priviledged for wild beastes and foules of Forest Chase and Warren to rest and abide in, in the safe protection of the King, for his princely delight and pleasure, which territorie of ground, so priviledged, is meered and bounded with irremoueable markes, meres, and boundaries, wether knowen by matter of record or else by prescription.[1]

Passing from ancient law in England to present conditions in the United States of America, we find that recreation uses on the National Forests are rapidly increasing, and that they have reached a stage where more definite and systematic provision must be made for them in the plan of administration. In view of this situation, the Forester, early in 1917, commissioned the writer to make an extended examination in the field and to report to him as to existing conditions of recreation, with recommendations of methods and general policies.

The present report is based on a five months' field study of existing condi-

*Frank A. Waugh, *Recreation Uses on the National Forests* (Washington, D.C.: Government Printing Office, 1918), 3–11, 23–28.
[1] Townley, "English Woodlands," p. 1. London, 1910.

tions. Visits were made to all the Forest districts, and to a considerable number of individual Forests. Special attention was naturally given to those regions where recreational developments appear to be most pressing. In this way it was possible to hold extended consultations with Forest officers having supervision of the lands thus used, and also with those private citizens who are using them.

It should be said that the point of view of the writer is that of the professional landscape engineer. From this standpoint the landscape of the wide Forest areas has very great esthetic and human value. The mountains, glaciers, lakes, streams, woods, and natural parks contribute largely and effectively to human health and enjoyment. This contribution has a demonstrable value. The fundamental problem of the landscape engineer would then be to release these values, to make the human resources of the Forests accessible to visitors, and not merely accessible but intelligible and effective.

The moment that recreation (using this word in a very liberal meaning) is recognized as a legitimate Forest utility the way is opened for a more intelligent administration of the National Forests. Recreation then takes its proper place along with all other utilities. In each particular case these utilities are weighed against one another and a plan of administration devised to adjust and harmonize, to the utmost point practicable, the various forms of use so that the largest net total of public good may be secured. Where one must be subordinated to another, preference is given to that of highest value to the public.

With these general considerations in mind we may take a look at the National Forests, observing the extent and nature of current recreation activites.

The simplest form of recreation is found in hiking, packing, or automobiling through the Forests. There have already been provided for administrative uses (fire protection, etc.), thousands of miles of trails. These are built to standardized specifications, the most popular type ("Class A trails") providing for a safe, clean footway, 4 feet wide, laid at a maximum gradient of 6 per cent. Admirable examples of this kind of trail were examined in the Natural Bridge Area of the Appalachian Forest in Virginia. Here, in a mountain country readily accessible to the large eastern centers of population, these trails lead through splendid forests with inspiring landscape outlooks, across delightful streams and amidst surroundings well adapted to camping and all the more rigorous forms of outdoor exploration.

Yet this is merely a sample. Similar trails by hundreds of miles are found in the Forests of Colorado, California, Oregon, Washington, Montana, and indeed wherever the Forest Service has established its administration.

Besides these trails, suitable for foot passengers and pack animals, there are within the Forests other hundreds of miles of roadway fit for wagon traffic and for automobiling. Much of this mileage has been built by the Forest Service, usually in cooperation with local (country or State) authorities. But, however financed, the finished roads lie far and tempting through the Forests. Thither the camper in his wagon and the tourist in his automobile take their way, and here they linger for days and weeks at a time. The mountains, streams and woodlands are laid open to thousands of persons in this way, and no one counting their crowding procession can doubt their appreciation of the opportunity.

A typical example of this provision for public service is found in the "Park-to-Park Highway" running between the Yellowstone National Park and Glacier National Park, constructed by Forest engineers and passing over the Great Divide and through the Beaverhead and the Bitterroot Forests. The most famous example is certainly the Columbia River Highway which, though not designed or built by the Forest Service, passes for miles through the Oregon National Forest.

Along these automobile and wagon trails camps are in strong demand. Many trail tourists do not mind patronizing the hotels a part of the time, but for the rest they greatly prefer the tent and the camp fire. To meet their needs the Forest Service has laid out and equipped a large number of camps. These are always located where good water is available, and usually a practicable wood supply is an item of the equipment. Simple provisions are made for sanitation, and cement fireplaces are often installed. Sometimes telephone service is made available. Such camps are extensively used by travelers, especially along the more popular through routes. To a certain degree they prove a protection for the Forests, since the camp fires of the tourists, instead of being set in out-of-the-way and dangerous places, are made in safe areas. It is found, moreover, that the campers, once their interest and cooperation is aroused, become a volunteer fire guard of no mean efficiency. In hundreds of instances these tourists report incipient fires or assist in putting them out.

On the forest areas are many spots which, for special local reasons, have come to be popular as picnic grounds The Big Hole battle field, near Wisdom, Mont., is a fair example. Here the old settlers hold an annual reunion, and parties congregate at other times.

*　*　*

Probably the most notable example of this form of recreation is found at Eagle Creek on the Oregon Forest, on the Columbia River Highway. Here the mountains open to the picturesque Eagle Creek gorge, through which a beautiful mountain stream flows down from the snows of Mount Hood. At the mouth of the stream, where it is crossed by the Columbia River Highway, the canyon widens into a small natural park surrounded by big trees. This spot is approximately 40 miles east of Portland, just the convenient distance to make an acceptable stopping place for automobiles running out from the city. Here the Forest Service has installed sanitary conveniences, a good water supply, a number of fireplaces, and picnic tables, with certain other practical accommodations for campers.

And here the picnickers come literally by the thousands. On any pleasant

Sunday in summer every table and camp fire is crowded and the grounds take on the appearance of circus day.

Hunting and fishing are perhaps the sports most typically associated with the Forests. In the great public forests of the Old World the rearing of game for food is often practiced on a large scale. The propriety of using our National Forests to multiply game for sport, for food, or for its own sake seems obvious. To these problems the Forest Service has already given considerable study. Specialists from the United States Biological Survey have also assisted materially in this field.

Several large areas within the National Forests have been set aside through State legislation and Federal proclamation as game sanctuaries. In these areas various species of wild fowl, deer, elk, and bison are protected at all times. Hundreds of square miles adjoining the Yellowstone National Park are reserved in this way for the pasturage and protection of the elk. In the Wichita Mountains of Oklahoma is a very successful preserve devoted especially to the buffalo. Here there is a considerable herd of these animals, and they are thriving and multiplying in a very satisfactory manner.

Forest officers everywhere cooperate with other Federal officials and with State and local authorities in stocking streams with trout or lakes with other fish and in their protection under State game laws. Indeed it is almost the rule that the local forest rangers shall be also State game wardens and shall assist everywhere in the enforcement of game laws.

Some of the noblest landscape in the wide world is to be found within the National Forests. No argument is required to show that where such landscapes can be preserved for human use without sacrifice of other interests they should be firmly protected. And if in special areas this direct human value of the landscape can be shown to outweigh other economic values it obviously becomes good public policy to sacrifice the lesser interest to the greater.

Actually this is the situation which arises in many restricted areas. In the White Mountains of New Hampshire, for example, are a number of very beautiful neighborhoods the charm of which could be quickly annihilated by heedless stripping of the forests. These specific localities have a high recreation value enjoyed by thousands of persons annually—a value immeasurably greater than that to be reaped from a sale of the lumber. The preservation of such tracts for their purely scenic and recreational values seems hardly open to debate. The only questions are just what areas must be preserved for their landscape beauty, how they shall be defined, and how they shall be managed to secure their largest contribution to the beauty of the landscape. An early study should be made in the White Mountain Forest to determine these very matters.

There are hundreds of areas within the National Forests where similar reservations should be made for the same ends and on the basis of similar investigations. One other outstanding example deserves special mention. This is the scenery of Lake Chelan in central Washington. Here we have an ancient glacial gorge now dammed by the moraine at its mouth and filled with the deep blue waters of many glaciers. These glaciers hanging on the steep alpine heights which shut in the lake are reflected, along with the white rolling clouds upon the mountain summits, in the glassy waters below. If one had the wildest fjord of Norway brought inland and filled with sweet and quiet waters, or if one had Lake Brienz of Switzerland extended to a length of 50 miles, one would have a possible competitor for Lake Chelan; but until such improvements in terrestrial topography can be made this lake is unique. It is in short, and without exaggeration or qualification, one of the best landscapes in the world.

Having now enumerated the principal forms which recreation assumes on the National Forests, and having in view the question as to what policies should prevail in the administration of these interests, it seems desirable to form the clearest possible conception of the extent and value of this recreation.

In the summer of 1916 forest officers in the field were directed to report upon the number of recreation visitors with a rough classification of their activities— camping, fishing, hunting, motoring, hiking, etc. As the investigation was new, the specifications somewhat vague, and the census officers were preoccupied with other duties, the results when compiled could not be too freely accepted as decisive. Personal examination convinces me that the numbers reported were generally too low. Nevertheless, the summary figures indicated that approximately two and a half million persons during the summer of 1916 entered upon the National Forests for some kind of recreation.[1] During the summer of 1917 the census, which it had been planned to continue, was seriously impaired through the depletion of the Forest staff by enlistment in the Army. However, a certain number of Forests were able to report the count of recreation visitors for the year, and these reports indicate very clearly a substantial increase over the year 1916. A conservative estimate for 1917 would place the total of recreation visitors at 3,000,000.

If these figures seem large it must be remembered that the National Forests are large. They cover three and one-half times the area of all New England. There are 151 different Forests, with an area of about 156,000,000 acres, occupying territory in 22 different States and Territories.

A further estimate made by the forest officers on the ground indicates that the average stay of these visitors was two and one-half days. This gives us a basis for a more accurate measurement of the total recreation product, since students of this subject generally agree that the hour is the proper unit by which to measure recreation. If, then, the average visitor spent two and one-half days in the Forests, and if we call these 10-hour days, thus converting the time per person to

---

[1] It seems probable that in these totals a good many individuals were counted twice. Thus a single person might pass through 10 different Forests and be separately counted in each of them. This fact, however, does not affect our computation.

25 hours; and if we multiply this factor by the number of visitors (3,000,000) we reach the considerable total of 75,000,000 recreation hours. While the factors here used are all estimates, they are carefully made upon actual counts, and the final product is not far from the truth.

The further matter as to the market value of this body of recreation can be determined within reasonable limits. Mr. G. A. Parker, superintendent of parks in Hartford, Conn., the recognized authority on such matters, computes that park recreation as managed in the United States costs on the average 2 cents an hour. This, however, is cost, not value.

The human value of an hour spent in skating in a city park or fishing in a National Forest would be hard to estimate; but ultimate human values are seldom estimated in dollars and cents. Our usual figures indicate merely commercial values, i.e., market prices. Now the commercial value or market price of recreation is determinable quite as easily and exactly as the price of beans or books or tobacco. Enormous quantities of recreation are daily bought and sold in the open market, and the prices are as well recognized as for any commodity of commerce. The movies cost 10 cents or 15 cents; the vaudeville theaters cost 25 cents or 50 cents; the "legitimate drama" costs 50 cents to $2 a hearing; concerts cost from 25 cents to $2; grand opera, $2 to $5; a baseball game costs 50 cents; the circus costs 50 cents for the big tent, 10 cents for the concert, and 10 cents for the side show.

A moment's thought will show that 5 cents an hour represents the absolutely minimum cost of commercialized recreation. In some towns a person can buy the mild entertainment of an hour's ride on the street cars for a nickel. There still are streets where the movies perform indescribable rubbish for 5 cents.

On the whole, however, it is perfectly clear that very few and very questionable forms of recreation are offered at the price of 5 cents an hour. If we go up to 10 cents an hour the availabilities improve. The movies are better; we can occasionally get into a skating rink for a dime; we can buy an hour's reading in a cheap magazine; we can ride out to the park and back; or we can get 10 cents' worth of fishhooks and go fishing. Our choice is still much restricted.

If we seek a comparison with forms of recreation more nearly like those offered by the Forests, our results are less precise but no less convinving. A few men are able to maintain private hunting and fishing clubs in the Adirondacks, in Maine, or on the Restigouche. The time they pass at these resorts costs them anywhere from $1 to $10 an hour. To take a vacation at any public seaside or mountain resort costs from $2 to $10 a day.

These figures, though somewhat sketchy, are a statement of plain facts. In view of them the following generalizations are self-evident:

1. The minimum market cost to the consumer of wholesome recreation privately provided is 10 cents an hour.

2. The average cost of commercial recreation is much higher, probably lying somewhere between 25 cents and $1 an hour.

It ought to be self-evident, further, that the great bulk of such recreation is worth all it costs. If it isn't, the large majority of our whole population are being daily robbed in their recreation bills. One more premise hardly needs an argument, viz, that the average recreation in the National Forests is as valuable in all human ways as the average of commercial recreations.

Now if we take even the minimum of these estimates and apply the figures to the problem in hand the results are fairly sobering. For 75,000,000 recreation hours annually yielded by the National Forests (and these figures will be quickly and widely exceeded in years to come), valued at the minimum of 10 cents an hour, amounts to $7,500,000—a pretty penny.

Stated in general terms it appears that *the recreation use of the National Forests has a very substantial commercial value, and that recreation stands clearly as one of the major Forest utilities.*

* * *

We have seen the wide extent and variety of recreation uses on the National Forests, and we have considered briefly the commercial value of this product. We are now in a position to discuss some of the questions of public policy as implied in these data. Such questions of policy must inevitably have a considerable influence on the practical administrative operations of the Forest Service.

It would seem that the following principles may be safely adopted:

1. Recreation upon the Forest areas is a social utility of large dimensions and very substantial value.

2. Recreation of many kinds, all legitimate, develops on practically all areas of the National Forests. It is inherent in the character of the Forests and must be recognized as a permanent and universal factor in Forest administration. Only by the most drastic and extraordinary administrative measures could recreation be excluded from particular Forest areas.

3. Being a public utility of great value and being inevitable to the Forest administration, recreation should be developed by the Forest Service on the same basis as any other Forest utility.

The most logical statement of the situation is made by saying that recreation stands on a par with other major uses of the Forest areas, and is to be managed on its merits precisely like the others. These major uses are—

Timber production
Grazing
Watershed protection
Recreation

And from the figures given it would appear that recreation is by no means an unworthy member of this group.

Now the policy with respect to handling these several utilities on the Forest areas has never been obscure. Where two or more of these main uses can be served at the same time on the same area they are carried forward side by side,

[383]

sometimes in actual cooperation. Whenever two of these uses come into conflict, some authority determines which is likely to render the greater public service. This then becomes the paramount use on the area in question; other uses are secondary, and, if they interfere seriously with the primary use, they are altogether excluded from the area. This policy is so obvious, simple, and practical that it needs no defense.

Moreover this policy need not be changed in the slightest when recreation comes to be recognized in the list of major utilities. It is, in fact, the policy already and inevitably adopted. *On the principal areas of the National Forests recreation is an incidental use; on some it is a paramount use; on a few it becomes the exclusive use.*

With respect to this matter as it affects the internal workings of the Forest Service alone, some emphasis should be placed on the fact, frequently not recognized, that the recreation use on Forest lands only rarely interferes with other uses. In general the natural development and protection of the Forests operates directly to enhance the recreation values. On the other hand recreation, except where it becomes intensive at certain points, seldom infringes upon other uses of the Forest. The development of this fact has been, in some cases, rather surprising. For example, it has been found, contrary to common expectation, that the presence of campers and summer-home permittees in considerable numbers, instead of increasing the fire risk has in some cases actually assisted in fire protection. Any general argument therefore which alleges a conflict between the recreation uses and other Forest utilities starts from a premise which is not true.

REPORT OF THE FORESTER*
1920

By 1920, outdoor recreation had assumed enough importance to merit a section in the Forest Service Annual Report.

RECREATION AND GAME

The use of the National Forests for recreation purposes is increasing rapidly. This use is not confined to a few well-advertised regions of special attractiveness, but is noticable in almost all of the 152 Forests. It is common to the White Mountains, the southern Appalachians, the forests of Minnesota, the Rocky Mountains, the Cascade and Sierras, and the alluring tablelands of Arizona and New Mexico. As an important use it bids fair to rank third among the major services performed by the National Forests, with only timber production and stream-flow regulation taking precedence of it.

* * *

The use of the National Forests for recreation is being recognized by many communities as one of their greatest assets and privileges. This is resulting in the establishment of community camps under more or less formal organization. They take every form from the municipal vacation camps erected on the Angeles National Forest under permit from the Forest Service and maintained and managed by the city of Los Angeles to the improvement of some favorite picnic ground in the National Forest by local citizens in cooperation with the local forest officers. Space is provided for parking automobiles, simple permanent fireplaces are built, wood is made available for camp fires and cooking without endangering the Forest from fires, rustic tables and seats are located conveniently for different parties, signs indicate the direction and distance to attractive points, and public convenience is given thoughtful consideration. Similar improvements are made by the Forest Service when funds are available and local cooperation can not be obtained to meet a real public need. These camps are made available to the public without charge of any kind by the Forest Service. The vacation camps, such as those maintained by Los Angeles, require a charge merely sufficient to cover the expense of feeding and caring for the successive groups of city patrons who enjoy its privileges under municipal direction.

The appeal for local recreational facilities and the demand for summer-home sites are growing so rapidly that there is need for men of special training to direct and plan for the most effective development of this service. Many communities

*U.S. Dept. of Agriculture, U.S. Forest Service, *Report of the Forester—1920* (Washington, D.C.: Government Printing Office, 1920), 19–21.

are subscribing liberally for the erection of improvements upon the National Forests for public convenience. To bring about the fullest use of the National Forests and contribute their proper quota to the Nation's health, there is needed a special fund of $50,000 for recreational development. This will permit the employment of several trained landscape engineers, more rapid and at the same time more careful development, the improvement of additional camp grounds and provision of other public facilities and conveniences, and enlarged cooperation with local communities. This is certainly good business policy; the increased receipts from individual home sites, which is only one by-product of our recreational work, will return to the Treasury much more than the total amount to be expended for recreational development.

Closely related with the development of our recreational resources is the use of the National Forests as the habitat of fish and game and the protection of wild life as a great public resource. Game protection is one of the regular activities of the field officers of the Forest Service. Cooperation with the State and local authorities in enforcing the game laws has contributed in no small degree toward making our National Forests more attractive to visitors and conserving one of their most valuable resources. This work will be continued in the future along the same broad lines.

To make this work most effective and to secure better development of the fish and game resources of the National Forests, Congress should make provision for the establishment of game sanctuaries within which wild life may find security. These should be relatively limited in area, but should be established in considerable number. Their location will require careful preliminary field investigation and close cooperation with the State authorities. A favorable report has already been submitted to Congress upon one such measure, which would empower the President to establish such game sanctuaries within the National Forests of any State where their establishment is sanctioned by the State legislature.

In this connection special mention should be made of the necessity of additional protection for the harassed and decimated herds of elk using the Yellowstone National Park and the surrounding Forests. Famine and cold last winter took an unusually heavy toll from their number. Driven out of the high country by starvation and early deep snows, the northern herd suffered from hunters along the boundary line a percentage loss equal to that of a defeated army. Many that escaped the hunters perished from cold and starvation before spring. The southern herd also lost heavily. As a result, the total number of animals in these two herds is now estimated by the best qualified officers in the Forest Service to equal one-half of their number five years ago.

The Forest service, in close cooperation with the Biological Survey, will continue to do all in its power to help preserve these great herds from destruction by neglect. Congress should add to the Absaroka and Gallatin Forests the lands still in Government ownership now under withdrawal along the Yellowstone

River north of Gardiner. This land is urgently needed as winter range for the elk. Local settlers need not be excluded from the continued use of this range, for the small number of stock owned by them can easily be taken care of without materially affecting the well-being of the elk. If Congress makes the addition as recommended, its use by both game and domestic stock can be worked out without injury or injustice to any of the local residents. If this action is not taken the outlook for the northern elk herd is gloomy indeed. The prospects for the southern herd are more bright; but additional purchases of land for winter feeding grounds appear absolutely essential.

ROADS, TRAILS, AND OTHER IMPROVEMENTS

The mileage of road and trail construction during 1919 eclipsed all previous figures. This is the more notable in view of the high cost and scarcity of labor. The large amount of investigative and survey work carried on during 1918, when construction was restricted to projects that would contribute toward the prosecution of the war, aided materially in getting work under way early in 1919. This was particularly true of administrative and protective roads and trails. Special effort has been made to complete as quickly as possible the roads and trails essential to an effective system of fire protection; but although excellent progress has been made, a tremendous amount of transportation development remains to be accomplished before all danger points can be reached quickly. The accessibility of the forests for recreation has been greatly increased by the completion of many of the projects.

"THE WILDERNESS AND ITS PLACE
IN FOREST RECREATIONAL POLICY"*
1921

One of the first proponents of the wilderness concept was Aldo Leopold, a young forester, who wrote this article in 1921.

When the National Forests were created the first argument of those opposing a national forest policy was that the forests would remain a wilderness. Gifford Pinchot replied that on the contrary they would be opened up and developed as producing forests, and that such development would, in the long run, itself constitute the best assurance that they would neither remain a wilderness by "bottling up" their resources nor become one through devastation. At this time Pinchot enunciated the doctrine of "highest use," and its criterion, "the greatest good to the greatest number," which is and must remain the guiding principle by which democracies handle their natural resources.

Pinchot's promise of development has been made good. The process must, of course, continue indefinitely. But it has already gone far enough to raise the question of whether the policy of development (construed in the narrower sense of industrial development) should continue to govern in absolutely every instance, or whether the principle of highest use does not itself demand that representative portions of some forests be preserved as wilderness.

That some such question actually exists, both in the minds of some foresters and of part of the public, seems to me to be plainly implied in the recent trend of recreational use policies and in the tone of sporting and outdoor magazines. Recreational plans are leaning toward the segregation of certain areas from certain developments, so that having been led into the wilderness, the people may have some wilderness left to enjoy. Sporting magazines are groping toward some logical reconciliation between getting back to nature and preserving a little nature to get back to. Lamentations over this or that favorite vacation ground being "spoiled by tourists" are becoming more and more frequent. Very evidently we have here the old conflict between preservation and use, long since an issue with respect to timber, water power, and other purely economic resources, but just now coming to be an issue with respect to recreation. It is the fundamental function of foresters to reconcile these conflicts, and to give constructive direction to these issues as they arise. The purpose of this paper is to give definite form to the issue of wilderness conservation, and to suggest certain policies for meeting it, especially as applied to the Southwest.

It is quite possible that the serious discussion of this question will seem a far

*Aldo Leopold, "The Wilderness and Its Place in Forest Recreational Policy," *Journal of Forestry,* Vol. 19, No. 7 (Nov., 1921), 718–21.

cry in some unsettled regions, and rank heresy to some minds. Likewise did timber conservation seem a far cry in some regions, and rank heresy to some minds
of a generation ago. "The truth is that which prevails in the long run."

Some definitions are probably necessary at the outset. By "wilderness" I mean
a continuous stretch of country preserved in its natural state, open to lawful
hunting and fishing, big enough to absorb a two weeks' pack trip, and kept de-
void of roads, artificial trails, cottages, or other works of man. Several assumptions can be made at once without argument. First, such wilderness areas should
occupy only a small fraction of the total National Forest area—probably not to
exceed one in each State. Second, only areas naturally difficult of ordinary
industrial development should be chosen. Third, each area should be representative of some type of country of distinctive recreational value, or afford some
distinctive type of outdoor life, opportunity for which might disappear on other
forest lands open to industrial development.

The argument for such wilderness areas is premised wholly on highest recreational use. The recreational desires and needs of the public, whom the forests
must serve, vary greatly with the individual. Heretofore we have been inclined to
assume that our recreational development policy must be based on the desires
and needs of the majority only. The only new thing about the premise in this case
is the proposition that inasmuch as we have plenty of room and plenty of time, it
is our duty to vary our recreational development policy, in some places, to meet
the needs and desires of the minority also. The majority undoubtedly want all
the automobile roads, summer hotels, graded trails, and other modern conveniences that we can give them. It is already decided, and wisely, that they shall
have these things as rapidly as brains and money can provide them. But a very
substantial minority, I think, want just the opposite. It should be decided, as
soon as the existence of the demand can be definitely determined, to provide
what this minority wants. In fact, if we can foresee the demand, and make provision for it in advance, it will save much cash and hard feelings. It will be much
easier to keep wilderness areas than to create them. In fact, the latter alternative
may be dismissed as impossible. Right here is the whole reason for forehanded-
ness in the proposed wilderness area policy.

It is obvious to everyone who knows the National Forests that even with intensive future development, there will be a decreasing but inexhaustible number
of small patches of rough country which will remain practically in wilderness
condition. It is also generally recognized that these small patches have a high
and increasing recreational value. But will they obviate the need for a policy
such as here proposed? I think not. These patches are too small, and must grow
smaller. They will always be big enough for camping, but they will tend to grow
too small for a real wilderness trip. The public demands for camp sites and wilderness trips, respectively, are both legitimate and both strong, but nevertheless
distinct. The man who wants a wilderness trip wants not only scenery, hunting,

fishing, isolation, etc.—all of which can often be found within a mile of a paved auto highway—but also the horses, packing, riding, daily movement and variety found only in a trip through a big stretch of wild country. It would be pretty lame to forcibly import these features into a country from which the real need for them had disappeared.

It may also be asked whether the National Parks from which, let us hope, industrial development will continue to be excluded, do not fill the public demand here discussed. They do, in part. But hunting is not and should not be allowed within the Parks. Moreover, the Parks are being networked with roads and trails as rapidly as possible. This is right and proper. The Parks merely prove again that the recreational needs and desires of the public vary through a wide range of individual tastes, all of which should be met in due proportion to the number of individuals in each class. There is only one question involved—highest use. And we are beginning to see that highest use is a very varied use, requiring a very varied administration, in the recreational as well as in the industrial field.

An actual example is probably the best way to describe the workings of the proposed wilderness area policy.

The Southwest (meaning New Mexico and Arizona) is a distinct region. The original southwestern wilderness was the scene of several important chapters in our national history. The remainder of it is about as interesting, from about as large a number of angles, as any place on the continent. It has a high and varied recreational value. Under the policy advocated in this paper, a good big sample of it should be preserved. This could easily be done by selecting such an area as the headwaters of the Gila River on the Gila National Forest. This is an area of nearly half a million acres, topographically isolated by mountain ranges and box canyons. It has not yet been penetrated by railroads and to only a very limited extent by roads. On account of the natural obstacles to transportation and the absence of any considerable areas of agricultural land, no net economic loss would result from the policy of withholding further industrial development, except that the timber would remain inaccessible and available only for limited local consumption. The entire area is grazed by cattle, but the cattle ranches would be an asset from the recreational standpoint because of the interest which attaches to cattle grazing operations under frontier conditions. The apparent disadvantage thus imposed on the cattlemen might be nearly offset by the obvious advantage of freedom from new settlers, and from the hordes of motorists who will invade this region the minute it is opened up. The entire region is the natural habitat of deer, elk, turkey, grouse, and trout. If preserved in its semi-virgin state, it could absorb a hundred pack trains each year without overcrowding. It is the last typical wilderness in the southwestern mountains. Highest use demands its preservation.

The conservation of recreational resources here advocated has its historic counterpart in the conservation of timber resources lately become a national issue and expressed in the forestry program. Timber conservation began fifteen years ago with the same vague premonitions of impending shortage now discernible in the recreational press. Timber conservation encountered the same general rebuttal of "inexhaustible supplies" which recreational conservation will shortly encounter. After a period of milling and mulling, timber conservation established the principle that timber supplies are capable of qualitative as well as quantitative exhaustion, and that the existence of "inexhaustible" areas of trees did not necessarily insure the supply of bridge timber, naval stores, or pulp. So also will recreational resources be found in more danger of qualitative than quantitative exhaustion. We now recognize that the sprout forests of New England are no answer to the farmer's need for structural lumber, and we admit that the farmer's special needs must be taken care of in proportion to his numbers and importance. So also must we recognize that any number of small patches of uninhabited wood or mountains are no answer to the real sportsman's need for wilderness, and the day will come when we must admit that his special needs likewise must be taken care of in proportion to his numbers and importance. And as in forestry, it will be much easier and cheaper to preserve, by forethought, what he needs, than to create it after it is gone.

THE SHIPSTEAD-NOLAN ACT*
July 10, 1930

This landmark act, which grew out of a movement to protect the natural beauty and wilderness character of the many lakes in northern Minnesota, withdrew from entry all public lands north of Township 60 North in Cook and Lake Counties, Minnesota. It also required that the Forest Service conserve for recreation use the lakes in the Superior National Forest.

An Act to promote the better protection and highest public use of lands of the United States and adjacent lands and waters in northern Minnesota for the production of forest products, and for other purposes.

Be it enacted by the Senate and House of Representatives of the United States of America in Congress assembled, That all public lands of the United States situated north of Township 60 north in the Counties of Cook and Lake, State of Minnesota, including the natural shore lines of Lake Superior within such area; all public lands of the United States situated in that part of St. Louis County, State of Minnesota, lying north of a line beginning at the northeast corner of Township 63 north, Range 12 west, 4th P. M., thence westerly along the township line to the southwest corner of Township 64 north, Range 18 west, 4th P. M., thence northerly to the northwest corner of Township 65 north, Range 18 west, 4th P. M., thence westerly to the southwest corner, Township 66 north, Range 21 west, 4th P. M., thence northerly along the Township line to its intersection with the international boundary between the United States and the Dominion of Canada; all public lands of the United States on the shore lines of the lakes and streams forming the international boundary, so far as such lands lie within the areas heretofore described in this Act; all public lands of the United States in that part of the Superior National Forest located in Townships 61 and 62, Ranges 12 and 13 west, 4th P. M.; and all public lands of the United States on the shore lines of Burntside Lake and Lake Vermilion, State of Minnesota, are hereby withdrawn from all forms of entry or appropriation under the public land laws of the United States, subject to prior existing legal rights initiated under the public land laws, so long as such claims are maintained as required by the applicable law or laws and subject to such permits and licenses as may be granted or issued by the Department of Agriculture under laws or regulations generally applicable to national forests.

SEC. 2. That the principle of conserving the natural beauty of shore lines for recreational use shall apply to all Federal lands which border upon any boundary

*881 *Statutes at Large,* 1021.

lake or stream contiguous to this area, or any other lake or stream within this area which is now or eventually to be in general use for boat or canoe travel, and that for the purpose of carrying out this principle logging of all such shores to a depth of four hundred feet from the natural water line is hereby forbidden, except as the Forest Service of the Department of Agriculture may see fit in particular instances to vary the distance for practical reasons: *Provided,* That in no case shall logging of any timber other than diseased, insect infested, dying, or dead be permitted closer to the natural shore line than two hundred feet, except where necessary to open areas for banking grounds, landings, and other uses connected with logging operations.

Sec. 3. That in order to preserve the shore lines, rapids, waterfalls, beaches, and other natural features of the region in an unmodified state of nature, no further alteration of the natural water level of any lake or stream within or bordering upon the designated area shall be authorized by any permit, license, lease, or other authorization granted by any official or commission of the United States, which will result in flooding lands of the United States within or immediately adjacent to the Superior National Forest, unless and until specific authority for granting such permit, license, lease, or other authorization shall have first been obtained by special Act from the Congress of the United States covering each such project: *Provided,* That nothing in this section shall be construed as interfering with the duties of the International Joint Commission created pursuant to the convention concerning the boundary waters between the United States and Canada and concluded between the United States and Great Britain on January 11, 1909, and action taken or to be taken in accordance with provisions of the convention protocol and agreement between the United States and Canada, which were signed at Washington on February 24, 1925, for the purpose of regulating the levels of the Lake of the Woods: *Provided,* That with the written approval and consent of the Forest Service of the Department of Agriculture, reservoirs not exceeding one hundred acres in area may be constructed and maintained for the transportation of logs or in connection with authorized recreational uses of national-forest lands, and maximum water levels not higher than the normal high water mark may be maintained temporarily where essential strictly for logging purposes, in the streams between lakes by the construction and operation of small temporary dams: *Provided, however,* That nothing herein shall be construed to prevent the Secretary of Agriculture from listing for homestead entry under the provisions of the Act of June 11, 1906 (34 Stat. 233), any of the above-described lands found by him to be chiefly valuable for agriculture and not needed for public purposes: *Provided further,* That the provisions of this section shall not apply to any proposed development for water-power purposes for which an application for license was pending under the terms of the Federal Water Power Act on or before January 1, 1928.

Approved, July 10, 1930.

"A SUMMONS TO SAVE THE WILDERNESS"*
1935

By 1935, a Wilderness Society had been organized to try to preserve some of the wilderness areas that still remained. This article in the first issue of the society's publication, The Living Wilderness, *sets out the reasons for forming the society and its objectives.*

The Wilderness Society is born of an emergency in conservation which admits of no delay. It consists of persons distressed by the exceedingly swift passing of wilderness in a country which recently abounded in the richest and noblest of wilderness forms, the primitive, and who purpose to do all they can to safeguard what is left of it. This for transmission, a sacred charge, to its preservers of the future.

It is true that every conservation organization realizes the tragedy that is enacting in the mountains and plains and would help if it could, and that every conservationist is sick at heart of what he sees on every hand, but is helpless. Furthermore, we believe that the great majority of careless and casual enjoyers of out-of-doors (and what American does not enjoy his out-of-doors?) would join heartily in preservation if only he realized the exquisiteness of primeval nature, the majesty of much of it, and that, once destroyed, it can never be returned to its thrilling sequence from the infinite.

The reason for prevailing helplessness is failure in leadership. Each organization in federal lands has its own other major objective, for which it was created and financed, and, to achieve which in times like these, it has not sufficient men and money. Each sees the wilderness crashing around it, but is powerless against the pressure of its own specialties to more than cry aloud with pointed finger. All could help a little, but none could plan and lead without tragic sacrifice of its own responsibilities. This is true in the federal land field, which contains a fifth of the forest. The remaining four-fifths are in state and private lands with no protecting organizations except local groups of limited vision whose activities are necessarily affected by local interests.

Of this dire situation was born last January the Wilderness Society.

The group that started it on January 21 never for a moment dreamed of itself saving the wilderness, but of transmuting, perhaps, a nation's yearning into power, as the cheer-leader tunes the inchoate vocalism of a multitude into one great voice that makes for victory. The Wilderness Society does not plan a large membership or a fine establishment. A few hundred or thousand picked workers will suffice, represented in states where there is wilderness to save. We are pick-

*The Living Wilderness, Vol. 1, No. 1 (Sept., 1935), 1–2.

ing our members now, studying the field, planning methods, mapping opportunities, meantime spreading abroad, through every member, the intense need of wilderness salvation. This work will be backed, in time, by an ocean-to-ocean public opinion.

Among our members are already men widely known. This is, in a very special sense, an organization of youth. There is not a man in it who is not young in spirit, and few not young in years. They include executives of the most influential national conservation organizations.

Ten years of warfare in Congress saved the National Parks System from water power and irrigation, but left the primitive decimated elsewhere. What little of it is left is passing before a popular craze and an administrative fashion. The craze is to build all the highways possible everywhere while billions may yet be borrowed from the unlucky future. The fashion is to barber and manicure wild America as smartly as the modern girl. Our duty is clear.

THE WILDERNESS SOCIETY PLATFORM

1. That the wilderness (the environment of solitude) is a natural mental resource having the same basic relation to man's ultimate thought and culture as coal, timber, and other physical resources have to his material needs.

2. That the use of this resource should be considered a public utility and therefore its commercialization should not be tolerated.

3. That the time has come, with the brutalizing pressure of a spreading metropolitan civilization, to recognize wilderness environment as a human need rather than a luxury and plaything.

4. That this need is being sacrificed to the mechanical invasion in its various killing forms.

5. That scenery and solitude are intrinsically separate things, that the motorist is entitled to his full share of scenery, but that motorway and solitude together constitute a contradiction.

6. That outing areas in which people may enjoy the non-primitive forest are highly desirable for many pent-up city people who have no desire for solitude, but that such areas should not be confused in mental conception or administration with those reserved for the wilderness.

7. That, since primeval succession can never return once continuity has been severed, it is manifestly the duty of this generation to preserve under scientific care, for the observation, study, and appreciation of generations to come, as many, as large, and as varied examples of the remaining primitive as possible.

8. That the wilderness remaining in America has shrunk to such a small remnant of the country's total territory, that what area does remain is all-precious and its preservation a vital need.

9. That encroachment upon our remnant American wilderness in any one

locality is an attack upon the whole and creates an issue of national moment and not for local action alone.

10. That since the invasion of wilderness areas is generally boosted by powerful, country-wide organizations, it is essential that individuals and groups who desire to preserve the wilderness must unite in a country-wide defense.

11. That the means of achieving our objectives should be positive and creative as well as merely defensive, and hence that a long-range plan should be evolved toward bringing forth its mental and ultimate human uses.

THE TYPES OF WILDERNESS RECOGNIZED

In order to define more specifically what we want to preserve, it seems desirable to divide what might broadly be termed the wilderness into five types.

Extensive Wilderness Areas are regions which possess no means of mechanical conveyance and which are sufficiently spacious that a person may spend at least a week of travel in them without crossing his own tracks. They may include timber, range lands, bare rocks, snowfields, marshes, deserts, or water. The dominant attributes of such areas are: first, that visitors to them must depend largely on their own efforts and their own competence for survival; and second, that they be free from all mechanical disturbances.

Primeval Areas are virgin tracts in which human activities have never modified the normal processes of nature. They thus preserve the native vegetative and physiographic conditions which have existed for an inestimable period. They present the culmination of an unbroken series of natural events stretching infinitely into the past, and a richness of beauty beyond description or compare. Consequently, primeval areas not only are of surpassing value from the standpoint of scenery, but of great scientific value.

Superlatively Scenic Areas are localities with scenic values so surpassing and stupendous in their beauty as to affect almost everyone who sees them. They may also include natural features of unique scientific interest, such as the geysers of Yellowstone.

Restricted Wild Areas are tracts of land in regions of concentrated population which, even though not having great size, virgin conditions, or superlative scenery, are at least free from the sights and sounds of mechanization. They are the closest approximation to wilderness conditions available to millions of people.

Wilderness Zones are strips along the backbone of mountain ranges or rivers which, although they may be crossed here and there by railroads and highways, nevertheless maintain primitive travel conditions along their major axes. Such zones not only are primarily free from man-made sights and sounds, but also permit long journeys under the impetus of one's own energies instead of those of a machine.

"MULTIPLE USE—MULTIPLE BENEFITS"*
1953

National forests were first established, of course, to preserve forests for future use and to control runoff from forested watersheds. Prior to 1944, however, there was no formalized system for carrying out these purposes on a consistent and systematic basis over time. The Sustained-Yield Forest Management Act of March 29, 1944 (documented in Land and Water: 1900–1970, *p. 633) provided this system. The act is significant for our purposes mainly because preservation of wildlife was one of the stated objectives of "sustained yield."*

Grazing and wildlife preservation were very soon added to the primary uses or objectives, of the national forests; still later, outdoor recreation came to be recognized as a valid use. It is therefore clear that almost from the very beginning the national forests were managed under a multiple-use concept. Richard E. McArdle, Chief of the Forest Service, explained the concept of multiple-use in this speech to the North American Wildlife Conference in 1953.

Many different groups of people use the national forests—people who rightly feel that they have a proprietary interest in these great public properties. Every citizen of this country owns a share of stock in the national forests—one share only, no less and no more. But that one share is immensely valuable. It is becoming more valuable with every passing day.

The national forests are unique public properties—distinctive not only because they encompass 181 million acres of timber and range, jutting mountain peaks, and uncounted lakes and streams, but more particularly because of the management objectives applied in their administration. Most public lands are managed primarily for a single purpose, or in some instances for a dual purpose. The national forests are managed for many purposes.

Today, more than at any other time in the past, this concept of multiple-use management is being challenged. I do not recall seeing the challenge thrown down exactly as I have phrased it. But it can be seen none the less plainly in proposals to dedicate, legislatively or otherwise, large areas to one use or for the benefit of only one group of users. It can be seen in proposals to remove large areas from public ownership so as to benefit primarily one use or one group of users. It is evident in other proposals that would give this or that group exclusive or dominant rights in the use of these public lands.

A development such as this is inevitable in the growth of our country. We need to recognize the existence of this rapidly changing public-land use situation and to be aware of its implications. We need to look as far and as clearly into the

*Richard E. McArdle, "Multiple Use—Multiple Benefits," *Journal of Forestry,* Vol. 51, No. 5 (May, 1953), 323–25.

future as we possibly can. This is no penny-ante game; the stakes are tremendous.

In the management of the national forests, we of the Forest Service are having to face up to this problem every day, in more places and in more and more different ways. This is particularly true of the western national forests. Here are former hinterlands that only a few years ago were remote and inaccessible. Here are areas whose values have jumped as population has increased, as industrial and agricultural development has leaped ahead, as transportation and communication advances have erased barriers of space and time. The ever-increasing intensity of use of these national-forest lands brings conflicts that at times seem nearly impossible to resolve satisfactorily. Yet resolve them we must, for only by wise balancing of these diverse interests can these public properties be made to yield maximum benefit to all our people.

To help you see this picture more clearly, let me sketch for you some of the multiple uses of the national forests that by leaps and bounds are growing in volume and intensity.

RECREATIONAL USE

Take fishing and hunting, for example. More than 2 million hunters and some 4 million fishermen used the national forests last year. We are wholeheartedly in favor of this use of the national forests and want to see it increase.

As a matter of fact, all kinds of recreational uses of the national forests are on the increase. Last year the national forest had 30 million recreational visitors. Ten years ago there were only 10 million. Some of these millions of people want only a place to picnic. Others want to camp overnight. Some want summer homes. A lot of people just want to put a pack on their backs and hike up and down hill. Some want to experience the fascination and deep-seated satisfaction that comes with penetration of a vast wilderness far from sight and sound of civilization. And recently national-forest winter sports use has been increasing at an almost unbelievable rate. The present need for ski runs and lifts and so on is something we failed to foresee a quarter of a century ago. It makes me wonder if today we are seeing future recreational needs accurately—even for only ten or twenty years ahead.

At any rate, with better roads and more of them, with better automobiles and more of them, with a five-day week, longer vacations and more leisure time generally—whatever the reasons may be—more and more and still more people are using the national forests for recreational purposes. That's fine. We like it.

And we are not alone in approving this use of the national forests. Measured in terms of dollars spent, outdoor recreation is one of the biggest businesses in this country. Think of the people who make some or all of their living by selling food and lodging, souvenirs and soft drinks, fishing tackle, golf clubs, gasoline, and a thousand and one other items to recreationists. Think of the many others employed in manufacturing these articles or in transporting recreationists here and there or in serving them in countless other ways. The national forests produce a big chunk of this business.

But to me the commercial aspects of national-forest recreation are secondary to the opportunity for people to get away from the mental and emotional strains of present-day living. It is a safety valve which has great significance in keeping people healthy and happy—in helping them to keep a balance and a sense of values in a world increasingly beset with emotional strain. You can't put a dollar sign on this sort of thing, but we believe it is one of the great contributions the national forests make to the people who own them.

TIMBER MANAGEMENT

Now let's consider for a moment a quite different use of these same lands. More than half a century ago the Congress set forth, as a principal objective in establishing the national forests, the need to furnish "a continuous supply of timber for the use and necessities of citizens of the United States." For a great many years this use, like recreational use, was not very large. Today, as with recreational use, the picture has changed. The amount of timber cut on the national forests has doubled in less than ten years. Receipts from sale of timber were $64 million last year and will be even larger this year.

Harvesting national-forest timber under the sustained-yield principle has helped stabilize communities and local industries and has provided jobs for many thousands of people—not only in the wood-using industries but for butchers, bakers, doctors, lawyers, and merchants serving these industries and their employees. Local governments benefit too because 25 percent of all national-forest receipts go to the states for roads and schools in the counties having national-forest land.

We think this use of the national forests is all to the good. It's good for our country—for all of us. It's wise use of land. It's something that we want to see increase and prosper.

LIVESTOCK GRAZING

There is still another substantial use of the national forests. Last year permits were issued to about 20,000 ranchers to graze some 3 million sheep and nearly 1¼ million cattle and horses. Grazing fees total about $5 million a year, and this income, too, is shared with the states and counties.

This dollar income, however, does not tell the whole story. Much national-forest range is high-mountain summer range, usable for only part of the year. The home ranches of many livestock owners are at lower elevations with only winter range. We try to work with these stockmen to fit the private and public range together so as to provide the year-around operation required for this industry. We believe that livestock grazing is a proper use of many national-forest areas. Let no one tell you that we want to fence out grazing use of the national forests. By building up the grazing capacity of these ranges through reseeding and good management we can improve their value. We have already demonstrated that this can be done. We want to make this use play an even stronger part in our whole agricultural and industrial economy.

WATERSHED PROTECTION

There is another use of the national forests which in many respects is more important, more essential, than perhaps any other use. The basic legislation establishing these public forests provided, as a principal reason for their reservation in public ownership, the need to make certain of "favorable conditions of water flows." Our pioneer forefathers knew how important water is. It was the first thing they looked for when they selected a homesite or a place to establish a new community. As time passed, their children and great grandchildren hired other people to worry about their water supplies. It became a job for the superintendent of the city water works, not for the apartment dweller, the individual home or factory owner.

But today, we are again becoming aware—as individual citizens—of our water situation. In the past six months I have been in three cities where water use was temporarily being restricted. I was in another city when the reserve supply of water was sufficient for only a few hours of use. There are towns, both East and West, where futher industrial expansion depends on somehow finding an increase in current water supplies. Think of the great distances to which some cities are now reaching out for more adequate supplies of water—distances that only a relatively few years ago would have been considered incredible and probably impossible. These are not things that might happen; these are actualities.

No one knows precisely how much the national forests—and other public lands—are worth to the people of this country as major sources of clean, pure, usable water. I have seen estimates by competent authorities that, at current water prices, add up to hundreds of millions of dollars a year. I know of some national-forest watersheds that for water yield alone are estimated to be worth $2,000 an acre.

Dollar value alone is a poor criterion. Water is something that we must have; it is worth whatever we have to pay to get it. There are other ways to measure the value of this use of the national forests. There are more than 1,800 communities—some are cities of several hundred thousand population—that are dependent on national-forest watersheds for their domestic and industrial water. Thousands more are partly dependent on the national forests. Many—I believe

I could say most—of the major irrigated farm developments of the West depend on national forests for their water supplies. More than 600 hydroelectric power developments—including practically all of the major power projects in western states—depend on water from the national forests.

But valuable as our national forests are today for water production—valuable as these lands are today—it's small compared with the role they are going to play in years to come. If we want water tomorrow we must take care of our watersheds today.

LANDS OF MANY USES

Perhaps that's enough to show that the national forests are lands of many uses—and many users. The intensity of all these uses is increasing—and increasing rapidly.

As intensity of use increases we sometimes find one or more of these uses in conflict. It would be more accurate to say that there is conflict between the personal interests of the various groups of users. The wilderness enthusiasts, and there are many of them, naturally want timber cutting and other commercial uses excluded on substantial areas. Timber users object to taking too much commercial-quality timber off the market. The argument, of course, turns on how much is too much. Hunters want more wild game, but the livestock people say that too much big game takes forage away from domestic livestock. Again, we come up against how much is too much? Irrigated land farmers and other water users are beginning to protest vigorously any use of national-forest watersheds that may jeopardize their water supplies.

There are conflicts, too, between surface and subsurface uses. Development of the mineral resources of the national forests is legitimate, proper, and in the public interest. But it should be done with minimum disturbance of surface resources.

It all boils down to this: The practical workability of the multiple-use concept of national-forest administration is being tested on a scale and to an intensity greater than we have ever experienced. The Forest Service believes that many of the diverse uses of the national forests are reasonably compatible. If we had to deal with only one group of users, it would be somewhat easier to agree on a reasonable course of action. But since we must consider the interests of all the people, so also we usually find ourselves in the middle.

Let me make it completely clear that I think being in the middle is exactly where we ought to be. I believe that our inability to satisfy completely each and every group of national-forest users is a definite sign of success in doing the job assigned to us. When each group is somewhat dissatisfied, it is a sign that no one group is getting more than its fair share.

The guiding principle laid down for us nearly fifty years ago still hits the mark.

[401]

We were instructed to so administer these national forests that they would yield the "most productive use for the permanent good of the whole people, and not for the temporary benefit of individuals or companies;" and "where conflicting interests must be reconciled, the question will always be decided from the standpoint of the greatest good of the greatest number in the long run." That is still the guiding policy of the Forest Service, and I hope it always will be. It expresses the responsibility that we have to protect and build up not only your share of stock in these national forests but that of every one of your 150 million fellow Americans.

THE MULTIPLE USE ACT*
June 12, 1960

Congress approved and legitimatized the concept of multiple use in the Multiple Use Act. Lumbering, watershed protection, grazing and wildlife preservation had previously been recognized by Congress as legitimate uses of the national forests. Now for the first time Congress added outdoor recreation to the list as a valid use of all national forests (not only for specific designated areas). Because of its importance for outdoor recreation, the act is duplicated here.

> An Act to authorize and direct that the national forests be managed under principles of multiple use and to produce a sustained yield of products and services, and for other purposes.

Be it enacted by the Senate and House of Representatives of the United States of America in Congress assembled, That it is the policy of the Congress that the national forests are established and shall be administered for outdoor recreation, range, timber, watershed, and wildlife and fish purposes. The purposes of this Act are declared to be supplemental to, but not in derogation of, the purposes for which the national forests were established as set forth in the Act of June 4, 1897 (16 U.S.C. 475). Nothing herein shall be construed as affecting the jurisdiction or responsibilities of the several States with respect to wildlife and fish on the national forests. Nothing herein shall be construed so as to affect the use or administration of the mineral resources of national forest lands or to affect the use or administration of Federal lands not within national forests.

SEC. 2. The Secretary of Agriculture is authorized and directed to develop and administer the renewable surface resources of the national forests for multiple use and sustained yield of the several products and services obtained therefrom. In the administration of the national forests due consideration shall be given to the relative values of the various resources in particular areas. The establishment and maintenance of areas of wilderness are consistent with the purposes and provisions of this Act.

SEC. 3. In the effectuation of this Act the Secretary of Agriculture is authorized to cooperate with interested State and local governmental agencies and others in the development and management of the national forests.

SEC. 4. As used in this Act, the following terms shall have the following meanings:

(a) "Multiple use" means: The management of all the various renewable surface resources of the national forests so that they are utilized in the com-

*74 *Statutes at Large,* 215.

bination that will best meet the needs of the American people; making the most judicious use of the land for some or all of these resources or related services over areas large enough to provide sufficient latitude for periodic adjustments in use to conform to changing needs and conditions; that some land will be used for less than all of the resources; and harmonious and coordinated management of the various resources, each with the other, without impairment of the productivity of the land, with consideration being given to the relative values of the various resources, and not necessarily the combination of uses that will give the greatest dollar return or the greatest unit output.

(b) "Sustained yield of the several products and services" means the achievement and maintenance in perpetuity of a high-level annual or regular periodic output of the various renewable resources of the national forests without impairment of the productivity of the land.

Approved June 12, 1960.

THE WILDERNESS ACT*
September 3, 1964

The wilderness concept has great emotional appeal and both its proponents and opponents appear to have been well organized and well financed. Numerous "Wilderness Bills" were introduced in recent sessions of Congress—most of them had as their primary objective the protection of the status quo in order to prevent any encroachment on lands currently designated as wilderness. One such bill was the widely-supported S. 174 introduced by Senator Clinton P. Anderson in the 87th Congress. Restrictions on use of wilderness areas in S. 174 were generally the same as those imposed by the Forest Service, except that prospecting and mining were prohibited unless authorized by the President.

The bill was supported by the President, the Secretary of Agriculture, the Secretary of Interior, and by most conservation, wildlife, and wilderness organizations. Opposed, however, was a long roster of business interests, including the National Association of Manufacturers, the Chamber of Commerce of the United States, the American National Cattlemen's Association, the National Woolgrower's Association, the Industrial Forestry Association, the American Pulpwood Association, the National Lumber Manufacturers Association, the Northwest Mining Association, the Idaho Mining Association, the Independent Petroleum Association of America, the Utah Mining Association, and the American Mining Congress. The state legislatures of Idaho and Wyoming memorialized the Congress in opposition to the bill.

S. 174 passed the Senate by a substantial majority but failed in the House. A similar bill, S. 4, was introduced in the 88th Congress and passed the Senate by a vote of 73 to 12 on April 9, 1963. It was then referred to the House Committee on Interior and Insular Affairs, which held extensive field hearings and finally reported out an amended version which passed on September 3, 1964. The act placed 9.1 million acres of federally-owned land into a permanent wilderness system and authorized eventual inclusion of an additional 51.9 million acres. The act differs from the original Senate bill mainly in that such additions to a wilderness system require affirmative action by Congress and mining and mineral leasing laws in wilderness areas are extended through 1983.

An Act to establish a National Wilderness Preservation System for the permanent good of the whole people, and for other purposes.

Be it enacted by the Senate and House of Representatives of the United States of America in Congress assembled,

*78 Statutes at Large, 890.

SECTION 1. This Act may be cited as the "Wilderness Act".

WILDERNESS SYSTEM ESTABLISHED STATEMENT OF POLICY

SEC. 2. (a) In order to assure that an increasing population, accompanied by expanding settlement and growing mechanization, does not occupy and modify all areas within the United States and its possessions, leaving no lands designated for preservation and protection in their natural condition, it is hereby declared to be the policy of the Congress to secure for the American people of present and future generations the benefits of an enduring resource of wilderness. For this purpose there is hereby established a National Wilderness Preservation System to be composed of federally owned areas designated by Congress as "wilderness areas", and these shall be administered for the use and enjoyment of the American people in such manner as will leave them unimpaired for future use and enjoyment as wilderness, and so as to provide for the protection of these areas, the preservation of their wilderness character, and for the gathering and dissemination of information regarding their use and enjoyment as wilderness; and no Federal lands shall be designated as "wilderness areas" except as provided for in this Act or by a subsequent Act.

(b) The inclusion of an area in the National Wilderness Preservation System notwithstanding, the area shall continue to be managed by the Department and agency having jurisdiction thereover immediately before its inclusion in the National Wilderness Preservation System unless otherwise provided by Act of Congress. No appropriation shall be available for the payment of expenses or salaries for the administration of the National Wilderness Preservation System as a separate unit nor shall any appropriations be available for additional personnel stated as being required solely for the purpose of managing or administering areas solely because they are included within the National Wilderness Preservation System.

DEFINITION OF WILDERNESS

(c) A wilderness, in contrast with those areas where man and his own works dominate the landscape, is hereby recognized as an area where the earth and its community of life are untrammeled by man, where man himself is a visitor who does not remain. An area of wilderness is further defined to mean in this Act an area of undeveloped Federal land retaining its primeval character and influence, without permanent improvements or human habitation, which is protected and managed so as to preserve its natural conditions and which (1) generally appears to have been affected primarily by the forces of nature, with the imprint of man's work substantially unnoticeable; (2) has outstanding opportunities for solitude or a primitive and unconfined type of recreation; (3) has at least five thousand acres of land or is of sufficient size as to make practicable its preservation and use in an unimpaired condition; and (4) may also contain ecological, geological, or other features of scientific, educational, scenic, or historical value.

NATIONAL WILDERNESS PRESERVATION SYSTEM—EXTENT OF SYSTEM

SEC. 3. (a) All areas within the national forests classified at least 30 days before the effective date of this Act by the Secretary of Agriculture or the Chief of the Forest Service as "wilderness", "wild", or "canoe" are hereby designated as wilderness areas. The Secretary of Agriculture shall—

(1) Within one year after the effective date of this Act, file a map and legal description of each wilderness area with the Interior and Insular Affairs Committees of the United States Senate and the House of Representatives, and such descriptions shall have the same force and effect as if included in this Act: *Provided, however,* That correction of clerical and typographical errors in such legal descriptions and maps may be made.

(2) Maintain, available to the public, records pertaining to said wilderness areas, including maps and legal descriptions, copies of regulations governing them, copies of public notices of, and reports submitted to Congress regarding pending additions, eliminations, or modifications. Maps, legal descriptions, and regulations pertaining to wilderness areas within their respective jurisdictions also shall be available to the public in the offices of regional foresters, national forest supervisors, and forest rangers.

(b) The Secretary of Agriculture shall, within ten years after the enactment of this Act, review, as to its suitability or nonsuitability for preservation as wilderness, each area in the national forests classified on the effective date of this Act by the Secretary of Agriculture or the Chief of the Forest Service as "primitive" and report his findings to the President. The President shall advise the United States Senate and House of Representatives of his recommendations with respect to the designation as "wilderness" or other reclassification of each area on which review has been completed, together with maps and a definition of boundaries. Such advice shall be given with respect to not less than one-third of all the areas now classified as "primitive" within three years after the enactment of this Act, not less than two-thirds within seven years after the enactment of this Act, and the remaining areas within ten years after the enactment of this Act. Each recommendation of the President for designation as "wilderness" shall become effective only if so provided by an Act of Congress. Areas classified as "primitive" on the effective date of this Act shall continue to be administered under the rules and regulations affecting such areas on the effective date of this Act until Congress has determined otherwise. Any such area may be increased in size by the President at the time he submits his recommendations to the Congress by not more than five thousand acres with no more than one thousand two hundred and eighty acres of such increase in any one compact unit; if it is proposed to increase the size of any such area by more than five thousand acres or by more than one thousand two hundred and eighty acres in any one compact unit the increase in size shall not become effective until acted upon by Congress. Nothing herein contained shall limit the President in proposing, as part of his recommendations to Congress, the alteration of existing boundaries of primitive areas or recommending the addition of any contiguous area of national forest lands predominantly of wilderness value. Notwithstanding any other provisions of this Act, the Secretary of Agriculture may complete his review and delete such area as may be necessary, but not to exceed seven thousand acres, from the southern tip of the Gore Range-Eagles Nest Primitive Area, Colorado, if the Secretary determines that such action is in the public interest.

(c) Within ten years after the effective date of this Act the Secretary of the Interior shall review every roadless area of five thousand contiguous acres or more in the national parks, monuments and other units of the national park system and every such area of, and every roadless island within, the national wildlife refuges and game ranges, under his jurisdiction on the effective date of this Act and shall report to the President his recommendation as to the suitability or nonsuitability of each such area or island for preservation as wilderness. The President shall advise the President of the Senate and the Speaker of the House of Representatives of his recommendation with respect to the designation as wilderness of each such area or island on which review has been completed, together with a map thereof and a definition of its boundaries. Such advice shall be given with respect to not less than one-third of the areas and islands to be reviewed under this subsection within three years after enactment of this Act, not less than two-thirds within seven years of enactment of this Act, and the remainder within ten years of enactment of this Act. A recommendation of the President for designation as wilderness shall become effective only if so provided by an Act of Congress. Nothing contained herein shall, by implication or otherwise, be construed to lessen the present statutory authority of the Secretary of the Interior with respect to the maintenance of roadless areas within units of the national park system.

(d) (1) The Secretary of Agriculture and the Secretary of the Interior shall, prior to submitting any recommendations to the President with respect to the suitability of any area for preservation as wilderness—

    (A) give such public notice of the proposed action as they deem appropriate, including publication in the Federal Register and in a newspaper having general circulation in the area or areas in the vicinity of the affected land;

    (B) hold a public hearing or hearings at a location or locations convenient to the area affected. The hearings shall be announced through such means as the respective Secretaries involved deem appropriate, including notices in the Federal Register and in newspapers of general circulation in the area: *Provided,* That if the lands involved are located in more than one State, at least one hearing shall be held in each State in which a portion of the land lies;

(C) at least thirty days before the date of a hearing advise the Governor of each State and the governing board of each county, or in Alaska the borough, in which the lands are located, and Federal departments and agencies concerned, and invite such officials and Federal agencies to submit their views on the proposed action at the hearing or by no later than thirty days following the date of the hearing.

(2) Any views submitted to the appropriate Secretary under the provisions of (1) of this subsection with respect to any area shall be included with any recommendations to the President and to Congress with respect to such area.

(e) Any modification or adjustment of boundaries of any wilderness area shall be recommended by the appropriate Secretary after public notice of such proposal and public hearing or hearings as provided in subsection (d) of this section. The proposed modification or adjustment shall then be recommended with map and description thereof to the President. The President shall advise the United States Senate and the House of Representatives of his recommendations with respect to such modification or adjustment and such recommendations shall become effective only in the same manner as provided for in subsections (b) and (c) of this section.

USE OF WILDERNESS AREAS

Sec. 4. (a) The purposes of this Act are hereby declared to be within and supplemental to the purposes for which national forests and units of the national park and national wildlife refuge systems are established and administered and—

(1) Nothing in this Act shall be deemed to be in interference with the purpose for which national forests are established as set forth in the Act of June 4, 1897 (30 Stat. 11), and the Multiple-Use Sustained-Yield Act of June 12, 1960 (74 Stat. 215).

(2) Nothing in this Act shall modify the restrictions and provisions of the Shipstead-Nolan Act (Public Law 539, Seventy-first Congress, July 10, 1930; 46 Stat. 1020), the Thye-Blatnik Act (Public Law 733, Eightieth Congress, June 22, 1948; 62 Stat. 568), and the Humphrey-Thye-Blatnik-Andresen Act (Public Law 607, Eighty-fourth Congress, June 22, 1956; 70 Stat. 326), as applying to the Superior National Forest or the regulations of the Secretary of Agriculture.

(3) Nothing in this Act shall modify the statutory authority under which units of the national park system are created. Further, the designation of

any area of any park, monument, or other unit of the national park system as a wilderness area pursuant to this Act shall in no manner lower the standards evolved for the use and preservation of such park, monument, or other unit of the national park system in accordance with the Act of August 25, 1916, the statutory authority under which the area was created, or any other Act of Congress which might pertain to or affect such area, including, but not limited to, the Act of June 8, 1906 (34 Stat. 225; 16 U.S.C. 432 et seq.); section 3(2) of the Federal Power Act (16 U.S.C. 796(2)); and the Act of August 21, 1935 (49 Stat. 666; 16 U.S.C. 461 et seq.).

(b) Except as otherwise provided in this Act, each agency administering any area designated as wilderness shall be responsible for preserving the wilderness character of the area and shall so administer such area for such other purposes for which it may have been established as also to preserve its wilderness character. Except as otherwise provided in this Act, wilderness areas shall be devoted to the public purposes of recreational, scenic, scientific, educational, conservation, and historical use.

PROHIBITION OF CERTAIN USES

(c) Except as specifically provided for in this Act, and subject to existing private rights, there shall be no commercial enterprise and no permanent road within any wilderness area designated by this Act and, except as necessary to meet minimum requirements for the administration of the area for the purpose of this Act (including measures required in emergencies involving the health and safety of persons within the area), there shall be no temporary road, no use of motor vehicles, motorized equipment or motorboats, no landing of aircraft, no other form of mechanical transport, and no structure or installation within any such area.

SPECIAL PROVISIONS

(d) The following special provisions are hereby made:

(1) Within wilderness areas designated by this Act the use of aircraft or motorboats, where these uses have already become established, may be permitted to continue subject to such restrictions as the Secretary of Agriculture deems desirable. In addition, such measures may be taken as may be necessary in the control of fire, insects, and diseases, subject to such conditions as the Secretary deems desirable.

(2) Nothing in this Act shall prevent within national forest wilderness areas any activity, including prospecting, for the purpose of gathering information about mineral or other resources, if such activity is carried on in a manner compatible with the preservation of the wilderness environment. Furthermore, in accordance with such program as the Secretary of the Interior shall develop and conduct in consultation with the Secretary of Agriculture, such areas shall

be surveyed on a planned, recurring basis consistent with the concept of wilderness preservation by the Geological Survey and the Bureau of Mines to determine the mineral values, if any, that may be present; and the results of such surveys shall be made available to the public and submitted to the President and Congress.

(3) Notwithstanding any other provisions of this Act, until midnight December 31, 1983, the United States mining laws and all laws pertaining to mineral leasing shall, to the same extent as applicable prior to the effective date of this Act, extend to those national forest lands designated by this Act as "wilderness areas"; subject, however, to such reasonable regulations governing ingress and egress as may be prescribed by the Secretary of Agriculture consistent with the use of the land for mineral location and development and exploration, drilling, and production, and use of land for transmission lines, waterlines, telephone lines, or facilities necessary in exploring, drilling, producing, mining, and processing operations, including where essential the use of mechanized ground or air equipment and restoration as near as practicable of the surface of the land disturbed in performing prospecting, location, and, in oil and gas leasing, discovery work, exploration, drilling, and production, as soon as they have served their purpose. Mining locations lying within the boundaries of said wilderness areas shall be held and used solely for mining or processing operations and uses reasonably incident thereto; and hereafter, subject to valid existing rights, all patents issued under the mining laws of the United States affecting national forest lands designated by this Act as wilderness areas shall convey title to the mineral deposits within the claim, together with the right to cut and use so much of the mature timber therefrom as may be needed in the extraction, removal, and beneficiation of the mineral deposits, if needed timber is not otherwise reasonably available, and if the timber is cut under sound principles of forest management as defined by the national forest rules and regulations, but each such patent shall reserve to the United States all title in or to the surface of the lands and products thereof, and no use of the surface of the claim or the resources therefrom not reasonably required for carrying on mining or prospecting shall be allowed except as otherwise expressly provided in this Act: *Provided,* That, unless hereafter specifically authorized, no patent within wilderness areas designated by this Act shall issue after December 31, 1983, except for the valid claims existing on or before December 31, 1983. Mining claims located after the effective date of this Act within the boundaries of wilderness areas designated by this Act shall create no rights in excess of those rights which may be patented under the provisions of this subsection. Mineral leases, permits, and licenses covering lands within national forest wilderness areas designated by this Act shall contain such reasonable stipulations as may be prescribed by the Secretary of Agriculture for the protection of the wilderness character of the land consistent with the use of the land for the purposes for which they are

leased, permitted, or licensed. Subject to valid rights then existing, effective January 1, 1984, the minerals in lands designated by this Act as wilderness areas are withdrawn from all forms of appropriation under the mining laws and from disposition under all laws pertaining to mineral leasing and all amendments thereto.

(4) Within wilderness areas in the national forests designated by this Act, (1) the President may, within a specific area and in accordance with such regulations as he may deem desirable, authorize prospecting for water resources, the establishment and maintenance of reservoirs, water-conservation works, power projects, transmission lines, and other facilities needed in the public interest, including the road construction and maintenance essential to development and use thereof, upon his determination that such use or uses in the specific area will better serve the interests of the United States and the people thereof than will its denial; and (2) the grazing of livestock, where established prior to the effective date of this Act, shall be permitted to continue subject to such reasonable regulations as are deemed necessary by the Secretary of Agriculture.

(5) Other provisions of this Act to the contrary notwithstanding, the management of the Boundary Waters Canoe Area, formerly designated as the Superior, Little Indian Sioux, and Caribou Roadless Areas, in the Superior National Forest, Minnesota, shall be in accordance with regulations established by the Secretary of Agriculture in accordance with the general purpose of maintaining, without unnecessary restrictions on other uses, including that of timber, the primitive character of the area, particularly in the vicinity of lakes, streams, and portages: *Provided,* That nothing in this Act shall preclude the continuance within the area of any already established use of motorboats.

(6) Commercial services may be performed within the wilderness areas designated by this Act to the extent necessary for activities which are proper for realizing the recreational or other wilderness purposes of the areas.

(7) Nothing in this Act shall constitute an express or implied claim or denial on the part of the Federal Government as to exemption from State water laws.

(8) Nothing in this Act shall be construed as affecting the jurisdiction or responsibilities of the several States with respect to wildlife and fish in the national forests.

STATE AND PRIVATE LANDS WITHIN WILDERNESS AREAS

SEC. 5. (a) In any case where State-owned or privately owned land is completely surrounded by national forest lands within areas designated by this Act as wilderness, such State or private owner shall be given such rights as may be necessary to assure adequate access to such State-owned or privately owned land by such State or private owner and their successors in interest, or the State-owned land or privately owned land shall be exchanged for federally owned land in the same State of approximately equal value under authorities available to the Secretary of Agriculture: *Provided, however,* That the United States shall not transfer to a State or private owner any mineral interests unless the State or private owner relinquishes or causes to be relinquished to the United States the mineral interest in the surrounded land.

(b) In any case where valid mining claims or other valid occupancies are wholly within a designated national forest wilderness area, the Secretary of Agriculture shall, by reasonable regulations consistent with the preservation of the area as wilderness, permit ingress and egress to such surrounded areas by means which have been or are being customarily enjoyed with respect to other such areas similarly situated.

(c) Subject to the appropriation of funds by Congress, the Secretary of Agriculture is authorized to acquire privately owned land within the perimeter of any area designated by this Act as wilderness if (1) the owner concurs in such acquisition or (2) the acquisition is specifically authorized by Congress.

GIFTS, BEQUESTS, AND CONTRIBUTIONS

SEC. 6. (a) The Secretary of Agriculture may accept gifts or bequests of land within wilderness areas designated by this Act for preservation as wilderness. The Secretary of Agriculture may also accept gifts or bequests of land adjacent to wilderness areas designated by this Act for preservation as wilderness if he has given sixty days advance notice thereof to the President of the Senate and the Speaker of the House of Representatives. Land accepted by the Secretary of Agriculture under this section shall become part of the wilderness area involved. Regulations with regard to any such land may be in accordance with such agreements, consistent with the policy of this Act, as are made at the time of such gift, or such conditions, consistent with such policy, as may be included in, and accepted with, such bequest.

(b) The Secretary of Agriculture or the Secretary of the Interior is authorized to accept private contributions and gifts to be used to further the purposes of this Act.

ANNUAL REPORTS

SEC. 7. At the opening of each session of Congress, the Secretaries of Agriculture and Interior shall jointly report to the President for transmission to Congress on the status of the wilderness system, including a list and descriptions of the areas in the system, regulations in effect, and other pertinent information, together with any recommendations they may care to make.

Approved September 3, 1964.

"THE ROLE OF THE FOREST SERVICE
IN OUTDOOR RECREATION"*
1966

Edward P. Cliff, Chief of the Forest Service, summarized the problems and responsibilities of that organization in this report to the Society of American Foresters.

The theme of our session today is federal responsibility for outdoor recreation. It is my assignment to outline for you the role of the Forest Service in particular.

The story of outdoor recreation in the national forests is worth serious study by any professional forester interested in recreational use of forest resources. It is a long story; this is our 60th Anniversary Year. Although the past two decades or so are the most significant in this evolutionary period, recreational use of some of these lands took place even before 1905.

* * *

By way of perspective, I know of no better reference on federal responsibilities than the work published a few years ago by the Outdoor Recreation Resources Review Commission.

* * *

But much has happened in this field since the 1960 data were compiled for that report. For example, recreation visits to the national forests increased from 92.6 million in 1960, to 133.8 million in 1964; and the numbers of visits continue to rise. Also, in 1960, our Forest Service budget item for recreation resource development and management on the National Forests was $8.5 million. This fiscal year it is nearly four times larger. And this does not include wildlife habitat improvement, road and trail development, protection of the forests against fire, insects and disease, or other items related to recreational use of the national forests.

I think it is safe to say that in the period since the ORRRC Report, the federal sector has done much to keep pace with the ever-increasing number of people seeking outdoor recreation opportunities. To again use the national forests as an example, in 1960 the capacity of all developed facilities in the national forests was 747,000 persons at one time. Today these facilities can accommodate approximately a million people at one time.

We sometimes tend to think of outdoor recreation mainly in terms of activities which involve camp grounds, picnic sites, winter sports areas and other facil-

*Edward P. Cliff, "The Role of the Forest Service in Outdoor Recreation," *Proceedings of the Society of American Foresters Meeting, 1965: Forest Resource Decisions in a Changing Power Structure* (Washington, D.C.: Society of American Foresters, 1966), 131–32.

ities. Actually, about three out of every five recreational visits to the national forests are for hiking, riding, hunting, fishing, or other activities which do not require developed sites.

This spotlights what I think is an especially pertinent feature of the federal role in outdoor recreation. Large tracts of unposted public lands, open to all users for their enjoyment, is the essence of the opportunity that most federal lands hold for millions of Americans. The characteristics inherent in wide open spaces, and the special requirements of many forms of outdoor recreation, give these lands an added value and a function that is unlike municipal or other smaller, highly developed tracts. This value is often enhanced by adjacent large blocks of private land also made available for public use. And, of course, large state-owned tracts may offer similar opportunities.

An outstanding illustration of this particular role of federal lands is the National Wilderness Preservation System established by the Congress last year. Forest Service responsibilities in connection with that law are familiar to most of you, I am sure. All of the 9.1 million acres in the 54 areas blanketed into the Wilderness System were national forest areas that had been previously designated as "Wilderness" or "Wild." Another 34 national forest areas that had been designated as "Primitive" before the law was passed are to be studied, reviewed in public hearings, and acted upon by the Congress if recommended as additions to the Wilderness System. Undeveloped areas in the national parks and certain other federal lands are also to be reviewed and considered as possible additions to the system.

An even more recent example is the current interest in legislation to preserve so-called "Wild Rivers." Some of the most scenic free-flowing reaches of important rivers flow through the national forests and other public lands. This effort captures the essence of another aspect of the federal role: To speak and act for the people as a whole, for the generations unborn as well as for the living—and if need be, to balance the needs of the many against the wishes of the few.

Just as federal lands have special characteristics which make them especially suited for special purposes, so are federal agencies equipped, by law or otherwise, to fulfill special needs. The Forest Service and the national forests are no exception to this general rule.

However, responsibility for administration of vast public recreation resources, within the spirit and the letter of the many pertinent laws, carries with it rigorous technical and managerial demands. Again to use wilderness as an example, we have a complex law enacted to guide our policies and activities. Some of the requirements of that law, those which involve mining claims for example, put land managers on the horns of a dilemma. On one hand, we must act to preserve the wilderness environment without impairment while, on the other, we must allow prospecting for mineral resources and permit development and operation of valid mining claims without unreasonable restrictions. Federal agencies are not the only ones with knotty problems—but we have our share!

One of the most pressing of the technical demands facing us at this time is to accommodate increasingly heavy recreational use of wilderness areas without destruction or impairment of the primitive character and esthetic values which are the main attraction. This problem has many aspects: For example, meeting forage needs for pack stock when natural supplies are inadequate; building and maintaining trail systems to disperse and safeguard visitors; managing range resources in areas where livestock grazing is already established; preventing erosion or damage to vegetation from the trampling of people and horses on fragile sites; providing prompt clean-up services at reasonable cost; and, of course, keeping visitors dispersed in time and space so that a reasonable degree of solitude remains.

My point in this—the federal role, as represented by the Forest Service, involves the solution of many problems which have national significance. Some relate to situations which are not faced by managers of resources held in private ownership. In other cases, such as design and management of campgrounds, winter sports areas and other facilities, or in coordinating recreation with other uses of forest land, the results of our work have value "across the board." Thus, federal agencies have an opportunity and a challenge for leadership and research in the field of outdoor recreation that is unsurpassed in complexity or importance.

Our Forest Service program of research includes significant projects in this field that will have broad application. They range from facility planning and operation techniques to exploring problems and opportunities of income-producing recreation enterprises on private land; and from rehabilitation of resources to measurement of recreation use and coordination of the multiple forest uses. To a degree, forests are giant laboratories within which research scientists study and test and perfect many of their projects. Quite often, resource administrators, who may need the information even before the study is designed, are able to assist and thereby speed the project to conclusion. Cooperative studies dealing with state parks, industrial tracts, and other public or private forest lands are part of the picture.

And so this is another aspect of the federal role—to foster enjoyment of natural resources by providing information and technical services to other resource managers and to the public at large. For example, earlier this year we published a "how-to-do-it" booklet entitled "The American Outdoors—Management for Beauty and Use." This popular item offers a concise summary of much that we have learned about esthetics in tree planting, road and trail design, and so forth. Throughout the booklet is a philosophy that integrates beauty with managed use of natural resources. My talk at the opening session of this meeting on Monday suggested another way in which a federal agency can move to gain public understanding and thereby increased public enjoyment of the forest environment.

The close tie between forest recreation and enjoyment of natural beauty should not be overlooked. Pleasure from hiking and sightseeing and other activities is heightened by outstanding scenic vistas or close-up study of flowers, wildlife, and so forth. It seems to me that the role of a federal agency includes taking steps to promote landscape management and to safeguard esthetic values as well as meeting the commercial needs that are dependent upon forest resources.

To summarize: In addition to assuring the physical accommodations and enjoyment of millions of pleasure-seeking visitors on the national forests, the Forest Service role in outdoor recreation includes such things as:

1. Extending the benefits of our experience to all interested parties.

2. Making large tracts of land available to the public for recreation with as few restrictions as is possible.

3. Developing and applying improved practices in management of wilderness.

4. Acting on behalf of the nation as a whole in dealing with land use decisions of lasting significance.

5. Developing answers to difficult, unsolved resource management problems through research and administrative studies.

6. Helping recreation seekers understand the forest at work and gain a deeper appreciation of the elements of natural beauty.

These are some of the ways in which our agency can help to redeem federal responsibilities in the field of outdoor recreation. The list is not all-inclusive by any means, but perhaps the shape of the Forest Service role is evident.

* * *

MAN-MADE LAKES

The construction of dams and the reservoirs behind the dams have created a tremendous new outdoor recreation resource. Such dams were constructed mainly for flood control, for irrigation, for the development of hydro-electric power, as aids to navigation by maintaining water levels in rivers and streams. Frequently, a single project served two or more of these purposes, and until recently, recreational use of the reservoirs was an afterthought. This secondary activity was carried on according to the accessibility of the site and the requirements of the primary purposes of the project.

After World War II, however, Americans developed what has been called "aquamania"; boats were sold by the millions and boat trailers made it possible for boaters and fishermen to travel considerable distances in a relatively short time. The reservoirs were then available for fishing, boating, water skiing, and swimming. Around the shoreline people hiked, rode horseback, and held picnics, and frequently, the recreationist, or his family, engaged in two or more of these activities on the same outing. In many cases the reservoirs also provided habitat for some species of wild game or waterfowl.

If number of visits is used as the criteria, these man-made lakes are the nation's most important outdoor recreation resource; consequently, the water construction agencies have become involved with outdoor recreation. In fact, in terms of number of visits, the Army Corps of Engineers has become the world's largest outdoor recreation organization.

In addition to the major dam construction agencies, the Department of Agriculture has encouraged and helped finance the construction of smaller dams for stock watering, erosion control, and other purposes. On a flight over middle and western America on a clear day, the air traveler will see hundreds of these small man-made lakes or farm ponds. Both the major water impoundments and the farm ponds are especially important for outdoor recreation, not only because they are a new and additional resource, but because they frequently are located in areas where other bodies of water are few or non-existent.

Notwithstanding their many benefits, all water impoundments cannot be considered to be beneficial for outdoor recreation. In some cases the quantity of recreation opportunities may be increased but at the cost of diminished quality. This often occurs when a trout stream, a scenic river, or a stretch of "white water" is flooded. In other situations, valuable nesting grounds for waterfowl or habitat for other wildlife may be destroyed or scenic, historic, or archaeological sites may be flooded and closed off forever. Proposals that involve these kinds of choices have provoked intense political controversies with high emotional charges. This chapter will document the major policy decisions with respect to recreation use of man-made lakes.

THE TENNESSEE VALLEY AUTHORITY

The Tennessee Valley Authority (TVA) was the first federal water resources agency to seriously consider and plan for recreational use of impounded waters and shoreline. Former chairman of the Board of Directors of TVA, Herbert D. Vogel, described early recreation policy on TVA lakes in this statement.

> TVA was created in 1933 as a regional resource development agency, based on the concept that all the resources of a river basin are interrelated and should be developed under one unified plan for maximum effectiveness. To put the Tennessee River to work, TVA built a system of multipurpose dams.
>
> * * *
>
> Recreation potentials were carefully considered at all stages of reservoir construction and planning. As field engineers set the stakes to mark future shorelines, recreation technicians followed them closely, seeking likely spots for parks, boat harbors, bathing beaches and camps.
>
> Recognition of the lakes' recreation potential resulted in a decision to acquire such lands as might be necessary to guarantee public access to the impounded waters. Acquisition policies varied from project to project but never departed from the principle of including lands for public access.*

The lakes created by TVA impoundments cover some 600,000 acres and have shorelines totaling over 10,000 miles—longer than the combined shoreline of the Atlantic and Pacific coasts. These lakes attracted 42.3 million visitors in 1960. Fifty-one thousand pleasure boats were moored on their shores—an increase of 434 percent in the last 13 years. Investment in lakeshore recreation facilities during 1960 alone totaled almost $20 million.

Outdoor recreation is big business in the Tennessee Valley and is rapidly growing bigger. Since 1947 recreation visits have *increased* at an average rate of more than 2.5 million per year. Despite the magnitude of use, outdoor recreation is still considered to be a by-product of the primary purposes for which dams were constructed—flood control, navigation, and power. Nevertheless, even though recreation has been considered a by-product, it has obviously not been neglected. According to one TVA official, "We planned to maximize utilization of the recreation by-product from the very beginning." Suitable access sites, boat harbors, and park areas were acquired when lands were purchased for reservoirs. Recreation values have been given high priority by TVA board members since the inception of the project.

---

*Remarks of General Herbert D. Vogel, Chairman of the Board, Tennessee Valley Authority, at the Conference on Access to Recreational Waters, cosponsored by the Sport Fishing Institute and the Outdoor Boating Club of America, Chicago, Mar. 29, 1961.

Despite its long-time emphasis on outdoor recreation, TVA administers very few recreation sites directly. Consistent with its original policies of decentralization and transfer of functions to "grass roots" governments, TVA has encouraged local participation and operation of recreation areas. Within this framework of TVA-state-local relationship, lands were first leased and later sold for public recreation purposes. By 1961, 365 public access areas, 13 state parks and 66 county and municipal parks had been transferred to state and local agencies or had been created on the shores of TVA lakes. In addition, TVA has transferred more than 120,000 acres to the National Park Service, Bureau of Sport Fisheries and Wildlife, and the Forest Service. Some 330 fishing camps, boat docks, and resorts are operated by private businesses on TVA lakeshores and about seven thousand privately-owned vacation homes have been built on lakefront sites. Campsites and marinas have also been transferred to private clubs and to service organizations such as the Y.M.C.A. and Boy Scouts.

During the early years of its growth TVA experienced considerable difficulty in stimulating enough concern for recreation areas to cause state or local agencies to assume responsibility for their administration. By demonstration, assistance, and sometimes by coercion (TVA closed some recreation areas to the public), TVA induced local agencies to take an active interest in outdoor recreation areas. TVA has reasoned that recreation values on its lakes accrue mainly to local residents and that therefore it should be their responsibility to build and maintain such facilities as they desire. If they desire none, TVA considers it a local problem. On the other hand, some of the facilities constructed by state and local agencies probably far exceed in cost and conveniences anything a federal agency would dare construct.

THE CORPS OF ENGINEERS

The Corps of Engineers is probably the oldest and largest construction organization in the United States. First authorized by the Continental Congress in 1779, the original Corps of Engineers was dissolved in 1783. The present organization dates from an act of March 16, 1802 which authorized the establishment of a Corps of Engineers consisting of five officers and 10 cadets to be stationed at West Point, New York, to constitute a military academy.

Early in its history, the Corps became involved in nonmilitary engineering and construction projects through the enactment of the first Rivers and Harbors Act in 1824. By 1852 the Corps position in civil works had become established firmly enough to cause Congress to place river and harbor improvements under the Secretary of War. An act of 1917 extended the scope of activities of the Corps of Engineers to include a flood control project for the lower Mississippi River. Responsibility for flood control was more definitely assigned by the Flood Control Act of 1936 which also established a general policy for federal participation in flood control throughout the United States. The series of flood control acts which followed the 1936 legislation gradually broadened the Corps interest in water resource development to include power, recreation, fish and wildlife conservation, water supply, and pollution abatement. Finally in 1946, Congress extended Corps of Engineers functions by authorizing funds for beach and shoreline erosion control. These various functions are carried out by the Civil Works Division in the Office of the Chief of Engineers.

When the Corps of Engineers first built dams for flood control, it was recognized that some people would be interested in viewing the structure, so guard rails and other safety devices were constructed as part of the installation. If a highway ran nearby, a viewing turnout would also be constructed. These and similar basic facilities were provided on the early damsites for those persons who came to look at the dam, but little else was done for recreationists, and indeed little else was needed. In 1946, visits to Corps of Engineers projects totaled only 5 million. Then came the boats! By 1960, the number of visits ran over 106 million. Guardrails and scenic turnouts were no longer adequate; the Corps of Engineers was in the recreation business whether it liked it or not.

In 1967 the Corps operated 350 reservoirs in 44 states covering 8 million acres. Recreation use of Corps of Engineers projects totaled 128.6 million visitor-days in 1965, as compared with 109 million in 1960 and 63 million in 1955—a doubling of visitors in the last decade.

The Corps understands that it is responsible only for the installation of basic facilities for recreationists. Those facilities which are constructed near the project structure are considered to be necessary to minimize hazards and to prevent interference with the operation of the dam, so they are charged to project purposes—not to recreation. These include overlook stations for viewing the project, public toilets, parking areas, roads, guardrails, fences, and directional signs. Facilities provided around the shoreline and away from the project structure are classified as recreational facilities and include access roads, parking areas, camping and picnicking areas, water supply, sanitary facilities, boat launching ramps, overlook stations, and essential safety devices.

When additional services and facilities are desired, the Corps attempts to induce state or local governments to assume responsibility for construction and maintenance. Such non-federal agencies are included in the planning phase of the project, where possible, and have, in some instances, also financed the installation of the basic facilities listed above. Expenditures for both private and commercial recreation facilities on adjacent privately owned lands have been considerable and possibly exceed the amounts spent on project lands.

Licenses to develop and maintain recreational areas are issued to federal, state, and local governments as long-term leases and without monetary consideration. Similar licenses are also issued to quasi-public, non-profit organizations such as the Izaak Walton League, Boy Scouts, and church organizations at minimum rates. When none of the foregoing kinds of organizations are interested in developing a recreation site, the Corps may lease lands to private recreation organizations or to commercial concessionaires, but concessionaire's construction plans must be approved by the Corps. The concessionaire ordinarily pays a flat rental fee plus a percentage of gross receipts.

THE BUREAU OF RECLAMATION

By 1877 some Congressmen had come to realize that large areas in the West were unsuited to cultivation because of lack of water. The Desert Land Act of 1877 was passed to remedy this situation, and it provided that a settler might purchase 640 acres of desert land for $1.25 per acre provided he would irrigate it within three years after filing. The Desert Land Act was a farce and a failure because settlers ordinarily did not have sufficient capital to install an irrigation system, and, if they did, there was seldom any water available for irrigation. About 8 million acres were sold under this act; probably most of this land was purchased as strategic points to control public domain range or was tillable (not desert) land.

The Carey Act of 1894 was the next government attempt at irrigation of the West. It gave each of the western states a million acres of desert land to be irrigated and granted to individual settlers in blocks of 160 acres. Lack of adequate funds and engineering skill prevented any progress under the Carey Act, and by 1902, when the Reclamation Act was passed, only about 11,000 acres had been patented.

After these two failures, the Federal Government undertook direct responsibility for planning and constructing irrigation projects in the Reclamation Act of 1902. This act was sponsored by Senator Francis Newlands of Nevada and received the energetic support of President Theodore Roosevelt. The legislation was passed to reclaim arid western lands through irrigation, and irrigation remains the primary function and orientation of the bureau of Reclamation today. However, amendments to the act have given the Bureau additional responsibilities in flood control, hydroelectric power, navigation improvement, and related activities. Since the passage of the 1902 act, the Bureau has provided irrigation water to over 8 million acres in the 17 western states.

By 1965, the Bureau had constructed some 200 reservoirs with 10,000 miles of shoreline which supported 36.6 million recreation visitor-days. As with other federal resource management agencies, recreation use of Bureau of Reclamation facilities has increased rapidly during the past 15 years.

Unlike the Corps of Engineers, the Bureau did not have authority to consider recreation values as either a primary or secondary purpose of water development projects unless specifically authorized in particular reclamation acts. Aside from these specific authorizations, any recreation resources created by Bureau

Estimated Visitor-Days
Bureau of Reclamation Reservoirs*
1950-1965

1950	6,594,000
1955	10,702,000
1960	24,300,000
1965	36,604,000

*Unpublished data furnished by Bureau of Reclamation.

water impoundments were therefore coincidental. Since the Bureau had no general authority to develop the recreation potential of its reservoirs, it attempted to transfer this function to other government agencies. If the recreation resource was determined to be of national significance, management and development was transferred to the National Park Service. Recreation management of water impoundments within National Forests was assumed by the Forest Service. The Bureau of Sport Fisheries and Wildlife managed those areas which were designated as fish and wildlife reserves. When none of the above situations applied, the Bureau attempted to transfer management of the recreation resource to state or local governments. When it was impossible or impractical to transfer recreation management responsibility to another agency, the Bureau managed the recreation activity itself.

The Fish and Wildlife Coordination Act of 1958 (documented in the chapter on Fishing in this volume, pp. 119) provided for more effective integration of fish and wildlife conservation programs with water-resource development projects including those constructed by the Bureau of Reclamation. Recreation opportunities around reservoirs were also enhanced by an agreement of February 23, 1962 between the Departments of Interior and Army to increase the area of lands available for recreation. Previous to that time both the Corps of Engineers and Bureau of Reclamation had been restricted in land acquisition to a 300-foot strip (or five-year flood frequency line) around reservoirs. The new policy provided that both departments would seek to acquire land in fee title for public access, to meet present and future requirements for outdoor recreation in general.

THE SOIL CONSERVATION SERVICE

By 1960 about 1.7 million small storage-type dams had been constructed with assistance from the Department of Agriculture for stock watering, erosion control, and flood control. The reservoirs behind these impoundments created a tremendous new outdoor recreation resource, and were of great significance because there were so many of them; because a considerable number were close to population centers; and because many of them existed in areas where other water bodies were few or non-existent.

BOATING

Americans have gone "boat happy." In 1947, there were less than 2.5 million pleasure boats in the United States; by 1960 the number had vaulted to an estimated 8 million. In 1959, for example, Americans spent $2.5 billion on boats and boating, and in the same year, it was estimated that boaters used 490 million gallons of gasoline, 25.5 million gallons of oil, and 24.5 million gallons of diesel oil. During the same period, the boating industry consumed approximately 12 million gallons of paint, 50 million pounds of aluminum, and 75 million pounds of plastics.

Since the 8 million recreational boats carried some 39 million people, it can truly be said that boating has become a principal source of outdoor recreation. As one new boatowner expressed it, "I don't know how I ever lived before without a boat."

PRESIDENT FRANKLIN D. ROOSEVELT
ON RESERVOIR RECREATION*
1936

President Franklin D. Roosevelt was one of the first persons to recognize the recreation potential of reservoirs. In a 1936 memorandum to Edward M. Markham, Chief of Engineers, he said:

[Washington] June 20, 1936

MEMORANDUM FOR GENERAL MARKHAM: Sometime later on in the summer, will you speak to me about the possibility of the erection, in the distant future, of a low dam or dams across the upper Missouri in the Dakotas. It has been suggested to me that by creating a series of comparatively shallow lakes, a good deal of water could be backed up and conserved, and that as in the case of the upper Mississippi, extremely attractive recreational areas thus destroyed.

You might have someone in your office try to work out on the contour map one or two suggestions along this line, the idea being conservation of water in lakes and development of recreational areas.

F. D. R.

*Edgar B. Nixon, ed. *Franklin D. Roosevelt and Conservation: 1911–1945,* Vol. 1, (Washington, D.C.: Government Printing Office, 1957), 533.

THE FLOOD CONTROL ACT*
December 22, 1944

The Flood Control Act of 1944 is of particular significance to outdoor recreation because it was the first congressional action to recognize and authorize outdoor recreation on federal water projects. The relevant portion of the act follows.

Provided, That preference shall be given to Federal, State, or local governmental agencies, and licenses may be granted without monetary consideration, to such agencies for the use of areas suitable for public park and recreational purposes, when the Secretary of War determines such action to be in the public interest. The water areas of all such reservoirs shall be open to public use generally, without charge, for boating, swimming, bathing, fishing, and other recreational purposes, and ready access to and exit from such water areas along the shores of such reservoirs shall be maintained for general public use, when such use is determined by the Secretary of War not to be contrary to the public interest, all under such rules and regulations as the Secretary of War may deem necessary. No use of any area to which this section applies shall be permitted which is inconsistent with the laws for the protection of fish and game of the State in which such area is situated. All moneys received for leases or privileges shall be deposited in the Treasury of the United States as miscellaneous receipts.

*58 *Statutes at Large,* p. 890.

THE FLOOD CONTROL ACT OF 1954*
September 3, 1954

Recreation use of reservoirs was expanded and made more explicit by the Flood Control Act of 1954. The pertinent section follows.

SEC. 209. That section 4 of the Act approved July 24, 1946 (Public, Numbered 526, Seventy-ninth Congress), is amended to read as follows:

"The Chief of Engineers, under the supervision of the Secretary of the Army, is authorized to construct, maintain, and operate public park and recreational facilities in reservoir areas under the control of the Department of the Army, and to permit the construction, maintenance, and operation of such facilities. The Secretary of the Army is also authorized to grant leases of lands, including structures or facilities thereon, in reservoir areas for such periods, and upon such terms and for such purposes as he may deem reasonable in the public interest: *Provided,* That leases to nonprofit organizations for park or recreational purposes may be granted at reduced or nominal considerations in recognition of the public service to be rendered in utilizing the leased premises: *Provided further,* That preference shall be given to Federal, State, or local governmental agencies, and licenses, or leases where appropriate, may be granted without monetary considerations, to such agencies for the use of all or any portion of a reservoir area for any public purpose, when the Secretary of the Army determines such action to be in the public interest, and for such periods of time and upon such conditions as he may find advisable: *And provided further,* That in any such lease or license to a Federal, State, or local governmental agency which involves lands to be utilized for the development and conservation of fish and wildlife, forests, or other natural resources, the licensee or lessee may be authorized to cut timber and harvest crops as may be necessary to further such beneficial uses and to collect and utilize the proceeds of any sales of timber and crops in the development, conservation, maintenance and utilization of such lands. Any balance of proceeds not so utilized shall be paid to the United States at such time or times as the Secretary of the Army may determine appropriate. The water areas of all such reservoirs shall be open to public use generally, without charge, for boating, swimming, bathing, fishing, and other recreational purposes, and ready access to and exit from such water areas along the shores of such reservoirs shall be maintained for general public use, when such use is determined by the Secretary of the Army not to be contrary to the public interest, all under such rules and regulations as the Secretary of the Army may deem necessary. No use of any area to which this section applies shall be permitted which is inconsistent with the laws for the protection of fish and game

*68 *Statutes at Large,* 1266.

[427]

of the State in which such area is situated. All moneys received by the United States for leases or privileges shall be deposited in the Treasury of the United States as miscellaneous receipts."

Sec. 210. Title II may be cited as the "Flood Control Act of 1954." Approved September 3, 1954.

THE WATERSHED PROTECTION AND FLOOD PREVENTION ACT*
August 4, 1954

Perhaps the most significant action in developing "new water" through support of the Department of Agriculture, was the passage of the Watershed Protection and Flood Prevention Act of 1954. This act authorized the Secretary of Agriculture (Soil Conservation Service) to cooperate with state and local organization, in protecting small watersheds, of which there are about 13,000 in the United States. About 8,000 of these could probably profit from protective action—including the construction of small dams and reservoirs. The act follows.

An Act to authorize the Secretary of Agriculture to cooperate with States and local agencies in the planning and carrying out of works of improvement for soil conservation, and for other purposes.

Be it enacted by the Senate and House of Representatives of the United States of America in Congress assembled, That erosion, floodwater, and sediment damages in the watersheds of the rivers and streams of the United States, causing loss of life and damage to property, constitute a menace to the national welfare; and that it is the sense of Congress that the Federal Government should cooperate with States and their political subdivisions, soil or water conservation districts, flood prevention or control districts, and other local public agencies for the purpose of preventing such damages and of furthering the conservation, development, utilization, and disposal of water and thereby of preserving and protecting the Nation's land and water resources.

SEC. 2. For the purposes of this Act, the following terms shall mean:

The "Secretary"—the Secretary of Agriculture of the United States.

"Works of improvement"—any undertaking for—

(1) flood prevention (including structural and land-treatment measures) or

(2) agricultural phases of the conservation, development, utilization, and disposal of water

in watershed or subwatershed areas not exceeding two hundred and fifty thousand acres and not including any single structure which provides more than five thousand acre-feet of total capacity. No appropriation shall be made for any plan for works of improvement which includes any structure which provides more than twenty-five hundred acre-feet of total capacity unless such plan has been approved by resolutions adopted by the Committee on Agriculture and Forestry of the Senate and the Committee on Agriculture of the House of Representatives, respectively. A number of such subwatersheds when they are com-

*68 *Statutes at Large,* 666.

[429]

ponent parts of a larger watershed may be planned together when the local sponsoring organizations so desire.

"Local organization"—any State, political subdivision thereof, soil or water conservation district, flood prevention or control district, or combinations thereof, or any other agency having authority under State law to carry out, maintain and operate the works of improvement.

SEC. 3. In order to assist local organizations in preparing and carrying out plans for works of improvement, the Secretary is authorized, upon application of local organizations if such application has been submitted to, and not disapproved within 45 days by, the State agency having supervisory responsibility over programs provided for in this Act, or by the Governor if there is no State agency having such responsibility—

(1) to conduct such investigations and surveys as may be necessary to prepare plans for works of improvement;

(2) to make such studies as may be necessary for determining the physical and economic soundness of plans for works of improvement, including a determination as to whether benefits exceed costs;

(3) to cooperate and enter into agreements with and to furnish financial and other assistance to local organizations: *Provided,* That, for the land-treatment measures, the Federal assistance shall not exceed the rate of assistance for similar practices under existing national programs;

(4) to obtain the cooperation and assistance of other Federal agencies in carrying out the purposes of this section.

SEC. 4. The Secretary shall require as a condition to providing Federal assistance for the installation of works of improvement that local organizations shall—

(1) acquire without cost to the Federal Government such land, easements, or rights-of-way as will be needed in connection with works of improvement installed with Federal assistance;

(2) assume such proportionate share of the cost of installing any works of improvement involving Federal assistance as may be determined by the Secretary to be equitable in consideration of anticipated benefits from such improvements: *Provided,* That no part of the construction cost for providing any capacity in structures for purposes other than flood prevention and features related thereto shall be borne by the Federal Government under the provisions of this Act;

(3) make arrangements satisfactory to the Secretary for defraying costs of operating and maintaining such works of improvement, in accordance with regulations presented by the Secretary of Agriculture;

(4) acquire, or provide assurance that landowners have acquired, such water rights, pursuant to State law, as may be needed in the installation and operation of the work of improvement; and

(5) obtain agreements to carry out recommended soil conservation measures

and proper farm plans from owners of not less than 50 per centum of the lands situated in the drainage area above each retention reservoir to be installed with Federal assistance.

SEC. 5. At such time as the Secretary and the interested local organization have agreed on a plan for works of improvement, and the Secretary has determined that the benefits exceed the costs, and the local organization has met the requirements for participation in carrying out the works of improvement as set forth in section 4, the Secretary is authorized to assist such local organizations in developing specifications, in preparing contracts for construction, and to participate in the installation of such works of improvement in accordance with the plan: *Provided,* That, except as to the installation of works of improvement on Federal lands, the Secretary shall not construct or enter into any contract for the construction of any structure unless there is no local organization authorized by State law to undertake such construction or to enter into such contract, and in no event after July 1, 1956: *Provided,* That in participating in the installation of such works of improvement the Secretary, as far as practicable and consistent with his responsibilities for administering the overall national agricultural program, shall utilize the authority conferred upon him by the provisions of this Act: *Provided further,* That, at least forty-five days (counting only days occurring during any regular or special sessions of the Congress) before such installation involving Federal assistance is commenced, the Secretary shall transmit a copy of the plan and the justification therefor to the Congress through the President: *Provided further,* That any such plan (a) which includes reclamation or irrigation works or which affects public or other lands under the jurisdiction of the Secretary of the Interior, or (b) which includes Federal assistance for floodwater detention structures, shall be submitted to the Secretary of the Interior or the Secretary of the Army, respectively, for his views and recommendations at least sixty days prior to transmission of the plan to the Congress through the President. The views and recommendations of the Secretary of the Interior, and the Secretary of the Army, if received by the Secretary of Agriculture prior to the expiration of the above sixty-day period, shall accompany the plan transmitted by the Secretary of Agriculture to the Congress through the President: *Provided further,* That, prior to any Federal participation in the works of improvement under this Act, the President shall issue such rules and regulations as he deems necessary or desirable to carry out the purposes of this Act, and to assure the coordination of the work authorized under this Act and related work of other agencies including the Department of the Interior and the Department of the Army.

SEC. 6. The Secretary is authorized in cooperation with other Federal and with States and local agencies to make investigations and surveys of the watersheds of rivers and other waterways as a basis for the development of coordinated programs. In areas where the programs of the Secretary of Agriculture may affect public or other lands under the jurisdiction of the Secretary of the Interior, the Secretary of the Interior is authorized to cooperate with the Secretary of Agriculture in the planning and development of works or programs for such lands.

SEC. 7. The provisions of the Act of June 22, 1936 (49 Stat. 1570), as amended and supplemented, conferring authority upon the Department of Agriculture under the direction of the Secretary of Agriculture to make preliminary examinations and surveys and to prosecute works of improvement for runoff and waterflow retardation and soil erosion prevention on the watersheds of rivers and other waterways are hereby repealed: *Provided,* That (a) the authority of that Department of Agriculture, under the direction of the Secretary, to prosecute the works of improvement for runoff and waterflow retardation and soil erosion prevention authorized to be carried out by the Department by the Act of December 22, 1944 (58 Stat. 887), as amended, and (b) the authority of the Secretary of Agriculture to undertake emergency measures for runoff retardation and soil erosion prevention authorized to be carried out by section 7 of the Act of June 28, 1938 (52 Stat. 1215), as amended by section 216 of the Act of May 17, 1950 (64 Stat. 163), shall not be affected by the provisions of this section.

SEC. 8. There are hereby authorized to be appropriated such sums as may be necessary to carry out the purposes of this Act, such sums to remain available until expended.

SEC. 9. This Act may be cited as the "Watershed Protection and Flood Prevention Act".

Approved August 4, 1954.

THE FEDERAL BOATING ACT*
September 2, 1958

The large number of boats on the nation's waters (most of them operated by amateurs) created hazards not only for the boaters and their passengers but for other persons who were using the same waters for other purposes. In an effort to alleviate this problem, Congress passed the Federal Boating Act of 1958 which provides for a numbering and identification system for boats of over 10 horse-power and amends the Motorboat Act of 1940 (46 U.S.C., 526) so as to make possible more effective enforcement of the "rules of the road" and the safety measures embodied in that act.

Since its founding in 1790, the Coast Guard has been generally responsible for maritime safety and law enforcement. However, when the 1958 act was being considered, the Coast Guard did not have the facilities to become a water-going policeman for the nation's boaters. Furthermore there was a general inclination among congressmen to consider boating traffic regulation to be the responsibility of state governments. As a result, the House Merchant Marine and Fisheries Committee asked the Council of State Governments to review proposed boating safety legislation, and in addition, the Secretary of the Treasury held a national small-boat safety conference in December 1957 which presented some 19 conclusions and recommendations on small-boat safety regulation. Most of the recommendations of the Council of State Governments and the national small-boat safety conference were incorporated into a bill which became the Federal Boating Act of 1958.

In effect, the Federal Boating Act recognized a system of concurrent jurisdiction over boating regulation between the states and the Federal Government. The act provides for the assumption of boat enumeration by state governments under systems approved by the Coast Guard; amends the Motorboat Act of 1940 to provide for a civil penalty for reckless or negligent operation of a boat; establishes requirements for the reporting of accidents; directs the Coast Guard to compile and analyze such accident reports; and declares it to be the policy of Congress to encourage uniformity of boating laws among the states and the Federal Government. This important act follows.

An Act to promote boating safety on the navigable waters of the United States, its Territories, and the District of Columbia; to provide coordination and cooperation with the States in the interest of uniformity of boating laws; and for other purposes.

---

*72 *Statutes at Large,* 1754.

Be it enacted by the Senate and House of Representatives of the United States of America in Congress assembled, That this act may be cited as the "Federal Boating Act of 1958."

SEC. 2. As used in sections 3 to 5, inclusive, and sections 7 to 13, inclusive, of this act—

(1) The term "undocumented vessel" means any vessel which is not required to have, and does not have, a valid marine document issued by the Bureau of Customs.

(2) The word "vessel" includes every description of watercraft, other than a seaplane on the water, used or capable of being used as a means of transportation on water.

(3) The word "Secretary" means the Secretary of the Department in which the Coast Guard is operating.

(4) The word "owner" means the person who claims lawful possession of a vessel by virtue of legal title or equitable interest therein which entitles him to such possession.

(5) The term "State" means a State of the United States, a Territory of the United States, and the District of Columbia.

SEC. 3. (a) Every undocumented vessel propelled by machinery of more than 10 horsepower, whether or not such machinery is the principal source of propulsion, using the navigable water of the United States, its Territories and the District of Columbia, and every such vessel owned in a State and using the high seas, shall be numbered in accordance with this act, except—

(1) foreign vessels temporarily using the navigable waters of the United States, its Territories and the District of Columbia;

(2) public vessels of the United States;

(3) State and municipal vessels;

(4) ships' lifeboats; and

(5) vessels designated by the Secretary under section 7(b) of this act.

(b) The owner of an undocumented vessel required to be numbered under subsection (a) of this section shall secure a number for such vessel in the State in which it is principally used, in accordance with the State numbering system approved by the Secretary in accordance with subsection (c) of this section, or if no such numbering system has been approved by the Secretary for the State where such vessel is principally used, shall secure a number for such vessel in accordance with subsection (d) of this section.

(c) The Secretary shall establish an overall numbering system for the numbering of vessels required to be numbered under subsection (a) of this section. He shall approve any State system for numbering vessels which is submitted to him which meets the standards set forth below:

(1) The system of numbering shall be in accordance with the overall system of numbering established by the Secretary.

(2) The certificate of number and the number awarded shall be valid for a period not exceeding 3 years, unless canceled or surrendered, and may be renewed for additional periods.

(3) The number awarded shall be required to be painted on, or attached to, each side of the bow of the vessel for which it was issued, and shall be of such size, color, and type, as may be prescribed by the Secretary. No other number shall be permitted to be carried on the bow of such vessel.

(4) The certificate of number shall be pocket size and shall be required to be at all times available for inspection on the vessel for which issued, whenever such vessel is in use.

(5) The owner shall be required to furnish to a designated State official, notice of the transfer of all or any part of his interest in any numbered vessel, and of the destruction or abandonment of such vessel, within a reasonable time thereof. The owner shall be required to notify a designated State official of any change in his address within a reasonable time of such change.

(6) The State shall require that reports be made to it of accidents involving vessels numbered by it under its numbering system, and shall compile and transmit to the Secretary such statistics on such accidents.

(7) The State shall recognize the validity of a number awarded to any vessel by another State under a numbering system approved by the Secretary under this act, or awarded a number by the Secretary, for a period of at least 90 days.

(8) In the case of a State having its numbering system approved after April 1, 1960, such State shall accept and recognize any valid certificate of number awarded under subsection (d) of this section for so long as such certificate would otherwise be valid under such subsection (d), except that where such a certificate would remain valid for more than 1 year after the date when such State's numbering system was approved, the State may accept and recognize the validity of such certificate for a lesser period, but such period shall not end sooner than 1 year from the date of approval of such system.

(9) The State may exempt any vessel or class of vessels from the numbering provisions of its system if such vessel or class of vessels has been made exempt from the numbering provisions of section 3(d) by the Secretary under section 7(b) of this act.

(10) The States may charge fees in connection with the award of certificates of number and renewals thereof.

(11) The States may require that the operator of a vessel required to be numbered hereunder shall hold a valid safety certificate to be issued under such terms and conditions as may be provided by State law.

(d) The owner of an undocumented vessel required to be numbered under subsection (a) of this section who uses his vessel principally in a State which does not have a numbering system approved by the Secretary under subsection (c) of this section, shall make application to the Secretary, and upon payment of the fee established under section 5, such owner shall be granted a certificate of number containing the number awarded such vessel by the Secretary.

(e) The certificate of number initially awarded to an owner under subsection (d) of this section shall be valid for 3 years from the date of the owner's birthday next occurring after the date the certificate of number is issued, unless surrendered or canceled pursuant to regulations of the Secretary. If at the end of such period such ownership has remained unchanged, such owner shall, upon application and payment of the fee established under section 5 of this act, be granted a renewal of such certificate of number for an additional 3-year period.

(f) The number awarded under subsection (c) or (d) of this section shall be painted on, or attached to, each side of the bow of the vessel for which it was issued, and shall be of such size, color, and type as may be prescribed by the Secretary. No other number shall be carried on the bow of such vessel.

(g) The certificate of number granted under subsection (c) or (d) of this section shall be pocket size and shall be required to be at all times available for inspection on the vessel for which issued whenever such vessel is in use, and shall constitute a document in lieu of a marine document that sets forth an official number issued by the Bureau of Customs.

(h) Whenever the Secretary determines that a State is not administering its approval system for numbering vessels in accordance with the standards set forth under subsection (c) of this section, he may withdraw such approval. The Secretary shall not withdraw his approval of a State system of numbering until he has given notice in writing to the State setting forth specifically wherein the State has failed to maintain such standards.

SEC. 4. The owner of any vessel numbered under section 3(d) of this act shall furnish to the Secretary notice of the transfer of all or any part of his interest in any numbered vessel, and of the destruction, or abandonment of such vessel, within a reasonable time thereof. The owner shall notify the Secretary of any change in his address within a reasonable time of such change.

SEC. 5. The Secretary may prescribe reasonable fees or charges for the numbering of a vessel, or renewal thereof, under subsections (d) and (e) of section 3 of this act.

SEC. 6. (a) Section 13 of the act entitled "An act to amend laws for preventing collisions of vessels, to regulate equipment of certain motorboats on the navigable waters of the United States, and for other purposes," approved April 25, 1940 (46 U.S.C. 5261), is amended to read as follows:

"SEC. 13. (a) No person shall operate any motorboat or any vessel in a reckless or negligent manner so as to endanger the life, limb, or property of any person. To 'operate' means to navigate or otherwise use a motorboat or a vessel.

"(b) In the case of collision, accident, or other casualty involving a motorboat or other vessel subject to this act, it shall be the duty of the operator, if and so far as he can do so without serious danger to his own vessel, or persons aboard, to render such assistance as may be practicable and necessary to other persons affected by the collision, accident, or casualty in order to save them from danger caused by the collision, accident, or casualty. He shall also give his name, address, and identification of his vessel to any person injured and to the owner of any property damaged. The duties imposed by this subsection shall be in addition to any duties otherwise provided by law.

"(c) In the case of collision, accident, or other casualty involving a motorboat or other vessel subject to this act, the operator thereof, if the collision, accident, or other casualty results in the death or injury to any person, or damage to property in excess of $100, shall file with the Secretary of the Department within which the Coast Guard is operating, unless such operator is required to file an accident report with the State under section 3(c) (6) of the Federal Boating Act of 1958, a full description of the collision, accident, or other casualty, including such information as the Secretary may by regulation require."

(b) Section 16 of such act of April 25, 1940 (46 U.S.C. 5260), is amended by striking out "than that contained in section 14 of this act".

(c) Such act of April 25, 1940 (46 U.S.C. 526-526t), is further amended by adding at the end thereof the following new section:

"Sec. 22. (a) This act shall apply to every motorboat or vessel on the navigable waters of the United States, Guam, the Virgin Islands, the Commonwealth of Puerto Rico, and the District of Columbia, and every motorboat or vessel owned in a State and using the high seas.

"(b) As used in this act—

"The term 'State' means a State of the United States, Guam, the Virgin Islands, the Commonwealth of Puerto Rico, and the District of Columbia."

SEC. 7. (a) The Secretary shall make such rules and regulations as may be necessary to carry out the provisions of this act: *Provided,* That such rules and regulations shall be submitted to the Speaker of the House and the President of the Senate when Congress is in session, and shall not become effective until 60 days thereafter.

(b) The Secretary may, from time to time, and for such periods as he may prescribe, exempt any vessel or class of vessels from the numbering provisions of subsection (d) of section 3 of this act.

SEC. 8. (a) Whoever being the owner of a vessel required to be numbered under this act, violates section 3 or 4 of this act, or regulations established by the Secretary under section 7 of this act, shall be liable to a penalty of $50 for each violation. Whoever operates a vessel in violation of section 3 of this act, or regulations established by the Secretary under section 7 of this act, shall be liable to a penalty of $50 for each violation.

(b) The Secretary may assess and collect any penalty incurred under this act,

[437]

or any regulations prescribed pursuant to section 7 of this act. The Secretary may, in his discretion, remit or mitigate any penalty imposed under this section, or discontinue prosecution therefor on such terms as he may deem proper.

(c) Commissioned, warrant, and petty officers of the Coast Guard may board any vessel required to be numbered under this act at any time such vessel is found upon the navigable waters of the United States, its Territories, and the District of Columbia, or on the high seas, address inquiries to those on board, require appropriate proof of identification therefrom, examine the certificate of number issued under this act, or in the absence of such certificate require appropriate proof of identification of the owner of the vessel, and, in addition, examine such vessel in compliance with this act, the act of April 25, 1940, as amended, and the applicable rules of the road.

SEC. 9. It is hereby declared to be the policy of Congress to encourage uniformity of boating laws, rules, and regulations as among the several States and the Federal Government to the fullest extent practicable, subject to reasonable exceptions arising out of local conditions. In the interest of fostering the development, use, and enjoyment of all the waters of the United States it is further declared to be the policy of the Congress hereby to encourage the highest degree of reciprocity and comity among the several jurisdictions. The Secretary, acting under the authority of section 141 of title 14 of the United States Code, shall to the greatest possible extent enter into agreements and other arrangements with the States to insure that there shall be the fullest possible cooperation in the enforcement of both State and Federal statutes, rules, and regulations relating to recreational boating.

SEC. 10. The Secretary is authorized and directed to compile, analyze, and publish, either in summary or detailed form, the information obtained by him from the accident reports transmitted to him under section 3 (c) (6) of this act, and under section 13(c) of the act entitled "An act to amend laws for preventing collisions of vessels, to regulate equipment of certain motorboats on the navigable waters of the United States, and for other purposes," approved April 25, 1940 (46 U.S.C. 5261), together with such findings concerning the causes of such accidents and such recommendations for their prevention as he may deem necessary. Such information shall be made available for public inspection in such a manner as the Secretary may deem practicable.

SEC. 11. (a) Except section 3(d), this act shall take effect on the date of its enactment.

(b) Section 3(d) of this act shall take effect April 1, 1960.

SEC. 12. The act entitled "An act to require numbering and recording of undocumented vessels", approved June 7, 1918, as amended (46 U.S.C. 288), and section 21 of the act entitled "An act to amend laws for preventing collisions of vessels, to regulate equipment of certain motorboats on the navigable waters of the United States, and for other purposes," approved April 25, 1940, as amended (46 U.S.C. 526t), shall not be applicable in any State having a numbering system approved by the Secretary under section 3(c) of this act. Such act of June 7, 1918, and such section 21 of the act of April 25, 1940, are repealed effective April 1, 1960.

Sec. 13. The applicability and the jurisdiction for enforcement, upon the navigable waters of the United States, its Territories, and the District of Columbia, of the laws of the United States and of any State which require the numbering and otherwise regulate the use of undocumented vessels, shall be as follows:

(1) Such laws of the United States shall be applicable and enforced on such waters by law enforcement officers of the United States.

(2) Such laws of any State in a State having a numbering system approved by the Secretary under section 3(c) of this act shall be applicable and enforced on such waters by law enforcement officers of the State or by law enforcement officers of the appropriate subdivisions of the State.

(3) Nothing herein shall preclude enforcement of State or Federal laws pursuant to agreements or other arrangements entered into between the Secretary and any State within the contemplation of section 9 of this act.

(4) Nothing herein shall interfere with, abrogate or limit the jurisdiction of any State: *Provided, however,* That the Secretary shall not approve any State system for numbering which does not fully comply with the standards set forth in section 3(c).

Approved September 2, 1958.

THE FOOD AND AGRICULTURE ACT*
September 27, 1962

*The Watershed Protection and Flood Prevention Act of 1954 did not specific-
ally authorize Federal Government support for recreation so although the recreation benefits on small watersheds were substantial, they were incidental to the
primary purposes of the project. The Food and Agriculture Act of 1962 amended
that law to allow federal cost-sharing for recreation in the development of small
watershed projects. The pertinent section of the act is reproduced below.*

SEC. 103. The Watershed Protection and Flood Prevention Act (68 Stat. 666),
as amended, is amended as follows:
(1) Paragraph (1) of section 4 of said Act is amended by changing the semi-
colon at the end thereof to a colon and adding the following: *"Provided,* That
when a local organization agrees to operate and maintain any reservoir or other
area included in a plan for public fish and wildlife or recreational development,
the Secretary shall be authorized to bear not to exceed one-half of the costs of
(a) the land, easements, or rights-of-way acquired or to be acquired by the local
organization for such reservoir or other area, and (b) minimum basic facilities
needed for public health and safety, access to, and use of such reservoir or other
area for such purposes: *Provided further,* That the Secretary shall be authorized
to participate in recreational development in any watershed project only to the
extent that the need therefor is demonstrated in accordance with standards
established by him, taking into account the anticipated man-days of use of the
projected recreational development and giving consideration to the availability
within the region of existing water-based outdoor recreational developments:
Provided further, That the Secretary shall be authorized to participate in not
more than one recreational development in a watershed project containing
less than seventy-five thousand acres, or two such developments in a project
containing between seventy-five thousand and one hundred and fifty thousand
acres, or three such developments in projects exceeding one hundred and fifty
thousand acres: *Provided further,* That when the Secretary and a local organization have agreed that the immediate acquisition by the local organization of
land, easements, or rights-of-way is advisable for the preservation of sites for
works of improvement included in a plan from encroachment by residential,
commercial, industrial, or other development, the Secretary shall be authorized
to advance to the local organization from funds appropriated for construction of
works of improvement the amounts required for the acquisition of such land,
easements or rights-of-way; and, except where such costs are to be borne by the

---

*76 *Statutes at Large,* 608.

Secretary, such advance shall be repaid by the local organization, with interest, prior to construction of the works of improvement, for credit to such construction funds."

(2) Clause (A) of paragraph 2 of section 4 of said Act is amended to read as follows: "(A) such proportionate share, as is determined by the Secretary to be equitable in consideration of national needs and assistance authorized for similar purposes under other Federal programs, of the costs of installing any works of improvement, involving Federal assistance (excluding engineering costs), which is applicable to the argicultural phases of the conservation, development, utilization, and disposal of water or for fish and wildlife or recreational development, and".

THE RIVERS AND HARBORS ACT*
October 23, 1962

This act reiterated and expanded upon previous authorizations for outdoor recreation. Relevant sections of the act are reproduced below.

An Act authorizing the construction, repair, and preservation of certain public works on rivers and harbors for navigation, flood control, and for other purposes.

Be it enacted by the Senate and House of Representatives of the United States of America in Congress assembled,

TITLE I—RIVERS AND HARBORS

SEC. 101. That the following works of improvement of rivers and harbors and other waterways for navigation, flood control, and other purposes are hereby adopted and authorized to be prosecuted under the direction of the Secretary of the Army and supervision of the Chief of Engineers, in accordance with the plans and subject to the conditions recommended by the Chief of Engineers in the respective reports hereinafter designated: *Provided,* That the provisions of section 1 of the River and Harbor Act approved March 2, 1945 (Public Law Numbered 14, Seventy-ninth Congress, first session), shall govern with respect to projects authorized in this title; and the procedures therein set forth with respect to plans, proposals, or reports for works of improvement for navigation or flood control and for irrigation and purposes incidental thereto, shall apply as if herein set forth in full:

SEC. 207. Section 4 of the Act entitled "An Act authorizing the construction of certain public works on rivers and harbors for flood control, and for other purposes", approved December 22, 1944, as amended by section 4 of the Flood Control Act of July 24, 1946, and by section 209 of the Flood Control Act of 1954, is hereby further amended to read as follows:

"SEC. 4. The Chief of Engineers, under the supervision of the Secretary of the Army, is authorized to construct, maintain, and operate public park and recreational facilities at water resource development projects under the control of the Department of the Army, to permit the construction of such facilities by local interests (particularly those to be operated and maintained by such interests), and to permit the maintenance and operation of such facilities by local interests. The Secretary of the Army is also authorized to grant leases of lands, including structures or facilities thereon, at water resource development proj-

*76 *Statutes at Large,* 1173.

ects for such periods, and upon such terms and for such purposes as he may deem reasonable in the public interest: *Provided,* That leases to nonprofit organizations for park or recreational purposes may be granted at reduced or nominal considerations in recognition of the public service to be rendered in utilizing the leased premises: *Provided further,* That preference shall be given to Federal, State, or local governmental agencies, and licenses or leases where appropriate, may be granted without monetary considerations, to such agencies for the use of all or any portion of a project area for any public purpose, when the Secretary of the Army determines such action to be in the public interest, and for such periods of time and upon such conditions as he may find advisable: *And provided further,* That in any such lease or license to a Federal, State, or local governmental agency which involves lands to be utilized for the development and conservation of fish and wildlife, forests, and other natural resources, the licensee or lessee may be authorized to cut timber and harvest crops as may be necessary to further such beneficial uses and to collect and utilize the proceeds of any sales of timber and crops in the development, conservation, maintenance, and utilization of such lands. Any balance of proceeds not so utilized shall be paid to the United States at such time or times as the Secretary of the Army may determine appropriate. The water areas of all such projects shall be open to public use generally, without charge, for boating, swimming, bathing, fishing, and other recreational purposes, and ready access to and exit from such areas along the shores of such projects shall be maintained for general public use, when such use is determined by the Secretary of the Army not to be contrary to the public interest, all under such rules and regulations as the Secretary of the Army may deem necessary. No use of any area to which this section applies shall be permitted which is inconsistent with the laws for the protection of fish and game of the State in which such area is situated. All moneys received by the United States for leases or privileges shall be deposited in the Treasury of the United States as miscellaneous receipts."

THE RECREATION ADVISORY COUNCIL POLICY ON NATIONAL RECREATION AREAS*
March 26, 1963

National Recreation Areas are administered by the National Park Service, frequently in cooperation with other state or federal agencies. They are considered to be areas of national significance for recreation but lacking the superlative qualities that would qualify them to be called national parks. Most of the National Recreation Areas were based on a large reservoir, such as Shadow Mountain (formed by the Colorado-Big Thompson project); Lake Mead, the world's largest man-made lake (created by Hoover Dam on the Colorado River); and Coulee Dam (Franklin D. Roosevelt Lake formed by Grand Coulee Dam).

These areas receive very heavy recreation use. Coulee Dam, for example, had over one million visitor days in 1966 and Lake Mead had 3.6 million visitor-days. Because of the large and increasing number of recreation visits to National Recreation Areas and the need for establishing additional areas, the Recreation Advisory Council gave this matter first priority in its deliberations and issued its first policy directive on this subject. The document follows.

PREAMBLE

The Recreation Advisory Council believes that:

1. Greater efforts must be made by Federal, State, local governmental, and private interests to fulfill adequately the steeply mounting outdoor recreation demands of the American people;

2. The Federal Government should provide leadership and stimulus to this effort, but does not have sole or primary responsibility for providing recreation opportunities;

3. Present Federal progams should be augmented by a system of National Recreation Areas made up of a limited number of areas where the recreation demand is not being met through other programs.

The system of National Recreation Areas should:

1. Provide for Federal investment in outdoor recreation that is more clearly responsive to recreation demand than other investments that are based primarily upon considerations of preserving unique natural or historical resources, the need to develop and conserve public lands and forests, or the requirements of major water resource development undertakings;

2. Be areas which have natural endowments that are well above the ordinary in quality and recreation appeal, being of lesser significance than the unique

*Recreation Advisory Council, "Federal Executive Branch Policy Governing the Selection, Establishment, and Administration of National Recreation Areas" (Washington, D.C.: Mar. 26, 1963), 1–7.

scenic and historic elements of the National Park System, but affording a quality of recreation experience which transcends that normally associated with areas provided by State and local governments;

3. Be consistent with Federal progams relating to national parks, national forests, public lands, fish and wildlife, water resource development, grants for urban open space, recreation programs on private agricultural lands, and programs for financial assistance to States in providing recreation opportunity.

In order to provide a rational basis for planning and evaluating proposed projects where outdoor recreation use is the dominant or primary purpose, the Recreation Advisory Council hereby sets forth the guidelines it believes should govern the selection, establishment, and administration of National Recreation Areas.

Under authority bestowed upon the Council by Executive Order 11017, of April 27, 1962, the Council commends this policy to all concerned Federal agencies, and by mutual agreement makes it binding upon the member agencies of the Recreation Advisory Council. It shall be applied to the existing backlog of National Recreation Area proposals, as well as to all future proposals.

TERMINOLOGY AND DEFINITION OF SCOPE

Many names have been used in the past in describing areas to be acquired and developed, or to be administratively designated, predominantly for recreation use. Some of these are National Seashore, National Lakeshore, National Waterway, National Riverway, National Recreation Demonstration Areas, and similar names which embody either the physical resource base or the functional purpose to be served. This policy statement includes such areas.

The following criteria are not intended to apply to (a) the classical elements of the National Park System; (b) the standard recreation use areas designated under National Forest practices; (c) the normal scale of recreation development associated with Federal multiple purpose impoundments; (d) the National Wildlife Refuges, Game Ranges, and National Fish Hatcheries; (e) military and national defense installations; and (f) sites within the zone of metropolitan responsibility, such as provided through the Open Space program of the Housing and Home Finance Agency, or which primarily serve massive day use requirements that properly should be met by local and State agencies of government. On the other hand, it is conceivable that National Recreation Areas may include within their boundaries portions of any existing Federal real property.

PRIMARY CRITERIA FOR SELECTION OF
NATIONAL RECREATION AREAS

These criteria represent an essential test. National Recreation Areas are conceived of as consisting of a limited number of areas. Therefore, the Council

[445]

recognizes that a high degree of judgment will have to be exercised in the choice of priorities among qualifying areas.

Application of the following seven primary criteria shall be mandatory for all proposals:

1. National Recreation Areas should be spacious areas, including within their perimeter an aggregate gross area of not less than 20,000 acres of land and water surface, except for riverways, narrow coastal strips, or areas where total population within a 250-mile radius is in excess of 30 million people.

2. National Recreation Areas should be located and designed to achieve a comparatively high recreation carrying capacity, in relation to type of recreation primarily to be served.

3. National Recreation Areas should provide recreation opportunities significant enough to assure interstate patronage within its region of service, and to a limited extent should attract patronage from outside of its normal service region.

4. The scale of investment, development, and operational responsibility should be sufficiently high to require either direct Federal involvement, or substantial Federal participation to assure optimum public benefit.

5. Although nonurban in character, National Recreation Areas should nevertheless be strategically located within easy driving distance, i.e., not more than 250 miles from urban population centers which are to be served. Such areas should be readily accessible at all times, for all-purpose recreational use.

6. Within National Recreation Areas, outdoor recreation shall be recognized as the dominant or primary resource management purpose. If additional natural resource utilization is carried on, such additional use shall be compatible with fulfilling the recreation mission, and none will be carried on that is significantly detrimental to it.

7. National Recreation Areas should be established in only those areas where other programs (Federal and non-Federal) will not fulfill high priority recreation needs in the foreseeable future.

SECONDARY CRITERIA FOR SELECTION OF NATIONAL RECREATION AREAS

Application of the following six secondary criteria will be given weight in situations where they bear a meaningful relationship to a specific proposal:

1. Preference should be given to proposed National Recreation Areas that:
   a. Are within or closely proximate to those official U.S. Census Divisions having the highest population densities;
   b. Are in areas which have a serious deficiency in supply of both private and public outdoor recreation areas and facilities as determined by the National Recreation Plan;

c. Are in areas which have a comparatively low amount of federally provided recreation carrying capacity;

d. Show an optimum ratio of carrying capacity to estimated cost.

2. National Recreation Areas may be based upon existing or proposed Federal water impoundments where it can be shown that significant increases in the scale of recreation development are required, beyond the level normally justified under standard multiple-purpose project development, in order to assure that full recreation potential is provided for projected needs.

3. National Recreation Areas may include within their boundaries scenic, historic, scientific, scarce or disappearing resources, provided the objectives of their preservation and enjoyment can be achieved on a basis compatible with the recreation mission.

4 National Recreation Areas should be in conformity with the National Recreation Plan prepared by the Bureau of Outdoor Recreation, and shall take into consideration State, regional, and local comprehensive plans.

5. Whenever possible, National Recreation Areas should be selected, developed, and managed to provide maximum compatibility with the recreation potential of adjacent rural areas in private ownership.

6. Preference should be given to areas within or proximate to a Redevelopment Area as officially designated by the Department of Commerce and deemed significant in the economic improvement of such a Redevelopment Area.

ESTABLISHMENT OF NATIONAL RECREATION AREAS

National Recreation Areas shall be established by an Act of Congress, Legislation to establish National Recreation Areas will be processed in accordance with established procedures for handling legislation. Upon request of the Executive Office of the President, the Recreation Advisory Council will review specific National Recreation Area proposals, based upon studies made or prescribed by the Bureau of Outdoor Recreation. For those proposals referred to it, the Council will recommend appropriate action regarding authorization; modification; priority of establishment; and the responsible management agency or agencies.

ADMINISTRATION OF NATIONAL RECREATION AREAS

National Recreation Area proposals should include recommendations as to the agency or agencies responsible for their management. In making this recommendation, sponsoring organizations should take into account the proximity of the proposed area to other publicly administered areas, along with such other factors as will assure effective and economical administration of the new area. Where deemed feasible and desirable, a joint Federal-State management arrangement may be recommended.

ACTIVATION OF POLICY CIRCULAR NO. 1

Upon approval by signature of this policy circular by members of the Recreation Advisory Council, the member agencies will become responsible for observing the foregoing policies and procedures, and will undertake immediately to give this circular force and effect by issuing an appropriate internal administrative directive, over the signature of the agency head or other responsible officer. The Council recommends the adoption of the foregoing policies and procedures by other Federal agencies.

THE LAND BETWEEN THE LAKES
1963* & 1964†

The Land Between the Lakes project, considered by Dr. Milton A. Gabrielson to be "potentially the most significant single development in the field of outdoor recreation and education that has happened in this century" was announced by President Kennedy in the following news release. A "Concept Statement" which describes the project is documented here immediately after the President's news release.

The President today announced that the Tennessee Valley Authority will develop a National Recreation Area as a demonstration in resource development in the 170,000 acre Between-the-Lakes area which lies between TVA's Kentucky Reservoir on the Tennessee River and the Army Corps of Engineers' Barkley Reservoir just across the divide on the Cumberland River. Two-thirds of the area involved lies in western Kentucky, the remainder in Tennessee.

For a distance of some 40 miles above each dam the shorelines of the two lakes lie only six to twelve miles apart. They enclose a narrow strip of wooded ridges rising up to 300 feet above the broad stretches of reservoir on either side.

The President noted that the Between-the-Lakes area is within 200 miles of nearly 10 million people living in the midwest and thus the development of a national recreation area in that location meets the recommendation made by the Outdoor Recreation Resources Review Commission, and endorsed by the President in his Special Message to Congress last year, that recreation facilities for our more densely populated areas merit high priority.

Nearly half the land under consideration for the recreation area already is in Federal ownership, under control of the Department of the Interior, TVA and the Corps of Engineers.

The decision to proceed with the Between-the-Lakes project followed notification by Secretary of the Interior Stewart L. Udall that the Department of the Interior would enter into an agreement with TVA whereby lands administered by the Department would be turned over to TVA for the project. Other Federal lands will likewise be transferred.

Development of the project will demonstrate how an area with limited timber, agricultural, and industrial resources can be converted into a recreation asset that will stimulate economic growth of the region. It will also help establish and define guidelines for the acquisition, development, and operation of other outdoor recreation areas.

*Office of the White House Press Secretary, "News Release of June 14, 1963."
†Tennessee Valley Authority, *The Land Between the Lakes: A Demonstration in Recreation Resource Development* (Knoxville: Apr., 1964) 1–8.

The area will include provision for development of new waterfowl wintering grounds in cooperation with the Bureau of Sport Fisheries and Wildlife and for management of upland game, including improvement of public hunting.

TVA expects to start on the project at an early date. The agency will administer the area for the period required to complete the demonstration, estimated at about 10 years. At the end of that period, arrangements for permanent administration of the area for outdoor recreation will be determined.

SUMMARY AND INTRODUCTION

The United States has always been a land of outdoor recreation. People have hunted and fished for pleasure and adventure as well as for food. As we have learned to earn a livelihood from the land, we have also learned to return to it as a source of rest, relaxation, and pleasure during our leisure moments. Fields and forests, streams and lakes, mountains and prairies have been open to us for hunting, fishing, and other outdoor recreation pursuits. As long as most of us lived on farms, we found our recreation close at home in the "lower forty" or the upland pasture. Even when we moved to town, we could find open space at the foot of main street or at the end of the carline—or even in one of the vacant lots in the block.

But, no longer does the end of the carline indicate open fields, and seldom do young "cowboys and Indians" find empty lots on the block where they can imitate their legendary heroes.

As more and more of the American countryside has become urbanized or industrialized, as more of us have acquired automobiles, we are becoming more and more accustomed, as a people, to seeking to fulfill these outdoor recreation needs on public lands and waters. The Land Between the Lakes will be such an area. It will encompass some 170,000 acres of field and forest in west Tennessee and Kentucky and will be surrounded by 300 miles of shoreline fronting on two of the largest man-made lakes in the United States. It is to be developed as a demonstration showing ways to meet the mounting needs of our industrializing society for adequate recreation facilities in the out-of-doors.

On June 14, 1963, President John F. Kennedy announced that TVA would have the mission of developing the Land Between the Lakes. Officially, the project was launched in January 1964 immediately after President Lyndon B. Johnson signed the public works appropriation bill of 1964. It meant that for the first time under Federal administration all of the resources of an area of this size would be managed and cultivated to produce the most favorable possible environment for outdoor recreation. As part of this cultivation, the area's rolling acres and scenic shorelines will be furnished with roads, trails, beaches, campgrounds, picnic areas, and other facilities that will convert the area into a magnificent setting for outdoor recreation. Also, to maintain this magnificent setting, techniques of multiple use land management will be employed to improve the area's forest cover and to provide food and shelter for wildlife.

The demonstration will contribute to economic development of the Tennessee Valley region and of the Nation. It will show that an area having only limited natural resources for conventional forms of economic use and development can help stimulate economic growth when developed as a public recreation area. TVA's policies with regard to the operation of the area will encourage private enterprise to invest in motels, resorts, restaurants, and other commercial facilities on the opposite shores of both lakes and along approach highways leading to the area. Within the next decade or so, the project is expected to create opportunities for private investment of as much as $25,000,000 in such "bed and board" facilities and other recreation services and attractions. This investment, in turn, will create 1,500 or more jobs in food and housing facilities to serve visitors to the Land Between the Lakes.

At the same time, the demonstration will provide a unique outdoor classroom and laboratory for those who like to lace their outdoor recreation pursuits with an educational flavor. This is an area to which people will be invited to come and do, as well as to come and look; where the urban dweller can renew and maintain his contact with the land, the forest, and wildlife in its natural habitat—factors which are ingrained in the American tradition but which could easily be lost in the rapid urbanization and industrialization of the American countryside. The Land Between the Lakes will be an area where groups of young people and adults can spend some of their leisure planting trees to help heal the scars of erosion. They will also be able to develop or renew their skills with axes and hand tools and learn to help provide food and shelter for wildlife.

THE AREA

General Location. The Land Between the Lakes is a peninsula in western Kentucky and Tennessee between TVA's Kentucky Lake, impounded in 1944, and the Corps of Engineers' Barkley Lake, impounded about twenty years later, in 1964 and 1965. The area includes parts of three counties, Trigg and Lyon Counties in Kentucky and Stewart County in Tennessee. It is less than 150 miles from the center of population of the United States near Centralia, Illinois. A 500-mile circle described around the Land Between the Lakes encompasses an estimated 70 million people; a 200-mile circle, 10 million people.

Boundaries. Kentucky and Barkley Lakes and the canal connecting them form natural boundaries on the west, east, and north sides of the area. The southern boundary is based on U.S. Highway 79 between Paris and Dover, Tennessee. Early plans of the state to relocate this highway and the urgent need of the city of Dover for room in which to expand have influenced the location of the southern boundary.

[451]

The entire area between Kentucky and Barkley Lakes from the southern boundary north to the canal will be purchased. No privately owned inholdings will remain within these boundaries.

The area's 300 miles of shoreline are its most precious asset for outdoor recreation. This shoreline has been, or is being, created as the result of Federal investment of some $300 million in public funds in the Kentucky and Barkley projects. All of it is needed for public use and development. Campgrounds, boat harbors, swimming areas, and other water access facilities will occupy many of the coves. Shallower reaches will provide desirable habitat for waterfowl. The remainder of the shoreline will round out the natural setting and provide a base for water sports and a backdrop for scenic roads and trails.

Interior lands are needed for access and administrative control and for service facilities. Wide expanses of the interior area will be developed to provide and maintain habitat for upland game and birds, and to supply the natural environment so desirable for the kinds of recreation activities visualized for the area.

Because of its elongated shape, no part of the area is very far from the outside despite the isolation afforded by the two bodies of water. By automobile, no point within the Land Between the Lakes is more than thirty minutes from one of the four principal entrances. Thus, visitors who base their recreation activities on their automobile—and most of them do—will find themselves close to the vacation services they need and the luxuries they desire. The need for services within the area where they would intrude upon the natural environment is limited and can be provided for on a minimum of demand basis.

About 30 percent of the users are expected to reach the area from the north over the new bridge crossing the canal, another 30 percent from the south via U.S. Highway 79, and the remaining 40 percent at the center of the area via U.S. Highway 68 at Golden Pond. (In future years, it is anticipated that U.S. Highway 68 across the area will need to be reconstructed as a four-lane dual highway.) Plans call for reception, overnight camping, administrative, and day-use facilities near these entrances. Here first-time visitors can become acquainted with the opportunities that the area affords and make a selection according to their individual desires and tastes.

USES AND USERS

The Land Between the Lakes offers an ideal setting for the Simple types of outdoor recreation activities that increasing thousands of American families are seeking—camping, picnicking, boating, swimming, fishing, hunting, hiking, riding, water-skiing, nature study, and conservation education. For many, most of these activities may be included within a weekend or vacation camping trip. Thousands of such families will find the Land Between the Lakes a convenient, economical objective for weekend and vacation camping trips by boat, car, trailer, or station wagon. Those who prefer not to camp but who still enjoy other activities in the out-of-doors may visit the area from their homes in the vicinity or from nearby motels and resorts. Plans for the area will be based on the anticipation of four to five million visitor-days in 1966; eight to ten million per year before the end of the demonstration.

The physical nature of the area lends itself to intensive development to supply facilities for a wide variety of recreation activities. The topography is rugged enough for interest but not so rugged as to require expensive construction.

* * *

The area will also serve many long-range uses. One such use will be studies to establish standards for future developers of recreation areas. Measures and experiments to determine optimum density of use of the entire area and of various kinds of facilities will be made. Results will be sought in terms of (1) user satisfaction, (2) carrying capacity of the resource, (3) development procedures, and (4) administrative methods.

The Land Between the Lakes will serve as a laboratory for students and educators working in the field of recreation and camping education. It will be a training ground for future specialists in outdoor recreation and education, and, through this media, will multiply the long-range effectiveness of the project. This work will be done in cooperation with colleges, universities, and other cooperating institutions.

DEVELOPMENT

All of the area's resources are to be administered and cultivated to produce the greatest possible outdoor recreation potential.

The area in its present state is aesthetically satisfying and offers a pleasant contrast to the surrounding rural-industrial environment, but it contains only a very few scenic or historic features which must be preserved against excessive recreation use. Consequently, facilities can be built to serve millions of visitors each year and still afford individual privacy or elbow room. Its forests can yield sawtimber, pulpwood, and other forest products while helping to create the most attractive forest possible for outdoor recreation prusuits. In short, policies can be followed in development of this area which will produce a maximum yield of outdoor recreation activities to which the area is suited in much the same way that an Iowa farmer manages his land to produce the maximum yield of corn, or a large paper company manages its forest holdings to produce the maximum yield of pulpwood.

THE FEDERAL WATER PROJECT RECREATION ACT*
July 9, 1965

This landmark act recognized outdoor recreation as a valid purpose in the construction of multiple-purpose water resource projects and provided for uniform policies in cost allocation. While the act applied to the Corps of Engineers as well as the Bureau of Reclamation, it was probably of greatest importance to the Bureau.

An Act to provide uniform policies with respect to recreation and fish and wildlife benefits and costs of Federal multiple-purpose water resource projects, and for other purposes.

Be it enacted by the Senate and House of Representatives of the United States of America in Congress assembled, That it is the policy of the Congress and the intent of this Act that (a) in investigating and planning any Federal navigation, flood control, reclamation, hydroelectric, or multiple-purpose water resource project, full consideration shall be given to the opportunities, if any, which the project affords for outdoor recreation and for fish and wildlife enahancement and that, wherever any such project can reasonably serve either or both of these purposes consistently with the provisions of this Act, is shall be contructed, operated, and maintained accordingly; (b) planning with respect to the development of the recreation potential of any such project shall be based on the coordination of the recreational use of the project area with the use of existing and planned Federal, State, or local public recreation developments; and (c) project construction agencies shall encourage non-Federal public bodies to administer project land and water areas for recreation and fish and wildlife enhancement purposes and operate, maintain, and replace facilities provided for those purposes unless such areas or facilities are included or proposed for inclusion within a national recreation area, or are appropriate for administration by a Federal agency as a part of the national forest system, as a part of the public lands classified for retention in Federal ownership, or in connection with an authorized Federal program for the conservation and development of fish and wildlife.

SEC. 2. (a) If, before authorization of a project, non-Federal public bodies indicate their intent in writing to agree to administer project land and water areas for recreation or fish and wildlife enhancement or for both of these purposes pursuant to the plan for the development of the project approved by the head of the agency having administrative jurisdiction over it and to bear not less than one-half the separable costs of the project allocated to either or both of said purposes, as the case may be, and all the costs of operation, maintenance, and replacement incurred therefor—

*79 *Statutes at Large,* 213.

(1) the benefits of the project to said purpose or purposes shall be taken into account in determining the economic benefits of the project;

(2) costs shall be allocated to said purpose or purposes and to other purposes in a manner which will insure that all project purposes share equitably in the advantages of multiple-purpose construction: *Provided,* That the costs allocated to recreation or fish and wildlife enhancement shall not exceed the lesser of the benefits from those functions or the costs of providing recreation or fish and wildlife enhancement benefits of reasonably equivalent use and location by the least costly alternative means; and

(3) not more than one-half the separable costs and all the joint costs of the project allocated to recreation and fish and wildlife enhancement shall be borne by the United States and be non-reimbursable.

Projects authorized during the calendar year 1965 may include recreation and fish and wildlife enhancement on the foregoing basis without the required indication of intent. Execution of an agreement as aforesaid shall be a prerequisite to commencement of construction of any project to which this subsection is applicable.

(b) The non-Federal share of the separable costs of the project allocated to recreation and fish and wildlife enhancement shall be borne by non-Federal interests, under either or both of the following methods as may be determined appropriate by the head of the Federal agency having jurisdiction over the project: (1) payment, or provision of lands, interests therein, or facilities for the project; or (2) repayment, with interest at a rate comparable to that for other interest-bearing functions of Federal water resource projects, within fifty years of first use of project recreation or fish and wildlife enhancement facilities: *Provided,* That the source of repayment may be limited to entrance and user fees or charges collected at the project by non-Federal interests if the fee schedule and the portion of fees dedicated to repayment are established on a basis calculated to achieve repayment as aforesaid and are made subject to review and renegotiation at intervals of not more than five years.

SEC. 3. (a) No facilities or project modifications which will furnish recreation or fish and wildlife enhancement benefits shall be provided in the absence of the indication of intent with respect thereto specified in subsection 2(a) of this Act unless (1) such facilities or modifications serve other project purposes and are justified thereby without regard to such incidental recreation or fish and wildlife enhancement benefits as they may have or (2) they are minimum facilities which are required for the public health and safety and are located at access points provided by roads existing at the time of project construction or constructed for the administration and management of the project. Calculation of the recreation and fish and wildlife enhancement benefits in any such case shall be based on the number of visitor-days anticipated in the absence of recreation and fish and wildlife enhancement facilities or modifications except as hereinbefore provided and on the value per visitor-day of the project without such facilities or modifications. Project costs allocated to recreation and fish and wildlife enhancement on this basis shall be nonreimbursable.

(b) Notwithstanding the absence of an indication of intent as specified in subsection 2(a), lands may be provided in connection with project construction to preserve the recreation and fish and wildlife enhancement potential of the project:

(1) If non-Federal public bodies execute an agreement within ten years after initial operation of the project (which agreement shall provide that the non-Federal public bodies will administer project land and water areas for recreation or fish and wildlife enhancement or both pursuant to the plan for the development of the project approved by the head of the agency having administrative jurisdiction over it and will bear not less than one-half the costs of lands, facilities, and project modifications provided for either or both or those purposes, as the case may be, and all costs of operation, maintenance, and replacement attributable thereto) the remainder of the costs of lands, facilities, and project modifications provided pursuant to this paragraph shall be nonreimbursable. Such agreement and subsequent development, however, shall not be the basis for any reallocation of joint costs of the project to recreation or fish and wildlife enhancement.

(2) If, within ten years after initial operation of the project, there is not an executed agreement as specified in paragraph (1) of this subsection, the head of the agency having jurisdiction over the project may utilize the lands for any lawful purpose within the jurisdiction of his agency, or may offer the land for sale to its immediate prior owner or his immediate heirs at its appraised fair market value as approved by the head of the agency at the time of offer or, if a firm agreement by said owner or his immediate heirs is not executed within ninety days of the date of the offer, may transfer custody of the lands to another Federal agency for use for any lawful purpose within the jurisdiction of that agency, or may lease the lands to a non-Federal public body, or may transfer the lands to the Administrator of General Services for disposition in accordance with the surplus property laws of the United States. In no case shall the lands be used or made available for use for any purpose in conflict with the purposes for which the project was constructed, and in every case except that of an offer to purchase made, as hereinbefore provided, by the prior owner or his heirs preference shall be given to uses which will preserve and promote the recreation and fish and wildlife enhancement potential of the project or, in the absence thereof, will not detract from that potential.

Sec. 4. At projects, the construction of which has commenced or been completed as of the effective date of this Act, where non-Federal public bodies agree to administer project land and water areas for recreation and fish and wildlife enhancement purposes and to bear the costs of operation, maintenance, and replacement of existing facilities serving those purposes, such facilities and appropriate project lands may be leased to non-Federal public bodies.

SEC. 5. Nothing herein shall be construed as preventing or discouraging post-authorization development of any project for recreation or fish and wildlife enhancement or both by non-Federal public bodies pursuant to agreement with the head of the Federal agency having jurisdiction over the project. Such development shall not be the basis for any allocation or reallocation of project costs to recreation or fish and wildlife enhancement.

SEC. 6. (a) The views of the Secretary of the Interior developed in accordance with section 3 of the Act of May 28, 1963 (77 Stat. 49), with respect to the outdoor recreation aspects shall be set forth in any report of any project or appropriate unit thereof within the purview of this Act. Such views shall include a report on the extent to which the proposed recreation and fish and wildlife development conforms to and is in accord with the State comprehensive plan developed pursuant to subsection 5(d) of the Land and Water Conservation Fund Act of 1965 (78 Stat. 897).

(b) The first proviso of subsection 2(d) of the Act of August 12, 1958 (72 Stat. 563; 16 U.S.C. 662(d), is amended to read as follows: "*Provided,* That such cost attributable to the development and improvement of wildlife shall not extend beyond that necessary for (1) land acquisition, (2) facilities as specifically recommended in water resource project reports, (3) modification of the project, and (4) modification of project operations, but shall not include the operation of wildlife facilities." The second proviso of subsection 2(d) of said Act is hereby repealed.

(c) Expenditures for lands or interests in lands hereafter acquired by project construction agencies for the establishment of migratory waterfowl refuges recommended by the Secretary of the Interior at Federal water resource projects, when such lands or interests in lands would not have been acquired but for the establishment of a migratory waterfowl refuge at the project, shall not exceed $28,000,000: *Provided,* That the aforementioned expenditure limitation in this subsection shall not apply to the costs of mitigating damages to migratory waterfowl caused by such water resource project.

(d) This Act shall not apply to the Tennessee Valley Authority, nor to projects constructed under authority of the Small Reclamation Projects Act, as amended, or under authority of the Watershed Protection and Flood Prevention Act, as amended.

(e) Sections 2, 3, 4 and 5 of this Act shall not apply to nonreservoir local flood control projects, beach erosion control projects, small boat harbor projects, hurricane protection projects, or to project areas or facilities authorized by law for inclusion within a national recreation area or appropriate for administration by a Federal agency as a part of the national forest system, as a part of the public lands classified for retention in Federal ownership, or in connection with an authorized Federal program for the conservation and development of fish and wild-life.

(f) As used in this Act, the term "nonreimbursable" shall not be construed to prohibit the imposition of entrance, admission, and other recreation user fees or charges.

(g) Subsection 6(a) (2) of the Land and Water Conservation Fund Act of 1965 (78 Stat. 897) shall not apply to costs allocated to recreation and fish and wild-life enhancement which are borne by the United States as a nonreimbursable project cost pursuant to subsection 2(a) or subsection 3(b) (1) of this Act.

(h) All payments and repayment by non-Federal public bodies under the provisions of this Act shall be deposited in the Treasury as miscellaneous receipts, and revenue from the conveyance by deed, lease, or otherwise, of lands under subsection 3(b) (2) of this Act shall be deposited in the Land and Water Conservation Fund.

SEC. 7. (a) The Secretary is authorized, in conjunction with any reservoir heretofore constructed by him pursuant to the Federal reclamation laws or any reservoir which is otherwise under his control, except reservoirs within national wildlife refuges, to investigate, plan, construct, operate and maintain, or otherwise provide for public outdoor recreation and fish and wildlife enhancement facilities, to acquire or otherwise make available such adjacent lands or interests therein as are necessary for public outdoor recreation or fish and wildlife use, and to provide for public use and enjoyment of project lands, facilities, and water areas in a manner coordinated with the other project purposes: *Provided,* That not more than $100,000 shall be available to carry out the provisions of this subsection at any one reservoir. Lands, facilities and project modifications for the purposes of this subsection may be provided only after an agreement in accordance with subsection 3(b) of this Act has been executed.

(b) The Secretary of the Interior is authorized to enter into agreements with Federal agencies or State or local public bodies for the administration of project land and water areas and the operation, maintenance, and replacement of facilities and to transfer project lands or facilities of Federal agencies or State or local public bodies by lease agreement or exchange upon such terms and conditions as will best promote the development and operation of such lands or facilities in the public interest for recreation and fish and wildlife enhancement purposes.

(c) No lands under the jurisdiction of any other Federal agency may be included for or devoted to recreation or fish and wildlife purposes under the authority of this section without the consent of the head of such agency; and the head of any such agency is authorized to transfer any such lands to the jurisdiction of the Secretary of the Interior for purposes of this section. The Secretary of the Interior is authorized to transfer jurisdiction over project lands within or adjacent to the exterior boundaries of national forests and facilities thereon to the

Secretary of Agriculture for recreation and other national forest system purposes; and such transfer shall be made in each case in which the project reservoir area is located wholly within the exterior boundaries of a national forest unless the Secretaries of Agriculture and Interior jointly determine otherwise. Where any project lands are transferred hereunder to the jurisdiction of the Secretary of Agriculture, the lands involved shall become national forest lands: *Provided,* That the lands and waters within the flow lines of any reservoir or otherwise needed or used for the operation of the project for other purposes shall continue to be administered by the Secretary of the Interior to the extent he determines to be necessary for such operation. Nothing herein shall limit the authority of the Secretary of the Interior granted by existing provisions of law relating to recreation or fish and wildlife development in connection with water resource projects or to disposition of public lands for such purposes.

Sec. 8. Effective on and after July 1, 1966, neither the Secretary of the Interior nor any bureau nor any person acting under his authority shall engage in the preparation of any feasibility report under reclamation law with respect to any water resource project unless the preparation of such feasibility report has been specifically authorized by law, any other provision of law to the contrary notwithstanding.

Sec. 9. Nothing contained in this Act shall be taken to authorize or to sanction the construction under the Federal reclamation laws or under any Rivers and Harbors or Flood Control Act of any project in which the sum of the allocations to recreation and fish and wildlife enhancement exceeds the sum of the allocations to irrigation, hydro-electric power, municipal, domestic and industrial water supply, navigation, and flood control, except that this section shall not apply to any such project for the enhancement of anadromous fisheries, shrimp, or for the conservation of migratory birds protected by treaty, when each of the other functions of such a project has, of itself, a favorable benefit-cost ratio.

Sec. 10. As use in this Act:

(a) The term "project" shall mean a project or any appropriate unit thereof.

(b) The term "separable costs," as applied to any project purpose, means the difference between the capital cost of the entire multiple-purpose project and the capital cost of the project with the purpose omitted.

(c) The term "joint costs" means the difference between the capital cost of the entire multiple-purpose project and the sum of the separable costs for all project purposes.

(d) The term "feasibility report" shall mean any report of the scope required by the Congress when formally considering autorization of the project of which the report treats.

(e) The term "capital cost" includes interest during construction, wherever appropriate.

Sec. 11. Section 2, subsection (a) of the Land and Water Conservation Fund Act of 1965 (78 Stat. 897) is hereby amended by striking out the words "nothwithstanding any provision of law that such proceeds shall be credited to miscellaneous receipts of the Treasury," and inserting in lieu thereof the words "nothwithstanding any other provision of law:" and striking out the words "or any provision of law that provides that any fees or charges collected at particular Federal areas shall be used for or credited to specific purposes or special funds as authorized by that provision of law" and inserting in lieu thereof "or affect any contract heretofore entered into by the United States that provides that such revenues collected at particular Federal areas shall be credited to specific purposes".

SEC. 12. This Act may be cited as the "Federal Water Project Recreation Act".

Approved July 9, 1965.

WATER POLLUTION AND OUTDOOR RECREATION

> The river Rhine, it is well known,
> Doth wash your city of Cologne;
> But tell me, nymphs! what power divine
> Shall henceforth wash the river Rhine?*

Polluted waters are hazards to human health; more than that they impair the quality of outdoor recreation and drastically reduce it in quantity. Because of increasing water pollution outdoor recreation opportunities for Americans are being sharply curtailed each year, and are rapidly becoming an effluent, as well as an affluent, society. Roger Revelle once likened the earth to a space ship equipped with facilities for man's use but from which he is unable to discharge anything. We cannot "throw it over the side." We may be able to hide or dilute our used materials for a time but eventually we must either devise means to re-use them or live in the refuse we have created.

The major portion of outdoor recreation activities takes place in water or adjacent to it. Swimming, boating, water skiing, fishing and some forms of hunting require unpolluted waters. It is also likely that most picnicking and camping takes place near water, and even hikers, bird watchers, and trail riders are likely to prefer areas close to water. All of these water-oriented recreation activities require that pollution be minimized for safety and enjoyment.

The demand for outdoor recreation opportunities has risen dramatically since World War II, and a continuation of this rising demand is anticipated for the future. However the pollution of recreational waters has increased at an alarming rate, and therefore as the demand for water-based recreation has risen, the supply has diminished. According to former Fish and Wildlife Commissioner Arnie J. Suomela, "It is considered that the amount of fish and wildlife habitat rendered unproductive each year (through pollution) is greater than that created by public agencies in carrying out programs of fish and wildlife restoration."* Similar observations could be made with reference to swimming, boating, and other water-based recreation.

Not only is the demand for outdoor recreation outstripping the rate of population growth, pollution of water because of increased industrialization and new

*Samuel Taylor Coleridge, from "Expectoration the Second," *The Works of Samuel Taylor Coleridge* (Philadelphia: Crissy and Markley, 1852), 228.
*Senate Select Committee on National Water Resources, *Water Resources Activities in the United States,* Committee Print No. 18, 86th Cong., 2nd sess. (Washington, D.C.: Government Printing Office), 25.

technological processes is also growing at a faster rate than the population. If the increasing rate of per capita use of water is added to these trends, it becomes obvious that we are on the threshold of a water crisis in the United States.

Until recent years there was, in most areas of the country, sufficient "original water" so that the discharge of pollutants into rivers, lakes, and harbors did not create either a serious health hazard or a serious threat to recreational and other uses of water. Consequently, the science of waste treatment and disposal is still in its infancy—it has a long way to go to catch up with industrial technology. There are, therefore, serious technical problems in waste disposal which need to be solved. The effects of many new "exotic" industrial wastes on human and animal life are as yet unknown. Some pathogens and so-called "nutrient" wastes are not removed by the usual sewage disposal processes. In the words of Justus H. Fugate, Chairman of the Committee on Water Resources of the American Municipal Association, "The scientific borderline we have set up between sewage water and drinking water is a precarious one. We live on the edge of a human or mechanical failure in our water purification works that could bring pestilence upon us and the danger grows every year."

Lack of uniformity in state anti-pollution laws will continue to create problems since weak pollution control laws may constitute a competitive industrial advantage. Nevertheless a high degree of uniformity is essential because water pollution is not a local problem. The movement of surface and ground waters does not respect local or state boundaries. Furthermore the increased mobility of people and the increasingly wide and rapid distribution of goods disperse the hazards of local polluted waters throughout the nation. Those who maintain that water pollution is a local problem are living in a day that has long since passed.

As the demand for water increases, it will become increasingly necessary that more water be used more than once. Already, according to former Secretary of Health, Education, and Welfare Abraham Ribicoff, the total flow of the Ohio River is used 3.7 times before it enters the Mississippi.* As more water is used more times, more hazards to health and recreation will be created and more funds will need to be expended in treating wastes or in purification plants, or both. Within limits, the problem can be attacked at either end. That is, the emphasis may be concentrated on the treatment of wastes before they enter a body of water or the emphasis may be placed on the purification of water before it is used. Neither category can be altogether effective alone, but if the only consideration is potable water, these may be considered as alternative or interchangeable approaches to the problem.

The controversy over treatment at entrance versus treatment at destination ignores recreational uses of the water between the two points. Recreationists

*Remarks of Abraham Ribicoff, Secretary of Health, Education, and Welfare, Hearings on H.R. 4036 before the Committee on Public Works, U.S. House, 87th Cong., 1st sess., 323.

and wildlife interests recognize that America's vanishing water-based recreation resources can only be protected by minimizing pollution at its entrance to water. According to the President's Council on Recreation and Natural Beauty:

> The problem is particularly acute in the major rivers that flow through the hearts of metropolitan areas. Waterborne wastes destroy beauty and make water-related recreation undesirable or impossible. The Potomac, the Hudson, and the Mississippi illustrate the problem. The Potomac's most serious pollution is in precisely the reach of the river with greatest potential for enjoyment by the 2½ million residents of the Washington, D.C., Metropolitan area. As the Potomac slowly flows through the Nation's Capital, its load of silt, filth, and acid from farms, mills, and mines blends with discharge from overloaded sewers to nourish an algae bloom and a summer stink that rises from the river for miles below the metropolis. The Hudson, from Albany to Manhattan, is an open sewer. Scavenger eels, one of the few animals that can live in waters loaded each day with 200 million gallons of raw sewage and the effluent of dozens of factories, have been known to attack sanitary engineers taking water samples. The Mississippi, at St. Louis, is so polluted that test fish placed in a sample of river water diluted with 10 parts of clean water die in minutes.
>
> In the future an expanding population will require more industry and agriculture. Each will produce more waste and at the same time require more clean water. In addition to the problem of coping with the increasing volumes involved, cleaning up water is becoming more complicated.
>
> Today's wastes from homes, industry, and agriculture include new and complex chemical compounds which are more difficult to identify and treat; detergents are only one example. The rapid pace of urbanization at suburban fringes results in siltation of water caused by erosion from lands stripped of vegetative cover. Runoff from city streets carries increasing volumes of wastes that are difficult to handle in treatment plants. Following heavy rain or snow, municipal sewer systems that carry combined storm water and sewage deliver substantial amounts of many communities' sewage raw to the receiving stream, lake, bay, or ocean. Coastal oil pollution, such as from the tragic spill from the tanker Torrey Canyon which blighted the coast of England in 1967, is a newly recognized hazard.
>
> Thermal pollution, caused by discharge of water at high temperatures from powerplants, also is cause for increasing concern as the number of nuclear powerplants along ocean and river shorelines increase.
>
> Electric power generation has doubled every 10 years since 1945. The rate of increase continues to jump so that some analysts estimate that the doubling time for increase in demands may now be as short as five years. More moderate estimates give 10 years to double the power demands. Either are staggering increases.
>
> About 70 percent of the industrial thermal pollution load in the United States today is caused by the steam electric power industry. Powerplants are now discharging into United States waterways 50 trillion gallons of heated water a year, in some cases with devastating effects on the environment and aquatic life.
>
> By 1980, the power industry will use one-fifth of the total fresh water runoff of the United States for cooling and is predicted to spew forth 100 trillion gallons of heated discharge.*

*The President's Council on Recreation and Natural Beauty, *From Sea to Shining Sea* (Washington, D.C.: Government Printing Office, 1968), 94–96.

GEORGE P. MARSH ON THE DANGERS OF WATER POLLUTION*
1885

While the dangers of water pollution have only lately received much public attention, there have been intermittent warnings of possible catastrophe for many years. Almost a century ago, George P. Marsh noted that:

Man has hitherto hardly anywhere produced such climatic or other changes as would suffice of themselves totally to banish the wild inhabitants of the dry land, and the disappearance of the native birds and quadrupeds from particular localities is to be ascribed quite as much to his direct persecutions as to the want of forest shelter, of appropriate food, or of other conditions indispensable to their existence. But almost all the processes of agriculture, and of mechanical and chemical industry, are fatally destructive to aquatic animals within reach of their influence. When in consequence of clearing the woods, the changes already described as thereby produced in the beds and currents of rivers, are in progress, the spawning grounds of fish are exposed from year to year to a succession of mechanical disturbances; the temperature of the water is higher in summer, colder in winter, than when it was shaded and protected by wood; the smaller organisms, which formed the sustenance of the young fry, disappear or are reduced in numbers, and new enemies are added to the old foes that preyed upon them; the increased turbidness of the water in the annual inundations chokes the fish; and, finally, the quickened velocity of its current sweeps them down into the larger rivers or into the sea, before they are yet strong enough to support so great a change of circumstances. Industrial operations are not less destructive to fish which live or spawn in fresh water. Milldams impede their migrations, if they do not absolutely prevent them, the sawdust from lumber mills clogs their gills, and the thousand deleterious mineral substances, discharged into rivers from metallurgical, chemical, and manufacturing establishments, poison them by shoals.

*George P. Marsh, *The Earth as Modified by Human Action* (New York: Charles Scribner's Sons, 1885), 106–07.

REPORT OF THE NATIONAL CONSERVATION COMMISSION*
1909

As long ago as 1909 the National Conservation Commission pointed out the need for research on the effects of pollutants on fishes in this brief statement:

The pollution of streams by sawdust, industrial wastes, and the discharge of water from mills, most of which abuses are preventable, has received some attention at the hands of this bureau, but should be the subject of further inquiry. That these pollutions do considerable injury to some of our minor fisheries is certain, and together with the results of deforestation they have ruined many streams formerly teeming with the best of our game fishes.

*Hugh M. Smith, "Fisheries of the United States," *Report of the National Conservation Commission,* Vol. III, Sen. Doc. 676, 60th Cong., 2nd sess. (Feb. 1909), 386.

THE OIL POLLUTION ACT*
June 7, 1924

As Americans became increasingly concerned with the dangers of water pollution Congress responded with a series of acts that have done much to lessen the amount of pollution. The Oil Pollution Act of 1924 was one of the first of these congressional attempts at pollution control.

An Act to protect navigation from obstruction and injury by preventing the discharge of oil into the coastal navigable waters of the United States.

Be it enacted by the Senate and House of Representatives of the United States of America in Congress assembled, That this Act may be cited as the "Oil Pollution Act, 1924."

SEC. 2. When used in this Act, unless the context otherwise requires—

(a) The term "oil" means oil of any kind or in any form, including fuel oil, oil sludge, and oil refuse;

(b) The term "person" means an individual, partnership, corporation, or association; any owner, master, officer or employee of a vessel; and any officer, agent, or employee of the United States;

(c) The term "coastal navigable waters of the United States" means all portions of the sea within the territorial jurisdiction of the United States, and all inland waters navigable in fact in which the tide ebbs and flows;

(d) The term "Secretary" means the Secretary of War.

SEC. 3. That, except in case of emergency imperiling life or property, or unavoidable accident, collision, or stranding, and except as otherwise permitted by regulations prescribed by the Secretary as herinafter authorized, it shall be unlawful for any person to discharge, or suffer, or permit the discharge of oil by any method, means, or manner into or upon the coastal navigable waters of the United States from any vessel using oil as fuel for the generation of propulsion power, or any vessel carrying or having oil theron in excess of that necessary for its lubricating requirements and such as may be required under the laws of the United States and the rules and regulations prescribed thereunder. The Secretary is authorized and empowered to prescribe regulations permitting the discharge of oil from vessels in such quantities, under such conditions, and at such times and places as in his opinion will not be deleterious to health or sea food, or a menace to navigation, or dangerous to persons or property engaged in commerce on such waters, and for the loading, handling, and unloading of oil.

SEC. 4. That any person who violates section 3 of this Act, or any regulation

*43 *Statutes at Large,* 604.

prescribed in pursuance therof, is guilty of a misdemeanor, and upon conviction shall be punished by a fine not exceeding $2,500 nor less than $500, or by imprisonment not exceeding one year nor less than thirty days, or by both such fine and imprisonment, for each offense. And any vessel (other than a vessel owned and operated by the United States) from which oil is discharged in violation of section 3 of this Act, or any regulation prescribed in pursuance therof, shall be liable for the pecuniary penalty specified in this section, and clearance of such vessel from a port of the United States may be withheld until the penalty is paid, and said penalty shall constitute a lien on such vessel which may be recovered in proceedings by libel in rem in the district court of the United States for any district within which the vessel may be.

SEC. 5. A board of local inspectors of vessels may, subject to the provisions of section 4450 of the Revised Statutes, and of the Act entitled "An Act to provide for appeals from decisions of local inspectors of vessels, and for other purposes," approved June 10, 1918, suspend or revoke a license issued by any such board to the master or other licensed officer of any vessel found violating the provisions of section 3 of this Act.

SEC. 6. That no penalty, or the withholding of clearance, or the suspension or revocation of licenses, provided for herein, shall be enforced for any violation of this Act occurring within three months after its passage.

SEC. 7. That in the administration of this Act the Secretary may make use of the organization, equipment, and agencies, including engineering, clerical, and other personnel, employed under his direction in the improvement of rivers and harbors, and in the enforcement of existing laws for the preservation and protection of navigable waters. And for the better enforcement of the provisions of this Act, the officers and agents of the United States in charge of river and harbor improvements, and the assistant engineers and inspectors employed under them by authority of the Secretary, and officers of the Customs and Coast Guard Service of the United States, shall have power and authority and it shall be their duty to swear out process and to arrest and take into custody, with or without process, any person who may violate any of said provisions: *Provided,* That no person shall be arrested without process for a violation not committed in the presence of some one of the aforesaid officials: *And provided further,* That whenever any arrest is made under the provisions of this Act the person so arrested shall be brought forthwith before a commissioner, judge, or court of the United States for examination of the offenses alleged against him; and such commissioner, judge, or court shall proceed in respect thereto as authorized by law in cases of crimes against the United States.

SEC. 8. That this Act shall be in addition to the existing laws for the preservation and protection of navigable waters and shall not be construed as repealing, modifying, or in any manner affecting the provisions of those laws.

SEC. 9. That the Secretary is authorized and directed to make such investigation as may be necessary to ascertain what polluting substances are being deposited into the navigable waters of the United States, or into nonnavigable waters connecting with navigable waters, to such an extent as to endanger or interfere with navigation or commerce upon such navigable waters or the fisheries therein; and with a view to ascertaining the sources of such pollutions and by what means they are deposited; and the Secretary shall report the results of his investigation to the Congress not later than two years after the passage of this Act, together with such recommendations for remedial legislation as he deems advisable: *Provided,* That funds appropriated for examinations, surveys, and contingencies of rivers and harbors may be applied to paying the cost of this investigation, and, to adequately provide therefor, the additional sum of not to exceed $50,000 is hereby authorized to be appropriated for examinations, surveys, and contingencies of rivers and harbors.

Approved, June 7, 1924.

THE WATER POLLUTION CONTROL ACT*
June 30, 1948

The Water Pollution Control Act was the first comprehensive attempt at water pollution control. The stated objectives of the act were "to conserve such waters for public water supplies, propagation of fish and aquatic life, recreational purposes, and agricultural, industrial, and other legitimate uses." The act follows.

An Act to provide for water pollution control activities in the Public Health Service of the Federal Security Agency and in the Federal Works Agency, and for other purposes.

Be it enacted by the Senate and House of Representatives of the United States of America in Congress assembled, That in connection with the exercise of jurisdiction over the waterways of the Nation and in consequence of the benefits resulting to the public health and welfare by the abatement of stream pollution, it is hereby declared to be the policy of Congress to recognize, preserve, and protect the primary responsibilities and rights of the States in controlling water pollution, to support and aid technical research to devise and perfect methods of treatment of industrial wastes which are not susceptible to known effective methods of treatment, and to provide Federal technical services to State and interstate agencies and to industries, and financial aid to State and interstate waters and tributaries thereof and improving the sanitary condition of their stream pollution abatement programs. To this end, the Surgeon General of the Public Health Service (under the supervision and direction of the Federal Security Administrator) and the Federal Works Administrator shall have the responsibilities and authority relating to water pollution control vested in them respectively by this Act.

SEC. 2. (a) The Surgeon General shall, after careful investigation, and in cooperation with other Federal agencies, with State water pollution agencies and interstate waters and tributaries thereof and improving the sanitary condition of or adopt comprehensive programs for eliminating or reducing the pollution of interstate waters and tributaries thereof and improving the sanitary condition of surface and underground waters. In the development of such comprehensive programs due regard shall be given to the improvements which are necessary to conserve such waters for public water supplies, propagation of fish and aquatic life, recreational purposes, and agricultural, industrial, and other legitimate uses. For the purpose of this subsection the Surgeon General is authorized to make joint investigations with any such agencies of the condition of any

*62 *Statutes at Large,* 1155.

waters in any State or States, and of the discharges of any sewage, industrial wastes, or substance which may deleteriously affect such waters.

(b) The Surgeon General shall encourage cooperative activities by the States for the prevention and abatement of water pollution; encourage the enactment of uniform State laws relating to water pollution; encourage compacts between States for the prevention and abatement of water pollution; collect and disseminate information relating to water pollution and the prevention and abatement thereof; support and aid technical research to devise and perfect methods of treatment of industrial wastes which are not susceptible to known effective methods of treatment; make available to State and interstate agencies, municipalities, industries, and individuals the results of surveys, studies, investigations, research, and experiments relating to water pollution and the prevention and abatement thereof conducted by the Surgeon General and by authorized cooperating agencies; and furnish such assistance to State agencies as may be authorized by law.

(c) The consent of the Congress is hereby given to two or more States to negotiate and enter into agreements or compacts, not in conflict with any law or treaty of the United States, for (1) cooperative effort and mutual assistance for the prevention and abatement of water pollution and the enforcement of their respective laws relating thereto, and (2) the establishment of such agencies, joint or otherwise, as they may deem desirable for making effective such agreements and compacts. No such agreement or compact shall be binding or obligatory upon any State a party therto unless and until it has been approved by the Congress.

(d) (1) The pollution of interstate waters in or adjacent to any State or States (whether the matter causing or contributing to such pollution is discharged directly into such waters or reaches such waters after discharge into a tributary of such waters), which endangers the health or welfare of persons in a State other than that in which the discharge originates, is hereby declared to be a public nuisance and subject to abatement as herein provided.

(2) Whenever the Surgeon General on the basis of reports, surveys, and studies, finds that any pollution declared to be a public nuisance by paragraph (1) of this subsection is occurring, he shall give formal notification thereof to the person or persons discharging any matter causing or contributing to such pollution and shall advise the water pollution agency or interstate agency of the State or States where such discharge or discharges originate of such notification. This notification may outline recommended remedial measures which are reasonable and equitable in that case and shall specify a reasonable time to secure abatement of the pollution. If action calculated to secure abatement of the pollution within the time specified is not commenced, this failure shall again be brought to the attention of the person or persons discharging the matter and of the water pollution agency or interstate agency of the State or States where such discharge

or discharges originate. The notification to such agency may be accompanied by a recommendation that it initiate a suit to abate the pollution in a court of proper jurisdiction.

(3) If, within a reasonable time after the second notification by the Surgeon General, the person or persons discharging the matter fail to initiate action to abate the pollution or the State water pollution agency or interstate agency fails to initiate a suit to secure abatement, the Federal Security Administrator is authorized to call a public hearing, to be held in or near one or more of the places where the discharge or discharges causing or contributing to such pollution originate, before a board of five or more persons appointed by the Administrator, who may be officers or employees of the Federal Security Agency or of the water pollution agency or interstate agency of the State or States where such discharge or discharges originate (except that at least one of the members of the board shall be a representative of the water pollution agency of the State or States where such discharge or discharges originate and at least one shall be a representative of the Department of Commerce, and not less than a majority of the board shall be persons other than officers or employees of the Federal Security Agency). On the basis of the evidence presented at such hearing the board shall make its recommendations to the Federal Security Administrator concerning the measures, if any, which it finds to be reasonable and equitable to secure abatement of such pollution.

(4) After affording the person or persons discharging the matter causing or contributing to the pollution reasonable opportunity to comply with the recommendations of the board, the Federal Security Adminsitrator may, with the consent of the water pollution agency (or of any officer or agency authorized to give such consent) of the State or States in which the matter causing or contributing to the pollution is discharged, request the Attorney General to bring a suit on behalf of the United States to secure abatement of the pollution.

(5) Before or after any suit authorized by paragraph (4) is commenced, any person who is alleged to be discharging matter contributing to the pollution, abatement of which is sought, may, with the consent of the water pollution agency (or of any officer or agency authorized to give such consent) of the State in which such matter is discharged, be joined as a defendant. The court shall have power to enforce its judgment against any such defendant.

(6) In any suit brought pursuant to paragraph (4) in which two or more persons in different judicial districts are originally joined as defendants, the suit may be commenced in the judicial district in which any discharge caused by any of the defendants occurs.

(7) The court shall receive in evidence in any such suit a transcript of the proceedings before the board and a copy of the board's recommendation; and may receive such further evidence as the court in its discretion deems proper. The court, giving due consideration to the practicability and to the physical and

[471]

economic feasibility of securing abatement of any pollution proved, shall have jurisdiction to enter such judgment, and orders enforcing such judgment, as the public interest and the equities of the case may require. The jurisdiction of the Surgeon General, or any other agency which has jurisdiction pursuant to the provisions of this Act, shall not extend to any region or areas nor shall it affect the rights or jurisdiction of any public body where there are in effect provisions for sewage disposal pursuant to agreement between the United States of America and any such public body by stipulation entered in the Supreme Court of the United States. While any such stipulation or modification thereof is in force and effect, no proceedings of any kind may be maintained by virtue of this Act against such public body or any public agency, corporation, or individual within its jurisdiction. Neither this provision nor any provision of this Act shall be construed to give to the Surgeon General or any other person or agency the right to intervene in the said proceedings wherein such stipulation was entered.

(8) As used in this subsection the term "person" includes an individual, corporation, partnership, association, a State, municipality, and a political subdivision of a State.

SEC. 3. The Surgeon General may, upon request of any State water pollution agency or interstate agency, conduct investigations and research and make surveys concerning any specific problem of water pollution confronting any State, interstate agency, community, municipality, or industrial plant, with a view to recommending a solution of such problem.

SEC. 4. The Surgeon General shall prepare and publish, from time to time, reports of such surveys, studies, investigations, research, and experiments made under the authority of this Act as he may consider desirable, together with appropriate recommendations with regard to the control of water pollution.

SEC. 5. The Federal Works Administrator is authorized, subject to the provisions of section 9 (c), to make loans to any State, municipality, or interstate agency for the construction of necessary treatment works to prevent the discharge by such State or municipality of untreated or inadequately treated sewage or other waste into interstate waters or into a tributary of such waters, and for the preparation (either by its engineering staff or by practicing engineers employed for that purpose) of engineering reports, plans and specifications in connection therewith. Such loans shall be subject, however, to the following limitations: (a) No loan shall be made for any project unless such project shall have been approved by the appropriate State water pollution agency or agencies and by the Surgeon General, and unless such project is included in a comprehensive program developed pursuant to this Act; (b) no loan shall be made for any project in an amount exceeding 33⅓ per centum of the estimated reasonable cost thereof, as determined by the Federal Works Administrator, or in an amount exceeding $250,000, whichever amount is the smaller; (c) every such loan shall bear interest at the rate of 2 per centum per annum, payable semiannually, and (d) the bonds or other obligations evidencing any such loan (1) must be duly authorized and issued pursuant to State and local law, and (2) may, as to the security thereof and the payment of principal thereof and interest thereon, be subordinated (to the extent deemed feasible and desirable by the Federal Works Administrator for facilitating the financing of such projects) to other bonds or obligations of the obligor issued to finance such project or that may then be outstanding.

SEC. 6. (a) The Surgeon General and the Federal Works Administrator, in carrying out their respective functions under this Act, shall provide for the review of all reports of examinations, research, investigations, plans, studies, and surveys, made pursuant to the provisions of this Act and all applications for loans under section 5. In determining the desirability of projects for treatment works and of approving loans in connection therewith, consideration shall be given to the public benefits to be derived by the construction thereof, the propriety of Federal aid in such construction, the relation of the ultimate cost of constructing and maintaining the works to the public interest and to the public necessity for the works, and the adequacy of the provisions made or proposed by the applicant for the loan for assuring proper and efficient operation and maintenance of the works after completion of the construction thereof.

(b) There is hereby established in the Public Health Service a Water Pollution Control Advisory Board to be composed as follows: The Surgeon General or a sanitary engineer officer designated by him, who shall be Chairman of the Board, a representative of the Department of the Army, a representative of the Department of the Interior, a representative of the Federal Works Agency, and a representative of the Department of Agriculture, designated by the Secretary of the Army, the Secretary of the Interior, the Federal Works Administrator, and the Secretary of Agriculture, respectively; and six persons (not officers or employees of the Federal Government) to be appointed annually by the President. One of the persons appointed by the President shall be an engineer who is expert in sewage and industrial-waste disposal, one shall be a person who shall have shown an active interest in the field of wildlife conservation, and, except as the President may determine that the purposes of this Act will be better furthered by different representation, one shall be a person representative of municipal government, one shall be a person representative of State government, and one shall be a person representative of affected industry. The members of the Board who are not officers or employees of the United States shall be entitled to receive compensation at a per diem rate to be fixed by the Federal Security Administrator, together with an allowance for actual and necessary traveling and subsistence expenses while engaged on the business of the Board. It shall be the duty of the Board to review the policies and program of the Public Health Service as undertaken under authority of this Act and to make recommendations thereon in reports to the Surgeon General. Such clerical and technical assistance as may be necessary to discharge the duties of the Board shall be provided from the personnel of the Public Health Service.

SEC. 7. There is hereby authorized to be appropriated to the Federal Security Agency for each of the five fiscal years during the period beginning July 1, 1948, and ending June 30, 1953, a sum not to exceed the sum of $22,500,000 for the purpose of making loans under section 5 of this Act. Sums so appropriated shall remain available until expended.

SEC. 8. (a) There is hereby authorized to be appropriated to the Federal Security Agency for each of the five fiscal years during the period beginning July 1, 1948, and ending June 30, 1953, the sum of $1,000,000, to be allotted equitably and paid to the States for expenditure by or under the direction of their respective State water pollution agencies, and to interstate agencies for expenditure by them, for the conduct of investigations, research, surveys, and studies related to the prevention and control of water pollution caused by industrial wastes. Sums appropriated pursuant to this subsection shall remain available until expended, shall be allotted by the Surgeon General in accordance with regulations prescribed by the Federal Security Administrator, and shall be paid prior to audit or settlement by the General Accounting Office.

(b) There is hereby authorized to be appropriated to the Federal Works Agency for each of the five fiscal years during the period beginning July 1, 1948, and ending June 30, 1953, a sum not to exceed $800,000 to enable the Federal Works Administrator to erect and to furnish and to equip such buildings and facilities at Cincinnati, Ohio, as may be necessary for the use of the Public Health Service in connection with the research and study of water pollution and the training of personnel in work related to the control of water pollution. The amount authorized for this purpose shall include the cost of preparation of drawings and specifications, supervison of construction and other administrative expenses incident to the work: *Provided,* That the Federal Works Agency shall prepare the plans and specifications, make all necessary contracts and supervise construction. Sums appropriated pursuant to this authorization shall remain available until expended.

(c) There is hereby authorized to be appropriated to the Federal Works Agency for each of the five fiscal years during the period beginning July 1, 1948, and ending June 30, 1953, a sum not to exceed the sum of $1,000,000 to enable the Federal Works Administrator to make grants to States, municipalities, or interstate agencies to aid in financing the cost of engineering, architectural, and economic investigations and studies, surveys, designs, plans, working drawings, specifications, procedures, and other action preliminary to the construction of projects approved by the appropriate State water pollution agency or agencies and by the Surgeon General. Grants made under this subsection with respect to any project shall not exceed whichever of the following amounts is the smaller:

(1) $20,000, or (2) 33⅓ per centum of the estimated reasonable cost (as determined by the Federal Works Administrator) of the action preliminary to the construction of such project. Sums appropriated pursuant to this subsection shall remain available until expended.

(d) There is hereby authorized to be appropriated to the Federal Security Agency for each of the five fiscal years during the period beginning July 1, 1948, and ending June 30, 1953, such sum (not to exceed the sum of $2,000,000) as may be necessary to enable it to carry out its functions under this Act.

(e) There is hereby authorized to be appropriated to the Federal Works Agency for each of the five fiscal years during the period beginning July 1, 1948, and ending June 30, 1953, such sum (not to exceed the sum of $500,000) as may be necessary to enable it to carry out its functions under this Act.

SEC. 9. (a) Five officers may be appointed to grades in the Regular Corps of the Public Health Service above that of senior assistant, but not to a grade above that of director, to assist in carrying out the purposes of this Act. Officers appointed pursuant to this subsection in any fiscal year shall not be counted as part of the 10 per centum of the original appointments authorized to be made in such year under section 207 (b) of the Public Health Service Act; but they shall for all other purposes be treated as though appointed pursuant to such section 207 (b).

(b) The Federal Security Administrator, with the consent of the head of any other agency of the Federal Government, may utilize such officers and employees of such agency as may be found necessary to assist in carrying out the purposes of this Act.

(c) (1) Upon written request of the Federal Works Administrator, from time to time submitted to the Federal Security Administrator, specifying (a) particular projects approved by the Surgeon General, (b) the total estimated costs of such projects, and (c) the total sum requested for loans which the Federal Works Administrator proposes to make for such projects, the Federal Security Administrator shall transfer such total sum (within the amount appropriated therefor) to the Federal Works Administrator for the making of loans for such projects pursuant to section 5 hereof. In making such loans, the Federal Works Administrator shall adhere to the order or sequence of priority for projects established by the Surgeon General and shall take such measures as, in his judgment, will assure that the engineering plans and specifications, the details of construction, and the completed treatment works conform to the project as approved by the Surgeon General; and the Federal Works Administrator shall furnish written reports to the Federal Security Administrator on the progress of the work.

(2) The Federal Works Administrator is hereby authorized (a) to hold, administer, exchange, refund, or sell at public or private sale any bonds or other obligations evidencing loans made under this Act; and (b) to collect, or provide

[475]

for the collection of, interest on and principal of such bonds or other obligations. All moneys received as proceeds from such sales, and all moneys so collected, shall be covered into the Treasury as miscellaneous receipts.

(d) The Surgeon General and the Federal Works Administrator are each authorized to prescribe such regulations as are necessary to carry out their respective functions under this Act.

SEC. 10. When used in this Act—

(a) The term "State water pollution agency" means the State health authority, except that, in the case of any State in which there is a single State agency, other than the State health authority, charged with responsibility for enforcing State laws relating to the abatement of water pollution, it means such other State agency;

(b) The term "interstate agency" means an agency of two or more States having powers or duties pertaining to the abatement of pollution of waters;

(c) The term "treatment works" means the various devices used in the treatment of sewage or industrial waste of a liquid nature, including the necessary intercepting sewers, outfall sewers, pumping, power, and other equipment, and their appurtenances, and includes any extensions, improvements, remodeling, additions, and alterations thereof;

(d) The term "State" means a State, the District of Columbia, Hawaii, Alaska, Puerto Rico, or the Virgin Islands;

(e) The term "interstate waters" means all rivers, lakes, and other waters that flow across, or form a part of, State boundaries; and

(f) The term "municipality" means a city, town, district, or other public body created by or pursuant to State law and having jurisdiction over disposal of sewage, industrial wastes, or other wastes.

SEC. 11. This Act shall not be construed as (1) superseding or limiting the functions, under any other law, of the Surgeon General or of the Public Health Service, or of any other officer or agency of the United States, relating to water pollution, or (2) affecting or impairing the provisions of the Oil Pollution Act, 1924, or sections 13 through 17 of the Act entitled "An Act making appropriations for the construction, repair, and preservation of certain public works on rivers and harbors and for other purposes", approved March 3, 1899, as amended, or (3) affecting or impairing the provisions of any treaty of the United States.

SEC. 12. If any provision of this Act, or the application of any provision of this Act to any person or circumstance, is held invalid, the application of such provision to other persons or circumstances, and the remainder of this Act, shall not be affected thereby.

SEC. 13. This Act may be cited as the "Water Pollution Control Act".

Approved June 30, 1948.

THE FEDERAL WATER POLLUTION CONTROL ACT*
June 9, 1956

This act amended and replaced the Water Pollution Control Act of 1948 with the stated objective: "To extend and strengthen the Water Pollution Control Act." Perhaps of greatest importance for outdoor recreation was the statement in Section 2, "In the development of such comprehensive programs due regard shall be given to the improvements which are necessary to conserve such waters for public water supplies, propagation of fish and aquatic life and wildlife, recreational purposes, and agricultural, industrial, and other legitimate uses."

Be it enacted by the Senate and House of Represenatives of the United States of America in Congress assembled, That the Water Pollution Control Act (33 U.S.C. 466–466j) is hereby amended to read as follows:

"DECLARATION OF POLICY

"SECTION 1. (a) In connection with the exercise of jurisdiction over the waterways of the Nation and in consequence of the benefits resulting to the public health and welfare by the prevention and control of water pollution, it is hereby declared to be the policy of Congress to recognize, preserve, and protect the primary responsibilities and rights of the States in preventing and controlling water pollution, to support and aid technical research relating to the prevention and control of water pollution, and to provide Federal technical services and financial aid to State and interstate agencies and to municipalities in connection with the prevention and control of water pollution. To this end, the Surgeon General of the Public Health Service shall administer this Act through the Public Health Service and under the supervision and direction of the Secretary of Health, Education, and Welfare.

"(b) Nothing in this Act shall be construed as impairing or in any manner affecting any right or jurisdiction of the States with respect to the waters (including boundary waters) of such States.

"COMPREHENSIVE PROGRAMS FOR WATER POLLUTION CONTROL

"SEC. 2. The Surgeon General shall, after careful investigation, and in cooperation with other Federal agencies, with State water pollution control agencies and interstate agencies, and with the municipalities and industries involved, prepare or develop comprehensive programs for eliminating or reducing the pollution of interstate waters and tributaries thereof and improving the sanitary condition of surface and underground waters. In the development of such comprehensive programs due regard shall be given to the improvements

*70 *Statutes at Large,* 498.

which are necessary to conserve such waters for public water supplies, propagation of fish and aquatic life and wildlife, recreational purposes, and agricultural, industrial, and other legitimate uses. For the purpose of this section, the Surgeon General is authorized to make joint investigations with any such agencies of the condition of any waters in any State or States, and of the discharges of any sewage, industrial wastes, or substance which may adversely affect such waters.

"INTERSTATE COOPERATION AND UNIFORM LAWS

"SEC. 3. (a) The Surgeon General shall encourage cooperative activites by the States for the prevention and control of water pollution; encourage the enactment of improved and, so far as practicable, uniform State laws relating to the prevention and control of water pollution; and encourage compacts between States for the prevention and control of water pollution.

"(b) The consent of the Congress is hereby given to two or more States to negotiate and enter into agreements or compacts, not in conflict with any law or treaty of the United States, for (1) cooperative effort and mutual assistance for the prevention and control of water pollution and the enforcement of their respective laws relating thereto, and (2) the establishment of such agencies, joint or otherwise, as they may deem desirable for making effective such agreements and compacts. No such agreement or compact shall be binding or obligatory upon any State a party thereto unless and until it has been approved by the Congress.

"RESEARCH, INVESTIGATIONS, TRAINING, AND INFORMATION

"SEC. 4. (a) The Surgeon General shall conduct in the Public Health Service and encourage, cooperate with, and render assistance to other appropriate public (whether Federal, State, interstate, or local) authorities, agencies, and institutions, private agencies and institutions, and individuals in the conduct of, and promote the coordination of, research, investigations, experiments, demonstrations, and studies relating to the causes, control, and prevention of water pollution. In carrying out the foregoing, the Surgeon General is authorized to—

"(1) collect and make available, through publications and other appropriate means, the results of and other information as to research, investigations, and demonstrations relating to the prevention and control of water pollution, including appropriate recommendations in connection therewith;

"(2) make grants-in-aid to public or private agencies and institutions and to individuals for research or training projects and for demonstrations, and provide for the conduct of research, training, and demonstrations by contract with public or private agencies and institutions and with individuals without regard to sections 3648 and 3709 of the Revised Statutes;

"(3) secure, from time to time and for such periods as he deems advisable, the assistance and advice of experts, scholars, and consultants as authorized by section 15 of the Administrative Expenses Act of 1946 (5 U.S.C. 55a);

"(4) establish and maintain research fellowships in the Public Health Service with such stipends and allowances, including traveling and subsistence expenses, as he may deem necessary to procure the assistance of the most promising research fellowhips: *Provided,* That the total sum authorized to be appropriated for any fiscal year for fellowships pursuant to this subparagraph shall not exceed $100,000; and

"(5) provide training in technical matters relating to the causes, prevention, and control of water pollution to personnel of public agencies and other persons with suitable qualifications.

"(b) The Surgeon General may, upon request of any State water pollution control agency, or interstate agency, conduct investigations and research and make surveys concerning any specific problem of water pollution confronting any State, interstate agency, community, municipality, or industrial plant, with a view of recommending a solution of such problem.

"(c) The Surgeon General shall, in cooperation with other Federal, State, and local agencies having related responsibilities, collect and disseminate basic data on chemical, physical, and biological water quality and other information insofar as such data or other information relate to water pollution and the prevention and control thereof.

"GRANTS FOR WATER POLLUTION CONTROL PROGRAMS

"SEC. 5. (a) There are hereby authorized to be appropriated for the fiscal year ending June 30, 1957, and for each succeeding fiscal year to and including the fiscal year ending June 30, 1961, $3,000,000 for grants to States and to interstate agencies to assist them in meeting the costs of establishing and maintaining adequate measures for the prevention and control of water pollution.

"(b) The portion of the sums appropriated pursuant to subsection (a) for a fiscal year which shall be available for grants to interstate agencies and the portion thereof which shall be available for grants to States shall be specified in the Act appropriating such sums.

"(c) From the sums available therefor for any fiscal year the Surgeon General shall from time to time make allotments to the several States, in accordance with regulations, on the basis of (1) the population, (2) the extent of the water pollution problem, and (3) the financial need of the respective States.

"(d) From each State's allotment under subsection (c) for any fiscal year the Surgeon General shall pay to such State an amount equal to its Federal share (as determined under subsection (h)) of the cost of carrying out its State plan approved under subsection (f), including the cost of training personnel for State and local water pollution control work and including the cost of administering the State plan.

"(e) From the sums available therefor for any fiscal year the Surgeon General shall from time to time make allotments to interstate agencies, in accordance with regulations, on such basis as the Surgeon General finds reasonable and equitable. He shall from time to time pay to each such agency, from its allotment, an amount equal to such portion of the cost of carrying out its plan approved under subsection (f) as may be determined in accordance with regulations, including the cost of training personnel for water pollution control work and including the cost of administering the interstate agency's plan. The regulations relating to the portion of the cost of carrying out the interstate agency's plan which shall be borne by the United States shall be designed to place such agencies, so far as practicable, on a basis similar to that of the States.

"(f) The Surgeon General shall approve any plan for the prevention and control of water pollution which is submitted by the State water pollution control agency or, in the case of an interstate agency, by such agency, if such plan—

"(1) provides for administration or for the supervision of administration of the plan by the State water pollution control agency or, in the case of a plan submitted by an interstate agency, by such interstate agency;

"(2) provides that such agency will make such reports, in such form and containing such information, as the Surgeon General may from time to time reasonably require to carry out his functions under this Act;

"(3) sets forth the plans, policies, and methods to be followed in carrying out the State (or interstate) plan and in its administration;

"(4) provides for extension or improvement of the State or interstate program for prevention and control of water pollution; and

"(5) provides such accounting, budgeting, and other fiscal methods and procedures as are necessary for the proper and efficient administration of the plan.

The Surgeon General shall not disapprove any plan without first giving reasonable notice and opportunity for hearing to the State water pollution control agency or interstate agency which has submitted such plan.

"(g) (1) Whenever the Surgeon General, after reasonable notice and opportunity for hearing to a State water pollution control agency or interstate agency finds that—

"(A) the plan submitted by such agency and approved under this section has been so changed that it no longer complies with a requirement of subsection (f) of this section; or

"(B) in the administration of the plan there is a failure to comply substantially with such a requirement,

the Surgeon General shall notify such agency that no further payments will be made to the State or to the interstate agency, as the case may be, under this section (or in his discretion that further payments will not be made to the State, or to the interstate agency, for projects under or parts of the plan affected by such failure) until he is satisfied that there will no longer be any such failure. Until he is so satisfied, the Surgeon General shall make no further payments to such State, or to such interstate agency, as the case may be, under this section (or shall limit payments to projects under or parts of the plan in which there is no such failure).

"(2) If any State or any interstate agency is dissatisfied with the Surgeon General's action with respect to it under this subsection, it may appeal to the United States court of appeals for the circuit in which such State (or any of the member States, in the case of an interstate agency) is located. The summons and notice of appeal may be served at any place in the United States. The findings of fact by the Surgeon General, unless contrary to the weight of the evidence, shall be conclusive; but the court, for good cause shown, may remand the case to the Surgeon General to take further evidence, and the Surgeon General may thereupon make new or modified findings of fact and may modify his previous action. Such new or modified findings of fact shall likewise be conclusive unless contrary to the weight of the evidence. The court shall have jurisdiction to affirm the action of the Surgeon General or to set it aside, in whole or in part. The judgment of the court shall be subject to review by the Supreme Court of the United States upon certiorari or certification as provided in title 28, United States Code, section 1254.

"(h) (1) The 'Federal share' for any State shall be 100 per centum less that percentage which bears the same ratio to 50 per centum as the per capita income of such State bears to the per capita income of the continental United States (excluding Alaska), except that (A) the Federal share shall in no case be more than 66⅔ per centum or less than 33⅓ per centum, and (B) the Federal share for Hawaii and Alaska shall be 50 per centum, and for Puerto Rico and the Virgin Islands shall be 66⅔ per centum.

"(2) The 'Federal shares' shall be promulgated by the Surgeon General between July 1 and September 30 of each even-numbered year, on the basis of the average of the per capita incomes of the States and of the continental United States for the three most recent consecutive years for which satisfactory data are available from the Department of Commerce. Such promulgation shall be conclusive for each of the two fiscal years in the period beginning July 1 next succeeding such promulgation: *Provided,* That the Federal shares promulgated by the Surgeon General pursuant to section 4 of the Water Pollution Control Act Amendments of 1956, shall be conclusive for the period beginning July 1, 1956, and ending June 30, 1959.

"(i) The population of the several States shall be determined on the basis of the latest figures furnished by the Department of Commerce.

"(j) The method of computing and paying amounts pursuant to subsection (d) or (e) shall be as follows:

"(1) The Surgeon General shall, prior to the beginning of each calendar quarter or other period prescribed by him, estimate the amount to be paid to each State (or to each interstate agency in the case of subsection (e)) under the provisions of such subsection for such period, such estimate to be based on such records of the State (or the interstate agency) and information furnished by it, and such other investigation, as the Surgeon General may find necessary.

"(2) The Surgeon General shall pay to the State (or to the interstate agency), from the allotment available therefor, the amount so estimated by him for any period, reduced or increased, as the case may be, by any sum (not previously adjusted under this paragraph) by which he finds that his estimate of the amount to be paid such State (or such interstate agency) for any prior period under such subsection was greater or less than the amount which should have been paid to such State (or such agency) for such prior period under such subsection. Such payments shall be made through the disbursing facilities of the Treasury Department, in such installments as the Surgeon General may determine.

"GRANTS FOR CONSTRUCTION

"Sec. 6. (a) The Surgeon General is authorized to make grants to any State, municipality, or intermunicipal or interstate agency for the construction of necessary treatment works to prevent the discharge of untreated or inadequately treated sewage or other waste into any waters and for the purpose of reports, plans, and specifications in connection therewith.

"(b) Federal grants under this section shall be subject to the following limitations: (1) No grant shall be made for any project pursuant to this section unless such project shall have been approved by the appropriate State water pollution control agency or agencies and by the Surgeon General and unless such project is included in a comprehensive program developed pursuant to this Act; (2) no grant shall be made for any project in an amount exceeding 30 per centum of the estimated reasonable cost thereof as determined by the Surgeon General or in an amount exceeding $250,000, whichever is the smaller: *Provided,* That the grantee agrees to pay the remaining cost; (3) no grant shall be made for any project under this section until the applicant has made provision satisfactory to the Surgeon General for assuring proper and efficient operation and maintenance of the treatment works after completion of the construction thereof; and (4) no grant shall be made for any project under this section unless such project is in conformity with the State water pollution control plan submitted pursuant to the provisions of section 5 and has been certified by the State water pollution control agency as entitled to priority over other eligible projects on the basis of financial as well as water pollution control needs.

"(c) In determining the desirability of projects for treatment works and of approving Federal financial aid in connection therewith, consideration shall be given by the Surgeon General to the public benefits to be derived by the construction and the propriety of Federal aid in such construction, the relation of the ultimate cost of constructing and maintaining the works to the public interest and to the public necessity for the works, and the adequacy of the provisions made or proposed by the applicant for such Federal financial aid for assuring proper and efficient operation and maintenance of the treatment works after completion of the construction thereof. The sums appropriated pursuant to subsection (d) for any fiscal year shall be allotted by the Surgeon General from time to time, in accordance with regulations, as follows: (1) 50 per centum of such sums in the ratio that the population of each State bears to the population of all the States, and (2) 50 per centum of such sums in the ratio that the quotient obtained by dividing the per capita income of the United States by the per capita income of each State bears to the sum of such quotients for all the States. The allotment of a State under the preceding sentence shall be available, in accordance with the provisions of this section, for payments with respect to projects in such State which have been approved under this section. For purposes of this section, population shall be determined on the basis of the latest decennial census for which figures are available, as certified by the Secretary of Commerce, and per capita income for each State and for the United States shall be determined on the basis of the average of the per capita incomes of the States and of the continental United States for the three most recent consecutive years for which satisfactory data are available from the Department of Commerce.

"(d) There are hereby authorized to be appropriated for each fiscal year the sum of $50,000,000 for the purpose of making grants under this section: *Provided,* That the aggregate of sums so appropriated shall not exceed $500,000,000. Sums so appropriated shall remain available until expended: *Provided,* That at least 50 per centum of the funds so appropriated for each fiscal year shall be used for grants for the construction of treatment works servicing municipalities of one hundred and twenty-five thousand population or under.

"(e) The Surgeon General shall make payments under this section through the disbursing facilities of the Department of the Treasury. Funds so paid shall be used exclusively to meet the cost of construction of the project for which the amount was paid. As used in this section the term 'construction' includes preliminary planning to determine the economic and engineering feasibility of treatment works, the engineering, architectural, legal, fiscal, and economic investigations and studies, surveys, designs, plans, working drawings, specifications, procedures, and other action necessary to the construction of treatment works; and the erection, building, acquisition, alteration, remodeling, improvement, or extension of treatment works; and the inspection and supervision of the constuction of treatment works.

"WATER POLLUTION CONTROL ADVISORY BOARD

"SEC. 7. (a) (1) There is hereby established in the Public Health Service a

Water Pollution Control Advisory Board, composed of the Surgeon General or a sanitary engineer officer designated by him, who shall be chairman, and nine members appointed by the President none of whom shall be Federal officers or employees. The appointed members, having due regard for the purposes of this Act, shall be slected from among representatives of various State, interstate and local governmental agencies, of public or private interests contributing to, affected by, or concerned with water pollution, and of other public and private agencies, organizations, or groups demonstrating an active interest in the field of water pollution prevention and control, as well as other individuals who are expert in this field.

"(2) (A) Each member appointed by the President shall hold office for a term of three years, except that (i) any member appointed to fill a vacancy occurring prior to the expiration of the term for which his predecessor was appointed shall be appointed for the remainder of such term, and (ii) the terms of office of the members first taking office after June 30, 1956, shall expire as follows: three at the end of one year after such date, three at the end of two years after such date, and three at the end of three years after such date, as designated by the President at the time of appointment. None of the members appointed by the President shall be eligible for reappointment within one year after the end of his preceding term, but terms commencing prior to the enactment of the Water Pollution Control Act Amendments of 1956 shall not be deemed 'preceding terms' for purposes of this sentence.

"(B) The members of the Board who are not officers or employees of the United States, while attending conferences or meetings of the Board or while otherwise serving at the request of the Surgeon General, shall be entitled to receive compensation at a rate to be fixed by the Secretary of Health, Education, and Welfare, but not exceeding $50 per diem, including travel time, and while away from their homes or regular places of business they may be allowed travel expenses, including per diem in lieu of subsistence, as authorized by law (5 U.S.C. 73b-2) for persons in the Government service employed intermittently.

"(b) The Board shall advise, consult with, and make recommendations to the Surgeon General on matters of policy relating to the activities and functions of the Surgeon General under this Act.

"(c) Such clerical and technical assistance as may be necessary to discharge the duties of the Board shall be provided from the personnel of the Public Health Service.

"ENFORCEMENT MEASURES AGAINST POLLUTION OF INTERSTATE WATERS

"SEC. 8. (a) The pollution of interstate waters in or adjacent to any State or States (whether the matter causing or contributing to such pollution is discharged directly into such waters or reaches such waters after discharge into a tributary of such waters), which endangers the health or welfare of persons in a

State other than that in which the discharge originates, shall be subject to abatement as herein provided.

"(b) Consistent with the policy declaration of this Act, State and interstate action to abate pollution of interstate waters shall be encouraged and shall not, except as otherwise provided by or pursuant to court order under subsection (g), be displaced by Federal enforcement action.

"(c) (1) Whenever the Surgeon General, on the basis of reports, surveys, or studies, has reason to believe that any pollution referred to in subsection (a) is occurring, or whenever requested by a State water pollution control agency or the Governor of any State, he shall give formal notification of any such pollution to the State water pollution control agency and interstate agency, if any, of the State or States where the discharge or discharges causing or contributing to such pollution originates and shall call promptly a conference of the State water pollution control agencies and interstate agencies, if any, of the State or States where the discharge or discharges causing or contributing to such pollution originates and of the State or States claiming to be adversely affected by such pollution.

"(2) The agencies called to attend such conference may bring such persons as they desire to the conference. Not less than three weeks' prior notice of the conference date shall be given to such agencies.

"(3) Following this conference, the Surgeon General shall prepare and forward to all the water pollution control agencies attending the conference a summary of conference discussions including (A) occurrence of pollution of interstate waters subject to abatement under this Act; (B) adequacy of measures taken toward abatement of the pollution; and (C) nature of delays, if any, being encountered in abating the pollution.

"(d) If the Surgeon General believes, upon the conclusion of the conference or thereafter, that effective progress toward abatement of such pollution is not being made and that the health or welfare of persons in a State other than that in which the discharge originates is being endangered, he shall recommend to the appropriate State water pollution control agency that it take necessary remedial action. The Surgeon General is to allow at least six months for the taking of such action.

"(e) If such remedial action is not taken or action reasonably calculated to secure abatement of such pollution is not taken, the Secretary of Health, Education, and Welfare shall call a public hearing, to be held in or near one or more of the places where the discharge or discharges causing or contributing to such pollution originated, before a board of five or more persons appointed by the Secretary. Each State in which any discharge causing or contributing to such pollution originates and each State claiming to be adversely affected by such pollution shall be given an opportunity to select one member of the board and at least one member shall be a representative of the Department of Commerce, and not less than a majority of the board shall be persons other than officers or employees of the Department of Health, Education, and Welfare. At least three weeks' prior notice of said hearing shall be given to the State water pollution control agencies and interstate agencies, if any, called to attend the aforesaid hearing and the alleged polluter or polluters. On the basis of the evidence presented at such hearing, the board shall make findings as to whether pollution referred to in subsection (a) is occurring and whether effective progress toward abatement thereof is being made. If the board finds such pollution is occurring and effective progress toward abatement is not being made it shall make recommendations to the Secretary of Health, Education, and Welfare concerning the measures, if any, which it finds to be reasonable and equitable to secure abatement of such pollution. The Secretary shall send such findings and recommendations to the person or persons discharging any matter causing or contributing to such pollution, together with a notice specifying a reasonable time (not less than six months) to secure abatement of such pollution, and shall also send such findings and recommendations and such notice to the State water pollution control agency, and to the interstate agency, if any, of the State or States where such discharge or discharges originate.

"(f) If action reasonably calculated to secure abatement of the pollution within the time specified in the notice following the public hearing is not taken, the Secretary of Health, Education, and Welfare, with the written consent of the State water pollution control agency (or any officer or employee authorized to give such consent) of the State or States where the matter causing or contributing to the pollution is discharged or at the written request of the State water pollution control agency (or any officer or employee authorized to make such request) of any other State or States where the health or welfare of persons is endangered by such pollution, may request the Attorney General to bring a suit on behalf of the United States to secure abatement of the pollution.

"(g) The court shall receive in evidence in any such suit a transcript of the proceedings before the Board and a copy of the Board's recommendations and shall receive such further evidence as the court in its discretion deems proper. The court, giving due consideration to the practicability and to the physical and economic feasibility of securing abatement of any pollution proved, shall have jurisdiction to enter such judgment, and orders enforcing such judgment, as the public interest and the equities of the case may require.

"(h) As used in this section, the term 'person' includes an individual, corporation, partnership, association, State, municipality, and political subdivision of the State.

"COOPERATION TO CONTROL POLLUTION FROM FEDERAL INSTALLATIONS

"SEC. 9. It is hereby declared to be the intent of the Congress that any Federal department or agency having jurisdiction over any building, installation, or other property shall, insofar as practicable and consistent with the interests of the

United States and within any available appropriations, cooperate with the Department of Health, Education, and Welfare, and with any State or interstate agency or municipality having jurisdiction over waters into which any matter is discharged from such property, in preventing or controlling the pollution of such waters.

"ADMINISTRATION

"Sec. 10. (a) The Surgeon General is authorized to prescribe such regulations as are necessary to carry out his functions under this Act. All regulations of the Surgeon General under this Act shall be subject to the approval of the Secretary of Health, Education, and Welfare. The Surgeon General may delegate to any officer or employee of the Public Health Service such of his powers and duties under this Act, except the making of regulations, as he may deem necessary or expedient.

"(b) The Secretary of Health, Education, and Welfare, with the consent of the head of any other agency of the United States, may utilize such officers and employees of such agency as may be found necessary to assist in carrying out the purposes of this Act.

"(c) There are hereby authorized to be appropriated to the Department of Health, Education, and Welfare such sums as may be necessary to enable it to carry out its functions under this Act.

"DEFINITIONS

"Sec. 11. When used in this Act—

"(a) The term 'State water pollution control agency' means the State health authority, except that, in the case of any State in which there is a single State agency, other than the State health authority, charged with responsibility for enforcing State laws relating to the abatement of water pollution, it means such other State agency.

"(b) The term 'interstate agency' means an agency of two or more States established by or pursuant to an agreement or compact approved by the Congress, or any other agency of two or more States, having substantial powers or duties pertaining to the control of pollution of waters.

"(c) The term 'treatment works' means the various devices used in the treatment of sewage or industrial wastes of a liquid nature, including the necessary intercepting sewers, outfall sewers, pumping, power, and other equipment, and their appurtenances, and includes any extensions, improvements, remodeling, additions, and alterations thereof.

"(d) The term 'State' means a State, the District of Columbia, Hawaii, Alaska, Puerto Rico, or the Virgin Islands.

"(e) The term 'interstate waters' means all rivers, lakes, and other waters that flow across, or form a part of, boundaries between two or more States.

"(f) The term 'municipality' means a city, town, borough, county, parish, district, or other public body created by or pursuant to State law and having jurisdiction over disposal of sewage, industrial wastes, or other wastes.

"OTHER AUTHORITY NOT AFFECTED

"SEC. 12. This Act shall not be construed as (1) superseding or limiting the functions, under any other law, of the Surgeon General or of the Public Health Service, or of any other officer or agency of the United States, relating to water pollution, or (2) affecting or impairing the provisions of the Oil Pollution Act, 1924, or sections 13 through 17 of the Act entitled 'An Act making appropriations for the construction, repair, and preservation of certain public works on rivers and harbors and for other purposes', approved March 3, 1899, as amended, or (3) affecting or impairing the provisions of any treaty of the United States.

"SEPARABILITY

"SEC. 13. If any provision of this Act, or the application of any provision of this Act to any person or circumstance, is held invalid, the application of such provision to other persons or circumstances, and the remainder of this Act, shall not be affected thereby.

"SHORT TITLE

"SEC. 14. This Act may be cited as the 'Federal Water Pollution Control Act'."

SEC. 2. The title of such Act is amended to read "An Act to provide for water pollution control activities in the Public Health Service of the Department of Health, Education, and Welfare, and for other purposes."

SEC. 3. Terms of office as members of the Water Pollution Control Advisory Board (established pursuant to section 6 (b) of the Water Pollution Control Act, as in effect prior to the enactment of this Act) subsisting on the date of enactment of this Act shall expire at the close of business on such date.

SEC. 4. As soon as possible after the date of enactment of this Act the Surgeon General shall promulgate Federal shares in the manner provided in subsection (h) of section 5 of the Water Pollution Control Act, as amended by this Act (and without regard to the date specified therein for such promulgation), such Federal shares to be conclusive for the purposes of section 5 of such Act for the period beginning July 1, 1956, and ending June 30, 1959.

SEC. 5. In the case of any discharge or discharges causing or contributing to water pollution with respect to which the actions by the Surgeon General prescribed under paragraph (2) of section 2 (d) of the Water Pollution Control Act, as in effect prior to the enactment of this Act, have already been completed prior to such enactment, the provisions of such section shall continue to be applicable; except that nothing in this section shall prevent action with respect to any such pollution under and in accordance with the provisions of the Water Pollution Control Act, as amended by this Act.

SEC. 6. This Act may be cited as the "Water Pollution Control Act Amendments of 1956".

Approved July 9, 1956.

THE FEDERAL WATER POLLUTION
CONTROL ACT AMENDMENTS*
July 20, 1961

On February 23, 1961 President Kennedy sent a Special Message to Congress on Natural Resources, in which he noted:

> *Our Nation has been blessed with a bountiful supply of water; but it is not a blessing we can regard with complacency. We now use over 300 billion gallons of water a day, much of it wastefully. By 1980 we will need 600 billion gallons a day.*
>
> *Pollution of our country's rivers and streams has—as a result of our rapid population and industrial growth and change—reached alarming proportions. To meet all needs—domestic, agricultural, industrial, recreational—we shall have to use and re-use the same water, maintaining quality as well as quantity. In many areas of the country we need new sources of supply—but in all areas we must protect the supplies we have.†*

President Kennedy then went on to outline his recommendations for congressional action. Congress responded to these directives with the Amendments to the Federal Water Pollution Control Act of 1956, which raised research funds to $5 million per year; raised grant-in-aid funds to states from $3 to $5 million per year; and authorized an aggregate of $570 million for construction grants through June 30, 1967. The act strengthened and expanded federal authority in pollution abatement enforcement by extending federal jurisdiction from "interstate" waters to "interstate or navigable" waters, which included coastal waters. Recreation was retained as one of the objectives of pollution abatement.

By 1961, water pollution had become, in the words of Senator Frank E. Moss, "a galloping national disease which must be met on a massive basis if we are to control it." The act of 1961 was a massive attempt but it was too little and too late.

An Act to amend the Federal Water Pollution Control Act to provide for a more effective program of water pollution control, and for other purposes.

Be it enacted by the Senate and House of Representatives of the United States of America in Congress assembled, That (a) the last sentence of section 1(a) of the Federal Water Pollution Control Act (33 U.S.C. 466(a)) is amended to read as follows: "To this end, the Secretary of Health, Education, and Welfare (hereinafter in this Act called the 'Secretary') shall administer this Act."

*75 *Statutes at Large,* 204.
†*Public Papers of the Presidents of the United States: John F. Kennedy, 1961* (Washington, D.C.: Government Printing Office, 1962), 120.

(b) Sections 2, 3, 4, 5, 6, 7, and 8(c) (3), and the first sentence of section 10(a), of such Act are each amended by striking out "Surgeon General" and "Surgeon General's" wherever they appear therein and inserting in lieu thereof "Secretary" and "Secretary's", respectively.

(c) Sections 4(a) and 7(c) of such Act are each amended by striking out "Public Health Service" and inserting in lieu thereof "Department of Health, Education, and Welfare".

(d) Sections 7(a) (2) (B) and 10 (b) of such Act are each amended by striking out "Secretary of Health, Education, and Welfare" and inserting in lieu thereof "Secretary".

(e) Section 10(a) of such Act is amended by striking out the second and third sentences thereof.

SEC. 2. Section 2 of the Federal Water Pollution Control Act is amended by inserting "(a)" after "Sec. 2." and by inserting at the end of such section the following:

"(b) (1) In the survey or planning of any reservoir by the Corps of Engineers, Bureau of Reclamation, or other Federal agency, consideration shall be given to inclusion of storage for regulation of streamflow for the purpose of water quality control, except that any such storage and water releases shall not be provided as a substitute for adequate treatment or other methods of controlling waste at the source.

"(2) The need for and the value of storage for this purpose shall be determined by these agencies, with the advice of the Secretary, and his views on these matters shall be set forth in any report or presentation to the Congress proposing authorization or construction of any reservoir including such storage.

"(3) The value of such storage shall be taken into account in determining the economic value of the entire project of which it is a part, and costs shall be allocated to the purpose of water quality control in a manner which will insure that all purposes share equitably in the benefits of multiple-purpose construction.

"(4) Costs of water quality control features incorporated in any Federal reservoir or other impoundment under the provisions of this Act shall be determined and the beneficiaries identified and if the benefits are widespread or national in scope, the costs of such features shall be nonreimbursable."

SEC. 3. (a) The proviso in paragraph (4) of subsection (a) of section 4 of the Federal Water Pollution Control Act is amended to read as follows: "*Provided,* That the Secretary shall report annually to the appropriate committees of Congress on his operations under this paragraph;".

(b) Section 4 of such Act is further amended by inserting at the end thereof the following new subsections:

"(d) (1) In carrying out the provisions of this section the Secretary shall develop and demonstrate under varied conditions (including conducting such basic and applied research, studies, and experiments as may be necessary):

[491]

"(A) Practicable means of treating municipal sewage and other water-borne wastes to remove the maximum possible amounts of physical, chemical, and biological pollutants in order to restore and maintain the maximum amount of the Nation's water at a quality suitable for repeated reuse;

"(B) Improved methods and procedures to identify and measure the effects of pollutants on water uses, including those pollutants created by new technological developments; and

"(C) Methods and procedures for evaluating the effects on water quality and water uses of augmented streamflows to control water pollution not susceptible to other means of abatement.

"(2) For the purposes of this subsection there is authorized to be appropriated not more than $5,000,000 for any fiscal year, and the total sum appropriated for such purposes shall not exceed $25,000,000.

"(e) The Secretary shall establish, equip, and maintain field laboratory and research facilities, including, but not limited to, one to be located in the northeastern area of the United States, one in the Middle Atlantic area, one in the southeastern area, one in the midwestern area, one in the southwestern area, one in the Pacific Northwest, and one in the State of Alaska, for the conduct of research, investigations, experiments, field demonstrations and studies, and training relating to the prevention and control of water pollution. Insofar as practicable, each such facility shall be located near institutions of higher learning in which graduate training in such research might be carried out.

"(f) The Secretary shall conduct research and technical development work, and make studies, with respect to the quality of the waters of the Great Lakes, including an analysis of the present and projected future water quality of the Great Lakes under varying conditions of waste treatment and disposal, an evaluation of the water quality needs of those to be served by such waters, an evaluation of municipal, industrial, and vessel waste treatment and disposal practices with respect to such waters, and a study of alternate means of solving water pollution problems (including additional waste treatment measures) with respect to such waters."

SEC. 4. (a) Subsection (a) of section 5 of the Federal Water Pollution Control Act is amended by inserting immediately following "June 30, 1961, $3,000,000" the following: ", and for each succeeding fiscal year to and including the fiscal year ending June 30, 1968, $5,000,000".

(b) Subsection (f) of section 5 of the Federal Water Pollution Control Act is amended by striking out "and" at the end of paragraph (4) thereof, by striking out the period at the end of paragraph (5) thereof and inserting in lieu thereof the following: "; and", and by adding after such paragraph (5) the following new paragraph:

"(6) sets forth the criteria used by the State in determining priority of projects as provided in section 6(b) (4)."

(c) The amendment made by subsection (a) of this section shall take effect July 1, 1961.

(d) The amendment made by subsection (b) of this section shall take effect July 1, 1962.

SEC. 5. (a) Clause (2) of subsection (b) of section 6 of the Federal Water Pollution Control Act is amended to read as follows:

"(2) except as otherwise provided in this clause, no grant shall be made for any project in an amount exceeding 30 per centum of the estimated reasonable cost thereof as determined by the Secretary, or in an amount exceeding $600,000, whichever is the smaller: *Provided,* That the grantee agrees to pay the remaining cost: *Provided further,* That, in the case of a project which will serve more than one municipality (A) the Secretary shall, on such basis as he determines to be reasonable and equitable, allocate to each municipality to be served by such project its share of the estimated reasonable cost of such project, and shall then apply the limitations provided in this clause (2) to each such share as if it were a separate project to determine the maximum amount of any grant which could be made under this section with respect to each such share, and the total of all the amounts so determined or $2,400,000, whichever is the smaller, shall be the maximum amount of the grant which may be made under this section on account of such project, and (B) for the purpose of the limitation in the last sentence of subsection (d), the share of each municipality so determined shall be regarded as a grant for the construction of treatment works;".

(b) Subsection (b) of such section 6 is further amended by striking out "and" at the end of clause (3) and by inserting before the period at the end of clause (4): "; and (5) no grant shall be made under this section for any project in any State in an amount exceeding $250,000 until a grant has been made thereunder for each project in such State (A) for which an application was filed with the appropriate State water pollution control agency prior to one year after the date of enactment of this clause and (B) which the Secretary determines met the requirements of this section and regulations thereunder as in effect prior to the date of enactment of this clause".

(c) The third sentence of subsection (c) of such section 6 is amended to read as follows: "Sums allotted to a State under the preceding sentence which are not obligated within six months following the end of the fiscal year for which they were allotted because of a lack of projects which have been approved by the State water pollution control agency under subsection (b) (1) of this section and certified as entitled to priority under subsection (b) (4) of this section, shall be reallotted by the Secretary, on such basis as he determines to be reasonable and equitable and in accordance with regulations promulgated by him, to States having projects approved under this section for which grants have not been made because of lack of funds: *Provided, however,* That whenever a State has funds subject to reallocation and the Secretary finds that the need for a project in a community in such State is due in part to any Federal institution or Federal construction activity, he may, prior to such reallocation, make an additional grant with respect to such project which will in his judgment reflect an equitable contribution for the need caused by such Federal institution or activity. Any sum made available to a State by reallotment under the preceding sentence shall be in addition to any funds otherwise allotted to such State under this Act. The allotments of a State under the second and third sentences of this subsection shall be available, in accordance with the provisions of this section, for payments with respect to projects in such State which have been approved under this section."

(d) Subsection (d) of such section 6 is amended to read as follows:

"(d) There are hereby authorized to be appropriated for each fiscal year through and including the fiscal year ending June 30, 1961, the sum of $50,000,000 per fiscal year for the purpose of making grants under this section. There are hereby authorized to be appropriated, for the purpose of making grants under this section, $80,000,000 for the fiscal year ending June 30, 1962, $90,000,000 for the fiscal year ending June 30, 1963, $100,000,000 for the fiscal year ending June 30, 1964, $100,000,000 for the fiscal year ending June 30, 1965, $100,000,000 for the fiscal year ending June 30, 1966, and $100,000,000 for the fiscal year ending June 30, 1967. Sums so appropriated shall remain available until expended: *Provided,* That at least 50 percent of the funds so appropriated for each fiscal year shall be used for grants for the construction of treatment works servicing municipalities of 125,000 population or under."

(e) Section 6 is further amended by adding at the end thereof the following new subsection:

"(f) The Secretary shall take such action as may be necessary to insure that all laborers and mechanics employed by contractors or subcontractors on projects for which grants are made under this section shall be paid wages at rates not less than those prevailing for the same type of work on similiar construction in the immediate locality, as determined by the Secretary of Labor, in accordance with the Act of March 3, 1931, as amended, known as the Davis-Bacon Act (46 Stat. 1494; 40 U.S.C., secs. 276a through 276a–5)."

SEC. 6. (a) The first sentence of subsection (a) (1) of section 7 of the Federal Water Pollution Control Act is amended to read as follows: "There is hereby established in the Department of Health, Education, and Welfare, a Water Pollution Control Advisory Board, composed of the Secretary or his designee, who shall be chairman, and nine members appointed by the President, none of whom shall be Federal officers or employees."

(b) The first sentence of subsection (a) (2) (A) of such section 7 is amended by inserting before the period at the end thereof: ", and (iii) the term of any member under the preceding provisions shall be extended until the date on which his successor's appointment is effective".

(c) Members of the Water Pollution Control Advisory Board (established pursuant to section 7(a) of the Federal Water Pollution Control Act as in effect prior to enactment of this Act) serving immediately before the date of enactment of this Act shall be members of the Water Pollution Control Advisory Board, established by the amendment made by subsection (a) of this section, until the expiration of the terms of office for which they were appointed.

SEC. 7. (a) Subsection (a) of section 8 of the Federal Water Pollution Control Act is amended to read as follows:

"ENFORCEMENT MEASURES AGAINST POLLUTION OF INTERSTATE OR
NAVIGABLE WATERS

"SEC. 8. (a) The pollution of interstate or navigable waters in or adjacent to any State or States (whether the matter causing or contributing to such pollution is discharged directly into such waters or reaches such waters after discharge into a tributary of such waters), which endangers the health or welfare of any persons, shall be subject to abatement as provided in this Act."

(b) Subsection (b) of such section 8 is amended by striking out "interstate waters" and inserting in lieu thereof "interstate or navigable waters".

(c) Paragraph (1) of subsection (c) of such section 8 is amended to read as follows:

"(c) (1) Whenever requested by the Governor of any State or a State water pollution control agency, or (with the concurrence of the Governor and of the State water pollution control agency for the State in which the municipality is situated) the governing body of any municipality, the Secretary shall, if such request refers to pollution of waters which is endangering the health or welfare of persons in a State other than that in which the discharge or discharges (causing or contributing to such pollution) originates, give formal notification thereof to the water pollution control agency and interstate agency, if any, of the State or States where such discharge or discharges originate and shall call promptly a conference of such agency or agencies and of the State water pollution control agency and interstate agency, if any, of the State or States, if any, which may be adversely affected by such pollution. Whenever requested by the Governor of any State, the Secretary shall, if such request refers to pollution of interstate or navigable waters which is endangering the health or welfare of persons only in the requesting State in which the discharge or discharges (causing or contributing to such pollution) originate, give formal notification thereof to the water pollution control agency and interstate agency, if any, of such State and shall promptly call a conference of such agency or agencies, unless, in the judgment of the Secretary, the effect of such pollution on the legitimate uses of the waters is not of sufficient significance to warrant exercise of Federal jurisdiction under this section. The Secretary shall also call such a conference whenever, on the basis of reports, surveys, or studies, he has reason to believe that any pollution referred to in subsection (a) and endangering the health or welfare of persons in a State other than that in which the discharge or discharges originate is occurring."

(d) Paragraph (3) (A) of subsection (c) of such section 8 is amended by striking out "interstate" and inserting in lieu thereof "interstate or navigable".

(e) Subsections (d), (e), and (f) of such section 8 are amended to read as follows:

"(d) If the Secretary believes, upon the conclusion of the conference or thereafter, that effective progress toward abatement of such pollution is not being made and that the health or welfare of any persons is being endangered, he shall recommend to the appropriate State water pollution control agency that it take necessary remedial action. The Secretary shall allow at least six months from the date he makes such recommendations for the taking of such recommended action.

"(e) If, at the conclusion of the period so allowed, such remedial action has not been taken or action which in the judgment of the Secretary is reasonably calculated to secure abatement of such pollution has not been taken, the Secretary shall call a public hearing, to be held in or near one or more of the places where the discharge or discharges causing or contributing to such pollution originated, before a Hearing Board of five or more persons appointed by the Secretary. Each State in which any discharge causing or contributing to such pollution originates and each State claiming to be adversely affected by such pollution shall be given an opportunity to select one member of the Hearing Board and at least one member shall be a representative of the Department of Commerce, and not less than a majority of the Hearing Board shall be persons other than officers or employees of the Department of Health, Education, and Welfare. At least three weeks' prior notice of such hearing shall be given to the State water pollution control agencies and interstate agencies, if any, called to attend the aforesaid hearing and the alleged polluter or polluters. On the basis of the evidence presented at such hearing, the Hearing Board shall make findings as to whether pollution referred to in subsection (a) is occurring and whether effective progress toward abatement thereof is being made. If the Hearing Board finds such pollution is occurring and effective progress toward abatement thereof is not being made it shall make recommendations to the Secretary concerning the measures, if any, which it finds to be reasonable and equitable to secure abatement of such pollution. The Secretary shall send such findings and recommendations to the person or persons discharging any matter causing or contributing to such pollution, together with a notice specifying a reasonable time (not less than six months) to secure abatement of such pollution, and shall also send such findings and recommendations and such notice to the State water pollution control agency and to the interstate agency, if any, of the State or States where such discharge or discharges originate.

"(f) If action reasonably calculated to secure abatement of the pollution within the time specified in the notice following the public hearing is not taken, the Secretary—

"(1) in the case of pollution of waters which is endangering the health or welfare of persons in a State other than that in which the discharge or discharges (causing or contributing to such pollution) originate, may request the Attorney General to bring a suit on behalf of the United States to secure abatement of pollution, and

"(2) in the case of pollution of waters which is endangering the health or welfare of persons only in the State in which the discharge or discharges (causing or contributing to such pollution) originate, may, with the written consent of the Governor of such State, request the Attorney General to bring a suit on behalf of the United States to secure abatement of the pollution."

(f) Subsection (h) of such section 8 is amended to read as follows:

"(h) Members of any Hearing Board appointed pursuant to subsection (e) who are not regular full-time officers or employees of the United States shall, while participating in the hearing conducted by such Board or otherwise engaged on the work of such Board, be entitled to receive compensation at a rate fixed by the Secretary, but not exceeding $100 per diem, including travel time, and while away from their homes or regular places of business they may be allowed travel expenses, including per diem in lieu of subsistence, as authorized by law (5 U.S.C. 73b–2) for persons in the Government service employed intermittently.

"(i) As used in this section the term—

"(1) 'person' includes an individual, corporation, partnership, association, State, municipality, and political subdivision of a State, and

"(2) 'municipality' means a city, town, borough, county, parish, district, or other public body created by or pursuant to State law."

SEC. 8. Section 9 of the Federal Water Pollution Control Act is amended by adding at the end thereof the following new sentences:

"In his summary of any conference pursuant to section 8(c) (3) of this Act, the Secretary shall include references to any discharges allegedly contributing to pollution from any Federal property. Notice of any hearing pursuant to section 8(e) involving any pollution alleged to be effected by any such discharges shall also be given to the Federal agency having jurisdiction over the property involved and the findings and recommendations of the Hearing Board conducting such hearing shall also include references to any such discharges which are contributing to the pollution found by such Hearing Board."

SEC. 9. Section 11 of the Federal Water Pollution Control Act is amended by striking out subsections (d) and (e) and inserting in lieu thereof the following:

"(d) The term 'State' means a State, the District of Columbia, the Commonwealth of Puerto Rico, the Virgin Islands, and Guam.

"(e) The term 'interstate waters' means all rivers, lakes, and other waters that flow across or form a part of State boundaries, including coastal waters."

SEC. 10. Section 301 (b) of the Water Supply Act of 1958 (72 Stat. 319), is amended by striking out all beginning with *"Provided,"* in the first proviso to the colon at the end of the second proviso and inserting in lieu thereof the following: *"Provided,* That the cost of any construction or modification authorized under the provisions of this section shall be determined on the basis that all authorized purposes served by the project shall share equitably in the benefits of multiple purpose construction, as determined by the Secretary of the Army or the Secretary of the Interior, as the case may be: *Provided further,* That before construction or modification of any project including water supply provisions for present demand is initiated, State or local interests shall agree to pay for the cost of such provisions in accordance with the provisions of this section: *And provided further,* That not to exceed 30 per centum of the total estimated cost of any project may be allocated to anticipated future demands where State or local interests give reasonable assurances, and there is reasonable evidence, that such demands for the use of such storage will be made within a period of time which will permit paying out the costs allocated to water supply within the life of the project".

SEC. 11. This Act may be cited as the "Federal Water Pollution Control Act Amendments of 1961".

Approved July 20, 1961, 12:25 p.m.

LOUIS S. CLAPPER ON WATER POLLUTION*
1963

Despite the efforts carried forward through legislation, and the independent efforts of local governments and industry, pollution became worse—not better. We had become, in the words of Joseph L. Fisher, "an effluent society." By 1963, Louis S. Clapper wrote:

A crow drifts slowly down the Missouri River riding a raft of solidified grease and animal tissue held together by a binder of hog hair. Only a carrion bird could stand the smell, yet many downstream cities take their drinking water from this river.

Live viruses, dumped into our coastal waters from sewers and dirty bilge tanks, have caused hepatitis in persons who ate clams harvested from sewage-laden waters on the Atlantic Coast, and oysters from the polluted Gulf.

Nitrochlorbenzene, an extremely poisonous organic chemical, is detected in the Mississippi at New Orleans—and followed a thousand miles upstream past many city water intakes to an industrial waste discharge in St. Louis. No one can yet guess the damage this might do to man and wildlife.

This is only a sampling of what is happening in many parts of this country. The detailed story is much longer, equally appalling, and adds up to America's shame—the pollution of our waters.

"Water pollution in the United States is a menace to our health and an economic burden which is robbing us of water we need," asserts G. E. McCallum, Chief of Water Supply and Pollution Control in the U.S. Public Health Service. "It is a destroyer of fish and wildlife habitat, a threat to outdoor recreation, and in many communities, an aesthetic horror."

Words, at least words that can be used in mixed company, cannot describe the filth we pour into many of our streams, lakes and oceans. Sewage, slaughterhouse offal, thousands of lethal chemicals, radioactive matter—these and other of man's wastes combine to form what sanitary engineers, for lack of a better term, call "gunk." Gunk defies analysis and perplexes health authorities who are desperately trying to keep up with its harmful effects on man and other living creatures.

We are faced with some inescapably gruesome facts:

■ Sewage treatment plants are, at best, only 90 percent efficient with organic material—and some inorganic wastes defy treatment.

■ The Public Health Service has isolated polio, infectious hepatitis and more than 30 other live viruses which may carry disease from treated sewage effluent.

*Louis S. Clapper, "Pollution," *National Wildlife,* Vol. I, No. 6 (Oct.–Nov., 1963), 9–11.

■ Because we increasingly re-use water, chances are four out of ten that the water you drink has passed through someone's household plumbing or an industrial plant sewer.

Then what prevents us all from being sick?

"The fact our water treatment plants are the best in the world," answers McCallum. So we have some of the worst pollution, but the safest drinking water—thanks to its being disinfected by chlorine and other chemicals which kill most bacteria, even though the water sometimes has a disagreeable taste and odor. But we are riding a thin edge.

The effects of water pollution are much broader than health. Industrial plants are rejecting water as unfit for their uses. Swimmers are finding beaches posted "UNSAFE FOR SWIMMING." Water skiing? Not when the coliform bacterial count *per drop of water* has reached 80 at the Detroit waterfront; 65 in the Androscoggin River; 20 in the Mississippi at St. Louis. (A count of five per drop is considered unsafe for swimming.)

Bad news for fishermen! Last year pollution killed 50 million fish in rivers and coastal waters. These are only the reported kills.

Radioactive wastes have been found in the Colorado River drainage, danger signals of more trouble to come as we enter the atomic age. Floating garbage and other filth clogs water supply intakes of many cities which take their water from open streams. Potent fumes from New Hampshire's Androscoggin River have peeled the paint from the walls of nearby buildings.

Detergent foam runs from water faucets in several states—you brush your teeth in someone else's dishwater. Acids, seeping from mines in Pennsylvania and West Virginia, have polluted streams and poisoned wildlife. Chemical pesticide sprays are lining lake and stream banks with dead fish. Unsewered septic tanks drain into underground waters, and farm chemicals are finding their way into subterranean streams. Oil spills have killed countless birds and spoiled many beaches.

Since time immemorial, water has been known as the natural purifier. Nearly all religions in one way or another use water as the symbol of purity. Yet two presidents of allegedly the most advanced nation on earth have called the pollution of American waters "a national disgrace." Why?

The problem hit with run-away speed. We were using only 160 billion gallons of water daily in 1945. Today, we use 355 billion gallons. The average home uses 60 gallons daily. It takes only three gallons of water to wash dinner dishes by hand, twice that amount by machine. It takes two gallons to flush garbage down the drain, five gallons a minute to take a shower.

The big jump in water usage has come with industrial growth. It takes 500 gallons of water to manufacture one yard of woolen cloth; 320,000 gallons to make a ton of aluminum; 500,000 to make a ton of synthetic rubber.

With a fixed supply of 315 billion gallons of fresh water available today, *we must re-use our water.* The Public Health Service estimates that the total flow of the Ohio River is being used 3.7 times before it reaches the Mississippi. By the time the water in the Mahoning River reaches Youngstown, Ohio, it has been re-used more than eight times. That's why water pollution is so dangerous to us all.

But most citizens are blissfully unaware of where their water comes from, and unconcerned about where it goes. As a result, both cities and industry have dragged their feet. "Of all our public works projects, waste treatment facilities are the least glamorous and the hardest to sell," says McCallum.

A few industries have exerted political pressure to evade anti-pollution laws. One popular claim is that "the plant will have to shut down" if forced to comply with the law, thereby throwing local people (who are also voters) out of work. "To the best of my knowledge, we have yet to shut down an industry or defeat a mayor," says James M. Quigley, assistant secretary of Health, Education, and Welfare.

All 50 states have water pollution laws, but enforcement is sometimes indifferent. You are more likely to be fined for throwing a candy wrapper out the car window in some states than for dumping poisons and ruining a stream.

The Federal Water Pollution Control Act passed in 1956 started the ball rolling with its powerful one-two punch: (1) construction grants to cities, and (2) threat of court action. Cities were spending less than $300 million annually on sewage treatment plants before the act was passed. But with the help of federal grants—first $50 million annually and then nearly double that figure—cities are now building at the $600 million rate per year.

The Division of Water Supply and Pollution Control has had 25 cases since it got more enforcement teeth. Fifteen were initiated by the Secretary of Health, Education and Welfare, and the rest by state governors. In none of these cases was a court injunction necessary. Mere threat of federal action caused offenders to clean up.

Dramatic progress has been made along the Missouri River where ten years ago not one major city treated its sewage. Today, Sioux City, Omaha, Kansas City and St. Joseph all have treatment plants in operation or under construction, and meat packing plants have really cleaned up. St. Louis recently voted a $95 million bond issue for waste treatment.

Many industries have invested millions and gone to much trouble to reduce water pollution. Through the National Technical Task Committee on Industrial Wastes, organized in 1950, major industries work with the federal government in task groups with mutual problems.

As a direct result, the Shell Oil Company plant at Anacortes, Washington, has installed a complete treatment system to avoid polluting the area's waters and to protect the local commercial and sport fisheries. Kaiser Steel at Fontana, California, reclaims integrated mill wastes with a settling and recycling system which keeps its water requirements at a minimum. The Allegheny County Sanitary Authority at Pittsburgh has a joint treatment operation in 68 communities and more than 100 industrial plants.

But despite all of these efforts, the pollution of our waters is the worst in history, most experts agree. We're making gains in some areas; in others, we appear to be losing. Our water, when doctored with chlorine and up to a half dozen other chemicals, has been about as safe as any in the world. But some responsible scientists are beginning to question: Is this safe enough?

As population skyrockets and industry expands, water intakes and sewage outlets are jammed closer and closer together. Sewage treatment plants are not the cure-all that most of us blissfully assume. A third of our cities use only primary treatment (screens and settling basins) which at best remove only 35 percent of the organic wastes. More efficient plants use a secondary treatment (bacterial action to eat up the dissolved organic matter) which removes up to 90 percent of this material, but leaves many other pollutants untouched.

Chicago, for example, has the best treatment available. Yet they pour an effluent into the Illinois River daily that is equal to the raw sewage from a city of a million people, containing 3,435 tons of solid wastes.

Moreover, our treatment processes are out of date. They cannot remove the complex wastes resulting from manufacture of such substances as plastics, detergents, synthetic fibers, pesticides, and medicines. Some synthetic chemical wastes cause tastes and odors. A large number are highly toxic to fish and aquatic life. Many do not respond to biological treatment and persist in streams for great distances. "We do not know how to detect most of these compounds in water, or how to treat or remove them in waste effluents. Nor do we know of their long range toxic effects on man," the Public Health Service warns.

Each year increasing amounts of these wastes come into our water supply intakes. Obviously, even with chlorine cocktails to kill bacteria, we are subjecting ourselves to increased exposure to harmful wastes, including radioactive substances and lethal pesticide chemicals.

Our future water needs are staggering. By 1980—just 17 years from now—we will be using 600 billion gallons of water daily. By the year 2,000 a trillion gallons. It would take a tank car train 600,000 miles long to haul it.

Unless we can find a cheap way to convert salt water to fresh, hydrologists estimate our maximum fresh water supply will be only 650 billion gallons a day. So re-use is a must. We'll need to re-use our water six times by 1980, according to some authorities.

These are the increased demands of the immediate future, yet we are barely holding our own today. "Even those states doing the best job on water pollution are doing an inadequate job," Assistant Secretary of Health, Education and Welfare Quigley told a Congressional committee. Last year, for the first time, we started gaining on municipal pollution, although we have a backlog of 5,831 projects which will cost $2.2 billion for treatment plants and sewers. Industry needs to build 6,000 plants. Federal institutions, too, need to clean up.

Some industrial groups have opposed the federal program of grants to cities on the grounds that pollution is a local and state problem. The reason for this attitude, it is suspected, is that once cities clean up pollution, the finger of guilt will inevitably point to the other polluters—mostly industrial plants. Organic wastes from industrial sources are *double* that from cities.

Water pollution is not an impossible problem. We know that the Ruhr River, which drains the heavily industrialized, heavily populated Ruhr Valley of western Germany, is managed so well it is still safe for boating and swimming. One possible reason—there's a tax on industrial wastes.

We have three big needs in the pollution fight: More money invested in city and industrial water treatment plants. More research to develop more efficient techniques of water treatment. And better enforcement of strong pollution laws—federal, state and local.

How clean and pure we attempt to maintain our streams is a matter of economics and realities, and of values, both tangible and intangible. But of these things we can be certain: Pollution *must* be kept below the levels of significant personal health damage. Pollution must not destroy recreational and wildlife values. Users of water do not have an inherent right to pollute—they must return it as nearly clean as possible.

POLICY GOVERNING THE WATER POLLUTION
ASPECTS OF OUTDOOR RECREATION*
April 9, 1964

The Recreation Advisory Council (composed of the Secretaries of the Interior, Commerce, Agriculture, Defense, Health, Education, and Welfare, and the Administrator of the Housing and Home Finance Agency) took note of the close relationship between water quality and outdoor recreation in their Circular No. 3, Policy Governing the Water Pollution and Public Health Aspects of Outdoor Recreation. *The preamble and policy statement is reproduced here.*

PREAMBLE

The conservation, development, and wise use of outdoor recreation resources are of great importance in satisfying the social and health goals of our population. For many people, outdoor recreation involves water; they swim and fish in it, hunt and boat on it, picnic beside it. The demands for water-based recreation are expected to expand materially in the next few years and more and more people will be competing for the privilege of using available water areas.

There is no question that increasing pollution is a major factor making water areas unsuitable for recreation and other uses. Pollution not only drives people away, it also destroys large areas of fish and wildlife habitat. There is also no question that the increasing number of visitors to outdoor recreation areas emphasizes the need for planning and constructing adequate sanitary facilities at public recreation areas, including the need for research which will assist in the solution of sanitary engineering problems peculiar to outdoor recreation activities.

The Recreation Advisory Council, recognizing the demand for water-oriented outdoor recreation and the need for immediate and positive action to protect not only the resource being used, but more importantly, the health and safety of the American people, hereby sets forth the guidelines it believes necessary (1) to prevent and control future water pollution and to restore existing bodies of polluted water to the highest quality practicable, and (2) to govern the planning, provision, and maintenance of sanitary facilities at outdoor recreation areas.[1]

I. WATER POLLUTION

A. DECLARATION OF POLICY

It shall be the Recreation Advisory Council policy that (1) recreation be recognized as a full partner with other beneficial water uses in water quality

---

*Recreation Advisory Council, *Policy Governing the Water Pollution and Public Health Aspects of Outdoor Recreation,* Circular No. 3 (Washington, D.C.: Government Printing Office, 1964), 1–4, 9.

[1] Recreation Advisory Council Circular No. 2, General Policy Guidelines for Outdoor Recreation, Federal Role, Item G, April 1964.

management policies and programs, (2) the water resources of the Nation be maintained as clean as possible in order to provide maximum recreation opportunities, and (3) all users of public waters have a responsibility for keeping these waters clean. This Declaration of Policy recognizes the primary responsibility of the Department of Health, Education, and Welfare for the enforcement of Federal laws relating to the prevention of water pollution.

All Federal agencies having responsibilities in the field of water pollution should coordinate such activities with each other. In turn, these activities should be coordinated wherever possible with State and local agencies having responsibilities in the field of water pollution in order to further a unified and effective effort in the following endeavors:

1. Development of comprehensive river basin water pollution control programs that protect outdoor recreation water uses;

2. Development of a set of principles for water quality standards for outdoor recreation, wildlife, fish, and other aquatic uses which could be applied where appropriate for the particular use involved;

3. Development of water quality monitoring systems for the protection of outdoor water recreation areas;

4. Development of water pollution research programs benefiting outdoor recreation, wildlife, fish, and other aquatic life;

5. Provision of technical services in water pollution prevention and control relating to outdoor recreation, wildlife, fish, and other aquatic life; and

6. Development of a set of principles as guides to the adoption of local standards by the appropriate State agencies to protect outdoor recreation uses and Federal investments for recreation in water resource developments.

B. POLICY IMPLEMENTATION

Federal, State, and local governments should assume their respective responsibilities for controlling water pollution to conserve and improve water for all uses, including recreation.

Federal agencies shall make every effort to implement the President's policy that ". . . the Government should set an example in the abatement of water pollution . . ."[2] by:

1. Demonstrating leadership in adopting pollution control programs to assure that Federal activity, or other activities on federally owned lands, does not pollute waters associated with such areas;

2. Promulgating effective rules and regulations for controlling water pollution on lands under their management;

3. Including adequate safeguards in comprehensive water resource developments to enhance and protect recreation waters and to assure that the recreation benefits assigned to the developments will not be impaired by pollution;

[2] Excerpt from letter from President Kennedy to the Secretary of Health, Education, and Welfare, dated December 14, 1962.

4. Utilizing acceptable principles of water quality standards in programing water pollution control measures and managing water pollution control programs benefiting recreation;

5. Establishing reliable monitoring systems to provide the data needed to make the water quality management decisions required to protect water recreation uses and investments;

6. Informing the public of damages to recreation values resulting from water pollution; and

7. Encouraging and supporting adequate State, interstate, and local water pollution control programs and cooperating fully with the appropriate agency in their implementation and management.

To discharge their responsibilities, State and local governments are encouraged to:

1. Enact and enforce adequate water pollution control legislation;

2. Develop programs to control pollution originating on publicly owned lands under their jurisdiction;

3. Participate in interstate or regional compacts to develop pollution control programs for interstate waters;

4. Cooperate with the responsible Federal water pollution control agency in the adoption and vigorous enforcement of adequate water quality standards for recreation and fish and wildlife; and

5. Develop and sustain a program of public information so that an enlightened public opinion can be brought to bear on the problems of pollution abatement and control.

* * *

III. ACTIVATION OF POLICY

Under authority bestowed upon the Council by Executive Order 11017, as amended, the Council commends this policy to all concerned Federal agencies. Upon approval of this statement, the member agencies of the Recreation Advisory Council become responsible for observing the foregoing policy and for giving it force and effect.

AN ACT TO ESTABLISH A FEDERAL WATER POLLUTION CONTROL ADMINISTRATION*
October 2, 1965

The Water Quality Act of 1965 continued and accelerated work on the pollution problem—which nevertheless continued to grow worse. The act created a Federal Water Pollution Control Administration, headed by an Assistant Secretary, in the Department of Health, Education, and Welfare. It provided for the establishment of water quality criteria and, once more, grants for sewage treatment plants were sharply increased.

An Act to amend the Federal Water Pollution Control Act to establish a Federal Water Pollution Control Administration, to provide grants for research and development, to increase grants for construction of sewage treatment works, to require establishment of water quality criteria, and for other purposes.

Be it enacted by the Senate and House of Representatives of the United States of America in Congress assembled, That (a) (1) section 1 of the Federal Water Pollution Control Act (33 U.S.C. 466) is amended by inserting after the words "SECTION 1." a new subsection (a) as follows:

"(a) The purpose of this Act is to enhance the quality and value of our water resources and to establish a national policy for the prevention, control, and abatement of water pollution."

(2) Such section is further amended by redesignating subsections (a) and (b) thereof as (b) and (c), respectively.

(3) Subsection (b) of such section (as redesignated by paragraph (2) of this subsection) is amended by striking out the last sentence thereof and inserting in lieu of such sentence the following: "The Secretary of Health, Education, and Welfare (hereinafter in this Act called 'Secretary') shall administer this Act through the Administration created by section 2 of this Act, and with the assistance of an Assistant Secretary of Health, Education, and Welfare designated by him, shall supervise and direct (1) the head of such Administration in administering this Act and (2) the administration of all other functions of the Department of Health, Education, and Welfare related to water pollution. Such Assistant Secretary shall perform such additional functions as the Secretary may prescribe."

(b) There shall be in the Department of Health, Education, and Welfare, in addition to the Assistant Secretaries now provided for by law, one additional Assistant Secretary of Health, Education, and Welfare who shall be appointed by the President, by and with the advice and consent of the Senate. The provisions of section 2 of Reorganization Plan Numbered 1 of 1953 (67 Stat. 631)

*79 *Statutes at Large,* 903.

[507]

shall be applicable to such additional Assistant Secretary to the same extent as they are applicable to the Assistant Secretaries authorized by that section. Paragraph (17) of section 303(d) of the Federal Executive Salary Act of 1964 (78 Stat. 418) is amended by striking out "(5)" before the period at the end thereof and inserting in lieu thereof "(6)."

SEC. 2. (a) Such Act is further amended by redesignating sections 2 through 4, and references thereto, as sections 3 through 5, respectively, sections 5 through 14, as sections 7 through 16, respectively, by inserting after section 1 the following new section:

"FEDERAL WATER POLLUTION CONTROL ADMINISTRATION

"SEC. 2. Effective ninety days after the date of enactment of this section there is created within the Department of Health, Education, and Welfare a Federal Water Pollution Control Administration (hereinafter in this Act referred to as the 'Administration'). The head of the Administration shall be appointed, and his compensation fixed, by the Secretary. The head of the Administration may, in addition to regular staff of the Administration, which shall be initially provided from the personnel of the Department, obtain, from within the Department or otherwise as authorized by law, such professional, technical, and clerical assistance as may be necessary to discharge the Administration's functions and may for that purpose use funds available for carrying out such functions; and he may delegate any of his functions to, or otherwise authorize their performance by, any officer or employee of, or assigned or detailed to, the Administration."

(b) Subject to such requirements as the Civil Service Commission may prescribe, any commissioned officer of the Public Health Service who, on the day before the effective date of the establishment of the Federal Water Pollution Control Administration, was, as such officer, performing functions relating to the Federal Water Pollution Control Act may acquire competitive civil service status and be transferred to a classified position in the Administration if he so transfers within six months (or such further period as the Secretary of Health, Education, and Welfare may find necessary in individual cases) after such effective date. No commissioned officer of the Public Health Service may be transferred to the Administration under this section if he does not consent to such transfer. As used in this section, the term "transferring officer" means an officer transferred in accordance with this subsection.

(c)(1) The Secretary shall deposit in the Treasury of the United States to the credit of the civil service retirement and disability fund, on behalf of and to the credit of each transferring officer, an amount equal to that which such individual would be required to deposit in such fund to cover the years of service credited to him for purposes of his retirement as a commissioned officer of the Public Health Service to the date of his transfer as provided in subsection (b), but only to the extent that such service is otherwise creditable under the Civil

Service Retirement Act. The amount so required to be deposited with respect to any transferring officer shall be computed on the basis of the sum of his basic pay, allowance for quarters, and allowance for subsistence and, in the case of a medical officer, his special pay, during the years of service so creditable, including all such years after June 30, 1960.

(2) The deposits which the Secretary of Health, Education, and Welfare is required to make under this subsection with respect to any transferring officer shall be made within two years after the date of his transfer as provided in subsection (b), and the amounts due under this subsection shall include interest computed from the period of service credited to the date of payment in accordance with section 4(e) of the Civil Service Retirement Act (5 U.S.C. 2254(e)).

(d) All past service of a transferring officer as a commissioned officer of the Public Health Service shall be considered as civilian service for all purposes under the Civil Service Retirement Act, effective as of the date any such transferring officer acquires civil service status as an employee of the Federal Water Pollution Control Administration; however, no transferring officer may become entitled to benefits under both the Civil Service Retirement Act and title II of the Social Security Act based on service as such a commissioned officer performed after 1956, but the individual (or his survivors) may irrevocably elect to waive benefit credit for the service under one Act to secure credit under the other.

(e) A transferring officer on whose behalf a deposit is required to be made by subsection (c) and who, after transfer to a classified position in the Federal Water Pollution Control Administration under subsection (b), is separated from Federal service or transfers to a position not covered by the Civil Service Retirement Act, shall not be entitled, nor shall his survivors be entitled, to a refund of any amount deposited on his behalf in accordance with this section. In the event he transfers, after transfer under subsection (b), to a position covered by another Government staff retirement system under which credit is allowable for service with respect to which a deposit is required under subsection (c), no credit shall be allowed under the Civil Service Retirement Act with respect to such service.

(f) Each transferring officer who prior to January 1, 1957, was insured pursuant to the Federal Employees' Group Life Insurance Act of 1954, and who subsequently waived such insurance, shall be entitled to become insured under such Act upon his transfer to the Federal Water Pollution Control Administration regardless of age and insurability.

(g) Any commissioned officer of the Public Health Service who, pursuant to subsection (b) of this section, is transferred to a position in the Federal Water Pollution Control Administration which is subject to the Classification Act of 1949, as amended, shall receive a salary rate of the General Schedule grade of such position which is nearest to but not less than the sum of (1) basic pay, quarters and subsistence allowances, and, in the case of a medical officer, special pay, to which he was entitled as a commissioned officer of the Public Health Service on the day immediately preceding his transfer, and (2) an amount equal to the equalization factor (as defined in this subsection); but in no event shall the rate so established exceed the maximum rate of such grade. As used in this section, the term "equalization factor" means an amount determined by the Secretary to be equal to the sum of (A) 6½ per centum of such basic pay and (B) the amount of Federal income tax which the transferring officer, had he remained a commissioned officer, would have been required to pay on such allowances for quarters and subsistence for the taxable year then current if they had not been tax free.

(h) A transferring officer who has had one or more years of commissioned service in the Public Health Service immediately prior to his transfer under subsection (b) shall, on the date of such transfer, be credited with thirteen days of sick leave.

(i) Notwithstanding the provisions of any other law, any commissioned officer of the United States Public Health Service with twenty-five or more years of service who has held the temporary rank of Assistant Surgeon General in the Division of Water Supply and Pollution Control of the United States Public Health Service for three or more years and whose position and duties are affected by this Act, may, with the approval of the President, voluntarily retire from the United States Public Health Service with the same retirement benefits that would accrue to him if he had held the rank of Assistant Surgeon General for a period of four years or more if he so retires within ninety days of the date of the establishment of the Federal Water Pollution Control Administration.

(j) Nothing contained in this section shall be construed to restrict or in any way limit the head of the Federal Water Pollution Control Administration in matters of organization or in otherwise carrying out his duties under section 2 of this Act as he deems appropriate to the discharge of the functions of such Administration.

(k) The Surgeon General shall be consulted by the head of the Administration on the public health aspects relating to water pollution over which the head of such Administration has administrative responsibility.

SEC. 3. Such Act is further amended by inserting after the section redesignated as section 5 a new section as follows:

"GRANTS FOR RESEARCH AND DEVELOPMENT

"SEC. 6. (a) The Secretary is authorized to make grants to any State, municipality, or intermunicipal or interstate agency for the purpose of assisting in the development of any project which will demonstrate a new or improved method of controlling the discharge into any waters of untreated or inadequately treated sewage or other waste from sewers which carry storm water or both storm water and sewage or other wastes, and for the purpose of reports, plans, and specifications in connection therewith. The Secretary is authorized to provide for the conduct of research and demonstrations relating to new or improved methods of controlling the discharge into any waters of untreated or inadequately treated sewage or other waste from sewers which carry storm water or both storm water and sewage or other wastes, by contract with public or private agencies and institutions and with individuals without regard to sections 3648 and 3709 of the Revised Statutes, except that not to exceed 25 per centum of the total amount appropriated under authority of this section for any fiscal year may be expended under authority of this sentence during such fiscal year.

"(b) Federal grants under this section shall be subject to the following limitations: (1) No grant shall be made for any project pursuant to this section unless such project shall have been approved by an appropriate State water pollution control agency or agencies and by the Secretary; (2) no grant shall be made for any project in an amount exceeding 50 per centum of the estimated reasonable cost thereof as determined by the Secretary; (3) no grant shall be made for any project under this section unless the Secretary determines that such project will serve as a useful demonstration of a new or improved method of controlling the discharge into any water of untreated or inadequately treated sewage or other waste from sewers which carry storm water or both storm water and sewage or other wastes.

"(c) There are hereby authorized to be appropriated for the fiscal year ending June 30, 1966, and for each of the next three succeeding fiscal years, the sum of $20,000,000 per fiscal year for the purposes of this section. Sums so appropriated shall remain available until expended. No grant or contract shall be made for any project in an amount exceeding 5 per centum of the total amount authorized by this section in any one fiscal year."

SEC. 4. (a) Clause (2) of subsection (b) of the section of the Federal Water Pollution Control Act herein redesignated as section 8 is amended by striking out "$600,000," and inserting in lieu thereof "$1,200,000,".

(b) The second proviso in clause (2) of subsection (b) of such redesignated section 8 is amended by striking out "$2,400,000," and inserting in lieu thereof "$4,800,000,".

(c) Subsection (b) of such redesignated section 8 is amended by adding at the end thereof the following: "The limitations of $1,200,000 and $4,800,000 imposed by clause (2) of this subsection shall not apply in the case of grants made under this section from funds allocated under the third sentence of subsection (c) of this section if the State agrees to match equally all Federal grants made from such allocation for projects in such State."

(d)(1) The second sentence of subsection (c) of such redesignated section 8 is amended by striking out "for any fiscal year" and inserting in lieu thereof "for each fiscal year ending on or before June 30, 1965, and the first $100,000,000 appropriated pursuant to subsection (d) for each fiscal year beginning on or after July 1, 1965,".

(2) Subsection (c) of such redesignated section 8 is amended by inserting immediately after the period at the end of the second sentence thereof the following: "All sums in excess of $100,000,000 appropriated pursuant to subsection (d) for each fiscal year beginning on or after July 1, 1965, shall be allotted by the Secretary from time to time, in accordance with regulations, in the ratio that the population of each State bears to the population of all States."

(3) The third sentence of subsection (c) of such redesignated section 8 is amended by striking out "the preceding sentence" and inserting in lieu thereof "the two preceding sentences".

(4) The next to the last sentence of subsection (c) of such redesignated section 8 is amended by striking out "and third" and inserting in lieu thereof ", third, and fourth".

(e) The last sentence of subsection (d) of such redesignated section 8 is amended to read as follows: "Sums so appropriated shall remain available until expended. At least 50 per centum of the funds so appropriated for each fiscal year ending on or before June 30, 1965, and at least 50 per centum of the first $100,000,000 so appropriated for each fiscal year beginning on or after July 1, 1965, shall be used for grants for the construction of treatment works servicing municipalities of one hundred and twenty-five thousand population or under."

(f) Subsection (d) of such redesignated section 8 is amended by striking out "$100,000,000 for the fiscal year ending June 30, 1966, and $100,000,000 for the fiscal year ending June 30, 1967." and inserting in lieu threreof "$150,000,000 for the fiscal year ending June 30, 1966, and $150,000,000 for the fiscal year ending June 30, 1967."

(g) Subsection (f) of such redesignated section 8 is redesignated as subsection (g) thereof and is amended by adding at the end thereof the following new sentence: "The Secretary of Labor shall have, with respect to the labor standards specified in this subsection, the authority and functions set forth in Reorganization Plan Numbered 14 of 1950 (15 F.R. 3176; 64 Stat. 1267; 5 U.S.C. 133z–15) and section 2 of the Act of June 13, 1934, as amended (48 Stat. 948; 40 U.S.C. 276c)."

(h) Such redesignated section 8 is further amended by inserting therein, immediately after subsection (e) thereof, the following new subsection:

"(f) Notwithstanding any other provisions of this section, the Secretary may increase the amount of a grant made under subsection (b) of this section by an additional 10 per centum of the amount of such grant for any project which has been certified to him by an official State, metropolitan, or regional planning agency empowered under State or local laws or interstate compact to perform metropolitan or regional planning for a metropolitan area within which the assistance is to be used, or other agency or instrumentality designated for such purposes by the Governor (or Governors in the case of interstate planning) as being in conformity with the comprehensive plan developed or in process of development for such metropolitan area. For the purposes of this subsection, the term 'metropolitan area' means either (1) a standard metropolitan statistical area as defined by the Bureau of the Budget, except as may be determined by the President as not being appropriate for the purposes hereof, or (2) any urban area, including those surrounding areas that form an economic and socially related region, taking into consideration such factors as present and future population trends and patterns of urban growth, location of transportation facilities and systems, and distribution of industrial, commercial, residential, governmental, institutional, and other activities, which in the opinion of the President lends itself as being appropriate for the purposes hereof."

SEC. 5. (a) Redesignated section 10 of the Federal Water Pollution Control Act is amended by redesignating subsections (c) through (i) as subsections (d) through (j), and by inserting after subsection (b) the following new subsection:

"(c)(1) If the Governor of a State or a State water pollution control agency files, within one year after the date of enactment of this subsection, a letter of intent that such State, after public hearings, will before June 30, 1967, adopt (A) water quality criteria applicable to interstate waters or portions thereof within such State, and (B) a plan for the implementation and enforcement of the water quality criteria adopted, and if such criteria and plan are established in accordance with the letter of intent, and if the Secretary determines that such State criteria and plan are consistent with paragraph (3) of this subsection, such State criteria and plan shall thereafter be the water quality standards applicable to such interstate waters or portions thereof.

"(2) If a State does not (A) file a letter of intent or (B) establish water quality standards in accordance with paragraph (1) of this subsection, or if the Secretary or the Governor of any State affected by water quality standards established pursuant to this subsection desires a revision in such standards, the Secretary may, after reasonable notice and a conference of representatives of appropriate Federal departments and agencies, interstate agencies, States, municipalities and industries involved, prepare regulations setting forth standards of water quality to be applicable to interstate waters or portions thereof. If, within six months from the date the Secretary publishes such regulations, the State has not adopted water quality standards found by the Secretary to be consistent with paragraph (3) of this subsection, or a petition for public hearing has not been filed under paragraph (4) of this subsection, the Secretary shall promulgate such standards.

"(3) Standards of quality established pursuant to this subsection shall be such as to protect the public health or welfare, enhance the quality of water and serve the purposes of this Act. In establishing such standards the Secretary,

[513]

the Hearing Board, or the appropriate State authority shall take into consideration their use and value for public water supplies, propagation of fish and wildlife, recreational purposes, and agricultural, industrial, and other legitimate uses.

"(4) If at any time prior to 30 days after standards have been promulgated under paragraph (2) of this subsection, the Governor of any State affected by such standards petitions the Secretary for a hearing, the Secretary shall call a public hearing, to be held in or near one or more of the places where the water quality standards will take effect, before a Hearing Board of five or more persons appointed by the Secretary. Each State which would be affected by such standards shall be given an opportunity to select one member of the Hearing Board. The Department of Commerce and other affected Federal departments and agencies shall each be given an opportunity to select a member of the Hearing Board and not less than a majority of the Hearing Board shall be persons other than officers of employees of the Department of Health, Education, and Welfare. The members of the Board who are not officers or employees of the United States, while participating in the hearing conducted by such Hearing Board or otherwise engaged on the work of such Hearing Board, shall be entitled to receive compensation at a rate fixed by the Secretary, but not exceeding $100 per diem, including travel time, and while away from their homes or regular places of business they may be allowed travel expenses, including per diem in lieu of subsistence, as authorized by law, (5 U.S.C. 73b–2) for persons in the Government service employed intermittently. Notice of such hearing shall be published in the Federal Register and given to the State water pollution control agencies, interstate agencies and municipalities involved at least 30 days prior to the date of such hearing. On the basis of the evidence presented at such hearing, the Hearing Board shall make findings as to whether the standards published or promulgated by the Secretary should be approved or modified and transmit its findings to the Secretary. If the Hearing Board approves the standards as published or promulgated by the Secretary, the standards shall take effect on receipt by the Secretary of the Hearing Board's recommendations. If the Hearing Board recommends modifications in the standards as published or promulgated by the Secretary, the Secretary shall promulgate revised regulations setting forth standards of water quality in accordance with the Hearing Board's recommendations which will become effective immediately upon promulgation.

"(5) The discharge of matter into such interstate waters or portions thereof, which reduces the quality of such waters below the water quality standards established under this subsection (whether the matter causing or contributing to such reduction is discharged directly into such waters or reaches such waters after discharge into tributaries of such waters), is subject to abatement in accordance with the provisions of paragraph (1) or (2) of subsection (g) of this section, except that at least 180 days before any abatement action is initiated under either paragraph (1) or (2) of subsection (g) as authorized by this subsection, the Secretary shall notify the violators and other interested parties of the violation of such standards. In any suit brought under the provisions of this subsection the court shall receive in evidence a transcript of the proceedings of the conference and hearing provided for in this subsection, together with the recommendations of the conference and Hearing Board and the recommendations and standards promulgated by the Secretary, and such additional evidence, including that relating to the alleged violation of the standards, as it deems necessary to a complete review of the standards and to a determination of all other issues relating to the alleged violation. The court, giving due consideration to the practicability and to the physical and economic feasibility of complying with such standards, shall have jurisdiction to enter such judgment and orders enforcing such judgment as the public interest and the equities of the case may require.

"(6) Nothing in this subsection shall (A) prevent the application of this section to any case to which subsection (a) of this section would otherwise be applicable, or (B) extend Federal jurisdiction over water not otherwise authorized by this Act.

"(7) In connection with any hearings under this section no witness or any other person shall be required to divulge trade secrets or secret processes."

(b) Paragraph (1) of subsection (d) of the section of the Federal Water Pollution Control Act herein redesignated as section 10 is amended by striking out the final period after the third sentence of such subsection and inserting the following in lieu thereof: "; or he finds that substantial economic injury results from the inability to market shellfish or shellfish products in interstate commerce because of pollution referred to in subsection (a) and action of Federal, State, or local authorities."

Sec. 6. The section of the Federal Water Pollution Control Act hereinbefore redesignated as section 12 is amended by adding at the end thereof the following new subsections:

"(d) Each recipient of assistance under this Act shall keep such records as the Secretary shall prescribe, including records which fully disclose the amount and disposition by such recipient of the proceeds of such assistance, the total cost of the project or undertaking in connection with which such assistance is given or used, and the amount of that portion of the cost of the project or undertaking supplied by other sources, and such other records as will facilitate an effective audit.

"(e) The Secretary of Health, Education, and Welfare and the Comptroller General of the United States, or any of their duly authorized representatives, shall have access for the purpose of audit and examination to any books, documents, papers, and records of the recipients that are pertinent to the grants received under this Act."

Sec. 7. (a) Section 7(f)(6) of the Federal Water Pollution Control Act, as that section is redesignated by this Act, is amended by striking out "section 6(b) (4)." as contained therein and inserting in lieu thereof "section 8(b)(4).".

(b) Section 8 of the Federal Water Pollution Control Act, as that section is redesignated by this Act, is amended by striking out "section 5" as contained therein and inserting in lieu thereof "section 7".

(c) Section 10(b) of the Federal Water Pollution Control Act, as that section is redesignated by this Act, is amended by striking out "subsection (g)" and inserting in lieu thereof "subsection (h)".

(d) Section 10(i) of the Federal Water Pollution Control Act, as that section is redesignated by this Act, is amended by striking out "subsection (e)" and inserting in lieu thereof "subsection (f)".

(e) Section 11 of the Federal Water Pollution Control Act, as that section is redesignated by this Act, is amended by striking out "section 8(c)(3)" and inserting in lieu thereof "section 10(d)(3)" and by striking out "section 8(e)" and inserting in lieu thereof "section 10(f)".

Sec. 8. This Act may be cited as the "Water Quality Act of 1965".

Approved October 2, 1965.

PRESIDENT LYNDON B. JOHNSON'S MESSAGE TO CONGRESS ON POLLUTION*
February 23, 1966

Early in 1966, President Johnson sent a message to Congress on "Programs for Controlling Pollution and Preserving Our Natural and Historical Heritage." Excerpts from that message follow:

To the Congress of the United States:

Albert Schweitzer said: "Man has lost the capacity to foresee and to forestall. He will end by destroying the earth."

The most affluent nation on earth may feel that it is immune from this indictment. A nation that offered its people—a century ago—uncharted forests, broad sparkling rivers, and prairies ripe for planting, may have expected that bounty to endure forever.

But we do not live alone with wishful expectations.

We live with history. It tells us of a hundred proud civilizations that have decayed through careless neglect of the nature that fed them.

We live with the certain future of multiplying populations, whose demands on the resources of nature will equal their numbers.

We are not immune. We are not endowed—any more than were those perished nations of the past—with a limitless natural bounty.

Yet we are endowed with their experience. We are able to see the magnitude of the choice before us, and its consequences for every child born on our continent from this day forward.

Economists estimate that this generation has already suffered losses from pollution that run into billions of dollars each year. But the ultimate cost of pollution is incalculable.

We see that we can corrupt and destroy our lands, our rivers, our forests, and the atmosphere itself—all in the name of progress and necessity. Such a course leads to a barren America, bereft of its beauty, and shorn of its sustenance.

We see that there is another course—more expensive today, more demanding. Down this course lies a natural America restored to her people. The promise is clear rivers, tall forests, and clean air—a sane environment for man.

I shall propose in this message one means to achieve that promise. It requires, first, an understanding of what has already happened to our waters.

THE POLLUTION OF OUR WATERS

"Pollution touches us all. We are at the same time pollutors and sufferers

*H. Doc. 387, 89th Cong., 2nd sess. (Feb. 23, 1966).

[517]

from pollution. Today, we are certain that pollution adversely affects the quality of our lives. In the future, it may affect their duration."

These are the words of the Environmental Pollution Panel of the President's Science Advisory Committee. They were written in November 1965.

At that time, every river system in America suffered some degree of pollution.

At that time, discharges into our rivers and streams—both treated and untreated—equaled the raw sewage from almost 50 million people. Animal wastes and waste from our cities and towns were making water unfit for any use.

At that time, rivers, lakes, and estuaries were receiving great quantities of industrial chemicals—acids from mine runoff, detergents and minerals that would not "break down" in the ordinary life of the water. These pollutants were reentering domestic and industrial water supplies. They were killing fish. They posed hazards to both human and animal life.

By that time, on Lake Erie 6 of 32 public recreation and swimming areas had been closed down because the water was unsafe for human beings. The blue pike catch in the lake had fallen from 20 million pounds in 1937 to 7,000 pounds in 1960. The oxygen that fish need for life was being rapidly devoured by blooms of algae fed by pollutants.

At that time, in the lower Arkansas Red River Basin, oilfield development and irrigation were dumping salt into rivers. The result was an additional annual expense of $13 million to bring in fresh water.

I have placed these comments in the past tense not because they are no longer true. *They are more tragically true today than they were 4 months ago.*

I seek instead to make them a benchmark in restoring America's precious heritage to her people.

I seek to make them that point in time when Americans determined to resist the flow of poison in their rivers and streams.

I seek to make them ancient history for the next generation.

And I believe the conditions they describe can become just that—if we begin now, together, to cleanse our rivers of the blight that burdens them.

A CREED TO PRESERVE OUR NATURAL HERITAGE

To sustain an environment suitable for man, we must fight on a thousand battlegrounds. Despite all of our wealth and knowledge, we cannot create a redwood forest, a wild river, or a gleaming seashore.

But we can keep those we have.

The science that has increased our abundance can find ways to restore and renew an environment equal to our needs.

The time is ripe to set forth a creed to preserve our natural heritage—principles which men and women of good will, will support in order to assure the beauty and bounty of their land. Conservation is ethically sound. It is rooted in our love of the land, our respect for the rights of others, our devotion to the rule of law.

Let us proclaim a creed to preserve our natural heritage with rights and the duties to respect those rights:

The right to clean water—and the duty not to pollute it.

The right to clean air—and the duty not to befoul it.

The right to surroundings reasonably free from manmade ugliness—and the duty not to blight.

The right of easy access to places of beauty and tranquillity where every family can find recreation and refreshment—and the duty to preserve such places clean and unspoiled.

The right to enjoy plants and animals in their natural habitats—and the duty not to eliminate them from the face of this earth.

These rights assert that no person, or company or government has a right in this day and age to pollute, to abuse resources, or to waste our common heritage.

The work to achieve these rights will not be easy. It cannot be completed in a year or 5 years. But there will never be a better time to begin.

Let us from this moment begin our work in earnest—so that future generations of Americans will look back and say: "1966 was the year of the new conservation, when farsighted men took farsighted steps to preserve the beauty that is the heritage of our Republic."

I urge the Congress to give favorable consideration to the proposals I have recommended in this message.

Lyndon B. Johnson

The White House
February 23, 1966

THE CLEAN WATER RESTORATION ACT*
November 3, 1966

This act continued the fight against water pollution by greatly increasing appropriations for federal grants to construct municipal waste-treatment facilities; by establishing a "clean rivers restoration" program; by increasing funds for research; and by doubling the amount of federal support available to state and interstate water pollution control agencies to strengthen their programs. In the meantime, the Water Pollution Control Administration had been transferred from the Department of Health, Education, and Welfare to the Department of the Interior—a change made to better facilitate coordination between such Department of the Interior agencies as the Bureau of Sport Fisheries and Wildlife, the Bureau of Commercial Fisheries, the Geological Survey, the Office of Water Resources Research, the Bureau of Reclamation, the Office of Saline Water, the Bureau of Mines, and the Bureau of Outdoor Recreation. Recreationists hoped that the new center of activity for pollution control would result in greater attention to the outdoor recreation aspects of polluted water.

An Act to amend the Federal Water Pollution Control Act in order to improve and make more effective certain programs pursuant to such Act.

Be it enacted by the Senate and House of Representatives of the United States of America in Congress assembled, That this Act may be cited as the "Clean Water Restoration Act of 1966".

TITLE I

SEC. 101. Section 3 of the Federal Water Pollution Control Act, as amended, is amended by adding at the end thereof the following:

"(c)(1) The Secretary shall, at the request of the Governor of a State, or a majority of the governors when more than one State is involved, make a grant to pay not to exceed 50 per centum of the administrative expenses of a planning agency for a period not to exceed 3 years, if such agency provides for adequate representation of appropriate State, interstate, local, or (when appropriate) international, interests in the basin or portion thereof involved and is capable of developing an effective, comprehensive water quality control and abatement plan for a basin.

"(2) Each planning agency receiving a grant under this subsection shall develop a comprehensive pollution control and abatement plan for the basin which—

*80 *Statutes at Large,* 1246.

[520]

"(A) is consistent with any applicable water quality standards established pursuant to current law within the basin;

"(B) recommends such treatment works and sewer systems as will provide the most effective and economical means of collection, storage, treatment, and purification of wastes and recommends means to encourage both municipal and industrial use of such works and systems; and

"(C) recommends maintenance and improvement of water quality standards within the basin or portion thereof and recommends methods of adequately financing those facilities as may be necessary to implement the plan.

"(3) For the purposes of this subsection the term 'basin' includes, but is not limited to, rivers and their tributaries, streams, coastal waters, sounds, estuaries, bays, lakes, and portions thereof, as well as the lands drained thereby."

TITLE II

Sec. 201. (a) Section 6 of the Federal Water Pollution Control Act is amended to read as follows:

"GRANTS FOR RESEARCH AND DEVELOPMENT

"Sec. 6. (a) The Secretary is authorized to make grants to any State, municipality, or intermunicipal or interstate agency for the purpose of—

"(1) assisting in the development of any project which will demonstrate a new or improved method of controlling the discharge into any waters of untreated or inadequately treated sewage or other wastes from sewers which carry storm water or both storm water and sewage or other wastes, or

"(2) assisting in the development of any project which will demonstrate advanced waste treatment and water purification methods (including the temporary use of new or improved chemical additives which provide substantial immediate improvement to existing treatment processes) or new or improved methods of joint treatment systems for municipal and industrial wastes,

and for the purpose of reports, plans, and specifications in connection therewith.

"(b) The Secretary is authorized to make grants to persons for research and demonstration projects for prevention of pollution of waters by industry including, but not limited to, treatment of industrial waste.

"(c) Federal grants under subsection (a) of this section shall be subject to the following limitations:

"(1) No grant shall be made for any project pursuant to this section unless such project shall have been approved by the appropriate State water pollution control agency or agencies and by the Secretary;

"(2) No grant shall be made for any project in an amount exceeding 75 per centum of the estimated reasonable cost thereof as determined by the Secretary; and

"(3) No grant shall be made for any project under this section unless the Secretary determines that such project will serve as a useful demonstration for the purpose set forth in clause (1) or (2) of subsection (a).

"(d) Federal grants under susbection (b) of this section shall be subject to the following limitations:

"(1) No grant shall be made under this section in excess of $1,000,000;

"(2) No grant shall be made for more than 70 per centum of the cost of the project; and

"(3) No grant shall be made for any project unless the Secretary determines that such project will serve a useful purpose in the development or demonstration of a new or improved method of treating industrial wastes or otherwise preventing pollution of waters by industry, which method shall have industry-wide application.

"(e) For the purposes of this section there are authorized to be appropriated—

"(1) for the fiscal year ending June 30, 1966, and for each of the next three succeeding fiscal years, the sum of $20,000,000 per fiscal year for the purposes set forth in subsections (a) and (b) of this section, including contracts pursuant to such subsections for such purposes;

"(2) for the fiscal year ending June 30, 1967, and for each of the next two succeeding fiscal years, the sum of $20,000,000 per fiscal year for the purpose set forth in clause (2) of subsection (a); and

"(3) for the fiscal year ending June 30, 1967, and for each of the next two succeeding fiscal years, the sum of $20,000,000 per fiscal year for the purpose set forth in subsection (b)."

(b) Section 5 of such Act is amended by adding at the end thereof the following new subsections:

"(g) (1) The Secretary shall, in cooperation with the Secretary of the Army, the Secretary of Agriculture, the Water Resources Council, and with other appropriate Federal, State, interstate, or local public bodies and private organizations, institutions, and individuals, conduct and promote, and encourage contributions to, a comprehensive study of the effects of pollution, including sedimentation, in the estuaries and estuarine zones of the United States on fish and wildlife, on sport and commercial fishing, on recreation, on water supply and water power, and on other beneficial purposes. Such study shall also consider the effect of demographic trends, the exploitation of mineral resources and fossil fuels, land and industrial development, navigation, flood and erosion control, and other uses of estuaries and estuarine zones upon the pollution of the waters therein.

"(2) In conducting the above study, the Secretary shall assemble, coordinate, and organize all existing pertinent information on the Nation's estuaries and estuarine zones; carry out a program of investigations and surveys to supplement existing information in representative estuaries and estuarine zones; and identify the problems and areas where further research and study are required.

"(3) The Secretary shall submit to the Congress a final report of the study authorized by this subsection not later than three years after the date of enactment of this subsection. Copies of the report shall be made available to all interested parties, public and private. The report shall include, but not be limited to—

"(A) an analysis of the importance of estuaries to the economic and social well-being of the people of the United States and of the effects of pollution upon the use and enjoyment of such estuaries;

"(B) a discussion of the major economic, social, and ecological trends occurring in the estuarine zones of the Nation;

"(C) recommendations for a comprehensive national program for the preservation, study, use, and development of estuaries of the Nation, and the respective responsibilities which should be assumed by Federal, State, and local governments and by public and private interests.

"(4) There is authorized to be appropriated the sum of $1,000,000 per fiscal year for the fiscal years ending June 30, 1967, June 30, 1968, and June 30, 1969, to carry out the purposes of this subsection.

"(5) For the purpose of this subsection, the term 'estuarine zones' means an environmental system consisting of an estuary and those transitional areas which are consistently influenced or affected by water from an estuary such as, but not limited to, salt marshes, coastal and intertidal areas, bays, harbors, lagoons, inshore waters, and channels, and the term 'estuary' means all or part of the mouth of a navigable or interstate river or stream or other body of water having unimpaired natural connection with open sea and within which the sea water is measurably diluted with fresh water derived from land drainage.

"(h) There is authorized to be appropriated to carry out this section, other than subsection (g), not to exceed $60,000,000 for the fiscal year ending June 30, 1968, and $65,000,000 for the fiscal year ending June 30, 1969. Sums so appropriated shall remain available until expended."

(c) (1) Subsection (d) of section 5 of the Federal Water Pollution Control Act is amended by striking out "(1)" and by striking out all of paragraph (2) of such subsection.

(2) The amendment made by this subsection shall take effect July 1, 1967.

SEC. 202. (a) Subsection (a) of section 7 of the Federal Water Pollution Control Act is amended by striking out "and for each succeeding fiscal year to and including the fiscal year ending June 30, 1968, $5,000,000" and inserting in lieu thereof "for each succeeding fiscal year to and including the fiscal year ending June 30, 1967, $5,000,000, and for each succeeding fiscal year to and including the fiscal year ending June 30, 1971, $10,000,000".

(b) Subsection (a) of section 7 of the Federal Water Pollution Control Act is further amended by striking out the period at the end thereof and inserting in lieu thereof a comma and the following: "including the training of personnel of public agencies."

SEC. 203. (a) Subsection (b) of section 8 of the Federal Water Pollution Control Act is amended to read as follows:

"(b) Federal grants under this section shall be subject to the following limitations: (1) No grant shall be made for any project pursuant to this section unless such project shall have been approved by the appropriate State water pollution control agency or agencies and by the Secretary and unless such project is included in a comprehensive program developed pursuant to this Act; (2) no grant shall be made for any project in an amount exceeding 30 per centum of the estimated reasonable cost thereof as determined by the Secretary; (3) no grant shall be made unless the grantee agrees to pay the remaining cost; (4) no grant shall be made for any project under this section until the applicant has made provision satisfactory to the Secretary for assuring proper and efficient operation and maintenance of the treatment works after completion of the construction thereof; and (5) no grant shall be made for any project under this section unless such project is in conformity with the State water pollution control plan submitted pursuant to the provisions of section 7 and has been certified by the appropriate State water pollution control agency as entitled to priority over other eligible projects on the basis of financial as well as water pollution control needs; (6) the percentage limitation of 30 per centum imposed by clause (2) of this subsection shall be increased to a maximum of 40 per centum in the case of grants made under this section from funds allocated for a fiscal year to a State under subsection (c) of this section if the State agrees to pay not less than 30 per centum of the estimated reasonable cost (as determined by the Secretary) of all projects for which Federal grants are to be made under this section from such allocation; (7) the percentage limitations imposed by clause (2) of this subsection shall be increased to a maximum of 50 per centum in the case of grants made under this section from funds allocated for a fiscal year to a State under subsection (c) of this section if the State agrees to pay not less than 25 per centum of the estimated reasonable costs (as determined by the Secretary) of all projects for which Federal grants are to be made under this section from such allocation and if enforceable water quality standards have been established for the waters into which the project discharges, in accordance with section 10(c) of this Act in the case of interstate waters, and under State law in the case of intrastate waters.

(b) The amendment made by subsection (a) of this section shall take effect July 1, 1967.

SEC. 204. The next to the last sentence of subsection (c) of section 8 of the Federal Water Pollution Control Act is amended by striking out the period at the end thereof and inserting in lieu thereof a comma and the following: "except that in the case of any project on which construction was initiated in such State after June 30, 1966, which was approved by the appropriate State water pollution control agency and which the Secretary finds meets the requirements of this section but was constructed without such assistance, such allotments for any fiscal year ending prior to July 1, 1971, shall also be available for payments in reimbursement of State or local funds used for such project prior to July 1, 1971, to the extent that assistance could have been provided under this section if such project had been approved pursuant to this section and adequate funds had been available. In the case of any project on which construction was initiated in such State after June 30, 1966, and which was constructed with assistance pursuant to this section but the amount of such assistance was a lesser per centum of the cost of construction than was allowable pursuant to this section, such allotments shall also be available for payments in reimbursement of State or local funds used for such project prior to July 1, 1971, to the extent that assistance could have been provided under this section if adequate funds had been available. Neither a finding by the Secretary that a project meets the requirements of this subsection, nor any other provision of this subsection, shall be construed to constitute a commitment or obligation of the United States to provide funds to make or pay any grant for such project."

SEC. 205. Subsection (d) of section 8 of the Federal Water Pollution Control Act is amended by striking out "and $150,000,000 for the fiscal year ending June 30, 1967." and inserting in lieu thereof the following: $150,000,000 for the fiscal year ending June 30, 1967; $450,000,000 for the fiscal year ending June 30, 1968; $700,000,000 for the fiscal year ending June 30, 1969; $1,000,000,000 for the fiscal year ending June 30, 1970; and $1,250,000,000 for the fiscal year ending June 30, 1971."

SEC. 206. Section 10(d) of the Federal Water Pollution Control Act is amended by redesignating paragraphs (2) and (3) as paragraphs (3) and (4), respectively, and by inserting immediately after paragraph (1) the following new paragraph:

"(2) Whenever the Secretary, upon receipt of reports, surveys, or studies from any duly constituted international agency, has reason to believe that any pollution referred to in subsection (a) of this section which endangers the health or welfare of persons in a foreign country is occurring, and the Secretary of State requests him to abate such pollution, he shall give formal notification thereof to the State water pollution control agency of the State in which such discharge or discharges originate and to the interstate water pollution control agency, if any, and shall call promptly a conference of such agency or agencies, if he believes that such pollution is occurring in sufficient quantity to warrant such action. The Secretary, through the Secretary of State, shall invite the foreign country which may be adversely affected by the pollution to attend and participate in the conference, and the representative of such country shall, for the purpose of the conference and any further proceeding resulting from such conference, have all the

[525]

rights of a State water pollution control agency. This paragraph shall apply only to a foreign country which the Secretary determines has given the United States essentially the same rights with respect to the prevention and control of water pollution occurring in that country as is given that country by this paragraph. Nothing in this paragraph shall be construed to modify, amend, repeal, or otherwise affect the provisions of the 1909 Boundary Waters Treaty between Canada and the United States or the Water Utilization Treaty of 1944 between Mexico and the United States (59 Stat. 1219), relative to the control and abatement of water pollution in waters covered by those treaties."

Sec. 207. Section 10(d) (3) of the Federal Water Pollution Control Act (as redesignated by this Act) is amended by inserting after the first sentence thereof the following: "In addition, it shall be the responsibility of the chairman of the conference to give every person contributing to the alleged pollution or affected by it an opportunity to make a full statement of his views to the conference."

Sec. 208. (a) Section 10 of the Federal Water Pollution Control Act is further amended by adding at the end thereof the following new subsection:

"(k) (1) At the request of a majority of the conferees in any conference called under this section the Secretary is authorized to request any person whose alleged activities result in discharges causing or contributing to water pollution, to file with him a report (in such form as may be prescribed in regulations promulgated by him) based on existing data, furnishing such information as may reasonably be requested as to the character, kind, and quantity of such discharges and the use of facilities or other means to prevent or reduce such discharges by the person filing such a report. No person shall be required in such report to divulge trade secrets or secret processes, and all information reported shall be considered confidential for the purposes of section 1905 of title 18 of the United States Code.

"(2) If any person required to file any report under this subsection shall fail to do so within the time fixed by regulations for filing the same, and such failure shall continue for thirty days after notice of such default, such person may, by order of a majority of the conferees, be subject to a forfeiture of $100 for each and every day of the continuance of such failure which forfeiture shall be payable into the Treasury of the United States and shall be recoverable in a civil suit in the name of the United States brought in the district where such person has his principal office or in any district in which he does business. The Secretary may upon application therefor remit or mitigate any forfeiture provided for under this subsection and he shall have authority to determine the facts upon all such applications.

"(3) It shall be the duty of the various United States attorneys, under the direction of the Attorney General of the United States, to prosecute for the recovery of such forfeitures."

(b) Subsection (f) of section 10 of the Federal Water Pollution Control Act is amended (1) by striking out "(f)" and inserting in lieu thereof "(f) (1)", (2) by inserting immediately after the third sentence thereof the following: "It shall be the responsibility of the Hearing Board to give every person contributing to the alleged pollution or affected by it an opportunity to make a full statement of his views to the Hearing Board.", and (3) by adding at the end thereof the following new paragraphs:

"(2) In connection with any hearing called under this section the Secretary is authorized to require any person whose alleged activities result in discharges causing or contributing to water pollution to file with him, in such form as he may prescribe, a report based on existing data, furnishing such information as may reasonably be required as to the character, kind, and quantity of such discharges and the use of facilities or other means to prevent or reduce such discharges by the person filing such a report. Such report shall be made under oath or otherwise, as the Secretary may prescribe, and shall be filed with the Secretary within such reasonable period as the Secretary may prescribe, unless additional time be granted by the Secretary. No person shall be required in such report to divulge trade secrets or secret processes, and all information reported shall be considered confidential for the purposes of section 1905 of title 18 of the United States Code.

"(3) If any person required to file any report under paragraph (2) of this subsection shall fail to do so within the time fixed by the Secretary for filing the same, and such failure shall continue for thirty days after notice of such default, such person shall forefeit to the United States the sum of $100 for each and every day of the continuance of such failure, which forfeiture shall be payable into the Treasury of the United States, and shall be recoverable in a civil suit in the name of the United States brought in the district where such person has his principal office or in any district in which he does business. The Secretary may upon application therefor remit or mitigate any forfeiture provided for under this paragraph and he shall have authority to determine the facts upon all such applications.

"(4) It shall be the duty of the various United States attorneys, under the direction of the Attorney General of the United States, to prosecute for the recovery of such forfeitures."

SEC. 209. Paragraph (f) of section 13 of the Federal Water Pollution Control Act is amended by striking out the period at the end thereof and inserting in lieu thereof a comma and the following: "and an Indian tribe or an authorized Indian tribal organization."

SEC. 210. The Federal Water Pollution Control Act, as amended, is amended by renumbering existing section 16 as section 19 and by adding immediately after section 15 the following new sections:

"SEC. 16. (a) In order to provide the basis for evaluating programs authorized by this Act, the development of new programs, and to furnish the Congress with the information necessary for authorization of appropriations for fiscal years beginning after June 30, 1968, the Secretary, in cooperation with State water pollution control agencies and other water pollution control planning agencies, shall make a detailed estimate of the cost of carrying out the provisions of this Act; a comprehensive study of the economic impact on affected units of government of the cost of installation of treatment facilities; and a comprehensive analysis of the national requirements for and the cost of treating municipal, industrial, and other effluent to attain such water quality standards as established pursuant to this Act or applicable State law. The Secretary shall submit such detailed estimate and such comprehensive study of such cost for the five-year period beginning July 1, 1968, to the Congress no later than January 10, 1968, such study to be updated each year thereafter.

"(b) The Secretary shall also make a complete investigation and study to determine (1) the need for additional trained State and local personnel to carry out programs assisted pursuant to this Act and other programs for the same purpose as this Act, and (2) means of using existing Federal training programs to train such personnel. He shall report the results of such investigation and study to the President and the Congress not later than July 1, 1967.

"Sec. 17. The Secretary of the Interior shall, in consultation with the Secretary of the Army, the Secretary of the department in which the Coast Guard is operating, the Secretary of Health, Education, and Welfare, and the Secretary of Commerce, conduct a full and complete investigation and study of the extent of the pollution of all navigable waters of the United States from litter and sewage discharged, dumped, or otherwise deposited into such waters from watercraft using such waters, and methods of abating either in whole or in part such pollution. The Secretary shall submit a report of such investigation to Congress, together with his recommendations for any necessary legislation, not later than July 1, 1967.

"Sec. 18. The Secretary of the Interior shall conduct a full and complete investigation and study of methods for providing incentives designed to assist in the construction of facilities and works by industry designed to reduce or abate water pollution. Such study shall include, but not be limited to, the possible use of tax incentives as well as other methods of financial assistance. In carrying out this study the Secretary shall consult with the Secretary of the Treasury as well as the head of any other appropriate department or agency of the Federal Government. The Secretary shall report the results of such investigation and study, together with his recommendations, to the Congress not later than January 30, 1968."

Sec. 211. (a) The Oil Pollution Act, 1924 (43 Stat. 604; 33 U.S.C. 431 et seq.), is amended to read as follows: "That this Act may be cited as the 'Oil Pollution Act, 1924'."

"Sec. 2. When used in this Act, unless the context otherwise requires—

"(1) 'oil' means oil of any kind or in any form, including fuel oil, sludge, and oil refuse;

"(2) 'person' means an individual, company, partnership, corporation, or association; any owner, operator, master, officer, or employee of a vessel; and any officer, agent or employee of the United States;

"(3) 'discharge' means any grossly negligent, or willful spilling, leaking, pumping, pouring, emitting, or emptying of oil;

"(4) 'navigable waters of the United States' means all portions of the sea within the territorial jurisdiction of the United States, and all inland waters navigable in fact; and

"(5) 'Secretary' means the Secretary of the Interior.

"Sec. 3. (a) Except in case of emergency imperiling life or property, or unavoidable accident, collision, or stranding, and except as otherwise permitted by regulations prescribed by the Secretary as hereinafter authorized, it is unlawful for any person to discharge or permit the discharge from any boat or vessel of oil by any method, means, or manner into or upon the navigable waters of the United States, and adjoining shorelines of the United States.

"(b) Any person discharging or permitting the discharge of oil from any boat or vessel, into or upon the navigable waters of the United States shall remove the same from the navigable waters of the United States, and adjoining shorelines immediately. If such person fails to do so, the Secretary may remove the oil or may arrange for its removal, and such person shall be liable to the United States, in addition to the penalties prescribed in section 4 of this Act, for all costs and expenses reasonably incurred by the Secretary in removing the oil from the navigable waters of the United States, and adjoining shorelines of the United States. These costs and expenses shall constitute a lien on such boat or vessel which may be recovered in proceedings by libel in rem.

"(c) The Secretary may prescribe regulations which—

"(1) permit the discharge of oil from boats or vessels in such quantities under such conditions, and at such times and places as in his opinion will not be deleterious to health or marine life or a menace to navigation, or dangerous to persons or property engaged in commerce on navigable waters of the United States; and

"(2) relate to the removal or cost or removal, or both, of oil from the navigable waters of the United States, and adjoining shorelines of the United States.

"Sec. 4. (a) Any person who violates section 3(a) of this Act shall, upon conviction thereof, be punished by a fine not exceeding $2,500, or by imprisonment not exceeding one year, or by both such fine and imprisonment for each offense.

"(b) Any boat or vessel other than a boat or vessel owned and operated by the United States from which oil is discharged in violation of section 3(a) of this Act shall be liable for a penalty of not more than $10,000. Clearance of a boat or

[529]

vessel liable for this penalty from a port of the United States may be withheld until the penalty is paid. The penalty shall constitute a lien on such boat or vessel which may be recovered in proceedings by libel in rem in the district court of the United States for any district within which such boat or vessel may be.

"SEC. 5. The Commandant of the Coast Guard may, subject to the provisions of section 4450 of the Revised Statutes, as amended (46 U.S.C. 239), suspend or revoke a license issued to the master or other licensed officer of any boat or vessel found violating the provisions of section 3 of this Act.

"SEC. 6. In the administration of this Act the Secretary may, with the consent of the Commandant of the Coast Guard or the Secretary of the Army, make use of the organization, equipment, and agencies, including engineering, clerical, and other personnel, employed by the Coast Guard or the Department of the Army, respectively, for the preservation and protection of navigable waters of the United States. For the better enforcement of the provisions of this Act, the officers and agents of the United States in charge of river and harbor improvements and persons employed under them by authority of the Secretary of the Army, and persons employed by the Secretary, and officers of the Customs and Coast Guard of the United States shall have the power and authority and it shall be their duty to swear out process and to arrest and take into custody, with or without process, any person who may violate any of such provisions, except that no person shall be arrested without process for a violation not committed in the presence of some one of the aforesaid persons. Whenever any arrest is made under the provisions of this Act the person so arrested shall be brought forthwith before a commissioner, judge, or court of the United States for examination of the offenses alleged against him, and such commissioner, judge or court shall proceed in respect thereto as authorized by law in cases of crimes against the United States.

"SEC. 7. This Act shall be in addition to other laws for the preservation and protection of navigable waters of the United States and shall not be construed as repealing, modifying, or in any manner affecting the provisions of such laws."

(b) The amendment made by subsection (a) of this section shall take effect on the thirtieth day which begins after the date of enactment of this Act.

Approved November 3, 1966

AN INQUEST ON OUR LAKES AND RIVERS*
1968

Supreme Court Justice William O. Douglas was for many years one of the nation's most fervent conservationists. In this wide-ranging and thoughtful article he surveyed the effects of pollution on the lakes and rivers of the United States and proposed some methods for solving the problem.

"It's too thick to drink and too thin to plow." The speaker was a tall, lean middle-aged man long identified with the University of Pennsylvania's crews who raced on the Schuylkill river in sculls. That day the water of the Schuylkill did, indeed, look like the viscous liquids of a cesspool as we peered at it from a Philadelphia bridge.

But the Schuylkill is pure, compared with some of our other waterways. Recently I revisited Houston, Texas, and the Buffalo Bayou, as fascinating a waterway as God ever made, which skirts the San Jacinto Battleground, famous in Texas history. Once it sparkled with myriads of life. The alligator was there and many species of fish. Birds without number frequented it, including great white pelicans and the water turkey that swims under water in pursuit of fish and has so little oil on its wings and body that it must spend long hours each day on the sunny side of a tree, drying its feathers. Then men dug out Buffalo Bayou, making it wider than a football field, deep enough for ocean liners and 50 miles long. As a result, Houston today is the nation's third largest port, supporting the largest industrial complex in the Southwest. But Buffalo Bayou today is a stinking open sewer and a disgrace to any area. It carries to the Gulf the sewage of about 2,000,000 people and 200 industries. One need not be an expert to detect both its chemical and its fecal odor. Buffalo Bayou is now a dead river, supporting only the gar, a symbol of ugliness. A red-brown scum covers the surface and occasionally streaks of white detergent foam. Fascinating Buffalo Bayou is now a smelly corpse.

Almost every community faces a substantial pollution problem. Rock Creek, once a sparkling stream fed by a spring in Maryland, was for years one of Washington, D.C.'s main attractions. Today it is a serious health hazard. It receives discharges from District sewers that are combined to carry both storm waters and sewage at time of heavy rain; people use it as a dump; the zoo puts its wastes into Rock Creek. The famous creek that Teddy Roosevelt tried to preserve is so heavy with silt from upstream construction projects that an old water wheel that once ran a gristmill will not work. And one who talks to the experts in the nation's capital learns that it will take until 2000 A.D. to convert Rock Creek into sanitary swimming holes for children.

The entire Potomac is so heavily polluted that it taxes the ingenuity of public-health experts to make the water both safe to drink and palatable. Every city in the several states the Potomac drains has a sewage-disposal plant, but the population explosion has made most of those plants inadequate to handle the supply. The Army Corps of Engineers, instead of coming up with an over-all sewage-disposal system that would clean up the Potomac and Chesapeake Bay as well, proposes a huge dam at Seneca that would destroy 80 miles of the river, produce a fluctuating water level that would expose long, ugly banks of mud and that would, the engineers say, provide a head of water adequate to flush the Potomac of sewage—at least in the environs of Washington.

Lake Erie, the fourth largest of the Great Lakes, is almost a dead lake. In addition to sewage from many cities, it receives over a ton of chemicals a minute from plants in four states. Beaches along the lake shore have had to be closed. Boating has dropped off because of the filth that accumulates on the hulls. Sport fishing has declined. Commercial fishing is only a small fraction of what it was. Pickerel and cisco disappeared and trash fish took their place. Large areas of the lake were found to have zero oxygen; plant life and fish life disappeared and the anaerobic, or nonoxygen, species of aquatic life (such as worms) took over. "What should be taking place over eons of time," one Public Health Service officer said, "is now vastly speeded up"—due to the pollutants. This expert says that Lake Erie is very sick and will have a convalescence running into many years.

Lake Michigan is sick, according to Secretary of the Interior Stewart L. Udall; and unless corrective steps are taken, it, too, will be dead. Michigan is, indeed, in a more precarious position than Erie; for while the latter is the beneficiary of a cleansing flow from Superior and Huron, Lake Michigan is isolated.

Some parts of the Ohio river have zero oxygen and not even the hardy trash fish can live there. At a zero oxygen level, a river becomes septic. A healthy river, the experts say, must have five parts of oxygen per million parts of water. When it has two parts per million, it has "the minimum quality which can be tolerated" for fish life.

The pollution of the Willamette river in Oregon is one of the nation's most notorious examples. I believe it was in 1946 that Stanley Jewett of the Fish and Wildlife Service and I took fresh, healthy rainbow trout and put them in a steel-mesh cage and lowered them at the mouth of the Willamette. We estimated that the oxygen content of the water at that point was probably 0 mg. The fish were, indeed, fairly inert within five minutes. The river has not improved since that time. As a matter of fact, its summer flow marks such a low concentration of dissolved oxygen that a salmon probably could never get through alive, whether it was going upstream or coming down. While there is very little upstream migration at that time, there is considerable downstream migration. Fish need a dissolved oxygen concentration of 5 mg. per liter to survive, and the Willamette studies indicate that the level in its lower reaches drops to somewhere between 0 mg. and 2 mg.

The problem of the Willamette is largely created by seven pulp mills. With two exceptions, these mills use a sulphite pulping process, rather than cooking chemicals by condensing and burning wastes as do plants with more modern processes. About 70 percent of the damaging pollutants in the Willamette comes from the pulp mills, and the pulp mills have pretty well controlled the state politics of Oregon when it comes to pollution control.

The St. Lawrence Seaway, which connects Duluth, Minnesota, with the ocean, is hailed as a great achievement. But there is already alarm over the pollution taking place (a) by vessels emptying their bilges in the Great Lakes, (b) by garbage disposal and (c) by the dumping of raw sewage.

The Merrimack in Massachusetts, to whose pollution Thoreau objected in 1839, has been getting progressively worse. It has turned a filthy brown and emits bubbles that carry nauseating gases.

In the lower Mississippi, millions of fish turn belly up and die. Near St. Louis, chicken feathers and viscera pile so high they stop a motorboat. In portions of the Hudson, only scavenger eels live.

The Presumpscot river near Portland, Maine, gives off malodorous hydrogen sulphide from paper-pulp sludge that has accumulated over the decades.

Beautiful Lake Tahoe—the sapphire that lies partly in Nevada and partly in California—seems doomed. I recently flew over it in a small plane; and the brown streaks of sewage had already possessed nearly half of the lake. The gambling casinos on the lake's edge attract tens of thousands, and it is largely their sewage that is doing the damage. Two hundred thousand gallons of sewage a day enters Lake Tahoe.

Progress seemed under way when a Federal abatement order in 1966 caused California and Nevada to sign an interstate agreement that would, among other things, export the sewage by pipeline out of the Tahoe drainage basin by 1970. But in 1967, Governor Reagan upset the settlement by turning over the problem "for study" during the next 18 months to two California and three Nevada counties.

The powerful forces that may turn the tide are the citizens' groups that are rallying public opinion. The case is, in a way, easy to plead, for the impending demise of Tahoe can be seen from almost any height.

The same story could be told about some stream or about some lake in every state of the Union, except possibly Alaska, where the total population is still only about 250,000. But where people pile up and industry takes hold, the problem of pollution multiplies.

A typical city of 100,000 produces every day of the year one ton of detergents,

17 tons of organic suspended solids, 16 tons of organic dissolved solids, 8 tons of inorganic dissolved solids and 60 cubic feet of grime.

While most cities have sewage-disposal plants, many communities do not; and the use of septic tanks and cesspools in congested areas has raised profound problems that affect the quality of the underground percolating waters. Indeed, the earth of an entire area may become so polluted that the natural processes of drainage purification and bacterial action are so overtaxed they are ineffective. Where the surface supply is also in jeopardy, the problem of a safe water supply then becomes almost insoluble. Some parts of the country, notably Suffolk County, New York, have approached this critical condition.

Of the cities and towns that have sewage-disposal plants, it is estimated that about 18 percent still discharge untreated waste into the country's waterways.

Some progress is being made. A compact of the six New England States plus New York has put all their waterways into various classes. Class A is uniformly excellent water. Class B is suitable for swimming, for fishing, for irrigation and for drinking after it is treated. Class C is suitable for boating, for fish life, for irrigation and for some industrial uses, while the other classes are largely available only for industrial uses. It is to the lower categories that the Merrimack, which I have already mentioned, has been relegated.

The Congress has been busy, and recent acts under the title of Federal Water Pollution Control have put into motion important machinery. Each state was given until June 30, 1967, to adopt water-quality criteria applicable "to interstate waters or portions thereof" within the state, and to submit a plan for the implementation and enforcement of those water-quality criteria. These standards are subject to Federal approval. In the absence of state action adopting water-quality criteria, the Federal Government can move and establish its own. After the standards are fixed, there are methods for policing and enforcing them. As this article is written, the hearings are going on across the country.

Why the program was put in the Department of the Interior is a mystery. For Interior harbors two of our worst polluters—the Bureau of Mines, which allows acid to despoil our waterways, and the Bureau of Reclamation, whose projects now fill our streams with salt.

Missouri recently held its hearings on standards for the Missouri River. Missouri has a water-pollution-control association that pointed out at the hearing that the Missouri River was an excellent water supply for half the people of the state and for a significant portion of its industries. The association, however, went on to say: "Use of the Missouri River for removal and ultimate disposal of the sewered wastes of cities and industries has economic value far greater than does use of the river as a source of municipal and industrial water supply. Without exception, cities and industries along the Missouri River could obtain adequate supplies of water of good quality from subsurface sources. Likewise, other means can be found for transportation, fish and wildlife propagation, livestock watering and recreation." In other words, this association proposes that everybody abandon the Missouri and, in the cause of economics, leave it to the polluters.

This association at the hearing predicted economic doom unless streams in Missouri are used for their capacity to assimilate wastes, saying that the failure to do so would "lower standards of living and the general economy and decrease employment."

In taking direct aim at those who like a clean river for its beauty, for its swimming holes, for its fishing, boating and canoeing, the association said at the hearing: "While the entire public will share in paying the cost of maintaining that water quality, only a fraction of the public will enjoy the benefits of those water uses for which water-quality requirements are most demanding."

The inertia of those who have a vested interest in pollution is one obstacle. These interests are powerful. They are represented by most of our vast industrial complex. They are made up of huge metropolitan areas like New York, and they have never made any attempt to treat their sewage. They are made up of many who still look upon a river as having no value except as a carrier of wastes.

In addition to the inertia is the cost of cleanup, and the cost is going to be staggering. For example, the city of St. Louis recently undertook a contract to build a sewage-disposal plant—not an up-to-date variety, but one of the most primitive nature. It will contain only a primary treatment process, which does little more than settle out the solids. This contract alone is estimated to cost at least $95,000,000. While the Federal share of these programs was promised for from 30 percent to 50 percent of the cost, the Federal budget has already been drastically cut, due to Vietnam expenditures; and the appropriation of the Federal Water Pollution Control Administration was cut by two thirds for the fiscal year ending June 30, 1968.

Industrial use frequently requires cool water for its processes, the water eventually returning to the river at a high degree of temperature. This process, if continued, may raise the temperature of the entire stream. A stream for trout must be a cool-water stream. Raising a stream's temperature may change its entire life, ruining not only its recreational potential but its commercial potential as well; e.g., its production of shellfish.

This has happened to several streams, notably the St. Croix in Minnesota and the lower Potomac in Virginia. The heating of the lower Potomac waters is apparently modifying vast populations of microscopic plants that start the food chain in the river. It has reduced the white perch and certain flatfish and caused the soft-shelled clams to disappear. It has killed tens of thousands of crabs.

The dangers of thermal pollution multiply fast; and with the oncoming use of nuclear power that demands great quantities of cooling water, the risks ahead are increasing.

[535]

Saving a stream from this fate means requiring industry to build cooling towers for its water and using the same water over and over again.

Strip mining for coal is another source of great infection. Strip mining uses massive machinery to remove coal near the surface. And it is a process notorious for desecrating wild land and poisoning pure water. There is sulphur in these Appalachian lands, and sulphur when wet produces sulphuric acid, which destroys all vegetation and all aquatic life in the streams and ponds that it reaches. At least 4000 miles of Appalachian streams are being poisoned in this way. TVA as well as private operators are the despoilers, TVA flying the Federal flag of conservation. It uses coal from strip mining to run its stand-by steam plants.

Why must we the people tolerate this ruination of our mountain waterways?

The problem has been neglected so long, the population has been increasing so fast, that the conditions across the country have reached an emergency status. So the crisis that has been developing around our waterways is one of the greatest we have had to face, at least since the Civil War.

And so the battle lines are being drawn in the late 1960s.

We in America have no monopoly on this pollution problem. Europe knows it intimately, and recently the conditions on the Rhine reached such desperate proportions that steps are under way to preserve the river.

The same awareness exists in the Soviet Union. We are told by the Soviet Academy of Science that in the heavily industrialized Ural Mountains area there is not "one single unpolluted river." Domestic and industrial water supplies have been greatly impaired. Fish have been deprived of spawning and feeding grounds and pollution has been so severe in spots that some Russian rivers have become impassable.

When I was in Siberia in 1965, I visited Lake Baikal. The lumber industry was getting under way and the cutting caused soil erosion that filled the river beds with mud and even brought it into the lake. Lake Baikal is unique in scientific circles. It has, it is said, the purest water in the world and it is the site of intense Russian scientific endeavors. When I was there, Russian pulp mills, newly constructed near Lake Baikal, were running their discharge pipes to the lake. The Russian scientists were up in arms and their power and prestige in the Soviet Union was so great they were able to get a change that might save the lake from pollution. The alternative they proposed was that there should be constructed a long pipeline that would carry the industrial wastes from the pulp mills through a small mountain range into a stream flowing north into the Arctic Ocean. By 1968, the Russian scientists had lost their battle and Lake Baikal was being polluted by the industrial waste from the new pulp mills.

The answer to the problem of pollution is no longer a mystery. Wherever and whenever it takes place, technology has most of the answers and the problem is to mobilize the people and the financial resources to clean up the lakes and rivers. Science is constantly putting these problems in new dimensions. Thus great progress made in desalting water from the ocean—an experiment headed up by Israel beginning about 20 years ago. While costs are still higher than those normally associated with the creation of municipal water supplies, they are within reach once the urgency is felt.

In 1964, when Fidel Castro decided to cut off all Cuban water on Guantánamo Bay, we decided to be independent of him and quietly installed a big desalting plant. Sea water is heated under pressure to 195 degrees F., when it flashes into steam. This process is repeated many times, the steam producing a condensate that is almost tasteless, since it contains no minerals. At Guantánamo we are producing one gallon of fresh water out of 16 gallons of sea water. Now, we produce at Guantánamo 2,250,000 gallons a day—more than enough to meet the needs of the base; and with the steam that is generated, we operate an electric power plant of 1500 kws.

The point of this is that not only is desalting useful to seacoast cities short of water but it is also useful to take the nutrients out of sewage, making it possible to return pure water to the river or the lake and to pipe the residue off to centers where it can be processed for industrial or agricultural use. The avenues leading to the solution of the pollution problem are numerous and science is constantly opening up new ones.

The problem of our rivers does not end with pollution. The erection of dams is probably our problem number two. Dams for hydroelectric power became a very popular political slogan about 30 years ago. Hydroelectric power is cheap power and it has become associated in the public mind in this country with *public* power. Whether a dam is built to generate public power on the one hand or private power on the other, it still ruins a river as a free-flowing stream. There is no turning back the clock by removing the dams that we already have built. But there is still opportunity to save what remains of our free-flowing rivers and seek our power from other sources. The remaining free-flowing rivers that we have are national treasures and should be cleaned up and preserved for their great recreational and spiritual values.

Sometimes these dams are proposed for flood control, sometimes for a water supply. There may be no alternative to one dam or a series of dams when it comes to flood control or for water supply. Yet even here, if the design is to save a free-flowing river, such dams as are needed can be put way upstream or on a tributary, saving the main waterway for fishermen, canoeists, swimmers, and the like.

A case in point is the Potomac river. As I have said, the Corps of Engineers has planned a dam to provide a head of water to flush the river of sewage. It has also proposed dams for a water supply, and there is no doubt but that the metropolitan area of the nation's capital needs prudent planning in that connection. But here again, alternatives are available. There is the estuary that runs for about 30 miles from Little Falls just above Chain Bridge down into Chesapeake

Bay. This part of the estuary is not salt or brackish water. It is tidal water that stays fresh. The technicians will probably deny that the water is fresh, because the water in the estuary contains tracings of salt. But those small portions of salt still leave the water potable, and it is potable water that is needed for the city's domestic use.

So in making plans for the city's future water supply, a pumping plant could easily be installed below Little Falls to move into action when the water above Little Falls becomes dangerouly low. The estuary contains 100 billion gallons of potable water and this, plus the flow of the river, is enough to keep the nation's capital supplied for the indefinite future, no matter how big it grows—*once the Potomac is cleaned up.*

Why does the Corps of Engineers therefore suggest dams instead of a pumping plant in the estuary plus complete sewage treatment and removal of all of the pollutants from the water? That remains a mystery. Many think it is because the Corps builds dams very well and does not do other things quite as well and, therefore, it imposes upon society its specialty, like the chef who imposes his own favorite dish on all the patrons! That has led some to say, "We pay the farmers not to plant crops. Why don't we pay the Corps of Engineers not to build dams?"

My point is that the free-flowing river usually can be saved by the use of alternatives and our search should be for those alternatives.

The reason for this is accentuated when one studies the history of the dams. In my state of Washington, there is a very fine dam on the Wenatchee that is now useless because it is sanded in. There have been suggestions that the dam be blown out so that the sand can escape. But the fish experts veto that proposal, because it would ruin spawning grounds for 20 or 30 miles downstream. So the dam stands as a white elephant.

Go to Texas and you will see dam after dam silted up and no longer useful, or fast becoming such, as at Lake Austin, Lake Kemp, Lake Corpus Christi, Lake Dallas, Lake Bridgeport, Eagle Lake, Lake Waco, Possum Kingdom Reservoir and Lake Brownwood.

The life of a dam there is shorter than the life of a dam in the Pacific Northwest, because rivers in Texas run heavy with silt.

Dams that ruin free-flowing rivers are temporary expedients for which we pay an awful price. The search, as I said, should be for other alternatives, whether the dam be used for power, public or private, water supply, flood control or irrigation.

I have mentioned the powerful Corps of Engineers as one of our despoilers. TVA is another. As this is written, TVA is promoting the building of a dam on the Little Tennessee—not for power, not for irrigation, not for flood control. The dam, it is said, will provide new industrial sites for industry. But TVA already has hundreds of industrial sites that go begging for purchasers or lessees. Why destroy the Little T? It is some 30 miles long and is the best trout stream in the Southeast. Its water is pure and cold. Its islands are wondrous campgrounds. Its valleys are rich and fertile, being some of the very best agricultural lands in the South. Here was the home of Sequoya, the great Cherokee chief. Here are the old Cherokee village sites never mined for their archaeological wonders. Here is the old Fort Loudoun, built by the British in 1756. All of these wonders will be destroyed forever and buried deep under water for all time. Why not save this recreational wonderland for our grandchildren? Why allow it to be destroyed in a real-estate promotion by TVA?

The truth is that our momentum is toward destroying our natural wonders, converting them into dollars. The modern Genghis Khans are not robber barons; they fly the "conservation" flag; they promote "employment" and "development" and "progress." They have many instruments at their command. Industrial waste and sewage is one; destruction of free-flowing rivers through the building of dams is another.

Yet in spite of this destructive trend, there are a few encouraging signs.

The cause of free-flowing rivers received new impetus in 1964 when Congress created the Ozark National Scenic Riverways, which will preserve in perpetuity portions of the Jack's Fork river in Missouri. By this law, Congress directed that the natural beauty of the landscape be preserved and enhanced, that the outdoor resources be conserved and that the Secretary of the Interior establish zones where hunting and fishing are permitted. A related idea is expressed in the Wild Rivers Bill that Senator Church of Idaho has been promoting. It passed the Senate in 1967 and is now pending in the House. This proposed National Wild River system would comprise large segments of the Salmon and Clearwater in Idaho, the Rogue in Oregon, the Eleven Point in Missouri, the Buffalo in Arkansas, the Cacapon and its tributary the Lost river in West Virginia, and the West Virginia portion of the Shenandoah. The Wild River area would be administered for water and wildlife conservation, and for outdoor-recreation values. Yet it would not interfere with other uses such as lumbering, livestock grazing, and the like, though it would bar industrial wastes and sewage. The idea is to hand down to the oncoming generation a few of our important free-flowing streams in a pleasing and relatively unaltered environment.

There is a growing interest among the states in the preservation of their free-flowing rivers. Maine has taken the lead in saving the Allagash, a famed canoe waterway even before Thoreau, which runs north through Telos Lake to the St. John. Most of this will now be preserved as a wilderness waterway, with a belt of land between 400 feet and 800 feet wide on each side that will be managed to maintain the wilderness character of the waterway. The electorate in November 1966 approved a bond issue to help finance the land- and water-rights acquisi-

[539]

tion. Federal funds will also help in the acquisition program. The state will control all campsites. Most motors will be barred, this being a canoe sanctuary for hunters, fishermen and those who like the thrill of white water.

In 1947, Congress approved a Water Pollution Control Compact between the New England States, and they have made considerable progress in providing water-quality standards and in classifying rivers. But sad to say, quite a number of the New England rivers, conspicuously the Merrimack and Nashua, are put in the lowest categories, which means they are little more than carriers of waste.

In 1961, Congress authorized the Delaware River Basin Compact between Delaware, New Jersey, New York and Pennsylvania. Some progress has been made in establishing water-quality standards for that river.

On September 26, 1966, the Hudson River Basin Compact became law, whereby Congress gave New York, New Jersey, Vermont, Massachusetts and Connecticut authority to preserve the natural, scenic, historical and recreational resources of the Hudson, to abate water pollution and develop water resources, to preserve and rehabilitate the scenic beauty of the river and to promote its fish and wildlife and other resources. Now the troublesome Hudson, saturated with raw sewage, can be surveyed in its entirety and over-all planning instituted that in time may make it safe, health-wise, even for swimming.

There is another interesting development—this one in the state of Washington. The Yakima river flows off the eastern slopes of the Cascades to form the Columbia near Pasco. In its upper reaches it is a clear, cold, free-flowing river filled with trout, excellent for swimming and a fine canoe waterway. Mrs. Douglas and I became disturbed at a creeping real-estate development. Real-estate operators are selling lots on the river front and it is plain that in time the river-bank will be packed with houses. Sewage from their cesspools and septic tanks will pollute the waters. Industry is moving in, and there are telltale signs that industrial wastes are beginning to poison the river. We helped form the Yakima River Conservancy to design state procedures for protecting this water-course. Others in the state capital took up the cause; and now there is a bill pending that would set aside this part of the Yakima and parts of several other rivers in Washington as wild rivers, putting under special zoning control a sanctuary belt that is one quarter of a mile wide on each side of each of these rivers. In this way, the natural state of a river will be preserved, its free-flowing character maintained, its scenic values and its purity honored, while no inconsistent use will be banned. In other words, agricultural uses could go on unimpaired; even some residential sites and campgrounds could be sanctioned. But the essential character of the stream will be kept inviolate; and 100 years from now, there will be unspoiled waterway wonders for our great-great-grandchildren.

Some ponds and swamps in national wildlife refuges and game ranges are under the jurisdiction of the U.S. Fish and Wildlife Service; and it is directed under the Wilderness Act of 1964 to make recommendations concerning their preservation as roadless wilderness areas. In 1967, numerous hearings of that character took place; one of the first concerned the Great Swamp in New Jersey, which harbors otter, beaver, and many other species of wildlife and many botanical wonders. Developers have had their eyes on it, especially for an airport. No decision has been reached by the agency on the Wilderness issue. The lands around the Great Swamp have been increasing in value and the speculators' appetites for the Great Swamp are keen. But for most of us, what Brooks Atkinson recently wrote is the essence of the cause: "In Great Swamp the property values are low because the land is good for nothing except life, knowledge, peace and hope."

The Forest Service and Park Service are also required by the Wilderness Act of 1964 to determine what roadless areas will be preserved in their respective domains. The hearings, now going on and to take place, will sometimes involve the fate of rivers. A notorious example is the Minam river in the Wallowa-Whitman National Forest of eastern Oregon, one of the very few rivers in the Pacific Northwest not paralleled by a road. Lumbermen are anxious to build such a road, not only to make money from timber sales but primarily to make a small fortune in building the road itself. The Minam—as crystal clear as any in the land—would be heavily silted by logging; the road would soon be clogged with cars; and the banks would be packed with people. The quiet and seclusion of the sanctuary would be lost forever and the natural character of the free-flowing Minam would disappear.

There will be a chance to save a number of waterways under the Wilderness Act from all pollution and all "development."

The same, of course, is true of many lakes in the high country. But as respects the lakes in our low country, we have made amazing progress. The Dust Bowl of the Twenties and Thirties taught us something of soil and water conservation. At that time, our natural ponds and marshes were fast being drained. The cycle has been reversed. Due largely to the Soil Conservation Service, about 1,500,000 new farm ponds have been formed. These have some recreational value, but their greatest impact probably has been on the duck population. Many are wonderful fish ponds. Over half of them have been a great boon to waterfowl. Those new ponds in the North Central States are in areas where several hundred million bushels of waste corn are commonly left in the fields. These are prized feeding grounds for waterfowl and probably have changed some of the ancient flyways.

In 1960, President Eisenhower vetoed the proposed Federal Water Pollution Control Act, which would have increased Federal grants for the construction of sewage-treatment works and such purposes. His veto was based on the fact that water pollution is "a uniquely local blight" that must be assumed by state and local governments.

That Federal attitude has changed under Presidents Kennedy and Johnson, so

[541]

that today there is a pervasive program for Federal control, in case the states fail to act promptly. The diminishing Federal funds available for cleanup of the rivers and lakes of the nation is part of the tragedy. Another is that the Eisenhower attitude still obtains in critical agencies such as the Bureau of the Budget. And in the absence of a tremendous popular drive, the critical conditions promise to get worse and worse.

One expert in the field of preservation of our streams and lakes recently said, "We can hardly expect to be as smart in the future as we've been stupid in the past." But with the mounting public concern evident on every hand, it may be possible by 2000 A.D. to restore some of our watercourses and lakes to their pristine condition.

PRESIDENT RICHARD M. NIXON'S
STATE OF THE UNION MESSAGE*
January 22, 1970

More than any other matter, concern for the environment held the attention of Americans in 1969, and within the broad context of "environment," we appeared to be most concerned with air and water pollution. President Nixon reflected this concern in devoting a considerable part of his State of the Union address to the problems of water pollution. The sections relating to water pollution follow.

In the next 10 years we shall increase our wealth by 50 percent. The profound question is—does this mean we will be 50 percent richer in a real sense, 50 percent better off, 50 percent happier?

Or, does it mean that in the year 1980 the President standing in this place will look back on a decade in which 70 percent of our people lived in metropolitan areas choked by traffic, suffocated by smog, poisoned by water, deafened by noise and terrorized by crime?

These are not the great questions that concern world leaders at summit conferences. But people do not live at the summit. They live in the foothills of everyday experience. It is time for us all to concern ourselves with the way real people live in real life.

The great question of the seventies is, shall we surrender to our surroundings, or shall we make our peace with nature and begin to make reparations for the damage we have done to our air, to our land and to our water?

Restoring nature to its natural state is a cause beyond party and beyond factions. It has become a common cause of all the people of this country. It is a cause of particular concern to young Americans—because they more than we will reap the grim consequences of our failure to act on programs which are needed now if we are to prevent disaster later.

Clean air, clean water, open spaces—these should once again be the birthright of every American. If we act now—they can be.

We still think of air as free. But clean air is not free, and neither is clean water. The price tag on pollution control is high. Through our years of past carelessness we incurred a debt to nature, and now that debt is being called.

The program I shall propose to Congress will be the most comprehensive and costly program in this field in America's history.

It is not a program for just a year. A year's plan in this field is no plan at all. This is a time to look ahead not a year, but 5 or 10 years—whatever time is required to do the job.

New York Times (Jan. 23, 1970), 22.

[543]

I shall propose to this Congress a $10 billion nationwide clean waters program to put modern municipal waste treatment plants in every place in America where they are needed to make our waters clean again, and to do it now.

We have the industrial capacity, if we begin now, to build them all within 5 years. This program will get them built within 5 years.

* * *

We no longer can afford to consider air and water common property, free to be abused by anyone without regard to the consequences. Instead, we should begin now to treat them as scarce resources, which we are no more free to contaminate than we are free to throw garbage in our neighbor's yard.

ORRRC AND BOR

During the 1950's, Americans became increasingly interested in outdoor recreation. Real incomes were high; people had more leisure time because of shortened work weeks, longer vacations, and more time in a retired status; and mobility was greater than it had ever been before. Furthermore, a new trend toward urbanization was apparently creating a growing demand for play-time in the out-of-doors.

At the same time that demand was increasing the supply of outdoor recreation resources was sharply and visibly decreasing because of water pollution, highway construction, drainage of wetlands, improper uses of pesticides, and many other factors. The increasing concern over outdoor recreation values eventually resulted in the creation of an Outdoor Recreation Resources Review Commission (ORRRC) to study the whole field of outdoor recreation and to submit a report of its findings and recommendations to the President and Congress. To many people ORRRC seemed to represent a revolutionary new concept of the importance of outdoor recreation but it was not a new idea. In fact there had been previous recommendations along the same lines and a National Conference on Recreation had functioned from 1924 to 1928. One of the ORRRC recommendations was the establishment of a new bureau of outdoor recreation and the means to finance and coordinate increased outdoor recreation.

This chapter documents early efforts at increasing outdoor recreation opportunities and the significant actions which led to the formation of the ORRRC and the Bureau of Outdoor Recreation.

"A CRISIS IN NATIONAL RECREATION"*
1920

Perhaps the first person to recognize the need for a nationwide study and the establishment of a nationwide policy on outdoor recreation was Henry S. Graves, Chief Forester of the United States. In this article Graves set forth his reasons for concern and his recommendations for solving what he thought to be a national crisis in outdoor recreation.

Widespread anxiety has been caused by the acute situation confronting the Government in its administration of the National Parks and other reservations which afford opportunities for recreation. The National Parks are threatened by proposals that would commercialize their natural resources. Already there are bills in Congress, well advanced toward passage, which would establish the precedent of industrial use of various resources in the Parks. There is no clear-cut policy regarding the relative functions of National Parks and National Forests, with the result that large transfers of land from the Forests to the Parks are advocated along lines that would jeopardize the whole system of National forestry. Conflicts have arisen as between the industrial and the recreation use of certain public properties. There is uncertainty regarding the real place of recreation in plans for road and trail development. The many federal activities in recreation are not adequately correlated. Friends of the recreation movement who look to the federal government for leadership and support of State and local effort are handicapped by the confusion of policies of the federal bureaus and deeply disturbed by the dangers to the National Parks created by the present legislative and administrative tendencies toward their commercialization.

It is only by the adoption of a sound national recreation policy that the public interests can be safeguarded. Such a policy should protect the integrity of the National Parks, should recognize the recreation functions of the National Forests and other permanent reservations, and should enable the Government, through its activities on the public properties and its co-operative and educational work outside, to take the leadership in forwarding the movement for outdoor recreation throughout the country.

Within the last few years there has been a widespread and spontaneous movement for outdoor recreation. Thousands who formerly spent their vacation days abroad or at some nearby resort are traveling long distances by rail or motor to visit the mountains, lakes, and forests of our own country.

In part this movement is explained by the betterment of roads, the wide ownership of automobiles, the diversion of travel from Europe by the circumstances

*Henry S. Graves, "A Crisis in National Recreation," *American Forestry,* Vol. 26, No. 319 (July, 1920), 391–400.

of the war, the advertising of our recreation opportunities, and by the prevailing prosperity. A deeper cause is the existence of a new appreciation of outdoor recreation, a new impulse to seek the wholesome environment of the hills and forests and to refresh mind and body through the vigors of mountain and camp life.

This movement is of great importance to the public, both because of the benefits to the people that come from outdoor recreation and because there must be a large participation by the public itself to provide facilities that can be enjoyed by all. That the opportunity for relaxation, exercise, and play out of doors means a factor in public health and in meeting social problems is well recognized in our larger cities and industrial centers. Millions of dollars are being expended on municipal parks, interior squares and breathing spaces, out-of-door playgrounds, public golf links, tennis courts, ball fields, bathing beaches, and the like. The benefits from such facilities in increased health, in mental stimulus, and in contentment and happiness can not be measured. The problem is absolutely basic to the social well being of our nation.

The new recreation movement reaches beyond the immediate problem of the city parks and playgrounds. It seeks to draw people to the country, to the fields, the forests, the lakes, and the mountains. It aims to afford opportunities not only for the well-to-do who can afford a long trip by rail or motor to an attractive resort, but also and especially for those of less means to have the refreshment that comes from days spent in natural woodlands and the open country.

Recreation has an important place in the new movement to enlarge the system of federal and state forest reservations and parks and to acquire woodland parks for municipalities. While the occasion for such reservations is frequently the protection of watersheds, timber production, or other public benefits, all of the areas afford opportunities for outdoor recreation. Equally true it is that recreation has an important place in the demand for a large program of road improvement and extension.

The federal Government has an important part to play in the movement for outdoor recreation. This is in part because the Nation owns large areas of forest and mountain land; in part also because many other federal activities contribute directly or indirectly to recreation. The work of the Government naturally centers in the public properties, the National Parks, National Forests, National Monuments, and wild life reservations, which include the National Game Preserves and Bird Reservations. In addition, the work of the Biological Survey in wild life conservation and of the Bureau of Fisheries in maintaining the stock of our streams are powerful factors in drawing people to the forest and field. The great work of road building under the direction of the Bureau of Public Roads is opening recreation areas heretofore inaccessible, developing highways that in themselves are objectives of the traveler, and creating by example and education an appreciation of the beautification of highways by planting and of the preservation of scenic values on and near the roads. The educational work in forestry by the Forest Service, in park development by the Park Service, in improvements of public grounds and planting about the home by the Bureau of Plant Industry, all serve to stimulate an interest in the out-of-doors, and aid in forwarding the great purpose of public health, contentment, and national efficiency that are back of the outdoor recreation movement.

A broad federal policy of recreation should include all of the permanent reservations, each performing a definite function in a comprehensive program. It should include also the various other activities, for each contributes in a large way to national recreation.

With the great public reservations used already by millions for recreation, with extensive field organizations each performing some function in recreation development, the federal Government should take the leadership in the movement, giving its moral support to the activities of other public and private agencies, and correlating their efforts where these touch those of the central Government.

* * *

A natural query is why the various bureaus in charge of the Federal reservations do not agree upon a common policy regarding the points discussed in the foregoing pages. Whatever the reasons, the fact remains that there is not a common policy and that legislation is repeatedly recommended to Congress by one department that is inconsistent with that recommended by another department, with resulting confusion to Congress and the general public. This is due in part to faulty departmental organization. A deeper cause is that there has been too much attention given to forms of reservations, to names, and to procedure, and not enough thought to the large recreation problem which includes the activities of all units of organization that are directly or indirectly concerned.

There is needed first of all a broad policy that sets forth the large public objectives of national recreation, the opportunities and needs of development, the basic principles underlying the establishment and purposes of the federal reservation and the functions of each in working out the large national program.

All friends of outdoor recreation, and all representatives of the federal bureaus have a single large objective. They ought to have no difficulty in agreeing upon the basis of a national policy. With the larger objectives and principles in mind comprehending the whole field of Government responsibilities taken together, the methods of working out a program become questions of lesser consequence, and would no longer tend to obscure the main public issues.

I have no doubt that if the President should request the formulation of such a policy by the departments concerned, it would be quickly worked out, with an agreement as to organization, methods, and procedure. With a basic policy which would become the policy of the whole Administration to be followed by all constituent members of the executive branch of the Government, order could be brought out of chaos.

OUTLINE OF A RECREATION POLICY

More specificially and in summary a national recreation policy should comprise the following points:

1. The formulation of a comprehensive base plan for all the Federal reservations, taken together, indicating:

(a) The recreation opportunities.

(b) The needs for the development of these opportunities.

(c) The relation of the recreation objectives in the various reservations to each other, regardless of the class of reservation, and the relation to similar points in State, municipal, and private areas outside.

(d) The relation of these to the plans for road and trail building within and outside the public properties.

(e) The function of each class of reservation and federal organization in carrying out a progressive plan of recreation development, with all working toward a common objective and each supporting the other.

2. On public properties not closed to industrial use, the correlation of the recreation development with the use of other natural resources, such as timber, forage, minerals, water for power and irrigation and domestic supply, and with wild life conservation.

3. A clear-cut policy regarding transfers of lands within National Forests to National Parks based on the principle that this will be done only in the case of areas of a character so unique as to justify their withdrawal from all economic and industrial development, and where they are large enough to necessitate a separate administration that can not be given under the present jurisdiction of the Forest Service.

4. A policy of administration of the National Parks that excludes economic development of natural resources like timber, grazing, etc.

5. As a corollary of the foregoing, not to include in new National Parks areas of merchantable timber and other resources which by their nature and location will inevitably be needed for industrial use.

6. Joining hands of the different federal agencies in promoting recreation development outside of the public properties. The activities would include encouragement of the establishment by States, municipalities, and quasi-public organizations, of reservations suitable for recreation use, the correlation of these with the federal properties where practicable, the encouragement by demonstration and education of preserving scenic values along highways and of roadside planting, and the stimulation of activities by States and other agencies in wild life

[549]

conservation. Through joint planning by the different federal agencies in this co-operative work, the part to be played by each of the bureaus would be clearly defined so that each would have its particular field of enterprise and there would be mutual support by all in the public leadership of each.

7. Encouragement of the organization outside of the federal service of a recreation council, representing the great associations of the country interested in outdoor recreation. Such a council would be able to render a public service through the education of its constituent members regarding the problems throughout the country, in bringing about harmonious and unified action in all recreation matters, by promoting sound principles of recreation development through federal, State, and municipal activities, and by its counsel to the public agencies as a spokesman of thousands of persons throughout the Nation interested in outdoor recreation.

8. The transfer of the National Park Service to the Department of Agriculture in order that its work may be more closely correlated with that of the Forest Service, the Biological Survey, the Bureau of Public Roads, and the Bureau of Plant Industry, which are the chief organizations, outside the Park Service, carrying on activities related to recreation. No single step of organization would be as effective as to bring under one departmental head all the main work of recreation. As a separate bureau the individuality of the work of the Park Service would be preserved. Under a single Cabinet officer, all bureaus could more readily unite in joint enterprises.

Aside from a better correlation of all recreation activities, the proposed action would enable the National Park Service to have the immediate services of the Bureau of Public Roads in its highway construction, and to coordinate more effectively than at present its forest fire protection with that of adjacent National Forests.

STATEMENT OF PRESIDENT CALVIN COOLIDGE CALLING
A NATIONAL CONFERENCE ON OUTDOOR RECREATION*
1924

Graves' ideas on the need for national attention to outdoor recreation problems were picked up by Charles Sheldon who was then chairman of the Game Preservation Committee of the Boone and Crockett Club. Sheldon incorporated Graves' proposals in a "Policy Statement" which was officially adopted by the Boone and Crockett Club. Sheldon's policy statement was in turn adopted by the Izaak Walton League of America and by the American Game Protective Association which was the forerunner of the Wildlife Management Institute.

These actions were brought to the attention of Theodore Roosevelt, Jr. who was then Assistant Secretary of the Navy. Roosevelt was sufficiently impressed to propose to President Calvin Coolidge that a national conference be organized to explore the whole field of outdoor recreation. Coolidge was apparently enthusiastic about the idea and promptly appointed a committee to organize such a conference. The membership of the committee gave some indication of the President's support, for it included: Assistant Secretary of the Navy Theodore Roosevelt, Jr., Secretary of War John W. Weeks, Secretary of Commerce Herbert C. Hoover, Secretary of the Interior Hubert Work, Secretary of Agriculture Henry Wallace, and Secretary of Labor James J. Davis.

On the advice of this committee, President Coolidge decided to hold a national conference on outdoor recreation in Washington, D.C. His statement follows.

Since the first announcement as to the needs of a national outdoor recreation policy, so many expressions of approval of such a project and so many offers of assistance in furthering it have been received by individual members of my committee that it is their unanimous opinion that a conference on this important subject should be called to meet in the city of Washington in the near future to assist the committee in forming a national program.

The proposed policy covers such a range of subjects, touches so many phases of our national life, and is the immediate mission of so many existing agencies, national, State, municipal, and private, that I feel that Federal leadership and support to coordinate this activity are desirable and I therefore heartily concur in the recommendations of my committee. May 22 to 24, inclusive, has been selected as the time for this conference and the New National Museum in Washington, D.C., as the place.

I have appointed Col. Theodore Roosevelt to act as executive chairman for

*Proceedings of the National Conference on Outdoor Recreation, Sen. Doc. 151, 68th Cong., 1st sess., 3–4.

the conference, and Secretaries Weeks, Works, Wallace, and Hoover as honorary chairmen. I have instructed Colonel Roosevelt to communicate with the national civilian organizations interested in this great subject, and ask them to send delegates to the conference. There is no all-embracing list of these organizations, and therefore it will be impossible to avoid unintentional omissions. Because of this I am going to ask those organizations that do not receive invitations, and that are embraced in the above-outlined category, to write at once to my chairman, Colonel Roosevelt, in regard to their representation.

In general, some of the topics which will be discussed and upon which it is hoped conclusions may be reached and constructive suggestions formulated are:

Encouragement of outdoor recreation as a Federal function; constitutional or legal authority for Federal participation; the bearing of outdoor recreation on mental, physical, social, and moral development; outdoor recreation as an influence in child welfare; the wild-life (game and fur-bearing animals, birds, fish, and plants) resources of the United States; the scenic resources of the United States, and major possibilities of national cooperation in promotion of recreation.

Under the last-named topic the following questions will be especially considered:

Formation of advisory councils on outdoor recreation; closer correlation of work of units of Government organization; closer correlation of agencies other than Federal, and their correlation with Federal agencies; formulation of an educational program for outdoor recreation; promotion and coordination of game preservation; and survey and classification of recreational resources.

This is not an effort to federalize recreation at the expense of State, municipal, local, or private interest therein. Individual effort should at all times be encouraged. Many of these interests, however, though working generally toward the same end, do not attain the maximum results because there is no coordination.

It will be the object of this conference, therefore, to assist in forming a national policy which will coordinate all these activities. The prime objective for which I feel we should strive is to endeavor to make available for the average American outdoor recreation, with all that it implies, and to preserve our facilities for outdoor recreation for our children and our children's children.

BARRINGTON MOORE ON PRINCIPLES AND POLICIES FOR OUTDOOR RECREATION*
1924

Barrington Moore, Secretary of the Council on National Parks, Forests, and Wildlife, delivered one of the most outstanding speeches at the National Conference on Outdoor Recreation in 1924. Partly for this reason and partly because most of his recommendations were followed 30 years later, Barrington Moore's speech is reproduced here.

Mr. MOORE. Mr. Chairman, ladies and gentlemen, In order to avoid misunderstanding I must point out that I am not speaking for all the organizations represented on the Council on National Parks, Forests, and Wild Life, but as an individual who has given a certain amount of thought to some of the matters before this conference, and who merely happens to be the secretary of the above-mentioned council. Many persons agree with what I will say; others with only parts of it.

PRINCIPLES

1. Since so much public money is being spent to acquire land for recreation, I think we can take it as axiomatic that the lands remaining in public ownership, which are primarily useful for recreation, should not be alienated.

2. Most of us will agree that land should serve its highest purpose, and that its resources should be developed to the fullest possible extent under the principle of coordinated use. Recreation is one of the resources of some lands, not all. Supreme works of nature, such as are found in the national parks, serve their highest purpose by complete preservation, free from commercialism. Coordinated use is a new term to some, though it has been applied to the national forests for nearly 20 years. It means weighing resources according to their highest usefulness, and developing each in such a way that a lower use will not injure the resource for a higher purpose. For example, the mature timber is harvested in such a way as not to injure scenic or recreation features. The trees around a camp ground, or around a lake, or along a road, are left standing. Cattle and sheep are not allowed to graze near camp grounds, so that the forage will be available for the campers' horses.

3. Practically speaking, recreation is not the sole use of any land outside of city parks and playgrounds. Even the national parks serve another and very high purpose besides recreation. They are of the utmost value in science and

*Proceedings of the National Conference on Outdoor Recreation, Sen. Doc. 151, 68th Cong., 1st sess., 49–54.

education as outdoor museums and laboratories where nature works out her problems unhampered by man. This is one of the strongest, if not the strongest, reason for keeping the national parks absolutely free from economic use, or other human interference, save what is absolutely necessary to permit of their enjoyment by the people.

Except on the national parks, a reasonable development of the resources—always under the principle of coordinated use—is not incompatible with recreation.

SURVEY OF RESOURCES

I would strongly recommend a detailed survey of all the natural resources, including recreation, on all lands remaining in public ownership. We already have a certain amount of information on the national forests, but practically nothing on the vast area of the public domain, and too little on Indian reservations. It should be understood that a survey of the resources of the Indian lands does not imply any intention of taking the resources away from the Indians. Knowledge of what their lands contain would be of value to the Indians themselves more than to anyone else, and it is understood that these resources would be administered for their benefit.

CLASSIFICATION AND USE OF FEDERAL LANDS

The next step would be to divide all Federal-owned lands into two broad classes: (1) Lands which it is in the public interest to dispose of under existing land laws. There is comparatively little land left which can be advantageously taken up for homesteads. (2) Lands which should be retained and administered.

It is important that the land which is kept in public ownership should be administered. The days have passed when we could afford to let it lie idle or be ruined by wasteful and short-sighted use. Administering these lands means developing the resources on vast areas of the public domain, especially in the semiarid parts of the West. It means developing water resources, improving the range, and controlling the grazing in such a way that the carrying capacity will be greatly increased. This can be done. The Department of Agriculture has already given an excellent demonstration on 202,000 acres of dry land in New Mexico during three years of a severe drought. In this period the losses on the Jornado Range Reserve, the experimental area, amounted to 3.5 per cent as against 35 cent, or ten times as much, on the neighboring lands managed in the usual way. Multiply this saving by the millions of cattle and sheep grazing on the public domain and you will have some conception of what administration will mean in terms of national wealth.

Administration will benefit not only the economic resources, but outdoor recreation. The outdoor recreation possibilities would also be administered, and would be managed under the principle of coordinate use.

The recreation resources on all public lands should be studied, and should be developed along the lines of a broad policy carefully worked out and laid down before development starts. I take it that the development of such a policy is one of the chief motives for calling this conference. Therefore a few recommendations would seem to be in order. I would suggest that recreation areas should be divided into three main classes:

1. Areas where land will be leased for permanent camp sites. Many people have an entirely legitimate desire for a summer camp in the mountains; and this desire should be permitted to find expression wherever not incompatible with the need of larger numbers of people. But these areas should be carefully selected, and limited in number and extent. Even on these areas it would probably be advisable to reserve certain spots for public camp grounds. Otherwise the place would be virtually closed to campers. It rather spoils the pleasure of a trip in the open to find the country filled up with summer cottages and private land. These areas should therefore be restricted to the smallest number compatible with legitimate demands. They can be added to later if absolutely essential. But once a place has been taken up for summer camps it remains in this class always, and can not be restored to its former condition of more general usefulness.

2. The second classification would be lands where no camp sites would be leased, but where camping facilities of an artificial nature, for the accommodation of considerable numbers, would be built. This means the construction of water-supply systems, of sanitary facilities with sewerage systems, and possibly of simple shelters. Such sites are already being developed on the national parks, and are of much use to a large number of tourists, especially motorists.

3. The third classification would include all the rest of the lands, which would be left without artificial dressing up, for those of us who like to get away from the crowd, and camp as simply as possible. The only needs in this case would be for patrols to prevent fires and to see that people do not ruin the country by leaving tin cans and other litter lying about.

Motor roads could be built into the first two classes, but not into the third, which should be accessible only by trails. Some places should be left even without trails. We do not want to altogether eliminate the exploring spirit.

ADMINISTRATION

Nobody imagines that the administration of the recreation and other natural resources on the lands owned by the Federal Government is a simple matter. The problem requires the best thought of those in the Government service and

[555]

in private life. But it can and will be solved. The guiding purpose, which should never be lost sight of, is to see that all the resources on all publicly owned land are administered, developed, and wisely used.

I can only suggest what seem to be practical and workable lines to follow. The machinery for carrying the proposals into effect will be considered in a moment. Reasonable effectiveness calls for full and hearty cooperation on the part of all the governmental agencies concerned. This need not preclude a spirit of healthy competition between departments, but it would preclude obstructive tactics.

Our public lands are so situated with regard to jurisdiction that pieces of country which should be developed under a single plan sometimes happen to fall under the jurisdiction of different agencies. Is it not logical for these two agencies to come to an agreement as to a workable plan of utilization? For example, roads, trails, and camp sites could be laid out where they are actually needed. Then each governmental agency could construct the road or trail up to its particular boundary, and the other authorities could build their part of the road to meet it. One State builds roads to meet those coming from another State. Why should not one branch of the Government do the same for another branch?

It has been proposed that special recreation reserves be set aside. It is said, and with reason, that there are a number of places suitable for outdoor recreation which can not be included in the national parks because they do not measure up to national park standards. All agree that these standards must be maintained. Furthermore, it would be impractical to restrict the economic utilization of resources on all recreation areas, and if areas on which economic use is permitted were included in the national parks it would undermine the entire system. Many of the areas of which we are speaking do not have timber which would justify their inclusion in the national forests. Why not, then, a third category, "national recreation reserves," in between the national parks and national forests?

The purpose of these recreational reserves would be to develop additional recreational facilities to supply the ever-increasing demand. Possibly they would succeed to a certain extent. But we must develop outdoor recreation on Government lands as a whole. If we merely spot the map with a few more reservations we fail of our purpose. I repeat that our aim is to insure the administration, development, and wise use of all resources, including recreation, on all public lands. Merely selecting a few national recreation reserves would be a superficial solution, indeed.

There is another and very practical objection to these reserves. Some of the lands best suited to outdoor sport are included within the Indian reservations, and others are on the national forests. We can not, in fairness, take away the Indians' lands for our sport. In some cases we could not, even if we were so inclined. The Canyon de Chelley, one of the finest bits of scenery in the United

States, belongs to the Navajo Indians by treaty, and can not even be made a national monument. As for the national forests, we already have in the making the best example of coordinated use in the country. It would be the height of folly to disrupt the unified administration of all resources in which outdoor recreation finds an increasingly prominent place to give over certain parts to recreation alone.

Still another aspect should be considered. As secretary of the Council on National Parks, Forests, and Wild Life I have come into contact with the public ignorance of the distinction between national parks and national forests. This widespread haziness is one of our greatest obstacles in defending the national parks against commercial invasion. If people are unable to distinguish between two such different classes, what would it be like if a third were added?

It might be desirable in certain cases for one governmental agency to make a temporary transfer of jurisdiction to another, such transfer to hold so long as the arrangement worked satisfactorily. The boundaries of our public reservations were mostly laid out along land lines for convenience. While convenient for purposes of description on the Land Office plats, it is anything but convenient in the field. The lines run straight north and south or east and west up and down hill, regardless of cliffs or torrents. Witness the northern boundary of the State of Arizona for a supreme example, with part of the State on the other side of the Grand Canyon. Therefore it is probable that here and there a ranger could extend his district to a natural feature, a ridge or stream, thereby insuring greater efficiency and economy of administration. These cases could be worked out directly on the ground in a mutually satisfactory manner. For this very practical suggestion, and for a considerable part of what follows, I am indebted to Mr. Frederick Law Olmsted.

MACHINERY FOR ADMINISTERING RECREATIONAL RESOURCES

FEDERAL RECREATION COMMISSION

It is evident that some sort of machinery must be set up to carry into effect the coordination of plans above suggested. We have a successful precedent in the Water Power Commission. Why not then form a recreational commission, made up of the secretaries of the departments concerned with administering lands containing recreational resources, or of persons designated by these secretaries. It would probably be unnecessary and unduly cumbersome to include departments which use or deal with, but do not administer, the lands, since every one uses them in one way or another.

This commission should have a salaried executive secretary and a small staff of experts. There should be a sufficient appropriation to cover travel expenses since a large part of the work of the staff would be done in the field.

It might be best for the commission and its staff to have no authority to issue orders. They could point out conditions to officers in the field, and even make suggestions if asked. But it would probably be necessary for the responsibility to rest with each department rather than with the commission. For the department must actually perform the work, not the commission. Furthermore, it would confuse the man in the field to have orders coming from different sources of authority. The experts could report to the secretary of the commission, who would lay the matters before the full commission, one of the members of which would be the particular secretary whose duty it would be to take whatever steps seemed necessary.

ADVISORY BOARD

It might be wise for an advisory board of nongovernmental persons to be created to assist the commission and the departments. The duties of such a board would, of course, be purely advisory. It would help in two important ways.

(1) It could supplement the work of the commission's staff by finding and calling attention to conditions in the field. By constructive suggestions it could assist in carrying out the policy adopted, furnish valuable information and increase efficiency. (2) It could serve as a link between the commission and the public to explain what the authorities are trying to do, to forestall and answer criticism, or when advisable pass on the criticism to the commission with a helpful suggestion for a remedy.

This Advisory Board should have to make an annual report to the commission, and should meet at least once a year, probably oftener. A small sum should be made available to defray the cost of attendance at meetings, since it is unfair to place this burden on the individuals or on the different organizations to which the individuals may belong. It would probably be better to select the board from among persons whose interest and willingness to serve could be counted upon and whose judgment could be trusted rather than from specified groups regardless of persons. Or, as with the National Research Council, a certain proportion could represent organizations and the remainder could be selected at large for particular qualifications. This is, however, a matter which can be worked out later. Such a board would not only help the commission but would bring the public in closer touch with the work; and after all it is the public that owns and uses the lands.

CHAUNCY J. HAMLIN'S "REVIEW OF PROJECT STUDIES"*
1928

The National Conference on Outdoor Recreation remained in operation until 1928. After four years of work, Chairman Chauncy J. Hamlin reviewed the studies undertaken by the Conference.

INTRODUCTION

Outdoor life has been characteristic of the American people whether expressed in adventure, work, or play. For nearly 300 years there has been a frontier to beckon the adventurer, a wilderness to conquer, and free soil to subdue. Each generation bred of a common stock and with common social ideals found its opportunity for the fullest expression of the pioneer spirit. The last half of the nineteenth century marked the climax. The discovery of gold, Civil War and the period of construction immediately following, the Indian wars, and the settlement of the vast public domain crowded within the short space of 50 years a sequence of romantic events without parallel in the making of a state.

The 25 years following the final close of the era of free soil has witnessed a remarkable transformation in the structure of American society. The individualism of the pioneer has been submerged in collective enterprise. A radical change in the distribution and make-up of the population has occurred coincident with a tremendous expansion of mechanization in industry. Population has become concentrated and heterogeneous in structure. More than half of the people are now classed as urban; that is, they live in towns of 2,500 or more. Farm population—that is, all persons actually living on farms—comprised less than 26 per cent of the total population in 1926. The homogeneity of the original stock has crumbled steadily since 1890 through the influx of great migrations from southern and eastern Europe.

The present increase in population indicates that within the lifetime of present children the population will approach 200,000,000. There is every reason to suppose, too, that the concentration of population will continue in marked degree. Individualism in industry is almost a thing of the past and is rapidly becoming so in the trades. There may be expected a concentration of the rural population in villages and towns as distinguished from isolated residence on the farm. The demands of modern agriculture, particularly in the production of basic crops, point to the widespread adoption of industrial methods and corporate management. What the social make-up of this population will be and the extent to which the homogeneity of the original stock will be broken down is a matter of speculation.

*Chauncey J. Hamlin, "Review of Project Studies," *Proceedings of the National Conference on Outdoor Recreation,* Sen. Doc. 158, 70th Cong., 1st sess., 1–5.

The exploitation of natural resources by a young and vigorous people has brought a level of unsurpassed well-being. Moreover, the development of science and improved organization in industry have made possible an unprecedented distribution of physical comforts and increasing periods of leisure to all classes. The picture of America to-day, then, is a country made prosperous through the exploitation of the stored natural capital of centuries—a population rapidly increasing in numbers, concentrating in cities, generally engaged in high-speed industry or collective enterprise, and with widely divergent social ideals and requirements.

The present stage of development is transitory—a period of flux intermediate between the initial acquisition and exploitation of virgin land and its resources and eventual disposition to satisfy the economic necessities and social requirements of a fast-growing population. The general level of prosperity has been made possible by the exploitation of natural resources of unparalleled variety and abundance, but manifestly this natural capital can not continue to be consumed without husbandry or replacement if accepted standards of living are to be sustained. And the present drain upon natural resources must take into account not only legitimate if extravagant consumption but insensate waste.

The objective to be sought is the attainment of a balanced system of national economy, a system that will adequately provide for an optimum population; that is, the number of people which the land and its resources can permanently maintain without lowering accepted standards of living, including a reasonable amount of leisure for all classes and opportunity for its useful enjoyment.

The attainment of this objective is dependent, first, upon the extent to which the quantitative and qualitative factors of immigration are controlled; second, upon the proper use of land.

A sound policy of restrictive immigration is dictated unless an unlimited and accumulative liability is to be charged against the resources of the land. Nation planning must be inaugurated to supplement and complement city and regional planning—a series of coordinated plans which in their total will allocate and dedicate all lands and their resources to highest service whether that be a factory zone in a city or a wild-life sanctuary in the Sierras. Within the compass of plan-wise land utilization and the future policy of immigration must be found the ultimate economic and social development of the Nation.

A reasonable amount of leisure and the opportunity for its enjoyment by all classes is a necessary complement of material well-being. Outdoor recreation is the most wholesome expression of leisure and a needful social force in the readjustments of American life to meet new conditions. It is a form of land utilization that must find its proportionate place in city, regional, and nation planning, if the vigor of the people and their productive efficiency is to be maintained. In the past economic influences in the use of land have outweighed social uses. This has been largely inevitable in the growth of a new country. A point in development has now been reached when economic and social factors must be brought into balance.

There is much to be done if the fact can be brought home that even to-day no center of population affords adequate provision for outdoor play and recreation; no State has as yet adequately provided for the recovery of its waste lands, for the purity of its streams, for the conservation of forests and wild life, and for necessary parks and recreation areas; and finally that the Nation as a whole is living on the principle of its natural capital and too complacent of its waste.

On April 14, 1924, President Coolidge issued the following statement stressing the importance of outdoor recreation and the need for a national policy:

> Particularly within the last decade, the outdoor recreation spirit among our people has increased rapidly. During this period there have been put forward projects—Federal, municipal, State, and private—to expand and conserve throughout the country our recreational opportunities. It is almost idle to emphasize their value to the country. The physical vigor, moral strength, and clean simplicity of mind of the American people can be immeasurably furthered by the properly developed opportunities for the life in the open afforded by our forests, mountains, and waterways. Life in the open is a great character builder. From such life much of the American spirit of freedom springs. Furthering the opportunities of all for such life ranks in the general class with education.
>
> Our aim in this country must be to try to put the change for out-of-door pleasure, with all that it means, within the grasp of the rank and file of our people, the poor man as well as the rich man. Country recreation for as many of our people as possible should be our objective.
>
> Though all are concerned in this matter, the lead must be and should be taken by the National Government. Our National Government is already concerned in many phases of it, but in an incoherent manner. In the administration of national parks, national forests, wild-life reserves, and unreserved domain the Government holds almost unlimited opportunities for this form of public service. The function of the Federal Government in the construction of highways, in the study of the propagation and protection of game animals, birds, and fish, has a very decided bearing upon the recreational facilities open to our people.
>
> At present outdoor recreation is fostered by State, municipal, and private agencies, and Federal bureaus—the National Park Service, the Forest Service, the Biological Survey, the Bureaus of Fisheries, Plants, Public Roads, and others. There are State parks in many of the States, State roads, State conservation commissions, and other like agencies. There are also many civilian organizations that impinge on this question; for example, the various sportsmen's associations, containing hundreds of thousands of members and spread through every State; the camp-fire associations, the boy and girl scouts, the conservation groups, and thousands of others. In order to handle this matter properly, to adjust the widely separated viewpoints, and interlock the interests concerned efficiently, there should be a definite and clearly prescribed national policy. The whole matter, being nation-wide in scope, demands such handling. The object to be secured should, therefore, be to promulgate a national policy which should not merely coordinate under Federal guidance all activities in behalf of outdoor recreation, but also formulate a program to serve as a guide for future action.
>
> I am asking, therefore, Secretary Weeks, Secretary Work, Secretary Wallace, Secretary Hoover, and Assistant Secretary Theodore Roosevelt to form a committee and to suggest to me how they think such a national policy can best be formulated and put into action.

It was the opinion of the President's committee that a national conference should be called to assist the committee in forming a national program and policy. With this recommendation the President expressed himself in hearty accord. . . .

One hundred and twenty-eight national organizations associated themselves into a conference at a meeting held in Washington, D.C., May 22–24, 1924. In the proceedings[1] that followed the present situation in the outdoor field was canvassed by the leading experts of the country. A permanent organization was formed and an executive committee appointed.

The executive committee after carefully reviewing and canvassing the field of outdoor recreation, and the various existing national organizations which have been devoting their efforts to various phases of the subject, announced the following declaration of policy:

> The National Conference on Outdoor Recreation believes that it is not its function to take over the exploitation of any part of the field of outdoor recreation, but rather to support, indorse, and seek assistance from the various national organizations already at work in this field.
>
> It is the intention of the conference to request national organizations to make surveys in the field of the social significance of outdoor recreation in its relation to child life, health, industrial workers, rural recreation needs, athletic games and sports, etc., and also in the field of the value of natural resources to outdoor recreation with particular reference to forests, game, and fur-bearing animals, fish, birds, plants and flowers, waters, etc.
>
> It is believed that through the close cooperation of such private agencies and Government agencies, Federal, State, county, and municipal, it will be possible eventually to evolve a national plan for outdoor recreation in which each agency, public and private, will have and play its part to the end that our country will be a happier, healthier place in which to live, and that opportunity may be open to all to gain abounding health, strength, wholesome enjoyment, understanding, and love of nature, good fellowship, and keen sportsmanship. Such opportunities will tend to the formation of that sturdy character by developing those qualities of self-control, endurance under hardship, reliance on self, and cooperation with others in teamwork which are so necessary to good citizenship.

Pursuant to this policy a series of fact-finding surveys and projects have been outlined which appear to the committee as fundamental to a national policy of outdoor recreation. Manifestly the complete picture can not be drawn at this time, but a number of surveys and projects have been completed and published and are here briefly reviewed to give a first perspective of the field. Ultimately a national policy of outdoor recreation contemplates nation planning so broad in scope that within congested centers of population there will be adequate provision for playgrounds for juveniles, athletic fields, recreation grounds and parks, boulevards and parkways; and connecting these centers of population there will be tree-lined rural highways flanked by public camp grounds, and county and State parks, forests, and game preserves of easy access for summer and winter recreation. The great mountain ranges—the White Mountains of New England, the Appalachians of the South, the northern and southern Rockies, the Sierras and the Cascades of the West, as well as the headwaters of the

[1]Proceedings of the National Conference on Outdoor Recreation. First Proceedings May 22–24, 1924, Senate Document No. 151, Sixty-eighth Congress, first session. Second Proceedings January 20–21, 1926, Senate Document No. 117, Sixty-ninth Congress, first session.

Mississippi in the Lake States, will supplement the State reservations and embrace the great national forests, parks, and game refuges.

In this there is nothing visionary. To-day the Nation's annual expenditures for outdoor pleasure participated in by millions of citizens are measured not in mere millions but billions and distributed through thousands of the channels of trade and industry. It is an astonishing index of present prosperity wholly apart from the social values involved. The economic significance is so great that outdoor recreation which at present is a development largely uncontrolled, unregulated, and often vulgar in expression must find a stable foundation in the Nation's economy because public welfare will demand it. And, moreover, there is a growing realization that wholesome leisure out of doors represents, as stated by Herbert Hoover, a fundamental need in American life and a fundamental desire to do something to escape the drabness of civilization.

Chauncey J. Hamlin
Chairman, National Conference on Outdoor Recreation

STATEMENT OF JOE PENFOLD BEFORE THE HOUSE COMMITTEE ON INTERIOR AND INSULAR AFFAIRS*
1957

Some time during the late 1940's, Joseph W. Penfold, then western representative of the Izaak Walton League of America, became acutely aware of the need for a nationwide inventory of outdoor recreation resources and the need for a survey of current and future outdoor recreation needs. Penfold discussed these ideas with many people including Senator Joseph C. O'Mahoney of Wyoming, who apparently first suggested that the best way to carry out such an undertaking would be through a joint congressional and presidentially appointed commission. In 1951, Penfold spoke with Colorado Congressman Wayne N. Aspinall who was also generally receptive to the proposal.

During the next few years Penfold continued to seek support and advice for his proposal from various government agencies and public officials. In 1956, David Brower and the Sierra Club proposed a national "Scenic Resources Review" which would, among other things, carry out an inventory of areas which would be suitable for park or wilderness status. It appeared that the time was ripe for congressional action.

By January 1957, eight senators and nine congressmen had introduced somewhat similar bills to provide for the establishment of an outdoor recreation resources review commission. Since Penfold was probably more influential in obtaining enactment of a recreation resources review law than any other single person, his testimony before the House Committee on Interior and Insular Affairs is especially significant.

Mr. PENFOLD. Madam Chairman, and gentlemen: We appreciate your consideration in calling this hearing, and particularly for timing it with the Senate hearing, which makes it a great deal more convenient to those of us from out of the city.

My name is Joseph W. Penfold of Wheatridge, Colo. I am conservation director of the Izaak Walton League of America, a national membership organization dedicated to the conservation and wise use of the Nation's natural resources. The league's headquarters is located in Chicago; I operate out of Denver.

The committee knows, I am sure, that the Izaak Walton League supports the outdoor recreation resources review legislation now before you. We had the

*Statement of J. W. Penfold, Director of Conservation, Izaak Walton League of America, *Establishment of a National Outdoor Recreation Resources Review Commission,* Hearings before the subcommittee on Public Lands of the Committee on Interior and Insular Affairs, U.S. House of Representatives, 85th Cong., 1st sess. (Washington, D.C.: Government Printing Office, 1957), 20–26.

privilege of working on it with some of you and with some of your distinguished colleagues who have introduced identical legislation in the Senate. There seems no real need, consequently, to elaborate on the many reasons why we believe that the outdoor recreation resources review should be authorized and implemented. Perhaps, however, I should summarize these reasons for the record.

1. Outdoor recreation is basic in the American scheme of things. It is essential to our physical and mental health. We shall recognize that fact more realistically in the future, as our civilization becomes still more complex, than we do today.

It is an interesting and frightening commentary on the times that the Senate committee studying juvenile delinquency has developed data that appears to indicate that economic well-being of itself is no deterrent to delinquency in young people. Further of interest is the committee's thought that outdoor activity, as in forestry camps, may be an effective means of combating delinquency and of rehabilitating offenders.

Outdoor recreation in my opinion, I hasten to add, is not a type of pill, a tranquilizer drug, which one can take and obtain an immediate cure of his troubles. Rather, outdoor recreation over a period of time, particularly during the formative years, helps develop confidence, a wholesome attitude toward life and certainly better perspective toward the world we live in.

Outdoor recreation opportunity for all people, then, has been and should continue to be a basic characteristic of our total culture.

2. Outdoor recreation requires space and the use, but not necessarily the consumption of basic natural resources. Recreation use of resources may conflict with other resources uses, but they are seldom mutually exclusive. When they become so, it is usually the result of poor planning or no planning at all.

3. Burgeoning cities, spiraling population, expanding industry, more efficient single purpose land and water management, coupled with increasing losses of land, water and production to such new developments as airports, superhighways and the like, crowd more heavily on resources available for outdoor recreation pursuits.

To illustrate: When we became a Nation, the citizens of the Original Thirteen Colonies could look westward clear across the continent, to space, lands, waters, and the resources of them amounting to just about 600 acres for each man, woman and child. Population had increased at such a rate, that when Alaska was added in 1867, the 600-acre figure had already been reduced to 60. Today, this has been further cut to about 13½. When my sons reach their most productive years their individual share will be but 10 acres each. Their sons will sustain a further reduction to about 8 acres each; 8 acres upon which they will be entirely dependent for everything that makes up their way of life; 8 acres for home, garage, schools, streets, heliports, factories, cornfields, wheatlands, forest products, minerals, and yes, hunting, fishing, camping, mountain climbing,

[565]

birdwatching, wilderness, adventure, and all the other wholesome, enjoyable, and rewarding activities we have available in the outdoors now.

What we are urging here today is that we make an intelligent, considered, and comprehensive start on a program which will assure future generations that the 8 acres will contain a relative abundance, undiminished in scope and quality, of the outdoor recreation opportunities we believe so essential.

We do not propose that there be an end to expanding suburbia, and it mushrooms around every city. At the same time I cannot forget that my home in Jefferson County occupies an acre which but a few years ago helped feed the city of Denver as well as producing a good annual crop of pheasants. As a result more intensive cultivation occurs on other agricultural lands, and the sportsman must travel farther afield for fewer and fewer birds.

We do not propose that there be an end to superhighways. After all they enable us to travel farther afield in the search for the outdoors. But we cannot forget, either, that the superhighway takes some 35 or 45 acres per mile out of production, and so exerting still greater pressure on remaining lands. Nor can we forget that just bumper to bumper parking of the cars and trucks today requires 600,000 acres for that single use.

We do not propose that there be an end to any constructive progress, each of us is an inescapable part of it. We do propose that a good start be made toward incorporating outdoor recreation opportunity into all our planning efforts.

4. Due to great improvement in basic economic conditions, in leisure, in transportation, more people are spending more time in outdoor recreation activity. The statistics are well known. Not included in the statistics, but very evident from my own observations, and I may add, very much to my deep personal satisfaction, the so-called underprivileged groups are participating in outdoor recreation activity at an equal or even higher rate of increase. Population increases prodigiously, and due to many factors more and more of them look to the outdoors for recreation opportunity; each of them is spending more time, almost twice as much, in the outdoors than he did just 10 years ago. What will be the impact when most of America is on the 4-day week.

5. These trends will continue, there will be no stopping them short of another world conflagration—God forbid. We must study carefully and analyze comprehensively these trends, that we can take them fully and intelligently into account as we make our plans for the future.

6. Outdoor recreation is, of course, no single activity, nor does the recreationist necessarily go afield with but a single objective in mind. To the fisherman, if his objective is simply to hoist a fish from the stream, or derrick a rainbow from the depths of Granby Reservoir, he could save time, money, and effort by catching his fish from the chicken wire ponds at so much per pound, with no gamble whatsoever involved.

If the hiker seeks only physical exertion, he can doubtless obtain it cheaper, more conveniently, and more scientifically at a gymnasium.

If the birdwatcher simply wishes to look at and identify birds, again he can do that cheaper and more conveniently at a city zoo or museum, with signs provided as well against which to check his identification.

The outdoor recreationist is not a single-purpose creature. He seeks a great many satisfactions on his trips, with the major objective frequently being little more than a socially acceptable excuse. There must be deep-seated anthropological reasons why society doesn't frown on fishing as a contagious form of loafing.

The stream fisherman wants the sound of the running water, the feel of the smooth rocks under his feet, the overhanging willows which give shade and cool the water, and intercept his backcast. He wants the chance to outwit the trout, and to enjoy the impertinent camp robber begging for part of his lunch. On Granby he wants the sun rising over the Front Range and absorbing the early morning mists, the slap of waves against the prow of his boat, the purr of his outboard, the leisurely lunch cooked on shore, and righteous wrath when he hooks bottom and loses his Pop Geer, leader, and length of line.

The birdwatcher wants all of nature and the feeling that he is not entirely an intruder in the natural scene.

So outdoor recreation cannot be measured just in terms of fish in the creel, game in the bag, or check marks on a bird list, any more than a forest can be measured solely in board-feet or a watershed in acre-feet of runoff.

7. Sound and scientific planning, of any type and for any purpose, can be achieved only when based on the facts with clear-cut objectives described with precise definitions. That is why we hire architects. Any competent craftsman can construct a house that will provide shelter and conform with the minimum building codes. The architect, however, can design into the structure those things and that precise layout which will give it the maximum livability as a home, and with provision for the addition of Junior and others as they come along. The real quality which he designs into the home has square feet as only one factor.

8. Outdoor recreation is not a matter strictly of public lands—Federal, State, and local. As has been suggested, 80 percent of all hunting occurs on private lands and waters. I am sure that a sizable portion of all other forms of outdoor recreation occur on private lands and waters or are basically dependent upon them. This is a particularly sensitive aspect of the whole problem we are discussing, and will become an increasingly important part of all our program objectives of the future.

9. Outdoor recreation is, of course, big business. Last year's survey revealed that hunting and fishing alone stimulate business to the tune of $3 billion annually. Add all other forms of outdoor recreation and the figure might be 3 or

4 times as much. The recreation we speak of does not exist to create business and industry. The economic benefits are byproducts of activities each with its own intrinsic value.

In essence, then, we can anticipate a far greater population, and a far greater need and demand for outdoor recreation opportunity. At the same time, we are faced with a diminishing supply of the resources upon which these opportunities depend. Moreover, in far too many areas there is deterioration in the remaining resources. It is time, as the chairman has said, that we stop and take a good hard look at the situation. That, as we see it, is the purpose and objective of this legislation—to stop and take a good hard look at outdoor recreation today and its potentials for tomorrow.

There are several fundamental reasons why we believe a commission, such as is proposed in this legislation, is required.

1. Outdoor recreation is not the sole concern of the Federal Government, the States, communities, or private groups and individuals. It is the concern of all.

2. The recreational use of resources is not something separate and apart from other resource uses and from the rest of our economic and social system.

3. Outdoor recreation is not a matter just of forests and parks, reservoirs and other public properties managed for the benefit of the public. It involves directly or indirectly all lands and waters.

4. The need at this time for the broadest and most comprehensive study precludes the possibility of its being carried out successfully by any one agency or group, or by any combination of several. It will require the thoughtful cooperation of all.

5. The study will provide the base upon which national policy may be developed and will be drawn upon as well by every kind of agency and group in the development of their own policies and programs.

6. As the Nation's first real effort in this aspect of long-range planning, it is imperative that the study, its evaluations and its recommendations reflect as accurately and realistically as possible the full national viewpoint.

We believe the Commission, with an advisory council as proposed, most nearly represents the quality and character of the body needed to make such an important study. Moreover, its makeup, at topmost level, will command respect and achieve the degree of cooperation necessary, will assure full use of existing data and avoid duplication and waste motion.

The several States have been making excellent progress in this general field the past few years. Primarily they have been rightly concerned in the first instance in attempting to provide for their own citizens. More and more, however, they are realizing that their outdoor recreation resources, opportunities, and potentials have regional and national significance. They have been groping for effective means to achieve greater coordination and cooperation among their various programs for the greater value to all. Such organizations as the International Association of Game, Fish, and Conservation Commissioners, similar regional associations, or the National Conference on States Parks evidence this need and this trend. This proposed legislation recognizes the importance of State responsibilities and programs, and I believe will provide a great opportunity for real assistance to the States at this critical juncture, and assistance available through no other means.

The legislation sets a target date for completion of the study and for publication of the Commission's report, with its evaluations and recommendations, and a date when all its affairs are to be wound up and closed. We are not interested in adding permanently to Government's already overcomplex structure.

At the same time we recognize fully that a short term "crash" program will not take care of our needs in this area forever. Outdoor recreation resources and opportunities will require continued study and analysis, just as any other aspect of the total resource picture. I believe that in the course of the review, as an inevitable byproduct, that the Commission will develop ideas about how the inventory, data, and evaluations may best be kept up to date and made universally available to those concerned with resource planning for recreation use.

Congress itself will have those determinations to make in the future, and the experience of this Commission would provide a much more sound basis of fact upon which to make them.

Important in the consideration of this legislation are the questions: How to implement the Commission; and how much will it cost?

It will cost money, that's for sure. Attached to this statement is a breakdown of principal costs—probably rather arbitrary, but at least drawn up with some relationship to the functions and responsibilities which the Commission would assume.

The figure at the bottom of the sheet totals $1,534,050. That sounds like a lot to me personally but spent over 3 fiscal years it represents about one-sixtieth of 1 percent of the economic value of hunting and fishing alone; and perhaps one two-hundredth of 1 percent of the economic value of all outdoor recreation with which it will be concerned.

Commission: There are seven members of the Commission eligible for a per diem allowance in lieu of salary when actually engaged in Commission business. I would estimate that this would average out at about 1½ Commissioner-days per day during the course of the review. Added to this would be travel costs, principally expended in carrying out field hearings.

Advisory council: Provision is made in the legislation to defray travel and subsistence costs of council members when attending the regular meetings of the council. It would likely be advantageous, as well, for them to attend some of the field hearings, particularly when held in their own areas. Many of the members, principally Bureau liaison officers, would be located in Washington where travel and subsistence expenses would be no particular factor.

Staff: An adequate and highly competent staff will be required, because on them will fall the brunt of a tremendous volume of paperwork, conferences, interviews, the specific development of questionnaires and other means of securing data and opinion; the endless compilations, the collating of material into form usable by the Commission itself.

Keymen on the staff would be the executive secretary, to whom the Commission would look for direction of staff and for administrative efficiency in getting the job done.

We have suggested 3 key assistants, 1 to take charge of fiscal matters, housekeeping functions, mimeographing, mailing, files, stenographic pool, and the like; and 2 general assistants to divide between them supervision of the regional specialists.

We have suggested that the study be made by regions, possibly 12 of them, placing a regional specialist in charge of each. This will serve for greater efficiency, better coordination of data originating within specific and comparable areas, and greatly simplify development of the final report in such form as will be of maximum usefulness to States and groups of States.

Staff people will attend field hearings, they will have other travel to perform in carrying out their assignments for the Commission.

Printing and office supplies will add up to a sizable amount, but correspondence is cheaper than travel and long-distance telephone, and should be used whenever possible.

A stenographic and clerical staff will be necessary.

The Commission and its staff operations will consume something more than half of this suggested budget. The balance to be expended in grants-in-aid to universities and colleges, State agencies, or other agencies or organizations when in the judgment of the Commission the data needed can best and most efficiently be secured in that way.

The amounts are arbitrary. The suggestion of grants to universities would finance 50 two-year fellowships, or the equivalent; that to State agencies would finance 50 technicians for 2 years, or the equivalent, to work on Commission assignments under State-agency supervision; other contracts might include financing the cost of a study to be made by the International Association of Game, Fish, and Conservation Commissioners at the request of the Commission, or investigations by such group as the economic research bureau of the University of Colorado.

As I say, it looks to me like a lot of money, but when I look at the size and importance of the task, which one way or another must be accomplished or be lost by default, I am sure that I am overly conservative.

The Izaak Walton League of America appreciates the privilege of presenting our views before this distinguished committee.

(The table referred to follows:)

Estimated costs: Outdoor Recreation Resources Review Commission, July 1, 1957– June 31, 1960

	Fiscal year 1958	Fiscal year 1959	Fiscal year 1960	Total
Commission members:				
Per diem	$35,000	$20,000	$20,000	$75,000
Travel	7,500	7,500	4,000	19,000
Subtotal	42,500	27,500	24,000	94,000
Staff:				
Executive secretary	13,750	15,000	10,000	38,750
Assistants (3)	27,500	30,000	16,500	74,000
Regional specialists (12)	80,000	96,000	43,000	224,000
Clerical (24)	86,000	103,000	51,600	240,000
Subtotal	207,250	244,200	126,100	577,550
Staff travel	7,500	7,500	4,000	19,000
Advisory council travel	12,000	10,000	8,000	30,000
Office space	7,500	7,500	3,750	18,750
Printing and supplies	7,500	7,500	3,750	18,750
Telephone and Telegraph	6,000	6,000	4,000	16,000
Miscellaneous	15,000	15,000	15,000	45,000
Publishing report	......	......	20,000	20,000
Commission operations total without grants-in-aid	305,250	325,200	209,600	839,050
Grants-in-aid:				
To universities	50,000	75,000	20,000	145,000
To State agencies	187,500	225,000	37,500	450,000
Other countracts	20,000	50,000	30,000	100,000
Subtotal	257,500	350,000	87,500	695,000
Grand total	562,750	675,200	296,100	1,534,050

AN ACT FOR THE ESTABLISHMENT OF THE OUTDOOR RECREATION RESOURCES REVIEW COMMISSION*
June 28, 1958

On June 19, 1957 the Senate passed S. 846, a bill to create an outdoor recreation resources review commission. This bill had been introduced by Senator Anderson of New Mexico and was co-sponsored by six other western senators. Within the next year, 10 similar or identical bills were introduced in the House of Representatives.

S. 846 was eventually reported out of the House Interior and Insular Affairs Committee with amendments which were accepted by the Senate. The amended bill passed the House on June 16, 1958 and was signed by the President on June 28, 1958.

> An Act for the establishment of a National Outdoor Recreation Resources Review Commission to study the outdoor recreation resources of the public lands and other land and water areas of the United States, and for other purposes.

Be it enacted by the Senate and House of Representatives of the United States of America in Congress assembled, That in order to preserve, develop, and assure accessibility to all American people of present and future generations such quality and quantity of outdoor recreation resources as will be necessary and desirable for individual enjoyment, and to assure the spiritual, cultural, and physical benefits that such outdoor recreation provides; in order to inventory and evaluate the outdoor recreation resources and opportunities of the Nation, to determine the types and location of such resources and opportunities which will be required by present and future generations; and in order to make comprehensive information and recommendations leading to these goals available to the President, the Congress, and the individual States and Territories, there is hereby authorized and created a bipartisan Outdoor Recreation Resources Review Commission.

SEC. 2. For the purposes of this Act—

(1) "Commission" shall mean the Outdoor Recreation Resources Review Commission;

(2) "Outdoor recreation resources" shall mean the land and water areas and associated resources of such areas in the United States, its Territories, and possessions which provide or may in the future provide opportunities for outdoor recreation, irrespective of ownership.

(3) "Outdoor recreation resources" shall not mean nor include recreation fa-

*72 *Statutes at Large,* 238.

cilities, programs, and opportunities usually associated with urban development such as playgrounds, stadia, golf courses, city parks, and zoos.

SEC. 3. (a) The Commission hereby authorized and created shall consist of fifteen members appointed as follows:

(1) Two majority and two minority members of the Senate Committee on Interior and Insular Affairs, to be appointed by the President of the Senate;

(2) Two majority and two minority members of the House Committee on Interior and Insular Affairs to be appointed by the Speaker of the House; and

(3) Seven citizens, known to be informed about and concerned with the preservation and development of outdoor recreation resources and opportunities, and experienced in resource conservation planning for multiple resources uses, who shall be appointed by the President, and one of whom shall be designated as chairman by the President.

Vacancies occurring on the Commission shall not affect the authority of the remaining members of the Commission to carry out the functions of the Commission, and shall be filled in the same manner as the original positions.

(b) The Commission members shall serve without compensation, except that each member shall be entitled to reimbursement for actual travel and subsistence expense incurred in the services of the Commission and each member appointed by the President shall be entitled to a per diem allowance not to exceed $50 per day when actually engaged in Commission business.

(c) The Commission shall convene as soon as practicable following appointment of its members, to implement the purposes and objectives of this Act.

SEC. 4. (a) The Commission is authorized, without regard to the civil-service laws and regulations, to appoint and fix the compensation of an executive secretary and such additional personnel as may be necessary to enable it to carry out its functions, except that any Federal employees subject to the civil service laws and regulations who may be assigned to the Commission shall retain civil service status without interruption or loss of status or privilege.

(b) The Commission shall establish headquarters in the District of Columbia and shall make such other arrangements as are necessary to carry out the purposes of this Act.

(c) The Commission shall request the Secretary of each Federal Department or head of any independent agency which, includes an agency or agencies with a direct interest and responsibility in any phase of outdoor recreation to appoint, and he shall appoint for each such agency a liaison officer who shall work closely with the Commission and its staff.

SEC. 5. (a) There is hereby established an advisory council which shall consist of the liaison officers appointed under section 4(c), together with twenty-five additional members appointed by the Commission who shall be representative of the various major geographical areas and citizen interest groups including the following: State game and fish departments, State park departments, State for-

[573]

estry departments, private organizations working in the field of outdoor recreation resources and opportunities, landowners, State water pollution control agencies, State water development agencies, private forestry interests, livestock interests, mining interests, State travel commissions, petroleum production interests, commercial fishing interests, commercial outdoor recreation interests, industry, education, labor, public utilities, and municipal governments.

(b) The functions of the advisory council shall be to advise and counsel the Commission in the development of ways, means, and procedures whereby maximum cooperation may be obtained from all agencies and groups whose assistance in accomplishing the purposes of this Act will be required in arriving at sound methods and criteria for evaluating outdoor recreation resources data assembled and otherwise to advise and assist the Commission in carrying out the purposes of the Act.

(c) Members of the advisory council, except those employed by the Federal Government and assigned to the Commission as liaison officers, shall serve without compensation except that each shall be entitled to reimbursement for actual travel and subsistence expenses incurred in attending meetings of the advisory council called by the Chairman of the Commission, or incurred in carrying out duties assigned by the Chairman of the Commission.

(d) The Chairman of the Commission shall call an initial organization meeting of the advisory council, a meeting of such council each six months thereafter, and a final meeting of such council prior to transmitting the final report to the President and the Congress.

SEC. 6. (a) The Commission shall proceed as soon as practicable to set in motion a nationwide inventory and evaluation of outdoor recreation resources and opportunities, directly and through the Federal agencies, the States, and private organizations and groups, utilizing to the fullest extent possible such studies, data, and reports previously prepared or concurrently in process by Federal agencies, States, private organizations, groups, and others.

(b) The Commission shall compile such data and in the light of the data so compiled and of information available concerning trends in population, leisure, transportation, and other factors shall determine the amount, kind, quality, and location of such outdoor recreation resources and opportunities as will be required by the year 1976 and the year 2000, and shall recommend what policies should best be adopted and what programs be initiated, at each level of government and by private organizations and other citizen groups and interests, to meet such future requirements.

(c) The Commission shall present not later than September 1, 1961, a report of its review, a compilation of its data, and its recommendations on a State by State, region by region, and national basis to the President and to the Congress, and shall cease to exist not later than one year thereafter. Such report, compilation, and recommendations shall be presented in such form as to make them of maximum value to the States and shall include recommendations as to means whereby the review may effectively be kept current in the future. The Commission, on its own initiative or on request of the President or the Congress, shall prepare interim or progress reports on particular phases of its review.

(d) The Commission is authorized to conduct public hearings and otherwise to secure data and expressions of opinion.

(e) The Commission is authorized to make direct grants to the States, and to transfer necessary funds to Federal agencies, from sums appropriated pursuant to section 8, to carry out such aspects of the review as the Commission may determine can best be carried out by the States, or Federal agencies, under such arrangements and agreements as are determined by the Commission; and may enter into contracts or agreements for studies and surveys with public or private agencies and organizations. The Commission is also authorized to reimburse Federal agencies for the expenses of liaison officers appointed under section 4 (c) and other cooperation.

SEC. 7. The Commission, in its inquiries, findings, and recommendations, shall recognize that present and future solutions to problems of outdoor recreation resources and opportunities are responsibilities at all levels of government, from local to Federal, and of individuals and private organizations as well. The Commission shall recognize that lands, waters, forest, rangelands, wetlands, wildlife and such other natural resources that serve economic purposes also serve to varying degrees and for varying uses outdoor recreation purposes, and that sound planning of resource utilization for the full future welfare of the Nation must include coordination and integration of all such multiple uses.

SEC. 8. There are hereby authorized to be appropriated not more than $2,500,000 to carry out the purposes of this Act, and such moneys as may be appropriated shall be available to the Commission until expended.

SEC 9. This Act may be cited as "the Outdoor Recreation Resources Review Act".

Approved June 28, 1958.

THE ORRRC RECOMMENDATIONS*
1962

The ORRRC, under the chairmanship of Laurance S. Rockefeller, published 27 detailed studies plus a summary report entitled Outdoor Recreation for America. *The commission also summarized their recommendations in the pages that follow.*

This report is a study of outdoor recreation in America—its history, its place in current American life, and its future. It represents a detailed investigation of what the public does in the out-of-doors, what factors affect its choices, what resources are available for its use, what are the present and future needs, and what the problems are in making new resources available. The investigation involves the present and to some extent the past, but its principal concern is for the future—between now and the year 2000. It is a plan for coming generations, one that must be started now and carried forward so that the outdoors may be available to the Americans of the future as it has been to those of the past.

Americans have long been concerned with the values of the outdoors. From Thoreau, Olmsted, and Muir in the middle of the past century to the leaders of today, there has been a continuing tradition of love of the outdoors and action to conserve its values. Yet one of the main currents of modern life has been the movement away from the outdoors. It no longer lies at the back door or at the end of Main Street. More and more, most Americans must traverse miles of crowded highways to know the outdoors. The prospect for the future is that this quest will be even more difficult.

Decade by decade, the expanding population has achieved more leisure time, more money to spend, and better travel facilities; and it has sought more and better opportunities to enjoy the outdoors. But the public has also demanded more of other things. In the years following World War II, this process greatly accelerated as an eager Nation, released from wartime restrictions, needed millions of new acres for subdivisions, industrial sites, highways, schools, and airports. The resources for outdoor recreation—shoreline, green acres, open space, and unpolluted waters—diminished in the face of demands for more of everything else.

In Washington, this created legislative issues in the Congress and administrative problems within the agencies responsible for providing opportunities for outdoor recreation. Similar problems were faced in many State capitals across the country. In some cases, they stemmed from conflicts among different interests vying for use of the same resources. In others, it was the matter of responsi-

*ORRRC, *Outdoor Recreation for America* (Washington, D.C.: Government Printing Office, 1962), 1-10.

bility—who should do the job, and who should pay the bill. Private landowners were faced with problems caused by the public seeking recreation on their land. The factors which brought about the increased need for outdoor recreation grew, and each year the problems intensified.

During the 1950's, the pressing nature of the problems of outdoor recreation had become a matter of deep concern for Members of Congress, State legislators, other public leaders, and many private citizens and organizations. Numerous problems, both foreign and domestic, were making demands upon the Nation's resources and energies. But it was felt that in making choices among these priorities, America must not neglect its heritage of the outdoors—for that heritage offers physical, spiritual, and educational benefits, which not only provide a better environment but help to achieve other national goals by adding to the health of the Nation.

By 1958, Congress had decided that an intensive nationwide study should be made of outdoor recreation, one involving all levels of government and the private contribution, and on June 28 of that year it established the Outdoor Recreation Resources Review Commission.

The authorizing act, Public Law 85–470, set forth the mission. It was essentially threefold:

To determine the outdoor recreation wants and needs of the American people now and what they will be in the years 1976 and 2000.

To determine the recreation resources of the Nation available to satisfy those needs now and in the years 1976 and 2000.

To determine what policies and programs should be recommended to ensure that the needs of the present and future are adequately and efficiently met.

The Commission that Congress established to carry out this task was composed of eight Congressional members, two representing each party from the Interior and Insular Affairs Committees of the Senate and of the House; and seven private citizens appointed by the President, one of whom was designated as Chairman.

In the fall of 1958, the Commission began recruiting a staff and in the following year launched its study program. The staff designed and coordinated the program and carried out some of the key studies, but many studies were assigned to outside contractors—Federal agencies, universities, and nonprofit research organizations—with particular skills, experience, or facilities. The reports resulting from these studies (listed in appendix C), with a full description of the techniques used in their conduct, are available in separate volumes because of their general public interest and potential value to officials at all levels of government and to others who may wish to pursue the subjects further. A few of the lines of investigation followed may be mentioned briefly.

To assess present resources for outdoor recreation, the Commission initiated an inventory of all the nonurban public designated recreation areas of the country. These numbered more than 24,000. Over a hundred items of information were analyzed in connection with 5,000 of the larger areas in order to evaluate present use and capacity and potential for development.

The Commission also carried out special studies to probe particular problems such as those connected with wilderness, water recreation, hunting and fishing, the densely populated Northeast, and sparsely populated Alaska.

To determine what the pressure is and will be on the resources, the Commission undertook a series of studies on the demand for outdoor recreation. At the base of these studies was a National Recreation Survey, conducted for the Commission by the Bureau of the Census. Some 16,000 persons were asked questions about their background, their economic status, what they presently do for outdoor recreation (if anything), what they would like to do more of, and why they do not do the things they want to do.

In further studies designed to complement and amplify the findings of the survey, the Commission investigated the effects on outdoor recreation of present and prospective changes—sectionally and nationally—in personal income, in population, in leisure time, and in travel facilities. To project future needs, the effects of such changes were applied to the present patterns as developed by the National Recreation Survey.

In order to have an effective method of working with the States, the Commission asked the Governor of each to appoint a State Contact Officer through whom it might channel all its requests. The Governors generally appointed the head of the State conservation, recreation, fish and game, or planning agency. These men and their associates made a major contribution in carrying out the inventory of State areas. This involved the laborious task of supplying detailed information on every area in the State. In other studies they provided financial, legal, and administrative data.

The Federal agencies in Washington and their field offices made available their valuable experience in the problems of outdoor recreation and provided specific data on their programs. In almost every study, the Commission began by consulting these agencies to determine what information was already available, and a great deal of valuable material was at hand.

The cooperation offered by the States and Federal agencies greatly expanded the reach of the Commission. Hundreds of people contributed significant time and effort and thus made it possible to do far more than otherwise could have been accomplished.

SOME FINDINGS OF THE STUDY

As results of the studies began flowing to the Commission, some old ideas were discarded, some were reinforced, and some new concepts evolved. The following are a few of the major conclusions.

The Simple Activities Are the
Most Popular.

Driving and walking for pleasure, swimming, and picnicking lead the list of the outdoor activities in which Americans participate, and driving for pleasure is most popular of all. This is generally true regardless of income, education, age, or occupation.

Outdoor Opportunities Are Most
Urgently Needed Near
Metropolitan Areas.

Three-quarters of the people will live in these areas by the turn of the century. They will have the greatest need for outdoor recreation, and their need will be the most difficult to satisfy as urban centers have the fewest facilities (per capita) and the sharpest competition for land use.

Across the Country, Considerable
Land Is Now Available for Outdoor
Recreation, But It Does Not
Effectively Meet the Need.

Over a quarter billion acres are public designated outdoor recreation areas. However, either the location of the land, or restrictive management policies, or both, greatly reduce the effectiveness of the land for recreation use by the bulk of the population. Much of the West and virtually all of Alaska are of little use to most Americans looking for a place in the sun for their families on a weekend, when the demand is overwhelming. At regional and State levels, most of the land is where people are not. Few places are near enough to metropolitan centers for a Sunday outing. The problem is not one of total acres but of *effective* acres.

Money Is Needed.

Most public agencies, particularly in the States, are faced with a lack of funds. Outdoor recreation opportunities can be created by acquiring new areas or by more intensive development of existing resources, but either course requires money. Federal, State, and local governments are now spending about $1 billion annually for outdoor recreation. More will be needed to meet the demand.

Outdoor Recreation Is Often
Compatible With Other
Resource Uses.

Fortunately, recreation need not be the exclusive use of an area, particularly the larger ones. Recreation can be another use in a development primarily managed for a different purpose, and it therefore should be considered in many kinds of planning—urban renewal, highway construction, water resource development, forest and range management, to name only a few.

Water Is a Focal Point of
Outdoor Recreation.

Most people seeking outdoor recreation want water—to sit by, to swim and to fish in, to ski across, to dive under, and to run their boats over. Swimming is now one of the most popular outdoor activities and is likely to be the most popular of all by the turn of the century. Boating and fishing are among the top 10 activities. Camping, picnicking, and hiking, also high on the list, are more attractive near water sites.

Outdoor Recreation Brings About
Economic Benefits.

Although the chief reason for providing outdoor recreation is the broad social and individual benefits it produces, it also brings about desirable economic effects. Its provision enhances community values by creating a better place to live and increasing land values. In some underdeveloped areas, it can be a mainstay of the local economy. And it is a basis for big business as the millions and millions of people seeking the outdoors generate an estimated $20 billion a year market for goods and services.

Outdoor Recreation Is a Major
Leisure Time Activity, and It Is
Growing in Importance.

About 90 percent of all Americans participated in some form of outdoor recreation in the summer of 1960. In total, they particpated in one activity or another on 4.4 billion separate occasions. It is anticipated that by 1976 the total will be 6.9 billion, and by the year 2000 it will be 12.4 billion—a threefold increase by the turn of the century.

More Needs To Be
Known About the
Values of Outdoor Recreation.

As outdoor recreation increases in importance, it will need more land, but much of this land can be used, and will be demanded, for other purposes. Yet there is little research to provide basic information on its relative importance. More needs to be established factually about the values of outdoor recreation to our society, so that sounder decisions on allocation of resources for it can be made. More must be known also about management techniques, so that the maximum social and economic benefit can be realized from these resources.

THE RECOMMENDATIONS

After 3 years of research, and an aggregate of some 50 days of discussion among the Commissioners, the Commission has developed specific recommendations for a recreation program. The 15 members brought differing political, social, and resource-use opinions to the meeting table, and proposed recommendations were put through the test of this range of opinions. During the course of the study and discussion, views of individual members developed, and the collective opinion crystallized. The final recommendations are a consensus of the Commission.

In the process of evolving recommendations, the Commission's Advisory Council played an important role. It consisted of 25 individuals representative of mining, timber, grazing, business, and labor interests as well as of recreation and conservation groups. The Council also included top-level representatives of 15 Federal agencies which have a responsibility relating to the provision of outdoor recreation. In five 2-day joint meetings with the Commission, the Council reviewed tentative proposals and suggested alternative courses of action on several occasions. The advice of the Council had a marked effect on the final product.

State Contact Officers also contributed to the decision-making process. In a series of regional meetings, at which the Commission sought their advice on pressing issues, they put forward practical and urgent suggestions for action.

In many cases the recommendations are general; in others they are specific. For various reasons, the recommendations tend to be more detailed and more extensive regarding the Federal Government. The Commission wishes to emphasize, however, that the key elements in the total effort to make outdoor recreation opportunities available are private enterprise, the States, and local government. In relation to them, the role of the Federal agencies should be not one of domination but of cooperation and assistance in meeting their respective needs.

The recommendations of the Commission fall into five general categeries—
A National Outdoor Recreation Policy.
Guidelines for the Management of Outdoor Recreation Resources.
Expansion, Modification, and Intensification of Present Programs to Meet Increasing Needs.
Establishment of a Bureau of Outdoor Recreation in the Federal Government.
A Federal Grants-in-Aid Program to States.

The body of this report presents the reasoning and significance of these recommendations. To those who would like a quick over-all picture of the recommendations, the following digest will prove helpful.

A NATIONAL OUTDOOR RECREATION POLICY

It shall be the national policy, through the conservation and wise use of resources, to preserve, develop, and make accessible to all American people such quantity and quality of outdoor recreation as will be necessary and desirable for individual enjoyment and to assure the physical, cultural, and spiritual benefits of outdoor recreation.

Implementation of this policy will require the cooperative participation of all levels of government and private enterprise. In some aspects, the government responsibility is greater; in others, private initiative is better equipped to do the job.

The role of the Federal Government should be—

1. Preservation of scenic areas, natural wonders, primitive areas, and historic sites of national significance.

2. Management of Federal lands for the broadest possible recreation benefit consistent with other essential uses.

3. Cooperation with the States through technical and financial assistance.

4. Promotion of interstate arrangements, including Federal participation where necessary.

5. Assumption of vigorous, cooperative leadership in a nationwide recreation effort.

The States should play a pivotal role in making outdoor recreation opportunities available by—

1. Acquisition of land, development of sites, and provision and maintenance of facilities of State or regional significance.

2. Assistance to local governments.

3. Provision of leadership and planning.

Local governments should expand their efforts to provide outdoor recreation opportunities, with particular emphasis upon securing open space and developing recreation areas in and around metropolitan and other urban areas.

Individual initiative and private enterprise should continue to be the most important force in outdoor recreation, providing many and varied opportunities for a vast number of people, as well as the goods and services used by people in their recreation activities. Government should encourage the work of nonprofit groups wherever possible. It should also stimulate desirable commercial development, which can be particularly effective in providing facilities and services where demand is sufficient to return a profit.

GUIDELINES FOR MANAGEMENT

All agencies administering outdoor recreation resources—public and private—are urged to adopt a system of classifying recreation lands designed to make the best possible use of available resources in the light of the needs of people. Present jurisdictional boundaries of agencies need not be disturbed, but where necessary, use should be changed in accordance with the classification.

Implementation of this system would be a major step forward in a coordinated national recreation effort. It would provide a consistent and effective method of planning for all land-managing agencies and would promote logical adjustment of the entire range of recreation activities to the entire range of available areas. Under this approach of recreation zoning, the qualities of the respective classes of recreation environment are identified and therefore more readily enhanced and protected.

The following system of classifying outdoor recreation resources is proposed—

Class I—High-Density Recreation Areas

Areas intensively developed and managed for mass use.

Class II—General Outdoor Recreation Areas

Areas subject to substantial development for a wide variety of specific recreation uses.

Class III—Natural Environment Areas

Various types of areas that are suitable for recreation in a natural environment and usually in combination with other uses.

Class IV—Unique Natural Areas

Areas of outstanding scenic splendor, natural wonder, or scientific importance.

Class V—Primitive Areas

Undisturbed roadless areas characterized by natural, wild conditions, including "wilderness areas."

Class VI—Historic and Cultural Sites

Sites of major historic or cultural significance; either local, regional, or national.

Recommendations for specific applications of the system appear in chapters 6 and 8.

EXPANSION, MODIFICATION, AND INTENSIFICATION OF PRESENT PROGRAMS

PLANNING, ACQUISITION, PROTECTION, AND ACCESS

1. Each State, through a central agency, should develop a long-range plan for outdoor recreation, to provide adequate opportunities for the public, to acquire additional areas where necessary, and to preserve outstanding natural sites.

2. Local governments should give greater emphasis to the needs of their citizens for outdoor recreation by considering it in all land-use planning, opening areas with recreation potential to use, and where necessary, acquiring new areas.

3. States should seek to work out interstate arrangements where the recreation-seeking public overflows political boundaries. The Federal Government should assist in meeting these interstate demand situations.

4. Systematic and continuing research, both fundamental and applied, should be promoted to provide the basis for sound planning and decisions.

5. Immediate action should be taken by Federal, State, and local governments to reserve or acquire additional water, beach, and shoreline areas, particularly near centers of population.

6. Full provision for acquiring shoreline lands for public access and use should be made in reservoir developments.

7. Surface rights to surplus Federal lands suitable for recreation should be transferred without cost to State or local governments with reversion clauses.

8. Open space programs for metropolitan areas should be continued.

9. Congress should enact legislation to provide for the establishment and preservation of certain primitive areas as "wilderness areas."

10. Certain rivers of unusual scientific, esthetic, and recreation value should be allowed to remain in their free-flowing state and natural setting without man-made alterations.

11. States should use their regulatory power to zone areas for maximum recreation benefit, maintain quality, and ensure public safety in conflicts between recreation and other uses and in conflicts among recreation uses.

12. Recreation areas should be strongly defended against encroachments from nonconforming uses, both public and private. Where recreation land must be taken for another public use, it should be replaced with other land of similar quality and comparable location.

13. Public agencies should assure adequate access to water-based recreation opportunities by acquisition of access areas, easements across private lands, zoning of shorelines, consideration of water access in road design and construction, and opening of now restricted waters such as municipal reservoirs.

14. Interpretive and educational programs should be intensified and broadened to promote appreciation and understanding of natural, scientific, and historic values.

PROMOTING RECREATION VALUES IN RELATED FIELDS

15. Outdoor recreation should be emphasized in federally constructed or licensed multipurpose water developments and thus granted full consideration in the planning, design, and construction of such projects.

16. Recreation should be recognized as a motivating purpose in programs and projects for pollution control and as a necessary objective in the allocation of funds therefor.

17. Flood-plain zoning should be used wherever possible as a method to preserve attractive reaches of rivers and streams for public recreation in addition to the other benefits from such zoning.

18. The Federal Government and the States should recognize the potential recreation values in highway construction programs and assure that they are developed.

19. Activities under watershed and other agricultural conservation programs should be oriented toward greater recreation benefits for the public.

20. The States should encourage the public use of private lands by taking the lead in working out such arrangements as leases for hunting and fishing, scenic easements, and providing protection for landowners who allow the public to use their lands.

MEETING THE COSTS

21. All levels of government must provide continuing and adequate funds for outdoor recreation. In most cases, this will require a substantial increase over present levels.

22. State and local governments should consider the use of general obligation and revenue bonds to finance land acquisition and capital improvements for outdoor recreation.

23. State and local governments should consider other financing devices such as season user fees, dedicated funds, and use of uncollected refunds of gasoline taxes paid by pleasure boat owners.

24. States should take the lead in extending technical and financial assistance to local governments to meet outdoor recreation requirements.

25. Public agencies should adopt a system of user fees designed to recapture at least a significant portion of the operation and maintenance costs of providing outdoor recreation activities that involve the exclusive use of a facility, or require special facilities.

26. In addition to outright acquisition, local governments should consider the use of such devices as easements, zoning, cluster developments, and open-land tax policies to supplement the supply of outdoor recreation opportunities.

27. Public agencies should stimulate desirable gifts of land and money from private individuals and groups for outdoor recreation purposes. The work of

private, nonprofit organizations in providing and enhancing opportunities should be encouraged.

28. Government should stimulate and encourage the provision of outdoor recreation opportunities by private enterprise.

29. Where feasible, concessioners should be encouraged to provide facilities and visitor services on Federal lands under appropriate supervision. Where this is not feasible, the Federal Government should build facilities and lease them to private business for operation.

A BUREAU OF OUTDOOR RECREATION

A Bureau of Outdoor Recreation should be established in the Department of the Interior. This Bureau would have over-all responsibility for leadership of a nationwide effort by coordinating the various Federal programs and assisting other levels of government to meet the demands for outdoor recreation. It would not manage any land. This would continue to be the function of the existing managerial agencies.

Specifically, the new Bureau would—

1. Coordinate the recreation activities of the more than 20 Federal agencies whose activities affect outdoor recreation.

2. Assist State and local governments with technical aid in planning and adminstration, including the development of standards for personnel, procedures, and operations.

3. Administer a grants-in-aid program to States for planning and for development and acquisition of needed areas.

4. Act as a clearinghouse for information and guide, stimulate, and sponsor research as needed.

5. Encourage interstate and regional cooperation, including Federal participation where necessary.

To assure that recreation policy and planning receive attention at a high level and to promote interdepartmental coordination, there should be established a Recreation Advisory Council, consisting of the Secretaries of Interior, Agriculture, and Defense, with the Secretary of the Interior as Chairman. Other agencies would be invited to participate on an *ad hoc* basis when matters affecting their interests are under consideration by the Council.

The Recreation Advisory Council would provide broad policy guidance on all matters affecting outdoor recreation activities and programs carried out by the Bureau of Outdoor Recreation. The Secretary of the Interior should be required to seek such guidance in the administration of the Bureau.

Initially the new Bureau should be staffed where possible by transfer of experienced personnel from existing Federal agencies. It should have regional offices.

A Research Advisory Committee consisting of professional people from government, academic life, and private business should be established to advise the Bureau on its research activities.

It is urged that each State designate a focal point within its governmental structure to work with the Bureau. This focal point, perhaps one of the existing State agencies, could also serve to coordinate State recreation planning and activities and be responsible for a comprehensive State outdoor recreation plan.

A GRANTS-IN-AID PROGRAM

A Federal grants-in-aid program should be established to stimulate and assist the States in meeting the demand for outdoor recreation. This program, administered by the proposed Bureau of Outdoor Recreation, would promote State planning and acquisition and development of areas to meet the demands of the public. Projects would be approved in accordance with a statewide plan. They would be subject to review by the proposed Bureau of Outdoor Recreation to ensure conformance with Federal standards. This program would complement and would be closely coordinated with the open space aid provisions of recent legislation.

Initial grants of up to 75 percent of the total cost for planning would be made the first year and a reduced percentage thereafter. Grants for acquisition or development would be made up to 40 percent of the total cost. Federal participation could be raised to 50 percent where the State acquisition or development was part of an interstate plan.

Funds for the program would be allocated on a basis which would take into account State population, area, needs, and the amount of Federal land and Federal recreation programs in the State and region.

The grants-in-aid program should be supplemented by a program of loans to the States. This would assist in projects where the States did not have matching funds available but where the need for acquisition or development was particularly urgent, or where funds were needed beyond those available as grants-in-aid.

PHILLIP O. FOSS ON THE NEED FOR A NEW
BUREAU OF OUTDOOR RECREATION*
1962

The ORRRC recommended that a new bureau of outdoor recreation be established. In his report to ORRRC, Federal Agencies and Outdoor Recreation, *Phillip O. Foss analyzed the need for a new bureau and reluctantly concluded that it was the best of the available alternatives. His summary statement follows.*

CHAPTER ONE

THE FEDERAL GOVERNMENT AND OUTDOOR RECREATION

ORIGINS OF THE PROBLEM

The Policy Vacuum

In 1960 there were some 425 to 450 million recreational visits to Government managed, financed, or licensed facilities but no agency of the Federal Government was established to provide recreation for the public. The U.S. Army Corps of Engineers was concerned with aids to navigation and flood control— yet it entertained 106 million visitors in 1960. The Forest Service was established to conserve the forests, but it played host to 92.5 million visitors. The Soil Conservation Service and the Agricultural Stabilization and Conservation Service were created to improve and conserve farm lands, but in the process they have helped farmers and ranchers construct 1.7 million farm ponds which provide outdoor recreation for uncounted millions each year. The Public Health Service was obviously not established to aid in providing recreational services to the public, but its water pollution abatement program may be of greatest benefit to fishermen. Even the National Park Service was not formed to provide recreation in the usual sense, but to preserve unique or exceptional scenic areas. None of these, or any other Federal agency, started out to provide public outdoor recreation, but they have had recreation and recreationists thrust upon them. Recreation has been an incidental, and almost an accidental, byproduct of the "primary" purposes of Federal agencies. Consequently there is no unified national policy on recreation, and few of the agencies have any real recreation policy. Agency practices have been established usually without adequate research and long-range planning and oftentimes as defensive measures against the recreationists. Lack of anything resembling a national recreational policy is therefore

*Phillip O. Foss, *Federal Agencies and Outdoor Recreation,* ORRRC Study Report No. 13 (Washington, D.C.: Government Printing Office, 1962), 1, 61, 67–68.

at the root of most of the recreation problems of the Federal Government. But the recreationists exist even if a policy does not.

"This thing is rolling over us"

A second major difficulty lies in the phenomenal growth of recreational use of Federal properties since World War II. Recreational visits to Corps of Engineers reservoirs grew from 5 million in 1946 to 106 million in 1960. Visits to the national forests rose from 18 to 92 million in the same 15-year period. Other resource-managing agencies experienced similar recreational growing pains. In the words of one official, "This thing is rolling over us."

RECREATIONAL VISITS TO SELECTED
FEDERAL PROPERTIES 1950–1960

Agency	1950	1960
National Park Service	32,780,000	72,288,000
Forest Service	27,368,000	92,595,000
Tennessee Valley Authority	16,645,000	42,349,000
Bureau of Reclamation	6,594,000	24,300,000
Corps of Engineers	16,000,000	106,000,000

By 1960, it was too late for the Federal Government to decide whether it should be, or wanted to be, in the recreation business. It was already in it.

* * *

With some few exceptions, the Federal Government has not officially recognized recreation as an activity for which it has any responsibility. No reference to recreation appears in the enabling acts of the Bureau of Land Management, Bureau of Reclamation, TVA, Bureau of Public Roads, and most other Federal agencies involved in recreational activities. Use of the national forests for recreation was recognized in the Multiple Use Act of 1960. The Flood Control Act of 1944 recognized recreational use as one of the multiple purposes to be served by Corps of Engineers reservoirs, and the Fletcher Act of 1932 amended previous River and Harbor Law to allow the corps to include recreational boating in planning navigation improvements. The Housing Act of 1961 makes reference to park and recreational purposes in its definition of open-space land. But these are exceptions to the general lack of official recognition of outdoor recreation by the Federal Government. The Bureau of Sport Fisheries and Wildlife supposedly operates to conserve fish and wildlife—not to provide a recreation resource. Similarly the appropriation act for 1962 authorizes cost-sharing benefits to farmers when the primary benefit is wildlife conservation—not recreation. Partly because of this lack of official recognition, there has been no attempt to define the term "recreation." Consequently we are spending considerable sums

[589]

for recreation and tagging the expenditure for irrigation, power, flood control, road construction, timber culture, soil conservation, wildlife conservation, and the like.

So long as outdoor recreation is not officially recognized and defined, no national policy is, or will be, forthcoming. The differing policies which now exist are largely individual agency practices which may, or may not, have received congressional approval in legislation. Since there is no national policy and since recreation demands are high and going higher, there has lately been a proliferation of unrelated and uncoordinated bills which have public recreation as their principal objective even if the word "recreation" does not appear in the bill. Because there is no general understanding or agreement as to what the role of the Federal Government is, or should be, in outdoor recreation, neither the Congress nor the Bureau of the Budget has any real basis or criteria for evaluating such bills.

It is time for the Federal Government to face up to the fact that it is already in the recreation business—too far in to withdraw—and that its recreation problems will not "go away" even if it continues to ignore them.

When it recognizes the existence of outdoor recreation, the Federal Government can then proceed to define its responsibilities and assign priorities of values. Until that time the present disjointed, unplanned, and generally chaotic situation in Federal administration of outdoor recreation can only grow worse.

* * *

Because recreational use of Federal facilities has grown so rapidly, because recreation has not been recognized or defined and hence has little status, because it ordinarily takes place along with, or as a consequence of, some other activity, and because it usually is subject to State and local influences, there has been little coordination in its administration. Since it operates through a complex web of legislative and administrative arrangements, through many agencies, at all levels of government, and since it is influenced by a myriad of extraneous factors, proper coordination is extremely difficult.

To further complicate an already confused situation are the differing allegiances and objectives of the various agencies and their supporting clientele groups.

Lack of coordination results in waste and duplication, but, more importantly, it prevents or postpones the accomplishment of public objectives.

No panacea is offered for the alleviation of this problem but a general observation may be ventured. The ideal method for accomplishing coordinated effort is to so organize that the process of coordination will take place automatically. Admittedly, this ideal is impossible of accomplishment, but further progress in that direction is possible. In the case of outdoor recreation, there are oftentimes several Federal agencies plus State and local agencies all engaged in administering what is essentially a single resource. In such a situation, there are really only two alternatives—complete reorganization or the addition of a separate coordinating body.

When agencies have been in existence for any considerable period, a real reorganization is extremely difficult to accomplish in a democratic society because of the political institutions and relationships which surround and support each agency. The establishment of a separate coordinating agency would thus appear to be the only remaining alternative.

A SPECIAL MESSAGE FROM PRESIDENT JOHN F. KENNEDY TO CONGRESS ON CONSERVATION*
March 1, 1962

Less than two months after ORRRC submitted its report President Kennedy sent a special message to Congress endorsing many of the ORRRC recommendations including the creation of a new bureau of outdoor recreation. That portion of the President's message which dealt specifically with outdoor recreation is documented here.

I. OUTDOOR RECREATION RESOURCES

Adequate outdoor recreational facilities are among the basic requirements of a sound national conservation program. The increased leisure time enjoyed by our growing population and the greater mobility made possible by improved highway networks have dramatically increased the Nation's need for additional recreational areas. The 341 million visits to Federal land and water areas recorded in 1960 are expected to double by 1970 and to increase fivefold by the end of the century. The need for an aggressive program of recreational development is both real and immediate.

The Outdoor Recreation Resources Review Commission, after a three-year study of our Nation's recreational demands and opportunities, has submitted a series of recommendations deserving the attention of governments at all levels and of the citizenry at large. Many of the Commission's suggestions have already been explored and developed to the point where we are prepared to recommend legislation implementing them. Others will be carefully considered and, where appropriate, put into effect by Executive action; where additional legislation is required, recommendations will be made to the Congress.

1. More than 20 different Federal Departments and Agencies have responsibilities of one sort or another in the field of recreation. It is essential that there be close coordination among these different groups and that all plans be fitted into a basic national policy. Accordingly, as recommended by the ORRRC Report, I shall appoint an Outdoor Recreation Advisory Council made up of the heads of Departments and Agencies principally concerned with recreation—to provide a proper forum for considering national recreation policy and to facilitate coordinated efforts among the various agencies.

2. Another organizational recommendation of the ORRRC Report to be adopted is the creation within the Department of the Interior of a Bureau of Outdoor Recreation. This Bureau will carry out planning functions already as-

Public Papers of the Presidents of the United States: John F. Kennedy, 1962 (Washington, D.C.: Government Printing Office, 1963), 178–80.

signed to the Department of the Interior and will administer the program of Federal assistance for State agencies I am proposing below. This new Bureau will serve as a focal point within the Federal Government for the many activities related to outdoor recreation, and will work and consult with the Departments of Agriculture, Army, and Health, Education, and Welfare, the Housing and Home Finance Agency and with other governmental agencies in implementing Federal outdoor recreation policies.

3. The interest and investment in recreational development by the various States have been irregular and uneven. Some have demonstrated outstanding organizational skills with corresponding benefits. The ORRRC recommendation that the States should be encouraged and aided in their efforts to understand and realize the full potential that lies within their boundaries rests on sound ground. Accordingly, I urge the Congress to enact legislation which will shortly be transmitted to establish a program of matching grants for the development of State plans for outdoor recreational programs. This program will supplement that enacted last year which authorized assistance to State and local governments in planning and acquiring open space lands in urban areas for recreation, conservation and other purposes.

4. In most cases the magnificent national parks, monuments, forests and wildlife refuges presently maintained and operated by the Federal Government have either been donated by States or private citizens or carved out of lands in the public domain. No longer can these sources be relied upon—we must move forward with an affirmative program of land acquisition for recreational purposes. For with each passing year, prime areas for outdoor recreation and fish and wildlife are pre-empted for suburban growth, industrial development or other uses. That expenditures for land resources is also a sound financial investment is clear from the multiplied value of those lands now devoted to parks, forests, and wildlife refuges which were acquired decades ago by the great conservationists—moreover, steadily rising land prices can in some cases serve to foreclose public acquisition. Expansion of our permanent recreational land base can best be achieved by investments in our future in the form of modest user payments from those who now enjoy our superb outdoor areas and from recreation and land related receipts.

To meet our national needs for adequate outdoor recreational lands, I propose creation of a "Land Conservation Fund" to be financed by (1) proceeds from entrance, admission, or user fees and charges at Federal recreation areas; (2) annual user charges on recreation boats; (3) diversion from the Highway Trust Fund of refundable, but unclaimed, taxes paid on gasoline used in motor boats; and (4) receipts from the sale of surplus Federal nonmilitary lands.

To prevent costly delay in beginning an acquisition program, I recommend authorization be granted to include advances from the Treasury not to exceed $500 million over an eight-year period in the proposed "Land Conservation

Fund" which will be repaid from the regular revenue sources of the Fund. Money would be made available from the Fund for land acquisition by annual appropriations by the Congress.

5. Last year's Congressional approval of the Cape Cod National Seashore Area should be regarded as the path-breaker for many other worthy park land proposals pending before the Congress. I urge favorable action on legislation to create Point Reyes National Seashore in California; Great Basin National Park in Nevada; Ozark Rivers National Monument in Missouri; Sagamore Hill National Historic Site in New York; Canyonlands National Park in Utah; Sleeping Bear Dunes National Lakeshore in Michigan; Prairie National Park in Kansas; Padre Island National Seashore in Texas; and a National Lakeshore Area in Northern Indiana. Acquisition of these park lands would be financed through the "Land Acquisition Fund."

6. In some sections of the United States—notably the East—available public lands do not meet the large recreational demands. These pent-up demands can be met in some instances through the disposal of lands surplus to Federal needs. I recommend that the Federal Surplus Property Disposal Act be amended to permit States and local governments to acquire surplus Federal lands for park, recreation or wildlife uses on more liberal terms. Furthermore as the ORRRC report pointed out, fishing, hiking, picnicking, riding, and camping activities on private lands can—and should be intensified and encouraged. One important step in this direction is the recommendation made in my Message on Agriculture which would permit the orderly movement of millions of acres of land not needed to produce food and fibers to recreational and other uses.

7. The special urgent recreation needs of our urban dwellers, first recognized by Congress in the Housing Act of 1961, are evident from the dramatic response to this Administration's open-space land programs on the part of States and cities throughout the Nation. In view of the known backlog of need for recreational lands, and the remarkable rate at which urban and suburban lands are being put to other uses, I have recommended that the present open-space grant authorization be increased by $50 million.

8. The fast-vanishing public shorelines of this country constitute a joint problem for the Federal Government and the States requiring a carefully conceived program of preservation. I recommend approval of legislation along the lines of S. 543, as approved by the Senate, to authorize a study of the ocean, lake and river shorelines of the Nation to develop a Federal-State shoreline preservation program.

9. Finally, we must protect and preserve our Nation's remaining wilderness areas. This key element of our Conservation program should have priority attention.

I therefore again strongly urge the Congress to enact legislation establishing a National Wilderness preservation system along the lines of S. 174, introduced by Senator Anderson.

A NEW BUREAU OF OUTDOOR RECREATION*
April 2, 1962

One month and one day after President Kennedy's message, Secretary of Interior Stewart L. Udall established a new Bureau of Outdoor Recreation under authority of Reorganization Plan No. 3 of 1950.

EXPLANATION OF MATERIAL TRANSMITTED:

This release 148 DM establishes the Bureau of Outdoor Recreation in the Department of the Interior.

All functions and responsibilities now exercised by the National Park Service under the Act of June 23, 1936 (49 Stat. 1894), except the study and planning of areas administered or proposals for areas to be administered by the National Park Service and planning and site surveys carried out by the National Park Service for specific recreation areas under jurisdiction of other bureaus of Interior and for other Federal agencies, are assigned to the Bureau of Outdoor Recreation.

All funds, personnel, records, and property utilized by the National Park Service for performing the functions assigned above are hereby transferred to the Bureau of Outdoor Recreation. This includes a proportionate share of the funds and personnel of the National Park Service engaged in executive direction, administrative services, program coordination, information, and other technical and administrative staff services. The detailed, specific determination of the funds, personnel, records and property to be transferred will be made by the Administrative Assistant Secretary with the concurrence of the Assistant Secretary—Public Land Management on the basis of recommendations of the Director of the Bureau of Outdoor Recreation and the Director, National Park Service.

The Director, Bureau of Outdoor Recreation will develop detailed plans for performance of functions and for the headquarters and field organization and staffing for submission to the Secretary.

> *Stewart L. Udall*
> Secretary of the Interior

ORGANIZATION
Part 148 Bureau of Outdoor Recreation

Chapter 1 Creation, Functions and Organization   148.1.1

*Dept. of the Interior, "Transmittal Sheet: Release No. 497," *Departmental Manual* (Apr. 2, 1962).

.1 *Creation.* The Bureau of Outdoor Recreation under the Assistant Secretary, Public Land Management performs those functions vested in the Secretary of the Interior by the Act of June 23, 1936 (49 Stat. 1894) and Reorganization Plan No. 3, of 1950 except for the study and planning of areas administered or proposed to be administered by National Park Service and planning and site surveys carried out by the National Park Service for specific recreation areas under the jurisdiction of other bureaus of Interior and for other Federal agencies; and assists the Secretary in carrying out the responsibilities assigned to him for the coordination of Federal recreation programs.

.2 *Functions.* The Bureau is responsible for the following functions:

    A. Coordination of related Federal programs

    B. Stimulation of and provision for assistance to the States

    C. Sponsorship and conduct of research

    D. Encouragement of interstate and regional cooperation

    E. Conduct of recreation resource surveys

    F. Formulation of a nationwide recreation plan on the basis of State, regional and Federal plans.

.3 *Organization.* The Bureau of Outdoor Recreation is composed of a headquarters staff in Washington, D.C. and several regional offices. The headquarters staff consists of Director, Associate Director, two Assistant Directors, and the Divisions of Federal Coordination, State and Local Cooperation, Research, Public Information, and Administration.

EDWARD C. CRAFTS' "GUIDELINES FOR OUTDOOR RECREATION"*
1962

Shortly after the new bureau was authorized, Dr. Edward C. Crafts was appointed as its first director. On June 21, 1962 he addressed the Fortieth Annual Convention and Conservation Conference of the Izaak Walton League of America in Portland, Oregon, and in this speech the new director outlined his policies and objectives for the Bureau of Outdoor Recreation. Shortly thereafter, Senator Maurine B. Neuberger asked to have part of Dr. Craft's remarks printed in the Congressional Record.

Mrs. NEUBERGER. Mr. President, at the recent annual convention of the Izaak Walton League of America in Portland, Oreg., the Director of the Department of Interior's new Bureau of Outdoor Recreation laid down some guidelines and basic principles for this agency. Many of us who have been active in development of the outdoor recreation program have high hopes for what can be accomplished. The Bureau's Director, Dr. Edward C. Crafts, clearly stated the policies which he will pursue. The policies which he has set forth clearly indicate that he has a firm grasp of the great potential for improving outdoor recreation throughout the United States.

I ask unanimous consent to have printed in the Appendix of the Record the list of 16 declarations of intent as Dr. Crafts presented them to the Izaak Walton League.

There being no objection, the statement was ordered to be printed in the Record, as follows:

These are the basic guidelines for the Bureau. Where do we stand with respect to progress?

I come now to 16 declarations of intent. These are my personal creed. They are what I believe. They are the policies I intend to pursue.

1. Outdoor recreation needs to be vigorously advocated across this land and in chambers where policy is made. I hope to be one of those advocates and to balance enthusiasm with realism. Sometimes a tinge of evangelism may even be in order. My old dean and mentor, Sam Dana, of the University of Michigan, once told me that the trouble with me was that I was all logic and no emotion. I hope to prove him wrong.

2. There needs to be national and nonpolitical leadership in recreation. The Bureau of Outdoor Recreation as a career service should provide that leadership. It should be intellectual leadership, not bureaucratic aggrandizement.

*Cong. Rec., 87th Cong., 2nd sess., 5224.

There needs to be effective articulation that reaches the public heart and mind. This we shall try to do.

3. There needs to be public understanding that recreation is not only a renewing experience but also serious business. It is serious national business both because of its economic impact and its beneficial effect on the physical, cultural, social, and moral well-being of the American people. It is a partial solution to the social problems created by urbanization and leisure time. It is a solution, at least in part, to the fact that man is not wholly suited physiologically to meet the technological demands placed upon him. Most of the hospitalizations in the country today are emotionally based. In this vein I like to think of the new organization as the Bureau of Outdoor Recreation. We have heard much of ORRRC. Now I like to think in terms of BORC for the Bureau of Outdoor Recreation.

4. The recreation business is the great hope for economic improvement of certain rural portions of this country that are otherwise depressed. Further the manufacture and marketing of recreation equipment and provision of recreation facilities have a major impact on our economy. Think for a moment of what is involved in the manufacture, use, and operation of sporting arms, fishing tackle, camping equipment, pleasure boats, winter sports equipment, pleasure trailers, recreation roads, resort hotels, motels, lodges and dude ranches, and the recreation press. All of this we recognize in the new Bureau.

5. There is need to professionalize recreation education in our colleges and universities and with the broad gage orientation which I am now trying to describe. Those currently engaged in the work of providing recreation for others are made up of a multitude of disciples—geographers, foresters, landscape architects, zoologists, physical education majors, engineers, and so on. I look forward to the day when recreation conservation may be recognized professionally as fully as forestry is today.

There is the other side of the coin too, namely the education of those who wish to partake intelligently and effectively of recreation opportunities. I think more is being done in this field than in the education of the professional technician in outdoor recreation.

6. This Bureau is and should continue to be small in terms of personnel and money. My hope is that though it be small in men and dollars, it may loom large in policy and in contribution to the welfare of the American people.

7. There will be no empire building in this Bureau. We have no intention to place the clammy hand of restraining bureaucracy on the initative of other Federal Bureaus, States, or the private sector. The primary emphasis of the Bureau should be on assistance to the States, to local instrumentalities of government, and to private enterprise. We hope to facilitate, to aid, and to be a catalytic agent.

8. This Bureau will not be a land-managing agency. Its duties will be policy

planning, long-range programs, and coordination. As it gains stature my hope is that it might function in the Federal hierarchy somewhat as an appellate court in the field of recreation. The emphasis should be on the quality, not quantity, improvement of standards and facilities, attraction of better personnel, and broadening of vision.

9. An unfortunate fact of life is that most of the people are where the land is not. This was dramatically impressed upon me recently as I flew nonstop from Anchorage to Chicago over Alaska and northern Canada with its tremendous scenery and millions of lakes but without a sign of human habitation or encroachment. Recreation opportunities need to be brought close to people, so much of the emphasis of the Bureau will necessarily be in the East and on the west coast where our population concentrations occur.

10. In the Federal area the Bureau function will be coordination, programing, and promotion of Federal acquisition of certain properties needed for the furtherance of the recreation aims of our national forest and park systems, our wildlife refuges and game ranges, and the Federal reservoirs.

11. "Coordination" is a difficult word and in many ways an onerous one. No power has been conferred on the Bureau by statute or by Executive fiat, to impose its will on any other Government entity. "Correlation" is perhaps a better word. This objective of correlation or coordination may be achieved through legislative review, budgetary review, conference, consultation, and the respect and stature which the Bureau may gain over a period of time as well as the force of public opinion which may develop behind it.

12. This Bureau is by no means another National Park Service or another Forest Service. Its orientation, its scope, its approach and objectives are quite different from any existing agency of Government, Federal or State. It is in a very real sense a new experiment in government.

13. There should be, in my opinion, a citizens advisory council to the Bureau and it is my hope to recommend one soon to Secretary Udall.

14. The emphasis of this Bureau needs to be on the needs of the people whereas too often in the past the emphasis in outdoor recreation has been on the utilization of a resource.

15. During the few years that I shall be Director of this Bureau I intend to push vigorously for the legislation, funds and policy that to me are in the public interest. There will be no pussyfooting around; but by the same token political expertise will be involved here and the meshing of goals with the art of the possible.

16. Finally, I should say I have little patience with plans that do not lead to action. I have no desire that this Bureau engage in academic or stratospheric planning which finds its use only in the libraries and with doctoral candidates. Planning and programing to me are primarily significant in direct relation to the results stemming from them.

In conclusion, let me remind you of two points which the President made in his talk at the recent White House Conference on Conservation. In emphasizing the need to apply science to conservation, the President said that the successful application of science to conservation may result in a great deal more lasting benefit to a particular country than being first in space. He also said: "I don't think there is anything that could occupy our attention with more distinction than trying to preserve for those who come after us this beautiful country which we have inherited."

EXECUTIVE ORDER ESTABLISHING
THE RECREATION ADVISORY COUNCIL*
April 27, 1962

One of the recommendations of ORRRC had been the establishment of a recreation advisory council. President Kennedy moved quickly and by Executive Order 11017 he created a national Recreation Advisory Council.

Executive Order 11017 providing for coordination with respect to outdoor recreation resources and establishing the recreation advisory council.

Whereas it is necessary, through the conservation and wise use of resources, to preserve, develop, and make accessible to all our people outdoor recreation of such quantity and quality as will make possible the individual enjoyment of, and will assure the physical, cultural, and spiritual benefits of, such recreation; and

Whereas the Federal Government has major nationwide responsibilities with respect to outdoor recreation resources; and

Whereas it is necessary to improve the effectiveness of Federal participation in the field of outdoor recreation; and

Whereas a new Bureau of Outdoor Recreation has recently been established in the Department of the Interior; and

Whereas improvements in the development of national outdoor recreation policies and the carrying out of national outdoor recreation programs will be facilitated by the provision of more adequate inter-agency consultation and advice:

Now, therefore, by virtue of the authority vested in me as President of the United States, it is ordered as follows:

SECTION 1. RECREATION ADVISORY COUNCIL. (a) There is hereby established the Recreation Advisory Council (hereinafter referred to as the Council). The Council shall be composed of the Secretary of the Interior, the Secretary of Agriculture, the Secretary of Defense, the Secretary of Health, Education, and Welfare, and the Administrator of the Housing and Home Finance Agency. The chairmanship of the Council shall rotate among these officials in the order named and for terms of two years each. Each of the foregoing officers may appoint a delegate to represent him in Council activity. When matters affecting the interests of Federal agencies (including, as used in this order, executive departments and other executive agencies) the heads of which are not members of the

*62 F. R. 1282.

Council are to be considered by the Council, the chairman of the Council shall invite such heads to participate in the deliberations of the Council.

(b) The Secretary of the Interior, in consultation with the other members of the Council, shall be responsible for developing methods and procedures for improved interagency coordination in the development and carrying out of national outdoor recreation policies and programs.

SEC. 2. FUNCTIONS OF THE COUNCIL. (a) The Council shall provide broad policy advice to the heads of Federal agencies on all important matters affecting outdoor recreation resources and shall facilitate coordinated efforts among the various Federal agencies.

(b) As far as may be practical, the Council, in carrying out the provisions of subsection (a) of this section, shall include advice to the Federal agencies concerned with respect to the following aspects of outdoor recreation resources: (1) the protection and appropriate management of scenic areas, natural wonders, primitive areas, historic sites, and recreation areas of national significance, (2) the management of Federal lands for the broadest possible recreation benefit consistent with other essential uses, (3) the management and improvement of fish and wildlife resources for recreational purposes, (4) cooperation with and assistance to the States and local governments, (5) interstate arrangements, including Federal participation where authorized and necessary, and (6) vigorous and cooperative leadership in a nationwide recreation effort.

SEC. 3. CONSTRUCTION. Nothing in this order shall be construed as subjecting any function vested by law in, or assigned pursuant to law to, any Federal agency or head thereof to the authority of any other agency or officer or as abrogating or restricting any such function in any manner.

SEC. 4. ASSISTANCE AND COOPERATION. (a) The Federal agencies headed by the officers composing the Council shall furnish necessary assistance to the Council in consonance with the provisions of Section 214 of the Act of May 3, 1945 (59 Stat. 134; 31 U.S.C. 691).

(b) In respect of duties of the Council and of the chairman of the Council, respectively, under this order, and insofar as practical, all Federal agencies shall upon request furnish information, data, and reports to, and shall otherwise cooperate with, the said Council and chairman.

John F. Kennedy

The White House
April 27, 1962

THE OUTDOOR RECREATION ACT*
May 28, 1963

A new Bureau of Outdoor Recreation had been established by the Secretary of the Interior and a Recreation Advisory Council had been created by executive order but some of the other recommendations of ORRRC required congressional action before they could be made operational. Among these were: the need to achieve better coordination among the 18 federal agencies directly involved with outdoor recreation; the need to cooperate with state recreation programs; and the requirement for a comprehensive and integrated nation-wide outdoor recreation plan.

These objectives were achieved in the Outdoor Recreation Act of 1963 which gave congressional approval to the establishment of the new bureau.

An Act to promote the coordination and development of effective programs relating to outdoor recreation, and for other purposes.

Be it enacted by the Senate and House of Representatives of the United States of America in Congress assembled, That the Congress finds and declares it to be desirable that all American people of present and future generations be assured adequate outdoor recreation resources, and that it is desirable for all levels of government and private interests to take prompt and coordinated action to the extent practicable without diminishing or affecting their respective powers and functions to conserve, develop, and utilize such resources for the benefit and enjoyment of the American people.

SEC. 2. In order to carry out the purposes of this Act, the Secretary of the Interior is authorized to perform the following functions and activities:

(a) Inventory.—Prepare and maintain a continuing inventory and evaluation of outdoor recreation needs and resources of the United States.

(b) Classification.—Prepare a system for classification of outdoor recreation resources to assist in the effective and beneficial use and management of such resources.

(c) Nationwide Plan.—Formulate and maintain a comprehensive nationwide outdoor recreation plan, taking into consideration the plans of the various Federal agencies, States, and their political subdivisions. The plan shall set forth the needs and demands of the public for outdoor recreation and the current and foreseeable availability in the future of outdoor recreation resources to meet those needs. The plan shall identify critical outdoor recreation problems, recommend solutions, and recommend desirable actions to be taken at each level of government and by private interests. The Secretary shall transmit the initial

*77 *Statutes at Large,* 49.

plan, which shall be prepared as soon as practicable within five years hereafter, to the President for transmittal to the Congress. Future revisions of the plan shall be similarly transmitted at succeeding five-year intervals. When a plan or revision is transmitted to the Congress, the Secretary shall transmit copies to the Governors of the several States.

(d) Technical Assistance.—Provide technical assistance and advice to and cooperate with States, political subdivisions, and private interests, including nonprofit organizations, with respect to outdoor recreation.

(e) Regional Cooperation.—Encourage interstate and regional cooperation in the planning, acquisition, and development of outdoor recreation resources.

(f) Research and Education.—(1) Sponsor, engage in, and assist in research relating to outdoor recreation, directly or by contract or cooperative agreements, and make payments for such purposes without regard to the limitations of section 3648 of the Revised Statutes (31 U.S.C. 529) concerning advances of funds when he considers such action in the public interest, (2) undertake studies and assemble information concerning outdoor recreation, directly or by contract or cooperative agreement, and disseminate such information without regard to the provisions of section 4154, title 39, United States Code, and (3) cooperate with educational institutions and others in order to assist in establishing education programs and activities and to encourage public use and benefits from outdoor recreation.

(g) Interdepartmental Cooperation.—(1) Cooperate with and provide technical assistance to Federal departments and agencies and obtain from them information, data, reports, advice, and assistance that are needed and can reasonably be furnished in carrying out the purposes of this Act, and (2) promote coordination of Federal plans and activities generally relating to outdoor recreation. Any department or agency furnishing advice or assistance hereunder may expend its own funds for such purposes, with or without reimbursement, as may be agreed to by that agency.

(h) Donations.—Accept and use donations of money, property, personal services, or facilities for the purposes of this Act.

SEC. 3. In order further to carry out the policy declared in section 1 of this Act, the heads of Federal departments and independent agencies having administrative responsibility over activities or resources the conduct or use of which is pertinent to fulfillment of that policy shall, either individually or as a group, (a) consult with and be consulted by the Secretary from time to time both with respect to their conduct of those activities and their use of those resources and with respect to the activities which the Secretary of the Interior carries on under authority of this Act which are pertinent to their work, and (b) carry out such responsibilities in general conformance with the nationwide plan authorized under section 2(c) of this Act.

Sec. 4. As used in this Act, the term "United States" shall include the District of Columbia and the terms "United States" and "States" may, to the extent practicable, include the Commonwealth of Puerto Rico, the Virgin Islands, Guam, and American Samoa.

Approved May 28, 1963, 10:13 a.m.

THE RECREATION ADVISORY COUNCIL'S
"GENERAL POLICY GUIDELINES FOR OUTDOOR RECREATION"*
1964

One of the most significant early actions of the Recreation Advisory Council was the publication of Circular No. 2, General Policy Guidelines for Outdoor Recreation. *These were especially important because they represented basic agreements among five executive departments and one agency (which shortly became a department) on outdoor recreation policy. Presumably, the policy guidelines had substantial impact because they were of greatest significance to a new agency, the Bureau of Outdoor Recreation, in the formative stages.*

In Public Law 88—29, approved May 28, 1963, the Congress promulgated the following outdoor recreation policy:

> That the Congress finds and declares it is desirable that all American people of present and future generations be assured adequate outdoor recreation resources, and that it is desirable for all levels of government and private interests to take prompt and coordinated action to the extent practicable without diminishing or affecting their respective powers and functions to conserve, develop, and utilize such resources for the benefit and enjoyment of the American people.

Other statements of outdoor recreation policy may be found in the following major Federal Statutes: National Park Service Act of 1916, National Park Administration Act, Public Health Service Act of 1944, Flood Control Acts of 1944 and 1962, Watershed Protection and Flood Prevention Act of 1954, Federal Water Pollution Control Act of 1956, Outdoor Recreation Resources Review Act of 1958, Federal Aid Highway Act of 1958, National Forests (Multiple Use Act), Housing Act of 1961, and Food and Agriculture Act of 1962.

One of the major factors that led to the declaration of the above quoted statement by the Congress was the increasing need for recreation opportunities as evidenced by the findings submitted to the President and the Congress in January 1962 by the Outdoor Recreation Resources Review Commission in its report entitled, "Outdoor Recreation for America."

The basic situation revealed in that report indicates that the United States is presently faced with serious imbalances, wherein existing recreation opportunities fall short of meeting current needs. Unless corrective action is taken soon, this condition will be further aggravated, since within the next 40 years the population of the United States is expected to double, while demands for outdoor recreation are expected at least to triple. These burgeoning requirements are accelerated by rising incomes, increased amounts of leisure time, increased

*Recreation Advisory Council, *General Policy Guidelines for Outdoor Recreation,* Circular No. 2 (Washington, D.C.: Government Printing Office, 1964), 1–13.

urbanization, and increased mobility on the part of the public. The need for an aggressive program of recreation development is both real and immediate and presents a challenge that must be met. This challenge consists of finding ways and means of assuring productive and creative outlets for the upsurge in outdoor recreation activity within the limited supply of physical land and water resources, and the increasing number of competing demands for such resources. The needs to be met involve all Americans, the hunters and fishermen, the wilderness visitor and the weekend vacationer, as well as the growing number of urban dwellers who seek relaxation from the pressures of everyday life in a variety of outdoor activities close to home.

The Recreation Advisory Council recognizes that outdoor recreation is a consequential activity of major social and economic significance in America today and the provision of opportunity for all to enjoy its advantages is a substantial responsibility of public and private interests. It believes that all of the initiative and imagination of public and private enterprise together with the best efforts of legislatures and public agencies will be required to plan and develop the far-seeing programs to meet tomorrow's needs for diversified recreation opportunity.

Accordingly, the Council hereby sets forth in this circular its views on the types of action needed and the division of responsibility it considers appropriate in carrying out the policy mandates of the Congress.

The Council hopes that its views will be helpful to all agencies, public and private, and to individuals concerned with meeting the common objective of providing adequate outdoor recreation for all Americans.

NATIONWIDE PLAN

High priority should be accorded to the directive by the Congress in Public Law 88—29 that the Secretary of the Interior formulate and maintain a comprehensive nationwide outdoor recreation plan.

The plan should provide an overall statement of the present and future nationwide needs for outdoor recreation and ways of meeting these needs. It should:

A. Provide for the preparation and maintenance of a continuing inventory and evaluation of outdoor recreation needs and resources in the United States.

B. Provide for a system for classification of outdoor recreation resources.

C. Describe the demand for all forms of outdoor recreation within and outside of urban areas. The inventory, classification, and study of the supply of recreation resources should take into account both public and private lands and facilities.

D. Recommend specific action programs to be undertaken by the Federal Government and identify specific actions that should be taken by State and local government and private interests in meeting the needs for outdoor recreation in the United States.

E. Contain provisions that will enable all agencies involved in providing outdoor recreation opportunities to carry out their responsibilities under their respective authorities such as providing technical assistance to State and local agencies and private interests and encouraging interstate and regional cooperation in the planning, acquisition, and development of outdoor recreation resources.

RESPONSIBILITY FOR MEETING OUTDOOR RECREATION NEEDS

Implementation of national outdoor recreation policy requires the cooperative participation of all levels of government and private enterprise. The most important single force in outdoor recreation is private endeavor–individual initiative, voluntary groups of many kinds, and commercial enterprise.

It is important, therefore, that full consideration be given to the private role. Since, however, private activities are carried out within the framework of public policy, the private role can best be discussed after a review of the roles suggested for the Federal, State, and local governments.

1. FEDERAL ROLE

The responsibility of the Federal Government in the field of outdoor recreation should be:

A. To develop a nationwide outdoor recreation plan, to coordinate action of the Federal agencies, and to promote coordinated action by all other interests in achieving its purpose.

B. To manage federally owned land and water resources for the broadest recreation use to the extent consistent with other uses of similar importance or priority.

C. To acquire and provide suitable management for land and water areas that represent an appropriate balance between unique areas without respect to location and areas near population centers. These should include scenic areas, natural wonders, wilderness areas, wild rivers, historic sites, wildlife refuges, wetlands, parks, parkways, scenic roads, shorelines, and National Recreation Areas.

D. To encourage the use of the concession system, where feasible, to provide services to the public on Federal lands as a means of encouraging private enterprise and reducing government expenditures and personnel.

E. To consider outdoor recreation one of the primary purposes in planning multiple-purpose water resource developments and to allocate an equitable share of the cost to outdoor recreation, including fish and wildlife enhancement.

F. To give full consideration to outdoor recreation in the planning and conduct of programs to which the Federal Government makes substantial financial contributions, such as highway construction, agricultural conservation, pollution abatement, open space, and urban renewal.

G. To assure provision of adequate measures for public health, safety, and pollution control in federally administered recreation areas, and to encourage the adoption of comparable measures by State, local, and private organizations.

H. To encourage continuing, active State and local official responsibility for recreation planning, development, and administration.

I. To provide grants-in-aid to States and local governments for the planning, acquisition, and development of outdoor recreation resources and facilities.

J. To provide in appropriate cases technical and financial assistance to the private sector and to State and local governments.

K. To promote interstate and regional agreements, including Federal participation when necessary or desirable.

L. To encourage private and public agencies to sponsor and conduct research in the broad field of outdoor recreation.

M. To encourage States and their political subdivisions, and semipublic and private groups, organizations, and individuals to construct and operate recreation facilities and programs on Federal land when, in the judgement of the administering agency, it is in the public interest to do so, taking into account the long-range plans of the States and the Federal Government.

N. To assure that appropriate consideration is given to the recreation potential of surplus real property proposed for disposal by any Federal agency.

O. To establish criteria for the imposition of reasonable user fees applicable to appropriate classes of federally administered recreation facilities and areas. A desirable Federal fee structure would take into consideration the variety of recreation opportunities and recognize the recreation requirements of special groups of individuals, while eliminating undue competition with the private sector, thereby encouraging the provision of additional recreation services by the private sector and reducing the burden placed upon direct appropriated funds.

P. To encourage development of recreation education both in the classroom and through such tools as workshops, interpretive programs, and nature centers.

Q. To encourage State and local governments to adopt liability, zoning, and taxing legislation which would encourage development of recreation areas on private lands.

R. To encourage the proper use of private consultants who are available to provide expert advice and services in connection with many aspects of recreation.

2. STATE ROLE

The States should play a pivotal role in recognizing, developing, and managing outdoor recreation resources that fall in the categories between national and local significance. In general, the States should exercise a role in relation to local and private interests analogous to that enumerated for the Federal Government. More specifically, the States should be encouraged to:

A. Develop a comprehensive statewide long-range plan for outdoor recreation as a significant element of State development plans, taking into account all Federal, State, local, and privately owned outdoor recreation resources and programs within the State.

B. Cooperate with local and private agencies as well as the Federal Government in the inventory and evaluation of outdoor recreation opportunities, and measuring the need for such opportunities.

C. Acquire, develop, manage, and maintain outdoor recreation resources of State significance.

D. Provide adequate financing for recreation through taxation, bond issues, user fees, and other means as appropriate.

E. Devote adequate consideration to zoning, the use of less-than-fee-acquisition such as easements, and regulatory powers in providing outdoor recreation opportunities.

F. Cooperate with other States and the Federal Government in the acquisition, development, and management of outdoor recreation resources having interstate significance.

G. Assist local governments and private enterprise in planning and developing recreation facilities at neighborhood, city, and metropolitan levels, with particular emphasis on comprehensive recreation developments serving metropolitan areas.

H. Provide legislative authority for local governments to issue bonds for the financing of recreation and give direct financial assistance where appropriate.

I. Review the effectiveness of State organizations and where necessary designate a central agency within each State to coordinate all State activities in the field of outdoor recreation.

J. Utilize a concession system, where feasible, to provide services to the public on State-owned lands. Use of such a system would act to stimulate private investment and to reduce Government expenditures for recreation development.

3. ROLE OF LOCAL GOVERNMENTS

As the level of government closest to the people, cities, counties, and other political subdivisions of the States are in the best position to know the needs and desires of their citizens and to gauge requirements for community and neighborhood outdoor recreation resources and facilities. They have an important responsibility for working closely with their citizens and local organizations in seeing that outdoor recreation needs are recognized, understood, and effectively met.

As our cities grow and metropolitan areas are formed, the patterns of recreation supply and demand increasingly cut across local governmental boundaries.

It is important, therefore, that the counties and other regional organizations be prepared to cope with the resulting problems of coordination.

In fulfilling their responsibilities, local governments should be encouraged to:

A. Cooperate with State and Federal agencies in the development of plans and programs for recreation as part of, or consistent with, overall State, regional, and local development plans.

B. Maintain an up-to-date inventory of existing and potential recreation resources.

C. Give greater consideration to outdoor recreation, playgrounds, municipal parks, and open-space requirements in developing plans for future urban expansion or renewal and in the construction of schools, highways, water supply and refuse disposal systems, and other public projects.

D. Provide adequate financing for recreation through taxation, bond issues, and user fees, as appropriate.

E. Acquire in fee or through easements those rights in land and water which will permit the protection, development, and management of public recreation use areas of adequate quality and carrying capacity conveniently located to major concentrations of people.

F. Make maximum use of such devices as land-use zoning, subdivision regulations, and assessment practices to encourage the provision of outdoor recreation opportunities and the protection of open space.

G. Encourage industrial firms, service clubs, youth groups, labor organizations, and other civic groups to invest in recreation sites and facilities for the enjoyment of members and their families.

H. Cooperate with private investors seeking to establish new commercial recreation enterprises consistent with the development plans for the area, by assisting in the search for suitable sites, negotiating to assure provision of utilities and services, securing road connections, providing buffer zones, and similar constructive measures.

I. Review internal organization and where necessary appoint or designate a central agency or person to take responsibility for coordination of all-recreation interests.

4. PRIVATE ROLE

The role of the private sector is by its nature different from that of government. The Council recognizes and welcomes the vital contribution to the public enjoyment of leisure time made through the provision of recreation programs and facilities by private organizations, both profit and nonprofit, and by individuals. An important role of government is to create and maintain a favorable climate within which private initiative, funds, and talent can successfully expand such efforts. This section, even though devoted to the private role, deals for the most part with actions that can be taken by government to encourage greater participation by the private sector. Among such actions, the following are suggested:

A. Government agencies should promote greater public recreation use of private lands—both large industrial holdings and smaller areas such as farms. In this connection, a well-considered system of reasonable user fees for certain classes of public recreation facilities would tend to encourage the provision of additional private facilities.

B. Government agencies should stimulate diversified commercial recreation investments on private lands and waters. Technical and financial assistance, in appropriate cases would help new enterprises to start and established ones to improve their operations.

C. Wherever feasible, all levels of government should utilize the concession system of private operation of recreation facilities on public roads. This would serve the dual purpose of encouraging private enterprise and conserving public funds.

D. Encouragement should be given to the efforts of noncommercial private groups, such as charitable, service, and civic organizations to acquire and conserve outdoor recreation resources that serve public needs.

E. All levels of government should encourage and stimulate donations of recreation resources to appropriate public agencies by private individuals, foundations, and other groups.

F. Educational institutions and foundations should be utilized in recreation studies and research. Such organizations should also be encouraged to expand their educational efforts in the field of outdoor recreation.

ACTIVATION OF POLICY CIRCULAR NO. 2

Upon approval of this statement, the member agencies of the Recreation Advisory Council become responsible for adhering to the foregoing policy, and for giving this policy force and effect. The Council recommends the adoption of this policy by other Federal agencies and its favorable consideration by other levels of government and by private agencies.

Approved:

Stewart L. Udall
Secretary of the Interior,
Chairman

Orville Freeman
Secretary of Agriculture

Anthony Celebrezze
Secretary of Health,
Education, and Welfare

Luther Hodges
Secretary of Commerce

Norman S. Paul
Asst. Secretary of Defense

Robert Weaver
Administrator, Housing
and Home Finance
Agency

Date: April 9, 1964

THE LAND AND WATER CONSERVATION FUND ACT*
September 3, 1964

No matter what form it takes, outdoor recreation is not free. Funds are needed to acquire land, to construct or develop facilities, and to manage both the resource and recreation programs. Congress had authorized the new Bureau of Outdoor Recreation and had charged it with certain responsibilities but no substantial funds were available to carry out these responsibilities.

The general policy of the Federal Government with reference to fees or charges for the use of government property had been set forth in Title V of the act of August 31, 1951. This brief, general policy directive stated:

> *It is the sense of the Congress that any work, service, publication, report, document, benefit, privilege, authority, use, franchise, license, permit, certificate, registration, or similar thing of value or utility performed, furnished, provided, granted, prepared, or issued by any Federal agency (including wholly owned Government corporations as defined in the Government Corporation Control Act of 1945) to or for any person (including groups, associations, organizations, partnerships, corporations, or businesses), except those engaged in the transaction of official business of the Government, shall be self-sustaining to the full extent possible, and the head of each Federal agency is authorized by regulation (which, in the case of agencies in the executive branch, shall be as uniform as practicable and subject to such policies as the President may prescribe) to prescribe therefor such fee, charge, or price, if any, as he shall determine, in case none exists, or redetermine, in case of an existing one, to be fair and equitable taking into consideration direct and indirect cost to the Government, value to the recipient, public policy or interest served, and other pertinent facts, and any amount so determined or redetermined shall be collected and paid into the Treasury as miscellaneous receipts:* Provided, *That nothing contained in this title shall repeal or modify existing statutes prohibiting the collection, fixing the amount, or directing the disposition of any fee, charge or price:* Provided further, *That nothing contained in this title shall repeal or modify existing statutes prescribing bases for calculation of any fee, charge or price, but this proviso shall not restrict the redetermination or recalculation in accordance with the prescribed bases of the amount of any such fee, charge or price.†*

In his message to Congress in 1962, President Kennedy had proposed the creation of a "Land Conservation Fund" to be financed by user fees, diversions from the Highway Trust Fund, annual charges on motorboats, and receipts from the sale of surplus federal non-military lands. On February 14, 1963, in a letter to President of the Senate Lyndon B. Johnson and Speaker of the House John W. McCormack, President Kennedy reiterated his recommendations of the previous year.

---

*78 *Statutes at Large*, 897.
†65 *Statutes at Large*, 290.

Four days later, on February 18, 1963, Congressman Aspinall introduced H.R. 3846 "to establish a land and water conservation fund." Several other similar or identical bills were introduced in the next few days in both the House and the Senate.

The land and water conservation fund bills encountered more opposition than had previous measures recommended by ORRRC, but H.R. 3846 eventually passed and was signed by the President on September 3, 1964. Sources of revenue for the Fund were to be derived from admissions and user fees for use of federal areas, the sale of surplus real property and from a federal tax on motorboat fuels. About 60 percent of the appropriations from the Fund were to go to the states with the other 40 percent to be used for federal purposes.

An Act to establish a land and water conservation fund to assist the States and Federal agencies in meeting present and future outdoor recreation demands and needs of the American people, and for other purposes.

Be it enacted by the Senate and House of Representatives of the United States of America in Congress assembled,

TITLE I—LAND AND WATER CONSERVATION PROVISIONS

SHORT TITLE AND STATEMENT OF PURPOSES

SECTION 1. (a) Citation; Effective Date.—This Act may be cited as the "Land and Water Conservation Fund Act of 1965" and shall become effective on January 1, 1965.

(b) Purposes.—The purposes of this Act are to assist in preserving, developing, and assuring accessibility to all citizens of the United States of America of present and future generations and visitors who are lawfully present within the boundaries of the United States of America such quality and quantity of outdoor recreation resources as may be available and are necessary and desirable for individual active participation in such recreation and to strengthen the health and vitality of the citizens of the United States by (1) providing funds for and authorizing Federal assistance to the States in planning, acquisition, and development of needed land and water areas and facilities and (2) providing funds for the Federal acquisition and development of certain lands and other areas.

CERTAIN REVENUES PLACED IN SEPARATE FUND

SEC. 2. Separate Fund.—During the period ending June 30, 1989, and during such additional period as may be required to repay any advances made pursuant to section 4(b) of this Act, there shall be covered into the land and water conservation fund in the Treasury of the United States, which fund is hereby established and is hereinafter referred to as the "fund", the following revenues and collections:

(a) Entrance and User Fees; Establishment; Regulations. — All proceeds from entrance, admission, and other recreation user fees or charges collected or received by the National Park Service, the Bureau of Land Management, the Bureau of Sport Fisheries and Wildlife, the Bureau of Reclamation, the Forest Service, the Corps of Engineers, the Tennessee Valley Authority, and the United States section of the International Boundary and Water Commission (United States and Mexico), notwithstanding any provision of law that such proceeds shall be credited to miscellaneous receipts of the Treasury: *Provided,* That nothing in this Act shall affect any rights or authority of the States with respect to fish and wildlife, nor shall this Act repeal any provision of law that permits States or political subdivisions to share in the revenues from Federal lands or any provision of law that provides that any fees or charges collected at particular Federal areas shall be used for or credited to specific purposes or special funds as authorized by that provision of law; but the proceeds from fees or charges established by the President pursuant to this subsection for entrance or admission generally to Federal areas shall be used solely for the purposes of this Act.

The President is authorized, to the extent and within the limits hereinafter set forth, to designate or provide for the designation of land or water areas administered by or under the authority of the Federal agencies listed in the preceding paragraph at which entrance, admission, and other forms of recreation user fees shall be charged and to establish and revise or provide for the establishment and revision of such fees as follows:

(i) An annual fee of not more than $7 payable by a person entering an area so designated by private noncommercial automobile which, if paid, shall excuse the person paying the same and anyone who accompanies him in such automobile from payment of any other fee for admission to that area and other areas administered by or under the authority of such agencies, except areas which are designated by the President as not being within the coverage of the fee, during the year for which the fee has been paid.

(ii) Fees for a single visit or a series of visits during a specified period of less than a year to an area so designated payable by persons who choose not to pay an annual fee under clause (i) of this paragraph or who enter such an area by means other than private noncommercial automobile.

(iii) Fees payable for admission to areas not within the coverage of a fee paid under clause (i) of this paragraph.

(iv) Fees for the use within an area of sites, facilities, equipment, or services provided by the United States.

Entrance and admission fees may be charged at areas administered primarily for scenic, scientific, historical, cultural, or recreational purposes. No entrance or admission fee shall be charged except at such areas or portions thereof ad-

[615]

ministered by a Federal agency where recreation facilities or services are provided at Federal expense. No fee of any kind shall be charged by a Federal agency under any provision of this Act for use of any waters. All fees established pursuant to this subsection shall be fair and equitable, taking into consideration direct and indirect cost to the Government, benefits to the recipient, public policy or interest served, and other pertinent factors. Nothing contained in this paragraph shall authorize Federal hunting or fishing licenses or fees or charges for commercial or other activities not related to recreation. No such fee shall be charged for travel by private noncommerical vehicle over any national parkway or any road or highway established as a part of the national Federal-aid system, as defined in section 101, title 23, United States Code, or any road within the National Forest system or a public land area which, though it is part of a larger area, is commonly used by the public as a means of travel between two places either or both of which are outside the area. No such fee shall be charged any person for travel by private noncommercial vehicle over any road or highway to any land in which such person has any property right if such land is within any such designated area.

No fees established under clause (ii) or clause (iii) of the second paragraph of this subsection shall become effective with respect to any area which embraces lands more than half of which have heretofore been acquired by contribution from the government of the State in which the area is located until sixty days after the officer of the United States who is charged with responsibility for establishing such fees has advised the Governor of this affected State, or an agency of the State designated by the Governor for this purpose, of his intention so to do, and said officer shall, before finally establishing such fees, give consideration to any recommendation that the Governor or his designee may make with respect thereto within said sixty days and to all obligations, legal or otherwise, that the United States may owe to the State concerned and to its citizens with respect to the area in question. In the Smoky Mountains National Park, unless fees are charged for entrance into said park on main highways and thoroughfares, fees shall not be charged for entrance on other routes into said park or any part thereof.

There is hereby repealed the third paragraph from the end of the division entitled "National Park Service" of section 1 of the Act of March 7, 1928 (45 Stat. 238) and the second paragraph from the end of the division entitled "National Park Service" of section 1 of the Act of March 4, 1929 (45 Stat. 1602; 16 U.S.C. 14). Section 4 of the Act entitled "An Act authorizing the construction of certain public works on rivers and harbors for flood control, and for other purposes", approved December 24, 1944 (16 U.S.C. 460d), as amended by the Flood Control Act of 1962 (76 Stat. 1195) is further amended by deleting ", without charge," in the third sentence from the end thereof. All other provisions of law that prohibit the collection of entrance, admission, or other recreation user fees or charges authorized by this Act or that restrict the expenditure of funds if such fees or charges are collected are hereby also repealed: *Provided,* That no provision of any law or treaty which extends to any person or class of persons a right of free access to the shoreline of any reservoir or other body of water, or to hunting and fishing along or on such shoreline, shall be affected by this repealer.

The heads of departments and agencies are authorized to prescribe rules and regulations for the collection of any entrance, admission, and other recreation user fees or charges established pursuant to this subsection for areas under their administration: *Provided further,* That no free passes shall be issued to any Member of Congress or other government official. Clear notice that a fee or charge has been established shall be posted at each area to which it is applicable. Any violation of any rules or regulations promulgated under this title at an area so posted shall be punishable by a fine of not more than $100. Any person charged with the violation of such rules and regulations may be tried and sentenced by any United States commissioner specially designated for that purpose by the court by which he was appointed, in the same manner and subject to the same conditions as provided for in title 18, United States Code, section 3401, subsections (b), (c), (d), and (e), as amended.

(b) Surplus Property Sales. — All proceeds (except so much thereof as may be otherwise obligated, credited, or paid under authority of those provisions of law set forth in section 485(b)–(e), title 40, United States Code, or the Independent Offices Appropriation Act, 1963 (76 Stat. 725) or in any later appropriation Act) hereafter received from any disposal of surplus real property and related personal property under the Federal Property and Administrative Services Act of 1949, as amended, notwithstanding any provision of law that such proceeds shall be credited to miscellaneous receipts of the Treasury. Nothing in this Act shall affect existing laws or regulations concerning disposal of real or personal surplus property to schools, hospitals, and States and their political subdivisions.

(c) Motorboat Fuels Tax. The amounts provided for in section 201 of this Act.

SEC. 3. Appropriations. — Moneys covered into the fund shall be available for expenditure for the purposes of this Act only when appropriated therefor. Such appropriations may be made without fiscal-year limitation. Moneys covered into this fund not subsequently authorized by the Congress for expenditures within two fiscal years following the fiscal year in which such moneys had been credited to the fund, shall be transferred to miscellaneous receipts of the Treasury.

ALLOCATION OF LAND AND WATER CONSERVATION FUND FOR STATE AND FEDERAL PURPOSES: AUTHORIZATION FOR ADVANCE APPROPRIATIONS

SEC. 4. (a) Allocation. — There shall be submitted with the annual budget of the United States a comprehensive statement of estimated requirements during the ensuing fiscal year for appropriations from the fund. In the absence of a provision to the contrary in the Act making an appropriation from the fund, (i) the appropriation therein made shall be available in the ratio of 60 per centum for State purposes and 40 per centum for Federal purposes, but (ii) the President may, during the first five years in which appropriations are made from the fund, vary said percentages by not more than 15 points either way to meet, as nearly as may be, the current relative needs of the States and the Federal Government.

(b) Advance Appropriations; Repayment.—Beginning with the third full fiscal year in which the fund is in operation, and for a total of eight years, advance appropriations are hereby authorized to be made to the fund from any moneys in the Treasury not otherwise appropriated in such amounts as to average not more than $60,000,000 for each fiscal year. Such advance appropriations shall be available for Federal and State purposes in the same manner and proportions as other moneys appropriated from the fund. Such advance appropriations shall be repaid without interest, beginning at the end of the next fiscal year after the first ten full fiscal years in which the fund has been in operation, by transferring, annually until fully repaid, to the general fund of the Treasury 50 per centum of the revenues received by the land and water conservation fund each year under section 2 of this Act prior to July 1, 1989, and 100 per centum of any revenues thereafter received by the fund. Revenues received from the sources specified in section 2 of this Act after July 1, 1989, or after payment has been completed as provided by this subsection, whichever occurs later, shall be credited to miscellaneous receipts of the Treasury. The moneys in the fund that are not required for repayment purposes may continue to be appropriated and allocated in accordance with the procedures prescribed by this Act.

FINANCIAL ASSISTANCE TO STATES

Sec. 5. General Authority; Purposes.—(a) The Secretary of the Interior (hereinafter referred to as the "Secretary") is authorized to provide financial assistance to the States from moneys available for State purposes. Payments may be made to the States by the Secretary as hereafter provided, subject to such terms and conditions as he considers appropriate and in the public interest to carry out the purposes of this Act, for outdoor recreation: (1) planning, (2) acquisition of land, waters, or interests in land or waters, or (3) development.

(b) Apportionment Among States; Notification.—Sums appropriated and available for State purposes for each fiscal year shall be apportioned among the several States by the Secretary, whose determination shall be final, in accordance with the following formula:

(1) two-fifths shall be apportioned equally among the several States; and

(2) three-fifths shall be apportioned on the basis of need to individual States by the Secretary in such amounts as in his judgment will best accomplish the purposes of this Act. The determination of need shall include among other

things a consideration of the proportion which the population of each State bears to the total population of the United States and of the use of outdoor recreation resources of individual States by persons from outside the State as well as a consideration of the Federal resources and programs in the particular States.

The total allocation to an individual State under paragraphs (1) and (2) of this subsection shall not exceed 7 per centum of the total amount allocated to the several States in any one year.

The Secretary shall notify each State of its apportionments; and the amounts thereof shall be available thereafter for payment to such State for planning, acquisition, or development projects as hereafter prescribed. Any amount of any apportionment that has not been paid or obligated by the Secretary during the fiscal year in which such notification is given and for two fiscal years thereafter shall be reapportioned by the Secretary in accordance with paragraph (2) of this subsection.

The District of Columbia, Puerto Rico, the Virgin Islands, Guam, and American Samoa shall be treated as States for the purposes of this title, except for the purpose of paragraph (1) of this subsection. Their population also shall be included as a part of the total population in computing the apportionment under paragraph (2) of this subsection.

(c) Matching Requirments.—Payments to any State shall cover not more than 50 per centum of the cost of planning, acquisition, or development projects that are undertaken by the State. The remaining share of the cost shall be borne by the State in a manner and with such funds or services as shall be satisfactory to the Secretary. No payment may be made to any State for or on account of any cost or obligation incurred or any service rendered prior to the date of approval of this Act.

(d) Comprehensive State Plan Required; Planning Projects.—A comprehensive statewide outdoor recreation plan shall be required prior to the consideration by the Secretary of financial assistance for acquisition or development projects. The plan shall be adequate if, in the judgment of the Secretary, it encompasses and will promote the purposes of this Act. The plan shall contain—

(1) the name of the State agency that will have authority to represent and act for the State in dealing with the Secretary for purposes of this Act;

(2) an evaluation of the demand for and supply of outdoor recreation resources and facilities in the State;

(3) a program for the implementation of the plan; and

(4) other necessary information, as may be determined by the Secretary. The plan shall take into account relevant Federal resources and programs and shall be correlated so far as practicable with other State, regional, and local plans. Where there exists or is in preparation for any particular State a comprehensive plan financed in part with funds supplied by the Housing and Home Fi-

nance Agency, any statewide outdoor recreation plan prepared for purposes of this Act shall be based upon the same population, growth, and other pertinent factors as are used in formulating the Housing and Home Finance Agency financed plans.

The Secretary may provide financial assistance to any State for projects for the preparation of a comprehensive statewide outdoor recreation plan when such plan is not otherwise available or for the maintenance of such plan.

(e) Projects for Land and Water Acquisition; Development.—In addition to assistance for planning projects, the Secretary may provide financial assistance to any State for the following types of projects or combinations thereof if they are in accordance with the State comprehensive plan:

(1) Acquisition of Land and Waters.—For the acquisition of land, waters, or interests in land or waters (other than land, waters, or interests inland or waters acquired from the United States for less than fair market value), but not including incidental costs relating to acquisition.

(2) Development.—For development, including but not limited to site planning and the development of Federal lands under lease to States for terms of twenty-five years or more.

(f) Requirements for Project Approval; Condition.—Payments may be made to States by the Secretary only for those planning, acquisition, or development projects that are approved by him. No payment may be made by the Secretary for or on account of any project with respect to which financial assistance has been given or promised under any other Federal program or activity, and no financial assistance may be given under any other Federal program or activity for or on account of any project with respect to which such assistance has been given or promised under this Act. The Secretary may make payments from time to time in keeping with the rate of progress toward the satisfactory completion of individual projects: *Provided,* That the approval of all projects and all payments, or any commitments relating thereto, shall be withheld until the Secretary receives appropriate written assurance from the State that the State has the ability and intention to finance its share of the cost of the particular project, and to operate and maintain by acceptable standards, at State expense, the particular properties or facilities acquired or developed for public outdoor recreation use.

Payments for all projects shall be made by the Secretary to the Governor of the State or to a State offical or agency designated by the Governor or by State law having authority and responsibility to accept and to administer funds paid hereunder for approved projects. If consistent with an approved project, funds may be transferred by the State to a political subdivision or other appropriate public agency.

No property acquired or developed with assistance under this section shall, without the approval of the Secretary, be converted to other than public outdoor recreation uses. The Secretary shall approve such conversion only if he finds it to be in accord with the then existing comprehensive statewide outdoor recreation plan and only upon such conditions as he deems necessary to assure the substitution of other recreation properties of at least equal fair market value and of reasonably equivalent usefulness and location.

No payment shall be made to any State until the State has agreed to (1) provide such reports to the Secretary, in such form and containing such information, as may be reasonably necessary to enable the Secretary to perform his duties under this Act, and (2) provide such fiscal control and fund accounting procedures as may be necessary to assure proper disbursement and accounting for Federal funds paid to the State under this Act.

Each recipient of assistance under this Act shall keep such records as the Secretary of the Interior shall prescribe, including records which fully disclose the amount and the disposition by such recipient of the proceeds of such assistance, the total cost of the project or undertaking in connection with which such assistance is given or used, and the amount and nature of that portion of the cost of the project or undertaking supplied by other sources, and such other records as will facilitate an effective audit.

The Secretary of the Interior, and the Comptroller General of the United States, or any of their duly authorized representatives, shall have access for the purpose of audit and examination to any books, documents, papers, and records of the recipient that are pertinent to assistance received under this Act.

(g) Coordination With Federal Agencies.—In order to assure consistency in policies and actions under this Act, with other related Federal programs and activities (including those conducted pursuant to title VII of the Housing Act of 1961 and section 701 of the Housing Act of 1954) and to assure coordination of the planning, acquisition, and development assistance to States under this section with other related Federal programs and activities, the President may issue such regulations with respect thereto as he deems desirable and such assistance may be provided only in accordance with such regulations.

ALLOCATION OF MONEYS FOR FEDERAL PURPOSES

SEC. 6. (a) Moneys appropriated from the fund for Federal purposes shall, unless otherwise allotted in the appropriation Act making them available, be allotted by the President to the following purposes and subpurposes in substantially the same proportion as the number of visitor-days in areas and projects hereinafter described for which admission fees are charged under section 2 of this Act:

(1) For the acquisition of land, waters, or interests in land or waters as follows:

National Park System; Recreation Areas.—Within the exterior boundaries of areas of the national park system now or hereafter authorized or established and of areas now or hereafter authorized to be administered by the Secretary of the Interior for outdoor recreation purposes.

National Forest System.—Inholdings within (a) wilderness areas of the National Forest System, and (b) other areas of national forests as the boundaries of those forests exist on the effective date of this Act which other areas are primarily of value for outdoor recreation purposes: *Provided,* That lands outside of but adjacent to an existing national forest boundary, not to exceed five hundred acres in the case of any one forest, which would comprise an integral part of a forest recreational management area may also be acquired with moneys appropriated from this fund: *Provided further,* That not more than 15 per centum of the acreage added to the National Forest System pursuant to this section shall be west of the 100th meridian.

Threatened Species.—For any national area which may be authorized for the preservation of species of fish or wildlife that are threatened with extinction.

Recreation at Refuges.—For the incidental recreation purposes of section 2 of the Act of September 28, 1962 (76 Stat. 653; 16 U.S.C. 460 k–1); and

(2) For payment into miscellaneous receipts of the Treasury as a partial offset for those capital costs, if any, of Federal water development projects hereafter authorized to be constructed by or pursuant to an Act of Congress which are allocated to public recreation and the enhancement of fish and wildlife values and financed through appropriations to water resources agencies.

(b) Acquisition Restriction.—Appropriations from the fund pursuant to this section shall not be used for acquisition unless such acquisition is otherwise authorized by law.

FUNDS NOT TO BE USED FOR PUBLICITY

SEC. 7. Moneys derived from the sources listed in section 2 of this Act shall not be available for publicity purposes.

TITLE II—MOTORBOAT FUEL TAX PROVISIONS

TRANSFERS TO AND FROM LAND AND WATER CONSERVATION FUND

SEC. 201. (a) There shall be set aside in the land and water conservation fund in the Treasury of the United States provided for in title I of this Act the amounts specified in section 209(f) (5) of the Highway Revenue Act of 1956 (relating to special motor fuels and gasoline used in motorboats).

(b) There shall be paid from time to time from the land and water conservation fund into the general fund of the Treasury amounts estimated by the Secretary of the Treasury as equivalent to—

(1) the amounts paid before July 1, 1973, under section 6421 of the Internal Revenue Code of 1954 (relating to amounts paid in respect of gasoline used for certain nonhighway purposes or by local transit systems) with respect to gasoline used after December 31, 1964, in motorboats, on the basis of claims filed for periods ending before October 1, 1972; and

(2) 80 percent of the floor stocks refunds made before July 1, 1973, under section 6412(a) (2) of such Code with respect to gasoline to be used in motorboats.

AMENDMENTS TO HIGHWAY REVENUE ACT OF 1956

SEC. 202. (a) Section 209(f) of the Highway Revenue Act of 1956 (relating to expenditures from highway trust fund) is amended by adding at the end thereof the following new paragraph:

"(5) Transfers from the trust fund for special motor fuels and gasoline used in motorboats.—The Secretary of the Treasury shall pay from time to time from the trust fund into the land and water conservation fund provided for in title I of the Land and Water Conservation fund provided for in title I of the Land and Water Conservation Fund Act of 1965 amounts as determined by him in consultation with the Secretary of Commerce equivalent to the taxes received, on or after January 1, 1965, under section 4041 (b) of the Internal Revenue Code of 1954 with respect to special motor fuels used as fuel for the propulsion of motorboats and under section 4081 of such Code with respect to gasoline used as fuel in motorboats."

(b) Section 209 (f) of such Act is further amended—

(1) by adding at the end of paragraph (3) the following new sentence: "This paragraph shall not apply to amounts estimated by the Secretary of the Treasury as paid under section 6421 of such Code with respect to gasoline used after December 31, 1964, in motorboats."; and

(2) by inserting after "such Code" in paragraph (4) (C) the following: "(other than gasoline to be used in motorboats, as estimated by the Secretary of the Treasury)".

Approved September 3, 1964.

DEMISE OF THE GOLDEN EAGLE:
AMENDMENT TO THE LAND AND WATER FUND ACT*
July 15, 1968

User fees under the Land and Water Conservation Fund Act were collected through sale of a "golden eagle" sticker at a uniform rate throughout the United States. Purchasers of the golden eagle could generally enter any federal properties and stay as long as they liked.

The sticker created considerable resentment among some recreationists and total revenues were considerably less than had been anticipated. For these, among other reasons, the uniform federal user fee was repealed. The amendment also had the effect of guaranteeing a total income to the fund of $200 million per year with shortages to come out of receipts from the Outer Continental Shelf Lands Act.

An Act to amend Title I of the Land and Water Conservation Fund Act of 1963, and for other purposes.

Be it enacted by the Senate and House of Representatives of the United States of America in Congress assembled, That (a) section 2, subsection (a), of the Land and Water Conservation Fund Act of 1965 (78 Stat. 897; 16 U.S.C. 460 1–5), except the fourth paragraph thereof, is repealed; said fourth paragraph is redesignated section 10 of said Act; and subsections (b) and (c) of said section 2 are redesignated (a) and (b), respectively.

(b) It is not the intent of the Congress by this repealer to indicate that Federal agencies which have under their administrative jurisdiction areas or facilities used or useful for outdoor recreation or which furnish services related to outdoor recreation shall not exercise any authority they may have, including authority under section 501 of the Act of August 31, 1951 (65 Stat. 290; 31 U.S.C. 483a), or any authority they may hereafter be given, to make reasonable charges for admission to such areas, for the use of such facilities, or for the furnishing of such services. Except as otherwise provided by law or as may be required by lawful contracts entered into prior to September 3, 1964, providing that revenues collected at particular Federal areas shall be credited to specific purposes, all fees so charged shall be covered into a special account under the Land and Water Conservation Fund and shall be available for appropriation, without prejudice to appropriations from other sources for the same purposes, for any authorized outdoor recreation function of the agency by which the fees were collected.

(c) Section 6, subsection (a), of said Act is amended by striking out the words "in substantially the same proportion as the number of visitor-days in areas and

---

*82 *Statutes at Large,* 354.

projects hereinafter described for which admission fees are charged under section 2 of this Act".

(d) The provisions of subsections (a) and (c) of this section shall be effective March 31, 1970. Until that date, revenues derived from the subsection (a) that is repealed by this section shall continue to be covered into the fund.

SEC. 2. The aforesaid section 2 of the Land and Water Conservation Fund Act of 1965 is further amended by adding at the end thereof the following new subsection:

"(c) (1) Other Revenues.—In addition to the sum of the revenues and collections estimated by the Secretary of the Interior to be covered into the fund pursuant to this section, as amended, there are authorized to be appropriated annually to the fund out of any money in the Treasury not otherwise appropriated such amounts as are necessary to make the income of the fund not less than $200,000,000 for each of the five fiscal years beginning July 1, 1968, and ending June 30, 1973.

"(2) To the extent that any such sums so appropriated are not sufficient to make the total annual income of the fund amount to $200,000,000 for each of such fiscal years, an amount sufficient to cover the remainder thereof shall be credited to the fund from revenues due and payable to the United States for deposit in the Treasury as miscellaneous receipts under the Outer Continental Shelf Lands Act, as amended (43 U.S.C. 1331 et seq.): *Provided,* That notwithstanding the provisions of section 3 of this Act, moneys covered into the fund under this paragraph shall remain in the fund until appropriated by the Congress to carry out the purpose of this Act."

SEC. 3. The first sentence of section 4, subsection (b), of the Land and Water Conservation Fund Act of 1965 is amended by deleting "for a total of eight years" and inserting in lieu thereof "until the end of fiscal year 1969".

SEC. 4. The Land and Water Conservation Fund Act of 1965 is further amended by adding thereto the following new sections:

"SEC. 8. Not to exceed $30,000,000 of the money authorized to be appropriated from the fund by section 3 of this Act may be obligated by contract during each of fiscal years 1969 and 1970 for the acquisition of lands, waters, or interests therein within areas specified in section 6(a)(1) of this Act. Any such contract may be executed by the head of the department concerned, within limitations prescribed by the Secretary of the Interior. Any such contract so entered into shall be deemed a contractual obligation of the United States and shall be liquidated with money appropriated from the fund specifically for liquidation of such contract obligation. No contract may be entered into for the acquisition of property pursuant to this section unless such acquisition is otherwise authorized by Federal law.

"SEC. 9. The Secretary of the Interior may enter into contracts for options to acquire lands, waters, or interests therein within the exterior boundaries of any area the acquisition of which is authorized by law for inclusion in the national park system. The minimum period of any such option shall be two years, and any sums expended for the purchase thereof shall be credited to the purchase price of said area. Not to exceed $500,000 of the sum authorized to be appropriated from the fund by section 3 of this Act may be expended by the Secretary in any one fiscal year for such options."

SEC. 5. (a) With respect to any property acquired by the Secretary of the Interior within a unit of the national park system or miscellaneous area, except property within national parks, or within national monuments of scientific significance, the Secretary may convey a freehold or leasehold interest therein, subject to such terms and conditions as will assure the use of the property in a manner which is, in the judgment of the Secretary, consistent with the purpose for which the area was authorized by the Congress. In any case in which the Secretary exercises his discretion to convey such interest, he shall do so to the highest bidder, in accordance with such regulations as the Secretary may prescribe, but such conveyance shall be at not less than the fair market value of the interest, as determined by the Secretary; except that if any such conveyance is proposed within two years after the property to be conveyed is acquired by the Secretary, he shall allow the last owner or owners of record of such property thirty days following the date on which they are notified by the Secretary in writing that such property is to be conveyed within which to notify the Secretary that such owners wish to acquire such interest. Upon receiving such timely request, the Secretary shall convey such interest to such person or persons, in accordance with such regulations as the Secretary may prescribe, upon payment or agreement to pay an amount equal to the highest bid price.

(b) The Secretary of the Interior is authorized to accept title to any non-Federal property or interest therein within a unit of the National Park System or miscellaneous area under his administration, and in exchange therefor he may convey to the grantor of such property or interest any Federally-owned property or interest therein under his jurisdiction which he determines is suitable for exchange or other disposal and which is located in the same State as the non-Federal property to be acquired: *Provided, however,* That timber lands subject to harvest under a sustained yield program shall not be so exchanged. Upon request of a State or a political subdivision thereof, or of a party in interest, prior to such exchange the Secretary or his designee shall hold a public hearing in the area where the lands to be exchanged are located. The values of the properties so exchanged either shall be approximately equal, or if they are not approximately equal, the values shall be equalized by the payment of cash to the grantor from funds appropriated for the acquisition of land for the area, or to the Secretary as the circumstances require.

(c) The proceeds received from any conveyance under this section shall be credited to the land and water conservation fund in the Treasury of the United States.

Approved July 15, 1968.

THE RACE FOR INNER SPACE

A clear stream, a long horizon,
a forest wilderness and open sky
—these are man's most ancient
possessions. In a modern society,
they are his most priceless.

Lyndon B. Johnson

The most dramatic news events of the decade of the sixties were the tentative probings of man into outer space. While these spectacular achievements were taking place, however, the quality of the environment on the earth's crust was rapidly degenerating. This chapter is concerned with some of the efforts to maintain that environment in terms of natural beauty, scenic highways and trails, and the preservation of historic sites.

NATURAL BEAUTY

A large portion of outdoor recreation does not involve any definite activity other than the enjoyment of natural beauty. But this is not restricted to sightseeing for all other outdoor recreation activities are enhanced by attractive natural surroundings.

It is probably correct to say that Americans have always enjoyed and appreciated natural beauty, but this facet of recreation has had low priority compared with other values commonly associated with the term "progress." Early attempts to preserve and enhance the beauties of nature as well as some recent governmental acts which indicated a reawakening of interest in natural beauty are documented in this chapter.

HIGHWAYS AND TRAILS

Most outdoor recreation requires travel, and presently this involves the private automobile most of all. Over 95 percent of the visitors to Yellowstone Glacier, Grand Canyon, and Great Smoky Mountains National Parks, for example, come by private automobile. The tremendous rise in the use of federally-owned recreation resources during the past few years has been made possible because of their accessibility via the public road system. Conversely, there remain many areas of great recreation potential which are used very little because of lack of adequate roads. The relationship is so close that by widening and improving roads we have, in some instances, exchanged congested roads for congested recreation sites.

In general we think of roads as being only a means to an end; we assume that recreation benefits do not begin until the site is reached and that time in transit is lost time or an unpleasant interlude to be endured in reaching the recreation area. All too often this may be true, but for many people the "trip" may provide as much enjoyment as the visit to the recreation site. Furthermore, there is a great deal of highway travel that is pleasurable in itself, that has no particular destination. Therefore, the highways themselves do, or could, provide a most valuable recreation resource. This becomes especially significant when we consider that streets and highways occupy 22 million acres of land—more than the entire area of the State of Maine. If multiple use is a valid concept for other kinds of lands, could it not also apply to road-lands? For example, some other uses of highways (besides providing a roadbed for vehicles) might include changes in routing and design to maximize the scenic values of the route, the consideration of wildlife values in planning route and construction, the establishment of more attractive roadside rest areas, the establishment of camp grounds at points easily accessible to main highways, and better control of outdoor advertising to improve both safety and scenic values.

As presently constructed, highways are designed to move freight—not people; there would be little change in route, design, or amenities if only truckers used the highways. This is not to suggest that highway planners have been unduly influenced by the trucking industry but simply to point out that highway engineers tend to think in terms of vehicles rather than people. Considering the increasing number of long passenger trips and the large amount of passenger traffic (including the high percentage of recreation travel), it is time for a reorientation in highway design in recognition of the fact that the principal function of highways is to move people—not freight.

THAT THE PAST SHALL LIVE:
THE PRESERVATION OF HISTORIC SITES

The race to conserve inner space is directly related to the effort to preserve historic sites; visits to the historic areas of the National Park system alone amounted to about 35 million in 1966. Americans have a rich historical legacy and they obviously wish to preserve outstanding evidences of the past, but such preservation is being threatened by the construction of highways and dams and the rapid growth of suburbs and industrial developments.

In the words of the National Park Service:

> The greatest threat, of course, results from our rapid population growth and the almost awesome mushrooming of urban development.

THE RACE FOR INNER SPACE

Everywhere across the land this swelling tide of people is demanding more living space—more subdivisions, more freeways, more supermarkets, more reservoirs, more pipelines, more parking lots, more irrigated land.

The public officials and private entrepreneurs who must meet these demands are understandably impatient with anything which stands in their way—particularly if those things happen to be old buildings or "worthless" historic or prehistoric sites.

The result—for those who feel that some of the old values of our nation deserve consideration with the new—is little short of appalling.

* * *

Few people fully realize the swiftness with which this trend toward severing our links with the past has been developing within the last brief span of years, nor the total cost in cultural losses that has been the end result. Unfortunately, those who advocate or endorse the spoiling or destruction of a single historic site that stands in the way of a particular new subdivision or commercial development have no way of observing the cumulative effect of the many thousands of such actions across the country.

Of course, no one maintains that every old house, every ancient Indian village site, or every rotting sailing vessel should be saved. Admittedly, many of the 100,000 or more historic places in this country are not as important as the new schools, new shopping centers, and new highways which will replace them. But many thousands of these sites and buildings do have something to say to the present and the future. They do throw light upon our history and the development of our culture. They do bring history to life by presenting the only possible authentic environment.*

---

*National Park Service, *That the Past Shall Live* (undated publication), 31.

HENRY DAVID THOREAU ON
THE SHRINES ON BAKER FARM*
1854

At a time when most Americans were primarily interested in taming the wilderness, Thoreau delighted in what was left of it. Here he speaks of visiting the "shrines" on Baker Farm.

Sometimes I rambled to pine groves, standing like temples, or like fleets at sea, full-rigged, with wavy boughs, and rippling with light, so soft and green and shady that the Druids would have forsaken their oaks to worship in them; or to the cedar wood beyond Flints' Pond, where the trees, covered with hoary blue berries, spiring higher and higher, are fit to stand before Valhalla, and the creeping juniper covers the ground with wreaths full of fruit; or to swamps where the usnea lichen hangs in festoons from the white-spruce trees, and toadstools, round tables of the swamp gods, cover the ground, and more beautiful fungi adorn the stumps, like butterflies or shells, vegetable winkles; where the swamp-pink and dogwood grow, the red alder-berry glows like eyes of imps, the wax-work grooves and crushes the hardest woods in its folds, and the wild-holly berries make the beholder forget his home with their beauty, and he is dazzled and tempted by nameless other wild forbidden fruits, too fair for mortal taste. Instead of calling on some scholar, I paid many a visit to particular trees, of kinds which are rare in this neighborhood, standing far away in the middle of some pasture, or in the depths of a wood or swamp, or on a hill-top; such as the black-birch, of which we have some handsome specimens two feet in diameter; its cousin, the yellow-birch, with its loose golden vest, perfumed like the first; the beech, which has so neat a bole and beautifully lichen-painted, perfect in all its details, of which, excepting scattered specimens, I know but one small grove of sizable trees left in the township, supposed by some to have been planted by the pigeons that were once baited with beech nuts near by; it is worth the while to see the silver grain sparkle when you split this wood; the bass; the hornbeam; the *celtis occidentalis,* or false elm, of which we have but one well-grown; some taller mast of a pine, a shingle tree, or a more perfect hemlock than usual, standing like a pagoda in the midst of the woods; and many others I could mention. These were the shrines I visited both summer and winter.

*Henry David Thoreau, *Walden,* Vol. 2 (Boston: Houghton, Mifflin & Co., 1854), 314–15.

THE ANTIQUITIES ACT*
June 8, 1906

The first general legislation to preserve historic or archeological sites was the landmark Antiquities Act of 1906 which follows.

An Act for the preservation of American antiquities.

Be it enacted by the Senate and House of Representatives of the United States of America in Congress assembled, That any person who shall appropriate, excavate, injure, or destroy any historic or prehistoric ruin or monument, or any object of antiquity, situated on lands owned or controlled by the Government of the United States, without the permission of the Secretary of the Department of the Government having jurisdiction over the lands on which said antiquities are situated, shall, upon conviction, be fined in a sum of not more than five hundred dollars or be imprisoned for a period of not more than ninety days, or shall suffer both fine and imprisonment, in the discretion of the court.

SEC. 2. That the President of the United States is hereby authorized, in his discretion, to declare by public proclamation historic landmarks, historic and prehistoric structures, and other objects of historic or scientific interest that are situated upon the lands owned or controlled by the Government of the United States to be national monuments, and may reserve as a part thereof parcels of land, the limits of which in all cases shall be confined to the smallest area compatible with the proper care and management of the objects to the protected: *Provided,* That when such objects are situated upon a tract covered by a bona fide unperfected claim or held in private ownership, the tract, or so much thereof as may be necessary for the proper care and management of the object, may be relinquished to the Government, and the Secretary of the Interior is hereby authorized to accept the relinquishment of such tracts in behalf of the Government of the United States.

SEC. 3. That permits for the examination of ruins, the excavation of archaeological sites, and the gathering of objects of antiquity upon the lands under their respective jurisdictions may be granted by the Secretaries of the Interior, Agriculture, and War to institutions which they may deem properly qualified to conduct such examination, excavation, or gathering, subject to such rules and regulations as they may prescribe: *Provided,* That the examinations, excavations, and gatherings are undertaken for the benefit of reputable museums, universities, colleges, or other recognized scientific or educational institutions, with a

*34 *Statutes at Large,* 225.

view to increasing the knowledge of such objects, and that the gatherings shall be made for permanent preservation in public museums.

SEC. 4. That the Secretaries of the Departments aforesaid shall make and publish from time to time uniform rules and regulations for the purpose of carrying out the provisions of this Act.

Approved, June 8, 1906.

A SPEECH BY J. HORACE McFARLAND ON NATURAL BEAUTY*
1908

One of the first public pleas for preservation of natural beauty was a speech by J. Horace McFarland, President of the American Civic Association, before the Conference of Governors of the United States in 1908.

Mr Chairman:

I would urge this august and influential assembly to consider the essential value of one of America's greatest resources—her unmatched natural scenery.

It is well that we should here take full account of the peril to our material prosperity which lies in further wasteful depletion of our waning resources of forest and mine, of water and soil. By the possibilities of conservation here discussed, the mind is quickened, the imagination fired. But the true glory of the United States must rest, and has rested, upon a deeper foundation than that of her purely material resources. It is the love of country that lights and keeps glowing the holy fire of patriotism. And this love is excited primarily by the beauty of the country. Truly inspired is our national hymn as it sings:

> My native country, thee,
> Land of the noble, free,
> Thy name I love;
> I love thy rocks and rills;
> Thy woods and templed hills
> My heart with rapture thrills,
> Like that above.

Paraphrasing a recent utterance of Mayor McClellan on city beauty, I insist that "The country healthy, the country wealthy, and the country wise may excite satisfaction, complaisance and pride; but it is the country beautiful that compels and retains the love of its citizens."

We can not destroy the scenery of our broad land, but we can utterly change its beneficial relation to our lives, and remove its stirring effect upon our love of country.

Scenery of some sort will continue as long as sight endures. It is for us to decide whether we shall permanently retain as a valuable national asset any considerable portion of the natural scenery which is so influential in our lives, or whether we shall continue to substitute the unnatural scenery of man's careless waste.

Shall we gaze on the smiling beauty of our island-dotted rivers, or look in dis-

*J. Horace McFarland, "Address," *Conference of the Governors of the United States,* Newton C. Blanchard, ed. (Washington, D.C.: Government Printing Office, 1909), 153–57.

gust on great open sewers, lined with careless commercial filth, and alternating between disastrous flood and painful drouth? Is the Grand Canyon of the Colorado to be really held as Nature's great temple of scenic color, or must we see that temple punctuated and profaned by trolley poles? Shall the White Mountains be for us a great natural sanitarium, or shall they stand as a greater monument to our folly and neglect?

It is certain that there has been but scant thought given to scenic preservation hitherto. I remember the contempt with which a lawyer of national renown alluded to the absurdity of any legislation by Congress in preservation of scenery, when, in response to the demand of the People, that body had chosen to give a measure of temporary protection to a part of Niagara's flood. [Applause]

Indeed, one of the potent forces of obstruction to the legislation now demanded by the country in belated protection to the almost destroyed mountain forests of the East has expressed itself in a contemptuous sneer at the very idea of national expenditures for the preservation of scenery.

Mr Chairman, we meet in a historic place, in a historic city. The Father of our Country was not only great in war and statesmanship, but great in esteem for natural beauty and in the desire to create urban beauty. George Washington loved the beauty of scenery, and his wisdom has provided, for all the world to see, a Federal city admirable in its adaptation to the public needs, and destined, as his plans are carried out, to be beautiful beyond compare.

What is the effect of the scenic beauty of Washington on the citizens of the Nation who come here? Is not their pride awakened, their patriotism quickened, their love of country increased? Consider wealthy Pittsburg, busy Cincinnati, with their wasteful smoke, their formless streets, their all-pervading billboards and grime—would one of these serve to stimulate love of country as the National Capital?

No; the unthinking and ofttimes unnecessary ugliness of civilization does not foster patriotism, nor does it promote the health and happiness which are at the very basis of good citizenship. When, in looking over the horrors of industrial civilization, William Morris urged humanitarian effort—"Until the contrast is less disgraceful between the fields where the beasts live and the streets where men live," he brought out a bitter truth. We have made our cities ugly for the most part; but we are learning the basis of happy citizenship, and while we can not altogether make over these centers of population we are bringing into them the scenic suggestion as well as the physical facilities of the open country—in our parks. In these parks lies the answer to the ignorant contempt for scenery to which I have alluded; for it is incontrovertible that peace and health and good order are fostered in parks in proportion as they represent scenic beauties.

Mr Chairman, there is, too, a vast economic reason for jealously guarding all of our scenic heritage in America. Visiting a quiet Canadian community on the shore of Lake Ontario a few days since, I was impressed by the number and the beauty of the summer homes there existing. Inquiry brought out the astonishing fact that they were almost exclusively owned by residents of a certain very wealthy and certainly very ugly American city where iron is king. The iron manufacturers flee from the all-pervading ugliness they have created, and the money they have earned in complete disregard of the naturally fine scenic conditions about their own homes is used in buying scenic beauty in a foreign country! Perhaps a certain form of needed protection is here suggested! [Applause]

It is authoritatively stated that the tourist-travel tribute paid annually to Europe exceeds half a billion dollars. Of this vast sum America contributes a full half, getting back a far smaller sum in return travel from all the world. No one will suggest that there is travel to Europe to see ugly things, or wasted scenery. No; this vast sum is expended almost entirely in travel to view agreeable scenic conditions, either natural or urban. The lumber king leaves the hills he has denuded into piteous ugliness, and takes his family to view the jealously guarded and economically beautiful Black Forest of Germany. [Laughter] The coal operator who has made a horror of a whole country-side, and who is responsible for the dreadful kennels among the culm-banks in which his imported labor lives, travels through beautiful France, or he may motor through the humble but sightly European villages from whence came his last invoice of workers.

Every instinct for permanent business prosperity should impel us not only to save in their natural beauty all our important scenic possessions, but also fully to safeguard the great and revolutionary development almost certain to follow this epoch-making Conference. We are assured by experience that the use of our great renewable resource of soil fertility is attended with the continuance of beautiful scenic conditions. The smiling farm, the glowing orchard, the waving wheatfield, the rustle of the corn—all these spell peaceful beauty as well as national wealth, which we can definitely continue and increase.

Can we not see to it that the further use of our unrenewable resources of minerals and primeval forest is no longer attended with a sad change of beautiful, restful, and truly valuable scenery into the blasted hillside and the painful ore-dump, ugly, disturbing, valueless?

The waters of our streams must furnish the "white coal" of the future and electrically turn the wheels of commerce in smokeless economy. Such a change can consider, retain and sometimes increase the beauty of the scenery; or it can introduce the sacrilegious ugliness of which the American gorge at Niagara is now so disgraceful an example. The banks of the waterways we are to develop can be such as will attract scenic travel rather than repel it. [Applause]

We can not, either, safely overlook the necessity for retaining, not only for ourselves but for our children's children, God's glory of mountain and vale, lake, forest and seaside, His refuge in the very bosom of nature, to which we may flee from the noise and strain of the market-place for that renewing of spirit and strength which can not be had elsewhere. True, we can continue and expand our travel tribute to the better scenic sense of the Eastern World; but that will not avail our toiling millions. "Beauty for the few, no more than freedom or education for the few," urges William Morris; and who shall say that our natural beauty of scenery is not the heritage of all and a plain necessity for good citizenship?

Every one of us recognizes the renewing of strength and spirit that comes from even a temporary sojourn amidst natural scenic delights. The President has but just returned from a "week-end" visit to his castle of rest in the Virginia Hills. Could he have had equal pleasure in Hoboken? [Laughter] Mr Carnegie's enterprise built Homestead—but he finds the scenery about Skibo Castle much more restful!

Who of us, tired with the pressure of Twentieth Century life, fails to take refuge amid the scenes of natural beauty, rather than to endeavor to find that needed rest in a mining village? The most blatant economist, who sneers at the thought of public beauty for all, is usually much interested in private beauty of scenery, of home and of person, accessible to him alone. Selfishly and inconsistently he recognizes in his own use the value of the natural resources he affects to despise!

I am convinced that the majority of my countrymen hold deep in their hearts sentiments of regard for the glorious natural beauty of America. If to my inadequate words there be any response among those here present, there may be future action.

May I, in conclusion, but hint at some things that might well result?

First, we must hold inviolate our greater scenic heritages. All the nations visit the Falls of Niagara as the wonder of the Western World; yet we are even now engaged in an attempt to see how closely we can pare its glories without complete destruction. Eminent authorities warn us that the danger line is now passed, and that a recurrence of a cycle of low water in the great lakes may completely extinguish the American Fall. A hundred other water-powers in New York and Ontario would together give as much wheel-turning electric energy, but all the world can not furnish forth the equivalent of Niagara in beneficent influence on the minds of men, if held as a scenic heritage. The glory of Niagara today hangs by a hair—and millions of money seek covetously to cut the hair.

The National Parks, all too few in number and extent, ought to be held absolutely inviolate, as intended by Congress. The Hetch-Hetchy valley of the Yosemite region belongs to all America, and not to San Francisco alone.

The scenic value of all the national domain yet remaining should be jealously guarded as a distinctly important natural resource, and not as a mere incidental increment. In giving access for wise economic purposes to forest and range, to valley and stream, the Federal Government should not for a moment overlook the safeguarding to the People of all the natural beauty now existing. That this may be done without preventing legitimate use of all the other natural resources is certain.

The Governors of sovereign States here assembled, the many organizations here represented, possess the power and have the opportunity so to change and guide legislation and public opinion as to foster the underlying desire for public beauty, both natural and urban. We have, for a century, Mr. Chairman, stood actually, if not ostensibly, for an uglier America; let us here and now resolve, for every patriotic and economic reason, to stand openly and solidly for a more beautiful, and therefore a more prosperous America!

BENTON MacKAYE ON THE APPALACHIAN TRAIL*
1924

In addition to more attractive highways, Americans need trails for hiking, horseback riding, and bicycling, for in most sections of the country these activities can be carried out only alongside streets and highways. The Appalachian Trail was one of the first large trail systems to be established in the United States. Benton MacKaye described the development of the Appalachian Trail in these remarks to the National Conference on Outdoor Recreation in 1924.

Mr. Chairman and members of the conference, I appreciate very much your request to hear about the project for an Appalachian Trail. This trail is, of course, a walking trail or path, and not an automobile road. Its route, as proposed and partly completed, follows the crest line of the Appalachian Mountain chain from Maine to Georgia. It traverses the White Mountains, the Green Mountains, and the Berkshire Hills in New England, the Hudson Highlands in New York and New Jersey, the Alleghenies from Delaware Water Gap to Harpers Ferry, the Blue Ridge through Virginia, and the ridges of the Carolina Highland in the States south. In all it embraces about 800 miles north and south from Harpers Ferry.

The Appalachian Trail is conceived as the backbone of a trail system to cover the general Appalachian territory. It is divided into about 40 links or sections, from gap to gap. Each link is being developed by a local group of workers as an independent unit or circuit to serve as an outlet from the adjacent cities and towns.

Thus the Palisades Interstate Park Section has been developed from Bear Mountain, N.Y., on the Hudson, to Arden, on the Ramapo River. This forms a circuit and outlet from New York City through rail or motor road connection. This Palisades Interstate Park Section, 18 miles long, has been completed by members of the New York-New Jersey Trail Conference. Maj. W. A. Welch is chairman of this conference and Mr. R. H. Torrey is secretary. Through the leadership of these men not only has the Palisades Interstate Park Section been scouted, cut through, and marked with the adopted "A. T." sign, but the whole route has been scouted, and in places cut through, from Delaware Water Gap to the Connecticut line.

Work in New England is being carried on through the general supervision of the New England Trail conference (under Mr. A. M. Turner in Connecticut, the Appalachian Mountain Club in Massachusetts and New Hampshire, and the Green Mountain Club in Vermont). Appalachian Trail committees have been

*Proceedings of the National Conference on Outdoor Recreation, Sen. Doc. 151, 68th Cong., 1st sess., 124–27.

formed in Pennsylvania, in the District of Columbia, and in Virginia. The route in the southern mountains follows in large part the trails of the United States Forest Service in the several national forests, the Forest Service having given invaluable assistance and encouragement to the work in this region.

The Appalachian Trail is being developed on the basis of two maxims—the strength of independence and the strength of union. Each link is an independent trail for local use, being scouted, cut, marked, and financed by some local group of volunteer workers. The idea is to stimulate local and individual interest capable of solving the local problems (topographic, legal, and otherwise) which arise in each locality. But each link is made part of a bigger whole. To obtain this "strength of union" the group is given in advance a definite objective—to connect two fixed points. These points mark the crossings of the general route of the Appalachian Trail. The local group also is requested to mark its link with the "A. T." symbol, choosing its own color, size, and local designation.

Thus the Appalachian Trail is a movement and not an organization. It is a loosely woven project for stimulating the building of local trails in harmony with a general plan or design. It is "a project in regional planning" (and so called in the title of the original article published in 1921 which set forth the idea). It is being fathered at this time by the Regional Planning Association of America.

The regional planning idea seems to be a development of the conservation movement of the Roosevelt-Pinchot days. It has been aptly defined as "the relating of man to his environment." It is the planning regionally of our life and work, so far as this may be seen upon the map. Very largely, therefore, it must be the planning of industrial plant. But it is planning the ends of industry as well as the means of industry. Assuming these "ends" (the object of industry and of work) to consist of vigorous human living as against mere drawn-out existence, it is just as important to have a regional living plant or "recreation plant" as to have an industrial plant. Hence the natural tendency, already pointed out by Professor Hubbard, to start regional planning (as we have started community planning) with the designing of recreational areas. We should first set down our objective, next lay out the method for attaining it. For unless the means are specifically adapted to achieve the ends, the ends themselves will be (as so often) defeated by an aimless mechanism.

And so this particular project in regional planning—the Appalachian Trail project—is conceived as one for setting down upon the map, and upon the actual ground, the framework of a regional recreational equipment. This framework would consist of a system of trails and camps providing economic, convenient, and practicable access to the environment of the natural resources and the forces of nature which lie at the roots of our life and work.

But this equipment is not an end in itself. It is merely a base for further action. The trail system is a skeleton, the body of which is the land itself. The land in this particular case is the Appalachian territory. This is a very significant territory in American life. It penetrates the most populous portion of the North American Continent. As Central Park is the breathing space for Manhattan Island, so the Appalachian Mountain territory is the breathing space for that eastern quarter of our country where more than half our population lives. Historically also this territory is vital; it is the hinterland and background of our pioneer tradition.

The big objective, therefore, behind the Appalachian Trail is the development of an Appalachian domain. This in large measure would be a public domain. We have the beginnings in the public forests and parks, both National and State. This domain should be developed by the people themselves and not merely by experts and officials. And the first suggested step in this development is the building of the "base line" along the range.

Several sections of this base line have been, in part at least, completed (as already noted), and within certain of these sections the second step of development has been begun. This second step consists in making a survey—what the geologists might call a "reconnaissance" survey. It consists of an amateur exploration of the topography along the line of route from gap to gap. It is something which though guided by technicians should be carried on by amateurs. For people seem to be more interested in something which they do themselves than in what some one else does for them.

The unit of this survey is the region adjacent to the line of trail between one major gap, or crossing, and the next. To illustrate by the projected Harpers Ferry section: This section of the trail (already partly scouted) extends from the Potomac River, crossing at Harpers Ferry southward along the Blue Ridge to Snickers Gap, above Bluemont, Va. The field of survey between these crossings would consist of the west slope of the Blue Ridge from the crest line to the channel of the Shenandoah River and of the east slope from the crest line to the foot of the range. A region of this type (called the "ridgeway") includes all forms of topography from mountain crest to valley bottom.

The point of view of the ridgeway survey is topography. What is the topography, what are its causes, what are its consequences? The United States Geological Survey, in the Geologic Folio, answers the first two of these questions. It presents a map of the region's topography, and then it presents a series of maps (and descriptions) showing the causes of the topography, i.e., the various geologic structures from which the features and soils of the region have resulted. The form sought for the ridgeway survey is a "folio" patterned somewhat on the United States Geologic Folio and adapted to the needs of the amateur.

But this folio would include more than geologic features; it would include the consequences as well as the causes of topography. It would show, for the region, the occurrence and possibilities of stream flow, of water power, of the various soils between crest and bottom, of forest growth, and of plant and animal life. It would show, under proper technical guidance, the basic facts and relations for the conservation, and the most all-around beneficial development, of the region's natural resources. The development itself of a series of such folios and surveys throughout the Appalachian domain, under thorough technical checking and under thorough popular discussion, might tend to visualize in the public mind some concrete but comprehensive program for dealing with our sources of life, on which in time all might agree.

So the Appalachian Trail is not an end within itself; it is a base for more fundamental needs. It is the equipment required for a certain line of badly needed social education, the power within a people's mind to see their common ends, not as a tangle of antagonistic parts but as a single, harmonized, integrated whole.

RECOMMENDATIONS OF THE NATIONAL CONFERENCE ON
OUTDOOR RECREATION REGARDING NATIONAL MONUMENTS*
1928

*Among other matters the National Conference on Outdoor Recreation in
1928 gave some attention to national monuments.*

A forward step in the protection of historic landmarks, historic, or prehistoric
structures and other objects of historic or scientific interest of national importance was the passage of the American antiquities act in 1906 authorizing the
President to permanently protect such objects as national monuments when
situated upon lands owned or controlled by the United States.

Under the provisions of the antiquities act 56 national monuments have been
established; 52 in the States aggregating in total area over 500,000 acres and four
in Alaska aggregating over 2,000,000 acres. The Interior Department administers 32, the Agricultural Department 15, and the War Department 9. Geo-
graphically 19 States and one Territory possess these national monuments, as
follows: Alaska, 4; Arizona, 11; California, 5; Colorado, 4; Georgia, 1; Florida,
2; Idaho, 1; Montana, 2; Nebraska, 1; New Mexico, 8; Nevada, 1; New York, 1;
North Dakota, 1; Ohio, 1; Oregon, 1; South Carolina, 1; South Dakota, 2; Tennessee, 1; Utah, 5; Washington, 1; and Wyoming, 2.

In the national-monuments system one finds five classes of exhibits: (a) Remains of prehistoric civilization, (b) historic relics, (c) geologic examples, (d)
botanic reservations, and (e) one reservation for wild animals. All are classed as
scientific. Although many monuments located on fine roads near through highways are much visited by sight-seeing motorists, the purpose for which they were
created is preservation for scientific and educational use. They are recreational
in the broadest sense of the word.

Of important immediate consideration is the meagerness of appropriations
which Congress makes for the protection of national monuments. Nearly all
monuments need improvements to make them accessible to visitors, to say nothing of protection, and every one of them should have a salaried custodian on
duty during seasons of visitation to prevent trespass and vandalism. Some of the
monuments have no custodian. Others have the slenderest kind of volunteer
service. The failure of the Federal Government to recognize national monuments as a system is responsible for the lamentable lack of development and
care, diversion of some of them to commonplace uses, for Congress recognizes

*Joint Committee on Recreational Survey of Federal Lands of the American Forestry Association
and the National Park Association, "Recreation Resources of Federal Lands," *National Conference
on Outdoor Recreation,* Sen. Doc. 158, 70th Cong., 1st sess., 65–66.

by general appropriations only those in the Interior Department, although several of the most important are under other administration.

In connection with the national monuments system consideration should be given to the system of national military parks under the administration of the War Department. These have been created by acts of Congress during a period covering 35 years. So far they consist of battle fields of the Civil War and include, too, the birthplace of Abraham Lincoln. Bills have been introduced in Congress to include battle fields of colonial times. The Secretary of War has now proposed that these military parks be administered by the National Park Service of the Interior Department. This logical proposal gives pertinency to the recommendation of Robert Sterling Yard, secretary of the National Parks Association, that a committee, comparable to that of the Coordinating Commission on National Parks and Forests appointed by the President's committee on outdoor recreation, be designated to survey and reclassify the national monument system and devise administrative standards for its proper maintenance. He is of the opinion that only archaeologic, geologic, and wild-life reservations should be retained in the national monument system, which has developed essentially as a scientific classification, and that all memorial areas in the Federal lands having to do with the white man's occupancy of America, including the national military parks, should be grouped into a system under the descriptive title of national historical parks.

The usefulness of the national monuments is practically limited to science and scientific study. In State and private lands, and in the Federal lands, scientific and historical examples are rapidly passing. Now is the time to preserve the best of them if they are to be preserved at all. In nearly all States societies are busy buying up for preservation spots of particular interest and value, and State funds are constantly sought and sometimes procured for this purpose. The National Government should set apart for preservation those scientific and historical places of real value which lie within its own immense lands.

FRANKLIN D. ROOSEVELT AND HIGHWAY TREE PLANTINGS*
1930

While he was still governor of New York, Franklin D. Roosevelt recommended that part of the state's highway maintenance money be used for "tree plantings." His letter to the New York legislature is reproduced below.

Albany, March 25, 1930

To the Legislature:

I recommend to your honorable bodies the authorization of the use of the sum of $10,000 from the highway maintenance money already appropriated, in order that the Department of Public Works with the cooperation of the Conservation Department may set out one stretch of highway tree planting in each of the ten highway districts. These plantings would be in part of an experimental nature but primarily for the purpose of demonstration to the people of the state that the highways could and should be more sightly. An increasingly large body of public opinion recognizes the beauty of tree-lined highways as well as their economic value.

If the state itself sets the example even in a small way, I am certain that communities and individuals will follow it in a large way. Perhaps, too, a greater realization of beauty by those who use our highways may lead us some day to the elimination of those excrescences on the landscape known as advertising signs.

Franklin D. Roosevelt

*Edgar B. Nixon, *Franklin D. Roosevelt and Conservation: 1911–1945,* Vol. 1 (Washington, D.C.: Government Printing Office, 1957), 71.

THE HISTORIC SITES ACT*
August 21, 1935

This act represented a real breakthrough because it authorized the National Park Service to acquire historic sites and buildings "by gift, purchase or otherwise," and in addition established an Advisory Board on National Parks, Historic Sites, Buildings and Monuments.

An Act to provide for the preservation of historic American sites, buildings, objects and antiquities of national significance, and for other purposes.

Be it enacted by the Senate and House of Representatives of the United States of America in Congress assembled, That it is hereby declared that it is a national policy to preserve for public use historic sites, buildings and objects of national significance for the inspiration and benefit of the people of the United States.

SEC. 2. The Secretary of the Interior (hereinafter referred to as the Secretary), through the National Park Service, for the purpose of effectuating the policy expressed in section 1 hereof, shall have the following powers and perform the following duties and functions:

(a) Secure, collate, and preserve drawings, plans, photographs, and other data of historic and archaeologic sites, buildings, and objects.

(b) Make a survey of historic and archaeologic sites, buildings, and objects for the purpose of determining which possess exceptional value as commemorating or illustrating the history of the United States.

(c) Make necessary investigations and researches in the United States relating to particular sites, buildings, or objects to obtain true and accurate historical and archaeological facts and information concerning the same.

(d) For the purpose of this Act, acquire in the name of the United States by gift, purchase, or otherwise any property, personal or real, or any interest or estate therein, title to any real property to be satisfactory to the Secretary: *Provided,* That no such property which is owned by any religious or educational institution, or which is owned or administered for the benefit of the public shall be so acquired without the consent of the owner: *Provided further,* That no such property shall be acquired or contract or agreement for the acquisition thereof made which will obligate the general fund of the Treasury for the payment of such property, unless or until Congress has appropriated money which is available for that purpose.

(e) Contract and make cooperative agreements with States, municipal subdivisions, corporations, associations, or individuals, with proper bond where

*49 *Statutes at Large,* 666.

deemed advisable, to protect, preserve, maintain, or operate any historic or archaeologic building, site, object, or property used in connection therewith for public use, regardless as to whether the title thereto is in the United States: *Provided,* That no contract or cooperative agreement shall be made or entered into which will obligate the general fund of the Treasury unless or until Congress has appropriated money for such purpose.

(f) Restore, reconstruct, rehabilitate, preserve, and maintain historic or prehistoric sites, buildings, objects, and properties of national historical or archaeological significance and where deemed desirable establish and maintain museums in connection therewith.

(g) Erect and maintain tablets to mark or commemorate historic or prehistoric places and events of national historical or archaeological significance.

(h) Operate and manage historic and archaeologic sites, buildings, and properties acquired under the provisions of this Act together with lands and subordinate buildings for the benefit of the public, such authority to include the power to charge reasonable visitation fees and grant concessions, leases, or permits for the use of land, building space, roads, or trails when necessary or desirable either to accommodate the public or to facilitate administration: *Provided,* That such concessions, leases, or permits, shall be let at competitive bidding, to the person making the highest and best bid.

(i) When the Secretary determines that it would be administratively burdensome to restore, reconstruct, operate, or maintain any particular historic or archaeologic site, building, or property donated to the United States through the National Park Service, he may cause the same to be done by organizing a corporation for that purpose under the laws of the District of Columbia or any State.

(j) Develop an educational program and service for the purpose of making available to the public facts and information pertaining to American historic and archaeologic sites, buildings, and properties of national significance. Reasonable charges may be made for the dissemination of any such facts or information.

(k) Perform any and all acts, and make such rules and regulations not inconsistent with this Act as may be necessary and proper to carry out the provisions thereof. Any person violating any of the rules and regulations authorized by this Act shall be punished by a fine of not more than $500 and be adjudged to pay all cost of the proceedings.

SEC. 3. A general advisory board to be known as the "Advisory Board on National Parks, Historic Sites, Buildings, and Monuments" is hereby established, to be composed of not to exceed eleven persons, citizens of the United States, to include representatives competent in the fields of history, archaeology, architecture, and human geography, who shall be appointed by the Secretary and serve at his pleasure. The members of such board shall receive no salary but may be paid expenses incidental to travel when engaged in discharging their duties as such members.

It shall be the duty of such board to advise on any matters relating to national parks and to the administration of this Act submitted to it for consideration by the Secretary. It may also recommend policies to the Secretary from time to time pertaining to national parks and to the restoration, reconstruction, conservation, and general administration of historic and archaeologic sites, buildings, and properties.

SEC. 4. The Secretary, in administering this Act, is authorized to cooperate with and may seek and accept the assistance of any Federal, State, or municipal department or agency, or any educational or scientific institution, or any patriotic association, or any individual.

(b) When deemed necessary, technical advisory committees may be established to act in an advisory capacity in connection with the restoration or reconstruction of any historic or prehistoric building or structure.

(c) Such professional and technical assistance may be employed without regard to the civil-service laws, and such service may be established as may be required to accomplish the purposes of this Act and for which money may be appropriated by Congress or made available by gifts for such purpose.

SEC. 5. Nothing in this Act shall be held to deprive any State, or political subdivision thereof, of its civil and criminal jurisdiction in and over lands acquired by the United States under this Act.

SEC. 6. There is authorized to be appropriated for carrying out the purposes of this Act such sums as the Congress may from time to time determine.

SEC. 7. The provisions of this Act shall control if any of them are in conflict with any other Act or Acts relating to the same subject matter.

Approved, August 21, 1935.

THE BLUE RIDGE PARKWAY ACT*
June 30, 1936

This landmark legislation, reproduced below, provided for one of America's first "recreation roads."

An Act to provide for the administration and maintenance of the
Blue Ridge Parkway, in the States of Virginia and North Carolina,
by the Secretary of the Interior, and for other purposes.

Be it enacted by the Senate and House of Representatives of the United States of America in Congress assembled, That hereafter all lands and easements conveyed or to be conveyed to the United States by the States of Virginia and North Carolina for the right-of-way for the projected parkway between the Shenandoah and Great Smoky Mountains National Parks, together with sites acquired or to be acquired for recreational areas in connection therewith, and a right-of-way for said parkway of a width sufficient to include the highway and all bridges, ditches, cuts, and fills appurtenant thereto, but not exceeding a maximum of two hundred feet through Government-owned lands as designated on maps heretofore or hereafter approved by the Secretary of the Interior, shall be known as the Blue Ridge Parkway and shall be administered and maintained by the Secretary of the Interior through the National Park Service, subject to the provisions of the Act of Congress approved August 25, 1916 (39 Stat. 535), entitled "An Act to establish a National Park Service, and for other purposes", the provisions of which Act, as amended and supplemented, are hereby extended over and made applicable to said parkway: *Provided,* That the Secretary of Agriculture is hereby authorized, with the concurrence of the Secretary of the Interior, to connect with the parkway such roads and trails as may be necessary for the protection, administration, or utilization of adjacent and nearby national forests and the resources thereof: *And provided further,* That the Forest Service and the National Park Service shall, insofar as practicable, coordinate and correlate such recreational development as each may plan, construct, or permit to be constructed, on lands within their respective jurisdictions which, by mutual agreement, should be given special treatment for recreational purposes.

Approved, June 30, 1936.

*49 *Statutes at Large,* 2041.

THE NATIONAL TRUST FOR HISTORIC PRESERVATION*
October 26, 1949

The act which follows created a "National Trust for Historic Preservation in the United States." The Trust was authorized to receive donations of historic sites and buildings and to preserve and administer them, and could also accept money and other gifts to help carry out its program.

An Act to further the policy enunciated in the Historic Sites Act (49 Stat. 666) and to facilitate public participation in the preservation of sites, buildings, and objects of national significance or interest and providing a national trust for historic preservation.

Be it enacted by the Senate and House of Representatives of the United States of America in Congress assembled, That, in order to further the policy enunciated in the Act of August 21, 1935 (49 Stat. 666), entitled "An Act to provide for the preservation of historic American sites, buildings, objects, and antiquities of national significance, and for other purposes", and to facilitate public participation in the preservation of sites, buildings, and objects of national significance or interest, there is hereby created a charitable, educational, and nonprofit corporation, to be known as the National Trust for Historic Preservation in the United States, hereafter referred to as the "National Trust". The purposes of the National Trust shall be to receive donations of sites, buildings, and objects significant in American history and culture, to preserve and administer them for public benefit, to accept, hold, and administer gifts of money, securities, or other property of whatsoever character for the purpose of carrying out the preservation program, and to execute such other functions as are vested in it by this Act.

SEC. 2. The National Trust shall have its principal office in the District of Columbia and shall be deemed, for purposes of venue in civil actions, to be an inhabitant and resident thereof. The National Trust may establish offices in such other place or places as it may deem necessary or appropriate in the conduct of its business.

SEC. 3. The affairs of the National Trust shall be under the general direction of a board of trustees composed as follows: The Attorney General of the United States; the Secretary of the Interior; and the Director of the National Gallery of Art, ex officio; and not less than six general trustees who shall be citizens of the United States, to be chosen as hereinafter provided. The Attorney General, and the Secretary of the Interior, when it appears desirable in the interest of the conduct of the business of the board and to such extent as they deem it advisable, may, by written notice to the National Trust, designate any officer of their

*63 *Statutes at Large,* 927.

respective departments to act for them in the discharge of their duties as a member of the board of trustees. The number of general trustees shall be fixed by the Executive Board of the National Council for Historic Sites and Buildings, a corporation of the District of Columbia, and the general trustees first taking office shall be chosen by a majority vote of the members of the Executive Board from the membership of the National Council. The respective terms of office of the first general trustees so chosen shall be as prescribed by the said Executive Board but in no case shall exceed a period of five years from the date of election. A successor to a general trustee shall be chosen in the same manner as the original trustees and shall have a term expiring five years from the date of the expiration of the term for which his predecessor was chosen, except that a successor chosen to fill a vacancy occuring prior to the expiration of such term shall be chosen only for the remainder of that term. The chairman of the board of trustees shall be elected by a majority vote of the members of the board. No compensation shall be paid to the members of the board of trustees for their services as such members, but they shall be reimbursed for travel and actual expenses necessarily incurred by them in attending board meetings and performing other official duties on behalf of the National Trust at the direction of the board.

Sec. 4. To the extent necessary to enable it to carry out the functions vested in it by this Act, the National Trust shall have the following general powers:

(a) To have succession until dissolved by Act of Congress, in which event title to the properties of the National Trust, both real and personal, shall, insofar as consistent with existing contractual obligations and subject to all other legally enforceable claims or demands by or against the National Trust, pass to and become vested in the United States of America.

(b) To sue and be sued in its corporate name.

(c) To adopt, alter, and use a corporate seal which shall be judicially noticed.

(d) To adopt a constitution and to make such bylaws, rules, and regulations, not inconsistent with the laws of the United States or of any State, as it deems necessary for the administration of its functions under this Act, including among other matter, bylaws, rules, and regulations governing visitation to historic properties, administration of corporate funds, and the organization and procedure of the board of trustees.

(e) To accept, hold, and administer gifts and bequests of money, securities, or other personal property of whatsoever character, absolutely or on trust, for the purposes for which the National Trust is created. Unless otherwise restricted by the terms of the gift or bequest, the National Trust is authorized to sell, exchange, or otherwise dispose of and to invest or reinvest in such investments as it may determine from time to time the moneys, securities, or other property given or bequeathed to it. The principal of such corporate funds, together with the income therefrom and all other revenues received by it from any source whatsoever, shall be placed in such depositories as the National Trust shall determine and shall be subject to expenditure by the National Trust for its corporate purposes.

(f) To acquire by gift, devise, purchase, or otherwise, absolutely or on trust, and to hold and, unless otherwise restricted by the terms of the gift or devise, to encumber, convey, or otherwise dispose of, any real property, or any estate or interest therein (except property within the exterior boundaries of national parks and national monuments), as may be necessary and proper in carrying into effect the purposes of the National Trust.

(g) To contract and make cooperative agreements with Federal, State, or municipal departments or agencies, corporations, associations or individuals, under such terms and conditions as it deems advisable, respecting the protection, preservation, maintenance, or operation of any historic site, building, object, or property used in connection therewith for public use, regardless of whether the National Trust has acquired title to such properties, or any interest therein.

(h) To enter into contracts generally and to execute all instruments necessary or appropriate to carry out its corporate purposes, which instruments shall include such concession contracts, leases, or permits for the use of lands, buildings, or other property deemed desirable either to accommodate the public or to facilitate administration.

(i) To appoint and prescribe the duties of such officers, agents, and employees as may be necessary to carry out its functions, and to fix and pay such compensation to them for their services as the National Trust may determine.

(j) And generally to do any and all lawful acts necessary or appropriate to carry out the purposes for which the National Trust is created.

SEC. 5. In carrying out its functions under this Act, the National Trust is authorized to consult with the Advisory Board on National Parks, Historic Sites, Buildings, and Monuments, on matters relating to the selection of sites, buildings, and objects to be preserved and protected pursuant hereto.

SEC. 6. The National Trust shall, on or before the 1st day of March in each year, transmit to Congress a report of its proceedings and activities for the preceding calendar year, including the full and complete statement of its receipts and expenditures.

SEC. 7. The right to repeal, alter or amend this Act at any time is hereby expressly reserved, but no contract or individual right made or acquired shall thereby be divested or impaired.

Approved October 26, 1949.

SPECIAL MESSAGE FROM PRESIDENT JOHN F. KENNEDY ON NATURAL RESOURCES*
February 23, 1961

One month and three days after he took office, President Kennedy sent his first message to Congress on natural resources—much of this volume is directly or indirectly concerned with the contents of that message. Throughout President Kennedy's speech there was a note of urgency; he stressed the need to act quickly in the race to preserve and improve the environment of the inner space in which we live. A major portion of the President's speech is reproduced below.

To the Congress of the United States:

From the beginning of civilization, every nation's basic wealth and progress has stemmed in large measure from its natural resources. This nation has been, and is now, especially fortunate in the blessings we have inherited. Our entire society rests upon—and is dependent upon—our water, our land, our forests, and our minerals. How we use these resources influences our health, security, economy, and well-being.

But if we fail to chart a proper course of conservation and development—if we fail to use these blessings prudently—we will be in trouble within a short time. In the resource field, predictions of future use have been consistently understated. But even under conservative projections, we face a future of critical shortages and handicaps. By the year 2000, a United States population of 300 million—nearly doubled in 40 years—will need far greater supplies of farm products, timber, water, minerals, fuels, energy, and opportunities for outdoor recreation. Present projections tell us that our water use will double in the next 20 years; that we are harvesting our supply of high-grade timber more rapidly than the development of new growth; that too much of our fertile topsoil is being washed away; that our minerals are being exhausted at increasing rates; and that the Nation's remaining undeveloped areas of great natural beauty are being rapidly preempted for other uses.

Wise investment in a resource program today will return vast dividends tomorrow, and failures to act now may be opportunities lost forever. Our country has been generous with us in this regard—and we cannot now ignore her needs for future development.

This is not a matter of concern for only one section of the country. All those who fish and hunt, who build industrial centers, who need electricity to light their homes and lighten their burdens, who require water for home, industrial, and recreational purposes—in short, every citizen of every state of the Union—

Public Papers of the Presidents of the United States: John F. Kennedy, 1961 (Washington, D.C.: Government Printing Office, 1962), p. 114–21.

all have a stake in a sound resources program under the progressive principles of national leadership first forged by Pinchot and Theodore Roosevelt, and backed by the essential cooperation of state and local governments.

This statement is designed to bring together in one message the widely scattered resource policies of the Federal Government. In the past, these policies have overlapped and often conflicted. Funds were wasted on competing efforts. Widely differing standards were applied to measure the Federal contribution to similar projects. Funds and attention devoted to annual appropriations or immediate pressures diverted energies away from long-range planning for national economic growth. Fees and user charges wholly inconsistent with each other, with value received, and with public policy have been imposed at some Federal developments.

To coordinate all of these matters among the various agencies, I will shortly issue one or more Executive Orders or directives:

(1) Redefining these responsibilities within the Executive Office and authorizing a strengthened Council of Economic Advisers to report to the President, the Congress and the public on the status of resource programs in relation to national needs;

(2) Establishing, under the Council of Economic Advisers, a Presidential Advisory Committee on Natural Resources, representing the Federal agencies concerned in this area and seeking the advice of experts outside of government; and

(3) Instructing the Budget Director, in consultation with the Departments and agencies concerned, to formulate within the next 90 days general principles for the application of fees, permits and other user charges at all types of Federal natural resource projects or areas; and to reevaluate current standards for appraising the feasibility of water resource projects.

In addition, to provide a coordinated framework for our research programs in this area, and to chart the course for the wisest and most efficient use of the research talent and facilities we possess, I shall ask the National Academy of Sciences to undertake a thorough and broadly based study and evaluation of the present state of research underlying the conservation, development, and use of natural resources, how they are formed, replenished and may be substituted for, and giving particular attention to needs for basic research and to projects that will provide a better basis for natural resources planning and policy formulation. Pending the recommendations of the Academy, I have directed my Science Advisor and the Federal Council for Science and Technology to review ongoing Federal research activities in the field of natural resources and to determine ways to strengthen the total government research effort relating to natural resources.

1. WATER RESOURCES

Our Nation has been blessed with a bountiful supply of water; but it is not a blessing we can regard with complacency. We now use over 300 billion gallons of water a day, much of it wastefully. By 1980 we will need 600 billion gallons a day.

Our supply of water is not always consistent with our needs of time and place. Floods one day in one section may be countered in other days or in other sections by the severe water shortages which are now afflicting many Eastern urban areas and particularly critical in the West. Our available water supply must be used to give maximum benefits for all purposes—hydroelectric power, irrigation and reclamation, navigation, recreation, health, home and industry. If all areas of the country are to enjoy a balanced growth, our Federal Reclamation and other water resource programs will have to give increased attention to municipal and industrial water and power supplies as well as irrigation and land redemption; and I am so instructing the Secretary of the Interior, in cooperation with the Secretary of Agriculture and the Secretary of the Army.

* * *

2. *WATER AND AIR POLLUTION CONTROL*

Pollution of our country's rivers and streams has—as a result of our rapid population and industrial growth and change—reached alarming proportions. To meet all needs—domestic, agricultural, industrial, recreational—we shall have to use and reuse the same water, maintaining quality as well as quantity. In many areas of the country we need new sources of supply—but in all areas we must protect the supplies we have.

Current corrective efforts are not adequate. This year a national total of $350 million will be spent from all sources on municipal waste treatment works. But $600 million of construction is required annually to keep pace with the growing rate of pollution. Industry is lagging far behind in its treatment of wastes.

* * *

3. *SALINE AND BRACKISH WATER CONVERSION*

No water resources program is of greater long-range importance—for relief not only of our shortages, but for arid nations the world over—than our efforts to find an effective and economical way to convert water from the world's greatest, cheapest natural resources—our oceans—into water fit for consumption in the home and by industry. Such a breakthrough would end bitter struggles between neighbors, states, and nations—and bring new hope for millions who live out their lives in dire shortage of usable water and all its physical and economical blessings, though living on the edge of a great body of water throughout that parched life-time.

This Administration is currently engaged in redoubled efforts to select the most promising approaches to economic desalinization of ocean and brackish waters, and then focus our energies more intensively on those approaches. At my request, a panel of the President's Science Advisory Committee has been working with the Secretary of the Interior to assure the most vigorous and effective research and development program possible in this field.

I now pledge that, when this know-how is achieved, it will immediately be made available to every nation in the world who wishes it, along with appropriate technical and other assistance for its use. Indeed the United States welcomes now the cooperation of all other nations who wish to join in this effort at present.

I urge the Congress to extend the current saline water conversion research program, and to increase the funds for its continuation to a level commensurate with the effort our current studies will show to be needed—now estimated to be at least twice the level previously requested.

II. ELECTRIC POWER

To keep pace with the growth of our economy and national defense requirements, expansion of this Nation's power facilities will require intensive effort by all segments of our power industry. Through 1980, according to present estimates of the Federal Power Commission, total installed capacity should triple if we are to meet our nation's need for essential economic growth. Sustained heavy expansion by all power suppliers—public, cooperative and private—is clearly needed.

The role of the Federal Government in supplying an important segment of this power is now long established and must continue. We will meet our responsibilities in this field.

—Hydroelectric sites remaining in this country will be utilized and hydroelectric power will be incorporated in all multiple-purpose river projects where optimum economic use of the water justifies such action.

—The Tennessee Valley Authority will continue to use the financing authority granted it by the last Congress to meet the power needs of the area it serves.

—Our efforts to achieve economically competitive nuclear power before the end of this decade in areas where fossil fuel costs are high will be encouraged through basic research, engineering developments, and construction of various prototype and full scale reactors by the Atomic Energy Commission in cooperation with industry.

* * *

III. FORESTS

Our forest lands present the sharpest challenge to our foresight. Trees planted today will not reach the minimum sizes needed for lumber until the year 2000. Most projections of future timber requirements predict a doubling of current consumption within forty years. At present cutting rates, we are using up our old growth timber in Western stands. Because of the time requirements involved, we must move now to meet anticipated future needs, and improve the productivity of our nearly 500 million acres of commerical forest land.

Unfortunately, the condition of our forest land area is substantially below par: 45 million acres are in need of reforestation; more than 150 million acres require thinnings, release cuttings and other timber stand improvement measures if growth rates are to be increased and quality timber produced; forest protection must be extended to areas now poorly protected. Losses in growth from insects and disease need to be reduced substantially by wider application of known detection and control measures.

(A) I urge the Congress to accelerate forest development on Federal public lands both as a long-term investment measure and as an immediate method of relieving unemployment in distressed areas.

(B) To make additional supplies of merchantable timber available to small businesses. I have directed the Secretaries of Agriculture and the Interior to accelerate the program of building approved access roads to public forests.

(C) A more difficult and unresolved forest situation lies in that half of our forest land held in small private ownerships. These lands, currently far below their productive potential, must be managed to produce a larger share of our future timber needs. Current forest owner assistance programs have proven inadquate. I am therefore directing the Secretary of Agriculture, in cooperation with appropriate Federal and State agencies, to develop a program to help small independent timber owners and processors attain better forest management standards and more efficient production and utilization of forest crops.

IV. PUBLIC LANDS

The Federal Government owns nearly 770 million acres of public land, much of it devoted to a variety of essential uses. But equally important are the vacant unappropriated and unreserved public domain lands, amounting to some 477 million acres—a vital national reserve that should be devoted to productive use now and maintained for future generations.

Much of this public domain suffers from uncontrolled use and a lack of proper management. More than 100 million acres of our Federal Grazing Districts are producing livestock forage well below their potential. We can no longer afford to sit by while our public domain assets so deteriorate.

I am, therefore, directing the Secretary of the Interior to

(1) accelerate an inventory and evaluation of the nation's public domain holdings to serve as a foundation for improved resource management;

(2) develop a program of balanced usage designed to reconcile the con-

flicting uses—grazing, forestry, recreation, wildlife, urban development and minerals; and

(3) accelerate the installation of soil conserving and water saving works and practices to reduce erosion and improve forage capacity; and to proceed with the revegetation of range lands on which the forage capacity has been badly depleted or destroyed.

V. OCEAN RESOURCES

The sea around us represents one of our most important but least understood and almost wholly undeveloped areas for extending our resource base. Continental shelves bordering the United States contain roughly 20 percent of our remaining reserves of crude oil and natural gas. The ocean floor contains large and valuable deposits of cobalt, copper, nickel, and manganese. Ocean waters themselves contain a wide variety of dissolved salts and minerals.

Salt (and fresh water) fisheries are among our most important but far from fully developed reservoirs of protein foods. At present levels of use, this country alone will need an additional 3 billion pounds of fish and shellfish annually by 1980, and many other countries with large-scale protein deficiency can be greatly helped by more extensive use of marine foodstuffs. But all this will require increased efforts, under Federal leadership, for rehabilitation of depleted stocks of salmon and sardines in the Pacific, groundfish and oysters in the Atlantic, Lake Trout and other desirable species in the Great Lakes, and many others through biological research, development of methods for passing fish over dams, and control of pollution.

This Administration intends to give concerted attention to our whole national effort in the basic and applied research of oceanography. Construction of ship and shore facilities for ocean research and survey, the development of new instruments for charting the seas and gathering data, and the training of new scientific manpower will require the coordinated efforts of many Federal agencies. It is my intention to send to the Congress for its information and use in considering the 1962 budget, a national program for oceanography, setting forth the responsibilities and requirements of all participating government agencies.

VI. RECREATION

America's health, morale and culture have long benefitted from our National Parks and Forests, and our fish and wildlife opportunities. Yet these facilities and resources are not now adequate to meet the needs of a fast-growing, more mobile population—and the millions of visitor days which are now spent in Federally-owned parks, forests, wildlife refuges and water reservoirs will triple well before the end of this century.

To meet the Federal Government's appropriate share of the responsibility for fulfilling these needs, the following steps are essential:

(A) To protect our remaining wilderness areas, I urge the Congress to enact a wilderness protection bill along the general lines of S. 174.

(B) To improve both the quality and quantity of public recreational opportunities, I urge the Congress to enact legislation leading to the establishment of seashore and shoreline areas such as Cape Cod, Padre Island and Point Reyes for the use and enjoyment of the public. Unnecessary delay in acquiring these shores so vital to an adequate public recreation system results in tremendously increased costs.

(C) For similar reasons, I am instructing the Secretary of the Interior, in cooperation with the Secretary of Agriculture and other appropriate Federal, state and local officials and private leaders to

— formulate a comprehensive Federal recreational lands program;

— conduct a survey to determine where additional national parks, forests and seashore areas should be proposed;

— take steps to insure that land acquired for the construction of Federally-financed reservoirs is sufficient to permit future development for recreational purposes; and

— establish a long-range program for planning and providing adequate open spaces for recreational facilities in urban areas.

I am also hopeful that consistent and coordinated Federal leadership can expand our fish and wildlife opportunities without the present conflicts of agencies and interests: One department paying to have wetlands drained for agricultural purposes while another is purchasing such lands for wildlife or water fowl refuges—one agency encouraging chemical pesticides that may harm the song birds and game birds whose preservation is encouraged by another agency—conflicts between private land owners and sportsmen—uncertain responsibility for the watershed and anti-pollution programs that are vital to our fish and wildlife opportunities.

I am directing the Secretary of the Interior to take the lead, with other Federal and state officials, to end these conflicts and develop a long-range wildlife conservation program—and to accelerate the acquisition of upper midwest wetlands through the sale of Federal duck stamps.

CONCLUSION

Problems of immediacy always have the advantage of attracting notice— those that lie in the future fare poorly in the competition for attention and money. It is not a task which should or can be done by the Federal Government alone. Only through the fullest participation and cooperation of State and local governments and private industry can it be done wisely and effectively. We cannot, however, delude ourselves—we must understand our resources problems, and we must face up to them now. The task is large but it will be done.

SPECIAL MESSAGE FROM PRESIDENT JOHN F. KENNEDY
ON THE FEDERAL HIGHWAY PROGRAM*
February 28, 1961

In a special message to Congress on the Federal Highway Program, President Kennedy spoke of the effect of billboads on the scenic values of highways. That portion of the message dealing with highway beautification is documented here.

V. BILLBOARD CONTROL

The Interstate Highway System was intended, among other purposes, to enable more Americans to more easily see more of their country. It is a beautiful country. The system was not intended to provide a large and unreimbursed measure of benefits to the billboard industry, whose structures tend to detract from both the beauty and the safety of the routes they line. Their messages are not, as so often claimed, primarily for the convenience of the motorist whose view they block. Some two-thirds of such advertising is for national products, and is dominated by a handful of large advertisers to whom the Interstate System has provided a great wind-fall.

The Congress took a wise though very modest step in 1958 by authorizing, through Section 122 of the 1958 Act, the control of outdoor advertising within designated limits of the routes of the Interstate System. States electing to comply with the Federal standards promulgated under that section were to receive an incentive payment of an extra one-half of 1 percent of the cost of interstate highway projects within the State.

Unfortunately that provision expires on June 30th of this year, and a variety of pressures has prevented all but one state (Maryland) from taking advantage of this provision. I urge the Congress to extend this billboard control section for four more years; and to increase the incentive bonus from ½ to 1% of a State's allotment. Should this measure still prove to be insufficient, it may be necessary to adopt more direct means of control, or to at least charge the billboard owners for the benefits they are receiving.

* * *

John F. Kennedy

Public Papers of the Presidents of the United States: John F. Kennedy, 1961 (Washington, D.C.: Government Printing Office, 1962), 126, 132–33.

SPECIAL MESSAGE FROM PRESIDENT LYNDON B. JOHNSON
ON CONSERVATION AND RESTORATION OF NATURAL BEAUTY*
February 8, 1965

President Johnson outlined a comprehensive program to restore natural beauty in this message to Congress. Within the next three years a substantial portion of the President's program was enacted into law.

To the Congress of the United States:

For centuries Americans have drawn strength and inspiration from the beauty of our country. It would be a neglectful generation indeed, indifferent alike to the judgment of history and the command of principle, which failed to preserve and extend such a heritage for its descendants.

Yet the storm of modern change is threatening to blight and diminish in a few decades what has been cherished and protected for generations.

A growing population is swallowing up areas of natural beauty with its demands for living space, and is placing increased demand on our overburdened areas of recreation and pleasure.

The increasing tempo of urbanization and growth is already depriving many Americans of the right to live in decent surroundings. More of our people are crowding into cities and being cut off from nature. Cities themselves reach out into the countryside, destroying streams and trees and meadows as they go. A modern highway may wipe out the equivalent of a fifty acre park with every mile. And people move out from the city to get closer to nature only to find that nature has moved farther from them.

The modern technology, which has added much to our lives can also have a darker side. Its uncontrolled waste products are menacing the world we live in, our enjoyment and our health. The air we breathe, our water, our soil and wildlife, are being blighted by the poisons and chemicals which are the by-products of technology and industry. The skeletons of discarded cars litter the countryside. The same society which receives the rewards of technology, must, as a co-operating whole, take responsibility for control.

To deal with these new problems will require a new conservation. We must not only protect the countryside and save it from destruction, we must restore what has been destroyed and salvage the beauty and charm of our cities. Our conservation must be not just the classic conservation of protection and development, but a creative conservation of restoration and innovation. Its concern is

Public Papers of the Presidents of the United States: Lyndon B. Johnson, 1965, Book 1 (Washington, D.C.: Government Printing Office, 1966), 155–65.

not with nature alone, but with the total relation between man and the world around him. Its object is not just man's welfare but the dignity of man's spirit.

In this conservation the protection and enhancement of man's opportunity to be in contact with beauty must play a major role.

This means that beauty must not be just a holiday treat, but a part of our daily life. It means not just easy physical access, but equal social access for rich and poor, Negro and white, city dweller and farmer.

Beauty is not an easy thing to measure. It does not show up in the gross national product, in a weekly pay check, or in profit and loss statements. But these things are not ends in themselves. They are a road to satisfaction and pleasure and the good life. Beauty makes its own direct contribution to these final ends. Therefore it is one of the most important components of our true national income, not to be left out simply because statisticians cannot calculate its worth.

And some things we do know. Association with beauty can enlarge man's imagination and revive his spirit. Ugliness can demean the people who live among it. What a citizen sees every day is his America. If it is attractive it adds to the quality of his life. If it is ugly it can degrade his existence.

Beauty has other immediate values. It adds to safety whether removing direct dangers to health or making highways less monotonous and dangerous. We also know that those who live in blighted and squalid conditions are more susceptible to anxieties and mental disease.

Ugliness is costly. It can be expensive to clean a soot smeared building, or to build new areas of recreation when the old landscape could have been preserved far more cheaply.

Certainly no one would hazard a national definition of beauty. But we do know that nature is nearly always beautiful. We do, for the most part, know what is ugly. And we can introduce, into all our planning, our programs, our building and our growth, a conscious and active concern for the values of beauty. If we do this then we can be successful in preserving a beautiful America.

There is much the federal government can do, through a range of specific programs, and as a force for public education. But a beautiful America will require the effort of government at every level, of business, and of private groups. Above all it will require the concern and action of individual citizens, alert to danger, determined to improve the quality of their surroundings, resisting blight, demanding and building beauty for themselves and their children.

I am hopeful that we can summon such a national effort. For we have not chosen to have an ugly America. We have been careless, and often neglectful. But now that the danger is clear and the hour is late this people can place themselves in the path of a tide of blight which is often irreversible and always destructive.

The Congress and the Executive branch have each produced conservation giants in the past. During the 88th Congress it was legislative executive teamwork that brought progress. It is this same kind of partnership that will ensure our continued progress.

In that spirit as a beginning and stimulus I make the following proposals:

THE CITIES

Thomas Jefferson wrote that communities "should be planned with an eye to the effect made upon the human spirit by being continually surrounded with a maximum of beauty."

We have often sadly neglected this advice in the modern American city. Yet this is where most of our people live. It is where the character of our young is formed. It is where American civilization will be increasingly concentrated in years to come.

Such a challenge will not be met with a few more parks or playgrounds. It requires attention to the architecture of building, the structure of our roads, preservation of historical buildings and monuments, careful planning of new suburbs. A concern for the enhancement of beauty must infuse every aspect of the growth and development of metropolitan areas. It must be a principal responsibility of local government, supported by active and concerned citizens.

Federal assistance can be a valuable stimulus and help to such local efforts.

I have recommended a community extension program which will bring the resources of the university to focus on problems of the community just as they have long been concerned with our rural areas. Among other things, this program will help provide training and technical assistance to aid in making our communities more attractive and vital. In addition, under the Housing Act of 1964, grants will be made to States for training of local governmental employees needed for community development. I am recommending a 1965 supplemental appropriation to implement this program.

We now have two programs which can be of special help in creating areas of recreation and beauty for our metropolitan area population: the Open Space Land Program, and the Land and Water Conservation Fund.

I have already proposed full funding of the Land and Water Conservation Fund, and directed the Secretary of the Interior to give priority attention to serving the needs of our growing urban population.

The primary purpose of the Open Space Program has been to help acquire and assure open spaces in urban areas. I propose a series of new matching grants for improving the natural beauty of urban open space.

The Open Space Program should be adequately financed, and broadened by permitting grants to be made to help city governments acquire and clear areas to create small parks, squares, pedestrian malls and playgrounds.

In addition I will request authority in this program for a matching program to cities for landscaping, installation of outdoor lights and benches, creating attractive cityscapes along roads and in business areas, and for other beautification purposes.

Our city parks have not, in many cases, realized their full potential as sources of pleasure and play. I recommend on a matching basis a series of federal demonstration projects in city parks to use the best thought and action to show how the appearance of these parks can better serve the people of our towns and metropolitan areas.

All of these programs should be operated on the same matching formula to avoid unnecessary competition among programs and increase the possibility of cooperative effort. I will propose such a standard formula.

In a future message on the cities I will recommend other changes in our housing programs designed to strengthen the sense of community of which natural beauty is an important component.

In almost every part of the country citizens are rallying to save landmarks of beauty and history. The government must also do its share to assist these local efforts which have an important national purpose. We will encourage and support the National Trust for Historic Preservation in the United States, chartered by Congress in 1949. I shall propose legislation to authorize supplementary grants to help local authorities acquire, develop and manage private properties for such purposes.

The Registry of National Historic Landmarks is a fine federal program with virtually no federal cost. I commend its work and the new wave of interest it has evoked in historical preservation.

THE COUNTRYSIDE

Our present system of parks, seashores and recreation areas—monuments to the dedication and labor of far-sighted men—do not meet the needs of a growing population.

The full funding of the Land and Water Conservation Fund will be an important step in making this a Parks-for-America decade.

I propose to use this fund to acquire lands needed to establish:

Assateague Island National Seashore, Maryland-Virginia
Tocks Island National Recreation Area, New Jersey-Pennsylvania
Cape Lookout National Seashore, North Carolina
Sleeping Bear Dunes National Lakeshore, Michigan
Indiana Dunes National Lakeshore, Indiana
Oregon Dunes National Seashore, Oregon
Great Basin National Park, Nevada
Guadalupe Mountains National Park, Texas
Spruce Knob, Seneca Rocks National Recreation Area, West Virginia

Bighorn Canyon National Recreation Area, Montana-Wyoming
Flaming Gorge National Recreation, Utah-Wyoming
Whiskeytown-Shasta-Trinity National Recreation Area, California.

In addition, I have requested the Secretary of Interior, working with interested groups, to conduct a study on the desirability of establishing a Redwood National Park in California.

I will also recommend that we add prime outdoor recreation areas to our National Forest system, particularly in the populous East; and proceed on schedule with studies required to define and enlarge the Wilderness System established by the 88th Congress. We will also continue progress on our refuge system for migratory waterfowl.

Faulty strip and surface mining practices have left ugly scars which mar the beauty of the landscape in many of our States. I urge your strong support of the nationwide strip and surface mining study provided by the Appalachian Regional legislation, which will furnish the factual basis for a fair and reasonable approach to the correction of these past errors.

I am asking the Secretary of Agriculture to work with State and local organizations in developing a cooperative program for improving the beauty of the privately owned rural lands which comprise three-fourths of the Nation's area. Much can be done within existing Department of Agriculture programs without adding to cost.

The 28 million acres of land presently held and used by our Armed Services is an important part of our public estate. Many thousands of these acres will soon become surplus to military needs. Much of this land has great potential for outdoor recreation, wildlife, and conservation uses consistent with military requirements. This potential must be realized through the fullest application of multiple-use principles. To this end I have directed the Secretaries of Defense and Interior to conduct a "conservation inventory" of all surplus lands.

HIGHWAYS

More than any country ours is an automobile society. For most Americans the automobile is a principal instrument of transportation, work, daily activity, recreation and pleasure. By making our roads highways to the enjoyment of nature and beauty we can greatly enrich the life of nearly all our people in city and countryside alike.

Our task is two-fold. First, to ensure that roads themselves are not destructive of nature and natural beauty. Second, to make our roads ways to recreation and pleasure.

I have asked the Secretary of Commerce to take a series of steps designed to meet this objective. This includes requiring landscaping on all federal interstate

[665]

primary and urban highways, encouraging the construction of rest and recreation areas along highways, and the preservation of natural beauty adjacent to highway rights-of-way.

Our present highway law permits the use of up to 3% of all federal-aid funds to be used without matching for the preservation of natural beauty. This authority has not been used for the purpose intended by Congress. I will take steps, including recommended legislation if necessary, to make sure these funds are, in fact, used to enhance beauty along our highway system. This will dedicate substantial resources to this purpose.

I will also recommend that a portion of the funds now used for secondary roads be set aside in order to provide access to areas of rest and recreation and scenic beauty along our nation's roads, and for rerouting or construction of highways for scenic or parkway purposes.

The Recreation Advisory Council is now completing a study of the role which scenic roads and parkways should play in meeting our highway and recreation needs. After receiving the report, I will make appropriate recommendations.

The authority for the existing program of outdoor advertising control expires on June 30, 1965 and its provisions have not been effective in achieving the desired goal. Accordingly, I will recommend legislation to ensure effective control of billboards along our highways.

In addition, we need urgently to work towards the elimination or screening of unsightly, beauty-destroying junkyards and auto graveyards along our highways. To this end, I will also recommend necessary legislation to achieve effective control, including Federal assistance in appropriate cases where necessary.

I hope that, at all levels of government, our planners and builders will remember that highway beautification is more than a matter of planting trees or setting aside scenic areas. The roads themselves must reflect, in location and design, increased respect for the natural and social integrity and unity of the landscape and communities through which they pass.

RIVERS

Those who first settled this continent found much to marvel at. Nothing was a greater source of wonder and amazement than the power and majesty of American rivers. They occupy a central place in myth and legend, folklore and literature.

They were our first highways, and some remain among the most important. We have had to control their ravages, harness their power, and use their water to help make whole regions prosper.

Yet even this seemingly indestructible natural resource is in danger.

Through our pollution control programs we can do much to restore our rivers. We will continue to conserve the water and power for tomorrow's needs with well-planned reservoirs and power dams. But the time has also come to identify and preserve free flowing stretches of our great scenic rivers before growth and development make the beauty of the unspoiled waterway a memory.

To this end I will shortly send to the Congress a Bill to establish a National Wild Rivers System.

THE POTOMAC

The river rich in history and memory which flows by our nation's capital should serve as a model of scenic and recreation values for the entire country. To meet this objective I am asking the Secretary of the Interior to review the Potomac River basin development plan now under review by the Chief of Army Engineers, and to work with the affected States and local governments, the District of Columbia and interested federal agencies to prepare a program for my consideration.

A program must be devised which will:

a. Clean up the river and keep it clean, so it can be used for boating, swimming and fishing.

b. Protect its natural beauties by the acquisition of scenic easements, zoning or other measures.

c. Provide adequate recreational facilities, and

d. Complete the presently authorized George Washington Memorial Parkway on both banks.

I hope action here will stimulate and inspire similar efforts by States and local governments on other urban rivers and waterfronts, such as the Hudson in New York. They are potentially the greatest single source of pleasure for those who live in most of our metropolitan areas.

TRAILS

The forgotten outdoorsmen of today are those who like to walk, hike, ride horseback or bicycle. For them we must have trails as well as highways. Nor should motor vehicles be permitted to tyrannize the more leisurely human traffic.

Old and young alike can participate. Our doctors recommend and encourage such activity for fitness and fun.

I am requesting, therefore, that the Secretary of the Interior work with his colleagues in the federal government and with state and local leaders and recommend to me a cooperative program to encourage a national system of trails, building up the more than hundred thousand miles of trails in our National Forests and Parks.

There are many new and exciting trail projects underway across the land. In

Arizona, a county has arranged for miles of irrigation canal banks to be used by riders and hikers. In Illinois, an abandoned railroad right of way is being developed as a "Prairie Path." In New Mexico utility rights of way are used as public trails.

As with so much of our quest for beauty and quality, each community has opportunities for action. We can and should have an abundance of trails for walking, cycling and horseback riding, in and close to our cities. In the back country we need to copy the great Appalachian Trail in all parts of America, and to make full use of rights of way and other public paths.

POLLUTION

One aspect of the advance of civilization is the evolution of responsibility for disposal of waste. Over many generations society gradually developed techniques for this purpose. State and local governments, landlords and private citizens have been held responsible for ensuring that sewage and garbage did not menace health or contaminate the environment.

In the last few decades entire new categories of waste have come to plague and menace the American scene. These are the technological wastes— the by-products of growth, industry, agriculture, and science. We cannot wait for slow evolution over generations to deal with them.

Pollution is growing at a rapid rate. Some pollutants are known to be harmful to health, while the effect of others is uncertain and unknown. In some cases we can control pollution with a larger effort. For other forms of pollution we still do not have effective means of control.

Pollution destroys beauty and menaces health. It cuts down on efficiency, reduces property values and raises taxes.

The longer we wait to act, the greater the dangers and the larger the problem.

Large-scale pollution of air and waterways is no respecter of political boundaries, and its effects extend far beyond those who cause it.

Air pollution is no longer confined to isolated places. This generation has altered the composition of the atmosphere on a global scale through radioactive materials and a steady increase in carbon dioxide from the burning of fossil fuels. Entire regional airsheds, crop plant environments, and river basins are heavy with noxious materials. Motor vehicles and home heating plants, municipal dumps and factories continually hurl pollutants into the air we breathe. Each day almost 50,000 tons of unpleasant, and sometimes poisonous, sulfur dioxide are added to the atmosphere, and our automobiles produce almost 300,000 tons of other pollutants.

In Donora, Pennsylvania in 1948, and New York City in 1953 serious illness and some deaths were produced by sharp increases in air pollution. In New Orleans, epidemic outbreaks of asthmatic attacks are associated with air pollutants. Three-fourths of the eight million people in the Los Angeles area are annoyed by severe eye irritation much of the year. And our health authorities are increasingly concerned with the damaging effects of the continual breathing of polluted air by all our people in every city in the country.

In addition to its health effects, air pollution creates filth and gloom and depreciates property values of entire neighborhoods. The White House itself is being dirtied with soot from polluted air.

Every major river system is now polluted. Waterways that were once sources of pleasure and beauty and recreation are forbidden to human contact and objectionable to sight and smell. Furthermore, this pollution is costly, requiring expensive treatment for drinking water and inhibiting the operation and growth of industry.

In spite of the efforts and many accomplishments of the past, water pollution is spreading. And new kinds of problems are being added to the old:

—Waterborne viruses, particularly hepatitis, are replacing typhoid fever as a significant health hazard.

—Mass deaths of fish have occurred in rivers over-burdened with wastes.

—Some of our rivers contain chemicals which, in concentrated form, produce abnormalities in animals.

—Last summer 2,600 square miles of Lake Erie—over a quarter of the entire Lake—were almost without oxygen and unable to support life because of algae and plant growths, fed by pollution from cities and farms.

In many older cities storm drains and sanitary sewers are interconnected. As a result, mixtures of storm water and sanitary waste overflow during rains and discharge directly into streams, bypassing treatment works and causing heavy pollution.

In addition to our air and water we must, each and every day, dispose of a half billion pounds of solid waste. These wastes—from discarded cans to discarded automobiles—litter our country, harbor vermin, and menace our health. Inefficient and improper methods of disposal increase pollution of our air and streams.

Almost all these wastes and pollutions are the result of activities carried on for the benefit of man. A prime national goal must be an environment that is pleasing to the senses and healthy to live in.

Our Government is already doing much in this field. We have made significant progress. But more must be done.

FEDERAL GOVERNMENT ACTIVITY

I am directing the heads of all agencies to improve measures to abate pollution caused by direct agency operation, contracts and cooperative agreements. Federal procurement practices must make sure that the Government equipment uses the most effective techniques for controlling pollution. The Administrator of General Services has already taken steps to assure that motor vehicles purchased by the Federal Government meet minimum standards of exhaust quality.

CLEAN WATER

Enforcement authority must be strengthened to provide positive controls over the discharge of pollutants into our interstate or navigable waters. I recommend enactment of legislation to:

—Provide, through the setting of effective water quality standards, combined with a swift and effective enforcement procedure, a national program to prevent water pollution at its source rather than attempting to cure pollution after it occurs.

—Increase project grant ceilings and provide additional incentives for multi-municipal projects under the waste treatment facilities construction program.

—Increase the ceilings for grants to State water pollution control programs.

—Provide a new research, and demonstration construction program leading to the solution of problems caused by the mixing of storm water runoff and sanitary wastes.

The Secretary of Health, Education, and Welfare will undertake an intensive program to clean up the Nation's most polluted rivers. With the cooperation of States and cities—using the tools of regulation, grant and incentives—we can bring the most serious problem of river pollution under control. We cannot afford to do less.

We will work with Canada to develop a pollution control program for the Great Lakes and other border waters.

Through an expanded program carried on by the Departments of Health, Education, and Welfare and Interior, we will continue to seek effective and economical methods for controlling pollution from acid mine drainage.

To improve the quality of our waters will require the fullest cooperation of our State and local governments. Working together, we can and will preserve and increase one of our most valuable national resources—clean water.

CLEAN AIR

The enactment of the Clean Air Act in December of 1963 represented a long step forward in our ability to understand and control the difficult problem of air pollution. The 1966 Budget request of 24 million dollars is almost double the amount spent on air pollution programs in the year prior to its enactment.

In addition, the Clean Air Act should be improved to permit the Secretary of Health, Education, and Welfare to investigate potential air pollution problems before pollution happens, rather than having to wait until the damage occurs, as is now the case, and to make recommendations leading to the prevention of such pollution.

One of the principal unchecked sources of air pollution is the automobile. I intend to institute discussions with industry officials and other interested groups leading to an effective elimination or substantial reduction of pollution from liquid fueled motor vehicles.

SOLID WASTES

Continuing technological progress and improvement in methods of manufacture, packaging and marketing of consumer products has resulted in an ever mounting increase of discarded material. We need to seek better solutions to the disposal of these wastes. I recommend legislation to:

—Assist the States in developing comprehensive programs for some forms of solid waste disposal.

—Provide for research and demonstration projects leading to more effective methods for disposing of or salvaging solid wastes.

—Launch a concentrated attack on the accumulation of junk cars by increasing research in the Department of the Interior leading to use of metal from scrap cars where promising leads already exist.

PESTICIDES

Pesticides may affect living organisms wherever they occur.

In order that we may better understand the effects of these compounds, I have included increased funds in the budget for use by the Secretaries of Agriculture, Interior, and Health, Education, and Welfare to increase their research efforts on pesticides so they can give special attention to the flow of pesticides through the environment; study the means by which pesticides break down and disappear in nature; and to keep a constant check on the level of pesticides in our water, air, soil and food supply.

I am recommending additional funds for the Secretary of Agriculture to reduce contamination from toxic chemicals through intensified research, regulatory control, and educational programs.

The Secretary of Agriculture will soon submit legislation to tighten control over the manufacture and use of agricultural chemcials, including licensing and factory inspection of manufacturers, clearly placing the burden of proof of safety on the proponent of the chemical rather than on the Government.

RESEARCH RESOURCES

Our needs for new knowledge and increasing application of existing knowledge demand a greater supply of trained manpower and research resources.

A National Center for Environmental Health Sciences is being planned as a

[671]

focal point for health research in this field. In addition, the 1966 budget includes funds for the establishment of university institutes to conduct research and training in environmental pollution problems.

Legislation recommended in my message on health has been introduced to increase Federal support for specialized research facilities of a national or regional character. This proposal, aimed at health research needs generally, would assist in the solution of environmental health problems and I urge its passage.

We need legislation to provide to the Departments of Agriculture and the Interior authority for grants for research in environmental pollution control in their areas of responsibility. I have asked the Secretary of Interior to submit legislation to eliminate the ceiling on pesticide research.

OTHER EFFORTS

In addition to these needed actions, other proposals are undergoing active study.

I have directed the Chairman of the Council of Economic Advisers, with the appropriate departments, to study the use of economic incentives as a technique to stimulate pollution prevention and abatement, and to recommend actions or legislation, if needed.

I have instructed the Director of the Bureau of the Budget and the Director of the Office of Science and Technology to explore the adequacy of the present organization of pollution control and research activities.

I have also asked the Director of the Office of Science and Technology and the Director of the Bureau of the Budget to recommend the best way in which the Federal government may direct efforts toward advancing our scientific understanding of natural plant and animal communities and their interaction with man and his activities.

The actions and proposals recommended in this message will take us a long way toward immediate reversal of the increase of pollutants in our environment. They will also give us time until new basic knowledge and trained manpower provide opportunities for more dramatic gains in the future.

WHITE HOUSE CONFERENCE

I intend to call a White House Conference on Natural Beauty to meet in mid-May of this year. Its chairman will be Mr. Laurance Rockefeller.

It is my hope that this Conference will produce new ideas and approaches for enhancing the beauty of America. Its scope will not be restricted to federal action. It will look for ways to help and encourage state and local governments, institutions and private citizens, in their own efforts. It can serve as a focal point for the large campaign of public education which is needed to alert Americans to the danger to their natural heritage and to the need for action.

In addition to other subjects which this Conference will consider, I recommend the following subjects for discussion in depth:

—Automobile junkyards. I am convinced that analysis of the technology and economics can help produce a creative solution to this vexing problem. The Bureau of Mines of the Interior Department can contribute technical advice to the conference, as can the scrap industry and the steel industry.

—Underground installation of utility transmission lines. Further research is badly needed to enable us to cope with this problem.

—The greatest single force that shapes the American landscape is private economic development. Our taxation policies should not penalize or discourage conservation and the preservation of beauty.

—Ways in which the Federal Government can, through information and technical assistance, help communities and states in their own programs of natural beauty.

—The possibilities of a national tree planting program carried on by government at every level, and private groups and citizens.

CONCLUSION

In my thirty-three years of public life I have seen the American system move to conserve the natural and human resources of our land.

TVA transformed an entire region that was "depressed." The rural electrification cooperatives brought electricity to lighten the burdens of rural America. We have seen the forests replanted by the CCC's, and watched Gifford Pinchot's sustained yield concept take hold on forestlands.

It is true that we have often been careless with our natural bounty. At times we have paid a heavy price for this neglect. But once our people were aroused to the danger, we have acted to preserve our resources for the enrichment of our country and the enjoyment of future generations.

The beauty of our land is a natural resource. Its preservation is linked to the inner prosperity of the human spirit.

The tradition of our past is equal to today's threat to that beauty. Our land will be attractive tomorrow only if we organize for action and rebuild and reclaim the beauty we inherited. Our stewardship will be judged by the foresight with which we carry out these programs. We must rescue our cities and countryside from blight with the same purpose and vigor with which, in other areas, we moved to save the forests and the soil.

Lyndon B. Johnson

The White House
February 8, 1965

REPORT OF THE PRESIDENT'S TASK FORCE
ON THE PRESERVATION OF NATURAL
BEAUTY: PRINCIPLES FOR ACTION*
1965

One of President Johnson's actions was to appoint a special task force on the preservation of natural beauty whose job was to review programs and progress in restoring natural beauty to America and to make recommendations for needed action. The summary and principles for action described in its report are reproduced here.

SUMMARY

The time was never better for action to conserve the natural beauty of this land.

The groundwork has been laid.

No vast proliferation of Federal activities or great new sums are needed.

Most of the money has already been funded.

Our great new conservation programs provide the machinery.

The States and local governments are primed to move.

With the spark of leadership, these elements can be harnessed for a powerful and invigorating program.

Thus, to our principal recommendations:

BUILD A FOCUS FOR NATURAL BEAUTY IN THE FEDERAL GOVERNMENT

Broaden the mandate of the Bureau of Outdoor Recreation to include natural beauty. Make it an independent agency under the Recreation Advisory Council.

Broaden the mandate of the Council and make it effective.

Write natural beauty into the statutes as a purpose of the various agencies. Create review boards to help them carry it out.

LAUNCH A NATIONAL PROGRAM OF LANDSCAPE AND TOWNSCAPE GRANTS

Provide seed money for local action: stir communities to put trees back on our streets and utility wires beneath them; to screen the desecration by auto junk-yards and gravel pits; to reclaim the once lovely streams that lie buried in refuse;

*The President's Task Force on Natural Beauty, *Report on the Preservation of Natural Beauty* (Washington, D.C.: Government Printing Office, 1965), 1–2, 27–28.

to open up the hidden beauty of our countrysides, and the riverfronts of our cities.

STRENGTHEN THE MAJOR FEDERAL
OPEN SPACE PROGRAMS

Give the HHFA program a good galvanic push.

Have BOR and HHFA agree on a concordat on their programs and get this news out to the States and local governments forthwith.

Stimulate a more aggressive use of new approaches to acquisition and development.

Earmark grants to promote regional open space action, streamside walkways and park strips, nature centers for children, conservation of private land through easements, better ways of landscaping and compressing parking areas.

OVERHAUL THE FEDERAL HIGHWAY PROGRAM SO THAT IT
WILL CREATE BEAUTY AND NOT DESTROY IT

Put teeth into Section 319 of the Highway Act so that the $100 million a year available for landscaping and recreation will be used for landscaping and recreation.

Start a national scenic highway program now.

Write natural beauty into the statutes as a major purpose of the highway program and make grants to States contingent on a practical recognition of this.

PUSH MEASURES THAT WILL MAKE OUR PARK AND
FOREST LANDS MORE USEFUL TO PEOPLE

Stimulate parks and forests managers to better land use by adoption of the classification system recommended by ORRRC.

Stop encroachment by establishing a board with power to veto Federal aid for projects which threaten park land.

Launch a program to reclaim the beauty of the riverways which run through our urban areas. Make the Potomac a major demonstration of what can be done.

HELP CITIES REHABILITATE THEIR
DETERIORATING PARK SYSTEMS

Use the anti-poverty program for training and expanding city park personnel. Put strong emphasis on neighborhood parks.

Right the Federal over-emphasis on capital improvement grants by providing more operating funds for city parks.

Establish Federal demonstration parks in the cities to introduce new ideas in design and uses.

[675]

Overhaul the sterile project approach of Federal agencies to the design of urban open spaces.

MAKE FEDERAL WATER RESOURCE PROJECTS
EMPHASIZE BEAUTY AS A MAJOR PURPOSE

Counter the engineering domination of the agencies by the addition of other professionals.

Overhaul standard cost benefit formulae so that they include beauty and other community benefits.

Step up Federal efforts for water and air pollution control.

STIMULATE PRIVATE EFFORTS FOR
CONSERVATION OF BEAUTY

Encourage the development of "civic trusts".

Review the tax policy to find the small but important changes that can encourage private expenditure.

Set up a system of awards to give recognition of outstanding examples of private and industrial efforts.

THE PRIVATE SECTOR

Every citizen should be enabled to express his concern with the quality of his environment.

. . . The President should invite private individuals and corporations to join in a campaign to promote natural beauty and to eliminate blight and ugliness by the suitable regulation of garbage dumps; auto junkyards; abandoned stripmines; scalped landscapes; gravel and sand pits; posts and overhead wires; trash heaps and litter.

A WHITE HOUSE CONFERENCE SHOULD BE CALLED AND
A PRESIDENTIAL PROCLAMATION SHOULD BE ISSUED

To identify and stimulate Federal, State and local levels of government in their respective responsibilities to preserve and improve the beauty of the Nation, the President should call a White House Conference on "America the Beautiful." The President should issue a declaration of the national purpose to incorporate considerations of natural beauty into the objectives of the programs by which the Federal Government affects the quality of the environment. Congress should be asked to approve a Joint Resolution embodying the principles of the Presidential Proclamation, and to amend statutory authorizations for Federal programs to make the enhancement of natural beauty a specific purpose of their planning and operation.

PRINCIPLES FOR ACTION

In conclusion, the Task Force presents the general findings which underlie its recommendations:

1. Even as a growing population with increasing leisure time makes ever greater demands for natural beauty in the United States, the supply is being depleted. There is a clear and present danger that our citizens will be denied their scenic, spiritual and historic patrimony.

2. The blight which spreads across our country does not represent a preference for the ugly, but rather a careless failure to grasp the potentialities of the beautiful. It can be remedied by encouraging greater awareness in Government of the day-by-day possibilities for improving the natural environment of the Nation.

3. The people of this democracy are making it clear that they reject an ugly America. States and cities have developed new programs for more parks, more open spaces, more recreational opportunities; and voters have authorized bond issues and heavier taxes to pay for such improvements of their environment.

The national government, in response to this popular demand and under the guidance of responsible leadership, has moved in the same direction. The 88th Congress, which will be remembered for its positive achievements in conservation, passed more than thirty significant conservation measures.

These laws build on a long tradition and a current consensus that authorize the Federal Government to preserve and restore the people's heritage of natural beauty.

4. The Federal Government has preserved a great treasure in its national parks, national forests, and wildlife preserves. We must now build upon these achievements. Conditions of the 20th century demand a New Conservation.

An overwhelming majority of Americans now live in cities or towns. Open space should be preserved where it is needed, near metropolitan areas; and far-away parks and forests, streams and beaches should be made more accessible. And the need for action is urgent, for open land is being built over at an incredible rate by the outward push of our great urban areas.

Natural beauty should be brought closer to the eye of the beholder; it should be carried into the sites where men spend their daily lives.

5. Achieving a more beautiful America does not require a vast proliferation of Federal activities. The problem is to refocus. The Federal Government, in the execution of its normal and unquestioned activities, is the greatest single builder and landowner in the country. As a consequence—though often without specific intent—it greatly influences the quality of our environment. Merely as a matter of good housekeeping, the Federal Government should ensure that its physical installations not only serve their immediate purposes efficiently but also enhance

the appearance of their general setting. The highway program is a striking example of how a pleasurable driving experience could be combined with an efficient engineering system.

Indifference to the environmental effect of a project constitutes a decision by default—that drabness is good enough.

6. The cost of achieving sound design and harmony with surroundings is often small. Even when it is not, it is a price which a great and wealthy society can well afford to pay. Furthermore, to burden the future with discordant installations that are not good neighbors to their environment is to impose on later generations a far greater cost in the achievement of beauty. They will not only have to build as we had the opportunity to do, but we will have forced them to tear down the eyesores which we have built.

7. Government by its own actions can create the conditions under which an harmonious environment is possible, but some affirmative Government action is necessary to reach this end. In a democracy the proper function of government is to extend the individual's range of opportunity to pursue his own style of life.

The American citizen cannot remedy pollution by himself. He may beautify his own home, he may tend his own garden; but he cannot control the other side of the street. He cannot shut his eyes to the ugliness of a withered landscape, nor can he close his nostrils to the pollution that he and his fellow citizens discharge into rivers.

The general beauty of the environment is something like the defense of a country. Defense expenditures pay for the defense of all citizens; everyone benefits all the time; but customers cannot buy one unit or two units of defense whenever they feel the need. Services of this sort must be paid for by government because they cannot be financed under any system of commercial pricing, but only from general tax revenues.

8. Natural beauty costs less than might be supposed, because it is linked with many of the most practical ends our society cherishes.

Beauty fosters safety; it dictates the control of flooding, and erosion, and the landscaping and careful planning of otherwise monotonous highways to avoid fatigue and accident. Beauty is a component of mental well-being. It provides relief and relaxation from the intensity of modern activity. The elements of natural beauty are essential as recreation resources. It provides creative and wholesome outlets for the leisure society. Beauty is associated with economic efficiency: the soot and sewage that make for ugliness also make for wasteful expenditure in cleaning; smogs cause illness as well as displeasure.

Beauty can be a weapon in the fight against poverty, because an attractive community and countryside draw new enterprise, gifted people, and income from tourism. Beauty contributes to the real national income, for a man can derive great satisfaction from seeing a mountain or from strolling in a fine city square, and this psychic income, even though statisticians do not know how to quantify it, contributes to his welfare.

9. The need for public action in maintaining and enhancing our environment is manifest. But there is, inevitably, a resistance from those who do not deny the need but are appalled at the thought of bureaucratic intervention in so delicate and personal matter as natural beauty. They fear an arbitrary imposition of a Government standard of taste. Yet many areas in which Government should act offer no threats to freedom of design—nobody prefers litter, car junkyards, and polluted streams. In its affirmative programs the Government does need to act with great care. It must not impose solutions, but rather facilitate the creative efforts of talented and skillful individuals. The very greatest variety of tastes and forms of expression must be and can be encouraged.

10. The Federal Government can appropriately seek to educate the public about the beauties of the Nation which are available but which many through lack of information never enjoy. It can help make available to society at large our land, air, and water resources. It should educate the public in the possibilities for development by recognizing and rewarding private, municipal and State contributions to the beauty of the Nation. In the long run, the beauty of the Nation must depend on men who are sensitive to their environment and proudly insistent that America be beautiful.

Finally, living and working in beautiful surroundings is an objective which justifies itself. It was Thomas Jefferson who first observed that communities "should be planned with an eye to the effect made upon the human spirit by being continuously surrounded with a maximum of beauty." Beauty helps to make life and work worthwhile. And this very circumstance makes natural beauty intensely practical, for a citizenry which is nurtured by a great environment will gain a heightened sense that its life is meaningful and ennobling.

REPORT OF THE PRESIDENT'S TASK FORCE
ON THE PRESERVATION OF NATURAL BEAUTY:
HIGHWAYS AND AUTOMOBILES*
1965

The President's Task Force issued this strongly-worded statement on high-ways and automobiles in 1965. Beauty, the Task Force said, must now be considered a principal aim of our highway program — not a by-product. The group also suggested that beauty was more important than was concrete.

HIGHWAYS AND AUTOMOBILES

The time is long overdue for a major shift of emphasis in our highway program. Fundamental to all the specifics that follow is our belief that beauty must now be considered a principal aim of our highway program, not a by-product — and that this concept be built into the operating procedures of our vast road building organizations.

They talk much of the importance of natural beauty. The fact remains that for most of them concrete comes first.

It was back in 1908 that the first limited access road in the U.S. was conceived, the Bronx River Parkway, and, it is still one of America's most beautiful road-ways. Since then we have made great progress in engineering, safety, and economic savings for motorists. We have made appallingly little progress as far as beauty goes, and in many respects we have been backtracking.

The enhancement of natural beauty should be written into the statutes as a major purpose of the Federal Interstate Highway Program and federal aid should be made contingent on a constructive recognition of this by the States.

One way of translating such a statute into action would be an overhauling of the benefit-cost formulae used to plan alignments. Community and aesthetic benefits should now be included. From a technical point of view it might be impossible to reduce such benefits to precise quantities. But surely there is some way of building into planning procedures a fuller consideration of these benefits. Recent memoranda of the Bureau of Public Roads are heartening. But it would be best to have a directive written into the statutes.

Put teeth into the Section 319 provision of the highway code for landscape and recreational areas in the Interstate system. — By providing up to 3 percent of the highway funds this provision can make effective all the tools for preserving the natural beauty of the scenic corridor: scenic easements, additional rights-of-way for turnouts, recreational areas for both pedestrians and motorists. This

*The President's Task Force on Natural Beauty, *Report on the Preservation of Natural Beauty* (Washington, D.C.: U.S. Government Printing Office, 1965), 8–10.

is the *people* aspect of highways that so needs emphasis. State highway commissioners regularly applaud Section 319 at their conferences. Highway user groups also applaud it. So do conservation groups.

And not one penny has been applied for. The trouble lies in one word: the States *"may"* use the funds for this purpose. But if they do not want to they can have the funds anyway for regular construction work. There is a sweetener in that the States do not have to put up matching money if they use funds for landscaping, but it is now quite obvious that to work, Section 319 needs to have the bugs taken out. We suggest two possibilities:

One is to change the word "may" to "shall." With this one word, some $100 million a year can be made available for natural beauty—and in a highly practical, immediate way.

We are aware of Commerce's fear that to ask for so much would antagonize those who want construction finished first. We do not understand why timidity should be in order. The original legislative expectation was that the 3 percent would be used for landscaping. We are only suggesting that the statute be cleaned up so that the program can do what was intended to be achieved in the first place. A good argument can be made, indeed, that the sum should be increased to 5 percent. (And that BOR oversee its expenditure.)

Another possibility would be to authorize additional grant monies for this purpose. This is the approach in S. 3173, 88th Congress, proposed by Senator Gaylord Nelson; up to 10 million a year would be authorized for 50 percent matching grants to the States for carrying out the Section 319 purposes, and these could be used in addition to the monies already available under the 3 percent allocation.

Section 319 should be reworded so that funds can be used for landscaping or increasing rights-of-way already acquired. Unless this is done, these very considerable funds would apply only to future highways.

A national program for scenic roads and parkways should be pushed now.— The key word is now. The Recreation Advisory Council has said some mildly encouraging things about scenic roads and has launched a study. This should prove very helpful. We do not see, however, why there should be a moratorium on legislative action until submission of the report in April, 1965. On a number of points the case for immediate action is pressing.

The Federal Government, for one thing, should encourage States to get their own scenic highway programs underway now. California has already made considerable progress on its scenic highway program, and the sheer setting up of the idea has encouraged some local governments to take advanced action; Monterey County, for example, has already secured scenic easements from developers to preserve the scenic corridor. In most States, however, the scenic road concept is unknown. With the present federal machinery there is quite enough leverage already to get States to go through the first motions of getting a program underway. The danger that States will be too precipitate does not seem a pressing one.

The Federal Government should take strong action on billboard control. — The one-half of one percent bonus now provided to States with billboard control has no punch; as of August, only 147 miles out of 1700 of the Federal Interstate Highway System were covered by agreements executed through the bonus. The bonus does not provide enough money and is too complicated. It applies only to rights-of-way acquired since July 1956 and it exempts many commercial areas.

The legislation, due to expire in 1965, should be extended and strengthened. To wit:

       Increase the bonus to two percent.

       Make the bonus apply to all of the Interstate system.

       Increase the setbacks for billboards to 1,000 feet.

       Direct the Bureau of Public Roads to apply Federal powers for regulating outdoor advertising along the Interstate System wherever effective State or local control is lacking.

       Direct the BOR, or National Park Service to designate the scenic sections of the Interstate System. Alignments tailored to the natural beauty of these areas would be mandatory; so would restriction against billboards or other encroachments.

Incentive awards should be given for outstanding examples of highway design. — The Bureau of Public Roads could establish a jury of distinguished architects, engineers, and landscape architects who each year would give awards for the outstanding demonstrations of how highway, bridge, and interchange design, and right-of-way landscaping can enhance the surrounding environment.

The Federal Government should take the lead in finding ways to solve the auto junkyard problem. — Abandoned automobiles are already one of our great scenic problems and they are likely to become far worse. There will be, for one thing, over 5 million cars each year to junk. Secondly, the demand for junked cars by the steel industry has been sharply lowered by oxygen processing of iron ore.

An immediate measure, noted in the Grant Section, is to screen the junkyards.

Other approaches would deal with the junking process. One would be a special tax levied on new cars, the proceeds to be applied to a program for auto disposal. Such a program might include establishment of a series of regional car smashing plants. New ways of processing the scrap more economically could help greatly; the possibility of federally insured loans might stimulate commercial efforts. The Bureau of Mines could be a logical agency to get some pilot research projects under way.

The Federal Government should encourage the States to couple highways with other resource projects. — Most highways seem to be planned in complete isolation from the plans of other land use agencies. Highway planners rarely seek out park and water resource planners in the initial phases, but neither do the latter seem to think of coupling their projects with the highways.

The few exceptions show how big is the potential to be grasped. The California West Side Program is an outstanding example. Spurred by a mandate from the legislature, State, local and Federal agencies joined forces to see how a projected interstate freeway and the new North-South Aqueduct through the central valley could be coupled. They found that not only could there be great economies in land acquisition, but that lakes, parks (public hunting and fishing areas) and roadside rests could be an integral part of the project.

Much greater effort should be made in the Federal Interstate Program to adapt the freeways to regional characteristics—and call on the talents of people within the region.—There is a wealth of capable professional talent, fully acquainted with local conditions, that should be called on but rarely is. These people can make a great contribution in tailoring the highway, its structures and landscaping to the local scene. By calling them in, furthermore, the highway agencies would go far to combat the prevalent feeling that they are invaders whose plans have been incubated far away and with little thought of regional characteristics.

One final note: Though transportation is outside our assignment, we believe that the movement of people and goods demands new techniques, and not a continued reliance on the automobile as the principal means.

There is a potential for beauty in our freeways. There would be an even bigger potential were freeways balanced by other methods in an overall system.

THE HIGHWAY BEAUTIFICATION ACT*
October 22, 1965

Finally, in 1965, some progress was made in highway beautification through the passage of the Highway Beautification Act which included measures for the control of outdoor advertising and junkyards adjacent to highways. The act also provided for the landscaping and scenic enhancement of roads and highways.

An Act to provide for scenic development and road beautification of the Federal-aid highway systems.

Be it enacted by the Senate and House of Representatives of the United States of America in Congress assembled,

TITLE I

SEC. 101. Section 131 of title 23, United States Code, is revised to read as follows:
"§ 131. Control of outdoor advertising
"(a) The Congress hereby finds and declares that the erection and maintenance of outdoor advertising signs, displays, and devices in areas adjacent to the Interstate System and the primary system should be controlled in order to protect the public investment in such highways, to promote the safety and recreational value of public travel, and to preserve natural beauty.
"(b) Federal-aid highway funds apportioned on or after January 1, 1968, to any State which the Secretary determines has not made provision for effective control of the erection and maintenance along the Interstate System and the primary system of outdoor advertising signs, displays, and devices which are within six hundred and sixty feet of the nearest edge of the right-of-way and visible from the main traveled way of the system, shall be reduced by amounts equal to 10 per centum of the amounts which would otherwise be apportioned to such State under section 104 of this title, until such time as such State shall provide for such effective control. Any amount which is withheld from apportionment to any State hereunder shall be reapportioned to the other States. Whenever he determines it to be in the public interest, the Secretary may suspend, for such periods as he deems necessary, the application of this subsection to a State.
"(c) Effective control means that after January 1, 1968, such signs, displays, and devices shall, pursuant to this section, be limited to (1) directional and other official signs and notices, which signs and notices shall include, but not be lim-

*79 *Statutes at Large,* 1028.

ited to, signs and notices pertaining to natural wonders, scenic and historical attractions, which are required or authorized by law, which shall conform to national standards hereby authorized to be promulgated by the Secretary hereunder, which standards shall contain provisions concerning the lighting, size, number, and spacing of signs, and such other requirements as may be appropriate to implement this section, (2) signs, displays, and devices advertising the sale or lease of property upon which they are located, and (3) signs, displays, and devices advertising activities conducted on the property on which they are located.

"(d) In order to promote the reasonable, orderly and effective display of outdoor advertising while remaining consistent with the purposes of this section, signs, displays, and devices whose size, lighting and spacing, consistent with customary use is to be determined by agreement between the several States and the Secretary, may be erected and maintained within six hundred and sixty feet of the nearest edge of the right-of-way within areas adjacent to the Interstate and primary systems which are zoned industrial or commercial under authority of State law, or in unzoned commercial or industrial areas as may be determined by agreement between the several States and the Secretary. The States shall have full authority under their own zoning laws to zone areas for commercial or industrial purposes, and the actions of the States in this regard will be accepted for the purposes of this Act. Nothing in this subsection shall apply to signs, displays, and devices referred to in clauses (2) and (3) of subsection (c) of this section.

"(e) Any sign, display, or device lawfully in existence along the Interstate System or the Federal-aid primary system on September 1, 1965, which does not conform to this section shall not be required to be removed until July 1, 1970. Any other sign, display, or device lawfully erected which does not conform to this section shall not be required to be removed until the end of the fifth year after it becomes nonconforming.

"(f) The Secretary shall, in consultation with the States, provide within the rights-of-way for areas at appropriate distances from interchanges on the Interstate System, on which signs, displays, and devices giving specific information in the interest of the traveling public may be erected and maintained. Such signs shall conform to national standards to be promulgated by the Secretary.

"(g) Just compensation shall be paid upon the removal of the following outdoor advertising signs, displays, and devices—

"(1) those lawfully in existence on the date of enactment of this subsection,

"(2) those lawfully on any highway made a part of the interstate or primary system on or after the date of enactment of this subsection and before January 1, 1968, and

"(3) those lawfully erected on or after January 1, 1968.

The Federal share of such compensation shall be 75 per centum. Such compensation shall be paid for the following:

"(A) The taking from the owner of such sign, display, or device of all right, title, leasehold, and interest in such sign, display, or device; and

"(B) The taking from the owner of the real property on which the sign, display, or device is located, of the right to erect and maintain such signs, displays, and devices thereon.

"(h) All public lands or reservations of the United States which are adjacent to any portion of the Interstate System and the primary system shall be controlled in accordance with the provisions of this section and the national standards promulgated by the Secretary.

"(i) In order to provide information in the specific interest of the traveling public, the State highway departments are authorized to maintain maps and to permit informational directories and advertising pamphlets to be made available at safety rest areas. Subject to the approval of the Secretary, a State may also establish information centers at safety rest areas for the purpose of informing the public of places of interest within the State and providing such other information as a State may consider desirable.

"(j) Any State highway department which has, under this section as in effect on June 30, 1965, entered into an agreement with the Secretary to control the erection and maintenance of outdoor advertising signs, displays, and devices in areas adjacent to the Interstate System shall be entitled to receive the bonus payments as set forth in the agreement, but no such State highway department shall be entitled to such payments unless the State maintains the control required under such agreement or the control required by this section, whichever control is stricter. Such payments shall be paid only from appropriations made to carry out this section. The provisions of this subsection shall not be construed to exempt any State from controlling outdoor advertising as otherwise provided in this section.

"(k) Nothing in this section shall prohibit a State from establishing standards imposing stricter limitations with respect to signs, displays, and devices on the Federal-aid highway systems than those established under this section.

"(1) Not less than sixty days before making a final determination to withhold funds from a State under subsection (b) of this section, or to do so under subsection (b) of section 136, or with respect to failing to agree as to the size, lighting, and spacing of signs, displays, and devices or as to unzoned commercial or industrial areas in which signs, displays, and devices may be erected and maintained under subsection (d) of this section, or with respect to failure to approve under subsection (g) of section 136, the Secretary shall give written notice to the State of his proposed determination and a statement of the reasons therefor, and during such period shall give the State an opportunity for a hearing on such determination. Following such hearing the Secretary shall issue a written order setting forth his final determination and shall furnish a copy of such order to the State. Within forty-five days of receipt of such order, the State may appeal such order to any United States district court for such State, and upon the filing of such appeal such order shall be stayed until final judgment has been entered on such appeal. Summons may be served at any place in the United States. The court shall have jurisdiction to affirm the determination of the Secretary or to set it aside, in whole or in part. The judgment of the court shall be subject to review by the United States court of appeals for the circuit in which the State is located and to the Supreme Court of the United States upon certiorari or certification as provided in title 28, United States Code, section 1254. If any part of an apportionment to a State is withheld by the Secretary under subsection (b) of this section or subsection (b) of section 136, the amount so withheld shall not be reapportioned to the other States as long as a suit brought by such State under this subsection is pending. Such amount shall remain available for apportionment in accordance with the final judgment and this subsection. Funds withheld from apportionment and subsequently apportioned or reapportioned under this section shall be available for expenditure for three full fiscal years after the date of such apportionment or reapportionment as the case may be.

"(m) There is authorized to be appropriated to carry out the provisions of this section, out of any money in the Treasury not otherwise appropriated, not to exceed $20,000,000 for the fiscal year ending June 30, 1966, and not to exceed $20,000,000 for the fiscal year ending June 30, 1967. No part of the Highway Trust fund shall be available to carry out this section."

SEC. 102. The table of sections of chapter 1 of title 23 of the United States Code is amended by striking out

"131. Areas adjacent to the Interstate System."

and inserting in lieu thereof

"131. Control of outdoor advertising."

TITLE II

SEC. 201. Chapter 1 of title 23, United States Code, is amended to add at the end thereof the following new section:
"§ 136. Control of junkyards

"(a) The Congress hereby finds and declares that the establishment and use and maintenance of junkyards in areas adjacent to the Interstate System and the primary system should be controlled in order to protect the public investment in such highways, to promote the safety and recreational value of public travel, and to preserve natural beauty.

"(b) Federal-aid highway funds apportioned on or after January 1, 1968, to any

[687]

State which the Secretary determines has not made provision for effective control of the establishment and maintenance along the Interstate System and the primary system of outdoor junkyards, which are within one thousand feet of the nearest edge of the right-of-way and visible from the main traveled way of the system, shall be reduced by amounts equal to 10 per centum of the amounts which would otherwise be apportioned to such State under section 104 of this title, until such time as such State shall provide for such effective control. Any amount which is withheld from apportionment to any State hereunder shall be reapportioned to the other States. Whenever he determines it to be in the public interest, the Secretary may suspend, for such periods as he deems necessary, the application of this subsection to a State.

"(c) Effective control means that by January 1, 1968, such junkyards shall be screened by natural objects, plantings, fences, or other appropriate means so as not to be visible from the main traveled way of the system, or shall be removed from sight.

"(d) The term 'junk' shall mean old or scrap copper, brass, rope, rags, batteries, paper, trash, rubber debris, waste, or junked, dismantled, or wrecked automobiles, or parts thereof, iron, steel, and other old or scrap ferrous or non-ferrous material.

"(e) The term 'automobile graveyard' shall mean any establishment or place of business which is maintained, used, or operated for storing, keeping, buying, or selling wrecked, scrapped, ruined, or dismantled motor vehicles or motor vehicle parts.

"(f) The term 'junkyard' shall mean an establishment or place of business which is maintained, operated, or used for storing, keeping, buying, or selling junk, or for the maintenance or operation of an automobile graveyard, and the term shall include garbage dumps and sanitary fills.

"(g) Notwithstanding any provision of this section, junkyards, auto graveyards, and scrap metal processing facilities may be operated within areas adjacent to the Interstate System and the primary system which are within one thousand feet of the nearest edge of the right-of-way and which are zoned industrial under authority of State law, or which are not zoned under authority of State law, but are used for industrial activities, as determined by the several States subject to approval by the Secretary.

"(h) Notwithstanding any provision of this section, any junkyard in existence on the date of enactment of this section which does not conform to the requirements of this section and which the Secretary finds as a practical matter cannot be screened, shall not be required to be removed until July 1, 1970.

"(i) The Federal share of landscaping and screening costs under this section shall be 75 per centum.

"(j) Just compensation shall be paid the owner for the relocation, removal, or disposal of the following junkyards—

THE RACE FOR INNER SPACE

"(1) those lawfully in existence on the date of enactment of this subsection,

"(2) those lawfully along any highway made a part of the interstate or primary system on or after the enactment of this subsection and before January 1, 1968, and

"(3) those lawfully established on or after January 1, 1968.
The Federal share of such compensation shall be 75 per centum.

"(k) All public lands or reservations of the United States which are adjacent to any portion of the interstate and primary systems shall be effectively controlled in accordance with the provisions of this section.

"(l) Nothing in this section shall prohibit a State from establishing standards imposing stricter limitations with respect to outdoor junkyards on the Federal-aid highway systems than those established under this section.

"(m) There is authorized to be appropriated to carry out this section, out of any money in the Treasury not otherwise appropriated, not to exceed $20,000,000 for the fiscal year ending June 30, 1966, and not to exceed $20,000,000 for the fiscal year ending June 30, 1967. No part of the Highway Trust Fund shall be available to carry out this section."

SEC. 202. The table of sections of chapter 1, title 23, United States Code, is amended by adding at the end thereof the following:

"136. Control of junkyards."

TITLE III

SEC. 301. (a) Section 319 of title 23, United States Code, is revised to read as follows:

"§ 319. Landscaping and scenic enhancement

"(a) The Secretary may approve as a part of the construction of Federal-aid highways the costs of landscape and roadside development, including acquisition and development of publicly owned and controlled rest and recreation areas and sanitary and other facilities reasonably necessary to accommodate the traveling public.

"(b) An amount equivalent to 3 per centum of the funds apportioned to a State for Federal-aid highways for any fiscal year shall be allocated to that State out of funds appropriated under authority of this subsection, which shall be used for landscape and roadside development within the highway right-of-way and for acquisition of interests in and improvement of strips of land necessary for the restoration, preservation, and enhancement of scenic beauty adjacent to such highways, including acquisition and development of publicly owned and controlled rest and recreation areas and sanitary and other facilities within or adjacent to the highway right-of-way reasonably necessary to accommodate the traveling public, without being matched by the State. The Secretary may authorize exceptions from this requirement, upon application of a State and upon a showing that such amount is in excess of the needs of the State for these purposes. Any funds not used as required by this subsection shall lapse. There is authorized to be appropriated to carry out this subsection, out of any money in the Treasury not otherwise appropriated, not to exceed $120,000,000 for the fiscal year ending June 30, 1966, and not to exceed $120,000,000 for the fiscal year ending June 30, 1967. No part of the Highway Trust Fund shall be available to carry out this subsection."

(b) The table of sections of chapter 3 of title 23 of the United States Code is amended by striking out

"319. Landscaping."

and inserting in lieu thereof

"319. Landscaping and scenic enhancement."

SEC. 302. In order to provide the basis for evaluating the continuing programs authorized by this Act, and to furnish the Congress with the information necessary for authorization of appropriations for fiscal years beginning after June 30, 1967, the Secretary, in cooperation with the State highway departments, shall make a detailed estimate of the cost of carrying out the provisions of this Act, and a comprehensive study of the economic impact of such programs on affected individuals and commercial and industrial enterprises, the effectiveness of such programs and the public and private benefits realized thereby, and alternate or improved methods of accomplishing the objectives of this Act. The Secretary shall submit such detailed estimate and a report concerning such comprehensive study to the Congress not later than January 10, 1967.

SEC. 303. (a) Before the promulgation of standards, criteria, and rules and regulations, necessary to carry out sections 131 and 136 of title 23 of the United States Code, the Secretary of Commerce shall hold public hearings in each State for the purpose of gathering all relevant information on which to base such standards, criteria, and rules and regulations.

(b) The Secretary of Commerce shall report to Congress, not later than January 10, 1967, all standards, criteria, and rules and regulations to be applied in carrying out sections 131 and 136 of title 23 of the United States Code.

SEC. 304. There is authorized to be appropriated the sum of $500,000 to enable the Secretary of Commerce to carry out his functions under section 135 of title 23 of the United States Code relating to highway safety programs.

SEC. 305. Nothing in this Act or the amendments made by this Act shall be construed to authorize the use of eminent domain to acquire any dwelling (including related buildings).

TITLE IV

SEC. 401. Nothing in this Act or the amendments made by this Act shall be construed to authorize private property to be taken or the reasonable and existing use restricted by such taking without just compensation as provided in this Act.

SEC. 402. In addition to any other amounts authorized by this Act and the amendments made by this Act, there is authorized to be appropriated, out of any money in the Treasury not otherwise appropriated, to the Secretary of Commerce not to exceed $5,000,000 for administrative expenses in carrying out this Act (including amendments made by this Act).

SEC. 403. This Act may be cited as the "Highway Beautification Act of 1965". Approved October 22, 1965, 2:30 p.m.

THE HISTORIC PROPERTIES ACT*
October 15, 1966

The Historic Properties Act was of special significance because it authorized matching grants to states and to the National Trust for Historic Preservation.

An Act to establish a program for the preservation of additional historic properties throughout the Nation, and for other purposes.

Be it enacted by the Senate and House of Representatives of the United States of America in Congress assembled,

The Congress finds and declares—

(a) that the spirit and direction of the Nation are founded upon and reflected in its historic past;

(b) that the historical and cultural foundations of the Nation should be preserved as a living part of our community life and development in order to give a sense of orientation to the American people;

(c) that, in the face of ever-increasing extensions of urban centers, highways, and residential, commercial, and industrial developments, the present governmental and nongovernmental historic preservation programs and activities are inadequate to insure future generations a genuine opportunity to appreciate and enjoy the rich heritage of our Nation; and

(d) that, although the major burdens of historic preservation have been borne and major efforts initiated by private agencies and individuals, and both should continue to play a vital role, it is nevertheless necessary and appropriate for the Federal Government to accelerate its historic preservation programs and activities, to give maximum encouragement to agencies and individuals undertaking preservation by private means, and to assist State and local governments and the National Trust for Historic Preservation in the United States to expand and accelerate their historic preservation programs and activites.

TITLE I

SEC. 101. (a) The Secretary of the Interior is authorized—

(1) to expand and maintain a national register of districts, sites, buildings, structures, and objects significant in American history, architecture, archeology, and culture, hereinafter referred to as the National Register, and to grant funds to States for the purpose of preparing comprehensive statewide historic surveys and plans, in accordance with criteria estab-

*80 *Statutes at Large,* 915.

lished by the Secretary, for the preservation, acquisition, and development of such properties;

(2) to establish a program of matching grants-in-aid to States for projects having as their purpose the preservation for public benefit of properties that are significant in American history, architecture, archeology, and culture; and

(3) to establish a program of matching grant-in-aid to the National Trust for Historic Preservation in the United States, chartered by act of Congress approved October 26, 1949 (63 Stat. 927), as amended, for the purpose of carrying out the responsibilities of the National Trust.

(b) As used in this Act—

(1) The term "State" includes, in addition to the several States of the Union, the District of Columbia, the Commonwealth of Puerto Rico, the Virgin Islands, Guam, and American Samoa.

(2) The term "project" means programs of State and local governments and other public bodies and private organizations and individuals for the acquisition of title or interests in, and for the development of, any district, site, building, structure, or object that is significant in American history, architecture, archeology, and culture, or property used in connection therewith, and for its development in order to assure the preservation for public benefit of any such historical properties.

(3) The term "historic preservation" includes the protection, rehabilitation, restoration, and reconstruction of districts, sites, buildings, structures, and objects significant in American history, architecture, archeology, or culture.

(4) The term "Secretary" means the Secretary of the Interior.

SEC. 102. (a) No grant may be made under this Act—

(1) unless application therefor is submitted to the Secretary in accordance with regulations and procedures prescribed by him;

(2) unless the application is in accordance with the comprehensive statewide historic preservation plan which has been approved by the Secretary after considering its relationship to the comprehensive statewide outdoor recreation plan prepared pursuant to the Land and Water Conservation Fund Act of 1965 (78 Stat. 897);

(3) for more than 50 per centum of the total cost involved, as determined by the Secretary and his determination shall be final;

(4) unless the grantee has agreed to make such reports, in such form and containing such information as the Secretary may from time to time require;

(5) unless the grantee has agreed to assume, after completion of the project, the total costs of the continued maintenance, repair, and administration of the property in a manner satisfactory to the Secretary; and

[693]

(6) until the grantee has complied with such further terms and conditions as the Secretary may deem necessary or advisable.

(b) The Secretary may in his discretion waive the requirements of subsection (a), paragraphs (2) and (5) of this section for any grant under this Act to the National Trust for Historic Preservation in the United States, in which case a grant to the National Trust may include funds for the maintenance, repair, and administration of the property in a manner satisfactory to the Secretary.

(c) No State shall be permitted to utilize the value of real property obtained before the date of approval of this Act in meeting the remaining cost of a project for which a grant is made under this Act.

SEC. 103. (a) The amounts appropriated and made available for grants to the States for comprehensive statewide historic surveys and plans under this Act shall be apportioned among the States by the Secretary on the basis of needs as determined by him: *Provided, however,* That the amount granted to any one State shall not exceed 50 per centum of the total cost of the comprehensive statewide historic survey and plan for that State, as determined by the Secretary.

(b) The amounts appropriated and made available for grants to the States for projects under this Act for each fiscal year shall be apportioned among the States by the Secretary in accordance with needs as disclosed in approved statewide historic preservation plans.

The Secretary shall notify each State of its apportionment, and the amounts thereof shall be available thereafter for payment to such State for projects in accordance with the provisions of this Act. Any amount of any apportionment that has not been paid or obligated by the Secretary during the fiscal year in which such notification is given, and for two fiscal years thereafter, shall be reapportioned by the Secretary in accordance with this subsection.

SEC. 104. (a) No grant may be made by the Secretary for or on account of any survey or project under this Act with respect to which financial assistance has been given or promised under any other Federal program or activity, and no financial assistance may be given under any other Federal program or activity for or on account of any survey or project with respect to which assistance has been given or promised under this Act.

(b) In order to assure consistency in policies and actions under this Act with other related Federal programs and activities, and to assure coordination of the planning acquisition, and development assistance to States under this Act with other related Federal programs and activities, the President may issue such regulations with respect thereto as he deems desirable, and such assistance may be provided only in accordance with such regulations.

SEC. 105. The beneficiary of assistance under this Act shall keep such records as the Secretary shall prescribe, including records which fully disclose the disposition by the beneficiary of the proceeds of such assistance, the total cost of the project or undertaking in connection with which such assistance is given or used, and the amount and nature of that portion of the cost of the project or undertaking supplied by other sources, and such other records as will facilitate an effective audit.

SEC. 106. The head of any Federal agency having direct or indirect jurisdiction over a proposed Federal or federally assisted undertaking in any State and the head of any Federal department or independent agency having authority to license any undertaking shall, prior to the approval of the expenditure of any Federal funds on the undertaking or prior to the issuance of any license, as the case may be, take into account the effect of the undertaking on any district, site, building, structure, or object that is included in the National Register. The head of any such Federal agency shall afford the Advisory Council on Historic Preservation established under title II of this Act a reasonable opportunity to comment with regard to such undertaking.

SEC. 107. Nothing in this Act shall be construed to be applicable to the White House and its grounds, the Supreme Court building and its grounds, or the United States Capitol and its related buildings and grounds.

SEC. 108. There are authorized to be appropriated not to exceed $2,000,000 to carry out the provisions of this Act for the fiscal year 1967, and not more than $10,000,000 for each of the three succeeding fiscal years. Such appropriations shall be available for the financial assistance authorized by this title and for the administrative expenses of the Secretary in connection therewith, and shall remain available until expended.

TITLE II

SEC. 201. (a) There is established an Advisory Council on Historic Preservation (hereinafter referred to as the "Council") which shall be composed of seventeen members as follows:

(1) The Secretary of the Interior.

(2) The Secretary of Housing and Urban Development.

(3) The Secretary of Commerce.

(4) The Administrator of the General Services Administration.

(5) The Secretary of the Treasury.

(6) The Attorney General.

(7) The Chairman of the National Trust for Historic Preservation.

(8) Ten appointed by the President from outside the Federal Government. In making these appointments, the President shall give due consideration to the selection of officers of State and local governments and individuals who are significantly interested and experienced in the matters to be considered by the Council.

(b) Each member of the Council specified in paragraphs (1) through (6) of subsection (a) may designate another officer of his department or agency to serve on the Council in his stead.

(c) Each member of the Council appointed under paragraph (8) of subsection (a) shall serve for a term of five years from the expiration of his predecessor's term; except that the members first appointed under that paragraph shall serve for terms of from one to five years, as designated by the President at the time of appointment, in such manner as to insure that the terms of not less than one nor more than two of them will expire in any one year.

(d) A vacancy in the Council shall not affect its powers, but shall be filled in the same manner as the original appointment (and for the balance of the unexpired term).

(e) The Chairman of the Council shall be designated by the President.

(f) Eight members of the Council shall constitute a quorum.

SEC. 202. (a) The Council shall—

(1) advise the President and the Congress on matters relating to historic preservation; recommend measures to coordinate activities of Federal, State, and local agencies and private institutions and individuals relating to historic preservation; and advise on the dissemination of information pertaining to such activities;

(2) encourage, in cooperation with the National Trust for Historic Preservation and appropriate private agencies, public interest and participation in historic preservation;

(3) recommend the conduct of studies in such areas as the adequacy of legislative and administrative statutes and regulations pertaining to historic preservation activities of State and local governments and the effects of tax policies at all levels of government on historic preservation;

(4) advise as to guidelines for the assistance of State and local governments in drafting legislation relating to historic preservation; and

(5) encourage, in cooperation with appropriate public and private agencies and institutions, training and education in the field of historic preservation.

(b) The Council shall submit annually a comprehensive report of its activities and the results of its studies to the President and the Congress and shall from time to time submit such additional and special reports as it deems advisable. Each report shall propose such legislative enactments and other actions as, in the judgment of the Council, are necessary and appropriate to carry out its recommendations.

SEC. 203. The Council is authorized to secure directly from any department, bureau, agency, board, commission, office, independent establishment or instrumentality of the executive branch of the Federal Government information, suggestions, estimates, and statistics for the purpose of this title; and each such department, bureau, agency, board, commission, office, independent establishment or instrumentality is authorized to furnish such information, suggestions, estimates, and statistics to the extent permitted by law and within available funds.

SEC. 204. The members of Council specified in paragraphs (1) through (7) of section 201(a) shall serve without additional compensation. The members of the Council appointed under paragraph (8) of section 201(a) shall receive $100 per diem when engaged in the performance of the duties of the Council. All members of the Council shall receive reimbursement for necessary traveling and subsistence expenses incurred by them in the performance of the duties of the Council.

SEC. 205. (a) The Director of the National Park Service or his designee shall be the Executive Director of the Council. Financial and administrative services (including those related to budgeting, accounting, financial reporting, personnel and procurement) shall be provided the Council by the Department of the Interior, for which payments shall be made in advance, or by reimbursement, from funds of the Council in such amounts as may be agreed upon by the Chairman of the Council and the Secretary of the Interior: *Provided,* That the regulations of the Department of the Interior for the collection of indebtedness of personnel resulting from erroneous payments (5 U.S.C. 46e) shall apply to the collection of erroneous payments made to or on behalf of a Council employee, and regulations of said Secretary for the administrative control of funds (31 U.S.C. 665 (g)) shall apply to appropriations of the Council: *And provided further,* That the Council shall not be required to prescribe such regulations.

(b) The Council shall have power to appoint and fix the compensation of such additional personnel as may be necessary to carry out its duties, without regard to the provisions of the civil service laws and the Classification Act of 1949.

(c) The Council may also procure, without regard to the civil service laws and the Classification Act of 1949, temporary and intermittent services to the same extent as is authorized for the executive departments by section 15 of the Administrative Expenses Act of 1946 (5 U.S.C. 55a), but at rates not to exceed $50 per diem for individuals.

(d) The members of the Council specified in paragraphs (1) through (6) of section 201(a) shall provide the Council, on a reimbursable basis, with such facilities and services under their jurisdiction and control as may be needed by the Council to carry out its duties, to the extent that such facilities and services are requested by the Council and are otherwise available for that purpose. To the extent of available appropriations, the Council may obtain, by purchase, rental, donation, or otherwise, such additional property, facilities, and services as may be needed to carry out its duties.

Approved October 15, 1966.

THE DEMONSTRATION CITIES AND METROPOLITAN DEVELOPMENT ACT*
November 3, 1966

The Demonstration Cities Act authorized grants for the preservation of historic structures among other things. Only the basic declaration of purpose and the sections dealing directly with the preservation of historic structures are reproduced here.

An Act to assist comprehensive city demonstration programs for rebuilding slum and blighted areas and for providing the public facilities and services necessary to improve the general welfare of the people who live in those areas, to assist and encourage planned metropolitan development, and for other purposes.

Be it enacted by the Senate and House of Representatives of the United States of America in Congress assembled, That this Act may be cited as the "Demonstration Cities and Metropolitan Development Act of 1966".

TITLE I
COMPREHENSIVE CITY DEMONSTRATION PROGRAMS

FINDINGS AND DECLARATION OF PURPOSE

SEC. 101. The Congress hereby finds and declares that improving the quality of urban life is the most critical domestic problem facing the United States. The persistence of widespread urban slums and blight, the concentration of persons of low income in older urban areas, and the unmet needs for additional housing and community facilities and services arising from rapid expansion of our urban population have resulted in a marked deterioration in the quality of the environment and the lives of large numbers of our people while the Nation as a whole prospers.

The Congress further finds and declares that cities, of all sizes, do not have adequate resources to deal effectively with the critical problems facing them, and that Federal assistance in addition to that now authorized by the urban renewal program and other existing Federal grant-in-aid programs is essential to enable cities to plan, develop, and conduct programs to improve their physical environment, increase their supply of adequate housing for low- and moderate-income people, and provide educational and social services vital to health and welfare.

*80 Statutes at Large, 1255.

The purposes of this title are to provide additional financial and technical assistance to enable cities of all sizes (with equal regard to the problems of small as well as large cities) to plan, develop, and carry out locally prepared and scheduled comprehensive city demonstration programs containing new and imaginative proposals to rebuild or revitalize large slum and blighted areas; to expand housing, job, and income opportunities; to reduce dependence on welfare payments; to improve educational facilities and programs; to combat disease and ill health; to reduce the incidence of crime and delinquency; to enhance recreational and cultural opportunities; to establish better access between homes and jobs; and generally to improve living conditions for the people who live in such areas, and to accomplish these objectives through the most effective and economical concentration and coordination of Federal, State, and local public and private efforts to improve the quality of urban life.

* * *

TITLE VI
PRESERVATION OF HISTORIC STRUCTURES

PRESERVATION OF HISTORIC STRUCTURES AS PART OF URBAN RENEWAL PROJECTS

SEC. 601. (a) Section 110(b) of the Housing Act of 1949 is amended by inserting "historic and architectural preservation," after "land acquisition,".

(b) Section 110(c) (6) of such Act is amended by inserting "to promote historic and architectural preservation," after "deterioration,".

(c) Section 110(c) of such Act is further amended by striking out "and" at the end of clause (8), and by striking out clause (9) and inserting in lieu thereof the following:

"(9) relocation within or outside the project area of structures which will be restored and maintained for architectural or historic purposes; and

"(10) restoration of acquired properties of historic or architectural value."

LOCAL GRANT-IN-AID CREDIT FOR RELOCATION AND RESTORATION OF HISTORIC STRUCTURES

SEC. 602. Clause (2) of section 110(d) of the Housing Act of 1949 is amended by striking out "clause (2) and clause (3)" and inserting in lieu thereof "clauses (2), (3), (9), and (10)".

GRANTS TO NATIONAL TRUST FOR HISTORIC PRESERVATION TO COVER RESTORATION COSTS

SEC. 603. (a) The Secretary of Housing and Urban Development is authorized to make grants to the National Trust for Historic Preservation, on such terms and conditions and in such amounts (not exceeding $90,000 with respect to any one structure) as he deems appropriate, to cover the costs incurred by such Trust in renovating or restoring structures which it considers to be of historic or architectural value and which it has accepted and will maintain (after such renovation or restoration) for historic purposes.

(b) There are authorized to be appropriated such sums as may be necessary for the grants to be made under subsection (a).

URBAN PLANNING GRANTS FOR SURVEYS OF HISTORIC STRUCTURES

SEC. 604. Section 701 of the Housing Act of 1954 is amended by adding at the end thereof the following new subsection:

"(h) In addition to the other grants authorized by this section, the Secretary is authorized to make grants to assist any city, other municipality, or county in making a survey of the structures and sites in such locality which are determined by its appropriate authorities to be of historic or architectural value. Any such survey shall be designed to identify the historic structures and sites in the locality, determine the cost of their rehabilitation or restoration, and provide such other information as may be necessary or appropriate to serve as a foundation for a balanced and effective program of historic preservation in such locality. The aspects of any such survey which relate to the identification of historic and architectural values shall be conducted in accordance with criteria found by the Secretary to be comparable to those used in establishing the National Register maintained by the Secretary of the Interior under other provisions of law; and the results of each such survey shall be made available to the Secretary of the Interior. A grant under this subsection shall not exceed two-thirds of the cost of the survey for which it is made, and shall be made to the appropriate agency or entity specified in paragraphs (1) through (9) of subsection (a) or, if there is no such agency or entity which is qualified and willing to receive the grant and provide for its utilization in accordance with this subsection, directly to the city, other municipality, or county involved."

GRANT FOR HISTORIC PRESERVATION

SEC. 605. (a) The heading of title VII of the Housing Act of 1961 is amended to read as follows:

"TITLE VII
OPEN-SPACE LAND, URBAN BEAUTIFICATION,
AND HISTORIC PRESERVATION".

(b) Section 701 of such Act is amended by redesignating subsection (c) as subsection (d), and by inserting after subsection (b) a new subsection as follows:

"(c) The Congress further finds that there is a need for timely action to preserve and restore areas, sites, and structures of historic or architectural value in order that these remaining evidences of our past history and heritage shall not be lost or destroyed through the expansion and development of the Nation's urban areas."

(c) Section 701(d) of such Act (as redesignated by subsection (b) of this section) is amended—

(1) by inserting after "urban development," the following: "to assist in preserving areas and properties of historic or architectural value,"; and

(2) by striking out "and (2)" and inserting in lieu thereof "(2) acquire, improve, and restore areas, sites, and structures of historic or architectural value, and (3)".

(d) Section 702(e) of such Act is amended to read as follows:

"(e) The Secretary shall consult with the Secretary of the Interior on the general policies to be followed in reviewing applications for grants under this title. To assist the Secretary in such review, the Secretary of the Interior shall furnish him (1) appropriate information on the status of national and statewide recreation and historic preservation planning as it affects the areas to be assisted with such grants, and (2) the current listing of any districts, sites, buildings, structures, and objects significant in American history, architecture, archeology, and culture which may be contained on a National Register maintained by the Secretary of the Interior pursuant to other provisions of law. The Secretary shall provide current information to the Secretary of the Interior from time to time on significant program developments."

(e) Section 706 of such Act is amended by striking out the proviso.

(f) Section 708 of such Act is amended by inserting "(a)" after "Sec 708.", by inserting "(b)" before "The" in the second paragraph, and by adding at the end thereof a new subsection as follows:

"(c) Notwithstanding any other provision of this title, the Secretary may use not to exceed $10,000,000 of the sum authorized for contracts under this title for the purpose of entering into contracts to make grants in amounts not to exceed 90 per centum of the cost of activities which he determines have special value in developing and demonstrating new and improved methods and materials for use in carrying out the purposes of this title."

(g) Title VII of such Act is amended by redesignating section 709 as section 710, and by adding after section 708 a new section as follows:

"GRANTS FOR HISTORIC PRESERVATION

"SEC. 709. The Secretary is authorized to enter into contracts to make grants to States and local public bodies to assist in the acquisition of title to or other permanent interests in areas, sites, and structures of historic or architectural value in urban areas, and in their restoration and improvement for public use and benefit, in accord with the comprehensively planned development of the locality. The amount of any such grant shall not exceed 50 per centum of the total cost, as approved by the Secretary, of the assisted activities. The remainder of such cost shall be provided from non-Federal sources."

(h) Commencing three years after the date of the enactment of this Act, no grant shall be made (except pursuant to a contract or commitment entered into less than three years after such date) under section 709 of the Housing Act of 1961 or section 701(h) of the Housing Act of 1954, or under section 103 of the Housing Act of 1949 to the extent that it is to be used for historic or architectural preservation, except with respect to districts, sites, buildings, structures, and objects which the Secretary of Housing and Urban Development finds meet criteria comparable to those used in establishing the National Register maintained by the Secretary of the Interior pursuant to other provisions of law.

"TO RENEW A NATION"*
March 8, 1968

On March 8, 1968, President Johnson reviewed some of the conservation achievements of his administration and set forth a "priority agenda" for further efforts. His broad and comprehensive special message to the Congress on conservation entitled "To Renew a Nation," refers to most of the major topics in this volume and is therefore reproduced here in its entirety.

To the Congress of the United States:

Theodore Roosevelt made conservation more than a political issue in America. He made it a moral imperative.

More than half a century ago, he sounded this warning:

> To skin and exhaust the land instead of using it so as to increase its usefulness, will result in undermining in the days of our children the very prosperity which we ought by right to hand down to them amplified and developed.

The conservation work that Roosevelt began was protection of our natural heritage for the enjoyment and enrichment of all the families of the land. That is work which never ends. It must be taken up anew by each succeeding generation, acting as trustees for the next.

But the conservation problems Theodore Roosevelt saw are dwarfed by the new ones of our own day.

An unfolding technology has increased our economic strength and added to the convenience of our lives.

But that same technology—we know now—carries danger with it.

From the great smoke stacks of industry and from the exhausts of motors and machines, 130 million tons of soot, carbon and grime settle over the people and shroud the Nation's cities each year.

From towns, factories, and stockyards, wastes pollute our rivers and streams, endangering the waters we drink and use.

The debris of civilization litters the landscapes and spoils the beaches.

Conservation's concern now is not only for man's enjoyment—but for man's survival.

Fortunately, we have recognized the threat in time, and we have begun to meet it.

Through the landmark legislation of the past few years we are moving to bring a safe environment—both to this generation, and to the America still unborn.

—The Water Quality Act of 1965 and the Clean Water Restoration Act of

Public Papers of the Presidents of the United States: Lyndon B. Johnson, 1968–69, Book 1 (Washington, D.C.: Government Printing Office, 1970), 355–70.

1966 provide the foundation of our first major efforts to curb the pollution blighting America's waters.

—The Clean Air Act of 1965 and the Air Quality Act of 1967 build a strong base from which we can begin to clean the air.

—The Solid Waste Disposal Act of 1965 launched a new program to find the most efficient ways of disposing of millions of tons of solid wastes that clog the city and the countryside.

—The Highway Beautification Act of 1965 laid the groundwork for scenic roads and enjoyable travels.

—Over 2.2 million acres have been authorized for addition to the Nation's Park System—and for the first time in generations more land is being preserved for the people than is being developed for industrial or urban purposes.

But the work of the new conservation, too—like the task we inherited from an earlier day—is unending. Technology is not something which happens once and then stands still. It grows and develops at an electric pace. And our efforts to keep it in harmony with human values must be intensified and accelerated. Indeed, technology itself is the tool with which these new environmental problems can be conquered.

In this Message I shall outline the steps which I believe America must take this year to preserve the natural heritage of its people—a broad hertiage that must include not only the wilderness of the unbroken forest, but a safe environment for the crowded city.

PRIORITY AGENDA

The dangers that threaten our environment are varied. To succeed in meeting their challenge requires a wide-ranging response, with special emphasis on the items of highest priority.

For Fiscal 1969, I propose a program to complete this vital agenda for action.

First, I recommend that we assure the people that their water supplies will be pure and plentiful now and in the years ahead by:

—Prosecuting the war on water pollution with conviction, combining federal, state and local efforts to finance the construction this year of $1.5 to $2 billion in community waste treatment plants.

—Creating a National Water Commission to plot the course of water resource management for the next century.

—Helping to assure the quality of community water supplies through the Safe Drinking Water Act of 1968.

—Meeting the water needs of one of America's fastest growing regions by authorizing the Central Arizona Project.

Second, I recommend that we guard the landscape against the waste products of modern life by:

—Protecting rivers, beaches and coastal areas against the devastation of oil spillage and other hazardous substances through strong legislation to control them.

—Preventing the future despoilment of thousands of acres of mining land through the Surface Mining Reclamation Act of 1968.

—Discovering efficient methods to dispose of the millions of tons of refuse and trash that threaten to engulf city and countryside, through an extension of the Solid Waste Disposal Act, and to accelerate the development of economical systems which will convert waste into useful by-products.

—Transforming our highways into corridors of beauty through prompt action to continue the Highway Beautification Program, and building new roadside parks for the traveling family.

Third, I recommend that we advance in the battle for clean air over America's cities by:

—Fully exploiting our vast technology to find new and effective pollution abatement methods.

—Investing $128 million as the federal share in pollution control and research, more than has ever been committed in a single year before.

—Organizing for action, through the designation of Air Quality Control Regions under the landmark Air Quality Act of 1967.

Fourth, I recommend that we bring a sense of fulfillment, outdoor recreation and serenity to all Americans by:

—Bringing new national parks closer to the people who live crowded city lives by development of the redwood groves of California, the Northern Cascades of Washington and the historic Potomac River.

—Adding thousands of new acres of unspoiled and primitive lands to the wilderness system.

—Completing action on the nationwide networks of scenic rivers and trails.

—Focusing now on the problem of noise and its impact on our daily lives.

Fifth, I recommend that we explore the peaceful promise of the ocean's depths by:

—Beginning to plan now with other nations to launch an International Decade of Ocean Exploration.

—Putting our most advanced marine technology to work in the development of improved buoys for better prediction of weather and ocean conditions.

WATER POLLUTION CONTROL

America's rivers, lakes and coastal waters have nourished her growth: irrigated the farms, powered the dynamos, and provided transport for commerce.

But we have not used our waters well.

Our major rivers are defiled by noxious debris. Pollutants from cities and industries kill the fish in our streams. Many waterways are covered with oil slicks and contain growths of algae that destroy productive life and make the water unfit for recreation. "Polluted Water—No Swimming" has become a familiar sign on too many beaches and rivers. A lake that has served many generations of men now can be destroyed by man in less than one generation.

Only recently have we begun to reverse this trend—to undertake a program to preserve waters that are still clean, and purify those that have become infested with pollution.

The conditions have worsened through decades of neglect and indifference. They affect entire industries. They involve thousands of miles of waterways and thousands of communities that border them.

We have discovered not only that the problems of pollution are formidable, but that their solutions must be interlocking.

—Water quality standards must be set for entire bodies of water, varying from place to place depending on the water's use.

—Standards must be enforceable and they must apply to both municipalities and industries.

—Waste treatment plants must be constructed and other methods developed to prevent pollutants from reaching the water.

—New methods of cooperation and enforcement must be established at all levels, for waters bearing poisons do not stop at city, county or state boundaries. Clearing one part of a stream is no answer. Water bodies must be cleaned in their entirety.

America took strong action to combat the problem in 1965 with the Water Quality Act, and took another major step a year later with the Clean Water Restoration Act. Under those measures, the long and difficult task of cleaning the waters of our land has begun.

WATER QUALITY STANDARDS

Now, for the first time in our history, all the states have taken inventory of their water resources, considered their future needs, and developed quality standards.

As the law requires, these standards, and the plans to carry them out, have been submitted to the Secretary of the Interior for approval.

Many of the plans have already been approved. This is welcome news for communities and businessmen alike. Now they can take action because they know the standards they must all meet.

I have asked the Secretary of the Interior to speed the review of the remaining standards and plans so the Federal Government can more effectively help the states and communities turn their blueprints into action.

TREATMENT PLANTS

The heart of a water pollution control program is the community waste treatment plant which prevents refuse, debris and filth from reaching the waters. To meet the Nation's critical needs calls for both the construction of new plants and the improvement of existing facilities.

Through the Clean Water Restoration Act, the Federal Government can provide financial help—from 30 to 55 percent of the cost—for the construction of municipal waste treatment works. Already, under that Act and earlier authority, 8,000 grants, totalling more than $1 billion, have been made. They have helped local communities build more than $4.5 billion worth of plants to control the pollution in 67,000 miles of water on which almost 66 million Americans depend.

More is required, however. The problem is pressing and the backlog of needed plants is great.

With accelerated federal help, we can stimulate the construction of $1.5 billion to $2 billion in waste treatment plants under the $700 million authorization approved by the Congress for Fiscal 1969.

This will be done in two ways.

First, I recommend an appropriation of $225 million for grants under the Clean Water Restoration Act. This should generate about $500 to $600 million of plant construction.

Second, I recommend legislation to allow the Secretary of the Interior to make annual installment payments in addition to the lump sum grants as is presently the practice. This would permit the Federal Government to make construction commitments up to a total of $475 million in Fiscal 1969.

Under this new financing method, the $475 million would generate a total of about $1 to $1.4 billion of construction. Communities would be able to build many of their urgently-needed plants without delay and get them into the fight against pollution now.

USER CHARGES

Capital and operating costs of treatment plants are expensive, and it is right that those costs be borne by those who receive the plant's benefits. Accordingly, the new financing programs will require, as one criterion for assistance, that municipalities impose a system of user charges on those who use the plants.

A system of user charges would not only provide an equitable way of sharing costs, but would accomplish other desirable purposes, as well. Such charges would:

—Provide an incentive for industries to curb pollution through improved manufacturing techniques.

—Relieve the pressure on the overloaded tax bases of local governments.

WATER SUPPLIES

As America's cities grew and developed their own water supply systems, cholera and typhoid posed a grim threat to health and safety.

That threat was countered long ago.

Now, we in America drink tap water without a thought as to its safety. And yet—that water is not always as safe as it should be.

We do not have enough information on the long-term health effects of substances in drinking water.

New hazards—chemical and industrial wastes, and other materials—are creating new problems.

The Nation's Public Health Service cannot respond fully to this danger. Its authority is limited by a law passed almost half a century ago.

A recent study has indicated that about 30 percent of the Nation's public drinking water systems may fall below federal standards.

To help the cities and communities of America assure citizens that the water they drink is safe, I propose the Safe Drinking Water Act of 1968.

This measure will strengthen the authority of the Secretary of Health, Education, and Welfare to:

    —Develop, adopt and enforce improved standards relating to chemical contaminants in drinking water.

    —Conduct a comprehensive study of the safety of public drinking water supplies in the United States.

    —Determine whether any additional steps are necessary in this area.

The new law will help move us toward this goal: That every glass of drinking water drawn from America's public water supply systems will meet proper health standards.

WATER MANAGEMENT

NATIONAL WATER COMMISSION

We will not have served the water needs of Americans if we meet only the requirements of today's population. A prudent nation must look ahead and plan for tomorrow.

First, we must continue our sound programs of water management, research, and advance planning to solve supply problems and to prepare for the future needs of farms and factories, and growing city populations.

Second, we must establish a board to develop long-range policy for water resources.

Last year I asked the Congress to establish a National Water Commission to:

    —Work with federal, state and private agencies in a survey of our long-term water needs.

    —Explore the effect of water development projects on regional growth.

    —Identify alternative policies and programs to meet national and regional water resources objectives.

Both the Senate and the House of Representatives have passed legislation to establish this Commission. The measure is now in conference.

I urge the Congress to complete its action and authorize this much-needed Commission.

CENTRAL ARIZONA PROJECT

A vast area of the Western United States is arid. Thousands of acres are in danger of becoming a barren wasteland as underground sources of water are used up or depleted.

We have the techniques and know-how to overcome this problem.

Now legislation is required to authorize a program to bring water from the Colorado River to meet the urgent needs of the people of Arizona.

Proposals affecting the canyons and the gorges of this mighty and historic river have been the subject of searching national debate. Out of this discussion, a plan has evolved that will require no dams on the Colorado River, preserve its scenic values, and at the same time permit the immediate construction of essential water supply facilities.

I ask the Congress to authorize the Central Arizona Project this year.

OIL POLLUTION ABATEMENT

Last year, when the TORREY CANYON sank off the coast of Cornwall, the 30 million gallons of oil it was carrying spread destruction throughout the coastal waters, killing fish and birds, and then the refuse of this devastation swept onto the beaches.

Only this week, at home, tragedy struck again. The tanker OCEAN EAGLE broke in half at the mouth of San Juan Bay, spewing some 1½ million gallons of oil over some of the finest beaches in the Western Hemisphere.

Major disasters rarely occur. But minor oil spills are frequent—and their combined effect, although less dramatic, can also be harmful.

Last year, I asked the Secretary of the Interior and the Secretary of Transportation to study the problem of oil pollution in American waters. Their report warns us that we must protect the beaches, places of recreation, coastal and inland waters, and our fisheries from spillage not only of oil, but of other hazardous substances as well.

We need a comprehensive system to control oil pollution and to provide for prompt clean-up.

We also must be able to cope with the spillage of large quantities of such substances as chlorine.

Last year the Senate passed S 2760 to deal with the problem of oil pollution.

I propose we build upon and strengthen that bill through the Oil Pollution and Hazardous Substances Control Act of 1968.

This Act, together with the earlier Senate legislation, would:

    —As a general rule, make the discharge of oil unlawful if it occurs from a

[709]

shore facility or a ship operating within 12 miles from shore. The 3-mile territorial and 9-mile contiguous zones are thus both covered. This greatly expands the previous standard of liability, which was limited to"gross or willful negligence" and to the 3-mile limit.

—Impose upon the oil pollutor responsibility for cleaning the beaches and waters.

—Empower the Federal Government to clean up oil spills whenever the owner or operator fails to act, but require the pollutor to reimburse the Government for the clean-up costs. Prior law limited the owner's liability to the salvage value of the ship. The proposal will make them liable for the full costs of clean-up.

—Authorize the Government to establish regulations for shipboard and related marine operations to reduce the possibility of oil leakage at the source.

—Provide protection against large and dangerous discharges of pollutants other than oil by requiring those responsible to take whatever clean-up or other action the Government considers necessary. If the pollutor fails to act, the Government will take the necessary steps, and hold the pollutor liable for the costs.

AIR POLLUTION

Metals corrode, fabrics weaken and fade, leather weakens and becomes brittle, rubber cracks and loses its elasticity, paint discolors, concrete and building stone discolor and erode, glass is etched and paper becomes brittle.

This is not a description of the effects of a new weapon.

It is a sobering report on the results of pollution in the air we breathe.

And that air is not divisible into convenient shares. Polluted air affects the lungs of all—rich and poor, manager and worker, farmer and urban dweller.

Of all the problems of conservation, none is more ugent than the polluted air which endangers the American people. We have been fortunate so far. But we have seen that when winds fail to blow, the concentrations of poisonous clouds over our cities can become perilous.

Air pollution is a threat to health, especially of older persons. It contributes significantly to the rising rates of chronic respiratory ailments.

It stains our cities and towns with ugliness, soiling and corroding whatever it touches. Its damage extends to our forests and farmlands as well.

The economic toll for our neglect amounts to billions of dollars each year.

The Clean Air Act of 1963 gave the Federal Government authority to help states and local communities plan effective programs to combat pollution.

In 1965, at my request, the Congress strengthened that Act by empowering the Secretary of Health, Education, and Welfare to set standards controlling automobile exhaust pollution—a major and mobile source of air contaminants.

Last year we took a giant step with the Air Quality Act of 1967. That Act:

—Will help our states abate pollution in the only practical way—on a regional basis. For air knows no man-made boundary.

—Gives the Government standby power to impose federal standards or enforce state standards, if the states do not act.

—Gives the Secretary of Health, Education, and Welfare a new power to stop serious cases of pollution that present a clear hazard to the public's health.

—Through accelerated research and testing, will help provide the technological answers to this baffling problem: How can we most economically and effectively prevent pollution at its source—in the fuels, while those fuels are being burned, or before the fumes reach the air?

To carry out our efforts to fight air pollution, I am seeking some $128 million for Fiscal 1969—more than we have committed in any past year.

I have directed the Secretary of Health, Education, and Welfare to designate the Nation's principal Air Quality Control Regions within the next few months, and to publish Air Quality criteria and related information on control techniques. This information will give states, local governments and industry the cost and control data they need to carry out their responsibilities.

One day we will have clean air over America—but only if all levels of Government and industry work closely and conscientiously. The legislation now on the books provides the framework for a partnership without precedent, matching the dimension of the need. The problem deeply affects us all, and all of us share the responsibility for solving it.

I am confident that those responsibilities will be carried out—and that we can return to the American people a fundamental right of their national heritage: the right to breathe clean air.

HARDSHIP CASES

We have looked carefully into the question whether water and air pollution control will have a serious economic impact on American industry.

According to recent studies, the cost should be small for most firms.

In some cases, however, pollution control costs may present undue financial hardships to both a business and a community. *I have asked the Secretary of Commerce and the Administrator of the Small Business Administration to give priority attention to providing assistance in these hardship situations.*

FEDERAL INSTALLATIONS

In the field of pollution, it is not enough for an enlightened Federal Government to stimulate the work of the states, localities and private industry. It must also set a good example for the Nation.

Across America, federal installations are adopting the latest air and water pollution control methods. During the coming year, that effort will be intensified.

We expect to devote $53 million to the task, for thirteen separate federal agencies and 360 air and water pollution abatement projects.

NOISE CONTROL

What was once critically described as "the busy hum of traffic" has now turned into an unbearable din for many city dwellers.

The crescendo of noise—whether it comes from truck or jackhammer, siren or airplane—is more than an irritating nuisance. It intrudes on privacy, shatters serenity and can inflict pain.

We dare not be complacent about this ever-mounting volume of noise. In the years ahead, it can bring even more discomfort—and worse—to the lives of people.

I am directing all departments of Government to take account of noise factors in choosing the location and design of buildings, highways and other facilities whose construction is assisted by federal funds.

I also urge the Congress to take prompt action on legislation to strengthen the authority of the Secretary of Transportation to deal with aircraft noise. We need greater capacity to deal with the rapidly growing noise problem created by our expanding air transportation system.

SURFACE MINING

An air traveler over some of the richest country in America can look down upon deep scars gouging the earth, acres of ravaged soil stretching out on either side.

Advances in mining technology have allowed us to extract the earth's minerals economically and swiftly.

But too often these new techniques have been used unwisely and stripping machines have torn coal and other minerals from the surface of the land, leaving 2 million acres of this Nation sterile and destroyed. The unsightly scars of strip mining blight the beauty of entire areas, and erosion of the damaged land pours silt and acid into our streams.

Under present practices, only one-third of the land being mined is also being reclaimed. This start has been made by responsible individuals, by mining companies, and by the states that have already enacted laws to regulate surface mining.

America needs a nationwide system to assure that all lands disturbed by surface mining in the future will be reclaimed. This can best be achieved through cooperative efforts between the states and the Federal Government.

I propose the Surface Mining Reclamation Act of 1968.

Under this Act:

—Criteria will be established which the states will use in developing their own regulatory plans.

—The states, assisted by federal grants, will develop their own plans within two years and submit them to the Secretary of the Interior for review and approval.

—The Secretary will impose federal standards if the state plans are inadequate or if they are not submitted.

Surface mining also occurs on federal lands. To enable Government to take the lead in this important conservation effort, I have directed that:

—Federal Agencies assure that their regulations require the reclamation of federal lands leased for surface mining.

—From now on, federal contracts for the purchase of coal and other surface-mined minerals contain effective reclamation clauses.

SOLID WASTE DISPOSAL

In 1965, I recommended and the Congress approved a national planning, research and development program to find ways to dispose of the annual discard of solid wastes—millions of tons of garbage and rubbish, old automobile hulks, abandoned refrigerators, slaughterhouse refuse. This waste—enough to fill the Panama Canal four times over—mars the landscapes in cities, suburbia and countryside alike. It breeds disease-carrying insects and rodents, and much of it finds its way into the air and water.

The problem is not only to learn how to get rid of these substances—but also how to convert waste economically into useful materials. Millions of dollars of useful by-products may go up in smoke, or be buried under the earth.

Already scientists working under the 1965 Act have learned much about how soils absorb and assimilate wastes. States and local communities have drawn up their plans for solid waste disposal.

That Act expires in June, 1969.

To continue our efforts, I recommend a one-year extension of the Solid Waste Disposal Act.

In addition, *I am directing the Director of the Office of Science and Technology working with the appropriate Cabinet officers to undertake a comprehensive review of current solid waste disposal technology.* We want to find the solutions to two key problems:

—How to bring down the present high costs of solid waste disposal.

—How to improve and strengthen government-wide research and development in this field.

AGRICULTURAL WASTES

The new agricultural and land management techniques that increase the productivity of our farms have also brought new problems:

—Soil and other substances polluting our streams are the result of the erosion of farmlands and other areas. This cause of pollution has never been fully controlled and rapidly expanding suburban development has aggravated it.

—Added amounts of animal wastes are generated from the efficient concentration of cattle, hogs and sheep in feed lots.

We must not permit harmful effects on fish, other wildlife and on drinking water supplies of chemicals from fertilizer and pesticides—whatever their source.

Many of these problems can be dealt with through existing programs. But some will require new research and new approaches.

I am instructing the Secretary of Agriculture to conduct a government-wide review of these problems.

SPLENDOR OF A CONTINENT

Before anything else, Americans had the splendor of a continent. Behind the facade of our cities, beyond the concrete ribbons that connect them, much of that splendor remains.

It is there because men of vision and foresight—men like Gifford Pinchot, Theodore Roosevelt and Franklin Roosevelt—determined that the people's oldest legacy, the inheritance of a spacious land, must be preserved.

It is for each generation to carry on that work.

In our time, the task has become more difficult—but ever more urgent. Our numbers grow, our cities become more crowded, the pace of our lives quickens—but man's need to raise his spirits and expand his vision still endures.

A clear stream, a long horizon, a forest wilderness and open sky—these are man's most ancient possessions. In a modern society, they are his most priceless.

NATIONAL PARKS

In the past several years, we have authorized the addition of more than 2.2 million acres to the Nation's Park System.

We are actually preserving more lands—over 1.7 million acres in 1967—for

[714]

*conservation and the recreation enjoyment of America's families than the bull-
dozer and power shovel are taking over.*

A park, however splendid, has little appeal to a family that cannot reach it.

The magnificent areas preserved in the early days of conservation were remote from the cities—and many Americans had to travel half a continent to visit
them.

The new conservation is built on a new promise—to bring parks closer to the
people. The man who works hard all week—the laborer, the shopkeeper, the
subway rider—deserves a chance to escape the city's crush and congestion. He
should have the opportunity to give his children a weekend of recreation and
beauty and fresh air.

To provide this chance is the purpose of our program.

In the last several years, 32 of 35 areas set aside by the new conservation—
seashores, lakeshores, and parks—were located near large urban centers—
North, West, East, and South, They are within easy driving distance of 120 million of our people. For example:

—The resident of New York City can within an hour or so reach the
beaches and waters of the Fire Island National Seashore, established in
1965.

—A family living in the Washington, D.C. area has—since 1965—been able
to enjoy the advantages and scenic wonders of Assateague Island National
Seashore, only three hours away by car.

—Citizens of Chicago will soon be able to visit the conveniently located
Indiana Dunes National Lakeshore, whose development began last year.

—A father in Kentucky can take his son hunting and camping in the new
"Land Between the Lakes" recreation area, which will serve millions of
of Americans in the Southeast.

—Boy Scout troops in the Southwest can explore and hike through the
Guadalupe National Park in Texas.

—People in North Carolina will have easy access to the Cape Lookout
National Seashore, now underway.

In 1967, almost 140 million visits were made to National Park areas. These visits are increasing steadily—a tribute to the quality and importance of our parks.
It is also a signal that more parks are needed.

Paramount among our last-chance conservation opportunities is the creation
of a Redwood National Park in Northern California to preserve the tallest, most
ancient sentinels of nature on the American continent. A park in this region
would benefit millions of Americans living on the West Coast who could reach
the park within an afternoon's drive.

*I urge the House to seize this opportunity and complete action on a Redwood
bill this year.*

[715]

I also recommend that the House complete action on two other major additions to the Park system that we sought and the Senate approved last year:

— North Cascades National Park in Washington State, the American Alps, an unsurpassed spectacle of mountain beauty in the great Northwest.

— Apostle Islands National Lakeshore, along Wisconsin's most scenic water areas.

We can achieve a new concept in conservation — greater than a park, more than the preservation of a river — by beginning this year to make the Potomac a living part of our national life.

That great river, coursing through Maryland, Virginia and West Virginia, cradles much of our early history. Five million people live within 50 miles of its shores, and its legend beckons millions more from every part of the Nation. For the Potomac is truly the American River.

I urge the Congress to authorize the development of a uniquely historic area — the Potomac National River. Failure to act now will make us the shame of generations to come.

SCENIC TRAILS, RIVERS AND WILDERNESS AREAS

The urgent work of conservation leads us into three other areas.

A citizen should be able to leave his car behind and explore a scenic trail on foot, by bicycle or horse. He can do that if we establish a nationwide network of scenic trails, many near our large cities and through historic areas. *Once again, I urge the Congress — as I did last year — to authorize a network of scenic trails.*

"The time has come," I said in 1965, "to identify and preserve free-flowing stretches of our great scenic rivers before growth and development make the beauty of the unspoiled waterway a memory."

Let this be the session of Congress that grasps the opportunity.

Last year the Senate passed a bill to save seven wild rivers and five scenic rivers. *I urge the Congress to complete action this year on legislation which would establish a scenic rivers system.*

One of the greatest delights for an American is to visit a primitive area of his land in its natural splendor.

In 1964, the Congress passed the Wilderness Act — a milestone in conservation policy. It permits the Government to set aside, at little cost to the taxpayer, some of the truly unspoiled areas of our continent.

Last year I asked the Congress to add the first four wilderness areas to the system: San Rafael in California, Mount Jefferson in Oregon, San Gabriel in California, and Washakie in Wyoming.

I urge the Congress to complete action on these wilderness areas.

I am today recommending the addition of seven new areas to the wilderness

[716]

system, embracing more than 400,000 acres of mountain and forest and lake. These new wilderness areas are:

  —Mt. Baldy in Arizona's Apache National Forest.

  —The Desolation Wilderness in California's Eldorado National Forest.

  —The Flat Tops, in Colorado's Routt and White River National Forests.

  —Pine Mountain in Arizona's Prescott and Tonto National Forests.

  —The Spanish Peaks, in Montana's Gallatin National Forest.

  —The Ventana Wilderness in California's Los Padres National Forest.

  —Sycamore Canyon in Arizona's Coconino, Kaibab, and Prescott National Forests.

We are now surveying unspoiled and primitive areas in Arkansas, Oklahoma, Georgia, and Florida as further possible additions to the Wilderness system.

THE LAND AND WATER CONSERVATION FUND

The machinery to finance the acquisition of federal recreation lands and to help the states plan, acquire and develop their own parks and forests is provided by the Land and Water Conservation Fund.

That Fund draws upon revenues from motorboat fuel taxes, federal recreation area admission charges, and proceeds from the sale of surplus federal lands.

For Fiscal 1969, I recommended new obligational authority of $130 million for the Land and Water Conservation Fund—an increase of $11 million over 1968.

But this alone may not be enough. The need for more recreation acreage to serve our growing population—along with rising land costs—requires that the Land and Water Conservation Fund be enlarged.

The longer we wait to acquire land for recreational purposes, the more those lands will cost.

A suitable addition to those sources of revenues now authorized can be found in the receipts from our mineral leases in the Outer Continental Shelf. That Shelf belongs to the people, and it is only right that revenues from it be used for the people's benefit. *I recommend that the Congress authorize the use of part of these revenues to augment the Land and Water Conservation Fund to raise it up to a level of $200 million a year for the next five years.*

HIGHWAYS

More than any other mark we make upon the land, the signature of mid-20th Century America is found in the more than 3 million miles of highways that cross and link a continent.

It is not enough that those highways be roads of utility. They must also be safe and pleasant to travel.

[717]

We have embarked on a major campaign to make them safe, in the Highway and Traffic Safety Acts of 1966.

In 1965—in the Highway Beautification Act—we set out to make them attractive. In partnership with the states, we determined to remove and control the eyesores that mar the landscape—auto graveyards, unsightly bill boards, junk heaps.

Early last year I asked the Congress to extend that Act—which expired on June 30, 1967—for two additional years. The Senate passed a one-year extension. It is still awaiting House action. The Highway Beautification Act represents an important item of unfinished business before the Congress. *I urge the Congress to complete action on the bill so that we can get on with the job of making America a more beautiful place to live.*

Our highways must be in harmony with the communities and countrysides of which they are part. Too often in the past, this need has received little more than lip service.

A distinguished Citizens' Advisory Committee on Recreation and Natural Beauty, under the Chairmanship of Mr. Laurance Rockefeller, has reported: "Highways have effects that reach far beyond those who drive on them; yet our present devices for choosing locations are still based mostly on requirements of the highway user rather than the community at large."

Under the new authority in the Department of Transportation Act, we are moving now to assure that natural beauty and recreational factors are woven into the highway and freeway planning process, along with traditional engineering and cost considerations.

— The Secretary of Transportation is requiring states to give full consideration to the views of local groups—and private citizens in preparing their route selections for federally-supported highways.

—The Secretaries of Transportation, Housing and Urban Development, Interior, and Agriculture will review exceptional cases which raise questions concerning a proposed highway route's impact on scenic and historic values.

ROADSIDE PARKS

A highway should not be an unending ribbon of concrete from point to point.

American families traveling on their roads should be able to stop, to stretch their legs, to open a picnic lunch and relax before going on their way.

A park along the roadside—with landscaped grounds, an outdoor stove and tables, a path to explore—should be part of every travel experience. These way stations are not expensive. But they can add immeasurably to the comfort and enjoyment of a family on a trip.

I have directed the Secretary of Transportation to work with the Governors and Highway Commissioners of each state on a priority program to increase sub-stantially the number and quality of rest and scenic areas along the Federal-aid Highway System.

VOLUNTEERS FOR CONSERVATION

All across America, men and women, boys and girls are making their cities and communities better places to live. In garden clubs and civic leagues, in Scout troops, 4-H clubs, and Junior Chambers of Commerce, they are planting and painting, cleaning and building, growing and repairing.

This is the army of conservation volunteers, and they number in the millions.

I propose this action program for volunteers to make America a place of beauty, enriching its communities and raising the spirits of their people, vol-unteers to:

— Increase local conservation efforts in every community, through the full participation of all citizens.

— Extend the National Paint-Up, Clean-Up, Fix-Up Week, now an annual event, to a seasonal event, four times a year.

— Encourage every city to beautify its approaches, through the planting of trees, shrubs and flowers native to the area.

— Impress upon every citizen the contribution he can make simply by ob-serving the "No Litter" signs as he drives along the highway and walks along the street. Clean-up is costly. For example, it takes $2,000 of the tax-payers' money each year to keep each mile of highway leading into the Na-tion's captial free of refuse.

— Call upon the news media to encourage the conservation work of local groups. Television and radio stations, which are granted the public air-ways, have a special obligation to highlight these worthy public events.

The volunteer work for conservation deserves recognition and honor. It de-serves help in mobilizing for greater efforts in the years ahead.

Accordingly, I am asking the President's Council on Recreation and Natural Beauty and the Secretary of the Interior in cooperation with the Governors and Mayors to join with private organizations in sponsoring a series of regional workshops to focus attention on those areas where greater private conservation efforts would be particularly productive.

OCEANS

The seas are the world's oldest frontiers. As Longfellow observed, they not only separate—but unite—mankind.

Even in the Age of Space, the sea remains our greatest mystery. But we know

[719]

that in its sunless depths, a richness is still locked which holds vast promise for the improvement of men's lives—in all nations.

Those ocean roads, which so often have been the path of conquest, can now be turned to the search for enduring peace.

The task of exploring the ocean's depth for its potential wealth—food, minerals, resources—is as vast as the seas themselves. No one nation can undertake that task alone. As we have learned from prior ventures in ocean exploration, cooperation is the only answer.

I have instructed the Secretary of State to consult with other nations on the steps that could be taken to launch an historic and unprecedented adventure— an International Decade of Ocean Exploration for the 1970s.

Together the countries which border the seas can survey the ocean's resources, reaching where man has never probed before.

We hope that those nations will join in this exciting and important work.

Already our marine technology gives us the ability to use the ocean as a new and promising source of information on weather and climate. We can now build and moor electronic buoys in deep water. Unattended, these scientific outposts can transmit to shore data for accurate long-range forecasts.

The benefits will be incalculable—to farmers, to businessmen, to all travelers.

This year we can begin development of improved ocean buoys. I urge the Congress to approve my request for $5 million in the Fiscal 1969 Coast Guard budget for this program.

As we turn more and more of our attention to the exploration and the promise of the seas, America must train more ocean scientists and engineers.

In 1966, I signed the National Sea Grant College and Program Act. This new partnership between the Federal Government and the Nation's universities will prepare men and women for careers in the Marine Sciences.

I recommend that the Congress appropriate $6 million in Fiscal 1969 to advance this program.

CRISIS OF CHOICE

Three years ago, I said to the Congress:

". . . beauty must not be just a holiday treat, but a part of our daily life."

I return to that theme in this message, which concerns the air we breathe, the water we drink and use, the oceans that surround us, the land on which we live.

These are the elements of beauty. They are the forces that shape the lives of all of us—housewife and farmer, worker and executive, whatever our income and wherever we are. They are the substance of The New Conservation.

Today, the crisis of conservation is no longer quiet. Relentless and insistent, it has surged into a crisis of choice.

Man—who has lived so long in harmony with nature—is now struggling to preserve its bounty.

Man—who developed technology to serve him—is now racing to prevent its wastes from endangering his very existence.

Our environment can sustain our growth and nourish our future. Or it can overwhelm us.

History will say that in the 1960s the Nation began to take action so long delayed.

But beginning is not enough. The America of the future will reflect not the wisdom with which we saw the problem, but the determination with which we saw it through.

If we fail now to complete the work so nobly begun, our children will have to pay more than the price of our inaction. They will have to bear the tragedy of our irresponsibility.

The new conservation is work not for some Americans—but for all Americans. All will share in its blessings—and all will suffer if the work is neglected. That work begins with the family. Its extends to all civic and community groups. It involves city hall and state capitol. And finally it must engage the concern of the Federal Government.

I urge the Congress to give prompt and favorable consideration to the proposals in this Message.

Lyndon B. Johnson

March 8, 1968

AN ACT TO ESTABLISH A NATIONAL TRAILS SYSTEM*
October 2, 1968

A first step in filling a long-felt need was taken when the National Trails System Act was passed in 1968 after the submission of a comprehensive report, Trails for America, *by the Bureau of Outdoor Recreation.*

Be it enacted by the Senate and House of Representatives of the United States of America in Congress assembled,

SHORT TITLE

SECTION 1. This Act may be cited as the "National Trails System Act".

STATEMENT OF POLICY

SEC. 2. (a) In order to provide for the ever-increasing outdoor recreation needs of an expanding population and in order to promote public access to, travel within, and enjoyment and appreciation of the open-air, outdoor areas of the Nation, trails should be established (i) primarily, near the urban areas of the Nation, and (ii) secondarily, within established scenic areas more remotely located.

(b) the purpose of this Act is to provide the means for attaining these objectives by instituting a national system of recreation and scenic trails, by designating the Appalachian Trail and the Pacific Crest Trail as the initial components of that system, and by prescribing the methods by which, and standards according to which, additional components may be added to the system.

NATIONAL TRAILS SYSTEM

SEC. 3. The national system of trails shall be composed of—

(a) National recreation trails, established as provided in section 4 of this Act, which will provide a variety of outdoor recreation uses in or reasonably accessible to urban areas.

(b) National scenic trails, established as provided in section 5 of this Act, which will be extended trails so located as to provide for maximum outdoor recreation potential and for the conservation and enjoyment of the nationally significant scenic, historic, natural, or cultural qualities of the areas through which such trails may pass.

(c) Connecting or side trails, established as provided in section 6 of this Act, which will provide additional points of public access to national recreation or national scenic trails or which will provide connections between such trails.

*82 Statutes at Large, 919.

The Secretary of the Interior and the Secretary of Agriculture, in consultation with appropriate governmental agencies and public and private organizations, shall establish a uniform marker for the national trails system.

NATIONAL RECREATION TRAILS

SEC. 4. (a) The Secretary of the Interior, or the Secretary of Agriculture where lands administered by him are involved, may establish and designate national recreation trails, with the consent of the Federal agency, State, or political subdivision having jurisdiction over the lands involved, upon finding that—

(i) such trails are reasonably accessible to urban areas, and, or

(ii) such trails meet the criteria established in this Act and such supplementary criteria as he may prescribe.

(b) As provided in this section, trails within park, forest, and other recreation areas administered by the Secretary of the Interior or the Secretary of Agriculture or in other federally administered areas may be established and designated as "National Recreation Trails" by the appropriate Secretary and, when no Federal land acquisition is involved—

(i) trails in or reasonably accessible to urban areas may be designated as "National Recreation Trails" by the Secretary of the Interior with the consent of the States, their political subdivisions, or other appropriate administering agencies, and

(ii) trails within park, forest, and other recreation areas owned or administered by States may be designated as "National Recreation Trails" by the Secretary of the Interior with the consent of the State.

NATIONAL SCENIC TRAILS

SEC. 5. (a) National scenic trails shall be authorized and designated only by Act of Congress. There are hereby established as the initial National Scenic Trails:

(1) The Appalachian Trail, a trail of approximately two thousand miles extending generally along the Appalachian Mountains from Mount Katahdin, Maine, to Springer Mountain, Georgia. Insofar as practicable, the right-of-way for such trail shall comprise the trail depicted on the maps identified as "Nationwide System of Trails, Proposed Appalachian Trail, NST—AT—101—May 1967", which shall be on file and available for public inspection in the office of the Director of the National Park Service. Where practicable, such rights-of-way shall include lands protected for it under agreements in effect as of the date of enactment of this Act, to which Federal agencies and States were parties. The Appalachian Trail shall be administered primarily as a footpath by the Secretary of the Interior, in consultation with the Secretary of Agriculture.

(2) The Pacific Crest Trail, a trail of approximately two thousand three hundred fifty miles, extending from the Mexican-California border northward

generally along the mountain ranges of the west coast States to the Canadian-Washington border near Lake Ross, following the route as generally depicted on the map, identified as "Nationwide System of Trails, Proposed Pacific Crest Trail, NST—PC—103—May 1967" which shall be on file and available for public inspection in the office of the Chief of the Forest Service. The Pacific Crest Trail shall be administered by the Secretary of Agriculture, in consultation with the Secretary of the Interior.

(3) The Secretary of the Interior shall establish an advisory council for the Appalachian National Scenic Trail, and the Secretary of Agriculture shall establish an advisory council for the Pacific Crest National Scenic Trail. The appropriate Secretary shall consult with such council from time to time with respect to matters relating to the trail, including the selection of rights-of-way, standards of the erection and maintenance of markers along the trail, and the administration of the trail. The members of each advisory council, which shall not exceed thirty-five in number, shall serve without compensation or expense to the Federal Government for a term of five years and shall be appointed by the appropriate Secretary as follows:

(i) A member appointed to represent each Federal department or independent agency administering lands through which the trail route passes and each appointee shall be the person designated by the head of such department or agency;

(ii) A member appointed to represent each State through which the trail passes and such appointments shall be made from recommendations of the Governors of such States;

(iii) One or more members appointed to represent private organizations, including landowners and land users, that, in the opinion of the Secretary, have an established and recognized interest in the trail and such appointments shall be made from recommendations of the heads of such organizations: *Provided,* That the Appalachian Trail Conference shall be represented by a sufficient number of persons to represent the various sections of the country through which the Appalachian Trail passes; and

(iv) The Secretary shall designate one member to be chairman and shall fill vacancies in the same manner as the original appointment.

(b) The Secretary of the Interior, and the Secretary of Agriculture where lands administered by him are involved, shall make such additional studies as are herein or may hereafter be authorized by the Congress for the purpose of determining the feasibility and desirability of designating other trails as national scenic trails. Such studies shall be made in consultation with the heads of other Federal agencies administering lands through which such additional proposed trails would pass and in cooperation with interested interstate, State, and local governmental agencies, public and private organizations, and landowners and land users concerned. When completed, such studies shall be the basis of appropriate proposals for additional national scenic trails which shall be submitted from time to time to the President and to the Congress. Such proposals shall be accompanied by a report, which shall be printed as a House or Senate document, showing among other things—

(1) the proposed route of such trail (including maps and illustrations);

(2) the areas adjacent to such trails, to be utilized for scenic, historic, natural, cultural, or developmental, purposes;

(3) the characteristics which, in the judgment of the appropriate Secretary, make the proposed trail worthy of designation as a national scenic trail;

(4) the current status of land ownership and current and potential use along the designated route;

(5) the estimated cost of acquisition of lands or interest in lands, if any;

(6) the plans for developing and maintaining the trail and the cost thereof;

(7) the proposed Federal administering agency (which, in the case of a national scenic trail wholly or substantially within a national forest, shall be the Department of Agriculture);

(8) the extent to which a State or its political subdivisions and public and private organizations might reasonably be expected to participate in acquiring the necessary lands and in the administration thereof; and

(9) the relative uses of the lands involved, including: the number of anticipated visitor-days for the entire length of, as well as for segments of, such trail; the number of months which such trail, or segments thereof, will be open for recreation purposes; the economic and social benefits which might accrue from alternate land uses; and the estimated man-years of civilian employment and expenditures expected for the purposes of maintenance, supervision, and regulation of such trail.

(c) The following routes shall be studied in accordance with the objectives outlined in subsection (b) of this section:

(1) Continental Divide Trail, a three-thousand-one-hundred-mile trail extending from near the Mexican border in southwestern New Mexico northward generally along the Continental Divide to the Canadian border in Glacier National Park.

(2) Potomac Heritage Trail, an eight-hundred-and-twenty-five-mile trail extending generally from the mouth of the Potomac River to its sources in Pennsylvania and West Virginia, including the one-hundred-and-seventy-mile Chesapeake and Ohio Canal towpath.

(3) Old Cattle Trails of the Southwest from the vicinity of San Antonio, Texas, approximately eight hundred miles through Oklahoma via Baxter Springs and

Chetopa, Kansas, to Fort Scott, Kansas, including the Chisholm Trail, from the vicinity of San Antonio or Cuero, Texas, approximately eight hundred miles north through Oklahoma to Abilene, Kansas.

(4) Lewis and Clark Trail, from Wood River, Illinois, to the Pacific Ocean in Oregon, following both the outbound and inbound routes of the Lewis and Clark Expedition.

(5) Natchez Trace, from Nashville, Tennessee, approximately six hundred miles to Natchez, Mississippi.

(6) North Country Trail, from the Appalachian Trail in Vermont, approximately three thousand two hundred miles through the States of New York, Pennsylvania, Ohio, Michigan, Wisconsin, and Minnesota, to the Lewis and Clark Trail in North Dakota.

(7) Kittanning Trail from Shirleysburg in Huntingdon County to Kittanning, Armstrong County, Pennsylvania.

(8) Oregon Trail, from Independence, Missouri, approximately two thousand miles to near Fort Vancouver, Washington.

(9) Santa Fe Trail, from Independence, Missouri, approximately eight hundred miles to Santa Fe, New Mexico.

(10) Long Trail, extending two hundred and fifty-five miles from the Massachusetts border northward through Vermont to the Canadian border.

(11) Mormon Trail, extending from Nauvoo, Illinois, to Salt Lake City, Utah, through the States of Iowa, Nebraska, and Wyoming.

(12) Gold Rush Trails in Alaska.

(13) Mormon Battalion Trail, extending two thousand miles from Mount Pisgah, Iowa, through Kansas, Colorado, New Mexico, and Arizona to Los Angeles, California.

(14) El Camino Real from St. Augustine to San Mateo, Florida, approximately 20 miles along the southern boundary of the St. Johns River from Fort Caroline National Memorial to the St. Augustine National Park Monument:

CONNECTING AND SIDE TRAILS

SEC. 6. Connecting or side trails within park, forest, and other recreation areas administered by the Secretary of the Interior or Secretary of Agriculture may be established, designated, and marked as components of a national recreation or national scenic trail. When no Federal land acquisition is involved, connecting or side trails may be located across lands administered by interstate, State, or local governmental agencies with their consent: *Provided,* That such trails provide additional points of public access to national recreation or scenic trails.

ADMINISTRATION AND DEVELOPMENT

SEC. 7. (a) Pursuant to section 5(a), the appropriate Secretary shall select the rights-of-way for National Scenic Trails and shall publish notice thereof in the

Federal Register, together with appropriate maps and descriptions: *Provided,* That in selecting the rights-of-way full consideration shall be given to minimizing the adverse effects upon the adjacent landowner or user and his operation. Development and management of each segment of the National Trails System shall be designed to harmonize with and complement any established multiple-use plans for that specific area in order to insure continued maximum benefits from the land. The location and width of such rights-of-way across Federal lands under the jurisdiction of another Federal agency shall be by agreement between the head of that agency and the appropriate Secretary. In selecting rights-of-way for trail purposes, the Secretary shall obtain the advice and assistance of the States, local governments, private organizations, and landowners and land users concerned.

(b) After publication of notice in the Federal Register, together with appropriate maps and descriptions, the Secretary charged with the administration of a national scenic trail may relocate segments of a national scenic trail right-of-way, with the concurrence of the head of the Federal agency having jurisdiction over the lands involved, upon a determination that: (i) such a relocation is necessary to preserve the purposes for which the trail was established, or (ii) the relocation is necessary to promote a sound land management program in accordance with established multiple-use principles: *Provided,* That a substantial relocation of the rights-of-way for such trail shall be by Act of Congress.

(c) National scenic trails may contain campsites, shelters, and related-public-use facilities. Other uses along the trail, which will not substantially interfere with the nature and purposes of the trail, may be permitted by the Secretary charged with the administration of the trail. Reasonable efforts shall be made to provide sufficient access opportunities to such trails and, to the extent practicable, efforts shall be made to avoid activities incompatible with the purposes for which such trails were established. The use of motorized vehicles by the general public along any national scenic trail shall be prohibited and nothing in this Act shall be construed as authorizing the use of motorized vehicles within the natural and historical areas of the national park system, the national wildlife refuge system, the national wilderness preservation system where they are presently prohibited or on other Federal lands where trails are designated as being closed to such use by the appropriate Secretary: *Provided,* That the Secretary charged with the administration of such trail shall establish regulations which shall authorize the use of motorized vehicles when, in his judgment, such vehicles are necessary to meet emergencies or to enable adjacent landowners or land users to have reasonable access to their lands or timber rights: *Provided further,* That private lands included in the national recreation or scenic trails by cooperative agreement of a landowner shall not preclude such owner from using motorized vehicles on or across such trails or adjacent lands from time to time in accordance with regulations to be established by the appropriate Secretary. The Secretary of the Interior and the Secretary of Agriculture, in consultation with appropriate governmental agencies and public and private organizations, shall establish a uniform marker, including thereon an appropriate and distinctive symbol for each national recreation and scenic trail. Where the trails cross lands administered by Federal agencies such markers shall be erected at appropriate points along the trails and maintained by the Federal agency administering the trail in accordance with standards established by the appropriate Secretary and where the trails cross non-Federal lands, in accordance with written cooperative agreements, the appropriate Secretary shall provide such uniform markers to cooperating agencies and shall require such agencies to erect and maintain them in accordance with the standards established.

(d) Within the exterior boundaries of areas under their administration that are included in the right-of-way selected for a national recreation or scenic trail, the heads of Federal agencies may use lands for trail purposes and may acquire lands or interests in lands by written cooperative agreement, donation, purchase with donated or appropriated funds or exchange: *Provided,* That not more than twenty-five acres in any one mile may be acquired without the consent of the owner.

(e) Where the lands included in a national scenic trail right-of-way are outside of the exterior boundaries of federally administered areas, the Secretary charged with the administration of such trail shall encourage the States or local governments involved (1) to enter into written cooperative agreements with landowners, private organizations, and individuals to provide the necessary trail right-of-way, or (2) to acquire such lands or interests therein to be utilized as segments of the national scenic trail: *Provided,* That if the State or local governments fail to enter into such written cooperative agreements or to acquire such lands or interests therein within two years after notice of the selection of the right-of-way is published, the appropriate Secretary may (i) enter into such agreements with landowners, States, local governments, private organizations, and individuals for the use of lands for trail purposes, or (ii) acquire private lands or interests therein by donation, purchase with donated or appropriated funds or exchange in accordance with the provisions of subsection (g) of this section. The lands involved in such rights-of-way should be acquired in fee, if other methods of public control are not sufficient to assure their use for the purpose for which they are acquired: *Provided,* That if the Secretary charged with the administration of such trail permanently relocates the right-of-way and disposes of all title or interest in the land, the original owner, or his heirs or assigns, shall be offered, by notice given at the former owner's last known address, the right of first refusal at the fair market price.

(f) The Secretary of the Interior, in the exercise of his exchange authority, may accept title to any non-Federal property within the right-of-way and in exchange therefor he may convey to the grantor of such property any federally owned property under his jurisdiction which is located in the State wherein such property is located and which he classifies as suitable for exchange or other disposal. The values of the properties so exchanged either shall be approximately equal, or if they are not approximately equal the values shall be equalized by the payment of cash to the grantor or to the Secretary as the circumstances require. The Secretary of Agriculture, in the exercise of his exchange authority, may utilize authorities and procedures available to him in connection with exchanges of national forest lands.

(g) The appropriate Secretary may utilize condemnation proceedings without the consent of the owner to acquire private lands or interests therein pursuant to this section only in cases where, in his judgment, all reasonable efforts to acquire such lands or interests therein by negotiation have failed, and in such cases he shall acquire only such title as, in his judgment, is reasonably necessary to provide passage across such lands: *Provided,* That condemnation proceedings may not be utilized to acquire fee title or lesser interests to more than twenty-five acres in any one miles and when used such authority shall be limited to the most direct or practicable connecting trail right-of-way: *Provided further,* That condemnation is prohibited with respect to all acquisition of lands or interest in lands for the purposes of the Pacific Crest Trail. Money appropriated for Federal purposes from the land and water conservation fund shall, without prejudice to appropriations from other sources, be available to Federal departments for the acquisition of lands or interests in lands for the purposes of this Act.

(h) The Secretary charged with the administration of a national recreation or scenic trail shall provide for the development and maintenance of such trails within federally administered areas and shall cooperate with and encourage the States to operate, develop, and maintain portions of such trails which are located outside the boundaries of federally administered areas. When deemed to be in the public interest, such Secretary may enter written cooperative agreements with the States or their political subdivisions, landowners, private organizations, or individuals to operate, develop, and maintain any portion of a national scenic trail either within or outside a federally administered area.

Whenever the Secretary of the Interior makes any conveyance of land under any of the public land laws, he may reserve a right-of-way for trails to the extent he deems necessary to carry out the purposes of this Act.

(i) The appropriate Secretary, with the concurrence of the heads of any other Federal agencies administering lands through which a national recreation or scenic trail passes, and after consultation with the States, local governments, and organizations concerned, may issue regulations, which may be revised from time to time, governing the use, protection, management, development, and administration of trails of the national trails system. In order to maintain good conduct on and along the trails located within federally administered areas and to provide for the proper government and protection of such trails, the Secretary of the Interior and the Secretary of Agriculture shall prescribe and publish such uniform regulations as they deem necessary and any person who violates such regulations shall be guilty of a misdemeanor, and may be punished by a fine of not more than $500, or by imprisonment not exceeding six months, or by both such fine and imprisonment.

STATE AND METROPOLITAN AREA TRAILS

SEC. 8. (a) The Secretary of the Interior is directed to encourage States to consider, in their comprehensive statewide outdoor recreation plans and proposals for financial assistance for State and local projects submitted pursuant to the Land and Water Conservation Fund Act, needs and opportunities for establishing park, forest, and other recreation trails on lands owned or administered by States, and recreation trails on lands in or near urban areas. He is further directed, in accordance with the authority contained in the Act of May 28, 1963 (77 Stat. 49), to encourage States, political subdivisions, and private interests, including nonprofit organizations, to establish such trails.

(b) The Secretary of Housing and Urban Development is directed, in administering the program of comprehensive urban planning and assistance under section 701 of the Housing Act of 1954, to encourage the planning of recreation trails in connection with the recreation and transportation planning for metropolitan and other urban areas. He is further directed, in administering the urban open-space program under title VII of the Housing Act of 1961, to encourage such recreation trails.

(c) The Secretary of Agriculture is directed, in accordance with authority vested in him, to encourage States and local agencies and private interests to establish such trails.

(d) Such trails may be designated and suitably marked as parts of the nationwide system of trails by the States, their political subdivisions, or other appropriate administering agencies with the approval of the Secretary of the Interior.

RIGHTS-OF-WAY AND OTHER PROPERTIES

SEC. 9. (a) The Secretary of the Interior or the Secretary of Agriculture as the case may be, may grant easements and rights-of-way upon, over, under, across, or along any component of the national trails system in accordance with the laws applicable to the national park system and the national forest system, respectively: *Provided,* That any conditions contained in such easements and rights-of-way shall be related to the policy and purposes of this Act.

(b) The Department of Defense, the Department of Transportation, the Interstate Commerce Commission, the Federal Communications Commission, the Federal Power Commission, and other Federal agencies having jurisdiction or control over or information concerning the use, abandonment, or disposition of roadways, utility rights-of-way, or other properties which may be suitable for the purpose of improving or expanding the national trails system shall cooperate with the Secretary of the Interior and the Secretary of Agriculture in order to assure, to the extent practicable, that any such properties having values suitable for trail purposes may be made available for such use.

AUTHORIZATION OF APPROPRIATIONS

SEC. 10. There are hereby authorized to be appropriated for the acquisition of lands or interests in lands not more than $5,000,000 for the Appalachian National Scenic Trail and not more than $500,000 for the Pacific Crest National Scenic Trail.

Approved October 2, 1968.

THE WILD AND SCENIC RIVERS ACT*
October 2, 1968

For many years there had been attempts to preserve some scenic American rivers in something approaching their natural state. The Wild and Scenic Rivers Act of 1968 was one of the last conservation measures of the Johnson administration and the culmination of many years of effort by outdoor recreation and conservationist groups.

An Act to provide for a National Wild and Scenic Rivers System, and for other purposes.

Be it enacted by the Senate and House of Representatives of the United States of America in Congress assembled, That (a) this Act may be cited as the "Wild and Scenic Rivers Act".

(b) It is hereby declared to be the policy of the United States that certain selected rivers of the Nation which, with their immediate environments, possess outstandingly remarkable scenic, recreational, geologic, fish and wildlife, historic, cultural, or other similar values, shall be preserved in free-flowing condition, and that they and their immediate environments shall be protected for the benefit and enjoyment of present and future generations. The Congress declares that the established national policy of dam and other construction at appropriate sections of the rivers of the United States needs to be complemented by a policy that would preserve other selected rivers or sections thereof in their free-flowing condition to protect the water quality of such rivers and to fulfill other vital national conservation purposes.

(c) The purpose of this Act is to implement this policy by instituting a national wild and scenic rivers system, by designating the initial components of that system, and by prescribing the methods by which and standards according to which additional components may be added to the system from time to time.

SEC. 2. (a) The national wild and scenic rivers system shall comprise rivers (i) that are authorized for inclusion therein by Act of Congress, or (ii) that are designated as wild, scenic or recreational rivers by or pursuant to an act of the legislature of the State or States through which they flow, that are to be permanently administered as wild, scenic or recreational rivers by an agency or political subdivision of the State or States concerned without expense to the United States, that are found by the Secretary of the Interior, upon application of the Governor of the State or the Governors of the States concerned, or a person or persons thereunto duly appointed by him or them, to meet the criteria established in this Act and such criteria supplementary thereto as he may prescribe,

*82 *Statutes at Large,* 906.

and that are approved by him for inclusion in the system, including, upon application of the Governor of the State concerned, the Allagash Wilderness Waterway, Maine, and that segment of the Wolf River, Wisconsin, which flows through Langlade County.

(b) A wild, scenic or recreational river area eligible to be included in the system is a free-flowing stream and the related adjacent land area that possesses one or more of the values referred to in section 1, subsection (b) of this Act. Every wild, scenic or recreational river in its free-flowing condition, or upon restoration to this condition, shall be considered eligible for inclusion in the national wild and scenic rivers system and, if included, shall be classified, designated, and administered as one of the following:

(1) Wild river areas—Those rivers or sections of rivers that are free of impoundments and generally inaccessible except by trail, with watersheds or shorelines essentially primitive and waters unpolluted. These represent vestiges of primitive America.

(2) Scenic river areas—Those rivers or sections of rivers that are free of impoundments, with shorelines or watersheds still largely primitive and shorelines largely undeveloped, but accessible in places by roads.

(3) Recreational river areas—Those rivers or sections of rivers that are readily accessible by road or railroad, that may have some development along their shorelines, and that may have undergone some impoundment or division in the past.

SEC. 3. (a) The following rivers and the land adjacent thereto are hereby designated as components of the national wild and scenic rivers system:

(1) CLEARWATER, MIDDLE FORK, IDAHO.—The Middle Fork from the town of Kooskia upstream to the town of Lowell; the Lochsa River from its junction with the Selway at Lowell forming the Middle Fork, upstream to the Powell Ranger Station; and the Selway River from Lowell upstream to its origin; to be administered by the Secretary of Agriculture.

(2) ELEVEN POINT, MISSOURI.—The segment of the river extending downstream from Thomasville to State Highway 142; to be administered by the Secretary of Agriculture.

(3) FEATHER, CALIFORNIA.—The entire Middle Fork: to be administered by the Secretary of Agriculture.

(4) RIO GRANDE, NEW MEXICO.—The segment extending from the Colorado State line downstream to the State Highway 96 crossing, and the lower four miles of the Red River; to be administered by the Secretary of the Interior.

(5) ROGUE, OREGON.—The segment of the river extending from the mouth of the Applegate River downstream to the Lobster Creek Bridge; to be administered by agencies of the Departments of the Interior or Agriculture as agreed upon by the Secretaries of said Departments or as directed by the President.

(6) SAINT CROIX, MINNESOTA AND WISCONSIN.—The segment between the

dam near Taylors Falls, Minnesota, and the dam near Gordon, Wisconsin, and its tributary, the Namekagon, from Lake Namekagon downstream to its confluence with the Saint Croix; to be administered by the Secretary of the Interior: *Provided,* That except as may be required in connection with items (a) and (b) of this paragraph, no funds available to carry out the provisions of this Act may be expended for the acquisition or development of lands in connection with, or for administration under this Act of, that portion of the Saint Croix River between the dam near Taylors Falls, Minnesota, and the upstream end of Big Island in Wisconsin, until sixty days after the date on which the Secretary has transmitted to the President of the Senate and Speaker of the House of Representatives a proposed cooperative agreement between the Northern States Power Company and the United States (a) whereby the company agrees to convey to the United States, without charge, appropriate interests in certain of its lands between the dam near Taylors Falls, Minnesota, and the upstream end of Big Island in Wisconsin, including the company's right, title, and interest to approximately one hundred acres per mile, and (b) providing for the use and development of other lands and interests in land retained by the company between said points adjacent to the river in a manner which shall complement and not be inconsistent with the purposes for which the lands and interests in land donated by the company are administered under this Act. Said agreement may also include provision for State or local governmental participation as authorized under subsection (e) of section 10 of this Act.

(7) SALMON, MIDDLE FORK, IDAHO.—From its origin to its confluence with the main Salmon River; to be administered by the Secretary of Agriculture.

(8) WOLF, WISCONSIN.—From the Langlade-Menominee County line downstream to Keshena Falls; to be administered by the Secretary of the Interior.

(b) The agency charged with the administration of each component of the national wild and scenic rivers system designated by subsection (a) of this section shall, within one year from the date of this Act, establish detailed boundaries therefor (which boundaries shall include an average of not more than three hundred and twenty acres per mile on both sides of the river); determine which of the classes outlined in section 2, subsection (b), of this Act best fit the river or its various segments; and prepare a plan for necessary developments in connection with its administration in accordance with such classification. Said boundaries, classification, and development plans shall be published in the Federal Register and shall not become effective until ninety days after they have been forwarded to the President of the Senate and the Speaker of the House of Representatives.

SEC. 4. (a) The Secretary of the Interior or, where national forest lands are involved, the Secretary of Agriculture or, in appropriate cases, the two Secretaries jointly shall study and from time to time submit to the President and the Congress proposals for the addition to the national wild and scenic rivers system of rivers which are designated herein or hereafter by the Congress as potential additions to such system; which, in his or their judgment, fall within one or more of the classes set out in section 2, subsection (b), of this Act: and which are proposed to be administered, wholly or partially, by an agency of the United States. Every such study and plan shall be coordinated with any water resources planning involving the same river which is being conducted pursuant to the Water Resources Planning Act (79 Stat. 244; 42 U.S.C. 1962 et seq.).

Each proposal shall be accompanied by a report, including maps and illustrations, showing among other things the area included within the proposal; the characteristics which make the area a worthy addition to the system; the current status of landownership and use in the area; the reasonably foreseeable potential uses of the land and water which would be enhanced, foreclosed, or curtailed if the area were included in the national wild and scenic rivers system; the Federal agency (which in the case of a river which is wholly or substantially within a national forest, shall be the Department of Agriculture) by which it is proposed the area be administered; the extent to which it is proposed that administration, including the costs thereof, be shared by State and local agencies; and the estimated cost to the United States of acquiring necessary lands and interests in land and of administering the area as a component of the system. Each such report shall be printed as a Senate or House Document.

(b) Before submitting any such report to the President and the Congress, copies of the proposed report shall, unless it was prepared jointly by the Secretary of the Interior and the Secretary of Agriculture, be submitted by the Secretary of the Interior to the Secretary of Agriculture or by the Secretary of Agriculture to the Secretary of the Interior, as the case may be, and to the Secretary of the Army, the Chairman of the Federal Power Commission, the head of any other affected Federal department or agency and, unless the lands proposed to be included in the area are already owned by the United States or have already been authorized for acquisition by Act of Congress, the Governor of the State or States in which they are located or an officer designated by the Governor to receive the same. Any recommendations or comments on the proposal which the said officials furnish the Secretary or Secretaries who prepared the report within ninety days of the date on which the report is submitted to them, together with the Secretary's or Secretaries' comments thereon, shall be included with the transmittal to the President and the Congress. No river or portion of any river shall be added to the national wild and scenic rivers system subsequent to enactment of this Act until the close of the next full session of the State legislature, or legislatures in case more than one State is involved, which begins following the submission of any recommendation to the President with respect to such addition as herein provided.

(c) Before approving or disapproving for inclusion in the national wild and scenic rivers system any river designated as a wild, scenic or recreational river by or pursuant to an act of a State legislature, the Secretary of the Interior shall submit the proposal to the Secretary of Agriculture, the Secretary of the Army, the Chairman of the Federal Power Commission, and the head of any other affected Federal department or agency and shall evaluate and give due weight to any recommendations or comments which the said officials furnish him within ninety days of the date on which it is submitted to them. If he approves the proposed inclusion, he shall publish notice thereof in the Federal Register.

SEC. 5. (a) The following rivers are hereby designated for potential addition to the national wild and scenic rivers system:

(1) Allegheny, Pennsylvania: The segment from its mouth to the town of East Brady, Pennsylvania.

(2) Bruneau, Idaho: The entire main stem.

(3) Buffalo, Tennessee: The entire river.

(4) Chattooga, North Carolina, South Carolina, and Georgia: The entire river.

(5) Clarion, Pennsylvania: The segment between Ridgway and its confluence with the Allegheny River.

(6) Delaware, Pennsylvania and New York: The segment from Hancock, New York, to Matamoras, Pennsylvania.

(7) Flathead, Montana: The North Fork from the Canadian border downstream to its confluence with the Middle Fork; the Middle Fork from its headwaters to its confluence with the South Fork; and the South Fork from its origin to Hungry Horse Reservoir.

(8) Gasconade, Missouri: The entire river.

(9) Illinois, Oregon: The entire river.

(10) Little Beaver, Ohio: The segment of the North and Middle Forks of the Little Beaver River in Columbiana County from a point in the vicinity of Negly and Elkton, Ohio, downstream to a point in the vicinity of East Liverpool, Ohio.

(11) Little Miami, Ohio: That segment of the main stem of the river, exclusive of its tributaries, from a point at the Warren-Clermont County line at Loveland, Ohio, upstream to the sources of Little Miami including North Fork.

(12) Maumee, Ohio and Indiana: The main stem from Perrysburg, Ohio, to Fort Wayne, Indiana, exclusive of its tributaries in Ohio and inclusive of its tributaries in Indiana.

(13) Missouri, Montana: The segment between Fort Benton and Ryan Island.

(14) Moyie, Idaho: The segment from the Canadian border to its confluence with the Kootenai River.

(15) Obed, Tennessee: The entire river and its tributaries, Clear Creek and Daddys Creek.

(16) Penobscot, Maine: Its east and west branches.

(17) Pere Marquette, Michigan: The entire river.

(18) Pine Creek, Pennsylvania: The segment from Ansonia to Waterville.

(19) Priest, Idaho: The entire main stem.

(20) Rio Grande, Texas: The portion of the river between the west boundary of Hudspeth County and the east boundary of Terrell County on the United States side of the river: *Provided,* That before undertaking any study of this potential scenic river, the Secretary of the Interior shall determine, through the channels of appropriate executive agencies, that Mexico has no objection to its being included among the studies authorized by this Act.

(21) Saint Croix, Minnesota and Wisconsin: The segment between the dam near Taylors Falls and its confluence with the Mississippi River.

(22) Saint Joe, Idaho: The entire main stem.

(23) Salmon, Idaho: The segment from the town of North Fork to its confluence with the Snake River.

(24) Skagit, Washington: The segment from the town of Mount Vernon to and including the mouth of Bacon Creek; the Cascade River between its mouth and the junction of its North and South Forks; the South Fork to the boundary of the Glacier Peak Wilderness Area; the Suiattle River from its mouth to the Glacier Peak Wilderness Area boundary at Milk Creek; the Sauk River from its mouth to its junction with Elliott Creek; the North Fork of the Sauk River from its junction with the South Fork of the Sauk to the Glacier Peak Wilderness Area boundary.

(25) Suwannee, Georgia and Florida: The entire river from its source in the Okefenokee Swamp in Georgia to the gulf and the outlying Ichetucknee Springs, Florida.

(26) Upper Iowa, Iowa: The entire river.

(27) Youghiogheny, Maryland and Pennsylvania: The segment from Oakland, Maryland, to the Youghiogheny Reservoir, and from the Youghiogheny Dam downstream to the town of Connellsville, Pennsylvania.

(b) The Secretary of the Interior and, where national forest lands are involved, the Secretary of Agriculture shall proceed as expeditiously as possible to study each of the rivers named in subsection (a) of this section in order to determine whether it should be included in the national wild and scenic rivers system. Such studies shall be completed and reports made thereon to the President and the Congress, as provided in section 4 of this Act, within ten years from the date of this Act: *Provided, however,* That with respect to the Suwannee River, Georgia and Florida, and the Upper Iowa River, Iowa, such study shall be completed and reports made thereon to the President and the Congress, as provided in section 4 of this Act, within two years from the date of enactment of this Act. In conducting these studies the Secretary of the Interior and the Secretary of Agriculture shall give priority to those rivers with respect to which there is the greatest likelihood of developments which, if undertaken, would render them unsuitable for inclusion in the national wild and scenic rivers system.

(c) The study of any of said rivers shall be pursued in as close cooperation with appropriate agencies of the affected State and its political subdivisions as possible, shall be carried on jointly with such agencies if request for such joint study is made by the State, and shall include a determination of the degree to which the State or its political subdivisions might participate in the preservation and administration of the river should it be proposed for inclusion in the national wild and scenic rivers system.

(d) In all planning for the use and development of water and related land resources, consideration shall be given by all Federal agencies involved to potential national wild, scenic and recreational river areas, and all river basin and project plan reports submitted to the Congress shall consider and discuss any such potentials. The Secretary of the Interior and the Secretary of Agriculture shall make specific studies and investigations to determine which additional wild, scenic and recreational river areas within the United States shall be evaluated in planning reports by all Federal agencies as potential alternative uses of the water and related land resources involved.

SEC. 6. (a) The Secretary of the Interior and the Secretary of Agriculture are each authorized to acquire lands and interests in land within the authorized boundaries of any component of the national wild and scenic rivers system designated in section 3 of this Act, or hereafter designated for inclusion in the system by Act of Congress, which is administered by him, but he shall not acquire fee title to an average of more than 100 acres per mile on both sides of the river. Lands owned by a State may be acquired only by donation, and lands owned by an Indian tribe or a political subdivision of a State may not be acquired without the consent of the appropriate governing body thereof as long as the Indian tribe or political subdivision is following a plan for management and protection of the lands which the Secretary finds protects the land and assures its use for purposes consistent with this Act. Money appropriated for Federal purposes from the land and water conservation fund shall, without prejudice to the use of appropriations from other sources, be available to Federal departments and agencies for the acquisition of property for the purposes of this Act.

(b) If 50 per centum or more of the entire acreage within a federally administered wild, scenic or recreational river area is owned by the United States, by the State or States within which it lies, or by political subdivisions of those States, neither Secretary shall acquire fee title to any lands by condemnation under authority of this Act. Nothing contained in this section, however, shall preclude the use of condemnation when necessary to clear title or to acquire scenic easements or such other easements as are reasonably necessary to give the public access to the river and to permit its members to traverse the length of the area or of selected segments thereof.

(c) Neither the Secretary of the Interior nor the Secretary of Agriculture may acquire lands by condemnation, for the purpose of including such lands in any national wild, scenic or recreational river area, if such lands are located within any incorporated city, village, or borough which has in force and applicable to such lands a duly adopted, valid zoning ordinance that conforms with the purposes of this Act. In order to carry out the provisions of this subsection the appropriate Secretary shall issue guidelines, specifying standards for local zoning ordinances, which are consistent with the purposes of this Act. The standards specified in such guidelines shall have the object of (A) prohibiting new commercial or industrial uses other than commercial or industrial uses which are consistent with the purposes of this Act, and (B) the protection of the bank lands by means of acreage, frontage, and setback requirements on development.

(d) The appropriate Secretary is authorized to accept title to non-Federal property within the authorized boundaries of any federally administered component of the national wild and scenic rivers system designated in section 3 of this Act or hereafter designated for inclusion in the system by Act of Congress and, in exchange therefor, convey to the grantor any federally owned property which is under his jurisdiction within the State in which the component lies and which he classifies as suitable for exchange or other disposal. The values of the properties so exchanged either shall be approximately equal or, if they are not approximately equal, shall be equalized by the payment of cash to the grantor or to the Secretary as the circumstances require.

(e) The head of any Federal department or agency having administrative jurisdiction over any lands or interests in land within the authorized boundaries of any federally administered component of the national wild and scenic rivers system designated in section 3 of this Act or hereafter designated for inclusion in the system by Act of Congress in authorized to transfer to the appropriate secretary jurisdiction over such lands for administration in accordance with the provisions of this Act. Lands acquired by or transferred to the Secretary of Agriculture for the purposes of this Act within or adjacent to a national forest shall upon such acquisition or transfer become national forest lands.

(f) The appropriate Secretary is authorized to accept donations of lands and interests in land, funds, and other property for use in connection with his administration of the national wild and scenic rivers system.

(g) (1) Any owner or owners (hereinafter in this subsection referred to as "owner") of improved property on the date of its acquisition, may retain for themselves and their successors or assigns a right of use and occupancy of the improved property for noncommercial residential purposes for a definite term not to exceed twenty-five years or, in lieu thereof, for a term ending at the death of the owner, or the death of his spouse, or the death of either or both of them. The owner shall elect the term to be reserved. The appropriate Secretary shall pay to the owner the fair market value of the property on the date of such acquisition less the fair market value on such date of the right retained by the owner.

(2) A right of use and occupancy retained pursuant to this subsection shall be subject to termination whenever the appropriate Secretary is given reasonable cause to find that such use and occupancy is being exercised in a manner which

[739]

conflicts with the purposes of this Act. In the event of such a finding, the Secretary shall tender to the holder of that right an amount equal to the fair market value of that portion of the right which remains unexpired on the date of termination. Such right of use or occupancy shall terminate by operation of law upon tender of the fair market price.

(3) The term "improved property", as used in this Act, means a detached, one-family dwelling (hereinafter referred to as "dwelling"), the construction of which was begun before January 1, 1967, together with so much of the land on which the dwelling is situated, the said land being in the same ownership as the dwelling, as the appropriate Secretary shall designate to be reasonably necessary for the enjoyment of the dwelling for the sole purpose of noncommercial residential use, together with any structures accessory to the dwelling which are situated on the land so designated.

SEC. 7. (a) The Federal Power Commission shall not license the construction of any dam, water conduit, reservoir, powerhouse, transmission line, or other project works under the Federal Power Act (41 Stat. 1063), as amended (16 U.S.C. 791a et seq.), on or directly affecting any river which is designated in section 3 of this Act as a component of the national wild and scenic rivers system or which is hereafter designated for inclusion in that system, and no department or agency of the United States shall assist by loan, grant, license, or otherwise in the construction of any water resources project that would have a direct and adverse effect on the values for which such river was established, as determined by the Secretary charged with its administration. Nothing contained in the foregoing sentence, however, shall preclude licensing of, or assistance to, developments below or above a wild, scenic or recreational river area or on any stream tributary thereto which will not invade the area or unreasonably diminish the scenic, recreational, and fish and wildlife values present in the area on the date of approval of this Act. No department or agency of the United States shall recommend authorization of any water resources project that would have a direct and adverse effect on the values for which such river was established, as determined by the Secretary charged with its administration, or request appropriations to begin construction of any such project, whether heretofore or hereafter authorized, without advising the Secretary of the Interior or the Secretary of Agriculture, as the case may be, in writing of its intention so to do at least sixty days in advance, and without specifically reporting to the Congress in writing at the time it makes its recommendation or request in what respect construction of such project would be in conflict with the purposes of this Act and would affect the component and the values to be protected by it under this Act.

(b) The Federal Power Commission shall not license the construction of any dam, water conduit, reservoir, powerhouse, transmission line, or other project works under the Federal Power Act, as amended, on or directly affecting any river which is listed in section 5, subsection (a), of this Act, and no department or agency of the United States shall assist by loan, grant, license, or otherwise in the construction of any water resources project that would have a direct and adverse effect on the values for which such river might be designated, as determined by the Secretary responsible for its study or approval—

(i) during the five-year period following enactment of this Act unless, prior to the expiration of said period, the Secretary of the Interior and, where national forest lands are involved, the Secretary of Agriculture, on the basis of study, conclude that such river should not be included in the national wild and scenic rivers system and publish notice to that effect in the Federal Register, and

(ii) during such additional period thereafter as, in the case of any river which is recommended to the President and the Congress for inclusion in the national wild and scenic rivers system, is necessary for congressional consideration thereof or, in the case of any river recommended to the Secretary of the Interior for inclusion in the national wild and scenic rivers system under section 2(a) (ii) of this Act, is necessary for the Secretary's consideration thereof, which additional period, however, shall not exceed three years in the first case and one year in the second.

Nothing contained in the foregoing sentence, however, shall preclude licensing of, or assistance to, developments below or above a potential wild, scenic or recreation river area or on any stream tributary thereto which will not invade the area or diminish the scenic, recreational, and fish and wildlife values present in the potential wild, scenic or recreational river area on the date of approval of this Act. No department or agency of the United States shall, during the periods hereinbefore specified, recommend authorization of any water resources project on any such river or request appropriations to begin construction of any such project, whether heretofore or hereafter authorized, without advising the Secretary of the Interior and, where national forest lands are involved, the Secretary of Agriculture in writing of its intention so to do at least sixty days in advance of doing so and without specifically reporting to the Congress in writing at the time it makes its recommendation or request in what respect construction of such project would be in conflict with the purposes of this Act and would affect the component and the values to be protected by it under this Act.

(c) The Federal Power Commission and all other Federal agencies shall, promptly upon enactment of this Act, inform the Secretary of the Interior and, where national forest lands are involved, the Secretary of Agriculture, of any proceedings, studies, or other activities within their jurisdiction which are now in progress and which affect or may affect any of the rivers specified in section 5, subsection (a), of this Act. They shall likewise inform him of any such proceedings, studies, or other activities which are hereafter commenced or resumed before they are commenced or resumed.

(d) Nothing in this section with respect to the making of a loan or grant shall apply to grants made under the Land and Water Conservation Fund Act of 1965 (78 Stat. 897; 16 U.S.C. 4601–5 et seq.).

Sec. 8. (a) All public lands within the authorized boundaries of any component of the national wild and scenic rivers system which is designated in section 3 of this Act or which is hereafter designated for inclusion in that system are hereby withdrawn from entry, sale, or other disposition under the public land laws of the United States.

(b) All public lands which constitute the bed or bank, or are within one-quarter mile of the bank, of any river which is listed in section 5, subsection (a), of this Act are hereby withdrawn from entry, sale, or other disposition under the public land laws of the United States for the periods specified in section 7, subsection (b), of this Act.

Sec. 9. (a) Nothing in this Act shall affect the applicability of the United States mining and mineral leasing laws within components of the national wild and scenic rivers system except that—

(i) all prospecting, mining operations, and other activities on mining claims which, in the case of a component of the system designated in section 3 of this Act, have not heretofore been perfected or which, in the case of a component hereafter designated pursuant to this Act or any other Act of Congress, are not perfected before its inclusion in the system and all mining operations and other activities under a mineral lease, license, or permit issued or renewed after inclusion of a component in the system shall be subject to such regulations as the Secretary of the Interior or, in the case of national forest lands, the Secretary of Agriculture may prescribe to effectuate the purposes of this Act;

(ii) subject to valid existing rights, the perfection of, or issuance of a patent to, any mining claim affecting lands within the system shall confer or convey a right or title only to the mineral deposits and such rights only to the use of the surface and the deposits and such rights only to the use of the surface and the surface resources as are reasonably required to carrying on prospecting or mining operations and are consistent with such regulations as may be prescribed by the Secretary of the Interior or, in the case of national forest lands, by the Secretary of Agriculture; and

(iii) subject to valid existing rights, the minerals in Federal lands which are part of the system and constitute the bed or bank or are situated within one-quarter mile of the bank of any river designated a wild river under this Act or any subsequent Act are hereby withdrawn from all forms of appropriation under the mining laws and from operation of the mineral leasing laws including, in both cases, amendments thereto.

Regulations issued pursuant to paragraphs (i) and (ii) of this subsection shall, among other things, provide safeguards against pollution of the river involved and unnecessary impairment of the scenery within the component in question.

(b) The minerals in any Federal lands which constitute the bed or bank or are situated within one-quarter mile of the bank of any river which is listed in section 5, subsection (a) of this Act are hereby withdrawn from all forms of appropriation under the mining laws during the periods specified in section 7, subsection (b) of this Act. Nothing contained in this subsection shall be construed to forbid prospecting or the issuance or leases, licenses, and permits under the mineral leasing laws subject to such conditions as the Secretary of the Interior and, in the case of national forest lands, the Secretary of Agriculture find appropriate to safeguard the area in the event it is subsequently included in the system.

SEC. 10. (a) Each component of the national wild and scenic rivers system shall be administered in such manner as to protect and enhance the values which caused it to be included in said system without, insofar as is consistent therewith, limiting other uses that do not substantially interfere with public use and enjoyment of these values. In such administration primary emphasis shall be given to protecting its esthetic, scenic, historic, archeologic, and scientific features. Management plans for any such component may establish varying degrees of intensity for its protection and development, based on the special attributes of the area.

(b) Any portion of a component of the national wild and scenic rivers system that is within the national wilderness preservation system, as established by or pursuant to the Act of September 3, 1964 (78 Stat. 890; 16 U.S.C. ch. 23), shall be subject to the provisions of both the Wilderness Act and this Act with respect to preservation of such river and its immediate environment, and in case of conflict between the provisions of these Acts the more restrictive provisions shall apply.

(c) Any component of the national wild and scenic rivers system that is administered by the Secretary of the Interior through the National Park Service shall become a part of the national park system, and any such component that is administered by the Secretary through the Fish and Wildlife Service shall become a part of the national wildlife refuge system. The lands involved shall be subject to the provisions of this Act and the Acts under which the national park system or national wildlife system, as the case may be, is administered, and in case of conflict between the provisions of these Acts, the more restrictive provisions shall apply. The Secretary of the Interior, in his administration of any component of the national wild and scenic rivers system, may utilize such general statutory authorities relating to areas of the national park system and such general statutory authorities otherwise available to him for recreation and preservation purposes and for the conservation and management of natural resources as he deems appropriate to carry out the purposes of this Act.

(d) The Secretary of Agriculture, in his administration of any component of the national wild and scenic rivers system area, may utilize the general statutory authorities relating to the national forests in such manner as he deems appropriate to carry out the purposes of this Act.

[743]

(e) The Federal agency charged with the administration of any component of the national wild and scenic rivers system may enter into written cooperative agreements with the Governor of a State, the head of any State agency, or the appropriate official of a political subdivision of a State for State or local governmental participation in the administration of the component. The States and their political subdivisions shall be encouraged to cooperate in the planning and administration of components of the system which include or adjoin State- or county-owned lands.

SEC. 11. (a) The Secretary of the Interior shall encourage and assist the States to consider, in formulating and carrying out their comprehensive statewide outdoor recreation plans and proposals for financing assistance for State and local projects submitted pursuant to the Land and Water Conservation Fund Act of 1965 (78 Stat. 897), needs and opportunities for establishing State and local wild, scenic and recreational river areas. He shall also, in accordance with the authority contained in the Act of May 28, 1963 (77 Stat. 49), provide technical assistance and advice to, and cooperate with, States, political subdivisions, and private interests, including nonprofit organizations, with respect to establishing such wild, scenic and recreational river areas.

(b) The Secretaries of Agriculture and of Health, Education, and Welfare shall likewise, in accordance with the authority vested in them, assist, advise, and cooperate with State and local agencies and private interests with respect to establishing such wild, scenic and recreational river areas.

SEC. 12. (a) The Secretary of the Interior, the Secretary of Agriculture, and heads of other Federal agencies shall review administrative and management policies, regulations, contracts, and plans affecting lands under their respective jurisdictions which include, border upon, or are adjacent to the rivers listed in subsection (a) of section 5 of this Act in order to determine what actions should be taken to protect such rivers during the period they are being considered for potential addition to the national wild and scenic rivers system. Particular attention shall be given to scheduled timber harvesting, road construction, and similar activities which might be contrary to the purpose of this Act.

(b) Nothing in this section shall be construed to abrogate any existing rights, privileges, or contracts affecting Federal lands held by any private party without the consent of said party.

(c) The head of any agency administering a component of the national wild and scenic rivers system shall cooperate with the Secretary of the Interior and with the appropriate State water pollution control agencies for the purpose of eliminating or diminishing the pollution of waters of the river.

SEC. 13. (a) Nothing in this Act shall affect the jurisdiction or responsibilities of the States with respect to fish and wildlife. Hunting and fishing shall be permitted on lands and waters administered as parts of the system under applicable State and Federal laws and regulations unless, in the case of hunting, those lands or waters are within a national park or monument. The administering Secretary may, however, designate zones where, and establish periods when, no hunting is permitted for reasons of public safety, administration, or public use and enjoyment and shall issue appropriate regulations after consultation with the wildlife agency of the State or States affected.

(b) The jurisdiction of the States and the United States over waters of any stream included in a national wild, scenic or recreational river area shall be determined by established principles of law. Under the provisions of this Act, any taking by the United States of a water right which is vested under either State or Federal law at the time such river is included in the national wild and scenic rivers system shall entitle the owner thereof to just compensation. Nothing in this Act shall constitute an express or implied claim or denial on the part of the Federal government as to exemption from State water laws.

(c) Designation of any stream or portion thereof as a national wild, scenic or recreational river area shall not be construed as a reservation of the waters of such streams for purposes other than those specified in this Act, or in quantities greater than necessary to accomplish these purposes.

(d) The jurisdiction of the States over waters of any stream included in a national wild, scenic or recreational river area shall be unaffected by this Act to the extent that such jurisdiction may be exercised without impairing the purposes of this Act or its administration.

(e) Nothing contained in this Act shall be construed to alter, amend, repeal, interpret, modify, or be in conflict with any interstate compact made by any States which contain any portion of the national wild and scenic rivers system.

(f) Nothing in this Act shall affect existing rights of any State, including the right of access, with respect to the beds of navigable streams, tributaries, or rivers (or segments thereof) located in a national wild, scenic or recreational river area.

(g) The Secretary of the Interior or the Secretary of Agriculture, as the case may be, may grant easements and rights-of-way upon, over, under, across, or through any component of the national wild and scenic rivers system in accordance with the laws applicable to the national park system and the national forest system, respectively: *Provided,* That any conditions precedent to granting such easements and rights-of-way shall be related to the policy and purpose of this Act.

SEC. 14. The claim and allowance of the value of an easement as a charitable contribution under section 170 of title 26, United States Code, or as a gift under section 2522 of said title shall constitute an agreement by the donor on behalf of himself, his heirs, and assigns that, if the terms of the instrument creating the easement are violated, the donee or the United States may acquire the servient estate at its fair market value as of the time the easement was donated minus the value of the easement claimed and allowed as a charitable contribution or gift.

[745]

SEC. 15. As used in this Act, the term—

(a) "River" means a flowing body of water or estuary or a section, portion, or tributary thereof, including rivers, streams, creeks, runs, kills, rills, and small lakes.

(b) "Free-flowing", as applied to any river or section of a river, means existing or flowing in natural condition without impoundment, diversion, straightening, rip-rapping, or other modification of the waterway. The existence, however, of low dams, diversion works, and other minor structures at the time any river is proposed for inclusion in the national wild and scenic rivers system shall not automatically bar its consideration for such inclusion: *Provided,* That this shall not be construed to authorize, intend, or encourage future construction of such structures within components of the national wild and scenic rivers system.

(c) "Scenic easement" means the right to control the use of land (including the air space above such land) for the purpose of protecting the scenic view from the river, but such control shall not affect, without the owner's consent, any regular use exercised prior to the acquisition of the easement.

SEC. 16. There are hereby authorized to be appropriated such sums as may be necessary, but not more than $17,000,000, for the acquisition of lands and interests in land under the provisions of this Act.

Approved October 2, 1968.

"THE RACE FOR INNER SPACE"*
1964

In 1964, the Department of the Interior published a special report to the nation entitled The Race for Inner Space, *one of the best statements written on the aspirations of Americans who would conserve and improve the quality of their environment. We may be involved in a race for outer space but the race to preserve the inner space that is our home is of greater importance and of equal urgency.*

The introduction to The Race for Inner Space *is reproduced here, for it is an appropriate closing document for this volume.*

One of the most absorbing enterprises of our time is the first tentative probing of earthlings into seemingly limitless outer space. Compared to the drama and glamor of this project, the race for inner space—the preservation of balance and sanity and solitude on our own planet—seems at first glance to be far less alluring.

In terms of fanfare, headlines, and expenditure, the wise development of resources and room for a steadily growing population has taken a back seat.

How many persons will leave this world during the next century to establish residence elsewhere in space we cannot know. But we do have a fair idea of how many people will be sharing this earth a century hence, and we can predict with a modicum of accuracy what will be their condition if we fail to turn our zeal and ingenuity to exploring the capabilities of the inner space which most of us will have to continue to occupy.

Our destiny depends more on the use of the space we now have than upon the acquisition of real estate on other planets. It depends upon the use we make of the outer crust of this earth and the atmosphere which wraps it.

DEPARTMENT'S RESPONSIBILITIES BASIC

The Department of the Interior, because of its basic natural resource responsibilities, is committed to a vision which looks beyond the superficial question "What can science do?" and makes a deeper, more fundamental query:

"What kind of a country do you want America to be?"

Science can provide the answers which will enable America to move ahead at a greatly accelerated rate. But if, when we "get there," we find only a shambles, it will then be too late to ask "What was the use of all that speed?"

The time to wonder and worry about what this country will look like 25 years

*U.S. Dept. of the Interior, *The Race for Inner Space* (Washington, D.C.: Government Printing Office, 1964), 5–21.

from now is today. And the attempt to take a clear look grows increasingly difficult because of mounting pressure from competing points of view. Our rivers for instance, belong to *all* the people. But agriculture, power, recreation, navigation, commercial fisheries—all these interests and more—must find ways of accommodating their special needs to the overall needs of the Nation.

MAN ALTERS FACE OF LAND

In the three hundred years since European man landed on North America, he has greatly altered the face of the land. There are few areas left where his heavy hand is not apparent. Many of the changes have lowered the quality of the land and most of these changes, unfortunately, are irreversible.

At first the problem of providing food, fiber, timber and other raw materials kept man closely related to the land. Today, specialized technology has cut the old intimate ties. Where farming was once a way of life, it is now an industry—one in which fewer and fewer individuals are engaged and almost entirely in a mechanized manner.

The shift of our Nation from a predominantly rural to an urban population has made a sinister sandwich of much of our land, buttering our soil with concrete and asphalt, piling people on people, and then hanging a pall of polluted air over all. Still, in spite of the voluntary switch to urbanity, people continue to seek the relaxation, the refreshment, and the "re-creation" which they find in land and water. Lately this search has developed into a $20 billion annual recreation industry.

We are assured by many technologists that shortages of space, food and essential raw materials are illusory. The proper application of scientific processes, we are told, can easily meet the needs of a population three times greater than present. It is still fair to ask what kind of world it will be—well fed but incredibly crowded?

With economists confidently predicting a Gross National Product of at least one trillion 72 billion dollars by 1980 it is fair again to ask—what will such affluence mean if, in the process of achieving this goal, we destroy most of the values that make for human well-being?

The nationwide race for inner space has its corollary inside each individual. This is the "inner space" concept that involves emotional balance and spiritual equilibrium. Americans have traditionally sought these things through their religious institutions and through close contact with the natural environment which challenged and nurtured them.

While the pace of civilization has stepped up dizzily, the progress of natural phenomena has maintained its age-old beat. The metronome of the heavens continues to wheel this planet at the same speed around the sun—the tides come and go at the call of a constant moon—the trees leaf and the sap rises under the steady baton of the seasons.

Something of this solid, elemental march—of seas and seasons and stars—communicates itself to the harried, hurried human being when he is able to find the time and the opportunity for outdoor leisure experiences. If these opportunities are to be a part of tomorrow's America, we must act to save them today.

In fiscal '63 the full force of the Presidency, the Administration, and Interior Department executive leadership was thrown into winning the race for inner space.

President Kennedy set the tone for his preservation-of-environment program when he delivered his historic Conservation message to the Congress in 1962, defining the relationships between man and the resources on which he depends. He reviewed his Administration's major conservation achievements and advanced new specifics toward which all America could work. Many of these had been accomplished before his death.

At the Department of the Interior the approach varied. But whether it was acquisition of wetlands for waterfowl habitat or drafting a Land and Water Conservation Fund Bill, the ultimate objective was improved total environment. Today offers both man's need and man's opportunity. Tomorrow the choice may have been stripped down to need only.

AGRICULTURE—INTERIOR COOPERATE

To remove all possible roadblocks to the Administration's outdoor recreation program, Secretary of the Interior Stewart L. Udall and Secretary of Agriculture Orville L. Freeman announced a sweeping agreement between the two departments, which ushered in "a new era of cooperation".

Out of the new harmony many conservation and recreation gains were born, including:

(1) Joint proposals for establishment of two National Recreation areas in California [2] and Utah [3], a National Seashore in Oregon [4], plus a whole group of special studies on other outstanding recreation areas [5].

(2) Formation of the President's Recreation Advisory Council, composed of the Secretaries of the Interior, Agriculture, Defense, Commerce and Health, Education and Welfare, plus the Administrator of the Housing and Home Finance Agency, to improve interagency coordination in national recreation policies.

(3) Establishment by the Council of guidelines for National Recreation Areas—a brand new category of Federal lands, requiring Congressional approval and which would embrace lands possessing above average natural endowment but less significance than the unique scenic and historic National Parks and

National Forests. Spaciousness (not less than 20,000 acres of land and water surface), high carrying capacity (located and designed to serve large numbers of people), and interstate use (opportunities significant enough to attract interstate recreation seekers from outside the normal service region) were the main criteria.

(4) Presidential announcement in June 1963 that the Department of the Interior and the Tennessee Valley Authority had reached an agreement which would make possible development of the Between-the-Lakes region [6] in Kentucky and Tennessee as "a Demonstration National Recreation Area."

Development of the 170,000 acres lying between TVA's Kentucky Reservoir on the Tennessee River and the Army Corps of Engineers' Barkley Reservoir across the divide on the Cumberland River will show how an area with limited timber, agricultural and industrial resources can be converted into a recreational asset which will stimulate regional economic growth. In addition, it will provide guidelines for acquisition, development and operation of other outdoor recreation areas.

(5) Launching, at the Council's direction, of a task force representing the Bureau of Public Roads, National Park Service, Forest Service and Bureau of Outdoor Recreation, on a study to determine the feasibility of a national system of scenic roads and parkways. A report is expected in time for Presidential recommendations to Congress in early 1964.

* * *

NEW CONSERVATION ETHIC CITED

In speeches and articles during fiscal '63 Interior spokesmen attempted to lay the groundwork for a whole new conservation ethic. Ironically, the very successes of science have presented a new set of problems in this decade. It began with the inrush to the cities at the onset of World War II, and intensified with each new advance of technology. Our accomplishments in minerals and energy, in electronics and aircraft, in autos and agriculture have lifted us to new heights of affluence, but in the process we have lost ground in the attempt to provide a habitat that will, each day, renew the meaning of the human enterprise.

A lopsided performance has allowed us to exercise dominion over the atom and to invade outer space, but we have sadly neglected the inner space that is our home.

We can produce a wide range of goods and machines, but our manipulations have multiplied waste products that befoul the land, and have introduced frightening new forms of erosion that diminish the quality of indispensable resources and even imperil human health.

The hazards appear on every hand; many new machines and processes corrupt the very air and water; in what Rachel Carson has called "an age of poisons," an indiscriminate use of pesticides threatens both men and wildlife; and the omnipresent symbol of the age, the auto, in satisfying our incessant demand for more mobility, has added to the congestion and unpleasantness of both cities and countrysides.

CONSERVATION PROGRAM ERRATIC

Countless illustrations attest to the erratic progress of conservation. With the passing of each year, neglect has piled new problems on the Nation's doorstep. Some brilliant successes encourage a false sense of well-being, but our massive ability to overpower the natural world also multiplied immeasurably our capacity to damage those resources that make up the total environment.

Our water husbandry methods typify these failures. At the same time that our requirements for fresh water were doubling, our national sloth more than doubled our water pollution. We now are faced with the need to spend six billion dollars and build 10,000 treatment plants to clean it up.

Wilderness is a vital part of the new conservation ethic. In the postwar period, unfortunately, most Americans took their out-of-doors for granted. It was a fact that pressures were growing each year to despoil our few remaining wilderness areas; Americans accustomed to outdoor recreation as a way of life, with access to public areas for hunting, fishing, hiking and swimming, found their opportunities narrowing by the month.

The status we give our wilderness and near-wilderness areas will measure the degree of our reverence for the land. If our stewardship fails, even our small scraps of wilderness will have to be rationed as to visitors, to preserve their wilderness quality—the rest of our outdoor experience may have to come from packed amusement parks, shoulder to shoulder beaches, and table-to-table picnic grounds.

OPTIMUM DEVELOPMENT NEEDED

What America must have is an optimum development of resources that will allow us to pluck the fruit of science without harming the trees of life.

We have developed a whole new generation of sedentary, city-bound citizens, wheedled by spectatorship and the air-conditioned advantages of glass-in living into acquiescing to the diminution of the spaciousness, the freshness, the green splendor of the American earth.

The dead myth of superabundance has been superseded by the myth of scientific supremacy. This is the myth which rests on the mistaken assumption that scientists can fix everything tomorrow. Instead of relying on this myth, we must require a day in and day out effort by business, by government and by vigorous volunteer movements to preserve the beauty and bounty of the American earth.

The fruits of such concerted effort will be to harness the tides of Passamaquoddy, interconnect the electric power systems of whole regions, economically extract fresh water from the seas, turn vast oil shale beds into oil, and at the same time allow us to preserve the beauty of our earth's surface, to provide pleasure and true re-creation on the "inner space" surface of the planet we call home.

HERITAGE IS JEOPARDIZED

Americans are the inheritors of a spacious, virgin continent and it is our relationship with the American earth that is being altered by the quiet crisis—our birthright of fresh landscapes and far horizons.

Unless we are to betray our heritage consciously, we must make an all-out effort now to acquire the public lands which present and future generations need. Only prompt action will save prime park and forest and shoreline and other recreation lands before they are preempted by other uses or prices beyond the public purse.

The Land and Water Conservation Fund proposed by President Kennedy may mark a turning point in conservation history. If the States are to provide leadership before it is too late, if the few remaining spacious seashores are to be preserved for all of the people, if wildlife values are to be permanently protected, and our National Park, Forest and Wildlife Refuge systems are to be rounded out by the addition of the remaining suitable lands, the task must begin immediately and be finished within the next three decades.

* * *

LONGTERM GAINS NECESSARY

The front line of conservation today extends from minerals to mallards, from salmon to soils, from wilderness to water, from lignite to lizards—and most of our major problems will not be resolved until resource inter-relationships are evaluated with an eye to longterm gains and values.

An urgent need exists today for a study of the "ecology of man," to determine the ideal relationship between human population and the land. We are heading for a standing-room-only environment. The amount of open space available per person is decreasing at a faster rate than the population increases. Eventually people will be piled on top of each other. They will have no alternative.

The conservation concept is ultimately something of the mind—a search for balance and order, a quest for new values, a striving for a land conscience that has meaning for the future.

THE CASE OF SCOTT TURNER

Out in California, a small boy had his personal search for balance and order interrupted, and the resulting correspondence made front page news from coast to coast. In November, 1962, Scott Turner, aged 7, went out to hunt lizards in "his" canyon, only to find that the previously open land was now occupied by a field restricted to organized play. The next canyon over was disappearing under home construction.

In complete defeat, anger and frustration, he ran home, demanded paper and pencil and put a determined hand to a letter of protest to the President.

Dear Mr. President
we Have no Place
to go when we
want to go out
in the canyon
Because there
ar going to Build
houses So could you
Set aside some
land, where we could
Play? thank you four listening
love SCOTT

"Dear Scott . . . We are trying as hard as we can, President Kennedy and I, to do just what you asked—'to set aside some land' where you can play—not in groups with supervision, but just roaming around by yourself and finding out how you relate to the earth and the sky. . . ."

[753]

Scott's letter and Interior's reply on behalf of the President received a blaze of attention—column upon column of newsprint testified to the effect that the Nation was in sympathy with one little boy's search for inner space.

As the race for inner space goes into the stretch, the United States has the opportunity to set an example of how to plan the best relationship of human beings to their environment. We should give solemn attention to the matter of developing the optimum man-land ratio—the ratio which would result not only in the highest and best use of the land, but the highest and best development of free men.

INDEX

A

accidents, boating, 435-38
acid, from mine drainage, 500, 518, 536, 670, 712
acreage, of national parks, 143
Act to Authorize Special-Use Permits for Land Adjacent to Mineral Springs (1899), 363
Act to Establish a National Park Service (1916), 183-84, 410
Act to Establish Redwood National Park (1968), 218-22
Act to Establish Yosemite National Park (1890), 154-56
Act for the Preservation of American Antiquities (1906), 11
Act for the Preservation of Historic American Sites (1935), 243
Act to Protect Endangered Species (1966), 85-91
Adirondack Forest Preserve, 10, 224, 241, 255, 259, 370, 382
Administrative Expenses Act (1946), 479, 697
advertising, outdoor see outdoor advertising
Advisory Board on National Parks, Historic Sites, Buildings, and Monuments, 196-97, 645-46, 651
Advisory Board on Wildlife Management, 197-99
Advisory Council on Historic Preservation, 695
Agricultural Appropriations Act (1915), 375
Agricultural Stabilization and Conservation Service, 588
agriculture, 10, 81, 90, 257, 273, 323, 341, 429, 431, 463, 566
  conservation in, for recreation, 585, 609
  needs of, balanced with conservation, 748-50
  as a polluter, 464
  preferential zoning for, 357
  water for, 469, 477-78, 514
Agriculture, Department of
  care of migratory birds, 39, 45-47, 49, 65
  conservation of natural resources, 654-58
  development of land, 123-24, 554
  fish conservation, 117, 135
  at the Hetch-Hetchy Dam, 167-77
  member, Migratory Bird Conservation Commission, 59-63
  and national forests, 132, 205, 364, 376, 392-93, 403
  national monuments of, 642
  national trail system, 723-26, 728-31
  in pollution control, 473, 522, 671-72, 714
  power to construct dikes, 56-58

preserving game, 13, 36
on Recreation Advisory Council, 586, 601
refuge lands of, 52-54, 59-63, 67, 73-76, 85, 98-99
research on pesticides, 671
rural lands beautification, 665
scenic roads, 648, 718
water development, 418, 423, 429-32
water for recreation, 459, 500
watersheds of, 431-32
wetland drainage, 82
wild rivers, 733-45
and wilderness areas, 407-13
wildlife functions pass to Department of Interior, 115
see also National Park Service
air
  clean, 517, 519, 705, 720
  pollution of, 323, 543-44, 654, 668-69, 676, 710-12
  space above rivers, 746
Air Quality Act (1967), 704-5, 711
airplanes, 410, 750
  noise of, 712
airports, 323, 337, 354-55, 541, 565, 576
Alabama, 21
Alaska, 77, 164-65, 186, 240, 249, 361, 409, 476, 481, 487, 492, 533, 565, 578, 599, 642, 726
  water resources of, 138-39
Alaska Game Commission, 110
Albright, Horace M., 144, 178-79, 183, 190
American Civic Association, 159, 179, 182
American Game Protective Association, 551
American Institute of Park Executives, 282
American Samoa, 269, 605, 619, 693
amusement parks, 256, 258-59, 751
Anadromous and Great Lakes Fish Act (1965), 93, 134-36
Anderson, Clinton P., 405, 572, 594
animals
  aquatic, 52-53, 97
  fur-bearing, 52-53, 99-100
  in national parks, 184, 187
  as property, 29-30, 54
  protection of, 88
anti-poverty program, 346-47, 675
antiquities, 630, 649
  see also historic sites
Antiquities Act (1906), 195, 631-32, 642-43
Appalachian Mountains, 203, 205, 359, 385, 536, 562
Appalachian Trail, 638-41, 668, 722-24, 726, 731
Appropriations Act (1922), 360

Fish and Wildlife Act (1956), 86, 111-18, 140
Fish and Wildlife Coordination Act (1934),
    67, 93, 98-99
Fish and Wildlife Coordination Act (1958),
    13, 86, 93, 119-25, 127, 136, 423
Fish and Wildlife Service, 12, 67, 101, 111, 113,
    540
  eradication of sea lamprey, 105
  funds for fisheries, 107-10, 140-41
  survey of fishery resources, 102-4
  two equal agencies in one (act of 1956),
    111-17, 119-21
  wild rivers, 743
Fisher, Joseph L., 499
Fisher, Walter L., 164, 179
fisheries
  anadromous, 459
  commercial, 10, 53, 102-5, 111-17, 132, 137,
    140-41, 501, 532, 574, 748
  federal bureau of, 96, 112
  loan fund for, 114
  resources, 102-4
  salt water, 657
Fisheries Research Act (1916), 97
fishing
  in city parks, 326-27, 336-37
  and conservation, 652
  economic value of, 569
  free along reservoirs, 617
  at Land Between the Lakes project, 452
  on military reservations, 17, 77-79
  in national forests, 361, 366-67, 374, 380-82,
    389-90, 398, 415
  in national parks, 187, 207-8
  night, 140
  on Potomac River, 667
  private clubs for, 382
  on private lands, 585, 594
  for recreation, 61, 84, 92, 94-95, 100, 102-8,
    126, 137-42, 418, 426-27, 443, 450, 461,
    566-67, 578, 580, 751
  regulations on, 6, 12-13, 21, 28, 30, 99, 93
  resources for, 138-42
  rights of colonists for, 138
  sport, 522, 532
  in state and county parks, 233, 237, 255,
    257-58, 289-90
  water quality for, 534-35, 537, 539-40
  on wild river lands, 744
Fletcher Act (1932), 589
flies, fishing, 94, 106-7
Flood Control Act (1936), 420
Flood Control Act (1944), 12, 426, 589, 606,
    616

Flood Control Act (1946), 442
Flood Control Act (1954), 427-28, 442
Flood Control Act (1962), 606, 616
floods, 8, 12, 205, 429, 654
  control of, 10, 81, 93, 127, 131-32, 139, 418-
    23, 429-31, 442, 457, 459, 522, 537-38
  control projects in parks, 159-60, 257, 323,
    327, 338
  control projects as a recreation resource,
    585, 590, 678
Florida, 6, 38, 278-79, 354, 642
flowers, 282, 417
  wild, conservation of, 52-54, 187
food
  birds as, 41, 47, 49, 51
  fish as, 102-4, 111
  for fish to eat, 139
  game as, 35
Food and Agriculture Act (1962), 440-41, 606
foreign countries, polluted by United States,
    525-26
forest rangers, 379-80
forestry, 143, 206, 220, 273
  education in, 598
forests
  in national parks, 192-94, 205
  need for, 3, 8-9
  primeval, 205-6, 218, 255, 366, 415-16, 635
  rain, 191, 202, 205
  for recreation, 13, 20, 363-64
  reserves of, 9-11, 20, 51, 154-56, 180, 182,
    360, 363-64
  sustained yield, 673
  in towns, 355
  trails in, 723-25
forests, national, 235, 250, 255, 260
  administration of, 546-47
  conservation in, 370-72, 427, 561, 655-56
  coordinated use of, 397-402, 553-58, 648
  future of, 750
  as game preserves, 51-52, 62, 80, 373-74
  and national parks, 123, 127, 131-32, 141,
    167, 184, 189, 199
  nurseries for, 368
  proposed additions to, 622, 665
  for recreation, 366-69, 377-84, 423, 443, 445,
    457-59, 599, 657-58
  statistics concerning, 359, 589
  summer homes in, 375
  transfer of land to national parks, 549
  and wild rivers, 734-35, 737, 739, 741-42, 745
  see also National Forest Service
forests, state, 10, 223, 253, 255, 562, 573
Foss, Phillip O., 588

impounded waters *see* dams, farm ponds, reservoirs

income, per capita, 322, 326, 353, 545, 578, 606

Independent Offices Appropriations Act (1963), 617

Indiana, 21, 224, 256

Indiana Dunes National Lakeshore, 664, 715

Indiana Nature Preserves Act (1967), 272-76

indians, 3, 38, 43, 79, 99
  lands of, 250, 554, 556-57, 738
  ruins from, 195
  wars with, 559

industrialism, 197, 440, 500, 503, 549, 559-60, 565, 574, 593, 628, 634

industry
  and conservation of natural resources, 652, 654
  contributing to pollution, 461-64
  plants for, 472, 479, 487, 500-1, 639
  use of land, 291, 320, 328, 337, 354, 416, 576
  wastes of, 254, 261, 469-70, 473-74, 476, 478, 488, 521-22, 539-40, 708
  water for, 469, 477-78, 514, 534-35

insects, 141, 186-87, 323, 410, 414, 656, 713

Inter-American Conference on Conservation of Renewable Natural Resources, 190

Interior, Department of
  conservation of natural resources, 12-13, 654-59, 719
  endangered species, interest in, 85-89
  established Bureau of Outdoor Recreation, 603
  fish and wildlife preservation, 78, 80, 82-84, 99-101, 112-26, 134-36
  funds for fisheries, 106-10
  Hetch-Hetchy Dam, 166-77
  highway beautification, 648, 718
  member, Migratory Bird Conservation Commission, 59
  member, Recreation Advisory Council, 586, 601-2
  and national forests, 363-64
  National Park Service established, 181-85, 193
  and national trail system, 723-24, 726, 728-31
  in outdoor recreation, 423, 449, 457-59, 593, 604, 607, 618-21, 625-26
  pollution control work, 473, 498, 520-30, 534, 539, 706-7, 709, 713
  preservation of historic sites, 631-32, 642-43, 649, 692-97, 700-2
  and public parks, 149, 157-58, 178-79, 196, 206, 208, 218
  The Race for Inner Space, 667, 670-73, 747-54

reclamation and irrigation projects, 431-32

Redwood National Park, 665

state park planning, 240, 243, 249-52, 268-71

and urban problems, 331, 334, 663

water resource development, 119-26, 130-33

wild rivers conservation, 732-46

and wilderness areas, 408, 410

Interior and Insular Affairs Committees of House and Senate, 572-73, 577

Internal Revenue Code (1954), 622-23

International Association of Game, Fish, and Conservation Commissioners, 569-70

International Boundary and Water Commission, 615

interstate commerce
  affecting wildlife protection, 25
  of fish, 117
  of game, 31-32, 34, 36-37
  of migratory birds, 39, 41, 48

Interstate Commerce Commission, 730

irrigation, 10, 93, 132, 139, 143
  Hetch-Hetchy Dam, 171-77
  projects for, in national parks, 160, 192, 395
  from public waters, 401, 549, 654
  as a recreation resource, 590, 668
  water projects for, 418, 422, 431, 442, 459, 538
  water quality for, 534

Itasca State Park, Minn., 224, 228, 258, 284

Izaak Walton League of America, 421, 551, 564, 571, 597

J

Jackson Hole National Monument, 191, 211

Jefferson, Thomas, 297, 663, 679

Johnson, Lyndon B., 218, 346, 352, 358, 450, 541, 613, 627, 674, 732
  on conservation, 661-73, 703-21
  on pollution, 517-19

Joint Resolution to Establish a Commission of Fish and Fisheries (1871), 96

Jones' Wood, N.Y., 254, 261, 305

junkyards, 666, 684, 687-89

Justice, Department of,
  role in historic preservation, 649, 695
  role in pollution control, 471, 486, 497, 527

juvenile delinquency, 565, 699

K

Kennedy, John F., 81, 330-31, 449-50, 590, 541, 592, 595, 601-2, 613, 749, 752-53

Wisconsin, 255, 354, 726
work
  ethic, 3-5, 9
  hours of, 14-15, 197, 216, 398, 545
World War II, 12, 102, 418, 461, 576, 589, 750
  national parks during, 190, 209, 225
Wyoming, 149, 186, 273, 374, 405, 642, 726

run by War Department, 178-79
Yosemite National Park, 9, 143-44, 146, 182, 191, 636
  established, 151-58
  and Hetch-Hetchy Dam, 159-77
  original state park, 224, 226-27
  poor condition of, 213-14
  run by War Department, 178

Y

Yellowstone National Park, 9, 254, 379, 386, 396, 627
  birth of, 147-50
  first national park, 143-44, 146
  guidelines of National Park Service, 184, 186, 188
  natural beauty of, 162, 182, 191, 195, 199, 207
  poor condition of, 213-14
  protection of elk in, 374, 380

Z

zoning
  for highways, 685
  for natural beauty, 667
  for open spaces, 320, 328-29, 332, 334, 337, 341, 356
  for parks, 264-65
  for recreation, 583-85, 610-11
  for scenic rivers, 739
zoos, 253, 279, 282, 310, 567, 573
  children's, 279